THE ATHENIAN DEMOCRACY IN
OF DEMOSTHENES

D1581751

Stephe Chambers

Cambridge
August 1991

𝕁𝔹

The Ancient World

GENERAL EDITOR: Oswyn Murray,
Fellow of Balliol College, Oxford

The classical age has exercised an enduring influence on the history and culture of Europe and the Middle East. **The Ancient World** series aims to further this process by publishing accounts of the ancient world and the classical tradition, written by leading scholars in the field. Volumes in the series embrace political, social and cultural history, philosophy and religion. Together they offer original interpretations of antiquity that are at once accessible and erudite.

Published

*out of print

THE ATHENIAN DEMOCRACY IN THE AGE OF DEMOSTHENES

Structure, Principles and Ideology

Mogens Herman Hansen

Translated by J. A. Crook

BLACKWELL
Oxford UK & Cambridge USA

Copyright © Mogens Herman Hansen 1991

First published 1991

Basil Blackwell Ltd
108 Cowley Road, Oxford, OX4 1JF, UK

Basil Blackwell, Inc.
3 Cambridge Center
Cambridge, Massachusetts 02142, USA

British Library Cataloguing in Publication Data

A CIP catalogue record for this book is available from the British Library.

Library of Congress Cataloging in Publication Data

Hansen, Mogens Herman, 1940–
    The Athenian democracy in the age of Demosthenes: structure, principles, and ideology/Mogens Herman Hansen.
      p. cm. — (The ancient world)
    Includes bibliographical references and indexes.
    ISBN 0–631–13822–6 — ISBN 0–631–18017–6 (pbk)
    1. Athens (Greece)   Politics and government. 2. Greece — Politics and government — To 146 B.C. 3. Democracy — History. I. Title.
II. Series.
JC79.ABH33   1991
320.438'5—dc20

                                        90–23832
                                          CIP

This book is printed on acid free paper

Typeset in 10 on 12 pt Garamond
by Photo·graphics, Honiton, Devon
Printed in Great Britain by T.J. Press, Padstow, Cornwall

Contents

Preface

This book is based on my Danish volumes *Det Athenske Demokrati i 4. årh. f. Kr.* I–VI (Copenhagen, 1977–81), but I have completely rewritten, reorganized and updated the work and changed it from a handbook (with discussions of problems and scores of source references in extremely long endnotes) into what I hope is a general and more accessible account. Thus, the present book is primarily intended not for specialists but for students of classics, history and political science, as well as for anyone else who takes an interest in the history of ancient Greece and of democracy. For the benefit of the non-specialist I have devoted much space and attention to description of the democratic institutions, and to a narrative account of how the Athenian democracy worked. I have also attempted to analyse the principles and ideals behind the institutions, but discussion of scholarly controversies has been eliminated. The result, for better or worse, presents my view of Athenian democracy. Since most readers will have no knowledge of Greek, quotations are given in translation and Greek terms in italicized transcription. Also all technical terms are explained in the Glossary (pp. 348–70). The notes have been kept as short as possible and consist exclusively of references to the sources and to the modern literature. Again, in each case I have restricted myself to one or two or at most three selected source references, followed by selected references to modern accounts where a fuller presentation of the evidence and a more detailed discussion of the problems can be found. References to scholars whose views I do not share are introduced by *pace* or *contra*, unless it is clear from the context that their views differ from mine. On the whole, however, I have preferred in the notes to refer directly to the sources rather than to modern treatments, and in the text to discuss the evidence rather than opposing modern interpretations of it. Chapter 2 presents the evidence on which the book is based, but this is an appropriate place to say something about the scope of the book and the method I have used.

The book is a systematic account of the Athenian democracy in the period 403/2–322/1. I do not share the belief that the fourth-century democracy was almost identical with the so-called 'radical' democracy of 462–411 and 410–404. On the contrary, I hold (1) that the democracy restored in 403 was different from fifth-century democracy in many important respects, and (2) that the democracy underwent many more changes and reforms during the years 403–322 than is usually assumed. More specifically I concentrate on the period 355–322, which is distinguished both by constitutional developments and by its relative abundance of sources. The defeats in the Social War, in 355, and in the second war against Philip of Macedon, in 338, seem to have entailed several major reforms of the democratic institutions as well as a revival of the ideals about the 'Solonian ancestral democracy', though democracy was replaced by oligarchy after the Macedonian conquest of Athens in 322. As for the sources, the greatest period of Attic rhetoric begins in 355, and for the next thirty-four years we have an unparalleled number of excellent sources relating to Athenian public life, primarily the speeches of Demosthenes, Aischines, Hypereides, Lykourgos and Deinarchos, as well as the late speeches of Isokrates. The systematic part of the Aristotelian *Constitution of Athens* describes the democratic institutions in the 330s, and the second half of the fourth century marks the peak of the epigraphical evidence. Not a single speech postdates Antipater's abolition of democracy in 322/1. The period 355–22 also coincides with Demosthenes' political career, which began in 355 with the prosecutions of Androtion and Leptines and was terminated by his suicide in 322. That is why I have chosen to call the book *The Athenian Democracy in the Age of Demosthenes*.

The account is based on contemporary sources, and unless specifically stated the sources are all treated as belonging to the same period. Occasionally, however, sources from other periods have been extrapolated and adduced in order to shed light on the fourth-century democracy: sources describing the democratic institutions in the age of Perikles are used in my description of the fourth-century institutions if there is supporting evidence that the institution in question had not been reformed in that particular respect; and, on the assumption that ideals change more slowly than institutions, the numerous fifth-century sources for democratic ideals are quite often referred to in the chapters on the ideology and the character of the Athenian democracy. Furthermore, in a few cases Hellenistic sources – always inscriptions – have been referred back to the fourth century to shed light especially on the working of the Assembly and the Council. Sources discussing the democratic *polis* in general are also sometimes used if there is reason to assume that the generalizations were inspired by and reflected Athenian institutions. The three most important sources in this category are Plato's *Laws* and *Republic* and Aristotle's *Politics*.

Like other historians I sometimes have to rely on analogies and *a priori* assumptions. But I avoid analogies with representative government in modern democracies and prefer analogies with the Swiss *Landsgemeinde*, which is an exceptional but outstanding example of direct democracy practised in a small society.

I have intentionally used modern terms such as 'constitution', 'state', 'decision-making', 'separation of powers', 'democracy', 'liberty' and 'equality', partly because it is unavoidable and partly because it is desirable. It is unavoidable because the only alternative would be to write about Roman history in Latin, Athenian history in Greek, and Babylonian history in cuneiform, which is simply impossible. But it is also desirable, because the historical perspective emerges by the clash between our concepts and the language of the sources we interpret. Only a bad historian will claim that he avoids contemporary concepts. On every page he will inevitably lead his readers astray. A historian must be Janus-faced and his analysis must move in two opposite directions: he must read and understand his sources in the original, but in his interpretation of them he must also analyse the modern concepts he *has* to use; the art of writing history lies in choosing, from among all the concepts we have at our disposal, those that lead to a meaningful description of ancient societies, while avoiding those that may mislead. I believe for example that 'city-state', 'constitution' and 'democracy' are usable equivalents of *polis*, *politeia* and *demokratia*, whereas concepts such as 'sovereignty', 'politician' and 'political party' are better avoided.

It remains for me to state my acknowledgements. First, I would like to thank Dr Oswyn Murray, who, on behalf of Blackwell, asked me to write this book. Next, I am grateful to my colleagues in the Department of Classics at Copenhagen University: Johnny Christensen, Minna Skafte Jensen, Jørgen Mejer, Helle Salskov Roberts and Christian Marinus Taisbak, who in the academic year 1989–90 took over my teaching and administration duties so that I could have a sabbatical year to finish the book. Next, I am grateful to the Carlsberg Foundation for awarding me the Carlsberg Fellowship at Churchill College, Cambridge, for the Lent term 1990. And that leads to by far the most important of my acknowledgements: my friend and colleague John Crook most generously undertook to translate my typescript into English (apart from this preface, for which I am responsible), during my stay in Cambridge he devoted almost all his time to the task, and my work has profited from his excellent understanding of Danish and his lively idiomatic English. What is more, besides translating the book he exposed its content to critical examination and helped to determine its structure. Weak arguments were sharpened, repetitions cut out, inaccuracies detected and exposed, and my interpret-ations of difficult passages in the sources accepted only after long dis-cussions with the Devil's advocate, and then often with some modifi-cation. It is my book – no doubt about it – but he has certainly left its mark on it, and for that I am especially grateful. The translated version was read by Dr Paul Cartledge and Dr Paul Millett, who made many helpful comments, and I am most grateful to my copy editor, Graham Eyre, who did such excellent work on the typescript. Thanks are due, finally, to Ollie, without whose assistance this book would never have been finished.

Abbreviations
for Classical Sources

Aeschin.	Aischines (*c*.390–322), *rhetor*
Aesch.	Aischylos (*c*.525–456), tragic poet
Supp.	*The Suppliant Women* (463?)
Agora XV	*The Athenian Agora XV. Inscriptions. The Athenian Councillors*, ed. B. D. Meritt and J. S. Traill (Princeton, NJ, 1974)
Agora XVII	*The Athenian Agora XVII. Inscriptions. The Funerary Monuments*, ed. D. W. Bradeen (Princeton, NJ, 1974)
Alc.	Alkaios (born *c*.620 BC), lyric poet
Alcid.	Alkidamas (fourth century BC), sophist
Andoc.	Andokides (*c*.440–*c*.390), *rhetor*
Androt.	Androtion (*c*.410–*c*.340), *rhetor* and Atthidographer
Ant.	Antiphon (*c*.480–411), *rhetor* and leader of the revolution in 411
Ar.	Aristophanes (*c*.445–*c*.385), poet of the old Attic comedy
Ach.	*Acharnians* (425)
Av.	*Birds* (414)
Eccl.	*Ekklesiazousai* (393 or 392)
Eq.	*Knights* (424)
Lys.	*Lysistrate* (411)
Nub.	*Clouds* (423)
Pax	*Peace* (421)
Plut.	*Ploutos* (388)
Ran.	*Frogs* (405)
Thesm.	*Thesmophoriazousai* (411)
Vesp.	*Wasps* (422)
Arist.	Aristotle (384–22), philosopher
Ath. Pol.	*Constitution of Athens*, composed in Aristotle's school *c*.330; his own involvement in dispute
Eth. Nic.	*Nicomachean Ethics*, 10 books
Hist. An.	*Historia Animalium*
Oec.	*Economics, 3 books: pseudonymous treatise ascribed to Aristotle*

Pol.	*Politics*, 8 books
Probl.	*Problems*
Rhet.	*Rhetoric*, 3 books
Rhet. ad Alex.	*Rhetoric to Alexander*, ascribed to Aristotle but probably composed by Anaximenes of Lampsakos (*c*.380–*c*.320)
Ath.	Athenaios (second century AD), sophist and literary historian
Clid.	Kleidemos (*c*.400–*c*.350), Atthidographer
Dem.	Demosthenes (384–22), *rhetor*
Ep.	Letters: 1–4 probably authentic; 5–6 spurious
Prooem.	*Introductions* to symbouleutic speeches
Din.	Deinarchos (*c*.360–*c*.290), logographer
Diod.	Diodoros from Sicily (first century BC), author of a world history in 40 books
Diog. Laert.	Diogenes Laertios (second century AD), author of compendium of lives of philosophers in 10 books
Dion. Hal.	Dionysios from Halikarnassos (born *c*.50 BC), author of essays on Lysias, Demosthenes and Deinarchos, and of
Ant. Rom.	*Antiquitates Romanae*
DK	H. Diels and W. Kranz, *Fragmente der Vorsokratiker* I–III, 6th edn (Berlin, 1952)
Etym. Magn.	*Etymologicum Magnum*: Byzantine lexicon of the twelfth century AD
Eur.	Euripides (*c*.485–*c*.406), tragic poet
Or.	*Orestes* (408)
Supp.	*The Suppliant Women* (422?)
FGrHist.	*Fragmente der griechischen Historiker*, ed. F. Jacoby (see endnote)
fr.	Fragment
Harp.	Harpokration (second century AD), lexicographer
Hdt.	Herodotos (*c*.484–*c*.425?), author of history of the Persian Wars in 9 books
Hell. Oxy.	(Papyrus) fragments (found in Oxyrhynchos) of a historical treatise of the fourth century BC
Hes.	Hesychios (fifth century AD), lexicographer.
Hom.	Homer (date uncertain), epic poet
Il.	*Iliad*
Od.	*Odyssey*
Hyp.	Hypereides (*c*.390–322), *rhetor*
hypoth.	*Hypothesis*: (Hellenistic) introduction to the work of a classical author
I. Délos	*Inscriptions de Délos*, ed. F. Durrbach, P. Roussel and M. Launey (Paris, 1926–37)
IG I^3	*Inscriptiones Graecae* I, 3rd edn., ed. D. M. Lewis (Berlin 1981): Attic inscriptions up to the archonship of Eukleides (403/2)

IG II²	*Inscriptiones Graecae* II, 2nd edn., ed. J. Kirchner (Berlin, 1913–40): Attic inscriptions after the archonship of Eukleides (403/2).
Is.	Isaios (*c*.420–*c*.350), logographer
Isoc.	Isokrates (436–338), author of rhetorical essays and political pamphlets
Lex. Cant.	*Lexicon Cantabrigiense*, lexicographical notes on technical terms in the Attic orators
Lex. Patm.	*Lexicon Patmense*, lexicographical notes on technical terms in Demosthenes
Lex. Seg.	Byzantine dictionary of Attic words
Lycurg.	Lykourgos (*c*.390–324), *rhetor*
Lys.	Lysias (*c*.445–*c*.380), logographer
M&L	*A Selection of Greek Historical Inscriptions to the End of the Fifth Century BC*, ed. R. Meiggs and D. M. Lewis, 2nd edn (Oxford, 1988)
Men.	Menander (342–*c*.290), poet of the new Attic comedy
P. Berol.	Papyri kept in Berlin
P. Oxy.	Papyri found in Oxyrhynchos (about 180 km south of Cairo)
P. Ryl.	John Rylands Papyri (in Manchester)
Paus.	Pausanias (*c*.AD115–*c*.180), author of a description of Greece in 10 books
Philoch.	Philochoros (*c*.340–*c*.260), Atthidographer
Phot.	Photios (*c*.AD820–91), patriarch of Constantinople and lexicographer
Pind.	Pindar (518–438), lyric poet
Pyth.	*Pythian Odes*
Pl.	Plato (427–347), philosopher
Ap.	*Apology* (of Sokrates)
Cri.	*Kriton*
Criti.	*Kritias*
Def.	*Definitiones*
Ep. 7	Seventh Letter
Euthphr.	*Euthyphron*
Grg.	*Gorgias*
Lg.	*Laws*, 12 books
Menex.	*Menexenos*
Phd.	*Phaidon*
Phdr.	*Phaidros*
Pol.	*The Statesman*
Prt.	*Protagoras*
Resp.	*The Republic*, 10 books
Tht.	*Theaitetos*
Plut.	Plutarch (*c*.AD45–*c*.125), author of lives of great men and of moral essays (*Moralia*)
Alc.	*Alkibiades*

Arist.	*Aristeides*
Cim.	*Kimon*
Dem.	*Demosthenes*
Mor.	*Moralia*
Nic.	*Nikias*
Per.	*Perikles*
Sol.	*Solon*
Them.	*Themistokles*
Poll.	Pollux (second century AD), professor of rhetoric in Athens and author of a work on the Attic vocabulary in 10 books
Polyb.	Polybios (*c*.200–*c*.118), author of a history in 40 books on the rise of Rome
Ps. Xen.	Pseudo-Xenophon
Ath. Pol.	*Constitution of Athens*: anonymous political pamphlet composed by an Athenian in the 420s (the 'Old Oligarch')
schol.	Scholia: Hellenistic or Byzantine notes on classical authors, written in the margins of the manuscript or published separately
SEG	*Supplementum Epigraphicum Graecum*, Leiden: annually published periodical on the progress in Greek epigraphy
*SIG*³	*Sylloge Inscriptionum Graecarum* I–IV, 3rd edn, ed. W. Dittenberger (Berlin, 1914–24)
Suda	Byzantine lexicon of the tenth century AD
Theop.	Theopompos of Chios (born *c*.375 BC), author of a history of the reign of Philip II in 58 books with digressions about Athenian demagogues
Theophr.	Theophrastos (*c*.370–*c*.285), pupil of Aristotle and after his death head of the Peripatetic School
Char.	*Characters*: 30 short character sketches
Thuc.	Thucydides (*c*.460–*c*.395), author of a history of the Peloponnesian war down to 411 in 8 books
Tod	*A Selection of Greek Historical Inscriptions II. From 403 to 323 BC*, ed. M. N. Tod (Oxford, 1948)
Xen.	Xenophon (*c*.425–*c*.355), historian and essayist
Apol.	*Apology* (of Sokrates)
Hell.	*Hellenika*, 7 books: history of Greece 411–362
Mem.	*Memorabilia*, 4 books: recollections of Sokrates
Oec.	*Oikonomikos*: treatise on how to manage a house.
Vect.	*Poroi*: treatise on revenue composed *c*.355.

References to fragments of the orators are to I. G. Baiter and H. Sauppe, *Oratores Attici* II (Zürich, 1850), unless otherwise stated. References to the fragments of the historians are to F. Jacoby, *Die Fragmente der griechischen Historiker* (Berlin and Leiden, 1923–58). References to the fragments of the comedies are to J. M. Edmonds, *The Fragments of Attic Comedy* I–III (Leiden, 1957–61). The speeches of Hypereides are numbered as in Chr. Jensen's Teubner edition (Stuttgart, 1963).

1

Direct Democracy in Historical Perspective

Almost everybody who writes about democracy begins with the distinction between 'direct' and 'indirect' or 'representative' democracy.[1] Those whose focus is on institutions sometimes put it in the form of 'assembly democracy' as opposed to 'parliamentary democracy'; but the distinction is the same: in a direct democracy the people actually govern themselves, i.e. all have the right to participate in decision-making, whereas in the other sort the only decision that all have the right to make is to choose the decision-makers.

Even structural analyses of democracy always claim a historical perspective (which is natural enough): it consists in asserting that direct democracy no longer exists,[2] at any rate in sovereign states as opposed to smaller units; and that undeniable truth tends to be followed by the assertion that such democracy *can* no longer exist because of the size of modern societies[3] (which is, actually, to ignore the fact that modern technology has made a return to direct democracy quite feasible – whether desirable or not is another matter[4]).

The historical perspective in the other direction, i.e. into the past, tends to vary with the nationality of the writer. The English-speaking world has looked to the Greek city-states and classical Athenian democracy[5] – except that Americans are also drawn irresistibly to their very own manifestation of direct democracy in the 'New England town meeting'.[6] The French, since Rousseau, have in addition lifted up their eyes to the Alps for inspiration,[7] while some German and Scandinavian scholars go on happily about the age-old direct democracy of the Germanic

---

[1] Holden (1974) 5, 26–9; Lively (1975) 29–32; Pennock (1979) 7; Lijphart (1984) 1; McLean (1989) 5.

[2] Sartori (1962) 252; Holden (1974) 5. [3] Sartori (1962) 255–6; Holden (1974) 27.

[4] Arterton (1987); McLean (1989). Cf. Hansen (1989b) 6.

[5] *The New Encylopaedia Britannica*, 15th edn (1975), s.v. Democracy.

[6] *Encyclopaedia Americana*, (1980 edn) s.v. Democracy.

[7] *Grand dictionnaire encyclopédique Larousse* (1982), s.v. Démocratie.

tribes.[8] A further historical case must, however, be dismissed without further ado: the Italian cities of the Renaissance. Venice, Florence, Milan, and so on, were unquestionably city-states, and can in that respect be usefully compared with the Greek *poleis*, but they were ruled by a monarchy or oligarchy;[9] democracy emerged in them only as a short-lived digression.[10] So they do not provide a historical parallel when the discussion is of democracy and the democratic state.

The four remaining historical examples of direct democracy demand a further word; and first German *Urdemokratie*. It goes back to a sentence in Tacitus' *Germania*, given currency by Montesquieu;[11] but historians and archaeologists in more modern times have been forced to abandon as a myth the notion of an age-old egalitarian system of government amongst the German tribes. As for Switzerland as the cradle of demo-cracy, that claim has two foundations, one much securer than the other. The first is that since the Middle Ages four Swiss cantons and four half-cantons have been governed by assemblies of the people (*Landsgemeinden*), five of which exist to this day:[12] as early as the sixteenth century Bodin drew attention to them as examples of democracy.[13] They constitute a real – indeed the only real – parallel to Athenian democracy; for, although nowadays the cantons are only subordinate units, with limited local powers, in their day they were sovereign states, governed by means of direct democracy. The other claim made for Switzerland rests mainly on Rousseau. He mentioned the true democracy of the little forest cantons only in passing,[14] and was mainly concerned with his native city of Geneva, which he mistakenly thought to be a democracy,[15] while at the same time equally wrongly claiming that Periklean Athens was not one.[16] In fact there is little to be said for Rousseau as a historian, even though his ideas have had a powerful influence on political thought. As for the New England town meeting,[17] it was direct democracy all right, but only on the municipal scale; so, although it is interesting to compare it with the Athenian People's Assembly, it provides no basis for a study of democracy as a form of state government. (More interesting, in fact, is

---

[8] Amira (1913) 126, 149ff; Ross (1946) 22–4.

[9] Plamenatz (1963) 9–11.   [10] Marks (1963).

[11] Tacitus *Germania* 11. Montesquieu, *De l'esprit des lois* 6.11 (p. 167 in the Garnier edn, Paris, 1961).

[12] Ryffel (1903); Stauffacher (1962); Kellenberger (1965); Carlen (1976).

[13] Bodin, *Les six livres de la république* 2.7.

[14] Rousseau, *Projet de constitution pour la Corse*, *Oeuvres*, Pléiade edn (Paris, 1967), III 906.

[15] Rousseau, 'Dédicace' to *Sur l'origine de l'inégalité*, *Oeuvres* III 111–21. Miller (1984).

[16] Rousseau, *Sur l'économie politique*, *Oeuvres* III 246.   [17] Sly (1930).

the 1647 'democraticall' constitution of Rhode Island, which has not attracted the attention it deserves.)[18]

We thus find ourselves brought back to Athens as the best case of a significant state governed by direct democracy. That form of government was introduced by Kleisthenes in 508/7 BC and abolished by the Macedonians when they conquered Athens in 322/1. We know that numerous other Greek city-states had democratic constitutions; but virtually all the evidence we have relates to Athens, so that is the only democracy of which we can give a proper description, even though it can be shown that in some important respects Athens was an anomaly, and that the Athenian type of popular rule was not the only one known to the Greeks. Aristotle in the *Politics* refers to a type of democracy where the only function of the assembly of the people is to choose the magistrates and call them to account for their conduct in office, while all political decisions are taken by the magistrates without the people having any say:[19] that, of course, is 'indirect' democracy, so we must reject as erroneous the common notion that Greek democracy was always 'direct'[20] while modern democracy is always 'indirect'. But Athens, at any rate, was a 'direct' democracy, the best known in history to date; and it is that direct democracy that will be described and discussed in the pages that follow.

---

[18] Ball, Farr and Hanson (1989) 72–3.
[19] Arist. *Pol.* 1318b21–2, 28ff, 1274a15–18, 1281b32–4. Hansen (1989c) 96–7.
[20] E.g. Meier (1990) 85, 165, 218.

2

Evidence

As in every historical inquiry, a first question in this book must be how much we know about our subject – the famous 'direct democracy' that is supposed to have been introduced at Athens by the aristocrat Kleisthenes some 2500 years ago;[1] how we know it; and, no less important, how much we do not know. Rather than give an indigestible list of 'sources', an attempt will be made here to furnish a more critical and explanatory account of the state of the evidence for Athenian democracy and to discuss some of the more important problems of its interpretation, especially its chronological distribution, which is the main reason why this book deals with Athenian democracy in the age of Demosthenes and not in the age of Perikles.

But, first, the extent and variety of the sources at our disposal, and at the same time their limitations, may be illustrated by a set of examples. These consist of seventeen small vignettes from Athenian history, in chronological order, each illuminated by a single source.

EXAMPLES

1 After Kleisthenes' introduction of democracy in 507, and perhaps as late as c.460, the Athenians constructed for themselves an assembly-place on the eminence called the Pnyx just across from the hill of the Areopagos; about 400 it was rebuilt and extended. Subsequently it was hidden under an enormous third rebuilding of the time of the emperor Hadrian (when it perhaps no longer served as an assembly-place), but in the course of excavations in the 1930s the classical foundations were rediscovered, and it proved possible to reconstruct the two earlier phases of the assembly-place of the Athenians, Pnyx I and Pnyx II.[2]

---

[1] 507 BC: Ostwald (1988) 306–7.

[2] Thompson (1982). See page 128 and maps 3-6 on pp. 3–6.

2   Ostracism, i.e. ten-year banishment imposed by a ballot in which the votes were written on *ostraka*, potsherds, was one of the Athenian democracy's most remarkable and criticized institutions. The first ostracism took place in 487, the last in about 416.[3] Some 11,000 *ostraka*, on which the citizens scratched (or had scratched for them) the name of the political leader they wished to see cast out, have been found on the slopes of the Akropolis, in the Agora, and in the cemetery of the Kerameikos.[4] No fewer than 4647 of the Kerameikos *ostraka* are inscribed with the same name, that of Kleisthenes' nephew Megakles, son of Hippokrates of the deme Alopeke (*Megakles Hippokratous Alopekethen*). He was actually ostracized twice,[5] the first time in 486,[6] but the Kerameikos *ostraka* seem to belong to his second ostracism, which probably occurred in the 470s.[7]

3   In the first years of the Peloponnesian War an unknown Athenian wrote a pamphlet in which the Athenian government of the people was described as an all-too-consistently worked-out product of a warped view of humanity and a mistaken concept of society. The *demos* is understood as 'the common people' and not 'the whole of the people', and the democracy is consequently seen as 'the government of the poor' instead of 'the government of the people'.[8] The pamphlet was falsely attributed to Xenophon and was transmitted amongst his writings; it has now become general[9] to call the author the 'Old Oligarch', because that is what he sounds like.[10]

4   Aristophanes' comedy *The Acharnians* was produced in 425. It begins with a scene in which Dikaiopolis the countryman is sitting alone in the assembly-place, complaining that the rest of the citizens are still chatting down in the Agora although the meeting ought to begin shortly after dawn. He watches the *prytaneis* (the presidents of the Assembly) come hurrying in late, pushing and shoving to sit on the front bench, while the other citizens down in the Agora are driven up on to the Pnyx by a line of policemen carrying between them a rope soaked in red paint.[11] In some of the manuscripts in which the play has come down to us there is a marginal note saying that any citizen who got red paint on his coat was liable to a fine.[12]

5   At the festival of the Dionysia in 422 (probably) a tragedy by Euripides was played, in which King Theseus appears as a champion of freedom and of government by the people. Supported by his people, he resists the demand of the tyrant of Thebes for the extradition of certain women

---

[3] Thomsen (1972). See p. 35.   [4] *M&L* 21.   [5] Lys. 14.39.
[6] Arist. *Ath.* Pol. 22.5.   [7] Lewis (1974b) 1–4.
[8] Ps. Xen. *Ath. Pol.* Frisch (1942); Treu (1967).   [9] Following Murray (1898).
[10] Gomme (1962a) 38–69.   [11] Ar. *Ach.* 1–42. See p. 150.   [12] Schol. Ar. *Ach.* 22.

from Argos who have sought asylum in Attica. King Theseus and the messenger from the tyrant of Thebes carry on for more than a hundred lines a fierce argument about constitutions, in which Theseus proclaims the freedom, equality and respect for the laws to be found in a people's government, as against the arbitrary rule of a tyrant.[13] The tragedy, called *The Suppliant Women* (Hiketides), is not regarded as one of Euripides' best, and the chance that has preserved for us this valuable testimony to the ideology of Athenian democracy in the age of Perikles is a curious one: out of an edition of the complete works of Euripides in alphabetical order there have survived by pure chance two sets of five tragedies each of whose titles begin with one of the letters *epsilon* to *eta* or *iota* to *kappa* (*Hiketides* begins with iota, as Greek does no represent *h* by a letter).[14]

6   Shortly before 411 the non-Athenian sophist Thrasymachos wrote a pamphlet about the 'ancestral constitution' of Athens, a piece of nostalgia for the alleged age when the young held their tongues and let the older and more experienced citizens do the talking.[15] The beginning of Thrasymachos' pamphlet is quoted in a Hellenistic rhetorical manual as a prize example of the eloquence of the old orators.[16]

7   Thucydides in his *History* quotes, though in his own words, the funeral speech given by Perikles in 430 at the annual state funeral of those who had died fighting for Athens. The core of the speech is an encomium of the fallen, of the forefathers, and of the *polis* of Athens and its constitution: in name it is a democracy, and in very fact it is a government by the majority, where all have equal rights before the law and individuals are respected and rewarded according to merit.[17]

8   At the end of the first book of his *History of Greece (Hellenika)* Xenophon has a description, ten pages long, of the notorious 'Trial of the Generals' in 406, when eight of the ten members of the Board of Generals were accused of having, after the victory in the naval battle at the Arginoussai islands, failed to pick up the survivors and the bodies of the fallen from the ships sunk by the enemy: they pleaded that a sudden storm had made it impossible, but the Assembly was convinced by the accusers that the generals were guilty of treason. They were sentenced to death collectively (which was actually illegal) and the six of them who were in Athens were executed. Xenophon finishes by saying that the Athenians shortly afterwards regretted their death sentence on the generals and proceeded to condemn the accusers and execute *them*.[18]

[13] Eur. *Supp.* 399–510.   [14] Snell (1935) 119–20.   [15] DK 85 B 1.
[16] Dion. Hal. *Dem.* 3.   [17] Thuc. 2.35–46. Loraux (1986). See p. 73.
[18] Xen. *Hell.* 1.7.1–35. Hansen (1975) cat. no. 66.

9   In 367 the Athenians concluded an alliance with Dionysios I, the tyrant of Syracuse. The treaty was passed by the Assembly and inscribed on a marble *stele* of which we still possess fragments.[19] The beginnings and ends of the lines are missing, but the middle is intact, and, because the inscription is written *stoichedon* as usual, i.e. like a chess-board with each letter under the one above and no blank spaces, it can be calculated that there were thirty-three letters per line.[20] Also, Athenian inscriptions were written in a formal style with invariable formulas, so that most of the Dionysios inscription can be restored with a high degree of probability. It says, *inter alia*, that the alliance is supposed to last 'for ever': as might be expected, its span of life was but brief.

10   A hundred years ago there was found near Spata in mid-Attica, in a grave of about 350 BC, a small bronze plaque measuring 11 cm by 2 cm by 3 mm thick. Three names had been incised in the bronze, but two of them had been erased again and can only be guessed at underneath the third and latest: 'Eupolemos Timodo(.ou) Erchieus'. The plaque also has a letter of the alphabet and a stamp representing an owl seen from the front.[21] Today we possess about a hundred such plaques, and we know that they were the identity tickets of the Athenian jurors: the owl is the same as occurs on the 3-obol coins,[22] and 3 obols precisely was the pay for a day's jury service.

11   The first seventeen of the sixty-one speeches that have come down to us under the name of Demosthenes purport to be published versions of speeches he delivered in the Assembly: nowadays fourteen of them are regarded as genuine speeches by the great orator.[23] They were spoken in the years 354–341, and most of them were directed against the arch-enemy of Athens in those years, Philip II of Macedon.[24] Demosthenes himself had his political speeches published, perhaps out of pique because the Athenians hardly ever took the advice he gave them. It is remarkable that Demosthenes gave up publishing his Assembly speeches in 341, just when that body began at last to pass the decrees he proposed and recognize him as the leading statesman in the struggle against Macedon.[25] The decrees he persuaded the Athenians to pass disappeared long ago and are only known from sporadic references in other sources, but his political speeches we can still read. It was by the brilliance of his rhetoric that the speaker Demosthenes succeeded in creating the myth of the statesman Demosthenes, which had its effect right down to the present century,[26] in which another statesman, Georges Clemenceau, used his

[19] *IG* II² 105 = Harding (1985) no. 52.   [20] Woodhead (1981) 29–34.

[21] Kroll (1972) 122–3 no. 16.   [22] Kroll (1972) 51–3.

[23] McCabe (1981). (Authenticity of 5, 8, 10 and 13 not beyond doubt.)

[24] Montgomery (1983) 39–65.   [25] Hansen (1989a) 296 n. 30.   [26] Drerup (1923).

otium to write a starry-eyed biography of Demosthenes as the champion of the democracy against the autocrat Philip.[27]

12 The *Laws* is the *magnum opus* of Plato's old age, and perhaps was not quite finished when he died, in 347. It is a dialogue in which an Athenian, a Spartan and a Cretan discuss not the best constitution but the best achievable constitution. This utopia is called Magnesia.[28] It is a city-state with 5040 (factorial 7) adult male citizens.[29] Its constitution and administration are described with an old man's minuteness; and many of the details are copied from contemporary Athens.[30]

13 In the excavations of the Agora there turned up the marble base of the statue erected by the Athenians in the 330s to the goddess Demo-kratia;[31] and later was found what is probably the torso of the statue itself.[32] From the same period, in the marble fragments of the accounts of the Treasurers of Athena, there are references to payments by generals in connection with offerings brought to that goddess.[33]

14 In 336 Ktesiphon, a henchman of Demosthenes, made the famous proposal for his chief to be honoured with a gold crown for his achievements in improving the city's defences after the defeat by Philip in 338. Aischines at once accused Ktesiphon of having proposed an unconstitutional decree, for Demosthenes had been a magistrate when the proposal was made and honours to a magistrate in office were forbidden by law. The case took a long time to come on, and was only heard by the jury in 330.[34] Demosthenes personally undertook the defence of his henchman, and for once we possess both speeches, for the prosecution and for the defence.[35] From a legal point of view Aischines was in the right,[36] but the trial developed into a battle over past history between the pro-Macedonian Aischines and the anti-Macedonian Demosthenes; and, though the latter had really lost Athens the war against Macedon, he nevertheless won the case and got more than four-fifths of the votes.[37]

15 Aristotle wrote a theoretical treatise on politics (the *Politics*) in eight books, and, as the empirical basis for the theory, he and his pupils wrote detailed descriptions of the actual systems of no fewer than 158 states,[38] of which the best-known were Athens[39] and Sparta.[40] The 158 descriptions were all subsequently lost, and were only known to exist from

[27] Clemenceau (1924).   [28] Pl. *Lg.* 848D.   [29] Pl. *Lg.* 737E.

[30] Chase (1933).   [31] Raubitschek (1962).   [32] Palagia (1982).

[33] *IG* II[2] 1496.131–2, 140–1.   [34] Hansen (1974) cat. no. 30; (1989a) 273 n. 11.

[35] Aeschin. 3; Dem. 18.   [36] Gwatkin (1957).

[37] Plut. *Mor.* 840C–D; *P. Oxy.* 1800 (*Lives of Orators*).

[38] Arist. *Eth. Nic.* 1181b17; Diog. Laert. 5.27; Arist. frr. xliv and 472–603.

[39] Arist. *Ath. Pol.*   [40] Arist. frr. 532–45.

scattered references; but in the 1880s in the sands of Egypt there were found four little papyrus rolls, on the reverses of which it was possible to read an almost complete surviving text of the Aristotelian treatise we call the *Constitution of Athens*.[41]

16   Sitting at home in his native Boiotia in the time of the emperor Trajan, the moral philosopher Plutarch wrote a long series of *Parallel Lives* of Greek and Roman statesmen, mostly in pairs, one Greek and one Roman. One of these pairs consists of Cato the Younger and the fourth-century Greek *rhetor* and general Phokion. According to Plutarch, Phokion was often in opposition to the popular will and had a poor view of the political judgement of the people, so when, one day, they spontaneously applauded a proposal of his he turned anxiously to his neighbour and asked whether he had said something silly.[42]

17   The Attic orators were still much read in Roman times, but readers often found it hard to understand the institutions and historical events, knowledge of which the orators took for granted in their audiences. So dictionaries and explanatory works came to be written. In the second century AD[43] a certain Harpokration wrote the first work of the kind know to us: it contains nearly 400 explanations, in alphabetical order, of difficult words and expressions in the ten Attic orators.

These seventeen little sketches show not only how rich our sources are but also how fortuitous they are and how many lacunae there are in our knowledge. If we had the corpus of laws that the Athenians inscribed on stone in 403/2[44] and all the more than 1000 speeches that were to be read in the Library of Alexandria in the Hellenistic period, we should be able to reconstruct the Assembly and the People's Court with much greater exactitude: in these cases we lack sources that existed but are lost. If we had census figures about the numbers of citizens and metics and slaves, we should have a much surer knowledge of the population of Athens; but in this case we lack sources because they never existed.

DIVISIONS OF THE EVIDENCE

According to content

The sources of evidence for Athenian democracy can be grouped in several ways, each with its particular usefulness. Let us consider first a division into what we may call 'survivals' of the democracy and 'accounts'

---

[41] Rhodes (1981a) 3.   [42] Plut. *Phocion* 8.5.
[43] Dated by *P. Ryl.* 532.   [44] See p. 164.

of the democracy. Survivals include not only archaeological remains and
inscriptions: they also include some literary sources, such as the speeches
of Demosthenes. The Athenian alliance with Dionysios and the *First
Philippic* are both 'survivals' from this point of view, for they were both
part of the domocratic process and without them history itself might have
taken a different turn. (Though it must be borne in mind that our
published texts are revised versions of the actual speeches, and can only
count as documentary evidence in so far as they do report what was
actually said: historians usually suppose that, but it cannot be proved.[45])
In contrast to that sort of documentary evidence must be put the accounts
of Athenian democracy in, for example, Aristotle and Plutarch: the former
is testimony to contemporary understanding of the democracy, the latter
to how it was seen in later times, but they are both 'accounts', not
'survivals'.

According to transmission

Another possible grouping of the evidence is by kinds of transmission:
in this arrangement we contrast the direct transmission of inscriptions
and other material survivals with the indirect transmission of the great
bulk of the literary sources. The latter are in large part known only from
manuscripts written in Byzantium from the ninth to the fifteenth century,
brought to Italy by scholars, lay and clerical, when Greek studies were
revived in the West in the fourteenth and fifteenth centuries, and now
preserved in the great European libraries.[46] Just a few texts survive in
fragments of papyrus from Egypt, preserved in the dry conditions of the
desert sands:[47] the most significant for us are the Aristotelian *Constitution
of Athens*, already referred to, and some of the speeches of the statesman
Hypereides – for, although forty of his speeches survived in a Byzantine
manuscript, it was destroyed by fire when the Turks captured Budapest
in 1526, and it had never been printed.[48] After that, Hypereides was
nothing but a name, until the papyrus discoveries in the last century,
when six speeches turned up, though five of them only in fragments.

Papyrus fragments have also been found of texts of which manuscripts
actually survive. Such fragments do not, of course, enlarge our source
material quantitatively, but they provide important corroboration; for a
comparison between the papyrus texts (which are always much the older
and nearer to the originals) and the manuscripts shows in most cases that
very few errors have crept in despite all the numerous recopyings that
must lie between them.[49] We can as a general rule assume, therefore,

---

[45] Adams (1912); Dorjahn (1935); Lavency (1964).
[46] Reynolds and Wilson (1974) 130–7.   [47] Pack (1965).
[48] Colin (1946) 52.   [49] Kenyon (1919) 3–4.

that our manuscripts are reasonably faithful reproductions of the original texts as they were first composed between 1000 and 1500 years earlier.

Putting together the two divisions, by content and by transmission, that we have so far considered, we can see that, as a general rule, the documents are directly transmitted and the accounts are indirectly transmitted. The one exception is the speeches, which partake of both kinds: they are documents, on a par with the inscriptions, but so far as transmission goes they are known only from the medieval manuscripts.

According to genre

In this grouping the inscriptions stand on one side and all the literary sources on the other, the latter being subdivided into speeches (but that includes pamphlets), history, philosophy and drama; other kinds of literature play no significant part from our point of view.

Inscriptions Publication was a prerequisite for a democracy, so the Athenians had to display everything they could in public. The style of publication had to correspond to the life-style of the Athenians. The ancient Greeks did not live much indoors: women certainly had to stay indoors most of the time, but male citizens spent the time when they were not working in agoras and porticos and palaestras. The Athenians did have a state archive in the Metroön in the Agora, where a copy of every public document, written on papyrus, was available to any citizen on request,[50] but what needed to be brought to the attention of the public had to be displayed in public places. As for the material, in a country where limestone and marble were everywhere available, whereas wood had since the Bronze Age been a rarity,[51] the natural form of publication was the inscribed marble slab (*stele*).

What sort of materials, then, did the Athenians feel the need to publish? Every year the Assembly passed probably more than 400 decrees.[52] In the fourth century the Board of Legislators, the *nomothetai*, had several times a year to deal with proposals to alter or expand the revised law-code of 403/2.[53] At the end of every year, boards of magistrates by the score had to answer for their administration and the funds in their control: the Treasurers of Athena (*tamiai*) for the temple treasury on the Akropolis, the Auctions Board (*poletai*) for the moneys obtained by public auctions, the Superintendents of the Dockyards (*epimeletai ton neorion*) for the naval vessels and all their gear, and so forth.[54] So magistrates had

---

[50] Harp, s.v. *Metroön*. Wycherley (1957) 150–60; Thomas (1989) 68–83.
[51] Larfeld (1898–1907) I 180–1.   [52] See p. 156.
[53] See p. 166.   [54] See p. 222–4.

to maintain inventories and accounts: the documents were doubtless first written on papyrus or on whitened boards, but many were also inscribed on stone. Also a good number of marble *stelai* are inscribed with lists of names – the list of debtors to the state that was kept on the Akropolis,[55] the lists of the administrative committee of the council (the *prytaneis*) and lists, even, of all the councillors of the year, kept in front of the Council house (the *bouleuterion*),[56] and the names of all citizens who had died in battle, inscribed year by year and kept (somewhere) in the Kerameikos cemetery.[57]

Over 20,000 inscriptions have been found just in Attica, most of them fragmentary, and several thousand of them are public documents from the golden age of democracy. For the fourth century alone we have some 500 decrees,[58] ten laws,[59] over 400 accounts and inventories,[60] and fifty-odd inscriptions with the names of *prytaneis* and other councillors. Documents on bronze are much rarer.[61] At the end of the year the little plaques of bronze were prepared for next year's jurymen,[62] and large bronze *stelai* were used to list the names of those liable for military service,[63] one for each year-class. As might be imagined, the valuable bronze *stelai* have long since vanished, but about a hundred of the jurymen's plaques have been found.[64]

Speeches   Athenian democracy was an assembly democracy; moreover, in the People's Court no less than in the Assembly, the numbers ensured that debates must necessarily consist of a series of speeches made by politically active citizens to an audience. Hence, political power was based on eloquence, and the demand for eloquence called into being an entirely new genre of prose, namely rhetoric.[65] Rhetoric was born in the middle of the fifth century in Syracuse and Athens, the two pillars of democracy in West and East, and all through the rest of antiquity the close connection between politics and rhetoric remained.[66] The three species of the genus were all political: the speech of advice, given before the Assembly or the Council; the forensic speech, before the People's Court; and the speech for special occasions, such as Perikles' funeral speech.[67] Soon it was well-nigh universal for political leaders to take lessons in rhetoric, often from travelling 'sophists',[68] and from about 420 BC some political figures

---

[55] Dem. 25.4, 70; 58.19, 48. *Hesperia* 5 (1936) 400 80–1. Harp. s.v. *pseudengraphe*.

[56] *SEG* 28 52.25–6.   [57] *Agora* XVII 1–25.   [58] See p. 156.

[59] Hansen (1987a) 174 n. 623.   [60] Most in *IG* II² 1370–1653.

[61] Larfeld (1898–1907) I 183–4.   [62] See p. 182.   [63] Arist. *Ath. Pol.* 53.4.

[64] Kroll (1972) cat. nos 1–19, 72–113; (1984) 1, 4–5.   [65] Kennedy (1963).

[66] Pl. *Grg.* 452E–453A; *Phdr.* 261A–C; Arist. *Rhet.* 1356a25–7; *Rhet. ad Alex.* 1421b7–11.

[67] Arist. *Rhet.* 1358b8–1359a5.

[68] Ar. *Nub.* 1105–11; Pl. *Prt.* 314E–316A; Isoc. 13.9.

started to publish their speeches.[69] The purpose may have been to keep the political pot boiling by fixing an oral contribution in written form; but, even when the political issues and the public trials had long lost their contemporaneity, the old speeches went on being read as literature and as school examples of eloquence. Like the architectural Seven Wonders of the World, there grew up a Top Ten list of the masters of oratory, who were all either Athenian citizens (Antiphon, Andokides, Isokrates, Demosthenes, Aischines, Lykourgos and Hypereides) or Athenian metics (Lysias, Isaios and Deinarchos).[70]

A total of about 150 speeches of those masters have come down to us, the earliest written in 419/18,[71] the latest in 322, just before the abolition of democracy.[72] Of them, seventeen are speeches to the people, almost all by Demosthenes; and more than a hundred are forensic speeches by all ten orators.[73] The majority were written for clients for a fee;[74] only a few were spoken by the orators themselves, and those usually in 'political' trials.[75] Especially important for us are the surviving prosecution speeches in the public prosecutions for having proposed unconstitutional decrees or undesirable laws,[76] for in them there are long passages about the structure and working of democratic institutions and well-formulated defences of the ideals of popular government. Finally, in addition to the 150 surviving speeches we have references to and titles of several hundred lost ones preserved by the lexicographers.[77]

Pamphlets A mere generation after the birth of rhetoric the Greeks invented another prose form, the political pamphlet: it was an extension of the political speeches, a speech that had never actually been delivered in a political gathering but was simply circulated in written copies to be read in private circles. Besides the fifth-century pamphlet of the Old Oligarch and the pamphlet of Thrasymachos, already referred to, there survive from the fourth century several long pamphlets from the hand of Isokrates (436–338). He seldom appeared in the Assembly, but preferred to write essays in which he gave Athens the benefit of his advice about political and constitutional matters: for the study of Athenian democracy the most important are the *Areopagitikos* (from about 357),[78] *On the Peace* (355) and the *Panathenaikos* (338). All these were works of his old age, in which he criticized his times and pleaded for a return to

---

[69] Pl. *Phdr*, 257D; Plut. *Mor.* 832D; *Per.* 8.7.   [70] Kennedy (1963) 125–6.
[71] Ant. 6.   Meritt (1928) 121–2; Dover (1950) 44.
[72] Dem. 56.   Isager and Hansen (1975) 208–9; Hansen (1981d) 173–5.
[73] Ober (1989) 341–9.   [74] Lavency (1964) 26–31.   [75] See p. 20.
[76] Dem. 20, 22, 23, 24; Aeschin. 3; Hyp. 4.   [77] Baiter and Sauppe II (1850).
[78] Wallace (1986).

the 'democracy of the forefathers', i.e. the constitution Athens was supposed to have had in the time of Solon.

Historical works Historiography began as a prose genre in Greece a generation earlier than rhetoric, in the first half of the fifth century, but when Herodotos is called the 'Father of History' that is very largely true. It is he who gives a long description of what is from our point of view the beginning of the tale, the civil strife that led to the introduction of democracy by Kleisthenes;[79] and in Book 3 he records (believing it to be authentic) the alleged debate of the Persian nobles in 522 BC about the three types of constitution – monarchy, oligarchy and the rule of the people – which is the earliest substantial piece of political theory we have in Greek prose.[80] The historians were mainly interested in political and military history, and social history, by and large, only caught their interest when they were describing foreign peoples; but, since war and peace were decided in Athens by the Assembly, there was every opportunity to bring in the process of decision-making in the Assembly or the course of a political trial in the People's Court against an allegedly corrupt political leader or an unlucky general. Such passages in the historians often took the form of invented Assembly speeches, which are the historians' counterparts to the real speeches of the orators.[81] For that reason there is plenty of useful material about the institutions of the democracy in Herodotos, Thucydides and Xenophon. The other historians who recorded Greek history down to the end of the fourth century are all lost, but in the case of the most important of them – Theopompos, Ephoros, Anaximenes of Lampsakos and Hieronymos of Kardia – their works formed the principal sources of the *World History* of Diodoros from Sicily, written in the time of the emperor Augustus, and Books 16–20 of that work have fortunately come down to us complete.

There were also writers who wrote specialist accounts of the history of Athens and Attica, known as *Atthides*.[82] They are known only in scanty fragments, but many of the pieces we do possess have a particular importance, because the Atthidographers often described constitutional features that lay outside the sphere of interest of the major historians. The most prominent Atthidographers were Androtion, who, after an active life in politics, wrote an *Atthis* in eight books in about 340–330, and Philochoros, who wrote the next substantial *Atthis* in the 260s, in no less than seventeen books.[83]

Finally, we must, as is traditionally done, count Plutarch (c. AD

---

[79] Hdt. 5.69ff, 6.131.   [80] Hdt. 3.80–3.   [81] Fornara (1983) 142–68.
[82] Pearson (1942); Jacoby (1949).
[83] *FGrHist.* 324 (Androtion), 328 (Philochoros).

50–125) amongst the historians, although his *Parallel Lives* are really essays in moral philosophy rather than history in the usual sense. The nine Athenian statesmen of whom he wrote biographies are Solon, Themistokles, Aristeides, Kimon, Perikles, Nikias, Alkibiades, Demosthenes and Phokion. Plutarch was very learned, and in contrast to the historians he often cited and discussed his sources; his *Lives* are therefore an important source for us, because they are often based on writings lost to us. His account is, however, strongly anecdotal, and, what is more, coloured by his own attitudes, which tell us more about the Roman Empire in the time of Trajan than about the Athenian constitution 500 years earlier: historians therefore ought to use him very critically.[84]

Philosophy The oldest of the prose genres was actually philosophy; but only in the fifth century did the philosophers start to consider the place of mankind in the universe. Men are social beings, they said; so of all the philosophical disciplines the study of the *polis* was the most important. (The first reflections on constitutions in the philosophers are to be found amongst the fragments of Demokritos – not earlier than, say, 430.[85]) That is why both Plato and Aristotle set as king-pin of their writings about morality their thoughts about the state and society, and, consequently, about the ideal society.[86] In his *Republic* Plato discusses the best imaginable city-state, in the *Laws* the best achievable one.[87] In the *Politics* Aristotle gives, in Book 1, what we should nowadays call a sociological analysis of the city-state, in Book 2 a historical survey of analyses of it, and in Books 3–6 an analysis in terms of political science; the whole is a background for the (unfinished) examination of how a city-state *ought* to be ordered (Books 7–8).

The problems of political thought are usually, in these authors, handled in a general way *via* the three main types of constitution – the rule of the one, the rule of the few and the rule of the many – each of which is found in both a positive and a negative variant. This sixfold model can be found already fully developed in Plato's *Statesman*.[88] It reappears in Book 3 of Aristotle's *Politics*,[89] and in our day Aristotle has had the credit for what in fact he took over from his old teacher. In Book 8 of Plato's *Republic* there is a detailed, but schematic, account of the development – or rather degeneration – of constitutions, in which democracy is painted as the worst but one of all constitutional types: worse than oligarchy but at least better than tyranny, which consequently is the one that replaces democracy.[90] By the time we get to the *Statesman*, democracy's stock has

---

[84] Gomme (1945) 59–60; Andrewes (1978) 1–2; Pelling (1980).
[85] Farrar (1988) 192–264.   [86] Pl. *Euthydemus* 291C–D; Arist. *Eth. Nic.* 1181b12–23.
[87] Pl. *Lg.* 739Bff; 807B.   [88] Pl. *Pol.* 291C–292A.
[89] Arist. *Pol.* 1279a22–b10.   [90] Pl. *Resp.* 555B–565D.

gone up a bit: it is now better than both oligarchy and tyranny, but it remains inferior to monarchy and aristocracy.[91] In the *Laws* the ideal has now become a mixed constitution with elements of monarchy and democracy[92] (and it is here that so many details reflect the actual institutions of Athens). In Aristotle's *Politics*, Books 4–6, democratic constitutions are divided into four variants, declining from the ancient moderate peasant democracy (type I) to the radical city democracy of his own day (type IV).[93]

Occasionally there can be found a more specific and critical evaluation of the particular democracy of Athens. Thus, Plato in the *Gorgias* has Sokrates the philosopher argue with the rhetoricians Gorgias, Polos and Kallikles, and demonstrate that in an assembly democracy such as Athens the rhetorical skill of the demagogue will always prevail over the expert knowledge of the statesman.[94] Even more important for us is the famous speech placed by Plato in the mouth of Sokrates, the *Apologia*, which for more than 2000 years has been read as a charge-sheet against Athenian democracy and its vaunted freedom of speech.[95] Lastly, in Book 2 of Aristotle's *Politics* there is a brief sketch of the historical development of the Athenian constitution, in which the moderate, mixed democracy such as Solon is supposed to have introduced in 594 is classified as the best variety, whereas that of Aristotle's own day has turned into an out-and-out radical democracy of the lowest variety.[96]

Drama European drama goes back to the festivals of Dionysos at Athens, at which, every year, tragedies and comedies were performed.[97] The plots of tragedies are usually mythological, but the ancient heroes who are their characters speak a language that reflects contemporary society;[98] so it is not surprising that we can find in all three of the great tragedians scenes in which Athenian democracy, in mythical guise, is praised by the characters. In the *Suppliant Women* (*Hiketides*) of Aischylos we have the earliest preserved picture of an assembly, at Argos (for which read 'Athens'): a majority of the people decide by a show of hands to give asylum to the daughters of Danaos (for which read 'protect those who have sought refuge in the free city of Athens'),[99] and the same scenario is found, as we have seen, in the tragedy of the same name by Euripides.[100] As for Sophokles, some historians believe that the political reson-

[91] Pl. *Pol.* 302E–303B.   [92] Pl. *Lg.* 693D–E, 756E. Aalders (1968) 38–49.

[93] Arist. *Pol.* 1291b30–1292a38 [four types, not five: see Papageorgiou (1990)], 1292b22–1293a10, 1298a10–34, 1318b6–1319b32.

[94] Pl. *Grg.* 452D–E, 455B–456A.   [95] Brickhouse and Smith (1989); Stone (1988).

[96] Arist. *Pol.* 1273b35–1274a21.   [97] Pickard-Cambridge (1968).

[98] Euben (1986); Ober and Strauss (1990).   [99] Aesch. *Supp.* 600–24.

[100] See pp. 5–6.

ance of his tragedies reflects his worries about the tyrannical aspects of Perikles' behaviour.[101]

In the tragedies it is always the ideals of democracy that are discussed; in the comedies it is often its working and institutions.[102] In fact, in the first century of comedy (down to c.390) the satirical handling of contemporary themes provides most of the jokes, and the democratic leaders are flayed alive, sometimes by name and sometimes under obvious disguises such as 'the tanner', for Kleon in the *Knights* (424). And in Aristophanes' *Acharnians* (425), *Wasps* (422) and *Ekklesiazousai* (?392)[103] are to be found the most amusing caricatures of the Assembly and the courts, and of the part played in them by the average Athenian.

Lexicography In the Hellenistic age there began a whole new epoch of European culture: it was the beginning of erudition and libraries and catalogues and literary research and commentaries on the Best Authors, and Alexandria, not Athens, was the home of erudition.[104] It was there that Kallimachos in the third century compiled the authorized edition of Demosthenes, which, besides authentic speeches, also contained a set of other original speeches from the fourth century that we now know not to have been by Demosthenes.[105] Book-collecting also brought with it deliberate literary forgeries, of which a word more will be said below. Anything but worthless, on the other hand, was the commentary on Demosthenes produced in the fifth century BC by Didymos (who was called *Bibliolathes*, the 'book-forgetter', because he could not remember his own books, they were so many).[106] A big papyrus fragment of Didymos' commentary on the *Fourth Philippic* has turned up, and it contains valuable insights into the historical background.[107]

In Hellenistic, Roman and Byzantine times learned commentaries were published as scholia or lexica. Scholia are point-by-point commentaries written in the margin (though in earlier times published separately); lexica are alphabetically arranged explications of words and names in the classical literature. The scholia to, especially, Aristophanes' comedies and the speeches of Demosthenes are treasure houses of enlightenment about Athenian institutions, on just the sorts of things that later generations needed to have explained in order to understand them. Of lexica the most significant are Harpokration's lexicon to the ten Attic orators, from the second century AD; that of the Byzantine patriarch Photios, from the ninth century; and the vast *Suda* (also Byzantine), from the tenth.

---

[101] Ehrenberg (1954).   [102] Henderson (1990).
[103] Ar. *Ach.* 1–173; *Vesp.* 760–1007; *Eccl.* 1–477.
[104] Pfeiffer (1968); Reynolds and Wilson (1974) 5–15.
[105] Goldstein (1968) 17–20; McCabe (1981).   [106] Ath. 139C.
[107] *P. Berol.* 9780, new Teubner edn 1983.

Apocryphal sources   Ancient historians always have to face the problem
of dubious sources. For the study of Athenian democracy in the age of
Demosthenes they are, fortunately, not a major issue; but the reader will
not expect them to be passed over in silence. The cases we are concerned
with are all apocrypha from antiquity itself: there are no relevant modern
falsifications. Consequently, the sources in question are not necessarily
bad evidence and to be rejected: they are simply not what they purport
to be, but correctly understood they may still be very valuable.

The only relevant actual forgeries are some alleged letters by well-
know people.[108] We possess letters purporting to be by Aischines,
Demosthenes and Isokrates, and some may be genuine, but detailed
stylistic analysis has shown that all the supposedly Aischinean ones[109]
and at least two of those attributed to Demosthenes[110] were written in
the Hellenistic age, probably by people in the business of supplying
collectors and librarians with celebrity letters.

There was a fashion in Hellenistic and later times for writing rhetorical
exercises in the style of a well-know orator, such as Lysias, and some
exercises of that kind were later taken for genuine speeches and included
in ancient editions of Lysias,[111] Andokides,[112] and so forth. In this case
also it is stylistic analysis that enables us to distinguish the exercises from
the real speeches; the former are apocryphal so far as the history of
Athens goes, although they are obviously not forgeries in the modern
sense.

Speeches in the Assembly and in the courts were often interspersed
with the reading of documents, such as laws and decrees, by the clerk,
and in a number of cases the medieval manuscripts retain the documents,
still in place in the midst of the rhetorical argument. Many of them are
demonstrably genuine[113] and have, for example, been confirmed by
inscriptional evidence.[114] Genuine are, certainly, the laws about the
legislative process quoted by Demosthenes in the speech against Timokrates.[115] But others are equally plainly false, like all the alleged decrees
in Demosthenes' speech *On the Crown* (where all the names of archons
are inventions);[116] the real documents were lost early on, but the speech
was so famous that people reconstructed them later as best they could –
which was not well enough to conceal from us that the alleged decrees
were written at the end of the second century BC. In a number of cases,
however, historians remain uncertain whether such inserted documents
are genuine or not – for example, the oath to be sworn by the jurors in

---

[108] Speyer (1971) 133, 137.   [109] Blass (1898) iii.2 185–6.   [110] Goldstein (1968).
[111] E.g. Lys. 11, 15. Dover (1968) 7, 11.   [112] Andoc. 4. Feraboli (1972).
[113] Drerup (1898).   [114] E.g. Dem. 43.57 and *M&L* 86 = Fornara (1977) no. 15B.
[115] Dem. 24.20–3, 33.   [116] Schläpfer (1939).

the People's Court, cited *in extenso* in the speech against Timokrates.[117]

In political pamphleteering literature from the end of the fifth century onwards, the writers often summoned up the spirit of 'ancestral democracy' to preside over their own models; and, because of the Athenians' lack of historical knowledge and perspective, there were very broad limits to what could be got away with by attributing things to the ancestors: an example would be Isokrates' picture of 'original democracy' from Theseus to Solon.[118] In that case we still possess the pamphlet, the *Panathenaikos* of 338, but in other cases the pamphlet is lost but its information was taken as good coin at the time and thus got inserted into the historical tradition as fact. The best-known example in relation to Athenian democracy is the 'constitution of Drakon' in chapter 4 of Aristotle's *Constitution of Athens*, where we are treated to such things as a Council of 401 whose members are selected by lot and are punished with a fine varying according to status if they do not turn up to meetings.[119] That Drakon's constitution is a chimera is evident not merely from the historical development of Athens, in terms of which it is an anachronism, but also on formal grounds: chapter 5 of the *Constitution of Athens* fits neatly on to the end of chapter 3, and in the summary of constitutions in chapter 41 the Drakonian constitution is an equally obvious insertion.[120] It must derive from a lost political pamphlet, perhaps from the time of the constitutional battles at the end of the fifth century.[121] Unfortunately, we cannot tell for certain when the insertion was made: maybe even in the very latest phase of composition of the *Constitution of Athens*.[122] As evidence for Athens in the archaic age it is, consequently, worthless, but it is of the highest value for understanding the democracy of the classical age; for better than most sources it shows the eagerness of the Athenians to anchor their institutions in the past, and it also shows which institutions were especially fought over during the crisis that led up to the 'new democracy' in 403/2.

CHRONOLOGICAL DISTRIBUTION OF THE EVIDENCE

It is from all the sources outlined above that we derive our knowledge both of the institutions of Athenian democracy and of its ideals; but the evidence for those two aspects of the democracy is very unevenly spread, both in genres and, still more importantly, in time.

---

[117] Dem. 24.149–50. Drerup (1898) 256–64; Lipsius (1905–15) 151–2.

[118] Isoc. 12.128–48.   [119] Arist. *Ath. Pol.* 4.3.   [120] Keaney (1969) 415–17.

[121] Hignett (1952) 5; Rhodes (1981a) 87, *pace* Fuks (1953) 84–101; Ruschenbusch (1958) 421–2.

[122] Von Fritz (1954).

Sources for the institutions of the democracy

The sources for the institutions of the democracy are mainly documentary,
i.e. partly inscriptions and partly speeches; of the other literary sources,
the only ones that shed much light on the institutions are the Aristotelian
Constitution of Athens, certain scenes in Aristophanes, and the scanty
fragments of the Atthidographers. And as soon as we concentrate on the
documents it becomes clear that they are unevenly spread chronologically,
their centre of gravity lying in the second half of the fourth century,
particularly the years 355–322.

Not a single speech survives from the period of the growth of Athenian
imperial power from the Persian Wars to the Peloponnesian War; and
that is not because we have lost them, but simply because nobody thought
of writing down and circulating his speeches until after the time of
Perikles. The earliest surviving speeches are Antiphon's law-court
speeches in homicide cases from about 420–411;[123] only two other complete speeches[124] go back before the restoration of democracy in 403.
From 400 to 380 there are some pearls of great price for constitutional
history in the speeches of Lysias and the essays of Isokrates, and then
there is another lacuna from 380 to 355, filled only by Isaios' inheritance-
law speeches. But then, suddenly, from 355 on we have a flood of
speeches, by Isokrates, Demosthenes, Aischines, Lykourgos, Hypereides
and Deinarchos, many of them dealing with the institutions of the
democracy because they were spoken in political prosecutions.

The inscriptions are more evenly distributed over the classical period,
but even in their case there is a distinct overbalance towards the fourth
century. Once again it is not the fortuitousness of survival that is playing
us tricks but the lateness of the transition from oral tradition to the
written document. As late as 411 the Athenians were in doubt whether
the constitutional laws of Kleisthenes existed anywhere in written form.[125]
A few years later a state archive was first established, perhaps in 409[126]
and doubtless in connection with the intended major revision of the laws
of Athens; six years later the revised code was inscribed on stone.[127]

The skewed distribution between the fifth and fourth centuries applies
to all types of inscriptions, and can be demonstrated by a brief survey
of the surviving laws and decrees. From the fifth century we have
fragments of 250 decrees that directly or indirectly cast light on the
democracy; but many of them concern the tribute from the allied cities,

---

[123] Dover (1950).   [124] Lys. 20; Andoc. 2.
[125] Arist. *Ath. Pol.* 29.3. Hansen (1989c) 85–6.
[126] Boegehold (1972); Thomas (1989) 39–40.   [127] Andoc. 1.83–5. See p. 164.

and so tell us more about the administration of the Delian League than about the democratic institutions of Athens.[128] From the fourth century, on the other hand, we have fragments of over 500 laws and decrees, and, what is more, the preambles to the decrees have become more detailed and are composed in a more uniform style, making it possible to restore the stages in the process of political decision-making with much greater certainty.[129]

One result of the uneven distribution is that the only democratic institution of the fifth century of which we have detailed knowledge is ostracism. Some 11,000 *ostraka* are preserved;[130] by pure chance, in two fragments of the Atthidographers (plus one source paraphrased by Plutarch)[131] we have descriptions of the procedure; and the political importance of ostracism ensured that it was mentioned more often by the historians than other institutions.[132] Apart from that, when we seek light on the democracy of Perikles' time we discover that even the Assembly, the Council and the courts remain in twilight owing to lack of evidence. Traces of the architectural framework of the institutions survive, but only the scantiest of traces of the institutions themselves. It is quite otherwise with the democracy of the fourth century, where a far greater number of inscriptions and all the speeches can be put alongside Aristotle's detailed descriptions of the institutions of his day to furnish an integrated picture of how the democracy worked in the time of Demosthenes.

Ancient historians have always preferred to focus on the age of Perikles, seeing it as the period of the real greatness of Athens in art and literature as well as politics; that philosophy and rhetoric reached their apogee in the fourth century counts for less. That has given especially to English and American accounts of the Athenian democracy a particular shape, namely a historical (diachronic) description of developments down to Ephialtes in 462, crowned by a systematic (synchronic) description of the democracy in the Periklean age, followed once again by a historical narrative of the oligarchical revolutions of 411 and 404, with a tailpiece in which the reader is given to understand that the democracy was restored in 403 and went on to 322.[133] And in the systematic part, on the institutions of the Periklean age, fourth-century sources are constantly called on, for want of better, and extrapolated back to the Athens of the fifth century. The method rests on two presuppositions that are seldom discussed: that in 403 the Periklean democracy was reintroduced with

---

[128] Schuller (1984) 87–101. [129] Henry (1977); Rhodes (1972) 64–81.

[130] *M&L* 21. Thomsen (1972) 68–70.

[131] Androt. fr. 6; Arist. *Ath. Pol.* 22; Philoch. fr. 30; Plut. *Arist.* 7.3–8.

[132] Thuc. 1.135.3, 8.73; Hdt. 8.79.1.

[133] E.g. Walker (1927); Glotz (1929) 128–262; Hignett (1952); Welwei (1983) 197–270.

very few and unimportant adjustments, and that the restored democracy maintained itself without further change until 322.

But the sources show that development and change to the Athenian constitution continued after 403, and, where chance permits a comparison of the fifth- and fourth-century democracies, it is often the differences rather than the similarities that leap to the eye. That is due not least to the fact that the democratic restoration of 403 was much more thorough-going than used to be thought:[134] in consequence, a description of Periklean democracy using, in part, fourth-century sources must be rejected as anachronistic. Equally, by stopping at 404, historians tear a great rent in a dynamic political system that in fact went on for the best part of 200 years, from the reforms of Kleisthenes in 507 to the death of Demosthenes in 322.

Instead, synchronic description of the democracy should be concentrated on the fourth century. Some attempts have been made to do this in recent years,[135] but tradition dies hard, and many people still want to bring the great days of Perikles into the description. Consequently, some historians take a different tack: they give a short diachronic description down to Ephialtes and then a synchronic one of the democratic institutions for the *whole* period 462–322.[136] The trouble with that is that a synchronic description of a period of 140 years is self-contradictory, and the result is confusion and the setting side-by-side of institutions that were really successive: for example, in the chapters about how political leaders were brought to book there turn up both ostracism and the *graphe paranomon*, although the last ostracism was in about 416 and the first attested *graphe paranomon* was in 415.[137] Further, the result of describing synchronically the democracies of the fifth and fourth centuries together is to trivialize the reforms of 403.[138]

The conclusion must be that we have to use the evidence in the following way: a synchronic description of the democracy in the age of Demosthenes, supplemented by a diachronic account of its development from the beginning till the beginning of the fourth century. Only thus can we avoid anachronistic backwards extrapolation of the sources and at the same time do justice to the 200-year-long history of Athenian democracy.

[134] See p. 000.   [135] Jones (1957); Ober (1989).
[136] Bleicken (1985); Sinclair (1988a); Stockton (1990).   [137] See p. 205.
[138] Hansen (1989d) 141–4; (1989e) 71–2.

Sources for the ideals of the democracy

The source material takes on a quite different appearance if we turn to describing Athenian democracy not as a political system but as a political ideology. Amongst the contemporary documents it is now the speeches that are much more important than the inscriptions, but we can also in this context bring into play important literary sources that do little to illumine the institutions of democracy: tragedy, philosophical dialogues, and pamphlets such as that of the Old Oligarch.

The sources are also more evenly distributed. The documents still mostly belong to the fourth century, but many literary sources belong to the earlier period: all the tragedies come from the fifth century, and so do Herodotos and Thucydides; and the pamphlet of the Old Oligarch, which is one of our major sources, happens also to be one of the oldest surviving texts in prose. Consequently, the study of the democracy in terms of political ideals can be taken back comfortably to the last three decades of the fifth century;[139] but, for the great period of the democracy before the beginning of the Peloponnesian War, the sources, even for ideology, still dry up, except for a few passages in Aischylos.[140] There is no historian before Herodotos, no orator before Antiphon, no political pamphlet before that of the Old Oligarch, no philosophy of politics before Demokritos, no surviving comedy earlier than those of Aristophanes. It is not inconceivable that a comedy from the first half of the fifth century might yet turn up, for there were such things, but in the other cases discoveries from this period are inconceivable, because the genres did not exist. The reconstructions by modern historians of the democratic ideals of the Athenians before 430 need to be taken with a pinch of salt, since they rest on the thinnest imaginable source material or even, sometimes, on none.[141]

Evaluations

As regards value-judgements, the sources for the political institutions of the democracy can be divided into three classes: neutral, in the case of descriptive sources; positive and negative, in the case of evaluative sources. For example, selection by lot is described neutrally by Aristotle in the *Constitution of Athens*, positively by Herodotos in the Debate on the Constitutions in Book 3, and negatively by the Sokrates of Xenophon's *Memorabilia*.[142] The sources for the political ideals of the Athenians are, by contrast, always evaluatory and never merely descriptive; always,

[139] Raaflaub (1989). [140] See p. 16. Raaflaub (1989) 50. [141] Hansen (1986a).
[142] Arist. *Ath. Pol.* 63–5; Hdt. 3.80.6; Xen. *Mem.* 1.2.9.

therefore, either positive or negative. There is a marked difference in value-judgements between our modern Western attitudes to democracy and that of the ancient Greeks to *demokratia*; for nowadays liberty, equality and democracy have become 'hurrah words', values that everyone rates positively – in public, at least.[143] Democracy in antiquity was the object of dispute, having its enemies as well as champions, and it was perfectly possible to assert, without causing eyebrows to be raised, that democracy was a bad form of government[144] and freedom[145] and equality[146] misconceived ideals capable of leading people astray.

Historians of antiquity often assert that the negative value-judgements predominate and that we have an astonishing lack of sources that give any praise to democracy as an ideal;[147] but that, though partly true, needs modification. It is correct that essayists such as the Old Oligarch, Xenophon and Isokrates take a poor view of democracy both as institution and as ideal, and it is also correct that the negative attitude prevails in the philosophers, such as Sokrates, Plato and Aristotle. Like their counterparts in all ages the philosophers took a particular delight in fouling their own nests: they sat in Athens and glorified Sparta to the detriment of Athens.[148] They took the natural view of philosophers that all states everywhere are badly governed,[149] but when it came to the point they preferred Spartan 'ancestral aristocracy' to Athenian democracy, though at a pinch they could at least give approval to what was supposed to be its original form, a kind of 'ancestral democracy' such as in the fourth century was often attributed to the lawgiver Solon.[150]

But over against the philosophers there stand other authors, with a quite different attitude. In the tragedies of Aischylos and Euripides the ideals of democracy are praised by the mythical kings of Athens; and weighty defence of popular sovereignty is expressed in the historians: wholeheartedly by Herodotos in the Debate on the Constitutions; less so by Thucydides, who personally took a critical view of his city's form of government[151] but has nevertheless introduced into his work speeches in which the democrats are allowed to say their piece – Perikles' funeral speech of 430[152] and that of Athenagoras at Syracuse in 415.[153] Our most important sources for the democratic ideal, however, are the surviving Assembly and court speeches, which contain an all-too-often-neglected treasury of passages praising 'rule of the people' as against 'rule of the one' and 'rule of the few'; and one category of speeches, the funeral

[143] Holden (1974) 2.   [144] Pl. *Pol.* 303A; Arist. *Pol.* 1279b4–10.
[145] Pl. *Resp.* 557B–558C; *Lg.* 698A–B; Theophr. *Char.* 28.6.
[146] Pl. *Resp.* 558C; Arist. *Pol.* 1301a28–35; Isoc. 7.20–1.
[147] Jones (1957) 41; Finley (1962) 9.   [148] Rawson (1969) 61–80.
[149] Pl. *Ep.* 7 326A; Arist. *Pol.* 1260b34–5.   [150] See p. 151.
[151] Hornblower (1987) 160ff.   [152] Thuc. 2.35–46.   [153] Thuc. 6.38–40.

speeches, had, of course, encomium of the democracy as an obligatory element in its composition.[154]

The supporters of democracy, be it remembered, were addressing a quite different public from its critics: Plato and Aristotle and Isokrates wrote for a small band of disciples or intellectuals, whereas the dramatists and the orators were talking in principle to the whole people. In the court speeches, indeed, reference to the democratic ideal is actually often used as a *captatio benevolentiae*;[155] and, surely, the ideas and attitudes of the orators must reflect what the majority of their audience were only too glad to hear.

Practically all our sources for Athenian democracy were written at Athens, and by Athenians. We possess no account of any democracy other than the Athenian, nor any evaluation of Athenian democracy by other Greeks (apart from one line of high praise in Herodotos).[156] Although we can read in Thucydides passages of evaluation of Athens by the Corinthians or the Spartans,[157] those passages were written by Thucydides the Athenian. There are writings by Lysias and Aristotle, who were not citizens but metics, and it is valuable to have the resident outsiders' view of the government of Athens; but Lysias was writing his speeches to be delivered by Athenian citizens, and Aristotle taught in the Lyceum at Athens. The nearest we can really come to a picture of the democracy seen from outside is the book *On the Athenian Demagogues* by Theopompos of Chios,[158] but even he had been a disciple of Isokrates' school at Athens – and, in any case, the book is lost except for a few scrappy fragments quoted by other authors.

The lack of outside evaluations of the democracy is somewhat compensated for by the fact that Athens was *par excellence* the state that celebrated freedom of speech as part of its ideals. In a speech of 355 Demosthenes rightly remarks that the most important difference between the political systems of Athens and Sparta is that at Athens it is permitted to praise that of Sparta and denigrate one's own, whereas at Sparta no one may praise any system other than the Spartan.[159] Many Athenians of critical temper exercised that freedom of speech, especially the philosophers. Sokrates, it is true, was condemned and executed in 399, *inter alia* for expressing his criticism of democracy in the aristocratic circles he frequented, whose members were involved in 411 and 404 in the overthrow of the democracy and the setting-up of an oligarchy.[160] Unfortunately, we do not possess the defence speeches made by Sokrates' advocates,[161] which presumably answered the political charges; even better

---

[154] Loraux (1986).   [155] Aeschin. 3.1–8.   [156] Hdt. 5.78.
[157] Thuc. 1.68–71, 80–85.   [158] *FGrHist.* 115; Connor (1968).   [159] Dem. 20.106–8.
[160] Brickhouse and Smith (1989) 71–3.   [161] Xen. *Apol.* 22.

would it have been if the speeches for the prosecution, especially that of Anytos, had survived.[162] But the prosecution of Socrates is an isolated occurrence in the history of Athens, and normally both citizens and foreigners living in Athens could exercise freedom of speech unhindered. It is Plato and Aristotle who give most of the unfavourable analyses of democracy in general and Athenian democracy in particular, and the criticism of democracy to be heard in Athenian sources is the strongest possible evidence that the Athenians' pride in their freedom of speech was not unfounded.

[162] Pl. *Ap.* 36A, cf. 23E.

3

The Athenian Constitution down to 403 BC: A Historical Sketch

The sketch that follows anticipates many important concepts, such as democracy itself, citizenship, and the political geography of Attica, that will only receive their proper treatment later. But, as explained in chapter 2, the principles of this book demand a chronological account of the beginnings and first century of Athenian democracy before we embark on the systematic study of its fourth-century form. What follows will also deal with Athenian political and imperial history only in so far as they are directly related to the constitution: for a brief account of the history of Athens in a more general sense the reader is recommended to turn to other books.[1] Some persistent controversies are also glossed over in this sketch in what may seem a somewhat bland manner; that is because they are of relatively minor importance for our purpose, for which it suffices to follow, up to 403/2, the traditional account of Athenian democracy, without too many 'ifs' and 'buts'. Four subjects, on the other hand, will be treated at rather greater length in excursuses at the end of the chapter, because full exposition of them is essential to all that follows: they concern (1) the Solonian propertied classes; (2) the Kleisthenic divisions of Attica; (3) the origins of selection by lot; and (4) the Periklean citizenship law.

THE ARCHAIC AGE

Democracy was introduced into Athens by Kleisthenes in 507 BC;[2] but in order to understand what he did we must go back more than a hundred years to an age when Athens was governed by magistrates (*archai*) picked by, and from, the Eupatridai (the 'well-born'), i.e. the leading clans.[3]

---

[1] Murray (1980), on the archaic period; Hornblower (1983), on the classical period; Schuller (1990), 'Forschungsbericht'.

[2] See p. 4.

[3] Arist. *Ath. Pol.* 3.1, cf. 13.2, 19.3; Poll. 8.111. Toepffer (1889); Wade-Gery (1958) 86–115; Roussel (1976) 55–8.

The most powerful magistrates were the nine archons,[4] of whom the chief gave his name to the year.[5] In the Athenians' own memory of the archon list – and perhaps it was accurate enough – that system went back to the archonship of one Kreon in 683.[6] An important political assembly was the Board of Chairmen of the forty-eight *naukrariai*;[7] but so limited is our knowledge of Athens in the archaic age that we have no idea what a *naukraria* was, nor even whether the word is connected with *naus* ('ship') or *naos* ('temple').[8] We do know that the Athenians were divided into four tribes,[9] that at the head of each was a 'king' (*phylobasileus*),[10] and that each tribe was subdivided into three ridings (*trittyes*, 'third parts')[11] and twelve *naukrariai*.[12] There is no evidence that Athens in that age had an assembly of the people: to claim that, we have to extrapolate from later evidence.[13] And the Athenians did not know themselves whether the Council of the Areopagos – composed of all ex-archons – had been instituted by Solon[14] or had existed long before his time,[15] originally as the king's council.[16] The laws remained unwritten, but were enshrined in the memories of the magistrates, who had to operate them so as to give judgement in lawsuits between citizens.[17]

Economically also the Eupatridai were the ruling class. Most of them were substantial landowners, and besides their own produce they received annual contributions from a large and growing group of smallholders (called *hektemoroi*, 'sixth-parters', because a *hektemoros* was obliged to make over a sixth of his produce every year to the large landowner whose dependant he was: if he failed in that obligation he could be sold into slavery).[18] There was a deepening gulf between rich and poor, perhaps mainly due to population growth:[19] the number of Athenians may well have doubled between 750 and 600, and, unlike other Greek states, Athens did not get rid of its surplus population by the founding of settlements abroad (*apoikiai*).[20] Amongst the smaller landowners, the rules of inheritance may have had the effect that the individual's plot

[4] Thuc. 1.126.8; Arist. *Ath. Pol.* 13.3.   [5] *M&L* 6 = Fornara (1977) no. 23.

[6] Hieronymus p. 93 (ed. R. Helm, Berlin, 1956); Cadoux (1948) 88. For alternative dates cf. Develin (1989) 27–8.

[7] Hdt. 5.71.2.   [8] Billigmeier and Dusing (1981); Gabrielsen (1985).

[9] Hdt. 5.66.2.

[10] Arist. *Ath. Pol.* 8.3. *Hesperia* 4 (1935) 19–32 no. 2.33–5 = Harding (1985) no. 9.

[11] Arist. *Ath. Pol.* fr. 3. *Hesperia* 4 (1935) 19–32 no. 2.37.36–7.

[12] Arist. *Ath. Pol.* 8.3, 21.5.   [13] Solon fr. 36.1–2. Andrewes (1982) 387.

[14] Plut. *Sol.* 19; Arist. *Pol.* 1273b35–41. Wallace (1989a) 3–47.

[15] Arist. *Ath. Pol.* 1273b41–1274a3.   [16] Andrewes (1982) 365.

[17] Busolt and Swoboda (1920–6) 488–9; Willetts (1967) 74.

[18] Arist. *Ath. Pol.* 2.2; Plut. *Sol.* 13.4–5. Rhodes (1981a) 90–7.

[19] Snodgrass (1980) 23–4 [but ct. Hansen (1982) 185 n. 8]; Morris (1987) 23.

[20] Graham (1982) 157.

became so small that its holder had to rely on help, or loans, from the big landowner in the neighbourhood; or that some sons had to leave their father's plot of land and cultivate marginal land or become tenants.[21] Population growth, however, is only one out of many possible explanations of how poor Athenians became *hektemoroi* and eventually indebted to the aristocrats.[22] What we know is only that a *hektemoros* in the end could end up as a slave, either in Attica or, by being sold, in some other city.[23] The impoverished smallholders began finally to agitate for the abolition of debt enslavement and the liabilities of the *hektemoroi*, and for a redistribution of the land. In the hundred years from about 630 to 530, those social and economic tensions produced a series of political crises, of which the most important resulted in the coup of Kylon, the laws of Drakon, the reforms of Solon and the tyranny of Peisistratos.

KYLON, DRAKON, SOLON

In 636 or 632[24] an Athenian called Kylon attempted to set himself up as *tyrannos* of the city.[25] (*Tyrannos* is not a Greek but probably a Phoenician word in origin.[26] At that time it just meant, neutrally, a 'ruler', and only a century later did it begin to mean a 'tyrant'.)[27] He was married to the daughter of the *tyrannos* of neighbouring Megara, and with the help of his father-in-law he and his friends attempted to lay siege to the Akropolis. The coup failed, and Kylon fled and his followers were put to death.

A few years later, in 621,[28] Athens acquired its first written code of laws, as a result of which the Eupatridai no longer had a monopoly of knowledge of the law and the convenience of remembering the clauses it suited them to remember.[29] The compiling of the laws was entrusted to one Drakon.[30] His law of homicide remained in force, with modifications, right down to the time of Demosthenes,[31] but the rest of his laws, whose penalties were said to have been 'written not in ink but in blood',[32] were superseded in the very next generation by those of Solon.[33]

Meanwhile, the socio-economic problems of the state remained unresolved, and only in 594 did rich and poor unite to give the archon Solon plenary power to dictate a compromise.[34] Solon was himself a Eupatrid,[35]

---

[21] E.g. French (1956).   [22] Cassola (1964).   [23] Solon fr. 36.8–15.
[24] Develin (1989) 30.
[25] Hdt. 5.71; Thuc. 1.126.3–12; Plut. *Sol.* 12; Schol. Ar. *Eq.* 445.
[26] Murray (1980) 132.   [27] Andrewes (1956) 20–30.   [28] Develin (1989) 31.
[29] Eur. *Supp.* 433–7; but see Eder (1986).
[30] Arist. *Ath. Pol.* 7.1; Arist. *Pol.* 1274b15–16. Stroud (1968) 74–5; Gagarin (1981).
[31] Andoc. 1.83; Dem. 20.158, 23.51.   [32] Plut. *Sol.* 17.3; Arist. *Pol.* 1274b15–18.
[33] Arist. *Ath. Pol.* 7.1.   [34] Diog. Laert. 1.62. Develin (1989) 37–8.
[35] Davies (1971) 322–4.

and he was probably not much over thirty when he was invested with power to reform his society. He began with a general amnesty,[36] then abolished enslavement for debt[37] and gave freedom to those so enslaved, even those who had been sold abroad[38] (however he managed that). Next, he freed the *hektemoroi* from the sixth-parts and allowed them to hold their land free of obligations;[39] but he set himself against a redistribution of the land,[40] and for ever after the archon on entering office had to proclaim that he would uphold the existing distribution of property.[41]

Besides his economic reforms Solon also reformed the administration of justice. According to later tradition he set up a people's court, called the Heliaia,[42] manned by sworn jurors,[43] and gave every party to any lawsuit the right to appeal to the Heliaia against the award of the magistrates;[44] two surviving laws prove, however, that the Heliaia was not only a court of appeal but could also hear new cases.[45] Solon also expanded the right of legal accusation, hitherto confined to the injured person, by giving every citizen the right to start a prosecution either on behalf of the injured person or simply in the public interest.[46]

In Solon's time Athenians were divided into three property classes: *hippeis* (cavalry), *zeugitai* (owners of a yoke of oxen) and *thetes* (literally 'menials', the day labourers). The fourth, top class, *pentakosiomedimnoi* (men worth 500 'measures' of natural produce) may have been added by Solon.[47] The *thetes* were excluded from all state offices,[48] and to the most important offices the electors (probably the People's Assembly)[49] could chose only citizens from the top class[50] or – as in the case of the nine archons – from the top two classes.[51] Thus, election now depended on wealth instead of birth, and by that means Solon created the conditions for a shift in Athenian society from the rule of aristocrats to the rule of the wealthy.

However, of Solon's constitutional reforms the most important, according to the tradition, was his creation of a Council of Four Hundred, 100 from each of the four tribes.[52] As to its functions nothing whatever is heard until Plutarch, who says that the Council had the task of preparing all matters to be decided by the Assembly,[53] exactly as the later Council

---

[36] Plut. *Sol.* 19.4.   [37] Arist. *Ath. Pol.* 6.1.   [38] Solon fr. 36.8–15.
[39] Arist. *Ath. Pol.* 6.1; Solon fr. 36.3–6.   [40] Solon fr. 34; Arist. *Ath. Pol.* 11.2.
[41] Arist. *Ath. Pol.* 56.2.   [42] Arist. *Pol.* 1373b35–a3; Arist. *Ath. Pol.* 7.3, 9.1.
[43] Arist. *Pol.* 1274a3. Hansen (1983a) 153–5; (1989a) 242–9, 258–61, *pace* Ostwald (1986) 10–11.
[44] Arist. *Ath. Pol.* 9.1.   [45] Dem. 23.28, 24.105. Hansen (1989a) 259–60.
[46] Arist. *Ath. Pol.* 9.1. Ruschenbusch (1968) 47–53; but see Hansen (1976) 115.
[47] Arist. *Ath. Pol.* 7.3. Rhodes (1981a) 137.   [48] Arist. *Ath. Pol.* 7.3–4.
[49] Solon fr. 5.1–2.   [50] Arist. *Ath. Pol.* 8.1, 47.1.
[51] Arist. *Ath. Pol.* 26.2. Hignett (1952) 101–2.   [52] Arist. *Ath. Pol.* 8.4.
[53] Plut. *Sol.* 19.1–2.

of Five Hundred had; and it is worrying that the earliest trace at all of Solon's Council in the sources is to be found in the revolutionary situation of 411, when the Athenians went over to an 'oligarchical' Council of Four Hundred and abolished the Council of Five Hundred.[54] There can be no doubt that the oligarchs in 411 claimed Solon's alleged Council as their paradigm,[55] and thus it is impossible to tell for certain whether the whole thing was just a propaganda invention that got taken afterwards as history or whether it really did once exist.[56]

Last but not least, Solon carried out a new codification of the laws,[57] and for hundreds of years 'the laws of Solon' were the juridical foundation of Athenian society:[58] they were not revised till 410–399,[59] when they were recodified;[60] and in that form they remained in force until the abolition of the democracy, Solon's law-code was, of course, not a comprehensive and systematic code in the modern sense, but a collection of laws, divided into sections not according to content but according to which magistrates were to administer them.[61] Moreover, like other codes, that of Solon most likely contained provisions only about what we would nowadays call private law, criminal law and the law of procedure;[62] only in the revision after the restoration of democracy in 403 were there added to the code provisions about the powers of the organs of state and detailed regulations about administration.[63] Hence the extreme difficulty of deciding whether particular constitutional reforms that were later attributed to Solon really do go back to the early sixth century.[64]

Solon's reforms underwent the usual fate of all sensible compromises: neither side was satisfied.[65] He tried to get the Athenians to maintain his laws unchanged for ten years,[66] and defended himself in verse pamphlets (prose being as yet unknown for literary purposes), of which substantial parts have come down to us, the first surviving reflections of a European statesman. He went abroad voluntarily for the ten years during which he hoped his laws would be respected,[67] and on his travels he is supposed to have visited King Kroisos of Lydia (560–546) and King Amasis of Egypt (570–526).[68] (The reigns of these monarchs are certain, which raises doubts as to whether the Athenians were remembering their archon list properly when they put Solon's archonship in 594.[69]) But the citizen

[54] Arist. *Ath. Pol.* 31.1.   [55] Hansen (1989c) 88–9.

[56] *Pro*: Cloché (1924) 1–26; Andrewes (1982) 387. *Contra*: Hignett (1952) 92–6.

[57] Solon fr. 36.18–20; Hdt. 1.29.1; Arist. *Ath. Pol.* 7.1. Rhodes (1981a) 130–5. Fragments in Ruschenbusch (1966).

[58] Schreiner (1913).   [59] Ruschenbusch (1966) 32–7.   [60] See p. 162.

[61] Stroud (1968) 32–3, *pace* Ruschenbusch (1966) 27–31.

[62] Von Fritz (1977); Hansen (1989c) 83–4.   [63] See p. 165.

[64] See p. 164.   [65] Solon frr. 34, 37.   [66] Hdt. 1.29.2.

[67] Hdt. 1.29.1; Arist. *Ath. Pol.* 11.1.   [68] Hdt. 1.30.1.   [69] Plommer (1969).

body was soon split into three competing factions: the 'Men of the Plain' (i.e. the plain around Athens), led by Lykourgos; the 'Men beyond the Mountains' (i.e. beyond Hymettos and Pentelikon), led by Peisistratos; and the 'Men of the Coast', led by the Alkmaionid Megakles.[70] All these leaders were, of course, themselves aristocrats, and now there happened at Athens, rather late, what had happened in many city-states in the previous hundred years: a leader of subsistence farmers got the upper hand over his fellow aristocrats and made himself tyrant.[71]

In Athens, as elsewhere in Greece, changes in the constitution were probably a corollary of changes in the fighting-forces. In most states the core of the army had ceased to be the mounted aristocrats and was now the foot soldiers with lance, shield, helmet, breastplate and greaves: the so-called *hoplitai*, mainly recruited from the farmers (i.e. in Athens the *zeugitai*). Military power led naturally to political power, so it was usually a commander of hoplites who turned against his peers and, with the help of the farmers, set himself up as tyrant.[72]

PEISISTRATOS AND HIPPIAS

In 561 Peisistratos became tyrant in a coup.[73] Formally, Solon's constitution remained unaltered:[74] Peisistratos merely saw to it that his supporters were elected archons[75] and kept a mercenary bodyguard about him always.[76] He was tyrant, barring two periods of exile, from 561 to 527;[77] his exiles were both due to the Men of the Coast allying themselves with the Men of the Plain to oust him,[78] but for most of the time he succeeded in obtaining the collaboration of the Men of the Coast under Megakles and of many of the aristocrats. The fourth-century Athenians also believed that Peisistratos championed the poor and so solved the land problem.[79] In any case he founded émigré communities in northern Asia Minor and the Hellespont,[80] and after his death there was never a movement for land reform.

Peisistratos was succeeded by his son Hippias (527 510), who met gradually increasing opposition from the aristocrats, and many of them were forced into exile.[81] Two of those who remained attempted a coup

---

[70] Hdt. 1.59.3; Arist. *Ath. Pol.* 13.4. Andrewes (1982) 393–8.
[71] Arist. *Pol.* 1305a21–4. Welwei (1983) 80–2, 164–6.
[72] Arist. *Pol.* 1310b12–31. Murray (1980) 120–52.
[73] Hdt. 1.59.4–6; Arist. *Ath. Pol.* 14.1.   [74] Hdt. 1.59.6; Arist. *Ath. Pol.* 16.8.
[75] Thuc. 6.54.6.   [76] Hdt. 1.59.5; Thuc. 6.57.1; Ar. *Eq.* 447.
[77] Rhodes (1981a) 191–9.   [78] Hdt. 1.60.1, 61.2; Arist. *Ath. Pol.* 14.3–15.5.
[79] Arist. *Ath Pol.* 16.2–3, 9.   [80] Hdt. 6.35–6.
[81] Hdt. 5.62.2; Thuc. 6.59.4; Arist. *Ath Pol.* 19.3. Lewis (1988) 299.

in 514: the young Harmodios and his lover Aristogeiton tried to murder Hippias at the Panathenaic festival, but only succeeded in killing Hippias' younger brother, Hipparchos. They were instantly put to death,[82] and were later regarded as democratic heroes, as martyrs and freedom-fighters: statues of the Tyrant-slayers were put up in 509 and again in 477,[83] a cult for Harmodios and Aristogeiton was instituted[84] and their descendants had dining-rights at public expense in the Prytaneion;[85] and many in later times were convinced that it was they who had unseated the tyrants and made Athens safe for democracy.[86] But the tyranny of Hippias lasted for four more years and was only really overthrown by the intervention of the Spartans: the aristocrats who had fled Athens had as their leader the Alkmaionid Kleisthenes, and he, with the help of Delphi, induced the Spartans to send a force into Attica under King Kleomenes. In 510 Athens was taken and Hippias and his associates besieged on the Akropolis: he soon capitulated on the promise of unhindered departure, and he and his family went into exile in Sigeion.[87]

ISAGORAS

No sooner was the tyrant driven out than a split developed between the newly returned aristocrats under Kleisthenes and those who had stayed behind, led by Isagoras who had been a supporter of Hippias until he joined the revolt.[88] Isagoras was elected archon for 508/7,[89] and Kleisthenes, finding that he had no hope of success with only his aristocratic faction to help him, 'took into his faction the ordinary people'.[90] Supported by the *demos* he successfully opposed Isagoras, whose name, ironically, signifies 'freedom of speech' (*isegoria*), the very ideal advocated by Kleisthenes and his supporters.[91] But Isagoras had a guest-friendship with King Kleomenes, and with the help of a Spartan army forced Kleisthenes and his followers into exile, whereupon the Athenian people rose in revolt. They booted the Spartans out, recalled Kleisthenes and condemned Isagoras to death in his absence.[92] In 507, only three years after the expulsion of the tyrants, the domination of the aristocrats, too,

[82] Hdt. 5.55–7; Thuc. 6.54–8; Arist. *Ath. Pol.* 18. Lewis (1988) 299–300.
[83] Plinius *Naturalis Historia* 34.17 (509); *Marmor Parium, FGrHist.* 239 A 54 (477). Brunnsåker (1955).
[84] Arist. *Ath. Pol.* 58.1. Kearns (1989) 55, 150.
[85] *IG* I³ 131.5–9 = Miller (1978) 139–40. no. 26; Is. 5.47.
[86] Thuc. 1.20.2, 6.53.3; Ath. 695B.
[87] Hdt. 5.62–5; Thuc. 6.59; Arist. *Ath. Pol.* 19.
[88] Hdt. 5.66.1; Arist. *Ath. Pol.* 20.1. Wade-Gery (1958) 136–9.
[89] Dion. Hal. *Ant. Rom.* 1.74.6. Develin (1989) 51.   [90] Hdt. 5.66.2.
[91] Hdt. 5.78.   [92] Hdt. 5.66, 69–70, 72; Arist. *Ath. Pol.* 20.2–3. Ostwald (1988) 305–8.

was abolished in favour of a new form of constitution, 'democracy',[93] which was actually arising in several Greek city-states at the time.[94]

KLEISTHENES

In order to break up the old social structure[95] and create a new, homogeneous one, Kleisthenes instituted a new organ of state, the Council of Five Hundred,[96] based on a new division of Attica into ten tribes, thirty ridings (*trittyes*) and 139 demes,[97] a new 'bouleutic' calendar based on the solar year,[98] and new cult associations based on the ten tribes.[99] It is worth comparing these innovations with the French Revolution, in which amongst the most wide-ranging reforms were the creation of an elected legislative assembly based on a new division of France into eighty-eight *départements* and over 500 districts, the introduction of a new religion, and a new calendar with new names for all the months. The religion and the calendar were speedily given up, but the legislative assembly and the divisions of France were permanent and far-reaching. Just so at Athens in 507: a hundred years later the new calendar had to be adjusted back to fit the old, lunar one,[100] and the new cult organizations never caught on, but the Council became one of the principal organs of state alongside the Assembly and the People's Court throughout the classical period, and the redistribution of Attica was the basis of a political structure that lasted, with modifications, for more than 700 years.[101]

That redivision is described in more detail below; here it is more important to list a series of reforms whose purpose was to secure the new democracy from enemies inside and out. Kleisthenes saw to it that many non-Athenians and even freed slaves were inscribed in the new demes, thus becoming Athenian citizens and firm adherents of the new regime.[102] The redivision of Attica was also probably undertaken at least in part with an eye to a New Model Army,[103] for each of the ten tribes was to supply a hoplite regiment; and not long afterwards, in 501,[104] the Board of Generals (*stratēgoi*) was first introduced, elected annually by the people

[93] See p. 69.   [94] Hdt. 3.142.2–5 [but see Raaflaub (1985) 139–40], 4.137.2, 6.43.
[95] Lévêque and Vidal-Naquet (1963) 13–24.
[96] Arist. *Ath. Pol.* 21.3. Rhodes (1972) 1–14.
[97] Hdt. 5.69; Arist. *Ath. Pol.* 21.2–4; Arist. *Pol.* 1319b19–27. Traill (1975, 1986).
[98] Ant. 6.44–5. Meritt (1928) 121–2.
[99] Hdt. 5.66.2; Arist. *Ath. Pol.* 21.6. Kron (1976); Kearns (1989) 80–92.
[100] Rhodes (1972) 224.   [101] Hansen et al. (1990) 30–2.
[102] Arist. *Pol.* 1275b34–7; Arist. *Ath. Pol.* 21.4. Newman (1887–1902) III 145–7.
[103] Effenterre (1976); Siewert (1982).   [104] Rhodes (1981a) 262–3.

and with ten members:[105] they commanded the army,[106] in the first period jointly with the polemarch,[107] and were the most important board of magistrates all through the fifth century. Finally, there was ostracism.

Ostracism is the best-known of all Kleisthenes' novelties.[108] In the years 510–507 he had had personal experience of how the rivalries of political leaders could split the state: to obviate such *stasis* in the future[109] he introduced a procedure by which a leader could be sent into banishment (but not penal exile, with no loss of status or property) for ten years.[110] It was called *ostrakismos* because voting was by means of *ostraka*, potsherds; but it was in fact a two-stage process. Each year the people voted in an Assembly meeting, by ordinary show of hands, whether they wanted an ostracism,[111] and if (and only if) they voted in favour of having one the ostracism took place some two months later in the Agora. The citizens went by tribes into an enclosure and there each cast a potsherd on which he had scratched the name of the leader he wanted to see banished.[112] The potsherds were counted, and if (and only if) there were at least 6000 they were then sorted by names, and that person whose name appeared most times (i.e. by a simple, not an overall, majority) had automatically, within ten days, to go into banishment for ten years.[113]

The law of ostracism is correctly attributed to Kleisthenes,[114] but it was twenty years before the Athenians actually used it, in order to banish Hipparchos, a relative of the former tyrant, in 487.[115] The following year the Alkmaionid Megakles was banished, and two years after that Xanthippos, the father of Perikles, and then, in 482, Aristeides,[116] whom people called 'the Just'.[117] Banishment by ostracism was used some fifteen times during the fifth century,[118] the last occasion being in one of the years 417–45,[119] when the victim was the 'demagogue' Hyperbolos.[120] The procedure was never abolished, but was a dead letter in the fourth century.

The reason for so many cases of ostracism in the 480s was connected with two especial dangers faced by the Athenians: the wish of the tyrants to get Athens back and that of the king of Persia to conquer the Greeks.

---

[105] Arist. *Ath. Pol.* 22.2; Hdt. 6.104.1.   [106] Hdt. 6.103.1.

[107] Hdt. 6.109.1–2, 111.1; *M&L* 18 = Fornara (1977) no. 49.   [108] See p. 21.

[109] Ostwald (1988) 344–6.   [110] Philoch. fr. 30.   [111] Arist. *Ath. Pol.* 43.5.

[112] Philoch. fr. 30.   [113] Plut. *Arist.* 7.6.   [114] Dover (1963); Thomsen (1972) 11–60.

[115] Arist. *Ath. Pol.* 22.3–4 = Androt. fr. 6.   [116] Arist. *Ath. Pol.* 22.5–7.

[117] Plut. *Arist.* 7.7.

[118] Rhodes (1981a) 271. Add Lys. 14.39: Megakles and Alkibiades were probably ostracized twice; see p. 5.

[119] Theophr. *Nomoi* fr. 18 (Szegedy-Maszak).

[120] Thuc. 8.73.3; Theop. fr. 96; Plut. *Nic.* 11.1–10; *Alc.* 13.4–9. Andoc. 4 is spurious; see p. 18.

The two threats were two sides of the same coin, because Hippias and his family and adherents had taken refuge in Sigeion and had powerful influence at the Persian Court.[121]

In 490 the Athenian army under Miltiades defeated the Persians at Marathon; a year later Miltiades was struck down in a political prosecution and died in prison.[122] In the following decade Themistokles was the leading figure at Athens, and his hand may well have been behind the ostracisms of the 480s by which his rivals were successively removed from the game.[123] Themistokles may also have been behind the reform of 487/6 by which the method of selection of the nine archons was changed from election to selection by lot (though from an elected shortlist).[124] Already in 493/2, as archon, he had got the Athenians to build a fortified harbour in the Piraeus,[125] and when in 483/2 a rich vein of silver was found at Maroneia in southern Attica he persuaded them to use the windfall to build a hundred naval vessels instead of distributing it equally among the citizens.[126] When King Xerxes invaded Greece in 480, Themistokles persuaded the people to evacuate Attica and meet the Persian onslaught at sea,[127] and the reward for his far-sighted policies came in late summer that year, when he led the Athenian contingent at the battle of Salamis. Yet, for all the honours Themistokles won, he soon shared the fate of Miltiades and was forced out by new leaders, Aristeides and Kimon, the son of Miltiades. About 471 he was ostracized,[128] and a few years later he was condemned to death *in absentia* for treason, since he, like Hippias, had become an honoured pensioner of the great king of Persia.[129]

EPHIALTES

By defeating the Persians and ostracizing the supporters of tyranny, and by creating the Delian League in 478 and consolidating the predominance of the Athenian fleet in the Aegean, the Athenians laid the groundwork for a further advance of democracy. The transformation of Athens from a land power to a sea power led to a shift in the internal balance of power, because the land forces (the hoplites) were recruited from the

---

[121] Ostwald (1988) 337–9.   [122] Hdt. 6.136. Hansen (1975) cat. no. 2; Ostwald (1986) 29.
[123] Ostwald (1988) 342–3.   [124] Arist. *Ath. Pol.* 22.5. Badian (1971) 21–6.
[125] Thuc. 1.93.3. Dickie (1973) 758–9.   [126] Arist. *Ath. Pol.* 22.7. Labarbe (1957).
[127] Hdt. 7.143–4; *M&L* 23 = Fornara (1977) no. 55.   [128] Thuc. 1.135.3. Lenardon (1959).
[129] Thuc. 1.135.2, 137.3ff; Krateros frr. 11–2. Hansen (1975) cat. no. 4; Carawan (1987) 196–200.

middle class[130] whereas the navy was manned by the poor (the *thetes*).[131] Furthermore, now that Athens had to lead and administer the League, the Assembly and Council and courts had far more and greater tasks to fulfil, so that the role of all three must have been significantly enlarged.[132] The result of these developments was the passing, on the motion of one Ephialtes, of a law transferring the political powers of the Areopagos to the democratic decision-making bodies.

The archaic Areopagos had had oversight of the laws, the magistrates, the politically active citizens, and the general conduct of all Athenians, and it could pronounce judgement, not excluding the death sentence, in political trials.[133] Kleisthenes had made no change in its powers except indirectly, by giving the Assembly too the right to hear political trials[134] and by allowing his new Council a hand in the control of the magistrates. But a group of democrats, led by Ephialtes[135] and his henchmen, the young Perikles[136] and Archestratos[137] (otherwise unknown), were keen to remove altogether the island of aristocratic power in the midst of a democratizing state, and in 462 they succeeded in reducing the Areopagos to the single function of being the court for homicide in cases where the deceased was an Athenian citizen.[138] It happened that just at that moment 4000 hoplites under Kimon were in the Peloponnese, where they had been sent to help the Spartans overcome a helot revolt,[139] so the poor citizens were in the majority in the Assembly.[140] Also, as we have seen, in 487/6 the Athenians had gone over to selecting the nine archons by lot from an elected short-list, and the result was that over a generation that body had ceased to be an assembly of leading political figures and turned into a more random cross-section of the upper class (for archons still had to be chosen from the richest citizens and *zeugitai* became eligible only after Ephialtes' reforms, in 458/7).[141] Thus, in 462 the perfect chance presented itself to curtail the powers of the Areopagos in order to make it correspond to its changed composition; the powers that it lost were divided between the Assembly, the Council and the People's Court.[142] On his return Kimon tried to get the new law reversed, but he drew the short straw and was himself ostracized in 461.[143]

[130] See p. 116.   [131] Arist. *Ath. Pol.* 24, 26.1; Ps. Xen. *Ath. Pol.* 1.2.
[132] Schuller (1984).
[133] Arist. *Ath. Pol.* 8.4. Hansen (1975) 19; Wallace (1989a) 64–9.
[134] Hansen (1975) 19; but see Sealey (1981).   [135] Arist. *Ath. Pol.* 25.1, 28.2, 41.2.
[136] Arist. *Ath. Pol.* 27.1; Plut. *Cim.* 15.2; *Per.* 9.5.   [137] Arist. *Ath. Pol.* 35.2.
[138] Arist. *Ath. Pol.* 25.2; Philoch. fr. 64.
[139] Thuc. 1.102; Ar. *Lys.* 1138–44; Plut. *Cim.* 16.8–17.4.
[140] Plut. *Cim.* 15.2. Cole (1974) 373–8; Martin (1974) 39.
[141] Arist. *Ath. Pol.* 26.2.   [142] Arist. *Ath. Pol.* 25.2.
[143] Plut. *Cim.* 15.3, 17.3; *Per.* 9.5.

PERIKLES

Ephialtes was, however, murdered[144] about the same time, and was succeeded as 'leader of the people' by Perikles the son of Xanthippos, who was connected with the Alkmaionids through his mother.[145] For the next thirty-two years Perikles was the acknowledged but not uncontested leader of Athens; a brief period of opposition led by Thucydides the son of Melesias ended when the latter was ostracized in 443.[146] Year after year Perikles was elected general,[147] and as speaker and proposer he so dominated the Assembly that Thucydides the historian was moved to coin the famous apophthegm that in those years Athens was 'in name a democracy but in fact under the rule of the first man';[148] but it was through, and as champion of, democracy that Perikles exercised his power. Under him democratic development was pushed further, especially on two fronts: citizens began to be paid for political activity,[149] and the criteria for citizenship were made more severe.

The first of those reforms was a natural consequence of Ephialtes' law. The new pressure of business, especially on the Council and courts, involved an increase in the number of meetings, but many citizens could only afford to participate if they received compensation for working-time lost. Perikles introduced daily pay, first for the jurors in the People's Court[150] and then for councillors and the rest of the magistrates.[151]

The second reform, the tightening of conditions for citizenship, followed naturally from the first: in 451/50 Perikles had a law passed confining citizenship for the future to those whose parents were both Athenian, i.e. the legitimate sons of an Athenian mother as well as father.[152] It is tempting to see Perikles' law in relation to the decision of the Athenians to give pay for jury service: once citizens had got an advantage out of political activity they were glad not to have too many others to share it with.[153] By Perikles' reforms the gulf that separated citizens from non-citizens was made deeper, and the citizenry became a closed population with a very limited potentiality for growth.[154]

---

[144] Ant. 5.68; Arist. *Ath. Pol.* 25.4, *pace* Stockton (1982).
[145] Hdt. 6.131.2. Davies (1971) 379, 455–6.   [146] Plut. *Per.* 14.
[147] Plut. *Per.* 16.3. Develin (1989) records twenty-two generalships.
[148] Thuc. 2.65.9.   [149] Arist. *Ath. Pol.* 1274a8–9; Pl. *Grg.* 515E.
[150] Arist. *Ath. Pol.* 27.3.
[151] *IG* I³ 82.20; Thuc. 8.69.4; Ps. Xen. *Ath. Pol.* 1.3. Hansen (1979a) 12–4.
[152] Arist. *Ath. Pol.* 26.4. See pp. 52–4.   [153] Walker (1927) 102–3.
[154] See p. 90.

THE SUCCESSORS OF PERIKLES

The growth of the Athenian Empire and the fear of it amongst the other states led to the Peloponnesian War. The major contestants were, of course, Athens and Sparta. Sparta was the land power, representing and supporting oligarchy; Athens the sea power, supporting democracy and exporting her own constitution to the allied states:[155] the ideological aspect was as important in the conflict as that of power politics. The war lasted twenty-seven years, 431–404; in the first two years Perikles still led Athens, but as a result particularly of the plague in 430–429 he for the first time failed to persuade the people to follow his policies, and was actually sentenced to a big fine in a political trial (429).[156] True enough, the Athenians elected him again to the generalship, but he died soon after entering office, perhaps a victim of the plague.[157]

His death brought a great change into Athenian politics;[158] historians have sometimes made too much of it, but it is authentic enough. Down to and including Perikles all Athenian leaders (except, perhaps, Ephialtes) had been aristocrats and landowners;[159] after him they were often of lower birth – just as wealthy, but their wealth based more on slave-manned workshops. The new leaders could still be elected generals,[160] but their power was based much more on their ability to persuade the people in the Assembly.[161] The best-known of them are the tannery-owner Kleon,[162] who fell at Amphipolis in 422, the lamp-manufacturer Hyperbolos,[163] the last Athenian leader to be ostracized, and the lyre-maker Kleophon,[164] condemned and executed in a political trial in the last year of the war.[165] They competed for power, and that was bad for the Athenian conduct of the war: the philosophers disdainfully called them 'demagogues'.[166] But the remaining leaders of the old type, Nikias and Alkibiades, also competed, and their competition was also disas-trous.[167] In 415 Alkibiades persuaded the Athenians into an expedition against Syracuse in the grand manner under his own leadership; but just as the fleet was due to sail he was denounced for having parodied and

[155] Thuc. 3.82.1; Ps. Xen. *Ath. Pol.* 1.14–6; Isoc. 4.104–6; Arist. *Ath. Pol.* 1307b22–4.
[156] Thuc. 2.65.3; Plut. *Per.* 32, 35. Hansen (1975) cat. no. 6.
[157] Thuc. 2.65.5; Plut. *Per.* 38.   [158] Thuc. 2.65.8–10.
[159] Eupolis fr. 103. Connor (1971) 10–2; Bicknell (1972).
[160] Hansen (1989a) 17 with n. 46.
[161] Connor (1971) 155, 159.   [162] Schol. Ar. *Eq.* 44; Critias DK 88 fr. 45.
[163] Schol. Ar. *Pax* 692 (= Cratinus fr. 196).   [164] Andoc. 1.146; Aeschin. 2.76.
[165] Lys. 30.10–3, 13.12. Hansen (1975) cat. no. 139.
[166] Arist. *Ath. Pol.* 41.2; *Pol.* 1313b40; Isoc. 8.129; Xen. *Hell.* 2.3.27.
[167] Connor (1971) 140ff.

profaned the Mysteries in nocturnal orgies,[168] and friends of his were denounced for mutilating the statues of Hermes that stood about the streets of Athens.[169] The culprits were found and sentenced to death, and several were executed: it is remarkable how many of them belonged to the circle of Sokrates.[170] The trial of Alkibiades was put off till after the campaign, but hardly had he departed with the fleet than he was summoned back to Athens. He escaped, instead, to Sparta and was condemned to death in his absence.[171]

OLIGARCHICAL REVOLUTIONS

The Sicilian expedition, 415–413, imposed on the Athenians by the persuasion of Alkibiades but commanded in his absence by Nikias, who had been against it, ended in catastrophe, and the effect was the rise of oligarchical opposition, putting all the blame on the leaders who had persuaded the people and on the people themselves for being cozened by them.[172] The leaders of the opposition were Peisander and Theramenes (with the general Phrynichos in command of the fleet at Samos and the orator Antiphon in the background);[173] the faction was organized through the clubs of the upper-class, the *hetaireiai*,[174] its programme a 'return to the constitution of Solon',[175] its method terrorism.[176] Contact was made with Alkibiades, now in exile in Persian territory, and he promised he could get an alliance with Persia if Athens would give up democracy and reverse his death sentence. The result was a constitutional somersault in 411: at an irregular meeting the Assembly voted to abolish the democracy and put the government in the hands of a Council of Four Hundred chosen by the oligarchs.[177] Why did the Assembly do such a thing? No doubt because the Athenians were weary of the war, the democratic leaders were intimidated by the terror, and many of the lower classes were with the naval forces stationed off Samos.

The rule of the Four Hundred lasted only four months:[178] Alkibiades could not deliver the promised alliance, and the fleet at Samos stuck to democracy; we, they said, are the people of Athens, and we do not

---

[168] Andoc. 1.11–14, 27; Thuc. 6.28–9. Hansen (1975) cat. no. 11.
[169] Andoc. 1.34–69; Thuc. 6.27–8, 60–1. Hansen (1975) cat. nos 43–60.
[170] Hansen (1980e) 73–5.
[171] Thuc. 6.53.1, 61.1.7; Plut. *Alc.* 19, 21–2. Hansen (1975) cat. no. 12.
[172] Thuc. 8.1.1.   [173] Thuc. 8.68; Arist. *Ath. Pol.* 32.2. Rhodes (1981a) 407–9.
[174] Thuc. 8.48.3–4, 65.2, 92.4; Xen. *Hell.* 2.3.46. Calhoun (1913) 97–147.
[175] Arist. *Ath. Pol.* 29.3. Hansen (1989c) 88–9.   [176] Thuc. 8.65.2.
[177] Thuc. 8.67.2–69.1; Arist. *Ath. Pol.* 29.4–5.   [178] Arist. *Ath. Pol.* 33.1.

recognize the regime at home.[179] Hoped-for peace with Spara failed and the Athenians were hard-pressed; so in autumn 411 the moderate oligarchs under Theramenes tried another constitutional switch: full political rights were to be given to all who could afford hoplite equipment – nominally 5000 men,[180] actually a good many more than that, perhaps more like 9000;[181] and they would form the Assembly.[182] The Four Hundred were punished with *atimia*,[183] Peisander fled to Sparta,[184] and Antiphon was condemned and executed.[185] But the 5000 also only lasted a few months: the Athenians won a badly needed naval victory, and, with morale restored, re-established democracy in spring 410[186] and started on the revision of the laws of Drakon and Solon (which was only to reach completion in 399).[187]

On the whole, however, Athens' difficulties in the war grew steadily greater. She won some more naval victories under Alkibiades, but after a minor defeat in 407 he went into exile. A naval battle in 406 off the Arginoussai islands was a further victory for the Athenian fleet, but its consequences, paradoxically, were a shattering blow to political morale; for the Athenian survivors were not picked up, and many drowned. The generals were held responsible, and eight of them were impeached for treason, tried (unconstitutionally) all together in the Assembly, and condemned: two were absent, the other six were executed forthwith.[188] The Trial of the Generals was cited by contemporaries as evidence that assembly democracy was a bad form of government.[189] The Athenians suffered definitive naval defeat at Aigos Potamoi in the following year, and endured four months' siege by the Spartans; and in spring 404 they capitulated, on various terms including the dissolution of the naval empire, the pulling down of the Long Walls and an amnesty for all exiles (which allowed the survivors of the 400 exiled oligarchs to return home).[190] The constitutional consequences were then spelt out: democracy, people said, was bankrupt. The oligarchs,[191] organized in *hetaireiai*,[192] came to the fore once again, this time under Theramenes[193] and Kritias, the uncle of Plato's mother.[194] They had the help of the Spartans, who by their naval presence under Lysander forced the people

---

[179] Thuc. 8.75–6.   [180] Thuc. 8.97.1–2; Arist. *Ath. Pol.* 33.1–2.
[181] Lys. 20.13.   [182] Rhodes (1981a) 412, *pace* Ste Croix (1956).
[183] Andoc. 1.78.   [184] Thuc. 8.98.1; Lys. 7.4.
[185] Thuc. 8.68.2; Ant. fr. 3 (Budé); Plut. *Mor.* 833D–834B. Hansen (1975) cat. no. 135–7.
[186] Arist. *Ath. Pol.* 34.1; Andoc. 1.96–8.   [187] See pp. 162–4.
[188] Xen. *Hell.* 1.7.1–35. Hansen (1975) cat. no. 66. See p. 6.
[189] Arist. *Ath. Pol.* 34.1; Diod. 13.102.5.
[190] Xen. *Hell.* 2.2.20; Arist. *Ath. Pol.* 34.2–3; Diod. 14.3.2–7. Bengtson (1962) no. 211.
[191] Whitehead (1982) 106 with n. 4.   [192] Lys. 12.55; Arist. *Ath. Pol.* 34.3.
[193] Xen. *Hell.* 2.3.15ff; Lys. 12.72–8.   [194] Xen. *Hell.* 2.3.15ff; Aeschin. 1.173.

to pass a decree appointing a Commission of Thirty to govern Athens and by a revision of the laws to restore the ancestral constitution.[195] The Thirty were duly appointed and acquired a short popularity by their stern measures against sycophants,[196] but they soon turned themselves into a ruling junta and fully earned the name they have always gone by, the 'Thirty Tyrants'.[197] Kritias led the extremist wing of the oligarchs, and when Theramenes protested against the severity of their actions he was executed on the spot.[198] A Spartan garrison held the Akropolis,[199] and more than 1500 citizens were put to death,[200] while the Eleven in charge of the prison, a board of ten in charge of the Piraeus, and a corps of 300 whip-bearers were all the law there was for those who remained;[201] and they were eventually reduced to 3000 full citizens,[202] while all the other Athenians were disfranchised, disarmed[203] and expelled from Athens.[204]

Of course, many loyal democrats had fled; and it was they who gathered and organized the resistance.[205] Early in 403 they entered the Piraeus again under their leader Thrasyboulos,[206] and in a pitched battle at Mounichia near the ruins of the Long Walls the forces of the oligarchs were defeated and Kritias fell.[207] The oligarchs tried a final sleight-of-hand by substituting a Commission of Ten for the Thirty:[208] they were supposed to mediate between oligarchs and democrats, but they merely stepped into the shoes of the Thirty. They appealed to Sparta, and Lysander was prepared to invade Athens again in their support, but his king, Pausanias, took things into his own hands, appeared in Attica with a Spartan force, and brought the *stasis* to an end with an enforced compromise: the Athenians could have their democracy back if they would let the oligarchs create their own little *polis* at Eleusis in north-west Attica.[209] In autumn 403 the democrats returned in triumphant procession to Athens and an amnesty was proclaimed;[210] two years later Eleusis was recovered and the remaining oligarchic leaders executed,

---

[195] Xen. *Hell.* 2.3.2; Lys. 12.72–5; Arist. *Ath. Pol.* 34.3–23.2. Fuks (1953) 52–83; Krentz (1982) 49–50.

[196] Lys. 25.19; Xen. *Hell.* 2.3.12; Arist. *Ath. Pol.* 35.2–3.   [197] Arist. *Ath. Pol.* 41.2.

[198] Xen. *Hell.* 2.3.23–56; Arist. *Ath. Pol.* 37.1.

[199] Xen. *Hell.* 2.3.13–14; Arist. *Ath. Pol.* 37.2

[200] Isoc. 20.11; Aeschin. 3.235; Arist. *Ath. Pol.* 35.4.

[201] Xen. *Hell.* 2.3.54–5; Pl. *Ep.* 7 324C; Arist. *Ath. Pol.* 35.1.

[202] Xen. *Hell.* 2.3.18; Arist. *Ath. Pol.* 36.1.

[203] Xen. *Hell.* 2.3.20; Arist. *Ath. Pol.* 37.2.

[204] Isoc. 7.67; Diod. 14.5.6–7.

[205] Xen. *Hell.* 2.4.2–7.

[206] Xen. *Hell.* 2.4.10; Arist. *Ath. Pol.* 38.1.

[207] Xen. *Hell.* 2.4.10–19; Arist. *Ath. Pol.* 38.1.

[208] Xen. *Hell.* 2.4.23–4; Arist. *Ath. Pol.* 38.1; Lys. 12.53–4.

[209] Xen. *Hell.* 2.4.38; Arist. *Ath. Pol.* 39.   [210] Lys. 13.80; Xen. *Hell.* 2.4.39.

without intervention by the Spartans.[211] A new amnesty was proclaimed – and this time it was largely respected.[212] Democracy was restored and even deified: in the fourth century offerings were made to the goddess Demokratia in Boedromion[213] – probably on the 12th of that month, i.e. on the anniversary of the restoration of democracy.[214] The date suggests that the cult of Demokratia, though not attested before the 330s, was in fact set up in 403, when the democrats returned to Athens after the civil war.

EXCURSUS 1   SOLON AND THE PROPERTY CLASSES

By Solon's reforms the Athenians were divided into four classes (*tele*) by property. The citizen who produced annually at least 500 'measures' (*metra*) of corn, wine or olives counted amongst the *pentakosiomedimnoi*; if he produced between 300 and 500 measures he was among the *hippeis*; if he produced between 200 and 300 he belonged to the *zeugitai*; and if he produced less than 200 he belonged to the *thetes*.[215] The first striking thing about this system is that wealth is measured in produce, not in capital, and the second is that the only relevant produce is crops. The word 'measures' (*metra*) covered both liquid and dry measures, i.e. *medimnoi* of 52 litres, by which corn was measured, and *metretai* of 39 litres, by which wine and olives were measured. The fact that Solon's first class were called *pentakosiomedimnoi* implies that his reform was brought in at a time when Attic farmers mainly grew corn and not wine or olives. Income from trade or manufacture was not taken into account, and there is no sign that the amounts were converted into a money value – which would have been absurd given that a measure of corn and a measure of wine or oil had different monetary values.[216] The division into classes must have been based on some kind of self-assessment. But was the basis a good year or a bad year? We do not know; and it is also impossible to say anything, on the evidence of the product, about the size of the estate it came from. For 200 measures of olives would have taken up a much greater area than the corresponding quantity of wine, though, on the other hand, the Athenians would have planted corn between olive-trees and got two crops off the same area.[217]

Historians have never reached agreement as to the purpose of Solon's

---

[211] Xen. *Hell.* 2.4.43; Arist. *Ath. Pol.* 40.4.   [212] Xen. *Hell.* 2.4.43.

[213] *IG* II² 1496.131–2, 140–1.   [214] Plut. *Mor.* 349F; Palagia (1982) 111.

[215] Arist. *Ath. Pol.* 7.3–4.   [216] Zimmermann (1974) 101–3.

[217] Skydsgaard (1988).

reforms and the significance of the four terms. The significance of the first term is plain enough. *Hippeus* is a 'horseman' and, according to Aristotle, means a man who can afford to keep a horse.[218] The lexicographers thought that *zeugites* came from *zeugos*, a span of oxen, and that *zeugites* was a citizen who owned such a span.[219] The etymology of *thes* is unknown, but in archaic and classical Greece it meant a day labourer, a propertyless man who had to work for another.[220]

In antiquity itself the Solonian property classes were always interpreted as a class division based on economic criteria; but many modern historians have wanted to connect the property classes with the organization of the army,[221] and for that reason have translated *zeugitai* differently. Both *zeugites* and *zeugos* are connected with *zygon*, a word that normally means a 'yoke' but can also mean a line of men in the hoplite phalanx;[222] so *zeugites*, it is held, could mean a man who serves in the ranks as a hoplite.[223] That fits in well, of course, with the interpretation of *hippeus* as a cavalryman. So the real purpose of the Solonian division, it is claimed, was as a basis for a new army organization resting no longer on cavalry but on hoplites. The theory finds support in the fact that in the fifth century the property classes were indeed the basis of conscription for military service; nevertheless it is dubious. First of all, the other two terms, *pentakosiomedimnoi* and *thetes*, are purely economic, with no verbal connection with military structure whatsoever. Secondly, whatever archaic, aristocratic cavalry force the Athenians may have had, the corps of *hippeis* as we know it was set up only in the middle of the fifth century,[224] so there is no evidence that the Solonian *hippeis* had anything to do with an archaic military structure.[225] As for the proposed etymology of *zeugites*, it is based on the erroneous assumption that the verbal substantive has to be interpreted as passive ('people who are all gathered under a yoke') rather than as active ('possessor of a *zeugos*'): the ancient etymology may perfectly well be right.[226] Finally, we have not the least evidence that Solon initiated any army reform at all.

What he surely did aim at was to add the wealthy to the well-born in the running of the state, by permitting only the well off to hold office. Some offices, such as those of the Treasurers of Athena, could be held only by *pentakosiomedimnoi*.[227] The highest magistrates, the nine archons, were chosen from the two top classes;[228] *zeugitai* only got access to the

---

[218] Arist. *Ath. Pol.* 7.4. Bugh (1988) 21–5.	[219] Poll. 8.132.

[220] Hom. *Od.* 11.489; Pl; *Euthphr.* 4C; Arist. *Pol.* 1278a12–13; Isoc. 14.48. Wyse (1904) 464–5.

[221] Whitehead (1981); Rhodes (1981a) 138; Andrewes (1982) 385.	[222] Thuc. 5.68.3.

[223] Plut. *Pelopidas* 23.4.	[224] Bugh (1988) 39–52.	[225] Bugh (1988) 20–34.

[226] Hansen (1985c) 56, *pace* Rhodes (1981a) 138.	[227] Arist. *Ath. Pol.* 47.1.

[228] Arist. *Ath. Pol.* 7.3, 26.2. Hignett (1952) 101–2.

archonships in 457/6,[229] thirty years after that magistracy had lost its predominance by being chosen by lot instead of election. *Thetes* were excluded from office altogether.[230] New offices, however, such as the Board of Generals (from 501) and the *Hellenotamiai* (from 478) were not, as far as we know, confined to the top two classes, which, taken with the fact that access to the archonships was extended in 457, suggests that the property classes began to lose some of their importance for office-holding after the introduction of democracy in 507.[231] Yet two dedications postdating 480 show that an Athenian might still think it important what property class he belonged to. One is a statue of Anthemion discussed by Aristotle, who also quotes the inscription: 'Anthemion son of Diphilos dedicated this statue to the gods having changed his status from *thes* to *hippeus*.'[232] The other is a fragmentary dedication on stone to Athena, and if the text is correctly restored it is a thank-offering from one of the *thetes* who had advanced to the status of *zeugites*.[233]

Moreover, in the fifth century there is evidence that the Solonian classes were still relevant to colonization and to military service. A decree of about 450 establishing a colony lays down that the colonists shall be drawn from *zeugitai* and *thetes* – i.e. not from the *plousioi* (the wealthy);[234] and the relationship of the classes to military service emerges from several passages in Thucydides about the Peloponnesian War. The Athenian army had three arms: the cavalry (*hippeis*), the heavy infantry (*hoplitai*) and the light infantry (*peltastai* or *psiloi*). Much the most important element were the hoplites, and for their call-up on each occasion a special muster-roll (*katalogos*) was drawn up[235] based on the population registers of the demes.[236] We know from Thucydides that a hoplite *katalogos* did not include *thetes*;[237] and Harpokration also says that *thetes* did not serve as hoplites.[238] Similarly with naval service: apart from trierarchs and officers (*hyperesia*), the naval vessels were manned by marines (*epibatai*) and oarsmen (*nautai*):[239] and in connection with the despatch of a fleet to Lesbos in 428 we learn that *pentakosiomedimnoi* and *hippeis* were not called up for naval service.[240] *Epibatai* may have had hoplite equipment, but two passages in Thucydides show that they were normally recruited from the *thetes*,[241] and received their equipment from the state.[242] Thus, social groups and types of national service corresponded: the upper class

[229] Arist. *Ath. Pol.* 26.2.   [230] Arist. *Ath. Pol.* 7.3–4.   [231] See pp. 107–8.
[232] Arist. *Ath. Pol.* 7.4. Rhodes (1981a) 145–6.
[233] Raubitschek (1949) no. 372 = no. 269 (P. A. Hansen).
[234] *IG* I³ 46.43–6 = M&L 49.39–42 and Fornara (1977) no. 100.
[235] Ar. *Eq.* 1369–71; Thuc. 7.16.1; Lys. 9.4. Hansen (1985a) 83–9.
[236] *IG* I³ 138; Meritt (1962) 22–34.   [237] Thuc. 6.43.1.
[238] Harp. s.v. *thetes kai thetikon*.   [239] Morrison (1984).   [240] Thuc. 3.16.1.
[241] Thuc. 6.43.1, 8.24.2.   [242] Gomme, Andrewes and Dover (1970) 310.

served in the cavalry, the middle class were the core of the army as hoplites, and the lower class, the *thetes*, dominated the fleet and served as light armed soldiers in the army.[243] In the fifth century and the first decades of the fourth the Solonian property classes went on playing this important role in the structure of Athenian society.

EXCURSUS 2   KLEISTHENES' REDIVISION OF ATTICA

We have seen that before Kleisthenes the Athenians were divided into four tribes (*phylai*), and each tribe into three ridings (*trittyes*) and twelve *naukrariai*.[244] There was also a quite different set of divisions: the tribes were divided into a number of phratries (*phratriai*), and the phratries were subdivided into a number of *gene*.[245] A *genos* was a clan,[246] but not necessarily an aristocratic kinship group, though that has been the accepted view until recently.[247] Perhaps the phratries were in origin military comrades' associations,[248] but in the classical period the Athenians preferred to regard them as groups of people very distantly related to each other,[249] centred round the cult of Zeus Phratrios, Athena Phratria,[250] Zeus Herkeios and Apollo Patroös.[251] They all celebrated the festival of Apatouria,[252] common to all Ionians,[253] and on the third day of the festival fathers had their three- to four-year old sons inscribed in their phratry.[254] A passage in Drakon's homicide law implies that every Athenian citizen was a member of a phratry.[255] A preserved list of phratry members records only twenty names[256] and another list indicates a membership of about 120.[257] Thus there must have been at least a hundred phratries, perhaps even several hundred. This whole archaic social structure was allowed to survive in classical times[258] (except the *naukrariai*, which were abolished either by Kleisthenes or at the beginning of the fifth century);[259] but the old tribes were reduced by Kleisthenes' reform to cult societies without significance for politics, and the condition for becoming a citizen was no longer membership of a phratry alone but registration in a Deme as well.[260]

[243] Arist. *Pol.* 1321a5–15.   [244] Arist. *Ath. Pol.* 8.3. Roussel (1976) 193–204.
[245] Arist. *Ath. Pol.* fr. 3.   [246] Bourriot (1976).   [247] Andrewes (1961a).
[248] Hom. *Il.* B 362–6. Andrewes (1961B) 140; Roussel (1976) 121.
[249] Philoch. fr. 35; Arist. *Pol.* 1252b16–18. Nilsson (1951) 65ff.   [250] *IG* II² 2344.1.
[251] Pl. *Euthydemus.* 302B–D; Arist. *Ath. Pol.* 55.3.
[252] Schol. Ar. *Ach.* 146. Deubner (1932) 232–4; Parke (1977) 88–92.   [253] Hdt. 1.147.2.
[254] *IG* II² 1237.26–9; *P. Oxy.* 2538 col. ii 25–7 (Lys).
[255] *IG* I³ 104.18 = *M&L* 86 and Fornara (1977) no. 15B.   [256] *IG* II² 2344. Flower (1985).
[257] *IG* II² 2345.
[258] Arist. *Ath. Pol.* 21.6; *Hesperia* 4 (1935) 19–32 no. 2 = Harding (1985) no. 9.
[259] Arist. *Ath. Pol.* 21.5; Clid. fr. 8.   [260] Isoc. 8.88; Dem. 57.46.

Kleisthenes' reform is described in two sources, Herodotos 5.69 and Aristotle, *Constitution of Athens* 21.2–6. Attica was divided first into three regions, the city (*asty*), the inland region (*mesogeios*) and the coast (*paralia*); each region was divided into ten ridings (*trittyes*);[261] and each riding comprised a number of demes, in the fourth century from one to ten demes per riding.[262]

The demes were the foundation of Kleisthenes' reform. A deme was a natural geographical entity: a country village plus its surrounding fields; a stretch of coast centred on a harbour; a valley at the foot of a mountain; a quarter in Athens itself, which was the only large conurbation.[263] But a deme was also a political entity, in that all the citizens living within the area of the deme were made members of it.[264] In fact, a deme was a society rather than a locality. Geographically speaking, it was first and foremost the place where its members met for purposes of politics and cult: it was a point rather than an area, and Strabo is evidence that there were no literal 'parish boundaries' between demes,[265] though accumulating discoveries of boundary stones between demes[266] are a warning that there must have been numerous exceptions to what Strabo says. In Kleisthenes' time, indeed, the members of a deme were all those citizens living in the neighbourhood of the place where the deme held its assembly, but prosopographical studies show that Kleisthenes made deme-membership hereditary,[267] thus building into his reform a feature that in the course of time was bound to break up the politico-geographical unity of the demes.

There is no evidence that any new demes were created before the Hellenistic age, and it is still universally believed that Kleisthenes created 139 demes in all.[268] The demes varied in size, but not until the fourth century do we acquire, from lists of the *prytaneis* and the Council, evidence for their representation on the Council and so for their relative sizes.[269] There must have been changes between the end of the sixth century and the beginning of the fourth;[270] but by cautious extrapolation we can conclude that several demes even in Kleisthenes' time were so

---

[261] Arist. *Ath. Pol.* 21.4. Hansen (1990d), *pace* Kinzl (1987), (1989) 348.

[262] The inland ridings of Oineis (VI) and Aiantis (IX) consisted of one deme only, i.e. Acharnai (VI) and Aphidna (IX), whereas the city riding of Aigeis (II) consisted of ten small demes.

[263] Traill (1986) 123–49.   [264] Arist. *Ath. Pol.* 21.4. Whitehead (1986) 16–38.

[265] Strabo 1.65. Thompson (1971) 72–9.   [266] Traill (1986) 116–22.

[267] E.g. Megakles Hippokratous of Alopeke (*IG* I² 908; Hdt. 6.131.2), father of Megakles Megakleous of Alopeke (*IG* I³ 322–4).

[268] Traill (1975) 73–6; Whitehead (1986) 21.   [269] *Agora* XV 2–56.

[270] Hansen et al. (1990) 30.

tiny that they only sent one representative to the Council, while others were ten or twenty times larger.[271]

The 139 demes were distributed among 30 ridings: we have no evidence as to Kleisthenes' basis for the distribution, but it is reasonable to suppose that the ridings were roughly equal in population, and that a riding was originally a geographical unit; the considerable geographical irregularities in the make-up of the ridings in the fourth century are likely to be due to adjustments made, perhaps, in 403/2, when so much else was redrawn.[272]

It was by the assignment of demes to tribes and ridings that Kleisthenes sought to break up the old social structures and create new political entities. In the north-east corner of Attica, for example, lay the Tetrapolis (the 'Four Towns') of Trikorynthos, Probalinthos, Oinoe and Marathon, which, in the *stasis* of the sixth century, had supported Peisistratos; so it is no chance that the Tetrapolis was broken up by Kleisthenes: Probalinthos was removed and became part of one tribe (Pandionis, tribe III), while the remaining three became part of another (Aiantis, tribe IX), along with the deme Rhamnous to the north, which had a quite different background and tradition.[273]

It has been suggested that Kleisthenes, who was a member of the Alkmaionids, arranged by his distribution to privilege the interest of his own clan and prevent others from gaining too great political influence.[274] That may well be so: the trouble is that we are not, by and large, in a position to know which irregularities in the structure go back to Kleisthenes and which are due to the probable later revision, which we may date about 403/2.

Each of the ten new tribes was composed of three ridings, one from the city, one from the inland region and one from the coast. According to Aristotle the distribution of the ridings into tribes was decided by lot,[275] and we have no reason to doubt him. If we suppose that Kleisthenes' desire was to break up the old groupings,[276] that purpose was sufficiently served by the use of the lot, and it was of secondary importance if it occasionally resulted in a tribe having, for example, an inland riding and a coastal riding geographically side by side. Precisely that situation can be detected on the east coast of Attica, where the coastal ridings of tribes IX, II, III and V bordered directly on the inland ridings of the same tribes. That configuration may perfectly well have been the outcome of the lot;[277] but it cannot, of course, be excluded that Kleisthenes gerrymandered the allotment in some way. With that reservation, how-

---

[271] See p. 102.
[272] Hansen (1990d) 53.   [273] Lewis (1963) 30–1.
[274] Lewis (1963); Stanton (1984).   [275] Arist. *Ath. Pol.* 21.4.   [276] Arist. *Ath. Pol.* 21.2.
[277] Hansen (1987b), *pace* Siewert (1982) 26.

ever, in general the system ensured that each tribe would consist of citizens from different parts of Attica.

The tribes were named after the heroes of Athens. The story is that Kleisthenes picked the names of 100 heroes and sent them to Delphi, and the Delphic oracle picked the ten heroes after whom the tribes were to be named: Erechtheis (I), Aigeis (II), Pandionis (III), Leontis (IV), Akamantis (V), Oineis (VI), Kekropis (VII), Hippothontis (VIII), Aiantis (IX) and Antiochis (X).[278] That order was official and was used, for example, in lists of councillors, citizens fallen in battle, and boards of magistrates.[279]

What, then, to sum up, was the purpose of these complexities? For what purposes of political organization was it needful to break up the old groupings and invent new ones that smack so strongly of the abstract drawing-board? What practical matters were artificial space and artificial time supposed to influence? For we can hardly suppose that Kleisthenes did it all, and that the Athenians accepted it, for merely academic satisfaction. Reflection suggests that two Athenian institutions above all were intended to be put beyond the reach of the old aristocratic influences: the army and the Council. The army was divided into ten regiments, of which each tribe supplied one, and the citizens of a tribe – coming from all over Attica – would henceforward fight side-by-side in the ranks, commanded by officers from their own tribe.[280] But still more important was the politico-geographical reform of Kleisthenes for the structure of his Council of Five Hundred, organized by tribes but related to the sizes of the demes, the basic unit of the whole democracy.[281]

EXCURSUS 3   SELECTION OF MAGISTRATES BY LOT

Deep disunity prevails amongst historians as to when the Athenians first began to select their magistrates by lot. The disunity has its roots in our principal source, the *Constitution of Athens*, where Aristotle sets out the development in five stages: selection by lot of minor magistrates (Drakon's alleged constitution of *c*.621);[282] selection of all magistrates by lot from an elected short-list (Solon, *c*.594);[283] election of archons (from the sixth century to 487);[284] selection by lot of archons from an elected short-list (487–403);[285] selection by lot of archons and other magistrates (403

---

[278] Arist. *Ath. Pol.* 21.6. Kearns (1989) 80–92.
[279] *Agora* XV 42; *Agora* XVII 23; *IG* II² 1388.1–12.
[280] Arist. *Ath. Pol.* 61.3; Thuc. 6.98.4.   [281] Traill (1975) 64–72.
[282] Arist. *Ath. Pol.* 4.3.   [283] Arist. *Ath. Pol.* 8.1.
[284] Arist. *Ath. Pol.* 22.5.
[285] Arist. *Ath. Pol.* 22.5.

onwards).[286] Aristotle's account exhibits a curious symmetry (A-B-C-B-A), which may delight a structuralist but is worrying to the historian; it takes one aback that the use of the lot, which is supposed to be *par excellence* the 'democratic' way of doing things,[287] should have been introduced as early as the end of the seventh century (minor magistrates) and the beginning of the sixth (archons). Aristotle, it is true, like many of his contemporaries, believed that Athenian democracy was invented by Solon, abolished by Peisistratos and reintroduced by Kleisthenes;[288] but alleged pre-Peisistratean democracy can only be a reflection of the constitutional conflicts between democrats and oligarchs at the end of the fifth century, when both factions claimed to be restoring the 'ancestral constitution'.[289] There can really be no doubt that Drakon's alleged constitution must be rejected as a reminiscence of a political pamphlet that has crept into history by mistake.[290] And can one rely to any greater degree on Aristotle's second stage, where he carries selection by lot back to Solon? He quotes, indeed, a law of Solon for the proposition that the Treasurers of Athena, one from each tribe, must be selected by lot from the *pentakosiomedimnoi*;[291] but the law in question can only have said that they must be chosen from that class: that they had to be chosen *by lot* and *one from each tribe* must be either Aristotle's own paraphrase of a genuine Solonian law (quite correctly understood from the standpoint of his own day) or a quotation from the Solonian law as revised in 403/2.[292]

Now, whether one believes or disbelieves that the Athenians were using the lot as early as Solon really depends on one's conception of the original purpose of the lot as a process of selection. Some think that it was only secondarily a democratic procedure, and that it was originally an institution reflecting the nexus of state and religion in archaic Greece: by using the lot you left to the gods the decision about who should run the community.[293] Only in the fifth century was it reinterpreted as the supremely democratic procedure for maintaining the equality of all and their equal right to rule.

Seeking the advice of the gods by means of the lot is, indeed, an age-old device in every country all over the world. If you wanted the gods to give sentence in a difficult case you could use the lot, or dice, just as well as ordeal; and, if you wanted to ask them for advice about the future, one well-known method was to offer them a set of alternatives to choose from by a drawing of lots by oracular priests.[294] On Germanic

[286] Arist. *Ath. Pol.* 8.1, 55.1, 62.1. Hansen (1986b), *pace* Abel (1983).
[287] Hdt. 3.80.6; Ps. Xen. *Ath. Pol.* 1.2–3; Arist. *Pol.* 1294b8–9.
[288] Arist. *Ath. Pol.* 41.2.   [289] See p. 40.   [290] See p. 19.
[291] Arist. *Ath. Pol.* 8.1, 47.1.   [292] Hansen (1990e) 57–8.
[293] Coulanges (1878) 613ff; Glotz (1907) 1401–8; Andrewes (1982) 386.
[294] Latte (1939) 831ff.

soil the ordeal was widespread but the lot oracle little used; by contrast, in ancient Greece there are only a few traces of ordeal,[295] whereas cleromancy, the lot oracle, flourished in archaic, classical and Hellenistic times.[296] In a fourth-century decree of the Athenian Assembly there is a minute description of the procedure of drawing lots where a matter is to be put to the Delphic oracle.[297] Priests were often selected by lot:[298] priests are the servants of the god; let him choose. Now, it is on that analogy that historians speculate that the lot was also used in archaic times in the choice of magistrates: archons had, after all, wide-ranging responsibilities in relation to cult. Aristotle, it is said, was quite right in his information that the archons were selected by lot in Solon's time, only wrong in his interpretation of it as a 'democratic' institution.

The theory is exciting, but weakly based. For one thing, the only text that unambiguously states that priests were selected by lot so as to leave the choice to the gods is a passage in Plato's *Laws*;[299] but in that very work Plato distinguishes between selection by lot of priests and election of magistrates[300] and insists on the distinction between sortition and divine decision.[301] What is more, those lot-chosen priests were subject to *dokimasia*, the scrutiny of qualifications before entry into office[302] – hardly a compliment to divine omniscience. All in all, there is not a single good source that straightforwardly testifies to the selection of magistrates by lot as having a religious character or origin,[303] whereas the connection of lot and democracy is a commonplace in the sources. Now, that could be simply due to the fact that the sources only begin to be abundant at a time when the lot had already come to be seen as a democratic procedure: the shortage of sources prior to 403 is so marked that the theory about the religious significance of sortition of officials can certainly not be ruled out by an argument from silence. More significant, however, is that other sources actually contradict the *Constitution of Athens*: in book 2 of the *Politics* Aristotle himself writes that Solon introduced the 'ancestral democracy' as a 'mixed' constitution in which election (as opposed to sortition) of magistrates was retained as the 'aristocratic' element;[304] and election was praised by Isokrates as just such an element in the 'original' democracy, introduced by Solon and reintroduced by Kleisthenes,[305] while in a forensic speech from the fourth

[295] Hom. *Il.* 3.316ff, 7.161ff. Glotz (1904); Ehrenberg (1921) 73ff; (1927) 1452.
[296] Latte (1939). [297] *IG* II² 204.23–54 = Harding (1985) no. 78.
[298] *IG* I³ 35.3–8 = *M&L* 44 and Fornara (1977) no. 93; *SEG* 12 80; Dem. 57.46ff. Feaver (1957).
[299] Pl. *Lg* 759B, cf. 741B. [300] Morrow (1960) 159–62.
[301] Pl. *Lg*. 757B.
[302] Pl. *Lg*. 759C.
[303] Headlam (1891) 78–87; Ehrenberg (1927) 1461–4; Staveley (1972) 34–6.
[304] Arist. *Pol*. 1273b35–41. [305] Isoc. 12.145, 153–4.

century it is asserted that the king archon under the 'ancestral democracy' was chosen by election from an elected short-list – double election and no lot at all.[306]

The sources are in conflict, which shows that the Athenians themselves had no clear knowledge how the archons were chosen in the seventh and sixth centuries; and the only form of selection by lot that can with any plausibility be thought to go back to Solon is the annual sortition of jurors for the People's Court. Against that, there is absolutely no doubt that the selection of the archons by lot in the classical age was a 'democratic' procedure, introduced twenty years after the reforms of Kleisthenes; and, if we ask how it was done before that, it can be said that archons were chosen by direct election in the period 501–487, while before that the evidence is contradictory.

But there is one powerful indication of election as the original procedure for choosing magistrates: in the classical age the Athenians held absolutely fast to the principle that military magistrates must be elected and not selected by lot. It is hardly conceivable that in the seventh and sixth centuries they put themselves in a position of fighting under commanders chosen by lot.[307] The Board of Generals was instituted in 502/1;[308] from then down to 487 the army was commanded by the polemarch and the generals together,[309] whereas before 501 it had been commanded by the polemarch alone. It is just possible that the nine elected archons in the period 501–487 drew lots for which of them should be archon and which king archon and which polemarch;[310] but it is extremely unlikely that Solon introduced the procedure by which the polemarch was chosen by lot from an elected short-list of forty, of whom only a few would have been likely to possess the necessary military experience.

These considerations should be sufficient to put out of court the notion that in the archaic age the Athenian magistrates were selected by lot.

EXCURSUS 4   PERIKLES' CITIZENSHIP LAW

By means of the democratic reform of 507 Kleisthenes had got a large number of metics and foreigners naturalized,[311] and down to the middle of the fifth century citizenship was given without question to *metroxenoi*, those whose fathers were citizens but their mothers not: Kleisthenes' own

[306] Dem. 59.75. Hansen (1986b) 225.   [307] Meyer (1937) 608 n. 2.
[308] Arist. *Ath. Pol.* 22.2. Rhodes (1981a) 262.   [309] Hdt. 6.109.2.
[310] Lang (1959) 88; Bicknell (1971) 147–9.
[311] Arist. *Pol.* 1275b35–7; Arist. *Ath. Pol.* 21.4.

mother was a daughter of Kleisthenes of Sikyon,[312] and both Themis-tokles[313] and Kimon[314] had Thracian mothers. It is even possible that citizens could have their offspring from slave women inscribed as citizens in their deme. In the first half of the fifth century the citizen population must have risen steadily, partly by natural increase (but that was never more than a few tenths of a percentage point a year), partly because of the *metroxenoi*, and partly, it must be concluded, because Athens attracted many metics, who somehow had no great difficulty in becoming citizens if they settled, especially if they married a citizen woman.[315] The result was that Athens simply had too many citizens to function properly as a *polis*: in 450 there may have been something like 60,000 adult male citizens.[316] One remedy employed by Perikles was to send thousands of poorer citizens, sometimes to start émigré communities as colonists, but more frequently to various subject cities, where they received plots of land and were called *klerouchoi* (possessors of a *kleros*), retaining their Athenian citizenship.[317] But a more important remedy was the citizenship law of 451, by which Athenian citizenship was made to depend on Athenian parentage on both sides, and the son of an Athenian citizen and a foreign woman could no longer be registered in his father's deme as a full citizen;[318] what is more, at least by Demosthenes' time, mixed marriages were actually heavily penalized.[319] Aristotle says explicitly that Perikles' law was enacted 'because of the number of citizens'.[320]

Perikles' citizenship law was not made retroactive, but those born of non-citizen mothers and not yet adult in 451/50 were probably excluded from citizenship.[321] When Prince Psammetichos of Egypt in 445/4 sent the Athenians 30,000 (or 40,000) *medimnoi* of corn to be distributed free among the citizens, opportunity was taken to look into who really possessed the citizenship, and it appears that the investigation led to the expulsion of no less than 5000 people from the registers.[322] This large number indicates that the citizenship law was at that time being applied as rigorously as possible. The Peloponnesian War, however, brought with it such a drastic reduction in citizen numbers that for a time the Athenians turned a blind eye to the Periklean law[323] and, what is more, on several occasions bestowed citizenship on larger groups of foreigners, for example the Plataians in 427[324] and the Samians in 405.[325] Upon the restoration

---

[312] Hdt. 6.130–1. [313] Plut. *Them.* 1.1.
[314] Hdt. 6.39.2; Plut. *Cim.* 4.1. [315] Davies (1977–8) 107; Patterson (1981) 70.
[316] Rhodes (1988) 275; Hansen (1988a) 14–28. [317] Jones (1957) 167–73.
[318] Arist. *Ath. Pol.* 26.4. [319] Dem. 59.16. [320] Arist. *Ath. Pol.* 26.4.
[321] Hignett (1952) 345; Humphreys (1974) 92–3. [322] Philoch. fr. 119; Plut. *Per.* 37.2.
[323] Isoc. 8.88. Humphreys (1974) 93–4.
[324] Dem. 59.104–5. Osborne (1981) D 1.
[325] *IG* II² 1.51–5 = Tod 97 and Fornara (1977) no. 166. Osborne (1981) D 4.

of democracy in 403/2, however, the law of Perikles was reintroduced by Aristophon and Nikomenes;[326] it remained unmodified all through the fourth century[327] and the Athenians no longer passed block grants of citizenship,[328] only individual grants, mostly as honours to foreigners who would not dream of taking up residence in Attica.[329]

Perikles' citizenship law had wide-ranging consequences, ideologically as well as demographically. The citizen population was, even more than before, a closed circle, deliberately isolated from the rest of the population; and demographically it had an effect perhaps much more drastic than had been foreseen: namely, that the natural increase in the citizen numbers was curtailed and at some periods could not even balance the numbers who left Attica to live elsewhere as metics or *klerouchoi*.[330] The citizen population of Athens had probably been halved in the Peloponnesian War,[331] and it never again approached the size it had been under Perikles, no doubt mainly because a juridically defined group, such as the Athenian citizen body was after 451, was incapable of recovering from the losses from the war (431–404), the plague (430–426), and the famine during the siege of 405/4. Throughout the fourth century, citizen numbers were stationary at about 30,000.[332]

The decline in citizen numbers must have affected all aspects of Athenian society. For one thing, in the fourth century there must, on average, have been twice as much land per citizen, and that may well be one of the reasons why redistribution of land, a major question in other democratic city-states, is never heard of as a problem at Athens. The introduction of pay for attending the Assembly in about 400 may have been another consequence: the Athenians upheld the requirement of a quorum of 6000 for certain types of decree and in the course of the century extended it, for example to citizenship decrees.[333] But, although, after the Peloponnesian War, it became more difficult to collect 6000 citizens, instead of lowering the quorum they preferred to stimulate attendance by paying for participation.[334]

It is often remarked that Spartan society suffered from lack of citizens (*oliganthropia*),[335] but it has not been often enough pointed out that fourth-century Athens also suffered from *oliganthropia*, which, though less severe than in Sparta, affected the democratic institutions and the society as a whole.

[326] Ath. 577B; Schol. Aeschin. 1.39.   [327] Hansen (1982) 177.
[328] Hansen (1982) 178.   [329] Osborne (1983) 147–50.
[330] Hansen (1982) 179–84; (1985) 8–9.   [331] Hansen (1988a) 26–8.
[332] See p. 92.   [333] See p. 130.   [334] See p. 150.
[335] Cartledge (1979) 307–18.

4

Athens as a City-State and as a Democracy

Polis

Classical Greece was divided into some 750 *poleis*[1] or 'city-states', as people like to call them. To the 750 must be added at least 300 more, founded by the Greeks as émigré communities outside Greece proper, mostly in the archaic age:[2] thus, historians have identified seventy-two *poleis* in Thrace alone between the Strymon and the Danube.[3] All round the coasts of the Mediterranean and the Black Sea sat Greek city-states 'like frogs round a pond', in Plato's vivid phrase.[4] Most of them were tiny, with an average territory of less than 100 sq. km and a citizen population of fewer than 1000 adult males; not more than a couple of hundred were larger than that, and even a powerful city-state such as Corinth only covered 900 sq. km, with a population in the classical period of about 10,000–15,000 adult male citizens.[5] Athens was in population the largest of all the *poleis* in Greece itself, and in territory the second largest next to Lakedaimon; and the town of Athens proper (the *asty*) along with the harbour town of the Piraeus was the only large conurbation in the territory of Attica, which had an area of about 2500 sq. km.[6] The size of the population as a whole is unknown, but it can be deduced from the evidence that there were some 60,000 male citizens when Perikles was the leader of Athens in the fifth century[7] and about 30,000 when Demosthenes was its leader against Philip of Macedon a hundred years later.[8] In fact, in some Greek eyes, Athens was actually too *large* to be a proper *polis*.

[1] Ruschenbusch (1978a) 3–17; (1985b) 253–63.
[2] Graham (1982) 160–2 (the best selection).   [3] Isaac (1986) xii, 283.
[4] Pl. *Phd.* 109B.   [5] Salmon (1984) 165–9.
[6] Busolt and Swoboda (1920–6) 758.   [7] Hansen (1988a) 14–28.
[8] See p. 92.

But what was a *polis*? The Greek word *polis* or *ptolis* (perhaps the Mycenean *po-te-ri-jo*) is related etymologically to Old Indian *púr* and Lithuanian *pilis*, and in all three languages its basic sense is 'stronghold'.[9] In older Greek, *polis* could be used as a synonym for *akropolis*, the 'stronghold on the height',[10] which was often a fortified hill with the royal residence and the principal shrines: thus, the *akropolis* was at once the centre of defence, government and cult. A town (*asty*) would grow up at the foot of the *akropolis*, new walls would be built around the whole town, and the whole would be called the *polis* (= *asty*),[11] as against the countryside, the *chora*. That is how *polis* came to mean a 'city',[12] and the development continued with its gradually coming to signify a city plus the countryside attached to it: *polis* was the generic term for *asty*-plus-*chora*,[13] i.e. a 'country', as we should say, or, in political terms, a 'state'.[14] By the fourth century the sense of 'stronghold' for *polis* had disappeared, and the sense 'country' too occurs very seldom even in quite early sources; by the time of Demosthenes *polis* was used almost exclusively in two senses: geographically to mean a 'city' and politically to mean a 'state'.[15] Hence the word 'city-state': it is a made-up word found only in history books, as a way of talking about a self-governing community of limited size consisting of a city plus a territory, in which the city is the political centre and the territory provides a measure of economic independence (*autarkeia*).[16]

When we nowadays talk of city-states we think at once of ancient Greece, but it must not be forgotten that city-states (not all of quite the same kind in all respects) existed in other places and in other ages. The oldest known are the Sumerian city-states in lower Mesopotamia between 3500 and 2300 BC, of which Uruk, Ur and Lagash were the most significant.[17] In the first millennium there flourished a whole group of Phoenician city-states, notably Arados, Byblos, Sidon and Tyre in the homeland and Carthage in North Africa.[18] The Etruscan people were divided into maybe twelve city-states until they were absorbed by the Romans in the fifth century BC.[19] So much for antiquity; but in the High Middle Ages northern Italy was entirely fragmented into city-states, with Florence, Milan and Venice vying for the primacy,[20] and at the

---

[9] Frisk (1970).

[10] Hom. *Il.* 6.327, 7.345. *IG¹* 3 40.60 = *M&L* 52 and Fornara (1977) no. 103. Lévy (1983) 57.

[11] Hom. *Od.* 6.262ff; Thuc. 6.45; Isoc. 14.7. Musiolek (1981).   [12] Thuc. 2.15.6.

[13] Pl. *Lg.* 746A; Arist. *Oec.* 1343a10.   [14] *M&L* 2 (seventh century BC); Ar. *Eccl.* 218.

[15] Aeneas Tacticus 1.1 (state), 2.1 (city).   [16] Arist. *Pol.* 1326b2ff.

[17] Griffeth and Thomas (1981) 1–30.   [18] Harden (1980).

[19] Pallottino (1975) 124–37.   [20] Waley (1978).

same time there existed seven free Swiss cities that were obviously city-states, and in Germany some eighty *Reichsstädte*: these, dotted about amongst the principalities and episcopal states, did not constitute a united territory and were, at least in principle, imperial cities, but otherwise met most of the criteria that define a city-state.[21] Or we can pass outside our own cultural sphere, and find city-states in Mexico under the Toltecs and Chichimecans from AD 1000 to 1300;[22] and in Africa south of the Sahara and east of the Niger, on the vast pastoral plain, the Hausa were organized in seven city-states between about 1450 and 1804.[23] In all these cases there was a large people sharing a common language and traditions but split up into little states, each centred on a city, each city-state jealously guarding its autonomy while at the same time attempting to subvert that of its neighbours. Apart, however, from a few short-lived conquests, no city-state ever succeeded in gaining sovereignty over the rest, and in every case the autonomy of the little states was finally brought to an end by the conquest of the whole area by some neighbouring great power.

State

So, a Greek *polis* was a self-governing community centred on a city: but was it a state in our sense? Well, yes and no. In the sources the word *polis* is used in all the sentences where we should use the word 'state': the *polis* legislated,[24] went to war,[25] levied taxes,[26] undertook public expenditures,[27] had frontiers with other *poleis*,[28] was damaged by treachery,[29] and so on. *Polis* is also used in a wider context for political entities that were certainly not city-states: Lakedaimon,[30] for example, which, including Messenia, covered 8000 sq. km and did not have a fortified city at its centre at all; and the Akarnanians, who were actually a federation of thirty-four different *poleis*.[31]

On the other hand, there are a number of important differences between the modern state and an ancient Greek *polis*, as can be seen as soon as we raise the question of what a 'state' is. The modern concept of a state is not discussed by historians, who take it for granted, nor by political scientists, who prefer to speak of 'political systems', but it is talked about by jurists studying international law, amongst whom there seems to be general agreement that three elements are involved in the concept of a

[21] Griffeth and Thomas (1981) 109–42. [22] Katz (1972) 127–33.
[23] Griffeth and Thomas (1981) 143–80. [24] Ar. *Vesp.* 467.
[25] Aeschin. 3.122. [26] *IG* II² 2492.25. [27] Thuc. 2.70.2.
[28] Aeschin. 3.133. [29] Hyp.3.8. [30] Thuc. 1.10.2.
[31] *IG* II² 43.106 = Tod 123 and Harding (1985) no. 35.

state: a territory, a people, and organs of government that exercise territorial sovereignty within the territory and authority over the individuals composing the people.[32] A state is, therefore, a government with the sole right to exercise a given legal order within a given area over a given population.

Territory

Now, according to the Greek conception, most clearly formulated by Aristotle, a *polis* was, 'a community [*koinonia*] of citizens [*politai*] with regard to the constitution [*politeia*]',[33] and *politeia* is further defined as the 'organization of political institutions, in particular the highest political institution'.[34] It is at once apparent that Aristotle only picks up two of the three elements that comprise the modern juristic idea of a state – the people and the constitution: the territory is left out altogether, and that is not by chance. For Aristotle asserts that no one is a citizen by mere domicile in a particular place,[35] and thus hits upon one fundamental difference between the *polis* and the modern state. We nowadays tend to equate a state with its territory – a state is a country; whereas the Greeks identified the state primarily with its people – a state is a people. Of course, the Greeks knew all about the territory of a state: the frequently used penalty of exile consisted precisely in the right of anyone to kill the outlaw if found within the territorial bounds,[36] so they were perfectly capable of saying 'the *polis* stretches to this-and-this point and not beyond'. But territory was not nearly as important for them as it is for us:[37] in all the sources, from documents and historical accounts to poetry and legend, it is the people who are stressed and not the territory,[38] a habit of thought that can be traced right back to the poet Alkaios round about 600 BC.[39] It was never Athens and Sparta that went to war but always 'the Athenians and the Lakedaimonians'.[40]

One of the corollaries of this difference between *polis* and state is that a high proportion of the population of a *polis* were liable to be not citizens of the *polis* but either free foreigners (often called metics) or slaves.[41] In a European state from the late Middle Ages on, virtually all the inhabitants were also citizens, so that one could identify the state with those domiciled in the territory and, consequently, with the territory. In a Greek *polis* it

---

[32] Starke (1989) 95 (Montevideo Convention of 1933).   [33] Arist. *Pol.* 1276b1.
[34] Arist. *Pol.* 1278b8–10.   [35] Arist. *Pol.* 1275a7.
[36] Dem. 23.37, 39ff; Philoch. fr. 30.
[37] Hampl (1939); Gschnitzer (1955). But see Osborne (1987) 51.
[38] Hdt. 8.61.2; Thuc. 7.77.7; Pl. *Def.* 415C.   [39] Alc. fr. 426. Smith (1907).
[40] Thuc. 5.25.1.   [41] Arist. *Pol.* 1326a16–20.

was not possible to identify the state with those domiciled in the territory and so with the territory: it was necessary to identify the state with the citizens (the *politai*),[42] who had in principle the exclusive right to own and use the territory. Louis XIV of France is supposed to have said, 'l 'état, c'est moi': the Athenian citizens could, with even greater justice, have said, 'The *polis* is *us*.'[43]

These two sayings actually bring out quite an important nuance in how a political community is regarded. A state can be looked at from two standpoints: either as a community of citizens manifesting itself in a set of organs with a government at the head,[44] or as a set of organs, typically a government, exercising rule over its citizens.[45] In modern states, even democracies, there is a tendency to identify the state with the executive and the government rather than with the people,[46] but in a democratic *polis*, especially Athens, government and citizens largely coincided,[47] primarily through the institution of the Assembly of the People,[48] and the dominant ideology was that the *polis* was the people (*demos*): it manifests itself, for example, in all the surviving treaties, where the state of Athens is called *ho demos ho Athenaion*, 'the people of the Athenians'.[49]

If we combine the geographical and political senses of the word *polis* we can see another difference between the Greek city-state and a European territorial state. In most modern European languages there are contrasting pairs of words for city and country: city/country, *Stadt*/*Land*, *cité*/*pays*, and so on; but, whereas in Greek it was the 'city' word that came to mean 'state', in most European languages the 'country' word has come to have that sense. The Greeks had small units with centralized government; feudal Europe in the Middle Ages had very decentralized government, and the kings travelled with their courts from castle to castle, so that it was not possible to identify the nation or the state with any specific locality: it could only be identified with the country as a whole. What is more, the political units were far bigger, so that every nation had numerous cities, instead of just one that was the national centre.

Size

And that is the next difference between *polis* and state: in population and geography the *polis* was a Lilliput.[50] Larger units the Greeks usually

---

[42] Arist. *Pol.* 1274b41, 1275b20.   [43] Dem. 43.72.

[44] Barker (1951) 91.   [45] Vincent (1987) 29–32.   [46] Holden (1988) 22.

[47] As in *IG*. I³ 101.49, 53 = *M&L* 89 and Fornara (1977) 156.   [48] Dem. 3.31.

[49] *IG* II² 96.9 = Tod 126; Dem. 9.42. Hansen (1983a) 142 n. 12.

[50] Arist. *Eth. Nic* 1170b30ff. Ruschenbusch (1978a) 7–13.

called *ethne* ('peoples'),[51] not *poleis*; and, because the Greek city-states were small, they did not normally need to think in terms of political representation: even in democracies the government could perfectly well be direct. All citizens could meet without difficulty in the People's Assembly and serve in the citizen militia.

A *polis* was a 'face-to-face society'; that is often asserted,[52] but if a *polis* spread over too large an area some citizens could not come regularly into the city and take part in the Assembly or the festivals, and if a *polis* acquired too many citizens it would have needed the voice of Stentor to summon them all to the levy or to the Assembly.[53] Experience seems to show that an assembly of 10,000 or more is too large for genuine debate,[54] and the Athenians could not live up to the ideal that everybody should know everybody else;[55] so Athens was not, in fact, a 'face-to-face society',[56] and the political community of the citizens could only function *because* out of the 30,000 full citizens not more than 6000, as a rule, turned up for the Assembly and the People's Courts.[57] The astonishing fact that it was possible to collect, on more than one day in two, as many as several thousand citizens for the courts, and, several times a month, more than 6000 for the Assembly is to be explained by several consider-ations. First, the Athenians were accustomed to travel long distances on foot or on a donkey: daily mobility was much greater than people now-adays suppose.[58] Secondly, political activity was regarded as a worthy expenditure of time in its own right and not just as a dreary duty.[59] Thirdly, most of the great religious festivals were held in the city,[60] which was also the centre of political life and of commerce. Because the soil of Attica was poor, many citizens had to come often into the city to sell their vegetables or wine or olives and buy corn or meal for their daily living;[61] at the same time, the territory of Attica was incredibly rich in a great variety of products, such as cheese, honey, hides, wool and charcoal, which required a central market. For citizens who lived beyond Pentelikon or Hymettos, smaller centres such as Thorikos in the south of Attica may have been the normal economic focus,[62] but for the vast majority it was Athens.

---

[51] Arist. *Pol.* 1326b4; *Hell. Oxy.* 16.4. Weil (1960) 367–415.
[52] Laslett (1956) 162; Finley (1983) 28–9.   [53] Arist. *Pol.* 1326b5–7.
[54] Hansen (1983a) 210.
[55] Thuc. 8.66.3; Isoc. 15.171–2; 11.2, cf. Hansen (1987a) 139 n. 60.
[56] Osborne (1985a) 64–5; Ober (1989) 31–3.   [57] See pp.130–2 and 189.
[58] Forrest (1966) 30–1; Harding (1981); Hansen (1987a) 140 n. 68.
[59] Rahe (1984); Murray (1987) 338 40.   [60] Parke (1977) 25, 174 5.
[61] Isager and Hansen (1975) 51.   [62] Osborne (1985a) 31.

City and country

In the Greek *polis* the contact between city and country was in any case much closer than in the other city-state cultures we know of. In the Greek *polis* citizenship was possessed by city-dwellers and country-dwellers alike, whereas in the medieval city-state it was an exclusive right of the city-dwellers; the country folk were subordinated to the city folk, and only a privileged countryman could ever migrate to the city and become a citizen.[63] The sharp division between city and country began at the gates, where in the daytime there were customs barriers and all traffic in and out was controlled, and by night every gate was locked and guarded.[64] In a Greek city such as Athens the gates were guarded only in time of war;[65] in peacetime, anyone could pass freely during the daylight hours, and, though at night the gates were shut, they seem not to have been guarded[66] and people could still get in and out.[67] The only evidence that customs were levied at the gates is a lexicographical note of doubtful value,[68] and quite certainly nothing was levied on produce brought by citizens into the market. In any case, a substantial number of farmers would have lived in the city and gone out to till their fields.[69]

The all-embracing state?

Was the *polis* just a political community? Many historians, since the famous *La cité antique* of Fustel de Coulanges in 1864, have held that the *polis* embraced *every* side of the existence of its citizens – religion, family, marriage, education, production and trade: the *polis* was a fusion of state and society,[70] so that our word 'state' is only a one-sided and limited translation of *polis*.[71] The belief is a curious mixture of ideal and actuality: Fustel's notion of a *polis* fits mainly the ideal states described in Plato's *Republic* and *Laws* and Aristotle's *Politics*. But those utopias were expressly written to commend to the Greeks how a city-state *ought* to be governed, and with their sharp criticism of contemporary *poleis* Plato and Aristotle are united in showing what a long distance there is between utopia and actuality.[72] When we turn from philosophy to history we can

---

[63] Griffeth and Thomas (1981) 127–8; Waley (1978) 55–66.

[64] Griffeth and Thomas (1981) 87; Bertelli (1978) 41–4.

[65] Aeneas Tacticus 28.1–4.   [66] Thuc. 2.2.3.

[67] Andoc. 1.38.   [68] Hes.s.v. *diapylion*.

[69] Xen. *Oec.* 5.9–11, 11.15–8; Lys. 20.11–2. Osborne (1985a) 47–63, (1987) 94–5; Hansen (1987a) 64 with nn. 413–15.

[70] Coulanges (1864) 3.17 pp. 284–5; Ostwald (1986) xix; Barker (1951) 5–7.

[71] Osborne (1985a) 8–10.   [72] Pl. *Ep.* 7 326A; Arist. *Pol.* 1260b34–5.

see that Fustel's concept of the *polis* properly applied only to Sparta[73] (which ties in neatly with the fact that Sparta was almost the only *polis* that found favour with the philosophers).[74] But there was a world of difference in the fourth century between oligarchic Sparta and democratic Athens. At Athens every citizen had an equal share in the political society, and Athens fulfilled the idea of a *polis* as a community more than did any oligarchy, where many of the poorer citizens were excluded from political rights. On the other hand, the Athenians distinguished between a public sphere, where every citizen took a part, and a private sphere, in which every citizen was entitled to live as he pleased, as long as he obeyed the laws and did not wrong his fellow citizens:[75] they were firmly against the notion that a *polis* ought to control every aspect of the lives of its citizens.

The concept of the *polis* as an essentially political entity emerges even more clearly if we consider the rights (or lack of them) of the different sections of the population of Athens. The *polis* was a society of *citizens*.[76] It was a male society from which women were excluded;[77] all foreigners were also excluded, and metics and slaves, though domiciled in the *polis*, were not members of it,[78] a fact of which they were reminded every day of their lives, when the citizens went off on their own to deal with affairs of state in the Assembly or the Council or the courts. If a metic or a slave was found participating in a political assembly, he was arrested and risked being condemned and executed.[79] Yet every day, when the meetings to deal with affairs of state were over, citizen, metic and slave went off to work side-by-side as artisans, traders or farmers: in the economic sphere the stranger was part of the society, though in the political sphere he was not.

Hence the *polis* was only to a small extent an economic community. The right to own landed property was confined to citizens,[80] yet metics and slaves took part in trade and crafts to the same extent as citizens and often on the same footing. A day's pay, for example, was the same irrespective of status: at the end of the fifth century a citizen, a metic and a slave were alike earning a drachma a day.[81] To a large extent the state involved itself in the economic life of the people only to collect taxes from them and to ensure that a citizen could get his daily bread at a

[73] Murray (1980) 167ff.
[74] Rawson (1969) 61–80.
[75] See p. 75.   [76] Arist. *Pol.* 1276b1–2; Pl. *Def.* 415C.
[77] Ar. *Eccl.* 210ff; Pl. *Resp.* 451C–57B. See pp. 88, 129.
[78] Arist. *Pol.* 1275a7–8, 1326a16–21; Dem. 9.3.   [79] Hansen (1976) 96–8.
[80] See p. 97.   [81] *IG* I³ 476. Austin and Vidal-Naquet (1977) no. 73.

manageable price; otherwise, trade and production were only tangential to the real matters with which the *polis* concerned itself.

In this respect also there was a fundamental difference between ancient Greece and, for example, the Italian city-states of the Middles Ages. In the latter the right to work at a craft or trade was a political right reserved to the citizens just as much as the right to participate in politics, and the political institutions were built directly upon the economic organization of the guilds and associations: economy and politics were interwoven in the activities of the artisans, merchants, jurists, doctors and bankers, through their professional organizations.[82] In the ancient city-state, commerce and crafts were not at all a monopoly of the citizens; on the contrary, the Athenians often tried to encourage foreign craftsmen to move to Athens,[83] and a not-unimportant section of the upper class of Athens (in economic terms) were metics, who lacked political rights. Guilds and associations were unknown in the Greek city-states before the Hellenistic period, when we meet, for example, the Dionysiac Artists, a fully organized association of actors.[84] The Athenians of the classical period had a complicated network of political institutions but, as far as we can tell from the sources, no parallel economic organizations. Recent research has done nothing to undermine what Max Weber asserted in 1921: the citizen of an ancient city-state was *homo politicus*, whereas the citizen of a medieval city-state was *homo oeconomicus*.[85]

The *polis* was, indeed, to a higher degree a religious community.[86] A good deal of cult was concentrated on the great state festivals organized by the magistrates, in which the citizens took part in their political groupings, their tribes and demes.[87] But it is important to stress that priests were never magistrates,[88] and it is also important that metics took part alongside citizens in nearly all the major festivals: they might have an inferior place, but in so far as it was a religious community they, too, could participate;[89] and even women[90] and slaves[91] were allowed to attend many of the ceremonies, including the theatre.[92] So it is misleading to say, as is from time to time said, that the audience in the theatre constituted a kind of political gathering on a par with the Assembly,[93]

---

[82] Griffeth and Thomas (1981) 129–34.

[83] Ps. Xen. *Ath. Pol.* 1.12; Xen. *Vect.* 2–3; Isoc. 8.21.

[84] *SIG*³ 399. Austin (1981) 214–17.

[85] Weber (1921) 756; Humphreys (1978) 159–74.   [86] Xen. *Hell.* 2.4.20–2.

[87] Dem. 44.37–8.   [88] Kahrstedt (1936) 3–4; Hansen (1980c) 170.

[89] *IG* I³ 82.23. Whitehead (1977) 86–9.

[90] Is. 8.19–20; Ar. *Ach.* 253ff. Gould (1980) 50–1.

[91] Philoch. fr. 97. Deubner (1969) 94, 96, 118, 135, 152.

[92] Ar. *Lys.* 1049; Pl. *Grg.* 502D; *Lg.* 658D. Schuller (1985) 52.

[93] Ober (1989) 152, 154.

for if that had been the case no one but citizens would have been there. In fact, the classical city-state was in its basic nature just as secular as the Italian ones, which actually emerged as episcopal jurisdiction gave way to that of the secular consuls.[94] There is no doubt that religion figured prominently in the life of a Greek *polis* just as in an Italian *città* or a German *Reichsstadt*, but in none of them did the state have its root or centre in religion. Anyone who wants to see a city-state that really was a religious community should look at the Sumerian cities, where everything was grouped round the temple and where the highest magistrate (called *ensi*) had as his principal duty that of presiding over the temple administration.[95]

To conclude, Aristotle is completely right in Book 3 of the *Politics* when he defines the *polis* as a 'community of citizens with respect to the constitution',[96] and modern historians are quite wrong when they try to contrast the ancient city-state's alleged fusion of state and society and the modern state's separation of the two.[97] Exactly the opposite can be maintained: in our day there is no longer a sharp distinction between state and society, for the state prevails over all – education, trade and production, the mass media, and so on and the difference between state and society diminishes all the time, notwithstanding the current fashion for privatization;[98] in classical Athens by contrast, the *polis*, which was the political community of the citizens, and the society as a whole, in which all groups participated, were clearly distinguished.

ATHENS AS A DEMOCRACY

Politeia

Aristotle, then, describes the *polis* as a 'community [*koinonia*] of citizens [*politai*] with respect to the constitution [*politeia*]'. At this point some further attention must be given to the last of these elements, *politeia*, for it is the most important in his definition. In Aristotle's conception the nature of a particular *polis* depends on the nature of its *politeia*:[99] a whole community may move to another site, but the *polis* will still be the same, because territory, as we have seen, was of little importance, and even the citizen population only determines the nature of the individual *polis* up to a point, since citizens come and go, die and are born, all the time. The only completely determining factor is the *politeia*. Aristotle uses a

---

[94] Waley (1978) 25.
[95] Griffeth and Thomas (1981) 17–22.
[96] Arist. *Pol.* 1276b1–2.   [97] Held (1987) 17–18; Vincent (1987) 22.
[98] Mannheim (1951) 44; Bobbio (1987) 111.   [99] Arist. *Pol.* 1276b2–9.

simile: the constitution is the course of a river and the citizens are the stream; the water in the river is changing all the time but the river stays the same.[100]

Politeia is always translated 'constitution', and that, on the whole, will do well enough.[101] Of course, the Greek word does not only mean a constitution in the American sense, although constitutions of that kind were not unknown in ancient Greece: for example, that of Kyrene (*c.*320 BC) was engraved on stone and is probably the oldest surviving written constitution in the world.[102] Nor does *politeia* simply mean the sum total of all the rules by which a state is governed. It means, rather, the total political *structure* of a *polis*:[103] the 'soul' of the *polis*, as it could be metaphorically called.[104] And, since a *polis* is, primarily, its citizens, *politeia* could also in appropriate contexts signify 'citizen rights',[105] or the political activity of an individual citizen,[106] or the whole citizen body as an entity.[107]

So the concept of *politeia* was in nature and origin much broader than what we mean by 'constitution'. Nevertheless, in practice it was used more narrowly to mean that which especially bound the citizens together into a society: namely, the political institutions of the state, and, in a specialized sense, the structure of the governing organs of the state – that is how Aristotle defines *politeia* in the *Politics*.[108] In that sense it was functionally divided under three heads: the process of political decision, the competence of magistrates, and the judiciary power.[109] And, being thus, primarily, the rules regulating the governing organs of the state, it was often distinguished from *nomoi*, 'the laws', which were *all* the rules of law in force in the society.[110]

Aristotle's theoretical treatment of *politeia* in the *Politics* has its counterpart in his empirical studies of the subject, in which, with his pupils, he assembled descriptions of 158 different *politeiai*.[111] From that series we possess the *Constitution of Athens* and fragments of others, from which it is plain that by *politeia* in that context Aristotle meant a description, both historical and systematic, of the political institutions of a city-state.

Typology of constitutions

In Greek political theory *politeiai* were divided into types according to how many people constituted and manned the principal organs of

[100] Arist. *Pol.* 1276a34–40.
[101] Meier (1989); Hansen (1989c) 86 n. 70; Wheare (1960) 1–13.
[102] *SEG* 9.1 = Austin (1981) no. 264. [103] Ps. Xen. *Ath. Pol.* 1.1; Dem. 20.105–6.
[104] Isoc. 7.14. [105] Dem. 23.89; Arist. *Ath. Pol.* 54.3.
[106] Dem. 19.184. [107] Arist. *Pol.* 1278b11.
[108] Arist. *Pol.* 1278b8–10, 1279a15. [109] Arist. *Pol.* 1297b37–1298a9.
[110] Pl. *Lg.* 734E–735A; Arist. *Pol.* 1289a15–20. [111] See pp. 8–9.

government. There were thus three constitutional types: the rule of the one, the rule of the few, and the rule of the many. The threefold division can be traced right back to Pindar;[112] it occurs in Herodotos in the Debate on the Constitutions,[113] and it was the foundation of almost every later discussion of the typology of states. In the fourth century the theory was further developed and extended by giving each of the three main types a positive and a negative variant (i.e. one a Good Thing and the other a Bad Thing). In the positive variant, government is in accordance with the laws and with all that is good; in the negative variant, the wielders of power are above the law, and power is exercised solely in the interest of the rulers. That theory can be found already in Plato's *Statesman*,[114] but it received its classic formulation in Book 3 of Aristotle's *Politics*.[115] A little chart will illustrate it.

	One	**Few**	**Many**
A good thing	Monarchy	Aristocracy	*Politeia*
A bad thing	Tyranny	Oligarchy	Democracy

Both the terminology and the content of this famous model of constitutions according to the number of the rulers influenced later political philosophy, from Marsilius of Padua,[116] Machiavelli,[117] Bodin,[118] Hobbes,[119] Locke,[120] Rousseau[121] and Bentham[122] to Kelsen[123] and Dahl.[124]

The most idiosyncratic aspect of Aristotle's analysis is that his 'positive' variant of the rule of the many is just called *politeia*, 'constitution', and not a specific form of constitution at all,[125] whereas Plato, his teacher, distinguishes between positive and negative democracy;[126] later on, in Polybios, the positive variant is called 'democracy' and the negative 'ochlocracy', the 'rule of the mob'.[127]

If we operate from a more historical and pragmatic standpoint Aristotle's sixfold model will appear both simpler and more complicated.[128] Simpler, because we can perform some eliminations in practice. Monarchy was virtually non-existent in Greece in the classical age: the Spartan double kingship was a unique exception. Most Greek tyrants had also been driven out by the time of the Persian wars, and tyranny only

---

[112] Pind. *Pyth.* 2.86–8.   [113] Hdt. 3.80–2.
[114] See p. 15. Pl. *Pol.* 291C–292A; Xen. *Mem.* 4.6.12.
[115] Arist. *Pol.* 1279a22–b10.   [116] Marsilius, *Defensor Pacis* 1.8.
[117] Machiavelli, *Discorsi* 1.2.   [118] Bodin, *Les six livres de la république*, 2.1.
[119] Hobbes, *De Cive* 7.   [120] Locke, *The Second Treatise of Government* 132.
[121] Rousseau, *Du contrat social* 3.3–6.   [122] Bentham *A Fragment on Government* 2.29–30.
[123] Kelsen (1946) 283ff.   [124] Dahl (1963) 26–8.   [125] Arist. *Pol.* 1279a37–9.
[126] Pl. *Pol.* 302D.   [127] Polyb. 6.4.6.   [128] Arist. *Pol.* 1286b8–22.

reappeared just at the very end of the fifth century and in the fourth, and then mainly in Sicily and southern Italy. In any case, Aristotle was mainly interested in Greek city-states and only peripherally in the king-doms of Persia and Macedon; so he contented himself with a very summary treatment of tyranny in Book 4 of the *Politics*[129] and with no further treatment of monarchy at all: instead he concentrates on the 'rule of the few' and the 'rule of the many'. Now, 'good' constitutions are always in short supply, and that was the case in fourth-century Greece.[130] Aristotle, always the realist, admits without fuss that there are not many examples of aristocracy or *politeia*:[131] oligarchy and democracy were overwhelmingly the commonest constitutions in Greece in his own day.[132]

On the other hand, the simple opposition between positive and negative forms of each constitutional type is too schematic and rigoristic to be applicable all round, so in Books 4 and 6 Aristotle often abandons the sixfold model and operates instead with the two basic types, oligarchy and democracy,[133] but divides those into subdivisions with a gradual passage from one variant to another.[134] Both oligarchy[135] and democ-racy[136] are typically divided each into four variants, the first being the most positive, i.e. the best (and least characteristic of its type): Democracy I and Oligarchy I are very nearly identical with *politeia* and aristocracy in the sixfold model. The fourth variant, by contrast, is the most negative, i.e. the worst, and most radical. Aristotle also allows that a constitution can include elements of both democracy and oligarchy;[137] in particular, elements of Democracy I and Oligarchy I tend to appear together in a 'mixed' constitution, in which case the word *politeia* may be used differ-ently to refer either to a 'golden mean' between democracy and oli-garchy[138] or to a mixture of the two:[139] if the mixture is predominantly democratic, the constitution is classified as a *politeia*; if predominantly oligarchical, the term 'aristocracy' can be used.[140] This model can be illustrated by the following chart.

	Aristocracy/*Politeia*	**Mixed**
Oligarchy I	Democracy I	
Oligarchy II	Democracy II	
Oligarchy III	Democracy III	
Oligarchy IV	Democracy IV	**Pure**

[129] Arist. *Pol.* 1295a1–24.   [130] Arist. *Pol.* 1260b34–5.
[131] Arist. *Pol.* 1293a39–42, 1301b40–1302a2.
[132] Arist. *Pol.* 1291b7–13, 1296a22–3, 1301b39–40.
[133] Arist. *Pol.* 1290a13–19.   [134] Arist. *Pol.* 1289a8–11, 1291b15–18.
[135] Arist. *Pol.* 1293a10–34, 1298a34–b5, 1320b17–1321a4.
[136] Arist. *Pol.* 1291b30–1292a38 [four types, not five: see Papageorgiou (1990)], 1292b22–1293a10, 1298a10–34, 1318b6–1319b32.
[137] Arist. *Pol.* 1316b39–1317a10.   [138] Arist. *Pol.* 1295a25–1296b12.
[139] Arist. *Pol.* 1293b31–4.   [140] Arist. *Pol.* 1293b34–8, 1317a2–3.

Typology of democracy

At the beginning of Book 6 Aristotle enumerates characteristic elements of a 'democratic' constitution.[141] They mostly relate to the magistrates, and prescribe rotation, limited powers, short duration, prohibition of a second term, and selection by lot (or sometimes by election, but in any case from and amongst all citizens). In addition, all citizens act as judges, all important decisions are taken by the assembly of the people, and all must be reimbursed for participation in political activity. Whereas oligarchy takes its character from the distinguished birth, wealth and good upbringing of the oligarchs, it is the common people, with their undistinguished birth, poverty and low upbringing, who determine the character of democracy. If all the above elements are present in fully developed form, the result is 'radical' democracy, type IV; if they are present only at the most basic level, the result is 'moderate' democracy, type I, which is also, thinks Aristotle, the original form, introduced into Athens, for example, by Solon. In four passages in the *Politics* Aristotle gives a detailed description of democracy in its four variants, but in all four Democracy I and Democracy IV predominate, while types II and III are only glanced at as transitional phases between I and IV.

In Democracy I citizen rights are confined to those born in lawful wedlock, and the community is basically agrarian, occupied with tilling the land and having little time for holding meetings of the assembly. The principal business of the assembly is to choose the magistrates and call them to account at the end of their tenure. All power is in the hands of the chosen magistrates, and there is often a property qualification (not a high one) for office-holding. There is no reimbursement for political activity. The laws are seldom changed, and they are respected as the true ultimate power in the state.[142]

In Democracy IV even illegitimates can receive citizen rights (at any rate, in the first phase of its establishment), and the state is dominated by artisans (*banausoi*), shopkeepers (*to agoraion plethos*) and especially day labourers (*thetes*), who all live in the city and so are forever holding assembly meetings. All decisions are taken by decrees of the assembly and only administrative competence is left to the magistrates (who are chosen, of course, by lot). All take a turn at being magistrates and there is no property qualification, while on the other hand there is full reimbursement for participation in the assembly. The laws are for ever being changed by decree and are seldom respected.[143]

---

[141] Arist. *Pol.* 1317b17–1318a3.
[142] Arist. *Pol.* 1291b30 41, 1292b25 34, 1298a12 19, 1318b6 1319a19.
[143] Arist. *Pol.* 1292a34–8, 1292b41–1293a10, 1298a28–33, 1319a24–b32.

Aristotle always treats democracy as the bad form of the 'rule of the many', though he does allow that compared with tyranny and oligarchy it is perhaps the least awful of the constitutions.[144] His critical stance is closely related to his interpretation of *demos*, the first element of the word 'democracy'. In book 3 he says that, although constitutions are divided, according to the number of power-holders, into the rule of the one, the rule of the few and the rule of the many, in practice it is the property of the power-holders that really makes the difference between the rule of the few and that of the many: oligarchy is the form of government in which power is exercised by the 'haves' – the *euporoi*, who are usually in a minority – while democracy is the form in which power is exercised by the 'have-nots' – the *aporoi*, who are usually the majority.[145] So for Aristotle democracy is really the rule of the poor rather than the rule of the many. *Demos* means 'the people', but there is the same ambiguity involved in the Greek word as in its English equivalent, because it can sometimes signify the people as a whole, but sometimes the 'ordinary' people as opposed to the upper class.[146]

The term demokratia

The constitution of Athens was a *demokratia* from Kleisthenes' reforms in 507 until the defeat in the Lamian War in 322. Herodotos, our oldest source, expressly says that Kleisthenes established *demokratia* in Athens,[147] and in 411 the Athenian Assembly passed a decree (which led to the rule of the Four Hundred) 'to investigate the ancestral laws that Kleisthenes gave when he introduced the *demokratia*'.[148]

It is true that the word *demokratia* only appears in our sources in the second half of the fifth century,[149] and many scholars have concluded that the term only began to be used in that period.[150] They have also held that it only received a positive evaluation (i.e. as a Good Thing) in the fourth century, whereas in the second half of the fifth it was used either pejoratively in political debate or at best neutrally in historical discussion – and in particular was not used in a good sense by democrats themselves,[151] who preferred as a slogan *isonomia*, equality of political rights.[152] The case for these views is, however, weak. To begin with, we *have* no sources from before 430 in which you would expect the word

---

[144] Arist. *Pol.* 1289b2–5.   [145] Arist. *Pol.* 1279b11–1280a6, 1290b1–3.
[146] See p. 125.   [147] Hdt. 6.131.1.   [148] Arist. *Ath. Pol.* 29.3.
[149] *IG* I³ 37.49(?); Hdt. 6.43.3; Democritus DK 68 fr. 251; Ps. Xen. *Ath. Pol.* 1.4; Ant. 6.45. Debrunner (1947) 21.
[150] Larsen (1948) 13; Bleicken (1985) 48; Sealey (1987) 98-102.   [151] Sealey (1974).
[152] Larsen (1948) 6; Vlastos (1953) 337–47; Pleket (1972) 80.

demokratia. It does not occur in inscriptions,[153] and before the middle of the fifth century almost all literature (except natural philosophy) was written in verse, in metres in which the word *demokratia* does not scan.[154] But from a surviving funeral *stele* it can be inferred that an Athenian citizen was given the name Demokrates no later than the 460s;[155] moreover a passage in Aischylos' *Suppliant Women* strongly indicates that the term *demokratia* was known to the poet;[156] so there is a good probability that *demokratia* was a current political word used in a favourable sense by democrats themselves before the reforms of Ephialtes. And one of the earliest examples of the term *demokratia* is in a speech of Antiphon of about 420, where it is said that before every meeting of the Council of Five Hundred a sacrifice is made 'on behalf of *demokratia*'.[157] There is no reason why that should not go back to the origin of the Council, and so no reason to doubt that *demokratia* was at least one word used by the Athenians in Kleisthenes' own time to describe their new constitution. As for *isonomia*, we shall see below that there is no adequate evidence that that term was a rallying-cry of the democrats in the first generations after Kleisthenes.[158]

Anyhow, as far back as our sources go there is no doubt that the Athenians, both officially and in ordinary speech, called their constitution a *demokratia*. In the two surviving laws against tyranny (410 and 336) outlawry is the penalty for overthrowing the *demokratia*,[159] and the law of 336 has carved above it the famous relief picture of the goddess Demokratia crowning an elderly bearded man representing *demos*, the people.[160] In 333/2 the Council caused a statue to that goddess to be put up in the Agora, and an inscription[161] shows that thereafter the generals made sacrifices to the goddess every year, perhaps on 12 Boedromion, the day on which in 403/2 the 'new democracy' was introduced.[162] In that same year a law was passed about state support for children whose fathers had fallen in defence of the *demokratia* in the civil war against the oligarchs.[163] Speeches in the Assembly and the courts praise the constitution of Athens as a *demokratia*,[164] and in his funeral speech in Thucydides Perikles expressly says that Athens is 'called a *demokratia*'.[165] Finally, it is not irrelevant to observe that numerous ships of the Athenian navy bore the name *Demokratia*.[166]

---

[153] Except as restored in *IG* I³ 37.49 = *M&L* 47 and Fornara (1977) no. 99.
[154] Hansen (1986a).   [155] *Hesperia* 53 (1984) 355–60.
[156] Aesch. *Supp.* 604. Ehrenberg (1950) 522; Lotze (1981).   [157] Ant. 6.45.
[158] See p. 83.   [159] Andoc. 1.96; *SEG* 12 87.9, 13, 16 = Harding (1985) no. 101.
[160] Meritt (1952).   [161] *IG* II² 1496.131–2, 140–1.
[162] Plut. *Mor.* 349F. Palagia (1982) 111.   [163] *SEG* 28.46 = Harding (1985) no. 45.
[164] E.g. Aeschin. 3.6–8, 23, 38, 145, 169, 196–202, 220, 234, 249–51, 157.
[165] Thuc. 2.37.1.   [166] *IG* II² 1604.24, 1606.59, 1620.32, 1623.326.

There does not appear to have been any conflict between the supporters of democracy and its opponents over what the system should be called. The word *demokratia* is frequently used by the Old Oligarch;[167] Plato's criticism of Athenian democracy is written with the trial of Sokrates in mind;[168] and both the *Politics* and the *Constitution of Athens* of Aristotle show that he classified Athens as a 'radical' democracy of type IV.[169]

Democracy as a political system

Athens was called a democracy by the Athenians themselves, and by everybody else in Greece, because that was the political system they lived under from 507 to 322 and because they cherished the ideals that went with that system. But when we call Athenian democracy a 'political system' we are giving that term a broader sense than the modern reader might, without some warning, expect; for nowadays the concept 'political' tends to refer primarily to the process of political decision-making,[170] and we distinguish (in principle at least) between politics and administration, including the administration of the law.[171] We expect administration under a democracy to be in principle pragmatic and apolitical (even if that is hardly so in practice),[172] and somebody who goes into the civil service or the law has not, in our parlance, chosen a 'political career' and would not be said to be engaged in 'political activity'. The Athenians saw things differently. For them, everything that had to do with the *polis* was 'political': they were quite capable of distinguishing between initiation, decision and execution,[173] but they did not distinguish between politics and administration, and in their view being a magistrate or a judge was just as much political activity as taking part in an Assembly meeting.[174] When Aristotle describes political freedom in a democratic state as 'to be ruled and rule by turns',[175] he is thinking of rotation of magistrates, not of any sort of rotation in attending the Assembly.[176]

So a description of Athenian democracy as a political system has to embrace all the city's political institutions: namely, the Assembly, the *nomothetai*, the People's Court, the boards of magistrates, the Council of Five Hundred (which was the most important of the boards), the Areopagos, and *ho boulomenos*, i.e. 'any citizen who wishes'. In what follows, after an account of the Athenian people, each of those seven institutions will be given a chapter to itself – a fact that calls for a word or two of

---

[167] Ps. Xen. *Ath. Pol.* 1.4–5.   [168] Pl. *Pol.* 299B–C; *Ep.* 7 325B–E, 326D.
[169] Arist. *Ath Pol.* 41.2; Arist. *Pol.* 1274a7–11, 1319b21.   [170] Miller (1987).
[171] Wilson (1887) 211; Dunsire (1973) 87ff.   [172] Vile (1967) 318–19.
[173] Arist. *Pol.* 1322b12–17.   [174] Dem. 25.20–3; Pl. *Tht* 173C–D.
[175] Arist. *Pol.* 1317b2–3.   [176] Hansen (1989b) 16–17.

commentary. In most history books the *nomothetai* are given a very cavalier treatment, just as an appendix to the Assembly,[177] doubtless because the books always concentrate on the fifth century, when legislation was indeed a function of the Assembly and no one else; but after 403/2 the texts of surviving laws show that the *nomothetai* were conceived of as a quite separate and independent political institution.[178] (Actually, if they were to be described along with another institution they would be better brigaded with the courts, for the *nomothetai* and the jurors of the courts were all drawn by lot from the same 6000 men who had sworn the Heliastic Oath.)[179] As for the Areopagos, that is usually treated along with the Council of Five Hundred (for it was indeed a 'Council', a *boule*)[180] or with the courts (because its powers were mainly judicial);[181] but it was a survival from archaic times, not really an integral part of the democracy, and so is better treated separately. The only relatively justifiable way of reducing our seven chapters would be to discuss the Council of Five Hundred along with the boards of magistrates, for in a sense the Council was just a very oversized board containing within it various sub-boards, and technically speaking the councillors were magistrates.[182] However, there are strong reasons for giving the Council its own chapter. First, it worked in harness with the Assembly and the *nomothetai* and had an important role in the process of decision-making, whereas the connection of the other magistrates was with the courts and the administration of justice, not with political decision-making.[183] Secondly, the Council was at the head of the entire system of public administration, and so had oversight of the other magistrates.[184] Finally, it was the only organ of state chosen deme by deme, so as to ensure that citizens from every part of Attica had a direct share in the running of things.[185]

What, finally, of *ho boulomenos*? He had no official position and no authority. Nevertheless he is recognized in our sources as a specific agent in the political process, and *ton Athenaion ho boulomenos hois exestin*, 'he of the Athenians who wishes from amongst those who may', frequently mentioned as the originator of laws, decrees and public prosecutions, was arguably the real protagonist of the Athenian democracy.[186]

---

[177] Busolt and Swoboda (1920–6) 1011–14; Rhodes (1972) 49–52; Sinclair (1988a) 83–4; Bleicken (1985) 118–20.

[178] See p. 167.   [179] See pp. 167 and 181.

[180] Busolt and Swoboda (1920–6) 1019–21; Bleicken (1985) 121.

[181] Glotz (1929) 234–5.   [182] See pp. 226–7.   [183] See p. 229.

[184] See p. 258.   [185] See p. 104.   [186] See pp. 266–8.

DEMOCRACY AS AN IDEOLOGY

Nowadays democracy is both a political system and a political ideology.[187] What links the two is the conviction that democratic ideals are promoted by democratic institutions more than by any other kind of government. Exactly the same two facets are to be seen in the ancient concept of democracy, which meant on the one hand 'government of the people' in the political sense and on the other the ideals characteristic of such a 'government of the people'.[188] The democratic institutions of Athens supplied the framework for a democratic ideology centred, as both supporters and opponents unanimously admitted, on the notions of freedom, equality and the pursuit of happiness. Where the two sides differed was in their *valuation* of this ideology, as two quotations make clear.

In Perikles' funeral speech Thucydides gives him the following famous characterization of the Athenian constitution:

> It has the name democracy because government is in the hands not of the few but of the majority.[189] In private disputes all are equal before the law; and when it comes to esteem in public affairs, a man is preferred according to his own reputation for something, not, on the whole, just turn and turn about,[190] but for excellence, and even in poverty no man is debarred by obscurity of reputation so long as he has it in him to do some good service to the state. Freedom is a feature of our public life; and as for suspicion of one another in our daily private pursuits, we do not frown on our neighbour if he behaves to please himself or set our faces in those expressions of disapproval that are so disagreeable, however harmless.[191]

Two generations later Isokrates in his *Areopagitikos* supplies a sour gloss to those same idealizing sentiments: the ancestors, he says, didn't have a *politeia* that 'brought up the citizens to think that unrestraint was democracy and lawlessness liberty and saying what you please equality, and that the licence to do all those things was happiness'.[192] Comparison of the two texts shows that the 'pursuit of happiness' in Isokrates corresponds to what Thucydides says about freedom in the pursuits of daily life. The three ideals are thus in fact two: liberty (subdivided into liberty in the political sphere and liberty in the personal sphere) and equality.

---

[187] Sartori (1968) 112; Pennock (1979) 14.
[188] Arist. *Pol.* 1310a28–33. Hansen (1989b) 3–4.
[189] Cf. Thuc. 5.81.2, 8.38.3, 8.53.3, 8.89.2.   [190] Gomme (1956) 108.
[191] Thuc. 2.37.1–3.   [192] Isoc. 7.20.

Another concept often treated separately from liberty and equality in modern discussions is the 'rule of law'. Democrats, in open polemic against supporters of the other two types of constitution, tried to monopolize that particular high ground, as can be seen from a passage in Aischines:

> It is acknowledged that there are three kinds of *politeia* in all the world, tyranny and oligarchy and democracy. Tyrannies and oligarchies are governed at the whim of the rulers, but democratic states are governed by the established laws. And as you are well aware, Athenians, in a democracy it is the laws that protect the individual and the *politeia*, whereas the tyrant and the oligarch are protected by mistrust and armed bodyguards. Oligarchs, and those who run unequal states, have to guard themselves against those who would overthrow the state by force: you who have an equal state based on the law have to punish those who speak or have led their lives contrary to the laws.[193]

What Aischines says shows that the 'rule of (democratic) law' is conceived as an aspect of democratic equality, so it remains the case that the basic ideals are really just two, freedom and equality. *Demokratia*, *eleutheria* and *to ison* were a kind of trio[194] in Athenian political ideology like democracy, liberty and equality in the liberal-democratic ideology of the nineteenth and twentieth centuries.[195]

Liberty

The fundamental democratic ideal, then, was *eleutheria*, liberty, which had two aspects: political liberty to participate in the democratic institutions, and private liberty to live as one pleased. The dual nature of *eleutheria* is most clearly described by Aristotle in the *Politics*:

> A basic principle of the democratic constitution is liberty. That is commonly said, and those who say it imply that only in this constitution do men share in liberty; for that, they say, is what every democracy aims at. Now, one aspect of liberty is being ruled and ruling in turn. . . . Another element is to live as you like. For this, they say, is what being free is about, since its opposite, living not as you like, is the condition of a slave. So this is the second defining principle of democracy, and from it has come the ideal of not being ruled, not by anybody at all if possible, or at least only in turn.[196]

[193] Aeschin. 1.4–5.   [194] Pl. *Resp.* 563B; Isoc. 7.20; Arist. *Pol.* 1310a28–33.
[195] Vacherot (1860) 7–8; Pennock (1979) 16; Holden (1988) 28.
[196] Arist. *Pol.* 1317a40–b17.

Aristotle's description of democratic liberty is stated in general terms and there is no explicit reference to Athens, but all the sources show that in this respect the Athenians conformed to the norm.[197] The ideal 'to live as one pleases' is praised as a fundamental democratic value by Otanes in the Constitutional Debate in Herodotos,[198] by Athenian statesmen in Thucydides' speeches,[199] and by the orators in the speeches they delivered before the People's Court.[200] And 'to rule in turn' is singled out by King Theseus in Euripides' *Suppliant Women* as an essential feature of Athenian democracy.[201]

For almost two centuries historians and philosophers have debated what relation, if any, there is between the Athenian ideal 'to live as one pleases' and the modern concept of individual freedom.[202] Strangely enough, the emphasis has been on the differences rather than on the similarities.[203]

It is often said that *eleutheria* was basically different from modern liberty because the principal aspect of being *eleutheros* was to be free as opposed to being a slave.[204] That is true, and modern studies confirm that *eleutheria* in the sense of self-determination was rooted in the opposition free/slave,[205] whereas the modern concept of liberty does not have slavery as its antonym (except in a metaphorical sense). But *eleutheria* had different shades of meaning according to context; at least three different meanings are attested in the sources in three different contexts, social, political and constitutional.

1 *Eleutheros* in the sense of being free as opposed to being a slave applied both to citizens and to foreigners, and it applied to all types of city-state, since slaves existed in all *poleis* independent of their constitutions.[206]

2 *Eleutheros* in the sense of autonomous as against being dominated by others was of course esteemed in both oligarchies and democracies. Of the thirty-one *poleis* that fought for freedom against the barbarians in the Persian Wars,[207] most were oligarchies; and a century later, when Demosthenes advocated *eleutheria* in his political speeches, he was defending the freedom of all Greek states, not just the democracies, from Macedonian domination.[208] *Eleutheria* in the sense of *autonomia* was the freedom *of* the *polis*, which is different from freedom *within* the *polis*.

3 As a constitutional concept, however, *eleutheria* was associated

---

[197] Pl. *Resp.* 557B; *Def.* 412D; Isoc. 7.20.   [198] Hdt. 3.83.2–3.
[199] Thuc. 2.37.2, 7.69.2.   [200] Lys. 26.5.   [201] Eur. *Supp.* 406–8; cf. Isoc. 20.20.
[202] Constant (1819).   [203] Berlin (1969) xl–xli.   [204] Mulgan (1984) 8–9.
[205] Meier (1975) 426; Raaflaub (1985) 29–70, 160–88.   [206] Arist. *Pol.* 1326a18–20.
[207] *M&L* 27 = Fornara (1977) no. 59; Hdt. 7.178.2.   [208] Dem. 18.305.

both with political participation in the public sphere and with personal freedom in the private sphere. Two considerations will suffice to show that *eleutheria* in the constitutional sense was different from *eleutheria* in the social sense (free *versus* slave) and in the political sense (city autonomy). First, as a constitutional ideal *eleutheria* was specifically democratic and not a value praised in oligarchies or monarchies; the oligarchs[209] (and the philosophers)[210] did not have an alternative interpretation of *eleutheria*, as we shall see they had of equality; they simply rejected *eleutheria* as a mistaken ideal.[211] Second, as a democratic ideal *eleutheria* (in the sense of personal freedom) applied not only to citizens, but also to metics and sometimes even to slaves. Thus, a slave, who in the social sphere was deprived of *eleutheria*, might well, in a democratic *polis*, be allowed a share in, for example, freedom of speech, though only privately and of course not in the political assemblies.[212]

To sum up, the social, political and constitutional meanings of *eleutheros* were interconnected and the idea of self-determination lies behind them all,[213] but the sources show that Greek democrats distinguished constitutional liberty from liberty in the two other senses and imposed the distinction on the rest, by inducing aristocrats and oligarchs to hate *eleutheria* as a mistaken democratic value.

Another alleged difference between individual liberty in ancient Athens and in modern liberal thought lies in the principles and arguments used to justify it. In modern democratic thought liberty is about the protection of individual rights against infringements by the state or by other people, whereas, it is held, Athenian liberty was not based on a clear notion of individual rights.[214] Again, the sources support a rather different view.

Several of the orators state with approval the rule that no citizen could be executed without due process of law.[215] Admittedly, thieves and robbers were not included: they could be put to death immediately if they were caught in the act and had to confess.[216] But that limitation, though important, does not seriously alter the fact that 'no execution without a trial' *(medena akriton apokteinai)* was felt to be a right which all citizens enjoyed.[217]

Another rule forbade torture of Athenian citizens.[218] It was warranted

[209] Ps. Xen. *Ath. Pol.* 1.8; Theophr. *Char.* 28.6.
[210] Pl. *Resp.* 557B–558C, 562B–564A; Arist. *Pol.* 1310a26–33, 1318b39–41.
[211] Hansen (1989b) 12, *pace* Mulgan (1984) 18–20.
[212] Dem. 9.3; Ps. Xen. *Ath. Pol.* 1.12.   [213] Democritus DK 68 fr. 251.
[214] Berlin (1969) xl–xli; Mulgan (1984) 13–14.
[215] Isoc. 15.22; Lys. 22.2. Hansen (1989b) 13.   [216] See p. 190.
[217] Carawan (1984); Hansen (1990a) 234 n. 93.   [218] Andoc. 1.43.

by a decree (*psephisma*) probably passed immediately after the expulsion of the tyrants in 510/9 before the introduction of the democracy.[219] It was nevertheless adopted by the democrats and, like the expulsion of the tyrants, was later associated with democracy. The principle that free men are exempt from corporal punishment is closely connected with democracy in Demosthenes' speech against Androtion.[220]

The Athenian democracy further provided some protection of a citizen's home. Demosthenes was severely criticized by Aischines for breaking into a house and arresting the alleged traitor, Antiphon, without a warrant, i.e. a *psephisma* of the people,[221] and in the Assembly Aeschines got his way and secured the man's release. Demosthenes, in his turn, accuses Androtion of having surpassed the Thirty in brutality: they had people arrested in the market-place, but, when exacting arrears of *eisphora*, Androtion conducted the Eleven to the debtors' houses and had them arrested there.[222]

Finally in Aristotle's *Constitution of Athens* we are told that, 'as soon as the archon enters upon his office, he proclaims through the public herald that whatever a person possessed before he entered upon his archonship he will have and possess until the end of his term'.[223] Like the ban on torture of citizens, this is probably a survival from the sixth century. It may even go back to Solon and have been a measure to reassure the Athenians that, after the *seisachtheia*, no further infringements of private property would take place.[224] But, even if the origin and original purpose of the proclamation are obscure, what we know for sure is that it was still made in the fourth century and understood as a guarantee that no redistribution of property would take place in Athens, as happened in other Greek *poleis*.

In addition to the protection of person, home and property, the most treasured of individual rights is freedom of speech, cherished by democrats but suppressed by supporters of authoritarian rule.[225] Once more we find the same ideal in democratic Athens,[226] as in Demosthenes' remark that a basic difference between Spartan oligarchy and Athenian democracy is that in Athens you are free to praise the Spartan constitution and way of life, if you so wish, whereas in Sparta it is prohibited to praise any other constitution than the Spartan.[227] The trial of Sokrates is evidence that the Athenians, for once, did not live up to their owns ideals,[228] but the sentence passed on Sokrates is unparalleled in the

---

[219] MacDowell (1962) 92–3.   [220] Dem. 22.55.   [221] Dem. 18.132.
[222] Dem. 22.51–2.   [223] Arist. *Ath. Pol.* 56.2. Mossé (1981).
[224] Rhodes (1981a) 622.   [225] Rawls (1987) 55–79.
[226] Eur. *Hippolytos* 421–3; Dem. 45.79; *Ep.* 3.13. Raaflaub (1980).
[227] Dem. 20.105–8.   [228] Hyp. fr. 59; Aeschin. 1.173. Hansen (1989b) 15.

history of Athenian democracy. A decree prohibiting the ridiculing of individuals in comedies was passed in 440 but abrogated four years later,[229] and the decree of Diopeithes, of about the same date, which laid down that there should be a criminal prosecution of 'atheists or astronomers'[230] may have led to a trial of Anaxagoras.[231] The evidence for the other public prosecutions of philosophers for impiety – the trial of Protagoras,[232] for instance – is anecdotal and dangerous to rely on without confirmation, and even the trial of Anaxagoras is not above suspicion:[233] after Sokrates it was an accolade for a philosopher to be charged with impiety, and the Hellenistic biographers were eager to bestow the honour on quite a few of Sokrates' contemporaries.[234]

It is not enough, however, to have laws and regulations protecting the citizens: there must also be ways of enforcing them when infringed by the democratic *polis* itself and its officials. Consequently the Athenians provided for both public and private prosecution of magistrates. For example, at the end of their term of office, any citizen could bring a private suit (*dike idia*) against a magistrate for having infringed his rights, and every summer thirty officials sat three entire days in the Agora to receive written complaints handed in by the citizens.[235] Since the magistrate was held to embody the *polis*,[236] private *euthynai* and other similar types of prosecution were litigation between a citizen and the *polis*, in which the citizen might defeat the *polis*. An example is Lysias' speech *On Behalf of the Property of Aristophanes against the Treasury*.[237] The title may be Hellenistic, perhaps even later, but the speech itself shows that the title is an accurate description of what the trial was about.

The champions of Athenian democracy emphasized that citizens were protected by the rule of law, and preferred to blame cases of violation on the magistrates and political leaders rather than the *demos* or the *polis* itself. An obvious example is Aischines' praise of the rule of law in democratic Athens quoted above,[238] where legal protection of the citizens is singled out as the hallmark of democracy. The comparison between the three constitutions in that passage leaves no doubt that the laws Aischines has in mind are laws binding the rulers, not the ruled. In oligarchies and tyrannies citizens are exposed to the whims of their rulers; in democracies the laws protect the citizens. Against whom? Obviously against the political leaders and the magistrates, who must respect the democratic laws in their dealings with the citizens.

[229] Schol. Ar. *Ach.* 67; Schol. *Av.* 1297.   [230] Plut. *Per.* 32.2.
[231] Diod. 12.39.2; Diog. Laert. 2.12ff. Plut. *Per.* 32.5.
[232] Arist. fr. 67; Timon fr. 3. Dover (1976) 142–6.
[233] Dover (1976) 138–42; but see Brickhouse and Smith (1989) 32–3.
[234] Derenne (1930).   [235] Arist. *Ath. Pol.* 48.3–5. See p. 223.
[236] Dem. 21.29–32.   [237] Lys. 19.   [238] Aeschin. 1.4–5. See p. 74.

Public and private

Like modern liberty, ancient democratic *eleutheria* had two sides: it was both freedom to participate in political life and freedom from political oppression. As has often been noted, these two aspects of liberty are mutually exclusive,[239] for 'to rule in turn' implies being sometimes ruled, so that if we maximize the principle of 'not being ruled' there is no room left for political decision-making in which to participate. The two opposed aspects of freedom are, however, compatible, but only if combined with a distinction between a public sphere, in which political freedom operates, and a private sphere, in which personal freedom is protected against interference by the state as well as by other people. The separation between a public and a private sphere is well known in the modern world, where it is a basic condition of democratic liberty;[240] but did the Athenians recognize a private sphere in which the *polis* did not interfere but allowed the citizens to live as they pleased? There are, indeed, historians who urge that in principle the Greek city-state was all-embracing, as we saw earlier in this chapter, and we must return to the theme now from a different standpoint.

Athenian sources debating about society regularly contrast the public and the private:[241] what is *idion* is set off against what is *demosion* or *koinon*.[242] The dichotomy of public and private is apparent in all aspects of life. The private person (*idiotes*) is opposed to the politically active citizen (*ho politeuomenos*);[243] citizens' homes to public buildings;[244] the national interest to private profit;[245] public finance to private means;[246] private litigation to administration of justice in public actions.[247] Forensic speeches are full of arguments such as 'this dispute is a private matter and not to be brought before the jurors by a public prosecution which concerns the *polis*'.[248] Or, conversely, as Demosthenes declares in *Against Meidias*, 'Meidias' assault on me is a public matter, since it was made on Demosthenes as representative of the *polis*, not on the person Demosthenes.'[249] Finally, the laws of the city are often subdivided into private (regulating the relations of private persons) and public (concerning the activities of government agencies).[250]

Thus, the Athenians did distinguish a public sphere from a private

---

[239] Constant (1819) 509; Kelsen (1946) 284–7.
[240] Berlin (1969) 124, 126; Holden (1988) 12–13, 140–1.
[241] Hansen (1989b) 18–19 with nn. 103–11; Musti (1985).
[242] Thuc. 2.37.1–2; Dem. 20.136.   [243] Aeschin. 1.195; Hyp. 3.27.
[244] Dem. 3.25–9, Arist. *Pol.* 1321b19–23.   [245] Xen. *Hell.* 1.4.13; Dem. 19.1.
[246] Isoc. 7.24; Din. 2.18.   [247] Pl. *Euthphr.* 2A; Dem. 46.26 (quoting a *nomos*).
[248] Hyp. 3.27–30.   [249] Dem. 21.26, 31–4.   [250] Dem. 24.192–3; 18.210.

sphere; but a note of warning is in order: the Athenian distinction is between the private (*to idion*) and the public (*to koinon* or *demosion*), which is not quite the same as our opposition between the individual and the state. First, in many modern discussions, of democratic freedom for instance, the contrast individual/state is itself somewhat twisted: the opposite of individual freedom is not state authority but public control.[251] Next, in the Greek sources, the public sphere is most identified with the *polis*,[252] whereas the private sphere is sometimes a social sphere without any emphasis on the individual: family life, business, industry and many types of religious association belonged in the private and not in the public sphere. The Athenians distinguished between the individual as a private person and the individual as a citizen rather than between the individual and the state. Thus, instead of *individual* freedom, it is preferable to speak about *personal* or *private* freedom, which was often individual in character, but not invariably so.

The point was made earlier that the public sphere (i.e. the *polis* sphere) was specifically a *political* sphere: the *polis* did not regulate all matters but only a limited range of social activities, and matters such as education, industry, agriculture and trade were left to private enterprise.[253] But, further, Athenians were regularly allowed to think and say what they liked about anything, as long as they did not, for example, profane the Mysteries,[254] or, without due permission, form new cults and religious societies.[255] That is not denied by those historians who emphasize the omnipotence of the *polis*, but they counter it by another observation: if the Athenians in their Assembly *decided* to interfere with education, production, or whatever, they were entitled to do so, and no one could plead that it was a violation of individual rights. Similarly, the people could at any time impose restrictions on freedom of speech, and sometimes did. So 'there were no theoretical limits to the power of the state, no activity, no sphere of human behaviour, in which the state could not legitimately intervene'.[256] But that correct observation ought not to be invoked to establish a difference between ancient and modern democratic ideology, because precisely the same observation applies, for example, to modern Britain: no aspect of human life is *in principle* outside the powers of Parliament and there is no constitutional protection of individual rights, though in practice they are highly regarded and mostly respected.[257]

[251] Taylor (1979) 175–7.   [252] Is. 7.30; Dem. 20.57.

[253] Hansen (1987a) 56, 118. See p. 158.

[254] Jacoby (1959) [Diagoras]; Hansen (1975) cat. nos 11–42 [profanation in 415].

[255] Hyp. frr. 202–10. Hansen (1989b) 40 n. 116.   [256] Finley (1973) 78.

[257] Waltman and Holland (1988) 108.

Not only was the public sphere a political sphere; the majority of the inhabitants of Attica were excluded from it, for the Greek *polis* was a community of citizens only. Metics and slaves lived in the *polis* without being members of it.[258] Freedom to participate in the democratic institutions applied only to citizens and only in the political sphere. Private freedom, however, to live as one pleased, applied to all who lived in Athens, including metics and sometimes slaves.[259] According to the critics of democracy that kind of freedom was extended even to women,[260] but that shocking charge was, of course, denied by the champions of the Athenian constitution.[261]

Equality

For equality[262] the Athenians had several terms, all compounds beginning with *iso-*. They include *isonomia* (equal political rights),[263] *isegoria* (equal right to address the political assemblies),[264] *isogonia* (equality of birth)[265] and *isokratia* (equality of power).[266] Historians agree that equality in Athens was a purely political concept that never spread to the social and economic spheres.[267] Equal distribution of land and cancellation of debts, for example, were hotly debated questions in other Greek city-states,[268] but never in democratic Athens.[269] Once again, it is worth noting, a basic democratic value was restricted to the political sphere and did not apply outside it.[270]

But what did political equality mean to the Athenians, and what does it mean today? In Western political thought there is a conflict between two different views of political equality. One view is that all men *are* essentially and by nature equal – that is, alike – and therefore all are entitled to an equal share of everything; the other is that all men *should* have equal opportunities – that is, should be all in a line at the starting-point. The first view is partly descriptive, i.e. an equality of nature is asserted in order to justify an equality of rights; the second view is purely prescriptive and claims on moral grounds an equality of opportunities, which – by the way – is perfectly compatible with an inequality of nature.[271] The first type is exemplified in the American Declaration of

---

[258] See p. 62.   [259] See p. 76.   [260] Pl. *Resp.* 563A–C.
[261] Thuc. 2.45.2.   [262] Kajanto (1984).   [263] Isoc. 7.20. Vlastos (1953, 1964).
[264] Dem. 15.18. Griffith (1966); Raaflaub (1980); Ober (1989) 296.
[265] Pl. *Menex.* 239A.   [266] Hdt. 5.92.1a.
[267] Ste Croix (1981) 285; Bleicken (1985) 206–8.
[268] Ste Croix (1981) 298–9 with n. 55 (608–9).
[269] Cf. Dem. 24.149. See. p. 54.   [270] But see Hansen (1989b) 41 n. 131.
[271] Sartori (1962) 328—33; Pennock (1979) 35–44.

Independence of 4 July 1776: 'We hold these truths to be self-evident, that all men are created equal, that they are endowed by their Creator with certain unalienable Rights, that among these are Life, Liberty and the pursuit of Happiness'. Here equality is asserted as a fact of human nature,[272] although we must not forget Lincoln's modification in his Springfield speech of 1857: 'the authors of that noble instrument did not intend to declare all men equal in all respects'. The obvious illustration of the second type is the first article of the French *Déclaration des droits de l'homme et du citoyen* of 29 August 1789: 'Les hommes naissent et demeurent libres et égaux en droits.' The two last words, 'en droits', are crucial and show that no natural equality was intended.[273] Historians discussing equality in democratic Athens hardly ever raise the question of whether the Athenian ideal was natural or normative equality; but the sources show that the Athenians were well aware of the distinction and that it was one of the main points in the debate for or against democracy. Critics of democracy, especially the philosophers, imputed to the democrats a descriptive interpretation of equality, as in Book 5 of Aristotle's *Politics*: 'Democracy arose from the idea that those who are equal in any respect are equal absolutely. All are alike free, therefore they claim that all are free absolutely. . . . The next is when the democrats, on the ground that they are all equal, claim equal participation in everything.'[274] Democrats themselves, however, stressed the other aspect of equality: that all men must have equal rights in order to have equal opportunities, as in the passage from Perikles' funeral speech quoted above;[275] and the same thought is expressed by Euripides in *The Suppliant Women*: '"Who is willing, having some good advice, to bring it before the city?" The man who will has glory; who will not keeps silence. What in the city can be more equal than that?'[276]

Admittedly, the democratic principle of 'one man one vote', the *isop-sephos polis* as Euripides says,[277] implies some kind of natural equality: all Athenians are so intelligent and valuable as human beings that they can (and ought to) be given an equal share in political decision-making. Hence, modern historians tend to emphasize *isonomia* as the central aspect of democratic equality and of democratic ideology altogether.[278] But the term *isonomia* is poorly attested in classical Athens.[279] First, it is never

---

[272] McDonald (1985) 53–5.
[273] Cf. Sieyès' first proposal of 20–1 July, in Rials (1988) 594.
[274] Arist. *Pol.* 1301a28–35; Pl. *Menex.* 239A. Harvey (1965) 113–20.
[275] See p. 73.   [276] Eur. *Supp.* 438–41.
[277] Eur. *Supp.* 353. Ste Croix (1981) 285.
[278] Finley (1976) 10; Mulgan (1984) 12; Bleicken (1985) 32, 191, 263, 312.
[279] Hansen (1989b) 42 n. 140.

used in symbouleutic and forensic speeches: of all the Athenian orators only Isokrates discusses *isonomia*, as a – misguided – democratic ideal advocated by radicals.[280] Second, the names a state gives its men-of-war often reflect the slogans and political values of the state in question. In the Athenian navy several triremes were called *Demokratia*[281] or *Eleutheria*;[282] one was called *Parrhesia* (Free Speech),[283] but there is no evidence that any trireme was ever called *Isonomia*.[284] Third, the political cults did not include *isonomia*: both *demokratia* and *eleutheria* were made divine and worshipped by the Athenians, Demokratia in its own right as a separate goddess,[285] Eleutheria in connection with the cult of Zeus Eleutherios;[286] but *isonomia* was never represented as a goddess and never connected with any form of worship. As for the positive evidence for *isonomia* as the basic democratic value in classical Athens, it is not very impressive. A drinking-song (*skolion*) composed in the years after the expulsion of the tyrants praises Harmodios and Aristogeiton for having made Athens *isonomos*,[287] but the *skolia* were performed in aristocratic *symposia*, and the song for Harmodios and Aristogeiton may well have been composed in the years 514–508 before the Athenians thought of popular rule.[288] Next, in Herodotos' Debate on the Constitutions, Otanes, the champion of popular rule, emphasizes *isonomia* as the principal democratic value.[289] But it is a pity that the principal evidence for *isonomia* as the basic democratic value in Athens should be Herodotos' Constitutional Debate, which undoubtedly reflects contemporary Greek political values, but is not specifically associated with Athens. When Herodotos describes the birth of Athenian democracy it is *isegoria* and not *isonomia* that he singles out as the principal form of democratic equality,[290] and his account conforms with what we find in Athenian sources: the aspect of equality most cherished by the Athenian democrats was *isegoria*, not *isonomia*. Now, whereas *isonomia* may imply natural equality as well as equality of opportunity, *isegoria* is really about equality of opportunity. No Athenian expected that every one of the 6000 citizens who attended a meeting of the Assembly could – or would – address his fellow citizens.[291] *Isegoria* was not for everyone, but for anyone who cared to exercise his political rights. Each citizen must have equal opportunity to demonstrate his

---

[280] Isoc. 7.20–1.

[281] *IG* II² 1604.24, 1606.59, 1620.32, 1623.326.

[282] *IG* II² 1604.49, 1607.85, 1627.202, 1631.488.   [283] *IG* II² 1624.81.

[284] Schmidt (1931); Hansen (1989b) 42. n. 142.   [285] See p. 70.

[286] Agora inventory no. 2483 = Wycherley (1957) no. 39; Xen. *Oec.* 7.1; Hdt. 3.142.4. Raaflaub (1985) 125–47.

[287] Ath. 695B.   [288] Pleket (1972) 68–72; Raaflaub (1985) 116.

[289] Hdt. 3.80.6.   [290] Hdt. 5.78.1.   [291] See p. 144.

excellence, but he deserved reward according to what he actually achieved. That is the argument in Perikles' funeral speech[292] and in the speech given to Athenagoras, the democratic leader in Syracuse;[293] and it is abundantly attested in the innumerable honorary decrees:[294] in the Athenian democracy the indispensable political initiative was stimulated by ambition (*philotimia*)[295] and competition (*hamilla*),[296] neither of which is compatible with natural equality. For the Athenians competition was an essential aspect of life in politics as well as in sport,[297] and the equality that mattered was, as in sport, that all must start in line, not that all were essentially equal.

Selection by lot was believed to be a more 'democratic' method of appointment than election.[298] Modern historians often connect the democratic preference for sortition with the democratic belief in equality:[299] but, once again, it is only the critics of democracy who connected sortition with equality,[300] whereas the democrats themselves seem to have preferred sortition not because of its being the obvious method of selection when all are alike, but because it safeguarded the powers of the people, prevented conflict and counteracted corruption.

There is one more aspect of political equality to discuss: equality before the law.[301] That is sometimes overlooked by historians, or only briefly described, perhaps because no slogan was coined for it as in the case of *isegoria* and *isonomia*. Equality before the law is mostly described in language using the adjective *isos* instead of an abstract noun. It is, however, a very important concept for the understanding of the Athenian democratic ideology and is a matter of normative, not natural, equality. The essence of it is that, however men may differ in wealth, power, social status, cleverness or eloquence, all ought to be equally treated by the laws[302] and by the jurors responsible for the meting out of justice.[303] In clear opposition to oligarchy, the emphasis of democrats is regularly on the distinction between the rich and the poor, who are said to deserve the same legal protection as the rich.[304] Equality before the law is closely connected with the rule of law as the distinguishing mark of democracy as against oligarchy or monarchy.[305]

The upshot of our discussion is that equality of nature was never an integral aspect of Athenian democratic ideology. It was imputed to the democrats by philosophers, but the various aspects of equality invoked

[292] Thuc. 2.37.1.   [293] Thuc. 6.39.1.   [294] See p. 157.
[295] Dem. 10.71. Whitehead (1983).   [296] Dem. 20.108, 18.320.   [297] Dover (1974) 229–34.
[298] See pp. 235–7.   [299] Jones (1957) 47–8; Finley (1976) 13.
[300] Isoc. 7.21–2; Pl. *Lg.* 757B.   [301] Thuc. 2.37.1; Eur. *Supp.* 429–34.
[302] Dem. 23.86.   [303] Dem. 18.6–7.   [304] Dem. 51.11; Isoc. 20.20.
[305] Aeschin., 1.5; Dem. 21.188; 25.16.

by democrats themselves were conceived of as equality of rights, by which all citizens might obtain equal opportunities and equal legal protection.

Liberty and equality

In political theory there is often an inherent opposition between equality and liberty.[306] But conflict develops only if equality is taken descriptively: if all, because they are by nature alike, ought to be treated equally in all respects, there is no longer liberty for anybody to develop and assert his personal merits. If, on the other hand, equality is understood in the sense of 'equality of opportunity', there is no opposition between liberty and equality; all men must be free and have equal opportunity to develop their talents.[307]

The connection between liberty and equality can also be established in another way. An analysis of equality inevitably leads to the question: equality of what? The answer given by liberal democrats in modern Europe has been 'equality of liberty':[308] the two concepts have tended to coalesce. A similar convergence of liberty and equality can be found in Greek democratic political theory. Rotation, for example, 'to rule and be ruled', is connected sometimes with liberty but sometimes with equality.[309] In Euripides' *Suppliant Women* everyone's right to address the people is described first as liberty but a few lines later as equality.[310] Similarly, *isegoria* is linked with *eleutheria* in Herodotos' description of Kleisthenes,[311] and everyone's right to say what he believes (*parrhesia*) is linked with liberty in Plato's *Republic*, but with equality in the pamphlet of the Old Oligarch.[312] The constant interplay of the two concepts is characteristic of Athenian democratic ideology and shows, once again, the close affinity between modern democracy and Athenian *demokratia* looked at as a political ideology rather than as a set of political institutions.

[306] Sartori (1962) 345–9; Pennock (1979) 46; Holden (1988) 28–32.
[307] Berlin (1969) 125; Pennock (1979) 45; Holden (1988) 33.
[308] Plamenatz (1956) 84; Sartori (1962) 348.
[309] Arist. *Pol.* 1317a40, 1332b25.
[310] Eur. *Supp.* 438, 441.
[311] Hdt. 5.78.1.
[312] Pl. *Resp.* 557B; Ps. Xen. *Ath. Pol.* 1.12.

5

The People of Athens

The three groups

The population of Athens, like that of every city-state, was divided into three clearly differentiated groups: citizens; resident foreigners, called metics (*metoikoi*); and slaves.[1] The division shows that Athens was a society based on 'orders' rather than 'classes', for the tripartition was by legal status, i.e. it was based on privileges, or otherwise, protected by law.[2] Membership of a group was typically inherited, and the groups were ordered hierarchically, in that by means of a constitutive act in due form a slave could become a metic (by manumission)[3] or a metic a citizen (by a citizenship decree),[4] while, on the other hand, a citizen could be penalized with loss of privilege (*atimia*) by which he forfeited all his rights and was virtually thrust out of the community,[5] and a metic could, for certain offences, be punished by being sold as a slave.[6] The citizens were the privileged order, which by law had the monopoly of landed property and political power; the metics were the underprivileged order of free people mostly making a living by crafts, trade and services;[7] the slaves were the unprivileged order, whose only right protected by law was that they could not be killed with impunity[8] (and the purpose of that regulation was undoubtedly to protect the master's property rather than the slave's life).

To analyse Athens in terms of a 'class society'[9] it would be necessary

---

[1] Ps. Xen. *Ath. Pol.* 1.12; Arist. *Pol.* 1326a18–20.
[2] Austin and Vidal-Naquet (1977) 103–6.
[3] Harp. s.v. *metoikion*. Whitehead (1977) 16–17.
[4] Din. 1.43. Osborne (1983) 141–54.   [5] Hansen (1976) 55–61.
[6] Phot. and *Suda* s.v. *poletai*.   [7] See p. 119.   [8] See pp. 120–1.
[9] Ste Croix (1981) 31–111.

to operate with a class of 'haves', comprising some of the citizens, some of the metics and even a few slaves,[10] over against a class of 'have-nots', comprising those citizens[11] and metics[12] who had to support themselves as day labourers,[13] plus the great majority of the slaves.[14] It would be a mistake to treat the slaves as a single class, because a few of them belonged to the exploiting class,[15] while the class of the exploited included, as well as most slaves, a significant number of citizens and metics; and it would be a mistake to identify the exploiting class with the citizens, because numerous citizens were 'have-nots'[16] and the exploiting class also included many metics and a few slaves. The largest Athenian business enterprise we hear of was a shield-manufactory with a hundred slaves or so, owned by Lysias and his brother Polemarchos, both metics;[17] and the richest man in all Athens at the beginning of the fourth century was Pasion the banker, who had been a slave, had become a metic, and, just in the last years of his life, achieved the status of citizen.[18]

The difference between citizens, metics and slaves does not correspond, either, to a division of the population of Athens according to social status (with all its psychological implications).[19] On the big public building-sites citizens, metics and slaves often worked side-by-side doing the same jobs for the same pay.[20] In the cemetery of the Kerameikos some of the grandest and some of the simplest gravestones stand randomly, erected by citizens and metics alike.[21] A passage in Xenophon is evidence that the metics were not confined to any sort of ghetto;[22] some of them were able to secure admission to the clubs of the sons of the wealthy,[23] the *hetaireiai*; and in Plato's dialogues metics and citizens turn up on an equal footing without the slightest trace of social demarcation.[24] But as soon as we come to the political sphere, though in that only, we meet the sharp division between metics and citizens. Such social differentiation as we do find in other spheres was a 'knock-on effect' from the political differentiation: metics and slaves could participate in the great festivals, but not on an equal footing,[25] and in times of crisis they were excluded

---

[10] Utchenko and Diakonoff (1970)
[11] Is. 5.39; Dem. 57.45; Xen. *Mem.* 2.8.1–2.   [12] *IG* II² 10 B 8 = Tod 100.
[13] Fuks (1951); Zimmermann (1974) 92–8.
[14] Finley (1973a) 49, *contra* Ste Croix (1981) 58–9.
[15] Lampis: Dem. 34.5–10. Pittalakos: Aeschin. 1.54.
[16] *Hypoth.* Lys. 34; Isoc. 7.54; Dem. 24.123.   [17] Lys. 12.8, 19.
[18] Dem. 36.48, 59.2.   [19] Finley (1973a) 49–51.
[20] *IG* I³ 474–6; *IG* II² 1672–3. Randall (1953).
[21] Garland (1982) 135–52; *IG* II² 6978, 7968.   [22] Xen. *Vect.* 2.6.
[23] Andoc. 1.15. Aurenche (1974) 111ff.   [24] Pl. *Resp.* 328B.
[25] See p. 63. Whitehead (1977) 86–9.

from sharing in the distributions of cheap or free corn that were made to the citizens.[26]

Athens, then, was, along with all other Greek city-states, a society based on 'orders', and, though, as in all such societies, there was some movement up and down the ladder, there was not the least tendency towards the evening-out of status: the citizens guarded their privileges fiercely, and the basic tripartition persisted undiminished throughout the classical age.

Metics and slaves lived alongside the citizens in a city-state, but the state itself was a community of citizens only, and of male citizens at that, for women were also excluded from political rights. Only an eccentric such as Plato[27] or a joker such as Aristophanes[28] could envisage giving women a role in running the state, just as only their crushing defeat by Philip in 338 induced the Athenians, for a few days, to grant citizen rights to the metics and freedom to the slaves; as soon as they learned that Philip was ready to conclude a peace on easy terms, they changed their minds and annulled the grant.[29]

On the other hand, political rights were possessed by all adult male citizens. It is true that at the restoration of the democracy in 403 one of the returning democrats, Phormisios, proposed the restriction of citizen rights to those who owned land, but the proposal was voted down.[30] In contrast to oligarchical city-states, fourth-century Athens had no property census. Solon did introduce a division of the citizen body into four census classes, and originally the right to hold magistracies was limited to the three top classes; that rule still applied in the time of Perikles, but by the fourth century it was a dead letter, and even the *thetes*, the lowest census class, could hold the magistracies that were supposed to be reserved for the top classes.[31] Political rights were not again made to depend on a property census until the democracy itself was abolished by the Macedonians when they conquered Athens in 322/1.[32] Under the democracy the only citizens excluded from the political community were the *atimoi*.

Age divisions of the citizens

But, if there was no division by property, another division was always maintained: that by age. An Athenian citizen came of age at eighteen, and was received into his deme and inscribed on the deme's population

---

[26] See pp. 98–9.

[27] Pl. *Resp.* 451C–457B.

[28] Ar. *Eccl.*   [29] Hyp. frr. 32–3. Hansen (1974) cat. no. 27.

[30] Lys. 34.   [31] Arist. *Ath. Pol.* 7.4, 47.1. See p. 107.

[32] Diod. 18.18.4; Plut. *Phocion* 27.5.

register (*lexiarchikon grammateion*);[33] but in the fourth century he only acquired political rights at the age of twenty. From the 370s at latest,[34] perhaps already in 403/2, the Athenians introduced a two-year military service for all eighteen- and nineteen-year-olds (who were called *hoi epheboi*),[35] on the model of the still-victorious Spartans; after the next grave defeat, at Chaironeia in 338, a law was passed to tighten up military training,[36] and from then at least, if not before, service as an ephebe involved garrison duty, which made the exercise of political rights temporarily *de facto* out of the question. So it may be conjectured that a young Athenian was only inscribed on the Assembly register of his deme (*pinax ekklesiastikos*) at the age of twenty.[37] And even then he had not attained to full citizen rights, for the right to be a juror in the People's Court (*dikastes*)[38] or a legislator (*nomothetes*)[39] or a magistrate (*arche*)[40] was reserved to citizens over thirty, a restriction that seems to have applied all through the fourth century. For certain magistracies the lower age-limit was actually forty;[41] and when a matter was about to be discussed in the Assembly it had originally been the rule for the crier to put the question 'Who wishes to speak, of those over fifty?'[42] We must remember, too, that the most revered court of law at Athens was the Areopagos, which had about 150 members, none under thirty-one (since they were ex-archons) and with a median age of about fifty-five;[43] and the arbitrators for private suits (*diaitetai*) were chosen from citizens in their last year of liability to conscription, when they were fifty-nine.[44]

The most important of those age-limits was undoubtedly the rule that jurors, legislators and magistrates must be over thirty. Given the low expectation of life of the Athenian population and its slow rate of growth, it can be conjectured that about one third of all adult citizens were in the age-bracket eighteen to thirty and that only two thirds of them were over thirty.[45] So the consequence of the thirty-year rule was that every third Athenian citizen had only limited citizen rights: he was old enough to attend the Assembly and move proposals and vote on the motions of others, but not old enough yet to be selected by lot to be a juror or a magistrate.

The reason for the higher age-limit for jurors and magistrates is nowhere expressly stated, but is not hard to guess. Everywhere in Greek literature we come across the idea that wisdom and experience grow with

---

[33] See p. 96.   [34] Aeschin. 2.167.
[35] Pélékidis (1962) 71–9; Reinmuth (1971) 123–38.   [36] Harp. s.v. *Epikrates*.
[37] Dem. 44.35.   [38] See p. 181.   [39] See p. 167.
[40] See p. 227.   [41] Arist. *Ath. Pol.* 42.2.
[42] Aeschin. 1.23, 3.4. See p. 142.   [43] See p. 289.
[44] Arist. *Ath. Pol.* 53.4.   [45] See p. 91.

age:[46] Aristotle says that the young have strength but the old have understanding, so the young ought to guard the state and the old steer it.[47] It is an idea whose analogy can be found in almost all old or 'primitive' societies: the power of judgement should be left to the oldest members.[48]

This division of the citizen body by age was both demographically and sociologically of the highest importance, yet it is, surprisingly, always overlooked by modern authors, who hastily equate the citizens in the Assembly with the citizens in the People's Court and say that both bodies constituted the same representative selection of the Athenian citizen body.[49] The fact is that they were not on all fours, because the Assembly was not representative at all – it *was* the citizen body; whereas the People's Court was a representative selection of a part of the citizen body.[50]

Numbers in the fourth century

How large was the citizen population of Attica, and how large or small was it in relation to the whole population, male and female, of all ages, inclusive of metics and slaves? The Athenians themselves would not have been able to answer either question with exactitude. Slaves were, as far as we know, never counted at all;[51] metics were counted, but only adult metics in so far as they had to pay a special 'metic tax'.[52] The lists of citizens were kept in the 139 separate demes, and there is nothing to suggest that there was a central citizen register.[53] Our only resource is to set certain figures (quoted or calculated) for the army and navy[54] alongside our general assumptions about the demographic structure.[55] The first thing to remember is that the citizen population of Athens had a special feature: after the citizenship law of Perikles in 451/50 citizenship was reserved to those born of parents who were both Athenian citizens,[56] and so from that time on the citizen body of Athens was a closed population, defined juridically and not geographically like other populations. Now, a geographical population depends on four factors – fertility, mortality, immigration and emigration – whereas a citizen population such as that of Athens depended on fertility, mortality,

---

[46] Dem. *Prooem.* 45.2; Thrasymachus DK 85 fr. 1; Aeschin. 1.23. Hansen (1990a) 223–4; Roussel (1951); Dover (1974) 102–8.

[47] Arist. *Pol* 1329a15; 1332b35–41.   [48] Newman (1983) 77–84.

[49] Rhodes (1981a) 525; Ostwald (1986) 34–5; Sinclair (1988) 70–1.

[50] Hansen (1983a) 159–60; (1989a) 213–18.   [51] Isager and Hansen (1975) 16.

[52] Whitehead (1977) 97.   [53] Hansen (1985a) 14.

[54] Hansen (1985a) 36–43.   [55] Hansen (1985a) 9–13.

[56] See pp. 52–4.

naturalization and loss of rights, but not on immigration or emigration. In the fourth century a few foreigners every year were admitted to citizenship by decree and a few citizens lost their rights by *atimia* or banishment; both groups were politically important, but demographically insignificant.[57] Nor, in the fourth century, did emigration have any effect on citizen numbers, because Athenians domiciled in other cities kept their Athenian citizenship; and immigration affected the general population but not the citizen population, since immigrants became only metics. So the increase of the citizen population depended *de facto* solely on fertility and mortality. But many Athenian citizens were domiciled away from Athens[58] and could not take part in political life. Thus we have to choose whether to try to calculate the number of Athenian citizens *tout court* or the number of Athenian citizens *domiciled in Attica*: from our point of view the latter is, naturally, the important figure.

Direct research into the demographic structure of the citizen population of Athens is unfortunately impossible, because the sources are wholly silent, and we are thrown back on analogies from other societies. The science of historical demography has made great strides in the last fifty years, and careful studies of hundreds of local communities in Europe have led to a new, and far more reductionist, picture of circumstances prior to about AD 1700. In the late Middle Ages and subsequently, a very high, though stable, fertility was combined with a very high, though strongly fluctuating, mortality; and the result was a modest growth of population in the short term, interrupted by crisis years in which there was a decline, so that in the long term the population remained roughly stationary. The expectation of life at birth was usually about twenty-five, at most thirty years, and even between crises a natural population increase of more than 1 per cent a year was out of the question.[59] Studies of the demography of the Roman Empire show roughly the same structure,[60] so it is reasonable to assume that the model can be used for the Greek city-states, and specifically for fourth-century Athens. That gives us a population of which about one third of all adult male citizens were under thirty, and no more than one tenth over sixty; and adult male citizens over eighteen represented only 30 per cent or so of all citizens, men, women, and children together.[61] In periods free from warfare or plague or famine there was doubtless some increase in the total of Athenian citizens, but, if we are considering those domiciled in Attica, any such increase must, by and large, have been neutralized by the constant emigration of citizens either as mercenaries,[62] or to live in other states

[57] Hansen (1982) 177–9.   [58] Hansen (1982) 179–83.
[59] Wrigley (1969); Flinn (1981).   [60] Hopkins (1966); Frier (1982, 1983).
[61] Hansen (1985a) 12.   [62] Is. 2.6; Pl. *Ep.*7 350A. Hansen (1982) 179–80.

(where of course they were metics)[63] or, occasionally, to colonize places overseas as *klerouchoi*, still retaining their citizenship.[64]

With these general considerations in mind we can approach the sources. The best we have relate to the military strength of Athens at the very end of our period.[65] In the last war against Macedon before the abolition of the democracy, the so-called Lamian War of 323–322, Athens put into the field a citizen army of 5500 men, and that was seven tenths of those in the twenty age-classes from twenty to thirty-nine: the rest were retained as a reserve.[66] So the whole Athenian army was 7800 men; but no society can ever call up 100 per cent of its menfolk,[67] so we must reckon that the army probably represented at most 80 per cent of the age classes called up, which must on that basis have been just about 10,000 in number. And, if we accept an average life-expectancy at birth of about twenty-five years and a population growth of 0.5 per cent,[68] 10,000 men between twenty and forty correspond to about 18,000 adult males over eighteen. Simultaneously with the land forces the Athenians sent out a fleet of at least 200 and perhaps 240 ships,[69] each of which should have had a crew of about 200.[70] Many ships were probably undermanned, but supposing (which is highly pessimistic) that only twenty men of every crew were Athenian,[71] we reach at least 4000 citizens on the ships, which, on the same principle as before, correspond to a population of about 9000 men. But while the Athenians had their army in Thessaly and their fleet in the Aegean they were still holding assemblies in which citizenship decrees were passed and ratified,[72] presumably with an attendance of 6000; and the Greater Dionysia were celebrated as usual in March–April 322,[73] and the whole machinery of state, with the Council of Five Hundred and hundreds of other magistrates, continued to function. Taking 18,000 plus 9000 plus all the Athenians who stayed in Athens throughout (and who cannot all have been senior citizens, invalids or shirkers), we shall have to reckon with an adult male citizen body of at least 30,000 – not the 20,000 or so that some historians in recent decades have suggested as the likely figure.[74] And 30,000 corresponds neatly to the census held on some occasion between 317 and 307 by Demetrios of Phaleron,[75] a census of male citizens and metics living in Attica (and fit

[63] *P. Oxy.* 2538. Hansen (1982) 180–2.
[64] *IG* II² 114 = Tod 146 and Harding (1985) no. 58. Hansen (1982) 182–3.
[65] Hansen (1985a) 37–40.   [66] Diod. 18.10.2, 11.3.
[67] Hansen (1985a) 16–21.
[68] Hansen (1985a) 12, based on Coale and Demeny (1983) 128.
[69] Diod. 18.10.2; *IG* II² 1631.167–74. Ashton (1972); but see Morrison (1987).
[70] Wallinga (1982).   [71] *IG* II² 398a, 493. Hansen (1985a) 101 n. 137.
[72] Osborne (1981) D 24–5.   [73] Edmonds (1957–61) II 433, 476–7, 581.
[74] Jones (1957) 75–96; Ruschenbusch (1984).   [75] Ath. 272C.

for the call-up),[76] which produced 21,000 Athenians and 10,000 metics.

A citizen population of 30,000 adult males corresponds to a total citizen population, including women and children, of about 100,000; but how about metics and slaves?[77] In contrast to the number of citizens, which was stable and roughly stationary, that of metics must have varied according to circumstances: peace and prosperity brought many metics to Athens, but they vanished again in any long war or crisis.[78] So it is not possible to say that in the fourth century there were so-and-so many metics. It has often been supposed that many of them were adult males without family,[79] but the gravestones show a percentage of women higher for metics than for citizens.[80] The only figure we have is Demetrios of Phaleron's census of 10,000 metics living in Attica in the period 317–307,[81] and if we take them to be a defence corps the total of adult male metics must have been about double that, and the total of all metics perhaps four times, and to them have to be added the metics who only stayed briefly in Attica without becoming domiciled there.

The slave population must have varied as greatly as that of metics. The majority were imported,[82] and slaves did not live longer than freeborn people, rather the other way round. In any long crisis people doubtless avoided buying new slaves, and in a few years the number of slaves would have fallen significantly.[83] We cannot name any absolute figure: in the source that records the census of Demetrios of Phaleron the figures of 21,000 adult male citizens and 10,000 metics are coupled with a figure of 400,000 slaves (men, women and children), which is incongruent and cannot come from the census but must have been supplied from some other source. What is more, it is impossible, and is quoted together with equally impossible figures for other cities, such as 470,000 slaves on the island of Aigina,[84] which is only 85 sq. km in size and would have had to have a density of 5500 per sq. km of slaves alone. Hypereides' surmise that there were 150,000 (adult male) slaves in his time,[85] however, fits a 400,000 total well. The Athenians did not know how many slaves there were: they guessed, and because they had no firm conception of very large numbers they guessed wrong; but they did have a conception that there were a lot of slaves, more than the free, and in that they may well have been right.[86] So there may have been over 150,000 slaves in Attica at certain times, and further than that we cannot get.

Putting all the figures together, we can conclude that the figure of

[76] Hansen (1985a) 28–36.
[77] Hansen (1988a) 10–12.　[78] Xen. *Vect.* 2.1–7; Isoc. 8.21.
[79] Whitehead (1977) 97–8 with n. 185.　[80] Hansen (1988a) 10.
[81] Ath. 272C.　[82] See p. 122.　[83] Xen. *Vect.* 4.4, 25, 28.
[84] Ath. 272C–D; Schol. Pind. I.244.22, 245.25.　[85] Hyp. fr. 33.
[86] Isager and Hansen (1975) 16–17.

30,000 adult male Athenian citizens represented no more than a tenth of the whole population of Attica and only a fifth of the whole adult population.

Acquisition of citizenship

Athenian citizenship was obtained either by birth or by naturalization, but, as the Athenians were extremely stingy about offering citizenship to foreigners, descent was overwhelmingly the main criterion.[87] There was a deep gulf between the Greek city-states and Rome, where, for example, a slave of a Roman citizen, manumitted in due form, automatically himself became a Roman citizen.[88] At Athens, in the fourth century at any rate, a citizen could be defined as someone whose parents were Athenian citizens.[89] It is hard to say whether illegitimate children of Athenian parents were citizens.[90] The positive evidence for that is slim,[91] and one source contradicts another. We know that being born in wedlock was a prerequisite for a child to be inscribed in a phratry,[92] and, since all Athenians in the fourth century were still, apparently, members of phratries,[93] it should follow that illegitimates did not have citizenship.

Citizenship by naturalization was a coveted privilege, only vouchsafed to a few favoured metics and foreigners. It had to be granted by a special procedure involving two Assembly meetings, of which the second was required to have a quorum of 6000 and the voting had to be by secret ballot.[94] The double procedure was introduced in about 370, and between 368 and 322 we have knowledge of fifty grants of citizenship, to sixty-four foreigners;[95] since the sources are fragmentary as usual, it may be conjectured that several hundred people obtained citizenship by naturaliz-ation in those forty-seven years, but that is no great number, and most of them were foreign princes and statesmen who had no intention of settling in Athens, so that their citizenship was in practice honorary.[96]

The Athenians guarded their privileges jealously, but illegitimates and foreigners must not infrequently have managed to insinuate themselves

---

[87] Cf. Arist. *Pol.* 1275b22–6.   [88] Nicholas (1962) 72–6.

[89] Arist. *Ath. Pol.* 42.1. See p. 53.

[90] Positive: Harrison (1968) 63–5; MacDowell (1976). Negative: Rhodes (1978); Hansen (1985a) 73–6.

[91] Plut. *Mor.* 834A–B; Lys. fr. vi; Is. 3.45. Hansen (1985a) 75–6.

[92] Ar. *Av.* 1661–70; Dem. 57.54. MacDowell (1976) 88.

[93] Hansen (1985a) 74; Lambert (1986) 6–18; Sealey (1987) 14, *pace* Osborne (1983) 176–83.

[94] Dem. 59.89–90.   [95] See p. 130.   [96] Osborne (1983) 147–50.

into the ranks of citizens and get themselves put on a deme register, for we often hear of the expulsion of such foreign bodies, either individually by a *graphe xenias* or collectively by a *diapsephismos*. The former, made against an individual, was a 'public prosecution for falsely representing himself as an Athenian' and was judged by the People's Court: condemnation resulted in the offender being sold into slavery by public auction.[97] *Diapsephismos* was a general revision of the citizen registers, deme by deme, each deme assembly voting on every member of the deme individually: a majority against anyone resulted in that person's being struck off the deme register. He could appeal to the court, in which the deme was represented by five elected accusers; but if he lost his appeal he was sold into slavery.[98] In addition to a comprehensive *diapsephismos* after the expulsion of the Tyrants in 510,[99] we hear of two other such revisions. The first was in 445/4, after the gift by Prince Psammetichos of Egypt of grain for free distribution amongst the citizens;[100] and a hundred years later, in 346/5, the Assembly once again passed a decree for a revision of all the registers, proposed by a man with the appropriate name of Demophilos, 'The People's Friend'.[101] The reason may perhaps have been that Philip of Macedon, a few years before, had turned a large number of Athenian *klerouchoi* out of Thrace and sent them back to Athens:[102] perhaps some of them had not been Athenian citizens at all.

In the bestowal of citizen rights Athens is an excellent example of what Aristotle in Books 3 and 6 of the *Politics* says about radical democracies in general: first of all they expand the number of citizens by taking in illegitimates, metics and slaves, until the ordinary people have secured a majority in the Assembly, after which they become extremely mean about granting citizenship to foreigners, and actually sharpen the criteria so that no more than absolutely necessary shall share in the benefits.[103] In a radical democracy even bare citizen rights carried far greater privileges than in an oligarchy, where property was the determinant of political rights; democracies were consequently even less willing than oligarchs and tyrants to offer citizenship to outsiders.

The vast majority of Athenian citizens were, then, citizens by birth, and in the great majority of cases a young Athenian in the second half of the fourth century would have had parents, grandparents and great-grandparents – fourteen persons – who were all Athenian citizens. Perhaps

---

[97] Is. 3.37; Dem. *Ep.* 3.29. Lipsius (1905–15) 416–17; Hansen (1982) 177 with n. 20.
[98] *Hypoth.* Dem. 57 and Is. 12. Lipsius (1905–15) 414–15.
[99] Arist. *Ath. Pol.* 13.5. Welwei (1967).
[100] Plut. *Per.* 37.4; Philoch. fr. 119. See p. 53.
[101] Dem. 57; Is. 12; Aeschin. 1.77, 86.   [102] Dem. 6.20. Hansen (1982) 183.
[103] Arist. *Pol.* 1278a26–34; 1319b6–18.

that does not much surprise a modern European, accustomed to the territory and the state being commensurate; but it is remarkable that such a principle could be maintained in ancient Greece, where the citizens were only a minority of all the inhabitants of the territory.

The Athenians had no central citizen register and citizens were listed in their phratries and in their demes. A male citizen was entered in his father's phratry when he was three to four years old,[104] and in his father's deme when he came of age.[105] Female citizens were not registered at all, but they were often presented to their fathers' phratries,[106] and the witness of the phratry-members must have been vital when a male Athenian had to prove that his mother was a citizen.[107] But it was inscription in the deme that really determined full citizenship. One of Kleisthenes' most important reforms was to link the exercise of political rights with membership of a deme, and in the fourth century the reference to a citizen's deme was as important a part of his full name as the patronymic:[108] every Athenian had a tripartite name, *onoma* (personal name), *patronymikon* (father's name), *demotikon* (name of deme): thus, 'Demosthenes, son of Demosthenes, of the deme Paiania'. The tripartite name applied in both the private and the public sphere: in the fourth century it is found both on the gravestones of citizens[109] and on their jury plaques.[110]

At the beginning of the year[111] all young men who had reached eighteen in the preceding year[112] were brought before their deme assemblies by their fathers or guardians.[113] Any member had the right to make objections against the young man's acceptance,[114] and even if no one raised an objection there still had to be a vote on every candidate. The assembly was put on oath and then voted twice: first whether the candidate was of age, i.e. eighteen, and then whether he was freeborn (i.e. his parents were citizens) and met the legal requirement (i.e. was born in wedlock).[115] If both votes were affirmative, the candidate was thereupon inscribed in the deme register;[116] if not, he had the right to appeal to the People's Court, in which case the deme was represented by five elected accusers and the young man presumably by his father. If he won in the court the deme had to accept him, but if the court ruled against him he was sold

---

[104] *P. Oxy.* 2538 col. ii 23–8 (Lys.).   [105] Arist. *Ath. Pol.* 42.1.

[106] Is. 3.73, 76, 79. Golden (1985), *pace* Gould (1980) 40–2.

[107] Dem. 57.40, 69.   [108] Arist. *Ath. Pol.* 21.4.

[109] Hansen et al, (1990) 25.   [110] Kroll (1972) 33–4.   [111] Dem. 30.15.

[112] Arist. *Ath. Pol.* 42.1. Golden (1979).   [113] Dem. 39.29.

[114] Dem. 44.40.   [115] Arist. *Ath. Pol.* 42.1. Wyse (1904) 281–2.

[116] Aeschin. 1.103; Harp. s.v. *lexiarchikon grammateion*. Kahrstedt (1934) 71 n. 2; Effenterre (1976).

into slavery.[117] After their registration in their demes all the new citizens of the year were then presented to the Council, which held a *dokimasia* in which their age was again scrutinized.[118]

Rights of citizenship

The principal privilege of an Athenian citizen was his political rights; in fact they were more than just a 'privilege': they constituted the essence of citizenship.[119] In contrast to metics and slaves, every adult male Athenian citizen had the right to attend the Assembly, and every Athenian citizen over thirty the further right to be a magistrate (*arche*) or a legislator (*nomothetes*) or a juror (*dikastes*). Magistrates were either elected or selected by lot from such persons as presented themselves as candidates;[120] legislators (who passed all laws)[121] and jurors (who manned the People's Court)[122] were selected by lot from a panel of 6000 citizens over thirty who had sworn a solemn oath. The panel of 6000 was itself selected by lot for one year at a time.[123] The actual legislators or jurors, numbering perhaps 500 or 1000, were selected by lot from the 6000 for a session lasting one day. On the other hand, the right to appear in court as a party or a witness was not confined to citizens: metics and in some cases even foreigners could do so.[124]

Besides their political rights, citizens had a set of advantages of a more economic sort. The right to own landed property in Attica was in principle reserved to them (trade and crafts were not so restricted, and agriculture was in any case regarded as the more honourable pursuit):[125] a metic could only acquire landed property if the Assembly had, by a special decree, granted him the privilege of *enktesis ges kai oikias*, 'right to acquire land and house'.[126] The minerals pertaining to the land were also reserved to the citizens. The foundation of the prosperity of Athens was the great silver-mines of Laureion in southern Attica. The Athenians held in principle that ownership of what lay beneath the soil was vested in the community, not the private persons under whose land it was found:[127] the state let out the exploitation of the mines to numerous concessionaires who bought by auction the right to mine silver for a fixed period of years.[128] But the right to hold such a concession was reserved to citizens

---

[117] Arist. *Ath. Pol.* 42.1.
[118] Arist. *Ath. Pol.* 42.2. Rhodes (1972) 171–4.
[119] Arist. *Pol.* 1275a22–6, b5–6.   [120] See pp. 230–5.   [121] See p. 167.
[122] See pp. 197–9.   [123] See pp. 181–3.   [124] See p. 118.
[125] Eur. *Or.* 917ff; Xen. *Oec.* 6.4–8; Arist. *Pol.* 1318b9ff.
[126] *IG* II² 80.9–11. Pecirka (1966); Henry (1983) 204–40.
[127] Hopper (1953) 206–9.   [128] Arist. *Ath. Pol.* 47.2. *Hesperia* 19 (1950) 189–312.

or to foreigners granted 'equal status' with citizens (*isoteleis*).[129] We know only two examples of foreigners being named in mine records, and they are both from Siphnos,[130] where there were also silver-mines; probably they were metics and had been given special privileges as experts of some kind.

Citizenship also carried with it financial advantages, as soon as the Athenians began to be paid for the exercise of their political rights. Every working day, *misthos* was paid to someone: on the relevant days to those who attended the Assembly,[131] more frequently to the jurors in the People's Court,[132] which met more often, and every working day to the councillors.[133] Other magistrates apparently received no regular reimbursement, but many of them could make a profit out of their office in the form of perquisites, some recognized and some not.[134] Furthermore, citizens of military age and fit for military service were paid for attending parades.[135] On festival days there were no meetings of any political bodies, but instead citizens received 'theatre money' (*theorika*).[136] The name derives from the fact that the payments, which did not begin till the mid fourth century,[137] were originally a subsidy towards entry into the theatre on those festival days when the tragedies and comedies were performed,[138] but the payment was gradually extended to other festivals;[139] and it can be surmised that in the second half of the fourth century many Athenian citizens, on most days of the year, could expect a state payment of one kind or another, *misthos* on working days and *theorikon* on festival days.[140]

The Athenians also had a sort of social security – limited to citizens, of course. Disabled persons with no means of support could be registered with the Council and receive a modest subsidy of first 1 obol[141] and later 2 obols a day;[142] and if a citizen had died in battle the state undertook the upbringing of any under-age sons.[143] Moreover, at times of food-crisis the state often distributed corn,[144] either subsidized or free; and, although the people who brought the corn to Athens were often metics and foreigners,[145] only citizens benefited from the distributions[146] – the

[129] Xen. *Vect.* 4.12.   [130] *Hesperia* 19 (1950) n. 20.3–5.
[131] See p. 150.   [132] See pp. 188–9.   [133] See pp. 253–5.
[134] See pp. 240–2.   [135] Isoc. 7.82.
[136] Dem. 3.11; Hyp. 1.26. Buchanan (1962).
[137] Harp. s.v. *Euboulos* and *Theorika* (Philinos). Ruschenbusch (1979a).
[138] Dem. 1 *hypoth* 4. Theophilus fr. 12 (Edmonds).
[139] Dem. 44.37; Plut. *Mor.* 818E–F.   [140] Dem. 13.2; Plut. *Mor.* 1011B.
[141] Lys. 24.26.   [142] Arist. *Ath. Pol.* 49.4; Aeschin. 1.103–4; Lys 24.
[143] Lys. fr. vi (Budé); *SEG* 28 46 = Harding (1985) no. 8; Aeschin. 3.154.
[144] Isager and Hansen (1975) 206–8.
[145] *IG* II² 360.8–12; *SEG* 21 298; *Hesperia* 43 (1974) 322–4 no. 3.
[146] Philoch. fr. 119; Dem. 34.37–9.

meritorious metics were fobbed off with an honorary decree. (So it is hardly likely to be coincidental that the revision of the citizen lists in 445/4 followed hard on the heels of Psammetichos' present of corn for free distribution amongst the citizens.)

Athenian citizens also had a privileged position at law. Murder of a citizen was held to be a more serious crime than murder of a metic or a slave. The penalty for intentional homicide was death, if the victim was an Athenian citizen,[147] lifelong banishment if the victim was a metic,[148] and only a fine if he was a slave.[149] Further, no citizen could be subjected to torture,[150] whereas metics could,[151] and slaves were obliged to be examined under torture before their testimony could be admitted in the courts.[152] And citizens were exempt from all corporal[153] (though not from capital) punishment, whereas slaves were often flogged.[154] For a citizen, the alternative to capital punishment was often *atimia*,[155] loss of all rights, which included loss of political rights and also a ban on appearing in the Agora or temples;[156] as the courts were situated in the Agora and a citizen under *atimia* was thus excluded from appearing before them,[157] the *atimos* was pretty well without rights.[158] The penalty was only used against citizens, especially any who had abused their citizen rights or failed to carry out their citizen duties.[159] One more privilege of an Athenian citizen was that he could not be sold into slavery, except if he had been ransomed as a prisoner of war and had not reimbursed his ransomer.[160]

Duties of citizenship

To rights correspond duties; but it is harder to give a precise description of the duties the Athenian state imposed on its citizens. Certainly, no duty was placed on any citizen to make use of his rights: no punishment was incurred if he held aloof from the Assembly and the courts and took no part in candidature for office,[161] and some citizens, even respected ones, in fact did decline to participate in the running of the political institutions.[162] There were, however, two duties: a duty to pay taxes and a duty of military service.[163] As to the former, the only direct tax was

[147] Lys. 1.50. [148] *Lex. Seg.* 194.12–13.
[149] Lycurg. 1.65. MacDowell (1963) 110–29. [150] Andoc. 1.43.
[151] Lys. 13.27, 54, 59–61. [152] Is. 8.12. Thür (1977). See p. 201.
[153] Dem. 22.55 = 24.167.
[154] *SEG* 26 72.30–2 = Harding (1985) no. 45; *IG* II² 333.7.
[155] Andoc. 1.73–9. Hansen (1976) 55–90. [156] Aeschin. 3.176.
[157] Lys. 6.24. [158] Hansen (1976) 55–60. [159] Hansen (1976) 72–4.
[160] Dem. 53.11. [161] Dem. 19.99. See pp. 233, 249.
[162] Isoc. 15.152. See p. 309. [163] Arist. *Ath. Pol.* 55.3.

eisphora, an (originally sporadic) tax on property;[164] but it was only levied on citizens above a certain property level.[165] As for military service, that was obligatory upon all citizens in good health and of military age.[166] Each year the new age-class of eighteen-year-olds swore a solemn oath, which is recorded in both literary[167] and epigraphical sources, and went as follows.[168]

> The ancestral ephebic oath which the ephebes must swear: 'I will not disgrace the sacred arms nor desert my neighbour wherever I may be stationed in the ranks. I will defend all things sacred and profane, and I will not pass on my native land diminished but greater and better, as far as in me lies and along with all others. And I will obey those in authority with due regard, and the laws, both those laid down and those which they shall afterwards lay down with due regard. And if anyone subverts the laws I will not permit it, as far as in me lies and along with all others, and I will honour the ancestral rites.'

Conscription included not only the ephebic service for the eighteen- and nineteen-year-olds,[169] but also liability to active service in time of war for all between twenty and fifty-eight; those aged fifty-nine were exempt from active service but had to be available in that year to act as *diaitetai*, arbitrators in private lawsuits.[170]

But neither military service nor liability to taxation was a duty exclusive to citizens, for metics also had to do military service and pay the property tax.[171] The only duties devolving exclusively on citizens were in the sphere of marriage, certain kinds of personal conduct and family life. Marriage between citizen and metic was null and void, and pretence of such a marriage was one of the offences punishable under the *graphe xenias*:[172] if an Athenian wished to live with a metic woman their children could not, for example, inherit from their father.[173] Male prostitution was forbidden to Athenian citizens: an Athenian who prostituted himself[174] or caused another citizen to prostitute himself[175] was punished with death[176] or *atimia*.[177] A citizen could also be punished with *atimia* if he squandered his ancestral inheritance or failed in his duties towards his parents: a son was obliged to provide food and accommodation for his parents when they grew old, and, when they died, to give them a proper funeral and

---

[164] Thomsen (1964); Brun (1983).   [165] Dem. 4.7.
[166] Busolt and Swoboda (1920–6) 1185.
[167] Lycurg. 1.77; Poll. 8.105–6; Stobaeus *Florilegium* 43.48.   [168] Tod 204.
[169] Arist. *Ath. Pol.* 42.2–5.   [170] Arist. *Ath. Pol.* 53.3–7.
[171] See pp. 118–19.   [172] Dem. 59.16, 52.   [173] Dem. 43.51.
[174] Aeschin. 1.19–20.   [175] Aeschin. 1.72.   [176] Aeschin. 1.87.
[177] Aeschin. 1.160.

maintain the cult at their graves; neglect of those duties was the crime of *kakosis goneon*, 'mistreating parents',[178] punished with *atimia*.[179] Although, strictly speaking, there is no evidence on the point, it is reasonable to hold that only citizens, and not metics, were liable for these two offences. Here the Athenian state was, indeed, legislating about private conduct, but these were all matters which, though private, directly affected the maintenance and quality of the citizen body.

THE POLITICAL GEOGRAPHY OF ATTICA

After Kleisthenes, the citizens of Athens were divided into ten tribes (*phylai*), thirty ridings (*trittyes*), three to each tribe, and 139 demes (*demoi*).[180] In the fourth century there were between one and ten demes in a riding and between six and twenty-one demes in a tribe.

Demes

A deme was originally a local community whose members were all those citizens living in the vicinity of the place where the deme assembly was held.[181] But Kleisthenes had made membership of the demes pass by inheritance,[182] and the political–geographical unity was broken as soon as more and more members of the demes moved to other parts of Attica (mostly to the city itself). In Athens and the Piraeus many gravestones have been found of citizens belonging to demes from all over Attica, whereas there are only a few graves round about Attica belonging to citizens from the city demes or the Piraeus: the direction of movement was evidently from country to city.[183] So a fourth-century deme must be defined as a hereditarily determined community of Athenian citizens meeting for purposes of politics and cult at a place where only some of them had their dwelling and family grave.[184] In certain cases the deme assembly was actually moved to Athens,[185] presumably because the deme was no longer the only natural assembly-point for its members. In the fourth century quite different people were politically active in the local affairs of the demes from those active in state politics;[186] and a reasonable explanation of the difference is that local politics was mainly carried on

[178] Xen. *Mem.* 2.2.13; Dem. 24.107.   [179] Aeschin. 1.28–32; Andoc. 1.74.
[180] Traill (1975) 75–6: 139 demes; (1986): 140 demes [Acharnai rated as a divided deme].
[181] Arist. *Ath. Pol.* 21.4.   [182] Arist. *Ath. Pol.* 42.1.
[183] Damsgaard-Madsen (1988); Nielsen et al. (1990); Hansen et al. (1990).
[184] *IG* II[2] 1180.21–5. Whitehead (1986) 86–90.
[185] Dem. 57.10; *SEG* 28 103.28.   [186] Osborne (1985) 83–92; Whitehead (1986) 313–26.

by those members of the demes who still lived in them, while politics in the Assembly and the Council was largely the sphere of those who had migrated into the city.[187]

The demes varied in size. In the middle of the fourth century many small demes sent only one representative each to the Council,[188] whereas the largest, Acharnai, to the north of the city, between Mount Aigaleos in the west and Pentelikon in the east, sent twenty-two. Examination of the evidence for how the Athenians manned the Council shows that in Demosthenes' time the number of representatives a deme sent to the Council must have corresponded quite closely to the number of citizens it contained,[189] and it follows that the smallest demes had no more than fifty or so adult males, while Acharnai would have had between 1000 and 1500. The 139 demes were distributed amongst the 30 ridings (*trittyes*).[190] We have no account of how Kleisthenes performed the distribution, but we know the pattern in the fourth century from numerous lists of the *prytaneis*, the Council's executive committee, and of the Council itself, in which the names of the fifty members from one tribe are often listed by demes and by ridings.[191] Most ridings sent either sixteen or seventeen men to the Council,[192] and it follows that they must have had roughly the same number of members (with the exception of Acharnai with its twenty-two councillors).[193] It further follows that the representation of the demes (and so the ridings) on the Council must have been changed after Kleisthenes but before about 350, when the inscriptions become numerous enough for us to reconstruct the pattern; for that after 150 years thirty demographic entities with hereditary membership could still be of equal size, as Kleisthenes had made them, is simply incredible.[194] Apart from other factors, the huge losses and shifts of population during the Peloponnesian War must have made adjustments necessary, and the obvious moment for the modification is 403/2, in connection with the re-establishment of the democracy.[195]

Ridings (*trittyes*)

It can be seen from the inscriptions that a riding was usually a geographical entity, but by no means always: sometimes a single deme stands isolated from the rest of the demes belonging to its riding,[196] and a set

---

[187] Hansen (1989a) 83, 89–90; (1990f) 352–3.   [188] See p. 104.

[189] Hansen (1985a) 60–4.   [190] Arist. *Ath. Pol.* 21.4.

[191] *Agora* XV 1–56; *Hesperia* 47 (1978) 269–331; 51 (1982) 204–6. Traill (1986) 197–235.

[192] Siewert (1982) 87–105; Kinzl (1989) 348–9.

[193] *Agora* XV 17.43–64, *pace* Traill (1986) 142–4 [see Whitehead in *Phoenix* 41 (1987) 442–3].

[194] Hansen et al. (1990) 30, *pace* Stanton (1984) 2 n. 2.   [195] Hansen (1989a) 77.

[196] Siewert (1982) 105–17.

of demes in north-east Attica were assigned to the city riding of their tribe instead of the inland or coastal riding that might have been expected from their location.[197] In the geographical distribution of the demes, the city zone was the smallest, with 130 places on the Council, while the coast had 196 and the inland zone 174;[198] and that may give a hint as to the background of our conjectured reform in 403/2. In all pre-industrial societies the death-rate has been higher in the towns than in the country, and any substantial growth of town populations has depended on a constant stream of immigrants,[199] so, whereas in Kleisthenes' time the whole city population of Athens very likely belonged to city demes, those demes may in the following period have lost in population compared with those of the inland and coastal zones.[200] A demographic shift in favour of the coastal and inland demes is, then, only what we should expect; and, in addition, plague and war may have hit the demes to a different degree. So in 403/2 (let us suppose) the Athenians would have made an adjustment to bring the ten city ridings up to their proper third of the membership of the Council by transferring a set of demes from inland and coastal ridings to the corresponding city ridings. However, apparently at the same time the deme Acharnai was allowed twenty-two councillors, and it is anything but certain that the adjustments were carried out with full rigour in all ridings.[201]

Tribes

Each of the ten Kleisthenic tribes was composed of three ridings, one from the city, one from the inland zone and one from the coast,[202] so a tribe included citizens from quite different parts of Attica, with widely differing traditions and economic bases. Thus, Hippothontis (tribe VIII) had farmers from Eleusis, craftsmen and traders from Koile in the city, and seamen from the Piraeus; and Akamantis (tribe V) had miners and fishermen from Thorikos in the south and farmers from Cholargos on the agricultural plain in the north. But all the tribes had their small assembly-places in the city of Athens or close to it.[203]

Organization of the demes, ridings and tribes

Kleisthenes' division of Attica was a necessary condition for the military and political organization of the citizen body. Athens, though a direct

---

[197] Siewert (1982) 107–9; Hansen (1990d) 52.
[198] Traill (1975) 71.   [199] Wrigley (1969) 97, 99; Hansen et al. (1990) 34.
[200] Hansen et al. (1990) 34.   [201] Hansen (1990d) 54.
[202] Arist. *Ath. Pol.* 21.4. Hansen (1990d), *pace* Kinzl (1987).   [203] Busolt and Swoboda (1926) 973–4 n. 1.

democracy, was much too large for the communication between the citizens and the central organs of government to be carried on without mediation; the way a citizen could exercise his political rights was through membership of a deme, and, *via* the deme, of a riding and a tribe.

Demes   The Athenian state was absolutely based on the 139 demes. Each deme had a *demarchos*, chosen for a year either by lot or by election in the deme assembly (*agora*),[204] where all members (*demotai*) met and took decisions about the affairs of the deme.[205] The *demarchoi* presided over local government only; they were not magistrates[206] (except the *demarchos* of the Piraeus, who was chosen by lot by the whole *polis* and not by his deme[207]). But a number of important aspects of central government were devolved upon the demes, of which the most important was the acceptance of new citizens and their registration by the *demarchos* in the population register of the deme, the *lexiarchikon grammateion*;[208] doubtless it was also he who kept the deme's other register, the assembly register or *pinax ekklesiastikos*.[209] Next, the demes were used for the call-up. The army was organized by tribes, not demes; but the levy was by demes, and was based on the *lexiarchikon grammateion* of each deme:[210] in the fourth century, at any rate, the *demarchos* was involved in the call-up for both the army and the navy.[211] But the Council, too, though organized by tribes, was chosen by demes; for, though each tribe sent fifty members to represent it,[212] the fifty were made up from the relevant demes according to population: thirty-eight demes had only one place on the Council,[213] and some of them were so small that in some years they were unable to send a representative.[214] Thirty-seven demes had two and twenty had three councillors, and only twenty-three demes were big enough to have seven or more representatives.[215] Demosthenes' deme, (Lower) Paiania, had eleven members: it is amazing how many known political figures belonged to that deme.[216]

Originally the demes had also played a part in the selection by lot of other magistrates (besides the councillors), but decentralization led to corruption and some demes actually took to selling offices. So in the fourth century it was decided that all magistrates must be selected cen-

---

[204] Arist. *Ath. Pol.* 21.5; Harp. s.v. *demarchos*. Damsgaard-Madsen (1973).
[205] Whitehead (1986) 86–120.   [206] Hansen (1980c) 173.
[207] Arist. *Ath. Pol.* 54.8.   [208] Dem. 57.60; Harp. s.v. *lexiarchikon grammateion*.
[209] Dem. 44.35.
[210] *IG* I[3] 138.5–6; *M&L* 23.29 = Fornara (1977) no. 55. Jameson (1963); Effenterre (1976).
[211] Dem. 50.6.   [212] Arist. *Ath. Pol.* 21.3.   [213] Traill (1975) 69–70.
[214] Traill (1975) 14, 19, etc.   [215] Traill (1975) 67–9.
[216] Develin (1989) 542.   [217] Arist. *Ath. Pol.* 62.1. Whitehead (1986) 279–90.

tra⌐   ⌐d the 500 Guardians of the Navy
Yard

Ridin⌐   much importance as independent
organs   each tribe's contingent of fifty,
who se⌐   year,[218] were divided by ridings
(two of ⌐)   ⌐),[219] and one riding picked by
the *epistᵤ*   ⌐ty in the Tholos for twenty-
four hour   ⌐he system of ridings had any
importanc⌐   ⌐] but boundary pillars (*horoi*)
from the f⌐   ⌐he Piraeus, which provide
evidence th⌐   ⌐anized by ridings,[222] and
Demosthene⌐   ⌐, rejected by the Assembly
in 354/3, sho⌐   ⌐used in the organization
of the navy in   ⌐the ridings did not play
a significant rol⌐   ⌐re naturally chosen one
from each riding   ⌐controlled entrance to
the meetings of t⌐   ⌐u), were picked three
per tribe without   ⌐d no importance for
the working of the

Tribes   The tribes w⌐   ⌐[227] and the members
of each tribe were u⌐   ⌐ero.[228] Each tribe
had a sanctuary in At⌐   ⌐ and for political
meetings. Common to ⌐   ⌐the Eponymous
Heroes, which stood in   ⌐⌐ (etroön) close to
the Council house (the   ⌐odging of the
prytaneis (the Tholos). T⌐   statues of all
the heroes on a high recta⌐   ⌐h was posted
all information requiring p⌐   – agendas for
the Assembly,[231] motions pr⌐   charge-sheets in public
prosecutions[233] and call-up li⌐   politically active citizen would have
needed to go daily to the Agora and study the new postings; and much

[218] Arist *Ath. Pol.* 43.2.

[219] W. E. Thompson (1966, 1969): the *trittyes* of the *boule* different from the Kleisthenic *trittyes*. Traill (1978, 1986); Siewert (1982): the bouleutic *trittyes* are the same as the Kleisthenic.

[220] Arist. *Ath. Pol.* 44.1.   [221] *Pace* Siewert (1982) 141–5.

[222] Siewert (1982) 10–13, 142.   [223] Dem. 14.23.

[224] *Hesperia* 5 (1936) 393–413 no. 10.167–70. Traill (1986) 79–92.

[225] *IG* II² 1749.79 = *Agora* XV 38.82. Hansen (1989a) 139.   [226] See p. 137.

[227] See p. 49.   [228] *IG* II² 1140. Kearns (1989) 80–92.

[229] Thompson and Wycherley (1972) 38–41.   [230] Wycherley (1957) 85–90.

[231] See p. 133.   [232] Aeschin. 3.39.   [233] Dem. 21.103.

[234] Ar. *Pax* 1183–4 with schol.

political argument at Athens would have taken place in front of the balustrade surrounding the Monument to the Heroes.

A tribe was under the presidency of three chosen *epimeletai tes phyles*, as we have seen – one from each of its ridings. The tribes were the basis of the magistracies, first and foremost the Council (which was a board of magistrates, albeit much the most important); for the Council was divided into ten sections, each of fifty persons from the same tribe. Many other magistrates were also picked by tribes: they were grouped in boards, and many boards comprised ten members, one per tribe.[235] In the fourth century, however, there grew a tendency to give up tribal representation and choose the boards from the whole citizen body (*ex hapanton*) irrespective of tribe.[236] Moreover, in some cases in which a board was composed of one representative per tribe, the tribal assembly also took part in the choice of its candidate.[237] Furthermore, the jurors in the People's Court were distributed by tribes,[238] and the panel of 6000 who, each year, swore the Heliastic Oath must have comprised 600 from each tribe.[239] Finally, the army organization was based on the tribes. The hoplite force was divided into ten regiments (*taxeis*), one from each tribe,[240] and the cavalry into ten squadrons (*phylai*), again one from each tribe.[241] A regiment was commanded by a *taxiarchos* and a squadron by a *phylarchos*.[242] Thus the citizens of a given tribe fought side by side in the ranks, officered by men from their own group: in the surviving lists of the fallen, officers and other ranks are listed tribe by tribe.[243] The fleet was also organized by tribes, but possibly, in that case, subdivided by ridings.[244]

THE PROPERTY CLASSES OF THE CITIZENS

The citizens of fourth-century Athens were still divided into the four Solonian property classes – *pentakosiomedimnoi*, *hippeis*, *zeugitai* and *thetes*[245] – which still had some practical applications. *Klerouchoi* were chosen from *zeugitai* and *thetes*,[246] a citizen had to state his property class when he was selected by lot to be a magistrate;[247] when a debtor to the state offered a surety, the surety had to be of the same property class as

---

[235] See p. 238.
[236] Arist. *Ath. Pol.* 61.1 (*strategoi*); *SIG*³ 298 (*epimeletai tou Amphiaraiou*).
[237] Aeschin. 3.27, 30.   [238] Arist. *Ath. Pol.* 63.2.   [239] Kroll (1972) 94–8.
[240] Xen. *Hell.* 4.2.19; Diod. 18.10.2.   [241] Arist. *Ath. Pol.* 61.5.
[242] Arist. *Ath. Pol.* 61.3, 5.   [243] *Agora* XVII 23.   [244] Dem. 14.23.
[245] See pp. 43–6.   [246] *IG* II² 30; *Hesperia* 40 (1971) 164 line 12.
[247] Arist. *Ath. Pol.* 7.4.

himself;[248] and a law about 'heiresses' (*epikleroi*) laid down that the guardian of an *epikleros* of the thetic class must provide her with a dowry out of his own funds, a *pentakosiomedimnos* paying 500 drachmas, a *hippeus* 300 and a *zeugites* 150.[249] As far as we can tell, the classes were in this age actually based on property and not on produce,[250] but we know nothing about how the property was assessed or how large a fortune was necessary to belong to the top three classes. When the democracy was abolished by the Macedonians in 322, Antipater imposed a new constitution with a property qualification of 2000 drachmas, which had the effect that only 9000 Athenians any longer had political rights and some 22,000 were disfranchised.[251] Some historians have built their socio-economic analysis of Athenian society in the fourth century on this passage, taking it that those 2000 drachmas were the property qualification for membership of the *zeugitai*, and hence that the 9000 represented all male adults in the top three classes, while the citizens excluded were those who had been *thetes*.[252] We have, however, not the slightest evidence that Antipater's property qualification was based on the Solonian classes at all; and if the assumption of those historians is followed, that the Athenian infantry went on being recruited only from the top three classes, thus producing a hoplite class of only 9000, it is utterly incompatible with what we know of the size of the Athenian army in the Lamian War in 323/2.[253]

The fact that there is no evidence to determine the size of the property classes in the fourth century no doubt coincides with the difficulty of assessing what real significance they had. The problem can be discussed under three heads: did the property classes have any significance for (1) the selection of magistrates, (2) liability to taxation, or (3) military service?

Selection of magistrates   For magistracies the former rule continued, that *thetes* were excluded from all offices; but two passages in Aristotle's *Constitution of Athens* show that it was a dead letter. At the drawing of lots for magistracies people were still asked what property class they belonged to, but the effect was simply that no one said he was a *thes*;[254] and, though the old rule still applied that the Treasurers of Athena had to be selected by lot from *pentakosiomedimnoi*, Aristotle comments that the man on whom the lot fell had to carry out the magistracy even if he was quite poor.[255] We know, too, that on one occasion a poor citizen

[248] Dem. 24.144.   [249] Dem. 43.54.
[250] Is. 7.39. Jones (1957) 142 n. 50.
[251] Diod. 18.18.4–5. Cf. Plut. *Phocion* 28.7: only 12,000 disfranchised.
[252] Jones (1957) 9, 81; Ruschenbush (1984) 259.   [253] See p. 92.
[254] Arist. *Ath. Pol.* 7.4.   [255] Arist. *Ath. Pol.* 47.1.

(with financial assistance from relatives) held the office of king archon;[256] and the Council itself could not have functioned if *thetes* had not supplied a large slice of its membership.[257] So the Solonian property classes did not any longer have practical significance for office-holding, and the Athenians had put into practice the democratic ideal that any citizen should be able to hold a magistracy.[258]

Liability to taxation   At the *dokimasia* before entry to the archonship, the candidate was asked whether he belonged to one of the top three classes, and the question was formulated as 'whether he paid his taxes'.[259] That could point to a time when there had been a tax (*telos*) graduated by property classes and paid by everybody; but in the fourth century the only direct tax on citizens was *eisphora*, and that was paid only by the well-off, certainly a smaller group than those in the top three classes.[260] In Deinarchos' speech against Aristogeiton the question about *telos* at the *dokimasia* is used as an opportunity to refer to payments of *eisphora* but no attempt is made to identify the two.[261] There is no other reliable evidence,[262] and not the least reason to suppose, that the *eisphora* in Demosthenes' time was linked to the Solonian classes.[263]

Military service   It is usual to believe that the Athenian army in the fourth century was based on property classes as it had been in the fifth; and in line with that belief many historians assume that ephebic service (which was either introduced or reformed in 403/2) was training in hoplite warfare, and was reserved to the top three classes.[264] On this model, the crucial gap in Athenian society remained that between the *zeugitai*, who, as hoplites, dominated the army, and the *thetes*, who mostly manned the ships but to a lesser degree served in the army as light-armed troops. But the sources point in a different direction, and suggest that there was a shift that may have begun as early as the beginning of the fourth century. Aristotle's detailed description of ephebic service gives no hint that it only applied to the top three classes,[265] and Lykourgos in his speech against Leokrates expressly says that all citizens swear the oath when they are inscribed in their *lexiarchikon grammateion* and are called

[256] Dem. 59.72.   [257] Rhodes (1972) 4–6.
[258] Arist. *Pol.* 1317b19–20.   [259] Arist. *Ath. Pol.* 55.3.
[260] See pp. 112–13.   [261] Din. 2.17–18.
[262] On Poll. 8.129–30 see Brun (1983) 11.   [263] Ste Croix (1953) 42–5.
[264] Gomme (1933) 8–12; Jones (1957) 82–3; Reinmuth (1972) 106–15, Rhodes (1981a) 503; Osborne (1985a) 44.
[265] Arist. *Ath. Pol.* 42.3–5.

up for ephebic service.[266] Moreover, the surviving lists of ephebes show that a year-class of conscripts was about 500 in the 330s but perhaps over 600 in the 320s; even 500 are too many to be confined to the top three classes, while 600 are too few to coincide with Lykourgos' assertion that all citizens are supposed to do ephebic service. The explanation must be that, from 336/5 at all events, ephebic service in principle applied to all citizens, but that it took a fair while for the principle to have full effect.[267]

If we assume that citizens of all four classes were called up as ephebes, Aristotle's description becomes much easier to understand. First, the ephebes are trained as both hoplites and peltasts, and there seems to be no 'division of labour': all the conscripts are trained in both techniques, and after the first year's training all of them receive a hoplite panoply at state expense.[268] At that date, therefore, there was no longer a gulf between the *zeugitai* who served as hoplites (because they could afford to pay for their outfit)[269] and the *thetes* who served as peltasts (for which service the outfit was much cheaper): it looks as if those called up were distributed between the two sorts of weaponry without reference to property classes.[270] And that system can, in essence, be traced back to the beginning of the fourth century; for it appears from Lysias' speech against the younger Alkibiades that many of the richest citizens of all, who were enrolled in the cavalry, had been called up as hoplites in the campaign of 395/4, and Lysias says that many of those called up as hoplites would have preferred to serve as cavalry – or as light-armed troops.[271]

Summing up, it can be said that, although the Solonian property classes persisted in the fourth century, they existed as a mere formality with no significance, other than in the few exceptional matters with which we began.

THE SOCIAL DIVISIONS OF THE CITIZENS ACCORDING TO WEALTH

Alongside the Solonian property classes there was another economic division of the citizens: between those, on the one hand, who were

---

[266] Lycurg. 1.76. Pélékidis (1962) 283–94; Vidal-Naquet (1968) 177–8; Ruschenbusch (1979b) 174.

[267] Hansen (1988a) 3–6; (1988d) 189–90; (1989f) 41–2, *pace* Ruschenbush (1988a) 139–40; (1988b) 194–6.

[268] Arist. *Ath. Pol.* 42.3, cf. Aeschin. 3.154.

[269] *IG* I³ 1.8–10 = M&L 14 and Fornara (1977) no. 44B.

[270] Dem. 13.4, 50.6, 16. Hansen (1985a) 87, 89.   [271] Lys. 14.7, 10–11, 14–15, 22.

required to pay property tax (*eisphora*) or perform public duties involving expenditure – 'liturgies' (*leitourgiai*) as they were called – or both, and those, on the other hand, who were exempt from such burdens.[272] As far as we know there was no correspondence between the two kinds of division, and, while the Solonian classes lost in importance in the fourth century, the division of the citizen body according to liability or otherwise for taxation or liturgies gradually became the decisive criterion for who counted as the 'upper class' at Athens. 'We who pay *eisphora*, we who perform liturgies', cries the wealthy Meidias from the speakers' platform in the Assembly;[273] and a mass of other sources chimes in with him.[274]

Liturgies

A liturgy[275] was a special sort of tax-payment, because coupled with the expenditure was the duty to administer something.[276] It was a traditional principle that some state expenditures were met not by state payments but by getting a rich man to perform the relevant expenditure[277] in a particular year.[278] Liturgies fell roughly into two classes: those related to festivals[279] and those related to the fleet.[280] (A third, less common kind of liturgy was *proeisphora*,[281] advance payment of taxation, to which we shall come.) In the first kind the rich man had to undertake an expense for one of the great cult festivals of the city and participate in its organization;[282] the best-known is the *choregia*, where the rich man had to be *choregos* and arrange for the training and equipment of the chorus that performed in the dithyrambs, tragedies and comedies at the festivals of Dionysos or Apollo or Athena.[283] In the second kind the rich man had to command a ship of the fleet and to maintain it partly at his own expense:[284] the liturgy was called *trierarchia* and the citizen *trierarchos*, captain of a trireme; he was under the command of the *strategoi* of the fleet, and was as a rule the actual captain of the ship he was required to maintain;[285] but he could also hire another man to perform the liturgy, thus transforming his trierarchy into a purely economic burden.[286] The trierarchy fell only upon citizens,[287] whereas the festival

---

[272] Xen. *Oec.* 2.3–6; Dem. 20.19.

[273] Dem. 21.153.

[274] Arist. *Pol.* 1291a33–4; Lys. 27.10.

[275] Böeckh (1886) I 533–54, 628–83; Kahrstedt (1934) 217–28. Davies (1967, 1971, 1981).

[276] Lys. 19.58.　　[277] Dem. 20.25.　　[278] Ps. Xen. *Ath. Pol.* 3.4.

[279] Dem. 20.21.　　[280] *Hesperia* 4 (1935) 1–2 p. 15; Dem. 4.36.

[281] Dem. 42.25.　　[282] Dem. 4.35–6. Davies (1967).

[283] Ps. Xen. *Ath. Pol.* 3.4; Ant. 6.11 14; Dem. 21.13–15.

[284] Dem. 51.4–7; *IG* II² 1604–32.　　[285] Xen. *Hell.* 1.7.5; Dem. 50.20.

[286] Dem. 21.80; 51.7.　　[287] Dem. 20.20.

liturgies could be imposed on metics as well.[288] For the festival liturgies
the man who had to perform them was chosen by the archon[289] or the
members of his tribe;[290] for the trierarchy, by the generals.[291] Those
chosen did not have to undergo any preliminary examination, *dokimasia*,
before entering on the duty, but they were naturally required to undergo
euthynai,[292] the examination of accounts at the end, because they were
always in a position of handling public property in addition to their own
expenditures.

Liturgies were a considerable economic burden on the well-to-do.[293]
A minor festival liturgy might not cost more than a few hundred
drachmas,[294] but a trierarchy could cost several thousand drachmas[295] or
as much as a talent.[296] No one was obliged to undertake more than one
liturgy in a year;[297] those who performed festival liturgies had every other
year off,[298] and trierarchs could even ask to be exempted for the two
following years.[299] But there were so many liturgies that even those who
availed themselves of the exemptions must have had to act with very few
years in between. It was common, however, for rich and ambitious
citizens to volunteer and to undertake more liturgies than required.[300]
Every year there were some 100 festival liturgies to perform,[301] and the
number of trierarchs must have risen with the size of the Athenian fleet
from less than a hundred in the first decades of the fourth century[302] to
some 400 in the age of Demosthenes.[303] Furthermore, a trierarchy could
be shared by two citizens.[304]

Since Athens possessed no bureaucracy capable of assessing and checking the property of its citizens, the system had to depend partly on self-
assessment and partly on the assessment of one citizen by another.
Both are characteristic of the psychology of the Athenians and of their
democratic principles. To undertake a liturgy gave status and distinction;
it was something that every citizen liked to pride himself on[305] and that
a politically active citizen would boast about before his audience,
especially if he were the accused in a political trial.[306] The Athenians
enhanced the status that accrued from carrying out liturgies by awarding
golden crowns and honorary decrees to the man who carried out his

---

[288] Dem. 20.18; Lys. 12.20.
[289] Arist. *Ath. Pol.* 56.3.
[290] Dem. 21.13.   [291] Dem. 39.8; Arist. *Ath. Pol.* 61.1. Jordan (1975) 61–70.
[292] Aeschin. 3.19.   [293] Isoc. 8.128; Theophr. *Char.* 26.6.
[294] Lys. 21.1–2.   [295] Lys. 21.2; Lys. 32.24, 27.   [296] Dem. 21.155.
[297] Dem. 50.9.   [298] Dem. 20.8.   [299] Is. 7.38.
[300] Lys. 19.29, 21.1–5; Dem. 21.13. Davies (1981) 26.   [301] Davies (1967).
[302] *IG* II² 1604. Sinclair (1978) 50.   [303] *IG* II² 1627.266–78. Morrison (1987) 92.
[304] Dem. 21.154, 47.22. Jordan (1975) 70–3.
[305] Isoc. 16.35; Is. 7.37–42; Davies (1971) xvii–xviii.   [306] Lys. 25.12–13.

liturgy best;[307] but they also satisfied the natural desire that those liable, at least sometimes had, to make somebody else undertake the burden. This they did by means of a special procedure called *antidosis* ('exchange of properties'):[308] if someone liable to a liturgy thought he knew someone else even better-off who ought to perform it, he could challenge that person either to undertake the liturgy in his place or to exchange properties with him.[309] The other man could accept the liturgy[310] or the challenge to exchange properties,[311] and in the latter case he could demand that the matter come before a court,[312] which decided which of the two of them ought to undertake the liturgy.[313] We have not a single example of an exchange of property actually taking place, but there are plenty of known cases of *antidosis* suits heard by the courts.[314]

Eisphora

The property tax, *eisphora*,[315] was originally a sporadically levied war tax[316] imposed by decree of the Assembly,[317] but from 347/6 it became a regular annual tax of 10 talents a year[318] and the Assembly could always impose extra *eisphorai*.[319] The tax was paid by both citizens and metics,[320] but only by the well-off.[321] It does not appear to have hit the rich particularly hard in the fourth century: in the ten years of Demosthenes' minority, when his property was administered by his guardians, they had to pay 1800 drachmas on a fortune that was assessed at 15 talents and was regarded as amongst the largest in Athens.[322]

We do not know for certain whether the group of liturgy-performers was identical with the group of *eisphora*-payers. In the *Leptines* speech of 355/4 Demosthenes takes for granted that there are more citizens liable to *eisphora* than to trierarchies,[323] and it has been held that not less than 6000 citizens must have been liable for *eisphora*.[324] But only a couple of years after the *Leptines* Isokrates in his speech *On the Antidosis* asserts that the same small group of 1200 citizens is liable to bear both burdens: to pay the *eisphorai* and to perform liturgies.[325] The explanation seems

---

[307] *IG* II² 1629.190–204, Dem. 51.1.   [308] *IG* I² 254.5–6, Dem. 42.1. Gabrielsen (1987a).
[309] Lys. 24.9.   [310] Dem. 21.80; 28.17.
[311] Dem. 42.19; Lys. 4.1–2. Lipsius (1905–15) 590–9, Gabrielsen (1987a) 15–16, *pace* Dittenberger (1872).
[312] Dem. 28.17. Goligher (1907), *pace* Gabrielsen (1987a) 23–4, 34ff.
[313] Isoc. 15.5; Dem. 42.4.   [314] Dem. 42; Isoc. 15; Lys. 3.20; Hyp. fr. 163.
[315] Ste Croix (1953); Thomsen (1964); Brun (1983).
[316] Thuc. 3.19.1; Xen. *Oec.* 2.6; Is. 5.45.   [317] Dem. 3.4.
[318] *IG* II² 244.12–13; 505.14–17.   [319] Din. 1.69. Brun (1983) 54–5.
[320] *IG* II² 244.19–20; 141.35–6.
[321] Harp. s.v. *symmoria*; Lys. 22.13, 27.10. Ste Croix (1953) 31–5.
[322] Dem. 27.37. Jones (1957) 29.   [323] Dem. 20.28.
[324] Jones (1957) 28: Strauss (1986) 43.   [325] Isoc. 15.145.

to be that Demosthenes focuses on *eisphora*-payers as against trierarchs only, to the exclusion of other liturgists, whereas Isokrates is talking about *eisphora* plus all the liturgies (comprising both the trierarchy and the festival liturgies). Since the trierarchy fell on the wealthiest citizens, who were thereby often exempted from festival liturgies,[326] the number of trierarchs was smaller than the total number of citizens performing liturgies (and paying *eisphora*).

The problem hangs together, however, with another: in Demosthenes' time both *eisphora*-payers and citizens liable for a trierarchy were formed into groups called 'symmories', (*symmoriai*); but were they the same symmories in both cases[327] or two separate sets?[328] An examination of the history of the symmories indicates that there was only one symmory system, but that it functioned differently in relation to the two types of obligation. Symmories were first established in 378/7[329] in order to systematize the payment of *eisphora*.[330] The rich citizens were divded into 100 symmories ('sharing-together groups'),[331] with, typically, fifteen men per symmory;[332] but the total number of symmory-members (*symmoritai*) need not have been more than some 1000,[333] and the taxable capital of the whole was assessed at 5750 talents.[334] They were also divided into classes according to their relative wealth,[335] and the richest of all were about 300 men,[336] divided amongst all the symmories.[337] Those 300 were required to act as *proeispherontes*, advance-payers,[338] for their respective symmories: they had to pay the whole tax immediately it was called for and make their own arrangements to reimburse themselves from the other members of the symmories.[339] The symmories were probably created in direct relation to the *proeisphora*, so that the actual payer could know exactly upon whom to call for reimbursement. *Proeisphora*, as noted above, was a liturgy, and to that extent the symmory system was connected to the liturgy system from the beginning.[340]

By a law proposed in about 358[341] by one Periandros, the symmory system was extended to cover the trierarchy as well as the payment of *eisphora*.[342] The rich citizens were now divided into twenty symmories, with, typically, sixty men per symmory;[343] but the exact number of

---

[326] Dem. 20.19.
[327] Mossé (1979b); Ruschenbush (1978b, 1987); MacDowell (1986).
[328] Jones (1957) 28; Rhodes (1985b). [329] Philoch. fr. 41.
[330] Dem. 22.44; Polyb. 2.62.6–7. Gabrielsen (1987b) 47–51.
[331] Clid. fr. 8. [332] Hyp. fr. 173, cf. *eispherein* in fr. 179.
[333] Lys. fr. 146; Is. fr. 106, *pace* Davies (1981) 140ff.
[334] Polyb. 2.62.6–7. Brun (1983) 8–13; Wallace (1989) 488–90. [335] Dem. 27.7.
[336] Is. 6.60. [337] Dem. 2.29. [338] Dem. 42.25.
[339] Dem. 37.37; 50.9. [340] Ste Croix (1953) 59; Wallace (1989b) 483–5.
[341] Dem. 47.44. Rhodes (1981a) 680. [342] Dem. 47.21. [343] Dem. 14.17.

members may have varied, both from symmory to symmory and also according to whether a particular symmory was being used as a tax group or a liturgy group, since *eisphora* fell on property but liturgies on persons.[344] Thus, both the duty to pay *eisphora*[345] and the duty to contribute to a trierarchy[346] were now confined to some 1200 citizens.[347] The same group of about 1200 citizens were also responsible for performing the festival liturgies;[348] but in that case they continued to serve as individuals and there was no organization into symmories.[349] Orphans, 'heiresses', and corporations such as phratries or demes were exempt from liturgies (because liturgies were a 'personal' service),[350] though liable for *eisphora*.[351] But we know that they were members of the symmories used for the trierarchy,[352] which indicates that there was only one system of symmories, not two.[353] What is in any case beyond doubt is that the same 300 persons were at the head of the symmories, whether for *proeisphora* or for trierarchies.[354] It is also evident that the 300 let the other 900 or so bear more than their fair share when it came to the trierarchy, for instead of serving as trierarchs themselves they farmed the duty out[355] and obliged five or six or even up to sixteen members of their symmories to pay the lion's share of the expense.[356] The unfortunate results of that system became apparent in time of war, when a fleet could not be despatched in proper order or in time because the members of a symmory were at odds over the distribution of the costs.[357]

So in 340, in the last major war of Athens against Philip, Demosthenes got another law passed concerning the trierarchy, which required the richest 300 to take full responsibility and bear the major part of the burden themselves.[358] Demosthenes' law is often interpreted to have meant that the duty of the trierarchy was (once more) confined to the 300,[359] divided into twenty symmories of fifteen men each;[360] but naval inscriptions from the 320s give evidence of symmories of about sixty persons,[361] so it must be concluded that all 1200 were still liable to

[344] Dem. 14.16 (20 × 60 persons), 14.19 (100 × 60 talents).   [345] Isoc. 15.145.

[346] Dem. 21.155.   [347] Is. fr. 74; Dem. 14.16; Philoch. fr. 45.

[348] Isoc. 15.145.   [349] Dem. 39.7–8.   [350] Dem. 14.16.

[351] Dem. 27.37; *IG* II² 2492.24–7.   [352] Dem. 14.16–17.

[353] Ruschenbusch (1987) 76–9.

[354] Dem. 42.5 [cf. Arist. *Ath. Pol.* 61.1], 42.25; Aeschin. 3.222; Hyp. fr. 160.

[355] Dem. 21.155.   [356] Dem. 18.104; Hyp. fr. 160.   [357] Dem. 4.36.

[358] Dem. 18.102–8; Hyp. fr. 160; Aeschin. 3.222; Din. 1.42.

[359] Davies (1971) xxix; Ruschenbusch (1978b) 283.   [360] Jones (1957) 88.

[361] *IG* II² 1632. Gabrielsen (1989) 153–8.

some degree for the trierarchy, though the burden was distributed more fairly.[362]

So the 'upper class' in fourth-century Athens was a group of some 1000–1200 rich citizens with, at their core, a smaller group of the 300 very rich. Studies that have been made of individual fortunes suggest that to be one of the rich citizens who performed liturgies a man would have had to have property of at least 3 or 4 talents.[363] 1 talent equals what an ordinary Athenian could earn in the course of more than ten years,[364] so the property of any one of the roughly 1200 liturgists would represent a lifetime's ordinary earnings.

Two social classes, or three?

Our sources speak in terms of two social groupings, which cut across each other somewhat. On economic criteria the citizen body is divided in two, into the 'have-plentys' (*euporoi* or *plousioi*) and the 'have-nots' (*aporoi* or *penetes*).[365] Where the boundary comes depends on context. The *euporoi* are mainly the liturgy-performers and *eisphora*-payers, i.e. in the fourth century the 1200 or so members of the symmories;[366] the *aporoi* are not just the destitute but all who have enough to live on but no surplus.[367] But in political terms *hoi aporoi* are usually equated with 'the majority' (*hoi polloi*),[368] or 'the many' (*to plethos*),[369] or sometimes 'the ordinary people' (*ho demos*).[370] That socio-political use of *demos* is only found amongst the critics of democracy, mostly the philosophers, and virtually never in speeches delivered in the Assembly or the courts.[371] On the other hand, in the orators there is a tendency to identify the rich with the critics of democracy or even saddle them with oligarchical sympathies.[372] A third or middle class is seldom referred to,[373] and then mainly by Aristotle,[374] which is not surprising, given his tendency to see everything good as the due mean between extremes. The twofold division into rich and poor is mainly asserted by the orators, who for their part have a tendency to polarize, not seldom perversely.

A quite different picture of the social classes in Athens emerges if we go back to the latter part of the fifth century, where our sources are the

---

[362] Gabrielsen (1989) 158–9.   [363] Davies (1971) xxiii–xxiv.
[364] Zimmermann (1974) 100.
[365] Lys. 24.17; Dem. 22.53, 51.11; Arist. *Pol.* 1279b10–1280a5, 1291b7–8. Ober (1989) 28, 195.
[366] Ps. Xen. *Ath. Pol.* 1.13; Dem. 21.153.
[367] Markle (1985) 267–71; Ober (1989) 195–6.   [368] Aeschin. 2.334; Isoc. 4.105.
[369] Dem. 24.124; Din. 3.19; Isoc. 20.19–21.   [370] Arist. *Ath. Pol.* 28.1–3; 41.2.
[371] See p. 125.   [372] Dem. 24.76, 112; Theophr. *Char.* 26.6.
[373] Ste Croix (1981) 71–4; Ober (1989) 134–6.   [374] Arist. *Pol.* 1295b1–3.

historians rather than the orators, and focus on the military instead of the purely economic aspect of the social structure. For this time we find a tripartition of the citizen body into cavalry (*hippeis*), recruited exclusively from the top two Solonian classes; hoplites, recruited mainly from the *zeugitai*; and light-armed troops recruited from the *thetes* (who also served in the navy, in part as marines [*epibatai*] and in part as rowers).[375] Here the hoplites are a middle class,[376] and the core of the middle class is the farmers[377] who can afford not only the hoplite panoply[378] but also the slave that a hoplite always has as his batman on campaigns.[379] This division into three classes with the hoplites in the middle emerges from numerous sources – for example Thucydides' description of the Athenian losses in the plague of 430–426: 'For no fewer than 4400 hoplites perished from the ranks and 300 cavalrymen, and a countless number of the mob [*tou allou ochlou*]',[380] i.e. the *thetes* are just part of the 'mob'.[381] And, in sources where the tripartition is simplified into a bipartition, the gap comes between the *thetes* and the top three Solonian classes,[382] who are sometimes lumped together as what modern historians like to call the 'hoplite class'.[383] But the distinction between the upper and the middle class is often maintained, as in the speeches of Lysias, where the pride of the upper class, the corps of *hippeis*, is contrasted with the hoplites.[384]

From the end of the fifth century to the middle of the fourth, Athens was a society at war, relieved by occasional short periods of peace, and the military division of the citizen body into three classes with the hoplites as the middle class consequently remained the most important social grouping. But the longer periods of peace in the last decades of the democracy produced a different situation: the Solonian classes seem to have lost their importance even for military service, so that even *thetes* were trained as hoplites,[385] and the alternative division into rich and poor on purely economic criteria came to have the greater importance.

METICS AND SLAVES

Metics

Whatever the etymology of the word *metoikos*,[386] it was used to signify in principle a freeborn person who had left his own city and lived in

---

[375] See pp. 45–6. [376] Thuc. 8.92.10–11; Arist. *Ath. Pol.* 33.1–2; *Pol.* 1297b1ff.
[377] Ar. *Arch.* 595ff. Vidal-Naquet (1968) 166–7. [378] *IG* I³ 1.8–10; Thuc. 8.97.1.
[379] Thuc. 3.17; Ar. *Ach.* 1132ff. Welwei (1974) 58–65. [380] Thuc. 3.87.3.
[381] Thuc. 2.31.2, 8.1.2. [382] Ps. Xen. *Ath. Pol.* 1.2; Xen. *Hell.* 2.3.48.
[383] Gomme (1933) 5, 26; Jones (1957) 81–2; Strauss (1986) 43. See Hansen (1981b) 24–9.
[384] Lys. 14.7–14; 16.13. [385] See pp. 108–9.
[386] 'Immigrant': Whitehead (1977) 6ff; Lévy (1988) 47–53. 'Mitwohner': Busolt and Swoboda (1920–6) 292.

another city-state without having citizen rights in that state:[387] metics were thus the most important element amongst the general body of *xenoi*, foreigners.[388] But in Athens not only domiciled foreigners were metics, for every foreigner had to have himself registered as a metic if he stayed in Athens even for a very short period – of days rather than months or years.[389] It was not a privilege to be a metic but a duty; and when the Athenians wanted to do foreigners a special favour they released them from the status of metic.[390] We do not know how long a foreigner could stay in Athens before being required to become a metic, nor how strictly the time-limit was enforced. In the city-states of Chaleion and Oianthea in Lokris the period was a month,[391] and there is some reason to attribute the same rule to Athens: the special tax on metics, the *metoikion*, was a fixed sum of 12 drachmas annually,[392] and could readily be divided into twelve monthly instalments of 1 drachma each, which gives colour to the hypothesis that any foreigner who stayed longer than a month was obliged to pay the tax.[393]

The name of a metic always included the deme he resided in, which shows that the registration of metics, as of citizens, took place not centrally but at deme level:[394] 'Kephisodoros dwelling in the Piraeus' was the official Athenian description of a metic.[395] On the other hand, the gravestones of metics show that they themselves preferred to be named after their home state,[396] where they had citizenship,[397] irrespective of how long they had been in Athens: 'Herodas son of Androkles, from Herakleia' is a typical metic grave inscription.[398] And, although officially a metic had the *demotikon* like a citizen, he was not a member of the deme; and, whereas deme membership was inherited, a metic probably had to change his *demotikon* if he went to live in a different area.[399]

Every metic had to choose an Athenian citizen as his sponsor and, perhaps, guardian (*prostates*),[400] and if he failed to do so he could be accused in a *dike aprostasiou*,[401] a 'private prosecution for failing to have a sponsor',[402] condemnation in which resulted in confiscation of the

[387] Harp. s.v. *metoikion*.   [388] Lys. 12.35; Lycurg. 1.39. Whitehead (1977) 10–1.

[389] Aristophanes Byzantinus fr. 38. Gauthier (1972) 117–18, (1988) 28–9, *pace* Lévy (1988) 53–61.

[390] *IG* II² 141.30–6 = Tod 139 and Harding (1985) no. 40.

[391] Tod 34.6–8 = Fornara (1977) no. 87.   [392] Harp. s.v. *metoikion*.

[393] Gauthier (1972) 122.   [394] Whitehead (1977) 72–5.

[395] *IG* I³ 421.33 = *M&L* 79A and Fornara (1977) no. 147D.   [396] Whitehead (1977) 33.

[397] Lys. 31.9; *IG* II² 141.30–6 = Tod 139 and Harding (1985) no. 40.

[398] *IG* II² 8678.   [399] Whitehead (1977) 74; (1986) 81–5.

[400] Hyp. fr. 26; Dem. 59.37; Harp. s.v. *prostates*.

[401] Arist. *Ath. Pol.* 58.3. Thür (1989) 120.

[402] Harp. s.v. *aprostasiou*; *Lex. Seg.* 201.12; Poll. 8.35

metic's property and his being sold into slavery by public auction.[403] The reason why the action was a private and not a public prosecution[404] may have been to give a potential prosecutor a profit from bringing the action, i.e. the proceeds of the auction of the foreigner and his property.[405] The procedure was, presumably, the Athenian way of ensuring that foreigners had themselves registered as metics if they stayed in Attica beyond the time-limit;[406] so it is plausible to connect choice of guardian with registration in a deme and conjecture that a foreigner chose his guardian from the deme he wanted to live in and got the guardian to help him acquire registration in it.[407]

Apart from that, we know nothing at all about the guardianship of metics. Aristotle says in the *Politics* that in many states a metic has to bring in a guardian in order to bring a lawsuit,[408] but we have no evidence that Athens was one of them. Private suits brought by metics[409] or against metics[410] came before the polemarch,[411] but public prosecutions were handled by the usual magistrates, whether the metic was accuser or accused, and the surviving speeches show that metics appeared in all courts in person[412] or had a friend, not their *prostates*, to assist them.[413]

Apart from the right to appear in court, metics had few rights and many burdens. They had no political rights and no share in the distributions and other economic advantages available to citizens.[414] As we have already seen, they could not own land or housing in Attica except by the special privilege of *enktesis*,[415] nor, without special leave, could they hold concessions in the silver-mines.[416] Marriage between a metic and an Athenian was null and void, and a metic who lived with an Athenian woman was punished more severely than an Athenian who lived with a metic woman.[417] Similarly, intentional homicide was less severely punished if the victim was a metic,[418] and metics could be made to give evidence under torture.[419] They were obliged to perform military service[420] and pay taxes: every metic had to pay the *metoikion*, at 12 drachmas a year for men and 6 for women;[421] and if rich enough they were liable, like

[403] Phot. and *Suda* s.v. *poletai*.   [404] See pp. 192–3.
[405] *Pace* Thür (1989) 120.   [406] MacDowell (1978) 78.
[407] Gauthier (1972) 126–36; Whitehead (1977) 90–1.   [408] Arist. *Pol.* 1275a7–14.
[409] Arist. *Ath. Pol.* 58.3.   [410] Lys. 23.3.   [411] Arist. *Ath. Pol.* 58.2.
[412] Lys. 12; Isoc. 17; Din. fr. xlii; Dem. 21.175, 59.64–9.
[413] Lys. 5.1–2; Is. fr. 66.   [414] Xen. *Vect.* 2.1. Gauthier (1976) 56–7.
[415] Pecirka (1966); Henry (1983) 204–40. See p. 97.   [416] See pp. 97–8.
[417] Dem. 59.16.   [418] *Lex. Seg.* 194.12–3.
[419] Lys. 13.27, 54, 59–61. Thür (1977) 15–25.
[420] Thuc. 2.13.7; Xen. *Vect.* 2.2. Whitehead (1977) 82–6.   [421] Harp. s.v. *metoikion*.

citizens, to *eisphora*[422] and to liturgies as their turn came.[423] Only by another special privilege, called *isoteleia*, 'equality of contributions', could they be released from payment of the *metoikion* and do their military service and pay their property tax alongside the citizens.[424]

The Athenian metics fell into two groups: on the one hand freeborn foreigners, who settled in Athens as artisans or traders[425] or as political refugees,[426] and on the other hand manumitted slaves, who became metics with their former master as their guardian.[427] The only legal difference between the two groups was that freedmen had a set of duties towards their former master; they could be accused in a *dike apostasiou* or 'private action for withdrawal' if they failed to fulfil such duties,[428] and their guardian inherited from them if they died without issue.[429] Heirs of freedmen seem to have counted as freeborn metics.

Xenophon remarks that a great many metics are 'barbarians' from Lydia, Phrygia, Syria and other distant places:[430] he must be thinking of freedmen, because the Athenians recruited their slaves from just those areas.[431] The freeborn metics, as their gravestones show, were mostly Greeks, indeed mostly from Greece proper, and only to a lesser degree from the distant Greek overseas communities.[432]

In spite of the disadvantages of metic status, foreigners streamed into Athens from all parts, and the reason no doubt is that citizen and metic were on an equal footing as traders and artisans in the largest city of Greece. The only limitation on the economic position of metics, as far as we know, was that they had to pay a special fee, the *xenikon telos*, to set up a stall in the market:[433] apart from that they could compete on equal terms with citizens.

In Plato's *Laws* we meet the utopia where all citizens work on the land[434] and all metics are artisans and traders,[435] and where not only are the metics forbidden to till the land but the citizens are forbidden to engage in trades or crafts.[436] The model was Sparta; Athens was not a bit like that. Ownership of land was certainly reserved to citizens, but they were not in the least prevented from being artisans and the like: on the contrary, the sources show that a high proportion of the citizen body were obliged to undertake such employment for their subsistence, and

---

[422] Dem. 22.61; *IG* II² 244.20. Ste Croix (1953) 32 n. 5.   [423] Dem. 20.18–21.
[424] Harp. s.v. *isoteles*; *IG* II² 360. 19–21.   [425] Isoc. 8.21; Dem. 35.1–2, 40–3.
[426] *IG* II² 237.22–31.   [427] Harp. s.v. *metoikion*.
[428] Arist. *Ath. Pol.* 58.3; Harp. s.v. *apostasiou*.   [429] Is. 4.9.
[430] Xen. *Vect.* 2.3.   [431] Isager and Hansen (1975) 33.
[432] Isager and Hansen (1975) 69–70, 217–19, 223.   [433] Dem. 57.34.
[434] Pl. *Lg.* 737Cff, 842D.   [435] Pl. *Lg.* 849B–D, 919C–920C.
[436] Pl. *Lg.* 846D–847B, 915D–920C.

that metics, though a significant factor, did not predominate in the manufacturing and mercantile fields.[437] What is more, many metics were farmers,[438] either as tenants (which they were not debarred from being) or in virtue of the special privilege of *enktesis*. Yet, in spite of all that, the Athenians would have preferred things to be as Plato outlines them in his utopia. We meet at every turn the idea that to occupy oneself in trade and manufacture is demeaning, and that agriculture is the only respectable way for a citizen to earn his living. Artisans are often called *banausoi*, and that was a pejorative term;[439] there was a special provision in the laws granting a suit for defamation if a citizen had been described in public in the Agora as a 'tradesman'.[440]

Slaves

It is out of the question to give, within the scope of this book, a full account of all aspects of slavery in the Greek city-state.[441] Everything down to the vocabulary for slaves has been the object of special studies, since the Greeks had as many words for slaves as the Arabs for camels and the Eskimos for seals: a slave was often called *doulos* (etymology unknown), but other common terms included *oiketes* ('household slave'), *pais* ('boy'). *therapon* ('servant') and *andrapodon* ('manfoot', as opposed to animals with four feet).[442] What follows is no more than a sketch of the legal status and conditions of slaves at Athens, with a few special words about the 'public slaves'. What little can be said as to the numbers of Athenian slaves has been said earlier in this chapter.

A slave was a piece of property just like animals, tools, money, land, and so on:[443] in Book 1 of the *Politics* Aristotle neatly defines a slave as *empsychon organon*, an 'animate tool'.[444] A slave was in the ownership of his master (*despotes*),[445] who could dispose freely of his slave, as of all his other property: sell him,[446] mortgage him,[447] hire him out,[448] and leave him by will.[449] The slave was at his master's mercy, with only two limitations, the first being that the master could not put him to death:[450] murder of a slave was judged in the court of the *ephetai* at the Palladion,[451] though in the case of slaves the penalty for murder was

---

[437] Isager and Hansen (1975) 70–4.   [438] *IG* II² 10 B = Tod 100.

[439] Hdt. 2.165–7; Pl. *Resp.* 590C; Arist. *Pol.* 1291a1–4; Xen. *Oec.* 4.2–3. Whitehead (1977) 116–21.

[440] Dem. 57.30.   [441] Finley (1980); Garlan (1988); *Actes du Colloque 1970–3* (1972–6).

[442] Klees (1975) 14–36.   [443] Arist. *Oec.* 1344a23–5.

[444] Arist. *Pol.* 1253b28–32.   [445] Arist. *Pol.* 1255b29–33.

[446] Hyp. 5.15.   [447] Dem. 27.9.   [448] Dem. 53.21.

[449] Diog. Laert. 3.42.   [450] Ant. 5.48.   [451] Schol. Aeschin. 2.87.

usually only a fine.[452] And mostly it was murder of someone else's slave that came before the court;[453] for if a master did kill his own slave there was as a rule no one to bring a charge, and the master would usually escape any public penalty (though he might make an atonement offering).[454] A master's right to punish his slave in any other way was unlimited: runaways were branded if caught,[455] and the disobedient could be, and constantly were, flogged,[456] or put in chains,[457] or sent to the mill.[458] Assault and battery upon someone else's slave could naturally be proceeded against, either by his master with a *dike blabes*, a civil suit for damage,[459] or by any citizen with a *graphe hybreos*, a public prosecution for injury.[460] The second limitation was that a slave could seek asylum in the shrine of the Erinyes or in the Temple of Theseus,[461] and could from there demand to be sold to another master:[462] as far as we know, his existing master could not force him out of the sanctuary and could certainly himself be forced to yield to the slave's demand and sell him.

A slave could own no property and could not marry without his (or her) master's consent;[463] any children slaves might have belonged to the master.[464] Slaves had, of course, no political rights, but they had the right to enter the temples, often took part in the great religious festivals,[465] and could even be initiated into the Mysteries.[466] They were excluded from the courts: a slave could not even appear as a witness, and testimony of a slave could only be submitted to the court if elicited by torture.[467] Lawbreakers could, naturally, be prosecuted and condemned, and, where a freeborn person was condemned to a fine, a slave would be flogged, sometimes on the basis of one stroke of the whip for every drachma the freeborn would have paid in fine.[468]

In principle, the conditions described above applied to all slaves whatsoever, but in practice things were much more differentiated. Some slaves (called *hoi choris oikountes*) lived not in their master's house under constant surveillance but in their own dwelling,[469] where they worked for their master on condition of making over to him a fixed part (*apophora*) of their income:[470] such a slave had, *de facto*, property of his own,[471] with which he could, for example, buy his freedom.[472] In one of the speeches attributed to Demosthenes we hear of a slave who is captain of a ship

---

[452] Lycurg. 1.65. [453] Isoc. 18.52. [454] Ant. 6.4.
[455] Schol. Aeschin. 2.79. [456] Ar. *Eq.* 64. [457] Xen. *Oec.* 3.4.
[458] Lys. 1.18. [459] Lys. in *Lex. Patm.* 150 s.v. *hekatompedon*.
[460] Dem. 21.46. [461] Schol. Ar. *Eq.* 1312. [462] Ar. fr. 567; Eupolis fr. 225.
[463] Men. *Heros* 42–4. [464] Xen. *Oec.* 9.5. [465] See p. 63.
[466] Dem. 59.21. [467] Dem. 49.55; Is. 8.12. See p. 201.
[468] *IG* II² 1362.9–15. [469] Aeschin. 1.97; Dem. 4.36. Perotti (1974).
[470] Andoc. 1.38; Hyp. 2.2. [471] Aeschin. 1.54. [472] Dem. 59.31.

and makes contracts with freeborn persons and grants a loan of 1000 drachmas to one of the merchants on board.[473] So in both economic and social terms there was a gulf between the thousands of slaves who worked in the mines of Laureion under the worst imaginable conditions, sometimes in chains,[474] and the minority of privileged slaves, who might be bankers[475] or foremen of workshops with other slaves under them,[476] or trusted administrators of their master's possessions.[477] The majority of slaves (and we should remind ourselves how many of them were women) were probably domestic slaves (*oiketai*),[478] who were, in a way, members of the household and worked for their masters in their houses[479] or workshops[480] or in the fields.[481]

Slaves were not used for armed service, except in direst emergencies,[482] in which case they often received their freedom as a reward;[483] but they always served in the army as batmen[484] and in the navy as oarsmen.[485] The Athenians, like the Greeks generally, shrank from putting weapons into the hands of slaves, but oarsmen bore no arms, and numerous sources testify that a significant proportion of rowers in the fleet were slaves.[486]

What was the provenance of the slave population of Athens? It was probably not profitable to breed slaves, and the vast majority were imported.[487] We know that there was a slave-market in the Agora[488] and that the duty on imported slaves was a substantial item of revenue in the fifth century.[489] Many must have been prisoners of war. After a battle between two Greek city-states it was normal for the prisoners to be ransomed by their family or friends. Early in the fifth century BC the ransom money seems usually to have been 200 drachmas, so that it was more profitable to let a prisoner be ransomed than to sell him.[490] When a city was sacked, however, it was not uncommon for all the inhabitants to be sold into slavery;[491] or the adult males might be put to death and the women and children sold.[492] When Greeks made war on barbarians prisoners were seldom ransomed, and when barbarians went to war among themselves Greek slave-dealers were often able to buy slaves from

[473] Dem. 34.5–10.   [474] Lauffer (1979) 1–117.
[475] Dem. 36.13–14. Bogaert (1968) 62ff.   [476] Aeschin. 1.97.
[477] Xen. *Oec.* 12.2–3.   [478] Finley (1959) 150.   [479] Arist. *Pol.* 1263a19–21.
[480] Dem. 27.9ff; Aeschin. 1.97.
[481] Philoch. fr. 97; Dem. 53.21. Jameson (1977), *contra* Wood (1983).
[482] Sargent (1927) 264–79; Amit (1965) 30ff.   [483] Paus. 7.15.7; Ar. *Ran.* 693–4.
[484] Thuc. 3.17. Welwei (1974) 61.   [485] *IG* II² 1951.
[486] Welwei (1974) 65–114.   [487] *M&L* 79 p. 247. Garlan (1988) 45–55.
[488] Harp. s.v. *kykloi*.   [489] Xen. *Vect.* 4.25.   [490] Hdt. 5.77.3; 6.79.1.
[491] Diod. 17.14.   [492] Thuc. 5.116.2.

the victors. The only Greek state to export slaves in any quantity was Thessaly,[493] where there was perpetual warfare between rival groups of aristocrats and so a constant supply of prisoners of war. And Greek prisoners were regularly brought to the market by pirates who had boarded Greek merchant ships[494] or made predatory landings on Greek coasts.[495] Most slaves, though, were barbarian, and the sources show that Athens usually imported hers from the north and the east: Thrace, the Black Sea, and the interior of Asia Minor and Syria; of western imports we hear only of slaves from Illyria and Sicily.[496]

Public slaves

While most slaves were owned by private individuals, the state itself owned a sizable number of slaves, not fewer than a thousand and maybe distinctly more.[497] These public slaves were called *demosioi*,[498] and fall into two groups: those who assisted the magistrates in the performance of their duties (*hyperetai*)[499] and those who worked as labourers (*ergatai*).[500] Another group was the force of Scythian slaves.

Magistrates' assistants   Several boards of magistrates had slaves at their disposal. The Eleven had a slave who was the public executioner (*demios*)[501] and helped with the torture of slaves whose testimony was required (*basanistai*).[502] The Council had at least eight slave assistants.[503] Aristotle says that at the selection of the jurors by lot the archons were assisted by public slaves.[504] And the coinage law of 375/4 contains a clause that two public slaves are to test the silver coinage used for payments in the markets of Athens and the Piraeus.[505]

Labourers   The state had several groups of slave workmen. We know that the streets of Athens were built and maintained by public slaves under the Board of Roads (*hodopoioi*)[506] and that the mint workers were also slaves.[507] In the Eleusinian accounts, seventeen public slaves with a foreman who is likewise a slave are engaged on jobs in the Eleusinion in 329/8.[508] How many workmen the state had altogether is not known, but

---

[493] Schol. Ar. *Plut.* 521.   [494] Andoc. 1.138; Dem. 53.6.
[495] Men. *Sicyonius.* 3ff, 354ff.
[496] Isager and Hansen (1975) 33; Jordan (1975) 264–7; Lévy (1974) 35.
[497] Jacob (1928).   [498] Harp. s.v.   [499] Arist. *Ath. Pol.* 50.2, 65.4.
[500] Arist. *Ath. Pol.* 54.1.   [501] Pl. *Resp.* 439E; *Theages* 129A.
[502] Aeschin. 2.126.   [503] *SEG* 24 163.   [504] Arist. *Ath. Pol.* 65.4.
[505] *SEG* 26 72.5, 37 = Harding (1985) no. 45.   [506] Arist. *Ath. Pol.* 54.1.
[507] Andoc. fr. 5 (Blass).   [508] *IG* II² 1672.4–5, etc. Glotz (1926) 211.

the scattered references give the impression that it must have been at least several hundred.

Scythians   In the period *c*.450–350 Athens had a force of 300 Scythian slaves, usually known as the 'archers' (*toxotai*) from the weapons they carried or the 'Scythians' from their nationality.[509] They were stationed on the hill of the Areopagos,[510] and their duties included keeping order in the Assembly[511] and the courts;[512] they were at the disposition of several boards of magistrates. It does not, however, seem that they were any kind of police force in the general modern sense.

From the Eleusinian accounts we learn that *demosioi* received an allowance and their clothing from the state,[513] and other sources show that some could live a relatively independent life, with their own dwelling and property and even the right to bring suits before the courts.[514]

---

[509] Andoc. 3.5 = Aeschin. 2.173.
[510] Schol. Ar. *Ach*. 54.
[511] Ar. *Ach*. 54; Pl. *Prt*. 319C.
[512] Poll. 8.131.
[513] *IG* II² 1572.4–5.
[514] Aeschin. 1.54, 58, 62.

6

The Assembly of the People

In the Assembly (*ekklesia*) the people of Athens (*demos*) met:[1] the word *demos* is often synonymous with *ekklesia*,[2] and decrees of the Assembly began with the formula *edoxe toi demoi*, 'It was decided by the people', or an equivalent.[3] When an Athenian democrat said '*demos*' he meant the whole body of citizens,[4] irrespective of the fact that only a minority were able to turn up to meetings;[5] critics of the democracy, on the other hand, especially philosophers, tended to regard the *demos* as the 'ordinary people' in contrast to the propertied class,[6] and in their eyes the Assembly was a political organ in which the city poor, the artisans, traders, day labourers and idlers could by their majority outvote the minority of countrymen and major property-owners.[7] This opposition between the supporters of democracy and its critics points to a problem that must be answered: how far did geographical, social or economic conditions influence the composition of the Assembly?[8]

The economic, social and geographical structure

Aristotle remarks that a good part of the Athenian *demos* is involved in the navy,[9] and that the ordinary people in the Piraeus are more democratic than the people in Athens.[10] His analysis corresponds closely to that of

---

[1] Dem. 18.169. [2] Dem. 24.80. Hansen (1983a) 142–3 with nn. 13–18.
[3] *IG* II² 28 = Tod 114. Rhodes (1972) 64–5.
[4] Aeschin. 3.224. Hansen (1987a) 138 n. 40. [5] See pp. 131–2.
[6] Arist. *Pol.* 1291b17–29. Hansen (1983a) 151 n. 30.
[7] Pl. *Resp.* 565A; Arist. *Pol.* 1319a25–32. [8] Kluwe (1976, 1977).
[9] Arist. *Pol.* 1291b24. [10] Arist. *Pol.* 1303b10.

the Old Oligarch a hundred years earlier, whose main thesis is that power is wielded by the *demos*, i.e. the poor, i.e. the rowers.[11] And the same point of view is found in the comedies of Aristophanes: 'a fleet is to be commissioned: the poor vote for and the rich countrymen vote against'.[12] Characteristic of these sources is the conflation of the society's social structure with the state's military structure; and in the *Politics* Aristotle notes the connection between social groups, constitutional forms, and types of weaponry: the upper class serve in the cavalry and support oligarchy, the middle class are hoplites and prefer a more moderate constitution with elements of democracy and oligarchy, while the propertyless are light-armed peltasts or row in the fleet, and agitate for democracy.[13]

Aristotle's generalization is borne out by consideration of two milestones in the history of the Athenian constitution in the fifth century. Radical democracy was introduced by Ephialtes' reforms in 462, which were passed by the Assembly when 4000 hoplites of the middle class were away fighting in Messenia.[14] Fifty-one years later the radical democracy was replaced by the oligarchic rule of the Four Hundred, and that constitutional change was passed by an Assembly in which the *thetes* were probably under-represented, because the meeting was held outside the walls[15] and because the entire Athenian navy was stationed off Samos.[16] These two episodes are a strong indication that Aristotle's analysis is not mere word-spinning: in the fifth century, at all events, there must have been a good deal of truth in the view that Athens was a radical democracy in which power was exercised by an Assembly in which the majority were *thetes*.

But it would be mistaken to imagine that the Assembly was limited anything like entirely to the workers and traders who lived in Athens and the Piraeus. Only two passages in the sources shed light on the economic status of those who attended: one is Plato's statement that speeches in the Assembly are made by blacksmiths, shoemakers, merchants, shippers, rich, poor, the grand and the humble;[17] the other is Xenophon's that the Assembly is manned by fullers, shoemakers, carpenters, smiths, countrymen, merchants and market traders.[18] Countrymen are here mentioned alongside the artisans and traders, and it would be an oversimplification to draw a sharp line between the country and the city people:[19] Aristophanes has a farmer who brings his wine to market

---

[11] Ps. Xen. *Ath. Pol.* 1.2.   [12] Ar. *Eccl.* 197–8. Strauss (1986) 61–3.
[13] Arist. *Pol.* 1321a5–15.
[14] See p. 37. Martin (1974) 39; Rhodes (1981a) 315.   [15] See p. 40.
[16] Thuc. 8.72–7.   [17] Pl. *Prt.* 319C–D.
[18] Xen. *Mem.* 3.7.6.
[19] See p. 61.

to sell it and buy flour, but he lives in Athens and has just had a conversation with his neighbour after an Assembly meeting.[20] Conversely, Theophrastos gives a satirical description of the countryman telling his day labourers in the field all about what he has heard in the city at the Assembly.[21] It need not be doubted that the meetings of the Assembly were dominated by the people from the city and its suburbs[22] and that the attendance of the country people did not match their proportion of the citizen population,[23] but the scanty sources present a less unbalanced picture than might at first be supposed.

The sources as to the social status of those attending the Assembly in the fourth century are also scanty, and the few that exist have been said to show that upper- and middle-class representation was much stronger in the Assembly than in the courts.[24] The only solid reason for such a belief comes down to two passages in speeches of Lysias, one spoken in the Assembly and one before a court, both in 389 and both about the same matter. In the speech to the Assembly there is a passage in which the speaker assumes that those present are taxpayers, and so belong to the upper class;[25] in the speech to the court the speaker in one place distinguishes between the taxpayers and the jurors he is talking to.[26] But in Demosthenes' speech *On the Symmories* he makes a distinction between the taxpayers and the members of the Assembly,[27] and in the *First Olynthiac* there is one passage where all the audience are lumped together as taxpayers[28] but another where apparently it is only the well-to-do amongst the audience who are liable.[29] Lysias' speech to the people may prove no more than that it was sometimes advantageous to an orator to attribute to his whole audience a status few of them actually possessed;[30] and more impressive are those passages in Isokrates[31] and Demosthenes[32] where we hear of the poor flocking to the entrances of the Assembly and the courts in their anxiety to secure their daily payment. There is, therefore, no good ground to postulate any marked difference between the Assembly and the courts in this regard: indeed, the crush to secure the daily payment indicates that the poorer group of citizens were the majority in both sorts of meeting, as they undoubtedly were in the population as a whole.

---

[20] Ar. *Eccl.* 817–22, cf. 372ff.   [21] Theophr. *Char.* 4.3.
[22] Ar. *Eccl.* 300.   [23] Kluwe (1976) 298; Forrest (1966) 30–1.
[24] Sinclair (1988a) 124–5, (1988b); Jones (1957) 36.   [25] Lys. 28.3. Sinclair (1988b) 61.
[26] Lys. 29.9.   [27] Dem. 14.25–6.   [28] Dem. 1.6.
[29] Dem. 1.28.   [30] Ober (1989) 224.   [31] Isoc. 8.130, 15.152.
[32] Dem. 24.123.

The Pnyx

Meetings of the Assembly were normally held on the Pnyx,[33] a low hill about 400 m south-west of the Agora; but the Pnyx was probably not used for that purpose before the reforms of Ephialtes:[34] before then, meetings were held in the Agora,[35] or in the Lykeion.[36] The Pnyx was excavated in the 1930s,[37] and the excavations uncovered three phases in its building history, Pnyx I (*c*.460–400), Pnyx II (*c*.400–AD 120) and Pnyx III (from AD 120 onwards).

In the fifth century[38] the people sat in a semicircle directly on the rocky surface,[39] where the worst unevennesses had been smoothed out, and on the north side there was a low wall which must have been the place of the speakers' platform (the *bema*): the audience therefore faced north. The area was about 2400 sq. m. The elevation sloped from south to north, and the auditorium was bounded on east, south and west only by the line where the smoothing of the rock stopped: there was nothing to prevent citizens at a heavily attended meeting from sitting or standing further to the south on the rough parts.[40]

The Pnyx was rebuilt about 400 BC.[41] The slope was eliminated by bringing thousands of tons of earth up the hillside and building a semi-circular retaining-wall to the north-east, and as a result Pnyx II had the opposite orientation from Pnyx I. The auditorium now sloped just a little from north-east to south-west.[42] On the south side, it seems, a good slice of the hill was cut away, and the speakers' platform thus stood in front of an escarpment.[43] The Assembly-place was now closed on all sides and had an area of some 2600–3200 sq. m. The citizens ascended to the site by two stairways built against the retaining wall at the north, and now sat, probably on wooden benches,[44] with their backs to the Agora, facing the sun. The Athenians used this Assembly-place all through the fourth century, until, about 300, the meetings were moved to the Theatre of Dionysos,[45] which had been rebuilt under Lykourgos and given marble seating. Only in Hadrian's time was the old Assembly-place on the Pnyx rebuilt once more: the remains now visible are those of the Hadrianic Pnyx.[46]

[33] Ar. *Eq.* 749–50; Aeschin. 3.34. Hansen (1983a) 4 n. 22.
[34] Thompson (1982) 136–7.   [35] Plut. *Sol.* 8.2, 30.1. Hansen (1983a) 4.
[36] *IG* I³ 105.34.   [37] Kourouniotes and Thompson (1932).
[38] Thompson (1982) 134–8.   [39] Ar. *Eq.* 783.
[40] Thompson (1982) 135; Hansen (1989a) 145.
[41] Plut. *Them.* 19.6. Moysey (1981) 35.
[42] Thompson (1982) 138–40.
[43] Hyp. 1.9. McDonald (1943) 71–6, *pace* Thompson (1982) 138–9.
[44] Ar. *Eccl.* 21, 86–7. McDonald (1943) 75f.
[45] *IG* II² 389, (*SEG* 21 354). McDonald (1943) 57–8.
[46] Kourouniotes and Thompson (1932) 181–90; Hansen (1989a) 141, *pace* Thompson and Scranton (1943) 298–9.

The Pnyx was almost a symbol for the Assembly, and even for the democracy itself: in Aristophanes' *Knights* the personification of the Athenian people is called 'Mr Demos of Pnyx',[47] and instead of saying 'go to the Assembly meeting' the Athenians usually said 'go up to the Assembly meeting', i.e. up to the Pnyx.[48] It is in itself remarkable that Athens had an independent Assembly-place, an *ekklesiasterion* as the Greeks called it, for in very few other cities have remains of such structures been found.[49] In some places the Agora was used for assemblies,[50] or more commonly the theatre,[51] which was built for a quite different purpose and where those attending can only have filled a fraction of the space. The importance to the Athenians of their Assembly is underlined by the special architectonic setting they gave it.

Admittance to the Assembly

The right to take part in meetings of the Assembly was reserved to adult male citizens, and it was necessary to have been inscribed in the Assembly register, *pinax ekklesiastikos*,[52] of one of the 139 demes, which, at least after 338, was only allowed at the age of twenty, when the young citizens had completed their ephebic service.[53] Excluded from the Assembly were not only Athenian women and metics and slaves[54] but also citizens who had forfeited their rights (*atimoi*).[55] Entry to the Assembly-place was originally controlled by six *lexiarchoi*,[56] but in Demosthenes' time the controllers were a committee of the Council called *syllogeis tou demou*: they were a board of thirty, three from each of the ten tribes.[57] If any unauthorized person was caught trying to participate in an Assembly meeting he was arrested and brought before the People's Court, which could, in particularly heinous cases, condemn him to death.[58] Foreigners could only be present as spectators,[59] and in Pnyx II they would presumably have had to stand or sit on the side of the hill behind the speakers' platform.[60] Almost all Assembly meetings were held on the Pnyx, apart from a session held in the precinct of Dionysos after the Greater Dionysia,[61] and sessions on naval matters, which could be held in the Piraeus.[62]

[47] Ar. *Eq.* 42.   [48] Dem. *Prooem.* 6.1.

[49] McDonald (1943) 80–4 (Argos), 91–6 (Delos); Miro (1967) 165–6 (Akragas); Mertens (1985) 93–124 (Metapontion); Hoepfner and Schwandner (1986) 102–3 (Kassope, erroneously classified as a *bouleuterion*). Other examples are extremely doubtful.

[50] *M&L* 32.3–4 = Fornara (1977) no. 70; Arist. *Pol.* 1331a30–5.

[51] Kolb (1981) 88–99.   [52] Dem. 44.35.

[53] Arist. *Ath. Pol.* 42.5. See p. 89.   [54] Dem. 9.3.

[55] Dem. 24.123.   [56] Poll. 8.104. Hansen (1980c) 162 n. 29.

[57] *IG* II² 1749.75–6 = *Agora* XV 38.78–81.   [58] Dem. 25.42, 92.

[59] Aeschin. 3.224.   [60] Hansen (1989a) 133.

[61] Dem. 21.8–9; *IG* II² 223 B 5–6.   [62] Dem. 19.60.

Numbers attending

Decrees of the Assembly were treated in principle as decisions of the entire Athenian people, but in practice not more than a fraction of the citizen population were ever present. The only direct testimony is a statement by some oligarchs in Thucydides that during the Peloponnesian War there were seldom more than 5000 present;[63] but that figure is tendentiously low and must be used with caution.[64] For the fourth century, though we have no direct evidence, the state of the sources is actually better: many specific decisions of the Assembly were required by law to be ratified with a quorum of 6000, voting by ballot and not by show of hands,[65] and the reason for the special voting-rule was doubtless so that the officials could count the votes and ascertain whether the quorum had been reached.[66] The most important quorum requirement we know is that which stipulated that grants of citizenship must be proposed at one Assembly meeting and ratified at the following one, the second time with a quorum of 6000:[67] it is attested first in 369/8[68] and may have been introduced shortly before that. Between 368 and the end of the democracy in 322 we hear of fifty grants of citizenship to sixty-four foreigners,[69] and in chapter 5 it was conjectured that some hundreds of foreigners received citizenship during that period. The ratifications were made individually and took place before the opening of a meeting, by the handing of *psephoi* to people as they arrived;[70] as nobody could have handled several sets of *psephoi* at a time, it would have been impracticable to deal with more than one – or at most two or three – ratifications at a single meeting,[71] so, to get through them all, there must have been numerous meetings every year at which grants of citizenship came up for ratification, and the surviving decrees show that the ratifications were not saved up for especially important meetings.[72] The conclusion must be that 6000 people were normally present at an Assembly meeting; and that is in line with the purpose of quorum requirements as we know them, which is to ensure that a normal and sufficient number of persons are present, not an especially high number.[73]

As to the maximum likely number of participants, what we know of the Assembly-place should tell us something. In the fifth century, as we have seen, the Pnyx had an area of about 2400 sq. m, in the fourth an

[63] Thuc. 8.72.   [64] Hansen (1983a) 9.
[65] Dem. 24.45. Hansen (1987a) 87–8.   [66] Hansen (1983a) 111.
[67] Dem. 59.89–90.   [68] *IG* II² 103 = Tod 133.
[69] Osborne (1981) D 10–28; (1983) T 39–82.   [70] Dem. 59.90.
[71] Hansen (1983a) 21–2.   [72] Hansen (1987a) 143 n. 124.
[73] Hansen (1983a) 13; Gauthier (1984) 98–9.

area of about 2600–3200. If participants at a big meeting sit on narrow benches or on cushions on the ground, the minimum space per participant, if they are not to be impossibly uncomfortable, is 0.4 sq. m;[74] and on the reasonable assumption that an Athenian took up more or less the same space as people do nowadays we can calculate that the smoothed-off space of Pnyx I could contain 6000 participants and the rather larger auditorium of Pnyx II between 6500 and 8000. It can hardly be coincidental that Pnyx I could just contain the prescribed quorum: ratification in an Assembly of 6000 must have been known already in the fifth century, and probably Pnyx I was actually so constructed that when the smoothed-off area on the hill was full to the last man they could be sure there was a quorum; if more came they could perfectly well stand or sit outside the auditorium. That was an ingenious practical device for checking a quorum, and in the salad days of democracy in the fifth century the Athenians were not as keen as they later became to count and check things at every opportunity.[75]

Pnyx II may have been as large as 3200 sq. m, though the view of the excavators was that it could hardly have been more than 2600, i.e. only 200 larger than its predecessor.[76] The enlargement does not necessarily mean that more people could get onto the Pnyx in its second period, because, whereas in the fifth century the citizens sat directly on the rock, in the fourth they probably sat on benches; so the auditorium perhaps still only accommodated 6000, only a bit more comfortably. But the new auditorium was closed on all sides and could not take more people than there was seating for on the benches. Now, just at that time, the Athenians introduced pay for attendance at the Assembly.[77] Aristotle says that this was done because in the years after the Peloponnesian War it was difficult to get the proper quorum, i.e. 6000, for ratifications.[78] Pay had the desired effect, for a few years later, in Aristophanes' *Ekklesiazousai*, we learn that now the rope with the red paint had to be used to prevent people from crowding in when the auditorium was already full,[79] whereas in the fifth century it had been used to drive people into the auditorium to begin with.[80] So after the introduction of pay there was normally a full house, and at least 6000 were present. The first 6000 to arrive were probably the ones who were paid, while those who came later got nothing, and some were perhaps refused entry. The building of a closed auditorium thus fits in with the introduction of pay, for there had to be a way, at the end of a meeting, of knowing who was entitled to his money.

[74] Hansen (1983a) 17, 213.   [75] Hansen (1983a) 26.
[76] Thompson (1982) 138–9.   [77] See p. 150.
[78] Arist. *Ath. Pol.* 41.3.   [79] Ar. *Eccl.* 378–9. Hansen (1983a) 27–8.
[80] Ar. *Ach.* 17–22 with schol.

As we said to begin with, a decree of the Assembly counted as having been taken by the whole people; but now the gulf between principle and actuality was even wider. Not only was the auditorium now – as it always had been – too small to contain the whole people; it was even too small to contain all those who turned up. Thus, in the fourth century the Athenians restricted entry to the Assembly, exactly as they had done already in the fifth century with the courts: if the total of adult male citizens was 30,000, the Assembly-place could only hold about a fifth of them, but that was, all the same, relatively many compared with the fifth century, when perhaps only a tenth turned up; and it is in any case a fact unique in history that the Athenians were able, forty times a year, to get a fifth of all those with civic rights to participate in the Assembly.

Aristotle's account

The most important source describing the meetings of the Assembly is a passage in the *Constitution of Athens*:

> The *prytaneis* summon both the Council and the people, the Council daily except for holidays, the Assembly four times a prytany. They prescribe how many items are to be put on the agenda of the Council, and what they are to be, and where the meeting is to be held. They also prescribe the meetings of the Assembly, one a *kyria* [*ekklesia*], in which a vote is to be taken whether the magistrates are doing their job properly [*epicheirotonia ton archon*], and the corn supply and the defence of the land are to be discussed, and anyone who wishes is to make a denunciation [*eisangelia*], and the lists of confiscated property are to be read out and the pleas concerning inheritances and 'heiresses' [*epikleroi*], so that no one shall be unaware that something is unclaimed. And in the sixth prytany, in addition to the above, they see that there is a vote about an ostracism, whether one is to be held or not, and also complaints [*probolai*] against sycophants, both Athenian and metic, up to three in each group, and if anyone has made a promise to the people and not fulfilled it. The second meeting is devoted to petitions, at which any person can submit a petition about anything he likes, public or private, and speak about it to the people. The remaining two are for other matters, at which the laws require that three items be devoted to religious affairs [*hiera*], three to heralds and deputations [*kerykes kai presbeiai*], and three to profane affairs [*hosia*]. Sometimes they deal with the business without a *procheirotonia* [an initial show of hands].[81]

---

[81] Arist. *Ath. Pol.* 43.3–6.

Many of the rules about the conduct of meetings of the Assembly can be described by reference to that central passage.

Summons to meetings

The Assembly was always summoned by the *prytaneis*.[82] They normally determined the agenda on their own initiative,[83] and it was published several days in advance, probably four,[84] and probably at the Monument to the Eponymous Heroes;[85] but the Council[86] or the Assembly itself[87] might decide that a meeting was to be held on a given day with a given time on the agenda. Such a decree took the form of an order to the *prytaneis*,[88] so they always had the responsibility for summoning the Assembly, if not always the initiative. We know that the Assembly was sometimes called at the behest of the generals; that presumably meant that the generals approached the Council and got it to pass a decree ordering the *prytaneis* to call the meeting,[89] for nothing suggests that the generals had authority to do so on their own account.

Number of meetings

Aristotle distinguishes two types of meetings: *ekklesia kyria*,[90] held once each prytany, i.e. ten times a year; and plain *ekklesia*,[91] three per prytany, i.e. thirty a year.[92] The number underwent several changes, but the two types are already found in decrees of the fifth century.[93] *Ekklesia kyria* means 'chief meeting', and it can be inferred from the term that at one time the Athenians had only ten fixed Assembly meetings a year, i.e. an *ekklesia kyria* in each prytany, and in addition called extra meetings *ad libitum*. That was probably the system prevailing still in the Peloponnesian War, for we read in Thucydides that in the summer of 431, during the Spartan invasion of Attica, i.e. during some forty days, Perikles avoided the calling of an Assembly – which would have been unconstitutional in Aristotle's time but seems to have been quite legitimate in that of Perikles.[94]

It is not known how many meetings were held over and above the obligatory *ekklesiai kyriai*; very likely it could not be laid down exactly,

---

[82] Arist. *Ath. Pol.* 43.3.   [83] Arist. *Ath. Pol.* 45.4.
[84] Phot. s.v. *propempta*. Hansen (1987a) 145 n. 160.
[85] Wycherley (1957) 85–90.   [86] Xen. *Hell.* 6.5.33.
[87] *IG* II² 554. Hansen (1983a) 74–6.   [88] Aeschin. 2.61.
[89] Thuc. 4.118.14; *SEG* 21 440.   [90] Cf. *IG* II² 336a.
[91] Cf. *IG* II² 330.   [92] Arist. *Ath. Pol.* 43.3.
[93] *IG* I³ 41.37; 61.54 = *M&L* 65 and Fornara (1977) no. 128.
[94] Thuc. 2.22.1. Christensen and Hansen (1983).

because in addition to political decisions the Assembly often had to pass sentence in political trials.[95] At such a meeting the hearing was the sole item on the agenda,[96] and our sources show that right down to the 360s the Assembly might have to meet several times a year for that purpose.[97] But about 355 all political trials were transferred to the People's Court;[98] and in a law of that period it is implied that there had to be three meetings in the first prytany of the year,[99] in which case (on the assumption that there was the same number of meetings in each prytany, as was true later), there were thirty meetings a year.[100] However, that rule evidently did not last long, since in Aristotle's account from the 330s the number is forty a year. From the detailed descriptions given by Demosthenes and Aischines of the peace negotiations between Athens and Philip of Macedon in spring 346 it emerges that in the eighth prytany of that year at least four Assembly meetings were called,[101] including one double one, i.e. a summons to two meetings on successive days but with a single agenda:[102] Demosthenes says that at the end of that prytany the Assembly had 'used up its meetings',[103] so it seems that by then there was a fixed maximum of meetings per prytany, presumably the four described by Aristotle. Perhaps three meetings per prytany had proved inadequate for the business.

Ekklesiai synkletoi

There turns up in the sources a third name for an Assembly meeting besides *ekklesia kyria* and plain *ekklesia*, namely *ekklesia synkletos*, which simply means an '*ekklesia* that has been summoned' – but of course all *ekklesiai* were 'summoned'. In inscriptions the term does not appear until the second century BC,[104] but it is already there in Aischines' description of the peace negotiations with Philip in the seventh and eighth prytanies of 346, where Aischines asserts that in that period more *ekklesiai synkletoi* were held than '*ekklesiai* prescribed by law';[105] and for the tenth prytany of the same year, when peace with Philip had been ratified, Demosthenes refers to the possibility of calling an *ekklesia synkletos*: it is evident that he is thinking of an Assembly meeting convened at short notice.[106]

On the basis of some obscure lexicographical references scholars have wished to interpret *ekklesia synkletos* as not just a meeting called at short

---

[95] See pp. 158–9.   [96] Aeschin. 3.197. Busolt and Swoboda (1920–6) 1161.
[97] Hansen (1975) 53.   [98] See p. 159.   [99] Dem. 24.21, 25.
[100] Hansen (1989a) 167–75.
[101] Hansen (1983a) 48–72; (1989a) 177–92, *pace* Harris (1986).
[102] Hansen (1989a) 185–6, *pace* Harris (1986) 371.   [103] Dem. 19.154.
[104] *SEG* 24 134. Tracy (1988).   [105] Aeschin. 2.72.   [106] Dem. 19.123.

notice but an 'extraordinary meeting'.[107] But the other sources give no support to that. Had it been the case, we should have to deduce from the Aischines passage referred to above that the Athenians, since they had four ordinary meetings, must have had at least five 'extraordinary meetings', i.e. at least nine altogether, in the eighth prytany of 346, which is incompatible with all our other evidence.[108] Moreover, we also know that there could be such a thing as an *ekklesia kyria synkletos*;[109] and other sources confirm that an *ekklesia synkletos* was not an extraordinary meeting called to discuss one especially pressing matter exclusively but could be used for routine business as well.[110] We may conclude that an *ekklesia synkletos* was one of the four ordinary Assembly meetings in a prytany, but was *summoned* in some way other than the usual – at short notice, or called by a decree of the Council or the Assembly. The Aischines passage can then be interpreted as meaning that at least five and possibly more of the summonses to meetings in the seventh and eighth prytanies of 346 were 'extraordinary', which ties in well with the other evidence: the famous double meeting in the eighth prytany at which the peace with Philip was discussed and ratified was called by special decree, and may have been one of the several *ekklesiai synkletoi* Aischines was thinking of. But a surviving decree shows that at that very meeting the Athenians transacted a lot of routine business before they passed to the discussion of peace with Philip.[111]

Days of meetings

The Athenians operated two different calendars: one which historians now call the 'festival calendar', in which the year was divided into twelve months with twenty-nine or thirty days each (from new moon to new moon); and one which is nowadays called the 'bouleutic' or 'conciliar' calendar, in which the year had ten prytanies of thirty-four days (prytanies 1–4) or thirty-five days (prytanies 5–10). Both calendars followed the lunar year of 354 days, and in both the year began at the first new moon after the summer solstice, i.e. in June or July. To bring the lunar year in line with the solar they intercalated a month of twenty-nine or thirty days roughly every third year, and in the intercalary years the prytanies were of thirty-nine days (1–4) and thirty-eight (5–10).[112]

Since the Assembly was called by the *prytaneis* of the Council, it naturally followed the bouleutic calendar. Meetings had to be called four

---

[107] Schol. Dem. 24.20. Hansen (1983a) 73; (1989a) 180.   [108] Hansen (1987a) 29–30.
[109] *IG* II² 359; Hansen (1983a) 88–9. *I. Délos* 1507; Tracy (1988).
[110] Hansen (1983a) 79.   [111] *IG* II² 212.53–7 = Tod 167 and Harding (1985) no. 82.
[112] Pritchett and Neugebauer (1947) 34–9; Mikalson (1975a) 8–10.

times in each prytany, though not on any particular day. There was some tendency for meetings to pile up at the end of a prytany, as a result of having to hold at least one available meeting in reserve in case an unforeseen situation called for a crisis meeting late in the prytany.[113] Meetings were usually announced at, probably, four days' notice, and the *prytaneis* did not regularly pass on their business,[114] so there were not likely to be meetings in the first four days of a prytany;[115] but otherwise the right of the *prytaneis* to summon an Assembly meeting when they thought fit was only limited by the rule that meetings must not be held on festival days,[116] nor, especially, on 'taboo-days', *hemerai apophrades*, such as when the Areopagos was judging murder cases.[117] Those days were polluted and must not be used at all: in crisis situations, but only then, Assembly meetings could be held on festival days, doubtless as *ekklesiai synkletoi*.[118] The laws also forbade the calling of the Assembly and the People's Court for the same day:[119] the *thesmothetai*, who summoned the courts, must have had to give way to the *prytaneis*.

Duration of meetings

A meeting of the Assembly could not go on beyond a day. It began at daybreak;[120] at what time did it finish?[121] When one remembers that the Athenians were notorious for argumentativeness and that every one of the 6000 was entitled to a say,[122] it would not be hard to imagine that they went on all day from dawn to dusk; and we have one example (but only one) of a meeting that did go on until darkness fell: the first of the two meetings in 406 that led to the collective death penalty on the eight generals had to come to an end because it was too dark to see the show of hands.[123] That was at the beginning of November, and the meeting may have lasted a good eleven hours. But a passage of Aischines provides an example of an ordinary Assembly meeting followed by a meeting of the Council.[124] Now, since we know from Aristotle that the *prytaneis* had to call the Council every day except *aphesimoi* (i.e. annual festival days plus 'taboo days'), we can combine those two sources and conclude that Assembly days were not *aphesimoi* and consequently that the Council regularly met after the Assembly was over. In fact, it is a reasonable guess that an Assembly meeting, like the meeting of a Swiss *Landsgemeinde*,[125] only lasted a few hours and was over by midday. It is true that people

---

[113] Hansen (1983a) 89–90.   [114] Hansen (1983a) 77 n. 22.   [115] Hansen (1983a) 87–8.
[116] Mikalson (1975a) 186–93.   [117] Mikalson (1975b) 26.   [118] Hansen (1983a) 78.
[119] Dem. 24.80.   [120] Ar. *Eccl.* 740–1.   [121] Hansen (1983a) 131–8.
[122] Thuc. 3.38.2–7.   [123] Xen. *Hell.* 1.7.7.   [124] Aeschin. 1.110–12.
[125] Hansen (1983a) 216–17.

brought their bread and wine onto the Pnyx;[126] but even a meeting of four to six hours in summer or three to five hours in winter was quite long enough to justify a snack. A meeting that began at daybreak and lasted till noon was, of course, shorter in winter than in summer; but that corresponds to the fact that the main area of business of the Assembly was foreign policy, and it is well known that wars and diplomatic moves were cut to a minimum in the winter months, so meetings could easily be shorter. Of those inscriptions where the precise date is preserved, the vast majority were passed in the summer months.[127] In the afternoon the Council was summoned to its daily meeting, and the rest of the citizens had time to discuss the results of the meeting amongst themselves or to do a half-day's work, at least if they lived in Athens or the Piraeus.

Seating-arrangements

We know that the citizens attended their Assembly meetings seated,[128] in the fifth century on the ground, or more likely on cushions.[129] in the fourth century probably on wooden benches.[130] The *prytaneis*[131] and, in the fourth century, also the *proedroi*[132] sat facing the audience. In 346/5 the Athenians passed a law that all members of one tribe should sit together in the part of the auditorium nearest the speakers' platform and be responsible for the orderly conduct of the meeting:[133] the tribes were to be taken in rotation. Perhaps the purpose was to prevent hecklers from getting too close to the speakers and disrupting their arguments.

A much-discussed question is whether the Athenians were seated in any kind of groups at Assembly meetings. There are three possible answers, and each has its adherents: they either sat by tribes[134] (and maybe actually by ridings[135]), in ten wedge-shaped sections, or else they sat wherever they liked, either entirely at random[136] or in groups supporting political leaders.[137] The theory that they sat by ridings does not square with the fact that the thirty *syllogeis* were divided by tribes but not by ridings;[138] and the theory that they sat by tribes in ten wedges is incompatible with the law that said that the members of one tribe must sit in the front.[139] No rule, therefore, obliged the citizens to sit in any particular order: they were free to sit at random or to form groups of

[126] Ar. *Eccl.* 306–8. [127] Hansen (1983a) 136. [128] Hyp. 1.9.
[129] Ar. *Eq.* 754, 783. [130] Ar. *Eccl.* 21, 86–7. Hansen (1983a) 28.
[131] Ar. *Ach.* 23ff. [132] Din. 2.13. On the *proedroi* see pp. 140–1.
[133] Aeschin. 1.33–4. [134] Staveley (1972) 81–2; Kolb (1981) 93.
[135] Siewert (1982) 10–3; Stanton and Bicknell (1987); Bicknell (1989).
[136] Gomme, Andrewes and Dover (1970) 238.
[137] Sealey (1956b) 241; Ober (1989) 88. [138] See p. 105.
[139] Hansen (1989a) 161–2, *pace* Stanton and Bicknell (1987) 63–5.

like-minded voters as they pleased, regularly or occasionally. Whether they did group politically is more difficult to answer, because the sources do not all tell the same tale. Plutarch has it that when in the 440s Perikles' policy was under attack by Thucydides the son of Melesias, who was leader of the 'better sort', the supporters of Thucydides were in a minority, but to compensate and give his group more clout he got them to collect around him in the Assembly.[140] On the other hand, the historian Thucydides (the son of Oloros) takes it for granted that in 415 the supporters of Alkibiades were scattered about the Pnyx side-by-side with the supporters of the more cautious policy of Nikias.[141] Plutarch's source may merely have said that Thucydides the son of Melesias was surrounded in the Assembly by close associates,[142] and the account of the historian Thucydides is corroborated by others, such as Theophrastos' sketch of the 'Oligarchical Man', who is ashamed to find himself in the Assembly seated beside a poor, hungry fellow-citizen.[143] Once again the Swiss *Landsgemeinde* provides an instructive parallel: although the Swiss have had well-organized political parties at federal level for over a hundred years, there is not the slightest evidence for any tendency of the burghers to stand together in party groups in the *Landsgemeinde*.[144]

The pre-Assembly stage in the Council of Five Hundred

The Assembly could only discuss and decide matters placed on its agenda by the *prytaneis*, and the latter could not put a matter on the agenda unless and until the Council had considered it and passed a preliminary decree[145] called a *probouleuma*, or sometimes *boules psephisma*.[146] The rule *meden aprobouleuton*, 'nothing without a *probouleuma*', seems to have been a fundamental principle of Athenian democracy.[147] The preliminary decree was either a 'concrete' *probouleuma*, fully worked out in detail, or an 'open' *probouleuma*, i.e. a simple order to the Assembly to discuss and decide a matter (which would thus depend on whatever proposals might be made from the floor of the Assembly).[148] This 'probouleumatic procedure', as historians like to call it, raises the question of whether Athenian policy was really made by the people by free debate in the Assembly,[149] or whether the Assembly only ratified (or rejected) decisions already taken by the Council and handed down as (concrete) *probouleumata*.[150]

---

[140] Plut. *Per.* 11.2.   [141] Thuc. 6.13.1. Gomme, Andrewes and Dover (1970) 238.
[142] Andrewes (1978) 1–2.   [143] Theophr. *Char.* 26.5; Ar. *Thesm.* 292.
[144] Hansen (1983a) 221–2.   [145] Arist. *Ath. Pol.* 45.4.   [146] Dem. 23.92.
[147] Dem. 22.5; 25, *hypoth.* 1.   [148] Rhodes (1972) 52–82.
[149] Jones (1957) 118.
[150] De Laix (1973) 192–4.

Some items on the Assembly's agenda were obligatory, and so made a *probouleuma* superfluous, and could probably be put to the people directly without any discussion in the Council.[151] That applies to some of the items for the *ekklesia kyria* mentioned by Aristotle, such as *epicheirotonia ton archon, eisangelia eis ton demon* and *probolai* against sycophants.[152] It applies also to the annual vote about the entire corpus of the laws (*epicheirotonia ton nomon*), which had to occur at the first Assembly meeting of the year.[153] But it is important to observe that the decrees passed by the Assembly on those matters were not conclusive, but only decisions to pass the matter on to the courts[154] or the *nomothetai*:[155] in such cases it was the Assembly's decree that was 'probouleumatic'.

More important is that the Council often avoided making a 'concrete' *probouleuma* and contented itself with an 'open' one; the discussion in the Assembly thus began with the question 'Who wishes to speak?' and the decree that the Assembly passed was upon a motion proposed by any of its members and, after 403, began with the words *edoxe toi demoi* or the like, without mention of the Council.[156]

In other cases the Council might put up a 'concrete' *probouleuma* which after discussion was voted down in favour of an alternative proposal by some member of the Assembly; in that case, too, the resulting decree began with *edoxe toi demoi*, without mention of the Council.[157]

But many decrees begin with the formula *edoxe tei boulei kai toi demoi*, 'It was decided by the Council and the people', and what follows after the preamble is set out as a decree of the Council introduced by the so-called 'probouleumatic formula': 'that the Council has determined that the *proedroi* chosen by lot to preside over the next Assembly of the People shall put on the agenda and shall present to the people the Council's decision that the Council thinks that . . . ', followed by the Council's *probouleuma* cited verbatim.[158] In these cases the people's decree is indeed only a ratification of one by the Council, and the Assembly's initiative is limited to minor modifications that can be appended to the *probouleuma* and begin with the formula 'For the rest as the Council, but . . . '.[159]

Many decrees of the Assembly were simple and uncontroversial ratifications of proposals by the Council; and, particularly in routine matters,

---

[151] Rhodes (1972) 55–6.   [152] Arist. *Ath. Pol.* 43.4–5. See p. 132.

[153] Dem. 24.20.

[154] Dem. 19.116–17; Hyp. 3.29–30 (*eisangelia*); Arist. *Ath. Pol.* 61.2 (*epicheirotonia*); Arist. *Ath. Pol.* 43.5, 59.2 (*probole*).

[155] Dem. 24.27.

[156] *IG* II² 240 = Tod 181; *IG* II² 337 = Tod 189 and Harding (1985) no. 111. Rhodes (1972) 67–8.

[157] *IG* II² 336. Rhodes (1972) 68.   [158] *IG* II² 206; Aeschin. 3.125.

[159] *IG* II² 206.27–8. Rhodes (1972) 71–3.

many of the Council's *probouleumata* were no doubt passed without debate and unanimously with thousands of votes for and none against, exactly as is often the case in the *Landsgemeinde*.[160] To shorten the proceedings, what was often done was to hold at the beginning of the meeting a *procheirotonia*, i.e. a preliminary show of hands, as to all the concrete *probouleumata* on the agenda.[161] If a *probouleuma* was passed unanimously it counted as ratified there and then and was not further discussed, but, if so much as a single hand was raised against it, it had to be discussed and voted upon in the normal way.[162]

The *psephismata* referred to in the literary sources never include the formulas that would show whether the decree was probouleumatic or non-probouleumatic. However, an exhaustive study of all the decrees that are preserved epigraphically[163] shows that some half of the Assembly's decrees were ratifications of concrete proposals by the Council, and the other half were proposed directly in the Assembly, either as a response to an open *probouleuma* or as an alternative to a concrete *probouleuma* from the Council. If we focus on the really important decisions and leave on one side standard business, especially honorary decrees, we come to much the same result: less than half the decrees of the Assembly were ratifications of *probouleumata*. Certainly the Council had a powerful influence, and the prior discussion of a matter by the Council was a precondition for the Assembly to function at all; but the process of deciding lay for the most part in the hands of the people in their Assembly. This epigraphical research is corroborated by the literary sources: all the political debates we hear about in the historians and the orators take place in the Assembly, hardly ever in the Council.[164] Thus the sources surely reflect reality, and testify that policy at Athens really was made by the Assembly rather than by the Council.

The presidents

In the fifth century it was the *prytaneis* and, in particular, their chairman, the *epistates ton prytaneon*, who presided over meetings of the Assembly.[165] At some time between 403/2[166] and 379/8[167] the presidency was transferred to a board of nine *proedroi*, one of whom was chosen to be chairman, *epistates ton proedron*.[168] The purpose of the reform was perhaps to obviate corruption: the *epistates ton prytaneon* was chosen at sunset to

---

[160] Dem. 59.5. Hansen (1983a) 215.   [161] Aeschin. 1.23; Harp. s.v.
[162] Hansen (1983a) 123–30.   [163] Rhodes (1972) 78–81.
[164] Gomme (1962b) 178.   [165] Ar. *Ach.* 23–6, 173; Xen. *Hell.* 1.7.14–15.
[166] *IG* II² 1.41–2.   [167] *CSCA* 5 (1972) 164–9.
[168] Arist. *Ath. Pol.* 44.2.

function for a night and a day,[169] whereas the *proedroi* were only picked (by lot) in the morning just before the meeting of the Assembly began: it would be just like the Athenians to invent the board of *proedroi* out of anxiety lest the chairman of the *prytaneis* should succumb to bribery in the middle of the night.[170] But they may have had other reasons as well. *Proedroi* had been introduced once before, by the oligarchs in 411, who established a board of five *proedroi* to set up the Council of Four Hundred.[171] The term *proedros* may well have been a favourite with the moderates and the new board of nine *proedroi* considered to be a desirable modification of the earlier democracy.

The *prytaneis* were one tribe's contingent of fifty members, and a different tribe served in each prytany. The nine *proedroi* were selected by lot from the 450 councillors not serving as *prytaneis*, one from each of the nine remaining tribes; and a second selection by lot from amongst the *proedroi* determined who was to be their *epistates*.[172] They were chosen just for one day, and their function was to preside over the meetings of the Council and the Assembly: it follows that no *proedroi* were chosen on days when there was no Council meeting. On most days the *proedroi* only presided over the Council, but on the forty Assembly days they had first to preside over the Assembly meeting and then, in the afternoon, over the Council. The selection of *proedroi* was performed by the *epistates ton prytaneon*, and that means that on Assembly days there must have been a short Council meeting before the Assembly convened.[173] When the *proedroi* had been selected they received the agenda for the Assembly from the *epistates ton prytaneon*,[174] and their duty was to see that all items on the agenda were dealt with.[175] A motion made in the Assembly had to be handed in to the *proedroi* in writing.[176] The *epistates ton proedron* had primary responsibility for controlling the discussion and, when it was over, putting the motion to the vote, and it was the duty of the *proedroi* to estimate the vote.[177]

DEBATE

The opening

Four days before a meeting the agenda was posted[178] and on the day itself some special sign was exhibited[179] (we do not know what) to show

---

[169] Arist. *Ath. Pol.* 44.1. [170] Aeschin. 3.3. Hansen (1983a) 135.
[171] Thuc. 8.67.3, cf. *IG* I³ 98 = *M&L* 80 and Fornara (1977) no. 149; cf. Thuc. 3.25.1.
[172] Arist. *Ath. Pol.* 44.2. [173] Dem. 18.169. Hansen (1983a) 76.
[174] Arist. *Ath. Pol.* 44.2. [175] Dem. 24.21–2. [176] Aeschin. 2.68.
[177] Arist. *Ath. Pol.* 44.2–3. [178] See p. 133.
[179] Ar. *Thesm.* 277–8; Andoc. 1.36.

everybody that it was an Assembly day. The countryfolk who intended to participate in the meeting must have left home long before dawn (unless they had come to the city the day before). At dawn people were already streaming up onto the Pnyx,[180] while the Council held its short meeting to select the *proedroi*. The citizens passed through the entrances to the Assembly-place under the eye of the thirty *syllogeis tou demou*, who handed to each a token (*symbolon*),[181] which had to be handed back when pay was distributed after the meeting. When the citizens had settled in the auditorium, proceedings began with a sacrifice: a pig was slaughtered and the *peristiarchos* dragged it round the Pnyx and purified the Assembly-place with its blood.[182] Then the crier (*keryx*) declaimed a prayer (*euche*)[183] and a curse (*ara*) upon any speaker (*rhetor*) who should attempt to lead the people astray;[184] but there was no oath-taking – a point of some importance, for in our sources the decisions of those who had sworn the oath (i.e. the jurors of the People's Court) are sometimes estimated above those of the Assembly, where there was no oath.[185] After the opening ceremonies the *procheirotonia* was held on all the concrete *probouleumata* on the agenda; and after that the Assembly proceeded to the first item that required debate, the crier putting the question 'Who wishes to speak?'[186] (Originally it was 'Who wishes to speak from amongst those over fifty?', and only when the seniors had had their say did the crier return to the simple 'Who wishes to speak?')[187]

Speeches

In an Assembly of 6000 people it is impossible to have a proper exchange of views in the form of a discussion: on the Pnyx, debate was necessarily in the form of a series of speeches of varied length. Sometimes the speeches were extempore, sometimes prepared, and in the latter case with or without a text.[188] It is not credible that a speaker read his entire speech verbatim: if a speaker used a text he probably had a prompter at hand,[189] but, also, the common idea that speakers learnt their speeches by heart is *a priori* unlikely, and has in fact no support in the sources – the systems of mnemonics recommended by the teachers of rhetoric indicate that an orator had to master the run of his arguments but only exceptionally had whole sections fully worked out.[190]

---

[180] Ar. *Eccl.* 20–1.
[181] *IG* II² 1749.76 = *Agora* XV 38.79; Ar. *Eccl.* 296–7. Svoronos (1900) 319–43; Lang and Crosby (1964) 78–80.
[182] Aeschin. 1.23 with schol. Parker (1983) 21–2.   [183] Din. 2.14.
[184] Dem. 19.70; Din. 2.16.   [185] Dem. 24.78.   [186] Dem. 18.170.
[187] Aeschin. 1.23, 3.4. Griffith (1966) 119.   [188] Dem. 1.1; Isoc. 13.9; Alcid. 2.11.
[189] Schol. Hom. *Il.* 19.77b/c (587 Erbse).   [190] Ar. *Eq.* 346–50; Alcid. 2.18; Quintilian *Inst. Or.* 11.2.1–51.

With the development of rhetoric as an independent discipline the Assembly speech (*demegorikos logos*), or speech of advice (*symbouleutikos logos*), as it was also called, became one of the three well-established rhetorical genres along with the forensic speech (*dikanikos logos*) and the 'display' speech (*epideiktikos logos*) spoken at Panhellenic festivals or the annual funeral service for the war-dead.[191] The well-known division of an oration into four sections is a direct inheritance from Greek rhetoric: preamble, narrative, arguments (usually in two subsections: positive arguments for one's own point of view and negative ones rebutting that of one's opponent) and peroration.[192] What is less often realized is that this arrangement only applied to forensic speeches, whereas Assembly speeches followed quite other rules. There was no narrative in an Assembly speech, since the subject was not a legal dispute where the jurors had to be put in the picture but a political situation that every citizen knew about already.[193] Instead, in the argumentative section, the speaker brought up the motion he wanted passed, and that section was thus divided into an introduction to the proposal, the proposal itself, and the justification of it;[194] and there was no rebuttal of the arguments of the other side.[195] For debate in the Assembly was carried on between any number of speakers, who might take the platform without warning and bring up quite unexpected points, whereas a lawsuit was a confrontation between just two parties who knew each other's points beforehand. Assembly speeches were, in consequence, shorter and more oral, whereas forensic speakers could work up their speeches in written form in advance. Moreover, forensic speeches were about the past and concerned right and wrong, whereas Assembly speeches were about the future and concerned the expedient and the inexpedient.[196] Nevertheless the purpose was ultimately the same: to persuade people and get as many votes as possible.

Speakers

The vast majority of the audience of 6000 were content to listen and vote, and only a tiny minority came forward to make speeches or propose motions. It is that minority that historians nowadays call the 'politicians';[197] the Athenians called them simply the 'speakers' (*rhetores*). The term was used for both speakers and proposers of motions,[198] and its twofold sense is mirrored in two other terms that are often used as synonyms of *rhetor*: *ho legon*, 'he who speaks' (to the people)[199] and *ho*

---

[191] Isoc. 13.9; Arist. *Rhet.* 1358b2–8. Kennedy (1963) 10–11.
[192] Arist. *Rhet.* 1414b19–1420a8. [193] Arist. *Rhet.* 1414a37–9.
[194] Dem. 1.1, 2–15, 16–20, 21–7, 28. [195] Arist. *Rhet.* 1414b1.
[196] Arist. *Rhet.* 1358b4ff, 20ff. [197] Perlman (1963).
[198] Aeschin. 2.74, 3.55. Hansen (1989a) 7. [199] Dem. 9.38.

graphon, 'he who writes' (a motion for a decree).[200] *Rhetor* was a technical term which in the language of the law referred to any citizen who appeared before the people with a speech or a proposal:[201] a citizen became a *rhetor* the moment he stepped onto the speakers' platform, and as a mark of his dignity a wreath was placed on his head like that worn by magistrates.[202] Being a *rhetor* was an *ad hoc* function, just as was being a member of an Assembly meeting (*ekklesiastes*): the difference was that a member of the Assembly could never be made to answer for the vote he had cast, whereas a *rhetor* was answerable for his speech or his motion. A speaker suspected of corruption or treachery could be denounced by an *eisangelia*,[203] and an unconstitutional proposal could be stopped by a *graphe paranomon*.[204]

To make a speech in the Assembly demanded some eloquence and rhetorical training, which not every citizen possessed. That is why debate was dominated by a small group of half- or fully-professional orators, some of whom had been trained by sophists or in the school of Isokrates[205] or in Plato's Academy:[206] Demosthenes, Hypereides, Demades and Lykourgos are names known not only in the history books but also in the histories of European literature, in the chapters about the early days of rhetoric. The Athenians' ideal Assembly speaker was, it is true, the plain man who spoke his honest mind with modest infrequency and without circumlocution: the fourth-century orators liked to praise that ideal, but with a rhetorical dexterity that gives away the professional.[207] The ideal *rhetor* was what we should call an amateur: the Athenians' term was *idiotes*, the 'private person'[208] as opposed to the 'professional' *rhetor* who took the platform at any opportunity and often made gain out of his political activity.[209] At any Assembly meeting there were, say, several hundred *rhetores* in the formal sense, i.e. people who might on occasion pluck up courage to come forward and propose something; but of *rhetores* in the political sense there can never have been more than a score or so – fewer than a hundred in the whole period from 403 to 322.[210]

The Athenians were ambivalent about the political leaders in the Assembly. On the one hand they were nervous that speakers might lead the people astray by their eloquence and be themselves led astray by gifts from foreign rulers or enemies of the democracy; so the term *rhetor* was often used pejoratively to mean a 'politician' who took the platform as a

[200] Dem. 18.219.
[201] Hyp. 3.8. Hansen (1987a) 61–3; (1990f) 354, *pace* Ober (1989) 110–11.
[202] Ar. *Eccl.* 131.   [203] See p. 213.   [204] See p. 205.
[205] Plut. *Mor.* 848D; Isoc. 15.101.   [206] Plut. *Phocion* 4.2.
[207] Aeschin. 3.220. Hansen (1987a) 61–3.   [208] Dem. *Prooem.* 13; Hyp. 3.13.
[209] Dem. 18.170; Din. 1.90.   [210] Hansen (1989a) 121–5; Ober (1989) 108. See p. 272.

professional and engaged in politics for gain.[211] But on the other hand the democracy could only function if a reasonable number of citizens were ready to take the platform and speak or propose motions; and the Athenians stimulated the political keenness of the citizenry every year by awarding honorary decrees and golden crowns to the man who 'always by his speeches and proposals does what is best for the people';[212] so the term *rhetor* was also used favourably, and Demosthenes proudly asserts that for a period, as a *rhetor*, he was the political leader of Athens.[213]

Proposers

Besides the political leaders there were a distinctly larger group of ordinary citizens and councillors who occasionally made a speech and not infrequently took it upon themselves to propose a motion. Makers of speeches in the Assembly, when the sources refer to them, are usually names we recognize, but many of the proposers of decrees in the literary and epigraphical sources are mere names, never heard of again in any other context.[214] There are at least two good explanations for the difference. In the first place, every other decree passed by the Assembly was probouleumatic, i.e. ratification of a decree of the Council proposed by a member of the Council.[215] Even a political leader could only be a councillor twice in his life, and not until he was thirty,[216] so if he wanted to have a motion passed by the Assembly he usually had to find a councillor to collaborate with him; the councillor would be the formal, answerable proposer and put the motion to the Council and then to the Assembly.[217] The probouleumatic procedure thus entailed that many decrees were put up by an ordinary councillor, whose name can be read today in the preamble to the decree (though it is never stated in the decree that the proposer is a councillor),[218] while the real initiator was a political leader who supported the motion (which was really his) in the Assembly, but whose speech was not published and so has not survived.[219] In the second place, anyone who proposed a motion was answerable for it, and, if convicted, for instance of making an unconstitutional proposal, might be mulcted with a gigantic fine that would leave him *atimos*.[220] So it was worthwhile for a political leader to get a man of straw, willing, for a consideration, to put the motion in the Assembly, where his principal would defend it: if the proposer was attacked by a *graphe paranomon* the political leader might defend him in court or at

---

[211] Dem. 23.201.   [212] Aeschin. 3.49–50; *IG* II² 223 A 11–12.
[213] Dem. 18.212.   [214] Hansen (1989a) 102–4.   [215] See pp. 140, 253.
[216] See p. 249.   [217] Xen. *Hell.* 1.7.8. Hansen (1987a) 163 n. 488.
[218] Hansen (1989a) 120–1.   [219] Aeschin. 3.125–6.   [220] See p. 207.

least write his speech for him.[221] In the speech against Neaira, Stephanos of the deme Eroiadai is described as a proposer of exactly that kind: 'Stephanos was . . . only a sycophant, one of those who flock round the speakers' platform and heckle, and proffer indictments and informations for hire and let their names be inscribed on the proposals of others.'[222]

The audience

Debate in the Assembly, then, consisted in a series of speeches unrelated to one another. Communication was only one-way, from speaker to audience: according to the letter of the law there was no communication from audience to speaker,[223] other than the vote itself, or between speaker and speaker, except that they could naturally refer to previous speeches,[224] or between members of the audience, except that a speaker might call upon, for example, the older citizens to confirm to the younger ones some historical reference,[225] and except for informal whispered consultations between political leaders in the body of the Assembly.[226] Having listened, the members of the Assembly voted on the motion without discussion.

In practice no Assembly meeting ever took place in which that stern principle was respected. At every meeting the audience interrupted[227] with applause[228] or protests[229] or laughter.[230] Applause, of course, a speaker might angle for, but sometimes, if he feared his thesis might not be immediately to their taste, he might beg his hearers not to interrupt;[231] it could even occur that a speaker was whistled off.[232] In other cases the reaction of the audience was a mixture of applause and protest.[233] Heckling from the auditorium was often unrehearsed,[234] but sometimes it consisted of questions or objections by a single citizen or a small group,[235] and there could even arise a bit of actual dialogue between the speaker and members of the audience, whose purpose might be to clarify something, though it might be just to bring the speaker to a halt, which was best achieved if the interruptor could carry the rest of the audience with him.[236] Interruption might be a deliberate strategy: there were a group of 'minor *rhetores*',[237] 300 or so according to Demosthenes,[238] who did not make regular speeches themselves, though they might act as proposers of motions for others, like Stephanos of Eroiadai. They tried to sit near

---

[221] Aeschin. 3.242–3. Hansen (1974) 53–4.   [222] Dem. 59.43.

[223] Aeschin. 3.2. Hansen (1990f) 350, *pace* Ober (1989) 104, 325.

[224] Aeschin. 2.51–2.   [225] Din. 1.42. Hansen (1987) 70 with n. 446.

[226] Aeschin. 2.64.   [227] Calhoun (1913) 121–3; Bers (1985); Hansen (1987a) 69–72.

[228] Dem. 21.14.   [229] Aeschin. 3.224.   [230] Aeschin. 1.80–4.

[231] Dem. 5.15.   [232] Xen. *Hell.* 6.5.49; Dem. 59.26–7.   [233] Aeschin. 2.51.

[234] Lys. 12.73.   [235] Dem. 8.38.   [236] Dem. 19.46.

[237] Hyp. 1.12.   [238] Dem. 2.29.

the speakers' platform,[239] where interruption would be most effective, which was what the law of 346/5, putting one tribe in the front, was presumably supposed to obviate.[240]

The vote

In fourth-century Athens there were two modes of voting: the Assembly voted by show of hands (*cheirotonia*),[241] the People's Court voted by ballot (*psephophoria*), i.e. by placing small discs of bronze in urns.[242] Nevertheless, the decisions of the Assembly were called *psephismata* and the procedure itself often *psephizesthai*[243] – both words are from *psephos* ('pebble'), which shows that at some earlier time the Assembly had voted in the same way as the courts;[244] but in the classical age voting by ballot only occurred in the Assembly in the few cases where a decision had to be reached with a quorum of 6000.[245]

The voting was directed by the *proedroi*. They first called for the 'ayes' to raise their hands and then the 'noes'.[246] Abstention was possible, but the number of those abstaining was never, it seems, estimated: the Athenians made no distinction between 'unanimous' and 'nem. con.'[247] The citizens voted from their places: there is no sign that voters were marshalled on different sides of the Pnyx to facilitate the estimation of the votes. We have very little evidence how that estimation was carried out. Study of votes by show of hands in assemblies of comparable size to the Athenian show that exact counting of hands is never undertaken. In the *Landsgemeinden*, for example, either the president of the assembly, the *Landammann*, or a board of officials (*Weibeln*) makes a rapid survey of the upraised hands and estimates whether the motion is passed or rejected: there is no counting for it is impossible. In cases of doubt the show of hands is repeated.[248] Such few sources as we have suggest that the Athenians used a similar procedure. Aristotle says in the *Constitution of Athens* that the nine *proedroi* 'judge' the show of hands:[249] the word he uses, *krinein*, does not naturally mean 'count', though it is usually so translated here. It implies that the *proedroi* made a judgement, a decision, which they could do not by counting but by assessing or estimating who had the majority. And the same is indirectly implied by Aristophanes in *The Wasps*: 'make a rough estimate, not with *psephoi* but with hands'[250]

---

[239] Dem. 59.43; Pl. *Resp.* 564D. [240] See p. 137.
[241] Dem. 20.3 (decrees), 4.26 (elections), 19.31 (judgements). [242] See p. 202.
[243] Isoc. 8.52. [244] Staveley (1972) 84–5.
[245] Dem. 59.89–90. Hansen (1983a) 11–12. [246] Dem. 22.9; Xen. *Hell.* 1.7.34.
[247] Lys. 12.75; Dem. 59.5. [248] Hansen (1983a) 213–15.
[249] Arist. *Ath. Pol.* 44.3. Hansen (1983a) 103–21. [250] Ar. *Vesp.* 655–7.

– a play between the judgements in the courts, which are by *psephoi* counted exactly, and those by show of hands, in which there is only an estimate. Naturally, the vote would have had to be repeated in a case of doubt: any citizen could lodge a protest under oath (*hypomosia*) and demand a second show of hands.[251] Once again the result was determined by an estimate made by the *proedroi*. On the other hand, if the *proedroi* were at odds over the result, perhaps there was a vote among the *proedroi* themselves,[252] settled by majority: it is not coincidental that the Assembly was presided over by a board of nine and not of ten, as might have been expected by comparison with other boards, since it assured that there would never be a tie.

A specimen decree

One complete decision of the Assembly may serve to draw together the threads of what has been said:[253]

> GODS. In the archonship of Phrynichos, in the prytany of [the tribe] Pandionis, being the tenth [prytany], in which Chairestratos the son of Ameinias of [the deme] Acharnai was secretary; the one of the *proedroi* who put the motion was Antiphanes of [the deme] Euonymon; Demades the son of Demeas of [the deme] Paiania proposed: May good luck attend the people of Athens; that it be a decision of the people that, since [name missing, evidently a Macedonian] is favourable to the people of Athens and looks after the Athenians who arrive to see Philip, achieving whatever good he can for the Athenians at the hand of Philip, he be *proxenos* and benefactor of the people of Athens, himself and his descendants, and the Council and the generals look after him in anything he requires. And that the proxeny [decree] be inscribed on a stone slab and the Secretary for the prytany set it up on the Akropolis. And for the inscribing of the slab let the Treasurer give 30 drachmas according to the law.

After a perfunctory-looking invocation of the gods and a date by archon and secretary (337/6) follows the preamble, whose principal purpose is the pinning of responsibility: the decision was made by the people but proposed by a named citizen and put to the vote by the board of nine *proedroi*, of whom only the chairman is named. The people could never be called to account, but the *proedroi* could, by a special public prosecution

---

[251] Xen. *Hell.* 1.7.34.
[252] Cf. Pl. *Lg.* 765B. Hansen (1983a) 110.
[253] *IG* II² 240 = Tod 181.

called *graphe proedrike* (which must have been set up as nine separate prosecutions), and so could the named chairman, by a *graphe epistatike*.[254] Those procedures are mere names to us, and were probably not much used, but the proposer himself could be charged by a *graphe paranomon*, and that was used on average several times a year.[255]

The substance of the decree follows, and then the decision for it to be published on stone. The original was presumably kept in the Metroön,[256] on papyrus or some other perishable material;[257] and decisions were only inscribed on stone if the people specifically so decided, as in this case. Publication was the responsibility of the secretary of the Council: he was a very important element in the working of the Assembly, because besides publication he also had the duty to produce the definitive text of all the people's decrees and archive them. Originally he was a councillor chosen by lot for a single prytany – which is how, oddly enough, he is still described in this specimen – but at some time between 368 and 363 the secretaryship was turned into a proper independent office, its holder chosen by lot from all Athenians and serving for the full year.[258] Finally, we note that payment was to be made by the Treasurer of the People, an office introduced at the beginning of the fourth century and probably manned by election like the other new financial offices.[259] The money for the decree had to be taken from the people's annual allowance under the *merismos*.[260]

Closure

After the vote the Assembly turned to the next item. There were probably at least nine items on a day's agenda,[261] and one item might involve the passing of several decrees.[262] But many concrete *probouleumata* needed no debate, and had already been decided at the *procheirotonia*. So an Assembly meeting could usually be got through in the morning, and as soon as all items had been dealt with the *proedroi* could declare the meeting closed.[263] (They could do so also in case of rain, even if not all items had been completed.[264]) The signal was taken down,[265] and the citizens left the Pnyx and received their pay upon handing back their *symbola*.

---

[254] Arist. *Ath. Pol.* 59.2.   [255] See p. 208.
[256] Aeschin. 3.187; Din. 1.86. Wycherley (1957) 150ff.   [257] Woodhead (1981) 37.
[258] Arist. *Ath. Pol.* 54.3. Rhodes (1972) 134–41.   [259] Kahrstedt (1936) 43.
[260] See p. 158.   [261] Arist. *Ath. Pol.* 43.6. Hansen (1989a) 98–9.
[262] Hansen (1989a) 99–100.   [263] Arist. *Ath. Pol.* 44.3.
[264] Ar. *Ach.* 170–3.   [265] Andoc. 1.36.

Pay

Aristotle in the *Politics* says that there are two ways of stimulating people to participate in political meetings: one is to punish those who absent themselves; the other to reward those who turn up. The former is the more oligarchical, the latter the radical-democratic way of proceeding.[266] In the fifth century, having not yet introduced Assembly pay, the Athenians sought to force people to attend the Assembly by the red rope and the penalty for having red paint on your coat.[267] In the fourth they turned to the alternative of paying people for participation, and that seems to have borne fruit straight away. Soon after the restoration of democracy in 403/2 Agyrrhios made a proposal for the payment of 1 obol to every participant; Herakleides raised the bid to 2 obols, and Agyrrhios promptly outbid him with 3, and that is how it was fixed.[268] Aristophanes in the *Ekklesiazousai* pokes fun at the effect of the three obols in inducing large numbers of citizens to attend the Assembly meetings.[269] Pay was presumably granted only to the first 6000[270] – which suddenly produced a good deal of pushing and shoving at the entrances to the Pnyx.[271] By Aristotle's time the rate was a drachma for a plain *ekklesia* and a drachma and a half for an *ekklesia kyria*:[272] calculation shows that the Assembly would have cost Athens in that age about 45 talents a year. At the same period a day's pay was $1\frac{1}{2}$–$2\frac{1}{2}$ drachmas;[273] but normally an Assembly meeting lasted only half a day, so the *ekklesiastikos misthos* was full compensation for half a day's lost employment, and we can reject the view that the poorer citizens were prevented *de facto* from attending the Assembly because of the inadequacy of the pay.[274]

POWERS

From the fifth to the fourth century

In virtually all modern accounts of Athenian democracy we meet the statement that the Assembly of the People was 'sovereign'.[275] The assertion is probably correct for the fifth century BC, when the people in their Assembly could pass decrees and laws and sit in judgement on

---

[266] Arist. *Pol.* 1297a35–8, 1298b17ff.   [267] Ar. *Ach.* 21–2 with schol. See p. 5.
[268] Arist. *Ath. Pol.* 41.3.   [269] Ar. *Eccl.* 300–3.
[270] Ar. *Eccl.* 282–4, 378–81. Hansen (1989a) 147–51.   [271] Ar. *Plut.* 329–30.
[272] Arist. *Ath. Pol.* 62.2.   [273] Zimmermann (1974) 99–100.
[274] Cloché (1951) 210; Ehrenberg (1960) 55; de Laix (1973) 176.
[275] Busolt and Swoboda (1920–6) 311–12; Glotz (1929) 162; Ehrenberg (1960) 58; Will (1972) 455–6; Finley (1983) 71; Bleicken (1985) 102–3.

all serious political trials; but in the fourth century the situation was different. After the two oligarchic revolutions of 411 and 404 the Athenians restored democracy in 403/2; but it was not Periklean democracy that they wanted to return to. Responsibility for the total defeat in the Peloponnesian War was largely laid at the door of the 'demagogues', who, by their misuse of the radical-democratic constitution, had induced the people to adopt false policies.[276] The concept of the 'ancestral constitution' continued to influence public sentiment, and in undertaking their codification of the laws the Athenians took a decision in principle as to the lines on which the new democracy should run: 'The Athenians shall govern themselves according to the custom of the ancestors and use the laws of Solon and Drakon as heretofore.'[277] That meant a 'moderate democracy'. Now, certainly, it was often hard to distinguish between 'moderate democracy' and no democracy at all; but the Athenians seem, by and large, to have held a decent balance. On the one side, they turned down Phormisios' proposal to confine citizen rights to those who owned land;[278] on the other, they limited the powers of the Assembly of the People. A principal trend in the development of the Athenian constitution in the fourth century is that legislation and jurisdiction came to be the monopoly of the 6000 persons each year who had sworn the Heliastic Oath, who served partly as *nomothetai* (legislators), and partly as *dikastai* (jurors). The powers of the Assembly were more and more confined to what we should nowadays call the executive sphere: foreign policy was still the business of the people, but in domestic policy the Assembly was an administrative body, mainly passing concrete measures for particular situations in accordance with the overriding principles laid down in the laws. Only in times of crisis, as for example the war against Philip in 340–338, did the Assembly recover the old omnicompetence it had had in the fifth century.[279]

A systematic account of the powers of the Assembly falls naturally into two sections: they can be described negatively, by listing the new limitations on the people's right to decide issues in the *ekklesia*, and positively, by surveying the decisions that *were* actually taken during the eighty-two years the 'new democracy' lasted.

Limits to the powers of the Assembly

The limitation of the Assembly's powers had two aspects: first, the scope of its powers was curtailed, so that the people's competence was reduced to passing decrees and electing magistrates; and, second, in both the fifth

---

[276] Thuc. 2.65.10–11; Isoc. 8.75; Aeschin. 2.176. Hansen (1987a) 94 with n. 603.
[277] Andoc. 1.83.   [278] Lys. 34.   [279] See pp. 172–3.

and the fourth centuries even that competence was limited by the fact that every matter that came before the Assembly had to be discussed first by the Council and could be, when decided, overturned by the People's Court. The limitations can be summed up in seven points.

1 By the codification of 403/2 the power of passing laws was transferred to the *nomothetai*:[280] the Assembly retained only the right to elect magistrates (*archairesia*), to give judgements in certain political prosecutions (*eisangeliai eis ton demon*) and to pass decrees (*psephismata*), i.e. decisions of foreign policy, including treaties, and concrete decisions about individual situations (administrative acts).

2 The decrees of the Assembly had to be consistent with the laws, which were of higher validity than decrees.[281]

3 The Assembly had much less influence over the finances of the state in the fourth century than before, because the rule of division that settled which revenues should be assigned to which exchequers, the *merismos*, was a law, so that the Assembly could only dispose of the state's revenues within the framework of that rule of division.[282]

4 Not long before the middle of the fourth century, probably about 355, the Assembly lost the last traces of its jurisdiction in political trials: thenceforeward all political prosecutions had to be judged by the People's Court.[283]

5 Every matter had to be considered by the Council before it could be put to the Assembly.[284]

6 Every decree of the Assembly could be appealed against to the People's Court by a *graphe paranomon*.[285]

7 Every election of a magistrate was subject to approval by the Court through the procedure of *dokimasia*; and in any case only about 100 of the magistrates were elected, the remaining 600 or so, plus the Council of Five Hundred, being selected by lot, a process over which the Assembly had no control.[286]

This summary of the limitations placed on the Assembly in the fourth century might give the impression that it was robbed of the major part of its powers and became only a secondary organ of government; but that would be mistaken, as can be shown if we return to our seven points with some further comments.

1 It was the Assembly which, by decree, decided on any given

[280] See p. 166.   [281] See pp. 173–4.   [282] See p. 158.   [283] See p. 159.
[284] See p. 138.   [285] See p. 207.   [286] See p. 230.

occasion to call *nomothetai* into being;[287] so it retained the initiative in legislation. (And we do have those exceptional situations mentioned above in which the Assembly passed decrees that counted as laws.)

2 The principle that decrees had to be consistent with the laws had no application in foreign policy, which was the Assembly's principal field of action.[288]

3 The Assembly could always vote an extraordinary property tax (*eisphora*), usually as a war measure.[289] It could also pass decrees overriding the *merismos* as long as the decree was ratified retrospectively by a board of *nomothetai*.[290]

4 Down to 355, i.e. half the period of the 'new democracy', the Assembly sat frequently as a court for political trials; and during the whole period it retained a certain control over political trials because prosecutions arising from *eisangelia* or *apophasis* could only go before the People's Court with the Assembly's sanction.[291]

5 As we have seen, the Council's *probouleumata* were often 'open' and merely introduced a subject to the Assembly with no influence on what it might decide;[292] what is more, the Assembly could always order the Council to put an item on its agenda,[293] and it could always throw out a 'concrete' *probouleuma* in favour of something proposed in its own meeting. And, finally, we have seen the numerous matters that were automatically on the agenda of the Assembly and needed no *probouleuma*, though in such cases the Assembly's decision was merely to pass the matter on to the courts or the *nomothetai*.[294]

6 The People's Court judged perhaps an average of one *graphe paranomon* a month,[295] but the Assembly must have passed something like 400 decrees a year, so only a small proportion of decrees were appealed against.

7 Although most magistrates were selected by lot, it was the most important of them that were elected, namely the generals and the chief financial officers.[296] Moreover, the sources show that *dokimasia* by the People's Court was almost always a pure formality; there is only a single known case where a general chosen by the Assembly was removed by that procedure.[297]

---

[287] See p. 168. [288] See pp. 156–7. [289] See p. 263. [290] See p. 173.
[291] See pp. 214, 292. [292] See p. 139.
[293] *IG* II² 125.6–9 = Tod 154 and Harding (1985) no. 66. Rhodes (1972) 65, 68.
[294] See pp. 168–9. [295] See p. 138. [296] See p. 233.
[297] Theramenes, Lys. 13.10.

'Sovereignty'?

Those historians who must at all costs defend the belief that the Assembly was still 'sovereign' in the fourth century are not, of course, unaware of the limitations of its competence sketched above; but to avoid the conclusion that surely has to be drawn from the sources they deploy two arguments.

1 That it is wrong to conceive the Assembly, the *nomothetai* and the People's Court as three different organs of government. Power at Athens belonged to the *demos*, which manifested itself institutionally in the Assembly, but the *demos* was not only the people in their Assembly: the 6000 who swore the Heliastic Oath each year constituted such a large section of the people that the *nomothetai* and the jurors were also a manifestation of the *demos*, the *demos* under another hat, and were not conceived of as separate organs opposed to the Assembly.[298]

2 That in so far as the jurors and the *nomothetai* were conceived of as separate organs it was as committees of the Assembly:[299] on practical grounds the people delegated part of their power to the jurors and the *nomothetai*,[300] so the powers of those bodies are no sign of any independent authority.

Of these two arguments, the former depends on a misunderstanding of the use of the term *demos*, the latter on a misinterpretation of constitutional relationships.

1 The Athenian concept of the *demos* can be deduced from innumerable passages in the sources, which support the following analysis: (a) when *demos* refers to an organ of state it is always synonymous with *ekklesia* and means the people in their Assembly;[301] (b) when *demos* is used (always by critics, never by democrats themselves) as a socio-political term for the Athenians in their Assembly or court[302] it always denotes 'the ordinary people', i.e. the poor, who are supposed to dominate those assemblies;[303] (c) there is no occurrence in any source of *demos* used to mean the People's Court as such;[304] (d) there are on the contrary many sources in which *dikasterion* is opposed to demos/ekklesia and praised to the detri-

---

[298] Will (1972) 456–8; Finley (1973b) 27; Rhodes (1972) 197–8; (1981a) 318; Bleicken (1985) 120, 142; Ostwald (1986) 34–5, 74; Sinclair (1988a) 70–1; Ober (1989) 145–7.
[299] Gomme (1962b) 188; Strauss (1986) 13.   [300] Glotz (1929) 166; Hignett (1952) 233.
[301] See p. 125 with nn. 1–3.   [302] Arist. *Ath. Pol.* 41.2.
[303] See p. 125 with nn. 6–7.   [304] Hansen (1989a) 214.

ment of the latter;[305] (e) whereas the *demos* in its *ekklesia* is often conceived of as the whole Athenian people assembled, the jurors in the People's Court are often conceived of as a section of the people.[306] Behind that there lay an important reality: *ekklesia* and *dikasteria* differed in membership and structure. The restriction of the courts to people over thirty meant that only two thirds of the citizen body could serve in them; and the oath, the debate and the voting-procedure in the courts distinguished them notably from the Assembly.[307]

2 Notions such as delegation and committees and subcommittees are based on modern experience and must not be applied automatically to the Greek city-states, especially when they are never defined by the historians who use them. In modern parlance a committee is chosen by a parent body, usually from amongst its own members, and must report to the parent body, and, if it makes decisions, they depend for validity on ratification by the parent body, and it can be stood down by the parent body. The People's Court and the *nomothetai* were plainly not committees of the Assembly in any such sense as that. And, if what is meant is something like a commission or agency with delegated powers, then, in the modern situation, even if the agency's acts are valid without ratification its activities as a whole are subject to review by the parent body; but no decision of the courts could be upset by the Assembly, whereas any decision of the Assembly could be upset by a court[308] (via the *graphe paranomon* and the *dokimasia*), and after 403/2 changes in the powers of the courts could not be achieved by decree of the Assembly but only by a law – which could only be passed by the *nomothetai*.

Decrees, judicial sentences and elections

We turn now to the positive side of the powers of the Athenian Assembly, to see what it in practice did in the period of the 'new democracy'. The decisions of the Assembly were of three types: decrees (*psephismata*), judicial sentences (*kriseis*) and elections (*hairesiai*).[309]

Decrees The discussion and passing of decrees was by far the most important – and time-consuming – job of the Assembly; that can be shown by a summary enumeration of all known decrees from the period

---

[305] Hansen (1983a) 146–7; (1990a) 241.   [306] Aeschin. 3.8. Hansen (1989a) 216.
[307] See pp. 209–10.   [308] Hansen (1974) 17.
[309] Hansen (1987a) 107–8.

403–322. The people met thirty to forty times a year and passed nine or ten decrees in a session.[310] In the eighty-two years of the 'new democracy' there were therefore some 3000 Assembly meetings, at which some 30,000 decrees were passed. We have trace of only about 800 of them, but they derive from two different types of source: 488 decrees are preserved on stone (even if often only in scanty fragments),[311] and those contain references to sixty-eight more;[312] and a further 219 decrees are quoted, paraphrased or referred to in the literary sources, some by the historians but most by the orators.[313] The two types seldom overlap: only nine out of 775 are known from both literary and epigraphical evidence.[314] Both types of source are biased, but in different ways: inscriptions are, fortunately, randomly preserved, but only special types, such as honorary decrees, were published on stone; the literary sources, by contrast, present a non-random selection, but at least in them all types of decree are referred to. Thus by combining the sources we can give a reasonable picture of the activities of the Assembly.

Of the 775 decrees 100 (preserved on stone) are so fragmentary that we cannot tell what they were about. The remaining 666 (675 minus the overlap of nine) can be divided by content thus: 362 about citizenship and honours; 192 about foreign and military policy; thirty-five about religion and festivals; seventeen about finance and public works; twenty about the administration of justice; sixteen about procedure in the Assembly itself; eleven decrees intended as laws; and thirteen miscellaneous. Virtually all of them are individual norms or norms with a time-limit to their validity – all except the eleven just mentioned, which were passed either before legislation was transferred to the *nomothetai* or in the crisis period during the war against Philip.[315] The conclusion is that, apart from those, between 403 and 322 the Assembly never passed decrees that were regarded as laws.

From this evidence we obtain the following picture: both the epigraphical and the literary sources show that foreign policy was the Assembly's most important field of action. The decrees on that subject include declarations of war[316] and peace,[317] alliances,[318] sending of envoys[319] – in fact all relations with foreign states. And by extension the field also includes defence of the land,[320] mobilization of armies,[321] despatch of fleets,[322] financing of expeditions,[323] orders to generals in the

---

[310] Hansen (1989a) 98–9.

[311] Hansen (1987a) 110–11; (1983a) 163 n. 6; (1987a) 183 n. 703.

[312] Hansen (1987a) 111.   [313] Hansen (1987a) 111–12; (1983a) 165 n. 15.

[314] Hansen (1987a) 183 n. 706.   [315] See pp. 172–3.   [316] Philoch. fr. 55.

[317] Aeschin. 3.54.   [318] *IG* II² 44 = Tod 124.   [319] Tod 137 = Harding (1985) no. 54.

[320] Lycurg. 1.16.   [321] Diod. 18.10.2.   [322] Dem. 50.4–6.

field,[324] and so on. No other organ of the Athenian state was competent in those matters: historians have sometimes argued that the Council, especially in the 390s, had an independent competence in foreign policy,[325] but the examples adduced are dubious and do not in any case invalidate the general principle, that foreign policy was the business of the people in their Assembly.[326]

Much the largest group of surviving decrees is, however, that comprising citizenship grants and honorary decrees.[327] They may be over-represented on stone, but the literary references are numerous enough to confirm that the appearance is not incorrect. The orators assert that rewards and punishments are two of the state's most important duties:[328] the Athenians left punishments mostly to the courts, but the rewarding of deserving foreigners, metics and citizens was a job for the Assembly. Thus, in a time of food shortage the Assembly's main task seems to have been to pass decrees honouring whoever brought corn to Athens and sold it cheaply or distributed it gratis.[329] Even more important was the stimulation of democratic participation: willingness to stand up and speak or make a proposal in the Assembly was encouraged by honorary decrees or by giving gold crowns worth 1000 drachmas to, for example, the best *rhetor* of the year[330] or the best board of *prytaneis*[331] or of *proedroi*.[332] A rough calculation shows that the cost to the state of these honorary decrees and the like was as great as the pay of the Council.[333] Also, of course, honorary decrees played a highly important part in diplomacy: alliances and treaties always end with honours to the other party's envoys,[334] and foreign rulers and statesmen were often rewarded with gold crowns or even with citizenship. Both Philip of Macedon[335] and Alexander the Great[336] were made Athenian citizens, though, naturally, neither of them migrated to Athens.

Decrees about cult and the religious festivals form a third numerically important group. They dealt essentially with details,[337] financial and otherwise, because the basic structure of the festivals was laid down by law, *inter alia* in the great sacrificial calendar.[338]

The number of decrees regulating state finances is surprisingly small,

[323] Dem. 50.8.   [324] Dem. 15.9.

[325] De Laix (1973) 78–84; Connor (1974); Hornblower (1983) 116–20.

[326] Hansen (1987a) 183–4 n. 724.   [327] Such as *IG* II² 240, quoted on p. 148.

[328] Dem. 20.154, 24.215.

[329] *Hesperia* 43 (1974) 322–4 n. 3. Isager and Hansen (1975) 207 n. 55.

[330] *IG* II² 223 A.   [331] *Agora* XV 13.1–2.   [332] Hyp. 4.4–5.

[333] Hansen (1987a) 115.   [334] Dem. 19.234; Tod 118.37–9. Henry (1983) 262.

[335] Plut. *Dem.* 22.4. Osborne (1983) T 68.

[336] Schol. Aristid. *Pan.* 178.16. Osborne (1983) T 69.   [337] E.g. *IG* II² 120.

[338] Dow (1959) 8–24.

but that is probably due to what we have already explained – that the *merismos*, with which the Assembly had nothing to do, settled the fixed budget for each board of magistrates. The people's power of decision in financial matters was limited to the imposition of *eisphorai*,[339] the provision of finance for public works[340] and the settling of the amount to be paid as *theorika*;[341] but it did also have its own fixed annual budget of 10 talents,[342] over which it had free disposal and which was used partly for various grants of honours and partly to defray the cost of publication on stone of many of the decrees.

The group of decrees about legislation and the administration of justice comprised two matters: every time a new law was to be promulgated the Assembly had to pass a decree for the appointment of *nomothetai*; and whenever a political prosecution was brought before the Assembly, for instance by *eisangelia* or *probole*, it had to pass a decree handing the case on to the People's Court. Thus, the Assembly retained to the end an important role in the initial phases of legislation and criminal proceedings.

If the surviving decrees give a true reflection of the business of the Assembly, it can be concluded that many important affairs of Athenian society lay outside or only on the margin of the Assembly's competence. There are no decrees about the silver-mines or customs or external trade (apart from grain-supply) or trade in the markets; there is nothing on the letting of public property or on manufacture or agriculture or town-planning, and nothing on education or schools. In some cases that is because the matter fell within the scope of another organ of state. The *nomothetai*, for example, passed laws about mining,[343] customs[344] and external trade;[345] and the Auctions Board (*poletai*) along with the Council, handled the letting of mining-concessions.[346] But in other cases the explanation is different: fields such as education, manufacture and land economy were outside the concern of a democratic *polis* such as Athens altogether: state regulation was at a minimum, limited mainly to fiscal considerations, and the rest was left to the private initiative of citizens and metics.

Judicial sentences   In the fifth century and the first half of the fourth the Assembly still had certain powers as a court of law, and its decisions in such cases were sentences (*kriseis*), not decrees (*psephismata*). Those powers probably existed only in relation to *eisangeliai*; but *eisangelia* was

---

[339] Dem. 3.4.   [340] *IG* II² 403.
[341] Dem. 44.37–8. Hansen (1983a) 199.
[342] *IG* II² 43.66–9 = Tod 123 and Harding (1985) no. 35. Jones (1957) 154 n. 33.
[343] Dem. 37.35, 38.   [344] Shear (1987) 8.   [345] Dem. 34.37.
[346] Arist. *Ath. Pol.* 47.2; *SEG* 12 100.

extremely important, because it was the procedure most used for the prosecution of generals and political leaders for alleged corruption and treachery.[347] It is clear from the evidence that in the first half of the fourth century the Assembly often decided to try such cases itself instead of passing them on to the courts,[348] but after 362 there is not a single example of the Assembly functioning as a court of law, and since we know that the law on *eisangelia* was reformed between 362 and 355[349] we may reasonably suppose that it was that reform which required all *eisangeliai* in future to be judged by the People's Court. We do not know the purpose of the reform, but both economic and constitutional considerations may have played a part. The trial of an *eisangelia* took a whole day,[350] and must have been the sole item on the agenda when it was judged by the Assembly; so it cost a whole talent (a drachma per man for all 6000 participants) to try an *eisangelia* in the Assembly,[351] whereas it cost only 250 drachmas (3 obols per man)[352] for a jury panel of 501, and not more than 500 drachmas or 750 drachmas if a double or triple panel of jurors was used. At the end of the Social War, in 355, the Athenians were bankrupt: that was just the year for thinking of economies and reducing the number of Assembly meetings.[353] By means of that reduction the Athenians also carried out one of the constitutional reforms recommended by Aristotle for turning a radical democracy into a more moderate one. Paying the whole people to take part in political activity, he says, makes radical democracy the most expensive of all constitutions: if the state's income declines it must be advised to cut down the number of meetings of its assembly.[354] Now, the reform of the law of *eisangelia*, by which the Assembly lost its last power to sit as a court, may be connected with the decision to hold three meetings a prytany.[355] Both changes can be narrowed down to the years around 355: they modified the constitution a little in the 'moderate' direction and fit in well with the demand at the end of the Social War for a return to the 'ancestral constitution'.

Elections The third power of the Assembly was the election of magistrates and other officials, such as envoys. The election of magistrates required a *probouleuma* of the Council,[356] but the election was not technically a *psephisma*.[357] The instructions given to envoys were, indeed, *psephismata*, but their election counted as a separate matter.

---

[347] See pp. 215–18.   [348] Dem. 49.10. Hansen (1975) 53 n. 15.
[349] Hansen (1975) 15–17.   [350] See p. 187.
[351] Perhaps two thirds of a talent. Hansen (1987a) 153 n. 317.
[352] Arist. *Ath. Pol.* 62.2.   [353] Hansen (1975) 55.   [354] Arist. *Pol.* 1320a22ff.
[355] See p. 134.   [356] Arist. *Ath. Pol.* 44.4.   [357] Hansen (1987a) 182 n. 698.

The vast majority of magistrates were selected by lot, but, as we have noted already, some of the most important ones were elected: the Athenians naturally had no desire to fight under a general picked out of the hat. It is more noteworthy that the new financial magistracies created in the fourth century were also manned with persons chosen by election: the treasurer of the Military Fund, the Board for the Theoric Fund, and the new post that Lykourgos held after 338, the Controller of the Finances (*ho epi tei dioikesei*).[358] It was in fact these elected financial magistrates who were more or less responsible for the revival of Athens after her defeats: Euboulos as a member of the Theoric Board after 355,[359] and Lykourgos as the Controller after the peace with Philip in 338.[360] In the same period Demosthenes served on the Theoric Board[361] and Demades as treasurer of the Military Fund.[362]

Magistrates were elected at a special Assembly meeting held in the spring.[363] The election was by show of hands,[364] but did not, as already noted, count as a *psephisma*; and that was not a merely formal difference, for a *psephisma* could always be challenged and brought before a court by a *graphe paranomon*, whereas the *graphe* could not be used (as far as we know) to challenge an election, and the citizen who proposed a candidate could not, like the proposer of a decree, be called to account for his proposal. Control over the Assembly was in principle achieved in that case through the *dokimasia* which every magistrate had to undergo before taking office.[365]

The procedure for filling magistracies is another of Aristotle's criteria for how radical a democracy is: in original 'moderate' democracy the magistrates are elected,[366] whereas selection by lot is a characteristic of the fully-formed radical democracy.[367] So, while the fact that the financial officers in fourth-century Athens were elected and not chosen by lot was certainly an increase in the powers of the Assembly, it was not a step on the road of radical democracy, because election was a hallmark of 'moderate' democracy: in this respect Athenian democracy, in Demosthenes' time, was something in between the two.[368]

---

[358] See pp. 263–4. [359] Aeschin. 3.25. Cawkwell (1963).
[360] Hyp. fr. 139. Mitchel (1970); Burke (1985). [361] Aeschin. 3.24.
[362] *IG* II² 1493–5 = *SEG* 21 552. [363] Arist. *Ath. Pol.* 44.4; *IG* II² 892.
[364] Din. 3.1. Hansen (1987a) 191 n. 781. [365] See pp. 218–20. [366] Arist. *Pol.* 1318b29.
[367] Arist. *Pol.* 1317b20–1. [368] See p. 233.

7

The Laws and the *Nomothetai*

In modern public-law theory a distinction is often made between 'general norms' without limit of duration and individual norms of limited duration – that is to say, emptied of validity once their concrete purpose has been fulfilled.[1] Like many other theories in public law, this distinction has roots in antiquity: it can be traced in Aristotle's writings,[2] it was taught in Plato's Academy,[3] and it was practised in fourth-century Athens.

In Attic Greek there are three words for what we nowadays call a law: *thesmos*, *nomos* and *psephisma*. *Thesmos* means something 'laid down' and is the oldest of the three. The distinction between *thesmos* and *nomos* is purely chronological: Drakon's laws in 621 and Solon's in 594 were *thesmoi*,[4] but Kleisthenes' laws in 507 were called *nomoi*. The new word *nomos* was probably brought into currency precisely by Kleisthenes when he established the democracy in Athens.[5] So in classical Attic there are only two words for a law: *nomos*, which means originally 'distribution', then 'custom', and finally 'law'; and *psephisma*, which means a decision, in principle one taken by means of *psephoi*, pebbles, which seem to have been used in voting at the beginning of the fifth century.[6] In all the sources for Athens in the fifth century *nomos* and *psephisma* can both properly be translated 'law', and both words can be used of the same norm. In Xenophon's description of the Trial of the Generals, for example, the law of Kannonos about trials for treason is described first as a *psephisma* and a line or two later on as a *nomos*.[7] Nevertheless, though both words refer to the same decision, some traces of a difference of meaning can be seen in the sources: the word *nomos* was used for

[1] Bentham (1816) 8.95; Wilson (1887) 209; Kelsen (1946) 258.
[2] Arist. *Eth. Nic.* 1137b13–14, 27–9; *Pol.* 1292a4–7, 32–7.
[3] Pl. *Def.* 415B.
[4] *IG* I³ 104 = *M&L* 86 and Fornara (1977) no. 15B; Plut. *Sol.* 19.4.
[5] Arist. *Ath. Pol.* 29.3. Ostwald (1968) 55–6.
[6] Staveley (1972) 84–5; Boegehold (1963) 367–8.   [7] Xen. *Hell.* 1.7.20, 23.

preference when the emphasis was on the content of a law, the word *psephisma* when the actual procedure of decision-making was being stressed.[8]

In the fourth century, however, the words were used in a quite different way: the purpose was now to distinguish between two different kinds of norm, and the words *nomos* and *psephisma* came to describe the two kinds. *Nomos* meant a general norm without limit of duration, whereas *psephisma* meant an individual norm which, once carried out, was emptied of its content.[9] For convenience, in what follows *nomoi* will be called 'laws' and *psephismata* will be called 'decrees'.

THE REVISION OF THE LAWS, 410–399 BC

410–404 BC

When Athens in the Peloponnesian War found itself in its first serious constitutional crisis since Kleisthenes, the Athenians were living, as always, under the laws of Drakon and Solon. The extensive constitutional developments of the sixth and fifth centuries had, of course, introduced many deep changes in the rules determining the powers of the various organs of state; but those changes had had only limited influence on the laws of Drakon and Solon, which concerned mainly what we should call private law, criminal law, and the law of procedure.[10] Nothing suggests that any attempt had been made to revise or recodify the laws before the end of the fifth century.[11]

The defeat of the Athenians in Sicily in 413 resulted in the oligarchical revolution of 411, and democracy was restored only in spring 410. In the course of those constitutional struggles both democrats and oligarchs had claimed for their side the 'ancestral constitution'.[12] All were agreed that the laws of Drakon and Solon were the basis on which the state of Athens ought to rely, but there was discord as to how far Drakon and Solon had been pioneers of democracy or advocates of oligarchy.[13] The lack of agreement resulted partly from lack of information and partly from ideological differences. The laws of Drakon and Solon probably contained no constitutional provisions,[14] and no one rightly knew what was the law in force when it had remained uncodified for the best part of 200 years. So one of the first decisions of the democrats in 410 was to set up a

---

[8] Quass (1971) 23–4; Hansen (1983a) 162–3.   [9] Hansen (1983a) 180–3.
[10] See p. 31.   [11] Ruschenbusch (1966) 32–7.
[12] Arist. *Ath. Pol.* 29.3 *versus* Thuc. 8.97.6. Fuks (1953); Lévy (1976) 173–208.
[13] Hansen (1989c) 76–7, 88–9.   [14] Von Fritz (1977) 245–7; Hansen (1989c) 83–5.

Codification Board (*anagrapheis ton nomon*) and give it the task of collecting and publishing the laws then in force, first and foremost the laws of Drakon and Solon.[15] The board was able quite quickly to republish Drakon's law of homicide and perhaps also an important law on the powers of the Council;[16] but the revision of Solon's laws must have been a hard job, for it took the board the six years from 410 to 404 to complete it[17] and to have the completed code inscribed on a wall of the Stoa Basileios, the portico of the king archon, in the Agora – from which it seems to have been removed shortly after, when the Thirty came to power.[18] The leading figure on the Codification Board was a man called Nikomachos; in 399/8 he was put on trial on a charge of manipulating the laws and of having helped the oligarchs to power in 404. The charge was probably false, for Nikomachos was set to carry on the work of codification after the restoration of full democracy in 403 and did so till the completion of the whole revision in 400/399.[19]

403–399 BC

After the restoration of democracy in 403 the Athenians decided that the laws of Drakon and Solon should be in force until further notice, but once again that they should be revised, ratified and republished. The principles to govern the codification were laid down in a decree proposed and carried by Teisamenos, cited *in extenso* in Andokides' speech *On the Mysteries*.[20] Two legislative boards (*nomothetai*) were set up, one elected by the Council of Five Hundred, the other, 500 strong, elected by the various demes in their deme assemblies. The former board was entrusted with the collection and preliminary publication of all the laws to be considered, and may well have been in practice the board of *anagrapheis*, revived and once again headed by Nikomachos;[21] The second board of *nomothetai* had to perform a 'test' (*dokimasia*) of all the laws,[22] i.e. after a hearing, to vote whether or not a particular law should be accepted and included in the revised code. The laws passed by the *nomothetai* were to be once again written up on the wall in the Stoa Basileios; and in future the Areopagos was to watch over the administration of the laws by the magistrates. It is important to notice that ratification of the laws was entrusted to the *nomothetai*, and the Assembly had absolutely no role in the work of legislation.[23] We must also understand that the revised law-

---

[15] *IG* I³ 104.5–6 = *M&L* 86 and Fornara (1977) no. 15B; Lys. 30.2, 25.
[16] *M&L* 86; *IG* I³ 105, cf. Lewis (1967) 132. [17] Lys. 30.2–3; Clinton (1982) 28.
[18] Andoc. 1.84; MacDowell (1962) 194–9; Fingarette (1971). [19] Lys. 30. Dow (1960).
[20] Andoc. 1.83–4. [21] Lys. 30.25. 28–9. Hansen (1990b) 68–9.
[22] Andoc. 1.84. [23] MacDowell (1962) 195; Hansen (1987a) 103 with n. 667.

code included a whole set of constitutional laws (i.e. rules defining the powers of the organs of state)[24] and no longer only private law, criminal law and law of procedure.

It appears from Andokides' speech that this time the revision of the laws was completed relatively quickly, and so was their inscription on the wall.[25] The revision included in addition to the laws of Solon and Drakon a number of laws passed under the democracy down to 404 and published on *stelai* put up in various places.[26] Even that was not the end of codification, for Nikomachos and his colleagues went on to codify all the sacrifices the state had to carry out and pay for during the year.[27] That took four years to complete, with the publication of a huge sacrificial calendar, of which we possess some fragments.[28]

Thereafter the law in force in Athens was those laws ratified by the *nomothetai* plus any new laws that might be passed after the revision was completed. They still talked of the 'laws of Drakon and Solon',[29] but that is not surprising, considering that numerous archaic laws, mostly about private law, went on unchanged throughout the fourth century, and so must have been received into the new code, with or without corrections. Homicide, for example, in the age of Demosthenes was still handled under Drakon's law of 621,[30] and inheritance law was still based on Solon's law of 594.[31] In everyday speech, even in speeches before the People's Court, 'law of Solon' was just a way of saying 'law at present in force',[32] and was used not only for genuine Solonian laws carried over into the new code, but even for new laws, such as the laws about the *nomothetai*, which were only passed in the years after 403.[33]

After Andokides' speech *On the Mysteries* we hear no more of the wall in the Stoa Basileios, and when a speaker names his source for a law he refers either to a *stele*[34] or to the state archive in the Metroön.[35] The explanation is no doubt that the new revised corpus of laws did not stay unchanged for many years after 400, and corrections became so extensive that the Athenians had to give up continually republishing them on stone. The original laws were, thereafter, written on papyrus and kept in the archive; some were also copied and published on stone, but the idea of a law-code stable enough to be worth engraving in marble was abandoned.

---

[24] E.g. Dem. 24.20–3, 33; Aeschin. 3.38–40. Lewis in *IG* I³ p. 125; Hansen (1985c) 61.
[25] Andoc. 1.85; Dem. 24.42. Hansen (1990b) 65.
[26] Andoc. 1.96–8; Dem. 24.42. Clinton (1982) 28–30.   [27] Lys. 30. Dow (1959, 1960).
[28] *Hesperia* 3 (1934) 46 no. 34; 4 (1935) 5–32 nos. 1–2; 10 (1941) 31–7 no. 2.
[29] Dem. 23.51, 24.142.
[30] Dem. 23.37; 43.57; *IG* I³ 104 = *M&L* 86 and Fornara (1977) no. 15B. MacDowell (1963) 6–7.
[31] Dem. 44.67–8, 46.14.   [32] Schreiner (1913) 12–60.
[33] Dem. 20.90; Hyp. 5.22.   [34] Dem. 59.75–6.   [35] Dem. 25.99; Lycurg. 1.66.

Organization of the law-code

The laws of Athens were written and grouped on quite different principles from those of today. Laws in a modern society are organized according to content; in Athens they were organized according to procedure, i.e. according to which magistrate was responsible for their administration. Nowadays we distinguish constitutional law, administrative law, criminal law, and so on; in Athens they distinguished the Council's laws, the archon's laws, the king archon's laws,[36] and so on. Rules of quite different content – according to our way of thinking – could thus be found side by side in the same section of the Athenian code. However, the law of the *nomothetai* cited at Demosthenes 24.20–3 shows that the whole corpus could be divided into four main sections: general laws, laws within the competence of the Council, laws within the competence of the nine archons, and laws for the other magistrates. And, since each magistrate had, up to a point, a competence determined on a material basis, the formal division of the laws did correspond roughly with a material order; thus, family and inheritance laws all came under the archon, much of the law about religion came under the king archon, and the polemarch must have had the whole law relating to metics and other non-Athenians.[37] The laws about the *nomothetai* and legislative procedure probably stood in the Council's group of laws, since it was the *prytaneis* and the Council who had to participate in the appointment of *nomothetai*.[38] In contradistinction to the original Solonian laws, the revised corpus of laws came to include quite a number of constitutional laws (i.e. norms defining the structure and powers of the organs of government).[39] They did not form a separate and especially protected part of the law-code; the Athenians had no constitution in the formal sense, and, though they sometimes used entrenchment clauses to make it more difficult to reverse a law or a decree,[40] such clauses were not attached to what we call constitutional laws.

LEGISLATION IN THE FOURTH CENTURY

Consequently upon the law-revision of 403/2 the Athenians acquired for themselves a new definition of a 'law', a new organ of legislation, a new

---

[36] Ath. 234F, 235C; Poll. 3.39, 6.35. Schöll (1886) 88–91; Stroud (1968) 32–3.
[37] Arist. *Ath. Pol.* 56–8.   [38] Dem. 24.27, 47–8.
[39] E.g. *IG* I³ 105; Andoc. 1.87; Aeschin. 1.34–5; Arist. *Ath. Pol.* 43.3–6.
[40] Dem. 23.62; *IG* II² 43.51–63 = Tod 123 and Harding (1985) no. 35. Lewis (1974a).

legislative procedure, and a new procedure for the scrutiny of the laws. Laws in future were to be sharply distinguished from decrees; they were to be made by the *nomothetai* and not the Assembly, they were to be passed by a procedure analogous to a trial, and if their validity was questioned they were to be scrutinized before the People's Court in a new procedure, the 'public action for having proposed and carried an unsuitable law' (*graphe nomon me epitedeion theinai*). The older institution for scrutinizing the laws, the *graphe paranomon*, was henceforward only to be used against decrees, and must therefore, after 403, be understood as a 'public prosecution for unconstitutional proposal of a *decree*'.

The laws about legislation

The new legislative procedure was regulated by a series of laws, of which we know three. (Whether there were more cannot be shown from the evidence at our disposal.[41])

1 *The 'review law'*[42] Demosthenes in his speech against Timokrates cites a law to the effect that the whole corpus of the laws, section by section, is to be put up for acceptance at the first Assembly meeting of each year. If a law in any section is rejected by the people, any citizen can make a proposal to change it. The people choose five representatives to defend the existing law, and both parties bring their arguments before a board of *nomothetai*, who decide by vote whether to uphold the existing provision unchanged or to substitute for it the alternative proposal.[43]

2 *The 'repeal law'* Another law cited in the same speech prescribes that any citizen, at any time in the year, can put up a proposal for changing an existing law, on condition only that he offer an alternative for a board of *nomothetai* to consider.[44]

3 *The 'inspection law'* In the speech *Against Ktesiphon* Aischines paraphrases a law that requires the *thesmothetai* to keep an eye on the laws of Athens: if they find invalid laws in the corpus, or inconsistent laws, or more than one law on the same point, the relevant laws are to be put before the people, who will set up a board of *nomothetai* to settle the matter.[45]

---

[41] MacDowell (1975) reconstructs five different laws, but see Hansen (1980a); Rhodes (1985a); Hansen (1985b) 346–52; Rhodes (1987) 16–20.

[42] MacDowell (1975) 66–9.   [43] Dem. 24.20–3; Schöll (1886) 84–110.

[44] Dem. 24.33; Dem. 20.89–94. Schöll (1886) 111–39; Hansen (1985b) 346–52.

[45] Aeschin. 3.38–40; Theophr. *Nomoi* fr. 1 (Szegedy-Maszak).

The nomothetai

From the laws and decrees that have survived epigraphically or in the literature we can draw the conclusion that the new legislative organ must have been set up at the beginning of the fourth century, or rather in 403/2 directly after the restoration of democracy.[46] The epigraphical record comprises several hundred decrees passed by the Assembly[47] and seven laws passed by the *nomothetai*.[48] The enormous difference in the number of surviving laws and decrees is something we shall return to: for the moment what is important is that the division of types of norm between the Assembly and the *nomothetai* was scrupulously maintained. If a decision is called a 'law' it begins with the formula 'It was decided by the *nomothetai*',[49] whereas in all cases where the decision is called a 'decree' we meet the formula 'It was decided by the people' or 'It was decided by the Council and the people'.[50] Examination of the terminology in the literary sources gives the same result. Only in five cases are we told that the Assembly has passed a 'law' as a decree; and, since all the cases are datable to the year 403/2, those laws were probably passed before the creation of the new legislative organ.[51] The fourth-century sources show without exception that the Athenians accepted the new distinction terminologically: *nomoi* are always passed by *nomothetai* and never by the Assembly. The question remains whether it was also accepted in substance, i.e. whether *nomoi* were always general norms without limit of duration and *psephismata* always individual or time-limited norms; this will be discussed below at pp. 172–3.

What persons were *nomothetai*? Demosthenes' speech against Timokrates informs us: in the review law we are told that *nomothetai* are to be taken from those who have sworn the Heliastic Oath.[52] In compliance with that law Timokrates in 354/3 had got a decree of the Assembly passed setting up a board of *nomothetai*, and in the decree it was laid down that 1001 *nomothetai* should be chosen from those who had sworn the Heliastic Oath and that the Council should assist the *nomothetai*.[53] *Hoi nomothetai* were therefore recruited from the panel of 6000 who had sworn the Heliastic Oath (*hoi omomokotes*), as were the jurors in the People's Court (*hoi dikastai*);[54] and by analogy with the jury court it may

---

[46] Hansen (1990b) 69.   [47] See p. 156.

[48] Hansen (1983a) 164 n. 7, 177.

[49] E.g. *SEG* 12 87.6–7. Hansen (1987a) 174 n. 623.

[50] E.g. *IG* II² 206 4–5, 28–30; 237.5, 31. Rhodes (1972) 64–5.

[51] Hansen (1983a) 165–6.   [52] Dem. 24.21. See pp. 182–3.   [53] Dem. 24.27.

[54] Hansen (1980a) 100; (1985b) 363–5; *pace* MacDowell (1975) 65 and Rhodes (1985a) 57.

be supposed that *nomothetai* were picked by lot for a given day from among those who presented themselves in the morning, and that the number of *nomothetai* varied according to the importance of the legislation proposed – perhaps at least 501, but for more important matters 1001, 1501, or even more.

The legislative procedure

It has often puzzled historians that the Athenians had at least three different laws prescribing each a different legislative procedure, and several reconstructions of the task of the *nomothetai* rest upon the supposition that the governing laws must have been passed in succession or have dealt with different kinds of law-revision.[55] There is no ground for such a supposition: on the contrary, it was typical of Athenian democracy to have several procedures available at the same time for the same thing. For example, in court procedure there were seven different ways of bringing a case against a corrupt magistrate; the procedures differed in the way they were begun, but they all resulted in a trial before the People's Court.[56] So it was with legislation; it was only the question of who took the initiative that distinguished the three laws: it could be taken (a) in the Assembly, or (b) by any citizen, or (c) by magistrates, namely the *thesmothetai*.[57] Apart from that the legislative procedure was in its principal characteristics the same, and can be described in the following points.

1 The procedure can be initiated in three different ways, as we have just seen.
2 Legislation seems always to have the character of a revision of the code, i.e. changing the law currently in force.[58] That goes, undoubtedly, with the adversarial nature of the procedure, every legislative proposal being seen as an accusation against the existing laws.
3 It is the Assembly that decides whether a revision of the code is needed,[59] and, if so, chooses the five advocates to defend the existing laws [60]
4 A proposal to change the existing laws must be published before the Monument to the Eponymous Heroes in the Agora, to enable any citizen who wishes to have a say in the matter.[61]

---

[55] MacDowell (1975); Rhodes (1985a); (1987) 15–20.
[56] See p. 193.   [57] (a) Dem. 24.20; (b) Dem. 24.33; (c) Aeschin. 3.38.
[58] (a) Dem. 24.21; (b) Dem. 24.33; (c) Aeschin. 3.39.
[59] (a) Dem. 24.21, 27; (b) Dem. 3.10–13; (c) Aeschin. 3.39.
[60] (a) Dem. 24.23; (b) Dem. 24.36; (c) see Hansen (1985b) 355.
[61] (a) Dem. 24.23; (b) Dem. 20.94, 24.36; (c) Aeschin. 3.39.

5 The Council is involved in the legislative procedure in so far as it calls and fixes the day's programme for the Assembly meetings which will prepare the setting-up of *nomothetai*, and brings the proposal for the new law before the Assembly. In every case the legislative procedure must have involved one or more (open) *probouleumata*.[62] Furthermore, the Council had a special legislation secretary,[63] which indicates that discussion of new laws took place in the Council as well as in the Assembly.

6 The proposal for the change of law must be read out in the Assembly, and apparently can be debated there.[64]

7 At a following Assembly the people decide by decree the setting-up of *nomothetai* and their number, and vote a consequential payment to the *nomothetai*.[65]

8 On the morning of the day fixed for the consideration of a legislative proposal the appropriate number of *nomothetai* are picked by lot from those who have sworn the Heliastic Oath.[66]

9 The meeting is chaired by a board of perhaps nine *proedroi*, one of them being chosen foreman of the board (*epistates ton proedron*).[67]

10 The act of legislation proceeds like a trial. The author of the proposal for change comes forward as the accuser of the existing laws. After he has spoken, the five advocates chosen by the people to defend the existing laws are given their turn.[68] When both parties have spoken, the *nomothetai* decide by show of hands.[69] If the majority is for the proposal for change, that proposal there and then becomes the law in force; if the majority is against change, the existing laws survive unchanged.

11 A meeting lasted only a single day; actually, it is likely that the *nomothetai* could deal with more than one proposal in the same meeting.[70] The *nomothetai* were paid for their services,[71] probably at the same rate as the jurors in the People's Court.

[62] (a) Dem. 24.21, 27; (b) see Hansen (1985b) 354; (c) Aeschin. 3.39, cf. Dem. 24.48. De Laix (1973) 66.

[63] Arist. *Ath. Pol.* 54.4; *Agora* XV 62.235–6. See p. 257.

[64] (a) Dem. 24.25; (b) Dem. 24.36; (c) Aeschin. 3.39. On (a) and (b) see Hansen (1985b) 355. Cf. Din. 1.42.

[65] (a) Dem. 24.21; (b) ?; (c) ?

[66] (a) Dem. 24.21, 27; (b) Dem. 20.93, see Hansen (1985b) 363–4; (c) ?

[67] *IG* II² 222.41–52; Dem. 24.71. Rhodes (1972) 28; MacDowell (1975) 63; Hansen (1980a) 103 n. 17.

[68] Dem. 24.23.

[69] Dem. 24.33. MacDowell (1975) 70; Hansen (1985b) 365–8, *pace* Rhodes (1985a) 58.

[70] Dem. 24.29. [71] Dem. 24.21.

The definition of a law

In the codification of 403/2 the Athenians passed a law to define what in the future would count as a 'law'. This fundamental rule, which for simplicity we shall call the 'law of definition', is cited or paraphrased in several sources. The fullest citation, which is also the earliest, is in Andokides' speech *On the Mysteries* (400/399), section 87:

> Law: magistrates must under no circumstances use unwritten law. No decree passed by the Council or the people may have higher validity than a law. No law may be passed that applies only to a single person. The same law shall apply to all Athenians, unless otherwise decided [in a meeting of the Assembly] with a quorum of 6000, by secret ballot.

This is of course a condensed version of the law, but it comprises three reforms of wide-ranging significance.

1 *The prohibition of unwritten law* By this provision the role of custom as a source of law was reduced. We have seen that in the fifth century *nomos* meant both custom and law; in the fourth century, in everyday speech, it continued to have both senses, but in legal contexts the concept of a 'law' came to be restricted to a written statute passed by the legislative organ of the state.[72] That is not to say that customary law played no part as a source of law. It is important to notice that the prohibition of unwritten law was directed against *magistrates*. The oath that the jurors of the People's Court took every year began as follows: 'I will cast my vote in consonance with the laws and with the decrees passed by the Assembly and by the Council.[73] But if there is no law [on a point] I will give judgement in consonance with my sense of what is most just.'[74] But the right to judge according to one's own sense of justice implies a right to use unwritten law and custom if there is no written law on a matter;[75] and, taken in conjunction with the Heliastic Oath, the law of definition reveals a fundamental feature of fourth-century democracy: the magistrates are *under* the law, but the jurors, being guardians of the law, though normally required to follow it, can in certain circumstances be regarded as *over* the law, and are vouchsafed a power denied to the magistrates.

---

[72] MacDowell (1978) 47.   [73] Dem. 19.179, 24.149–51.
[74] Dem. 20.118. See p. 182.
[75] Neither MacDowell (1978) 47 nor Clinton (1982) 35–7 discusses the distinction between magistrates and jurors.

2   *The distinction between laws and decrees*   By defining 'laws' as rules binding everyone the Athenians introduced a fundamental difference between general norms, passed as laws, and individual norms, passed as decrees (an individual norm is one that refers to a named person or a non-recurring matter). Equally fundamental is the duration of a law's validity, as indicated in the Platonic *Definitions*: '*nomos* [is] a decision in the affairs of the *polis* taken by the *plethos* (the majority) without limit of duration; *psephisma* [is] a decision in the affairs of the *polis* limited in duration'.[76] Actually, the question of duration is not referred to in the law of definition as we know it from Andokides; but the surviving laws and decrees from the fourth century show that the Athenians made use of the distinction between permanent and time-limited as a basis for their distinction between laws and decrees: from the restoration of democracy in 403/2 onwards, rules with a limited duration, which exhaust their content as soon as their purpose is fulfilled, are always passed as decrees, whereas a rule is only passed as a law if it is both general and without limit of duration. The distinction can be clarified by the following chart.

	Temporary	Permanent
General	*Psephisma* that forty triremes be launched, that all classes up to the age of forty-five be called up to man the ships and that an *eisphora* of 60 talents be imposed (Dem. 3.4)	*Nomos eisangeltikos* against anyone who attempts to overthrow the democracy or to betray the Athenian armed forces or to speak to the people after taking bribes (Hyperid. 3.7–8)
Individual	*Psephisma* that Demosthenes be crowned with a golden crown to be awarded in the theatre at the Greater Dionysia (Aeschin. 3.49)	*Psephisma* bestowing citizen rights on Dionysius I of Syracuse and all his descendants and granting permanent right of *prosodos* to the people and to the council (*IG* II² 103)

Now, theory is one thing and practice another: were the Athenians able to operate this distinction between general and individual norms, and did they respect the distinction during the eighty-two years that the new democracy lasted?

The first question, how easy or hard it was to distinguish between general and individual norms, can be answered first by an analogy and

[76] Pl. *Def.* 415B.

second by an argument from silence. The analogy is furnished by a constitutional change instituted in Obwalden in 1922, when it was decided that all laws (*Gesetze*), previously passed in the *Landsgemeinde* by a show of hands, would in future be submitted to a written vote, while all important decrees (*Verwaltungsakte*) would be passed in the *Landsgemeinde* as before. This Swiss distinction between *Gesetze* and *Verwaltungsakte* answers nicely to the Athenian distinction between *nomoi* and *psephismata*; and there has never, since 1922, been a problem about deciding which norms are *Gesetze* and which are *Verwaltungsakte*.[77] The argument from silence is the absence of any indication in the sources that the fourth-century Athenians were ever at odds whether a given norm should be passed as a law or as a decree. Nor is there any *a priori* reason to suppose that the distinction was particularly difficult to draw.

The question of how far the Athenians respected the distinction in practice can be divided into two: are there any cases of general norms without limit of duration being passed as decrees, and are there any cases of individual or time-limited norms being passed as laws?

In Athens all treaties were made by the Assembly as decrees,[78] even peace treaties claiming to be 'for ever'.[79] Today we should certainly say that a law is a rule binding the citizens of a state, whereas a treaty is a compact between two or more states.[80] Can we suppose that the Athenians had the same sense of the difference between treaties and laws? Well, in the *Politics* Aristotle specifically distinguishes between laws (*nomoi*) and decisions about war and peace and alliances.[81] He is not talking explicitly about Athens, but when all our surviving sources show that Athens always without exception passed declarations of war and peace and alliance as decrees and never as laws, that is a strong argument that the Athenians, like Aristotle, distinguished between laws and treaties.

Except for treaties there are very few cases of a general norm without limit of duration being passed as a decree. In the whole surviving epigraphical record – some hundreds of decrees – there is only one unambiguous example, the decision to undertake the public fostering of children whose fathers had fallen fighting for the democracy in the civil war of 404–403. The decision was probably taken in 403/2, i.e. before the introduction of the new definition of a law.[82] There are a couple more possible cases in the fourth century, but in none can it be determined with certainty that the Athenians legislated by decree. In the literary sources there are references to about 220 decrees, and they include a

---

[77] Hansen (1983a) 217–19.   [78] E.g. *IG* II² 98.6–7, 23–5.
[79] E.g. *IG* II² 97 = Tod 127.   [80] Starke (1989) 71ff. See Hansen (1983a) 183.
[81] Arist. *Pol.* 1298a4–5.
[82] *SEG* 28 46 = Harding (1985) no. 8. Hansen (1983a) 184.

dozen unmistakable cases of general norms with no limit of duration:[83] an example is Demosthenes' proposal that the Areopagos should have the right to judge all offences.[84] But it is striking that all those cases can be assigned to two short periods, the year 403/2, before the new definition of a law had come into force, and the years 340–338, when the Athenians were waging their last major war against Philip of Macedon, and may have been obliged, in a crisis, to pass laws as decrees because the ordinary legislative procedure was too time-consuming.

For the reverse case there are in the surviving inscriptions three examples of individual norms with time-limits being passed as laws.[85] All three cases are honorary decrees for named persons, in which the Assembly lays down that the decision about finding the money for the honours is to be put to the *nomothetai* for ratification and consequently passed as a law. This is, indeed, inescapable evidence that laws were not always general norms without limit of duration. But on the other side the point has to be made that this particular abandonment of the usual distinction between laws and decrees is expressly allowed in the law of definition, which prescribes that, exceptionally, a law (*nomos*) can be passed relating to a named individual, provided only that the Assembly has allowed it at a meeting with a quorum of 6000, by secret ballot.[86] One of the three decrees is a citizenship grant for one Peisitheides from Delos, and citizenship grants always had to be passed twice by the Assembly, the second time with a quorum of 6000 and secret ballot;[87] in the other two cases it is a reasonable guess that they also were passed in an Assembly with a quorum of 6000.

The reason why laws about individuals were sometimes allowed may well be that the Athenian budget in the fourth century was organized on the basis of the allocation of different sources of revenue to different exchequers; and the rule governing that allocation (called *merismos*) was a law. If a decree involved a breach of the *merismos* it had to have a dispensation, and that had necessarily to be by law, not just by decree, because by the reform of 403/2 a law was regarded as the higher norm and so could not be changed by decree alone.[88]

3 Laws as the higher norms The principle that no decree has greater validity than any law is often cited in the sources, either in that form[89] or in a variant, i.e. that decrees must be passed in consonance with the

[83] Hansen (1983a) 187–91.   [84] Din. 1.62, 82–3.
[85] *IG* II² 222.41–6, 330.18–23; *SIG*³ 298.35–41.   [86] Andoc. 1.87.
[87] *IG* II² 222. See p. 130.
[88] Hansen (1985b) 360–2, *pace* Rhodes (1985a) 59, (1987) 15.
[89] Hyp. 5.22.

laws.[90] By this provision laws became the higher norms in relation to decrees: it is powerful testimony to the Athenian effort to recover respect for the laws. Since Ephialtes' reforms in 462 the Assembly had more and more frequently used its increased power to legislate, and the traditional sense of the priority of the laws had given way to a sense that the people in their Assembly were the highest power in the state.[91] But in 403 the Athenians returned to the idea that the laws, not the people, must be the highest power and that the laws must be stable, even if not wholly entrenched.[92] Demosthenes in his speech against Timokrates tells admiringly the story of the Lokrians, who changed only one law in 200 years, because they had the marvellous custom that any proposal for a change of law must be made with a noose round the neck, and if the proposal was defeated the noose was drawn tight.[93]

It is no surprise that the Athenians created the distinction between general and individual norms in 403 when they were revising the whole corpus of laws. They started out with the mass of all decisions still in force from Drakon and Solon down to the last year of the Peloponnesian War, and the task was to settle which, out of all those decisions, merited inclusion in the code, so as to produce a new, well-defined and stable code suitable to be published on stone; doubtless it was that task that inspired them to introduce the distinction betwen *nomoi* and *psephismata* that prevailed in the fourth century.

The decision to raise laws to the status of higher norms had two effects: (1) if a new law was inconsistent with prior decrees, the decrees were invalid; and (2) if a new decree was inconsistent with the laws in force, the decree must at once be nullified.

The rule that new laws nullified older decrees is surprising, but well-documented: in the coinage law of 375/4 the final clause is an instruction to the Secretary of the Council to expunge forthwith any decree inconsistent with the new law.[94] Thus, decrees correctly passed by the people in the Assembly were, on the order of the *nomothetai*, expunged by a magistrate as an administrative act without the Council or Assembly even being asked about it.

In the case of a decree inconsistent with the laws in force, it was not left to a magistrate to expunge it: the initiative belonged to any citizen to start a 'public prosecution for unconstitutional proposal' (*graphe paranomon*) against the proposer, upon which the decision was taken by the People's Court.[95]

[90] Dem. 23.86.
[91] Ostwald (1986) 77–83.
[92] Romilly (1971) 139–54; Sealey (1982); Ostwald (1986) 497–524.
[93] Dem. 24.139–43.   [94] *SEG* 26 72.55–6 = Harding (1985) no. 45.   [95] Hyp. 4.4–5.

Procedure for the Scrutiny of Laws

In the fifth century any citizen could bring a *graphe paranomon* against any decision of the Assembly or the Council; it was in the form of an appeal to the People's Court to have the decision nullified and the proposer punished. Soon after the restoration of democracy in 403 there was established a new procedure for the scrutiny of laws, the 'public prosecution for having proposed and carried an unsuitable law' (*graphe nomon me epitedeion theinai*).[96] This reform resulted, no doubt, from the new division between laws and decrees: the *graphe paranomon* henceforward was used only against decrees, whereas laws that were contrary to the existing laws or inexpedient were brought before the People's Court by the new public action.[97] The main use of both kinds of accusation was if a law or decree was contrary to the existing laws, either formally, because the proper procedure had not been followed, or materially, because the proposal was in conflict with the laws in force. But they could also be used against laws or decrees that were perfectly in consonance with the rest of the laws and correctly passed, but which were regarded as unsuitable or, more bluntly, damaging to the democracy and the people. If the proposal was a decree it had to be quashed, because laws were the higher norms;[98] if it was a law it had to be invalidated by the People's Court on the principle that an older law had priority over more recent law.[99] (That viewpoint was in direct opposition to the modern principle of *lex posterior*,[100] but it is fully consistent with the Greeks' idea of the long-lost golden age and their encomiums of the 'ancestral constitution'.)

STABILITY OF THE LAWS

Aristotle, in his criticism of radical democracy in Books 4 and 6 of the *Politics*, claims that everything is settled by decrees and not by laws and that decrees have higher validity than laws.[101] Since the sources appear to show that the distinction between laws and decrees was upheld at Athens, Aristotle's assertion cannot apply to Athenian democracy in the fourth century; and in fact Aristotle does not claim that it does. There is a striking difference between his general criticism of radical democracy in the *Politics* and the description of Athenian democracy in the *Constitution of Athens*, where we are told that everything is settled 'by decrees

[96] Arist. *Ath. Pol.* 59.2; Dem. 24.33. See p. 212.
[97] Kahrstedt (1938) 24; Wolff (1970) 41; Hansen (1983a) 171–5.
[98] Andoc. 1.87.   [99] Dem. 24.33.   [100] Allen (1964) 474.
[101] Arist. *Pol.* 1292a4–7.

and *dikasteria'*, where 'the common people' have the power.[102] Here Aristotle puts the *dikasteria* alongside the Assembly (which passed decrees). The absence of a reference to the *nomothetai* is problematic, but it may be best explained by supposing that, since they, like the *dikastai*, were chosen from the 6000 who had sworn the Heliastic Oath, he intended them to be included in the notion of *dikasteria*.

A somewhat different criticism of Athenian legislation is made by Demosthenes in the speeches against Leptines and Timokrates. He asserts that far too many laws are passed,[103] that the legislative procedure is not upheld, and that decrees that ought to be passed on the authority of laws are often passed before the laws that were supposed to authorize them,[104] so that the laws lose their status as the higher norms. Demosthenes' criticism is rebutted by numerous other passages in the orators, who actually praise the procedure of legislation[105] and stress respect for the law,[106] and the importance of the laws for the preservation of democracy.[107] Assertion rebuts assertion, and it is astonishing how many scholars have put uncritical trust in that of Demosthenes.[108]

The allegation that the Athenians have passed too many laws is refuted by the epigraphical record, which consists of seven laws as against 488 decrees. It may be objected that perhaps laws were only exceptionally published on stone, so that it is inadmissible to draw any conclusion as to the number of laws from the epigraphical material. Nevertheless, it is striking that the epigraphy is consistent with the literary evidence for the procedure for scrutiny of the laws: in the orators we have thirty-nine examples of *graphe paranomon* against decrees as against six of *graphe nomon me epitedeion theinai* against laws.[109] There is no reason to suppose that the former should be better attested in the surviving speeches than the latter, and the numerical difference can be taken as an indication that laws were seldom under attack and that the corpus of Athenian laws was more stable than is often supposed.

The passing of laws *after* the decrees they are supposed to authorize is exemplified by the three honorary decrees spoken of above. But they were not in breach of the legislative procedure, because, as said above, though all three are individual norms, such norms *can*, exceptionally, be passed by the *nomothetai*.

It is conceivable that the legislative procedure was not always respected,

---

[102] Arist. *Ath. Pol.* 41.2.
[103] Dem. 24.142, cf. Isoc. 8.50.   [104] Dem. 20.91–2.
[105] Aeschin. 1.177–8.   [106] Dem. 25.20–4.   [107] Lycurg. 1.4.
[108] Busolt and Swoboda (1920–6) 458; Kahrstedt (1938) 12–18; Harrison (1955) 26–35; Ehrenberg (1960) 57.
[109] Hansen (1974) 46–7.

and Demosthenes may be right in both the cases where he attacks a law with this allegation. The speech against Timokrates is a *graphe nomon me epitedeion theinai* against a law passed by the *nomothetai* on 12 Hekatombaion 354/3, in accordance with Epikrates' decree for the establishment of 1001 *nomothetai* passed in the Assembly the day before. Demosthenes protests that the decision to appoint *nomothetai* had not been discussed in two Assembly meetings and that the legislative proposal had not been posted in front of the Monument to the Eponymous Heroes.[110] The speech against Leptines is another *graphe* against a law that Leptines had had passed by the *nomothetai*, but allegedly without debate, without the repeal of contrary laws, without the reading of the proposal before the Assembly, and without prior publication.[111] How much force there is in Demosthenes' strictures is difficult to estimate, but it is worth pointing out that even Demosthenes is obliged to admit that Leptines' law was passed by the *nomothetai* and not by the Assembly as a decree.[112]

There can be no doubt, however, that Demosthenes is exaggerating when he asserts generally that all laws come into being that way, and it is impossible to decide whether he is right in alleging that the procedure was unconstitutional. It must not be forgotten that the speeches against Leptines and Timokrates were speeches for the prosecution, in which Demosthenes was criticizing the legislation *ex officio*: our picture of *nomothesia* in Athens would certainly be very different if it were the defence speeches that had come down to us and the prosecution's speeches that were lost. It must also not be forgotten that the Athenians passed hundreds of laws that were never arraigned before the People's Court. Our sources are largely forensic speeches, which naturally give too large a place to defects in the society they describe: the historian has a duty to discount that impression.

[110] Dem. 24.17–38.
[111] Dem. 20.88–101.
[112] Dem. 20.94. Hansen (1985b) 368–71, *pace* Calabi Limentani (1981).

8

The People's Court

'People's Court' is a translation of the Greek word *dikasterion*, which in itself just means a court of law, but was mainly used in Athens for the great jury courts that were the hallmark of the democracy. Strictly speaking there were several different courts, and when the sources describe this institution the plural form *dikasteria* is much commoner than the singular;[1] but even when the plural is used it is clear that the Athenians saw their popular courts as a unity[2] and as an organ of state exactly on a par with the Assembly and the Council.[3]

In democratic city-states the People's Court was the most important organ of state, alongside the Assembly. Aristotle in the *Politics* defines a citizen in a democracy as one who has the right to be a juror (*dikastes*) and a participator in the Assembly (*ekklesiastes*);[4] and Aristotle's general analysis in the *Politics* coincides neatly with his specific analysis of Athenian democracy in the *Constitution of Athens*, where, in the introduction to the systematic description of the constitution, he classifies the Athenian democracy as one 'where power is wielded [by the Assembly], which passes decrees, and the People's Court [which declares judgements]'.[5] Other sources support Aristotle: the Old Oligarch says that the Athenians are notorious for having more litigation than all the other Greeks put together;[6] and in Thucydides' sketch of the prelude to the Peloponnesian War the Athenians themselves admit to that very charge.[7] In the *Clouds* of Aristophanes one of Socrates' pupils displays a map of the world to the would-be disciple Strepsiades and points out Athens, but Strepsiades refuses to believe him, for 'where', he says, 'are the courts?'[8] And in *The*

---

[1] E.g. Aeschin. 1.91; Arist. *Ath. Pol.* 62.2. [2] E.g. Dem. 57.56.
[3] Hansen (1990a) 216–17. [4] Arist. *Pol.* 1275a22–33, b5–6.
[5] Arist. *Ath. Pol.* 41.2. [6] Ps. Xen. *Ath. Pol.* 3.2, cf. 1.16–18.
[7] Thuc. 1.77.1.
[8] Ar. *Nub.* 206ff.

Wasps, when old, toothless Philokleon puts up a forceful defence of the
sovereignty of the courts, young Bdelykleon's only way of taking the bite
out of his arguments is by asserting that power is really in the hands of
the cunning demagogues who manipulate the jurors by their rhetorical
skill.[9] Finally, in the orators, too, the courts are always emphasized as
the highest organ of the democracy.[10]

From a modern standpoint it looks peculiar that the courts should be
treated as an organ of state on a par with the Assembly.[11] The difference
is largely due to the fact that, although the courts had roughly the same
tasks in Athens as in a modern society, the relative importance of the
tasks was different then from now. In a modern democracy the task of
the courts is mainly to settle legal differences between private individuals
and to judge criminal cases: they do usually also have the right and duty
to oversee the administration,[12] and sometimes to test the constitutionality
of parliamentary decisions,[13] but such functions take up only a fraction of
their time, especially in Great Britain, where judicial review is unknown.[14]
Consequently the courts play only a minor role in descriptions of the
constitution, and usually turn up only in the standard discussions of the
relation between legislature, executive and judiciary and the need to
preserve the alleged independence of the judges.[15]

At Athens things were otherwise. Many private legal quarrels were
settled by arbitration and only came before the courts if a party appealed
against the arbitrator's award;[16] and many criminal matters were also
dealt with without the courts being involved: homicide was usually
handled by the Areopagos and the *ephetai*,[17] and for the more blatant
attacks on property, such as burglary, the magistrates had the power in
certain circumstances to execute people without trial, and in such matters
the courts were again only brought in on appeal.[18] On the other hand
the courts had unlimited power to control the Assembly, the Council,
the magistrates and the political leaders: political trials were the largest
part of the business that came before them. Furthermore, the political
powers of the courts included a long series of administrative responsibilities. When public works were put out to auction, the auction took place
in the presence of a panel of jurors, who confirmed and witnessed the
contract;[19] when confiscated property was sold at public auction by the

[9] Ar. *Vesp.* 526–729.   [10] Dem. 57.56. Hansen (1990a) 241 nn. 124–6.
[11] Hansen (1990a) 228–9.   [12] Waltman and Holland (1988) 97, 118, 144–6.
[13] Abraham (1987) 66–93; Waltman and Holland (1988) 96–8, 140–4.
[14] Cane (1986) 12.   [15] Cane (1986) 17.
[16] Arist. *Ath. Pol.* 53.2. MacDowell (1978) 207–11; Ruschenbusch (1985a) 36–7.
[17] Arist. *Ath. Pol.* 57.2–4. MacDowell (1963).
[18] Aeschin. 1.91. Hansen (1990a) 234 n. 93, *pace* Carawan (1984).
[19] *IG* II² 1669.8ff, 1670.34ff.

Eleven, that, too, had to take place before a panel of jurors;[20] and, when a fleet was commissioned, a court had to deal with all the objections (*skepseis* and *antidoseis*) put up by the people selected for the trierarchy.[21] In the light of such considerations it is no longer surprising that the sources treat the People's Court as a political organ on a par with the Assembly, and that sometimes the court is even described as the highest organ of state.

Another singular feature of the Athenian courts is the complete absence from their working of professionals or experts. It arose, doubtless, from the wish to make the administration of justice democratic: if all citizens were to be able to take part, the whole legal system must be designed to be run by amateurs, and, if all citizens were in principle to have equal influence, it was necessary to inhibit the growth of a professional corps of advocates or magistrates, since if some are amateurs and others professionals the professionals will always get the upper hand and your democracy will turn into an oligarchy. This fundamental principle was applied to everyone involved in a lawsuit or trial at Athens.

1 Judgement was not given by a professional judge but by a jury of several hundred persons.[22]
2 The administration of the courts was in the hands of magistrates[23] selected by lot for one year without possibility of extension.
3 There was no state prosecutor, and every charge had to be brought and carried through by an ordinary citizen acting either on his own behalf or in the public interest.[24]
4 The parties were required to carry their suits through in person, and it was actually a punishable offence to pay someone else to appear as your advocate in court.[25]

Thus, a law-case at Athens was a play with three characters, all amateurs: the citizen who brought the charge, the magistrate who prepared the case and presided over the court, and the jury who heard the case and gave the judgement.

---

[20] Arist. *Ath. Pol.* 52.1; *Hesperia* 5 (1936) 393–413 no. 10.10–13.
[21] Arist. *Ath. Pol.* 61.1; IG II² 1629.204–17.
[22] Arist. *Pol.* 1301a11–12; *Ath. Pol.* 53.3, 68.1.
[23] Arist. *Pol.* 1298a30–2; Aeschin. 3.14.   [24] Lycurg. 1.4.
[25] Quintilian *Institutio Oratoria* 2.15.30; Dem. 46.26.

ORGANIZATION

Qualifications to be a juror

Whereas all male Athenian citizens over twenty could attend the Assembly, a juror in the People's Court had (1) to be at least thirty years old; (2) to have been picked by lot at the beginning of the year as a member of the panel of 6000 citizens from which the jury for each individual case would be drawn; (3) to have sworn the Heliastic Oath; and (4) to have been picked by lot on a given day to serve for that day.

1 *Age* In the *Constitution of Athens* it is stated that 'the right to be a juror belongs to persons over thirty years who are not in debt to the state and have not undergone loss of rights'.[26] Like innumerable other peoples the Athenians put the power of judging into the hands of the eldest and most experienced; and the thirty-years-of-age rule was a quite considerable limitation on the recruitment of jurors, seeing that out of the 30,000 adult male citizens there would not be more than 20,000 eligible for jury service.[27]

2 *Annual selection* Not all persons qualified by age served as jurymen. All citizens over thirty who cared to could certainly put themselves in, at the beginning of the year, for a drawing of lots, but out of them all there were drawn not more than 6000. Those selected then swore the Heliastic Oath, and were thenceforth entitled to turn up daily for meetings of the courts as potential jurors for the cases due to be heard on the relevant day.[28]

Every man who had sworn the oath was equipped with a personal 'ticket'; about a hundred such 'tickets' have turned up in excavations.[29] They take the form of a small bronze plaque, 11 cm × 2 cm and 2 mm thick, inscribed with the individual's full name and mostly stamped, either with an owl like that on the 3-obol coins or with a Gorgon's head. Some of the plaques have both stamps, whereas the latest have none at all: the stamped ones belong to *c*.375–350 and the unstamped ones to *c*.350–325.[30] The ones with an owl were used at the daily selection by lot of jurors, the ones with the Gorgon probably for the annual selection of magistrates; the ones with both may have been given to citizens who wanted to be both jurymen and magistrates.[31] As for the fact that after

[26] Arist. *Ath. Pol.* 63.3.   [27] See p. 91.
[28] Ar. *Vesp.* 662; Arist. *Ath. Pol.* 24.3; Andoc. 1.17. Lipsius (1905–15) 134–9; Hommel (1927) 109–15.
[29] See p. 7.   [30] Kroll (1972) 8–68.   [31] Kroll (1972) 51–68.

*c.*350 the surviving plaques are unstamped, what happened was that the jury plaques began to be made from boxwood[32] and the bronze plaques were used only for magistrates, so there was no need of stamps to distinguish the two functions. All the best-preserved plaques are from graves – a testimony to the Athenian mentality in the classical age, for in archaic times it was his weapons that a citizen took with him to the grave.

Detailed study of the surviving plaques shows that five out of six are palimpsests, i.e. that the name of the original holder has been hammered out and replaced with another name; moreover, most of the plaques are multi-palimpsests, and one can trace on them as many as six successive holders.[33] So they must have changed hands every few years, sometimes annually: it shows how much change went on in the composition of the 6000 jurors. The frequency of palimpsests also shows not merely that the panel of 6000 existed in the fourth century (it is only actually referrred to in the fifth-century sources) but also that there was competition for places:[34] the interest of Athenians in their democracy in the fourth century was greater than many scholars have tended to suppose.

3   *The Heliastic Oath*   When the 6000 had been selected they had to go up to the hill of Ardettos[35] outside the walls to the south-east and swear an oath called the Heliastic Oath (*ho heliastikos horkos*),[36] which traditionally went back to Solon:[37] that need not be taken too literally, for in the fourth century Solon was given the credit for everything relating to the People's Court.[38] The oath is quoted *in extenso* in Demosthenes' speech against Timokrates, and, though there is some doubt whether everything in our surviving text is authentic,[39] with the help of isolated quotations from various forensic speeches we can reconstruct its main lines:

> I will cast my vote in consonance with the laws and with the decrees passed by the Assembly and by the Council, but, if there is no law, in consonance with my sense of what is most just, without favour or enmity. I will vote only on the matters raised in the charge, and I will listen impartially to accusers and defenders alike.[40]

The oath was sworn in the names of Zeus, Apollo and Demeter, and ended with the juror uttering a curse against himself if he should break

[32] Arist. *Ath. Pol.* 63.4.   [33] Kroll (1972) 71.   [34] Kroll (1972) 69–90.
[35] Harp. s.v. *Ardettos.*   [36] Hyp. 3.40.   [37] Dem. 24.148.
[38] See p. 298.
[39] Dem. 24.149–51. Drerup (1898) 256–64 (authentic); Lipsius (1905–15) 151–2 (partly authentic, partly spurious).
[40] Fränkel (1878).

his oath. Looked at with modern eyes the Heliastic Oath might appear an empty formality: voting was secret, so no one could ever call a juror to account for breaking his oath. He could, however, suffer divine punishment,[41] and our evaluation of the oath must depend on our evaluation of religion in the Greek city-state.[42] The orators stress that a judgement by the sworn jurors has greater weight than a decision taken by the people in the Assembly who have sworn no oath;[43] and it can be argued that the oath was one of the very factors that caused the decisions of the People's Court to prevail over the decrees of the Assembly.

4 *Daily selection* The annual selection by lot of the jurors was supplemented by a selection by lot of such jurors as were needed on each particular day. The 6000 were divided into ten sections each of 600 men, and each section comprised sixty men from each tribe. In the fifth century, sections were allotted to particular magistrates and there was no selection on the day: the potential jurors formed a queue in the morning before the court-rooms and were let in in the order of their arrival until the required number of jurors was reached, at which point the doors were closed.[44] But in 403 (probably) there was introduced a daily selection by lot of jurors and allocation of them to different courts also by lot: each section received a letter from *alpha* to *kappa*, and on the morning letters were picked by lot to determine which sections would be called to serve on that day, and a second choice by lot was made to determine which magistrates should preside over which courts.[45] In 378/7 or shortly afterwards the daily selection of jurors was again reformed.[46] First there was a selection by lot, man by man, of who were to serve as jurors of the day, and then of which court each individual was to serve in. The process is valuable testimony to the complexity of the democratic constitution: it must undoubtedly have succeeded in its twofold purpose, to ensure a good measure of rotation among the jurors and to foil any attempt to bribe them.

Domicile, social standing and age distribution of jurors

Domicile, status and age are a bit better known in the case of the jurors than in that of the Assembly, partly because far more court speeches

---

[41] Lycurg. 1.79, 146.   [42] Dover (1974) 248–54.

[43] Dem. 24.78.

[44] Ar. *Vesp.* 233–4, 240, 303–5, 400, 689–90, 1107–9; Ant. 6.21–3. Lipsius (1905–15) 137–9; Hommel (1927) 110–15.

[45] Ar. *Eccl.* 681–90; *Plut.* 277, 972, 1167. Lipsius (1905–15) 139–43; Hommel (1927) 115–26.

[46] See pp. 197–9.

have survived than Assembly speeches and partly because the personal plaques provide useful prosopographical evidence.

A priori it might be assumed that the country population was less well represented in the courts than in the Assembly: there were far more meetings, a meeting went on all day, and the pay was less. Were citizens from beyond Aigaleos, Pentelikon and Hymettos cut off by distance from regular attendance at the courts? That belief is confirmed in so far as most of the jury plaques come from graves in Athens and the Piraeus;[47] however, one of them is from Erchia, 20 km east of Athens,[48] and it would be mistaken to believe that the jurors were exclusively drawn from the city population. In many cases the plaques are so well preserved that we can read the deme-names of the successive holders; and, astonishingly, it turns out that people from the coastal demes (*paralia*) and the inland demes (*mesogeios*) actually prevail over people from the city demes (*asty*).[49] Part of the explanation is, naturally, emigration from the country into the city: in the fourth century many people from the coastal and inland demes actually resided in Athens and the Piraeus.[50] But the geographical spread revealed by the jury plaques is so striking that the growth of the city population cannot be the whole story. We must allow that some jurors came on foot from the most distant demes; somebody in the *Birds* of Aristophanes remarks that the 'Unheliast' plant is rare, though it can sometimes still be found in the country if you look (i.e. that most people even in the country have taken the Heliastic Oath),[51] and Demosthenes in his speech against Kallikles takes it for granted that most of the jurors possess a smallholding in the country[52] – though in the latter case we must remember again that the divide between city and country population was not nearly as sharp in ancient Greece as in modern Europe.[53]

The few sources that say anything direct as to the social position of the jurors all point in one direction: that it was mainly the poor who manned the People's Court,[54] and that the daily pay of 3 obols constituted for many jurors their sole living. 'It must pierce every right-thinking person to the heart', intones Isokrates, 'to see before the court-room masses of citizens undergoing a selection by lot that determines whether they will get their daily bread or not.'[55] In his speech *Against Meidias* Demosthenes tells the story of Pyrrhos the *atimos*, whose poverty drove

---

[47] Kroll (1972) 9 n. 2.   [48] Kroll (1972) cat. no. 16. See p. 7.
[49] Hansen (1989a) 75, 87.
[50] Gomme (1933) 44–5; Damsgaard-Madsen (1988). See p. 101.
[51] Ar. *Av.* 109ff with schol. *ad* 111.   [52] Dem. 55.26.
[53] See p. 61.
[54] E.g. Ar. *Vesp.* 303ff; Ps. Xen. *Ath. Pol.* 1.18; Dem. 24.123. Markle (1985) 282–9.
[55] Isoc. 7.54.

him to flout the rule forbidding him to exercise his citizen rights: he tried to earn 3 obols by getting himself put down as a juror, but he was caught, denounced and condemned to death for failing to respect his *atimia*.[56] Also important is Aristotle's assertion that in the Athenian courts it is the *demos* that has the power; because here, as elsewhere in Aristotle's political writings, *demos* means 'the ordinary people, who are identified with the poor (*hoi aporoi*).[57]

In spite of all this, several modern historians have asserted that the juries, at least in the fourth century, were mainly recruited from the middle and upper class.[58] The assertion rests always on two arguments: (1) in several speeches in the orators it is taken for granted by the speaker that the jurors belong to the 'better sort'; and (2) the pay of 3 obols per meeting was too small to maintain a family, and many people simply could not afford to serve as jurors when they could make much more by working. Now, it is true that a speaker does often assume that his audience belongs to the higher social class;[59] but sometimes he is expressly addressing a restricted group of jurors,[60] and in the other cases we must remember that it was always good rhetoric to talk up to the jury, which could be done *inter alia* by attributing to all the jurors the social position that only a minority really had.[61] It is also true that jury pay was a poor substitute for a day's wages, which could run from $1\frac{1}{2}$ to $2\frac{1}{2}$ drachmas.[62] But 3 obols was perhaps enough to meet the necessities of a small family,[63] and for the elderly, the invalid and the unemployed it was very likely their only chance to earn anything at all for their subsistence. Which leads us to the question of the age-distribution of the jurors.

The rule that a person had to be at least thirty to be a juror must have resulted in a big difference from the Assembly: far more grey beards and bald heads would have been seen amongst the jurors in the Agora than on the Pnyx in the Assembly. The question is whether factors other than that rule also played a part in raising the average age of the jurors.

A meeting of the court lasted all day but was only rewarded with half a drachma, as compared to an Assembly meeting, which was over in half a day but carried with it a whole drachma. That must have dampened the ardour for attendance at the courts of anyone capable of working, who could earn or produce at least three times the jury pay; but it must have been a stimulus to those who could not, so that one can imagine that most of the jurors were older citizens who could no longer do hard physical work but could still sit on a bench and listen to speeches. And

[56] Dem. 21.182.　　[57] Arist. *Ath. Pol.* 41.2. See p. 125.
[58] E.g. Jones (1957) 36–7, 124.　　[59] E.g. Dem. 21.83, 95. Jones (1957) 36.
[60] Din. 1.42; Lys. 29.9. Sinclair (1988a) 124–7, (1988b) 63.　　[61] Ober (1989) 224.
[62] Zimmermann (1974) 98ff.　　[63] Markle (1985) 277–81.

that guess is borne out in Aristophanes' *Wasps*, where the chorus are represented as a swarm of 'senior citizens' on their way to the courts,[64] ready to sting any defendant. Some of them are being helped along by their young sons, so their physical age cannot be all that great; but even if they are not old they are at least no youngsters. What is more, they are poor, and will go hungry to bed if the court is dismissed or if they arrive at the back of the queue.[65] Aristophanes' grotesque satire has to be corrected by reference to the speeches of the orators, where the audience is sometimes divided into 'the young' and 'the old', and everybody who can remember back twenty or at most thirty years belongs in the latter class.[66] A speaker can also assume that most of the jurors took part in a campaign four or five years ago,[67] and so must be at most a bit over fifty. Nevertheless, however much Aristophanes' parody is modified, it retains its kernel of truth: the poor and the elderly were the majority in the courts.

Frequency of court days, size of juries, and number of jurors, courts and trials

The courts did not meet on Assembly days,[68] nor on taboo days (*hemerai apophrades*, when the Areopagos was judging trials for homicide),[69] nor on annual festival days,[70] but they did meet on monthly-recurring festival days,[71] like the Council but unlike the Assembly. The Attic year had about 195 ordinary working days (of which forty were given over to Assembly meetings), about eighty monthly festival days, and about sixty annual festival days;[72] the number of taboo days is not known but may have been something like fifteen. The courts met on monthly festival days perhaps because there were just not enough ordinary days; so from all this we can calculate that the courts must have been summoned at least 150 times a year (195 minus 40 minus 15, plus a few) and at most 240 times (354 minus 60 minus 40 minus 15); since it was left to the *thesmothetai* to decide when the courts should be summoned,[73] the actual number of court days must have been less than the maximum, say between 175 and 225 a year.[74]

How big was a jury panel for a court day, and how many panels were the jurors divided into? If we can answer those two questions we are in

---

[64] Ar. *Vesp.* 230ff.   [65] Ar. *Vesp.* 300ff.

[66] Lycurg. 1.93; Dem. 20.77. Bruck (1894) 312.   [67] Dem. 50.3; Lys. 21.10.

[68] Dem. 24.80.   [69] *Etym. Magn.* s.v. *apophrades*. Mikalson (1975b) 25–6.

[70] Ps. Xen. *Ath. Pol.* 3.8.   [71] Dem. 42.5; *IG II²* 1678.27–8. Hansen (1979b) 245.

[72] Mikalson (1975a).   [73] Arist. *Ath. Pol.* 59.1.   [74] Hansen (1979b).

a position to state how many jurors were chosen from the 6000 on a normal day.

In Aristotle's time private lawsuits were judged by a panel of 201 if the sum at issue was less than 1000 drachmas, or 401 if it was more,[75] and public prosecutions were usually judged by a panel of 501;[76] but the most important political cases (*graphe paranomon, eisangelia, apophasis*) were sometimes judged by a jury of several panels of 500 put together:[77] we have examples of panels of 1001, 1501, 2001 and 2501,[78] and the first known example of a *graphe paranomon* was actually judged by all the jurors at once (i.e. all those who had turned up on the day concerned).[79]

Aristotle's description of the allotment procedure by which the magistrates were distributed between courts[80] indicates that on an ordinary day there must have been at least three courts, and probably four or more. Since the magistrates and the cases to be judged were distributed between courts by lot, it follows that all courts must have been of the same size on a given day,[81] i.e. that juries were selected so as to be all of either 201 or 401 or 501 men: if several panels were to form a single court of (say) 1501, no other courts can have been set up for that day. On days when the higher-rate private suits were to be heard, 1600 or more jurors must have been selected, and on the days of public prosecutions the number selected must have been at least 1500 and more often probably 2000. The astonishing implications of these figures will be discussed further on.

A public prosecution took a whole day,[82] but in Greece the length of day varies from $9\frac{1}{2}$ hours at the winter solstice to $14\frac{1}{2}$ at the summer solstice.[83] A defendant's chance of presenting his case fully could naturally not be made to depend on whether it came to court in June or December, so the rule was that a day in court, all the year round, corresponded with the shortest day in the year, i.e. about $9\frac{1}{2}$ hours.[84] In public prosecutions the period was divided into three equal parts, so that the accuser had about three hours for his speech, the accused three hours to answer it, and the remaining three hours were for the selection of jurors, reading of the charge, voting, new speeches for meting-out of punishment, a further vote on the punishment, and so forth.[85] In private suits the time for speeches varied according to the value of the suit: suits for over 5000 drachmas got the longest time and perhaps lasted more than two hours,

---

[75] Arist. *Ath. Pol.* 53.3.   [76] Arist. *Ath. Pol.* 68.1. Hommel (1927) 24.
[77] Dem. 24.9.   [78] Hansen (1975) 10 n. 14. See pp. 207, 215, 293.
[79] Andoc. 1.17. Hansen (1989a) 230.   [80] Arist. *Ath. Pol.* 66.1.
[81] Arist. *Ath. Pol.* 66.1. Hommel (1927) 72–7.   [82] Aeschin. 2.126.
[83] Kubitschek (1928) 182.   [84] Arist. *Ath. Pol.* 67.4.
[85] Xen. *Hell.* 1.7.23; Aeschin. 3.197. Hommel (1927) 86ff.

suits for less than 1000 drachmas could perhaps be heard and judged in less than an hour.[86] Aristotle shows that a panel of 401 jurors was expected to hear and judge a total of four cases in a day;[87] so even in that case a session lasted about nine hours. Thus, on an ordinary day the courts could get through at least three public prosecutions or at least twelve private suits for the larger sum or an unknown number of smaller private suits. The passion of the Athenians for litigating and sitting in judgement is truly astonishing.

Pay for jury service

For one meeting, lasting a whole day, each juror got 3 obols.[88] In Aristotle's *Politics* pay for the jury courts is singled out as one of the foundations of the radical democracy,[89] and it is striking that payment for jury service (*to dikastikon*) was introduced at Athens more than half a century before pay for the Assembly. Aristotle says that the dikastic pay was started by Perikles as a counterpoise to Kimon,[90] who was so rich that he could buy himself a following with his private fortune.[91] Be that as it may, there is probably a connection between dikastic pay and the reforms of Ephialtes, for it was in 462 that the People's Court had its powers importantly enlarged, and it may well have been increased pressure on the courts that obliged the state to pay citizens in order to get them to serve. In any case, there is a presumption that dikastic pay must have been introduced before Perikles' citizenship law of 451, for pay for jury service for the first time made Athenian citizenship profitable, and it was bound to be in the interest of the citizens to ensure that not too many people got in on the act.

The original rate of pay is unknown: we know that Kleon in the first years of the Peloponnesian War raised it from 2 obols to 3;[92] pay was abolished under the oligarchic regimes in 411[93] and probably in 404[94] but reintroduced in 403,[95] after which the rate was always 3 obols, and was still so when Aristotle wrote the *Constitution of Athens* in the 320s.[96] During that period prices and wages had gone up a good deal: a day's pay from 1 drachma at the end of the fifth century to $1\frac{1}{2}$–$2\frac{1}{2}$ drachmas in the second half of the fourth, and Assembly pay, correspondingly, from 1–3 obols in the 390s to 1–$1\frac{1}{2}$ drachmas in the 320s. So for a meeting that went on all day the juror got less than someone who attended the

[86] Arist. *Ath. Pol.* 67.2–68.1. Rhodes (1981a) 719–28; MacDowell (1985) 525–6.
[87] Arist. *Ath. Pol.* 67.1.   [88] Ar. *Eq.* 255; Arist. *Ath. Pol.* 62.2.
[89] Arist. *Pol.* 1294a37–41, 1320a22ff.   [90] Arist. *Ath. Pol.* 27.3; *Pol.* 1274a8–9.
[91] Theop. fr. 89; Plut. *Cim.* 10.   [92] Schol. Ar. *Vesp.* 88, 300.
[93] Thuc. 8.67.3.   [94] Ar. *Ran.* 140–1 with schol.
[95] Ar. *Eccl.* 687–8; *Plut.* 277.   [96] Arist. *Ath. Pol.* 62.2.

Assembly, whose meetings usually lasted only a few hours. We do not know why this anomaly remained, but a modest guess may be worth making. On a normal court day the Athenians had to use 2000–3000 men from the jury list to pick up by lot 1500–2000 jurors; for an Assembly they had normally to use 6000 participants to get the prescribed quorum.[97] Possibly, while 3 obols were enough to ensure that on any court day enough qualified people turned up for allotment, it was harder to get 6000 to turn up regularly for the Assembly.

The annual cost to the state of jury pay must have been between 22 and 37 talents; one cannot be more precise, but that is enough to give an idea of its significance in the Athenian budget. The courts cost more than the Council but less than the Assembly, and the whole jury pay for a year was only a fraction of the cost of a single campaign of a few months.[98] That did not, indeed, prevent the Athenians from often getting into such severe difficulties, owing to their endless wars, that for whole periods they had to make cuts in the activities of the courts: if we can believe Demosthenes, all private suits were suspended for several years in the 360s,[99] and in 348 the courts were shut again for a shorter period,[100] because there was no money to pay jurors after the Euboian campaign. It was usually private suits that were suspended: a court could always be found for public prosecutions, and the Athenians seem never to have restricted the possibility of impeaching Assembly speakers or generals for a failed policy or a lost campaign.

The magistrates and the courts

In early times the magistrates had the power to judge all law-cases,[101] but later that power was limited by the introduction of appeal to the People's Court (*ephesis eis to dikasterion*):[102] if one of the parties was dissatisifed with the magistrate's ruling he could bring the matter before the court and have the case tried anew. That development is traditionally ascribed to Solon,[103] with how good reason we do not know: it is certainly an anachronism when Aristotle calls *ephesis eis to dikasterion* one of Solon's three most 'democratic' reforms. In the fourth century appeal to the People's Court was replaced by the absolute requirement to go before the court as a court of first instance, and the role of the magistrates was reduced to the preliminary investigation of cases (*anakrisis*)[104] plus the right to preside over all trials (*hegemonia tou dikasteriou*).[105]

---

[97] Arist. *Ath. Pol.* 41.3. Hansen (1987a) 143 n. 132.   [98] See p. 316.
[99] Dem. 45.4.   [100] Dem. 39.17.   [101] Arist. *Ath. Pol.* 3.5.
[102] Harrison (1971) 72–4; MacDowell (1978) 30, *pace* Ruschenbush (1961).
[103] Arist. *Ath. Pol.* 9.1. Rhodes (1981a) 160–2.   [104] E.g. Is 6.12, 10.2.
[105] Aeschin. 3.14, 27, 29.

There was, however, one sphere in which magistrates still had unlimited judicial authority, even in the fourth century: for some blatant offences, mostly against property, an ancient rule applied, that the Eleven had the right to execute a criminal without trial if he was caught in the act and confessed.[106] Criminals liable to execution without trial were called *kakourgoi*; they included kidnappers (of slaves), cutpurses, thieves, muggers, housebreakers, temple-robbers, pirates, adulterers, and certain classes of murderer.[107] A fundamental principle of Athenian democracy was that no citizen could be put to death without trial (*medena akriton apokteinai*).[108] That fine principle was somewhat undermined by the right of the Eleven to put *kakourgoi* to death without trial: the Athenians behaved in the matter as does the traditional order in many societies, considering that thieves and robbers belonged as a rule to the lowest section of society, which deserved the least legal protection while being liable to the sternest legal punishments.

Apart from that special power of the Eleven, the independent judicial power of the magistrates was reduced to a minimum in the fourth century. They had independent jurisdiction (were *autoteleis*) in all cases where the sum at issue did not exceed 10 drachmas,[109] and they could impose fines (*epibolai*):[110] if the fine was less than (perhaps) 50 drachmas[111] there was no appeal to the courts, but if it was more there had to be a trial before a court.[112]

The right to receive charges and preside over the courts belonged in principle to all magistrates,[113] but in practice the vast majority of cases came under a small group of magistrates and boards of magistrates, first and foremost the nine archons: family and inheritance came under the archon, homicide and sacrilege under the king archon, the affairs of metics and other non-Athenians under the polemarch, and all political trials under the six *thesmothetai*;[114] most private suits belonged to the Forty (*hoi tettarakonta*,[115] a board of four from each tribe), and the *strategoi* dealt with military law.[116]

Certain magistrates had a particular connection with the courts and with justice over and above their right to preside over the courts. The administration of the courts was the duty of the *thesmothetai*,[117] and the daily allotment of juries was controlled by the nine archons plus the

---

[106] Arist. *Ath. Pol.* 52.1. Hansen (1976) 18, 114; (1981a) 22–4.
[107] Aeschin. 1.90–1. Hansen (1976) 36–48.
[108] Lys. 19.7; Dem. 25.87. Carawan (1984); Hansen (1989b) 13.
[109] Arist. *Ath. Pol.* 53.2; *SEG* 26.72.23–5 = Harding (1985) no. 45.
[110] Aeschin. 3.27. Harrison (1971) 4 n. 1.   [111] *IG* I³ 82.26.
[112] Dem. 43.75.   [113] Aeschin. 3.14.   [114] Arist. *Ath. Pol.* 56–9.
[115] Arist. *Ath. Pol.* 53.1.   [116] Lys. 15.1.   [117] Arist. *Ath. Pol.* 59.1.

secretary of the *thesmothetai*.[118] The prison was administered by the Eleven,[119] who also had responsibility for condemned prisoners and (as we have seen) for *kakourgoi* caught in the act.[120]

Each board of magistrates seems to have had its own named court: that of the *thesmothetai* was called 'Heliaia',[121] that of the Eleven 'Parabyston'.[122] Sometimes the word Heliaia is used just in a general sense to mean People's Court, as a synonym for *dikasterion*:[123] possibly in archaic times the Heliaia had been the only court, borrowed from the *thesmothetai* by the other magistrates when they had a case to try.[124] In the fourth century the Heliaia was always the largest of the courts, in which all political trials took place under the presidency of the *thesmothetai*, sometimes with reinforced panels of up to 2501 jurors.[125]

To date, no trace has been found of the location of the Heliaia, the Athenians' oldest and most important court.[126] Most of the courts probably lay in the Agora: exactly where they were is nowhere stated in the extant sources. In the course of its excavation archaeologists have identified a series of successive building-complexes to the north-east,[127] the latest buildings being identified with the courts, which, according to Aristotle, were situated together behind an enclosure.[128] The identification is based on the fact that large finds of the objects used by jurors, such as the small bronze disks used in voting, occurred in just this area. However, more recent studies show that those buildings are Hellenistic in date.[129] With the exception of those for homicide, the court-rooms were roofed,[130] so that the activity of the jurors never needed to be interrupted by the weather.

The parties

At Athens in classical times there was no public prosecutor: the system was 'accusatorial', i.e. based on accusations by private individuals. The political leader Lykourgos openly states that illegalities would go unpunished unless some citizen took it upon himself to bring a case: 'without an accuser the laws and the courts are worth nothing'.[131] Such an 'accusatorial' system could only function because an astoundingly large number of citizens took an active part in the law, not only as jurors but also as prosecutors or plaintiffs.

---

[118] Arist. *Ath. Pol.* 63.1.   [119] Arist. *Ath. Pol.* 52.1.   [120] Dem. 24.113.
[121] Ant. 6.21.   [122] Harp. s.v.; *IG* II² 1646.12.   [123] Dem. 23.97.
[124] *M&L* 52.75 = Fornara (1977) no. 103; Dem. 43.75, quoting the archaic law.
[125] Arist. *Ath. Pol.* 68.1; Din 1.52.   [126] Hansen (1989a) 232–7.
[127] Thompson and Wycherley (1972) 52–72.   [128] Arist. *Ath. Pol.* 63.2.
[129] Forthcoming study by R. Townsend.   [130] Ant. 5.10–11. Hansen (1989a) 226–8.
[131] Lycurg. 1.4; Dem. 59.109.

Originally only the injured party had the right to bring a case,[132] except for homicide, where for obvious reasons it was the deceased's family who had the right.[133] Tradition ascribed to Solon a vital reform: henceforward any citizen was to have the right to bring a case on behalf of an injured person.[134] But the new rule was not followed in all cases, only if the injured person could not, for one reason or another, obtain justice himself, or in cases of injury to the whole society.[135] This limitation of the right of every citizen to bring a case lasted all through the classical age; and it was the reason for a twofold division of legal cases: private suits (*dikai idiai* or just *dikai*) and public prosecutions (*dikai demosiai* or *graphai*).[136] The difference between a *dike* and a *graphe* can be summed up in eight points, as follows.

1 *Dikai* could be brought only by the injured party,[137] *graphai* by any citizen.[138]

2 A private suit could always be terminated by a settlement,[139] whereas withdrawal of the accuser from a public prosecution was punishable by a fine of 1000 drachmas and loss of the right ever again to prosecute in the same kind of trial – a penalty known as 'partial *atimia*'.[140]

3 Correspondingly, there was usually no risk for a private plaintiff if he lost his case, but the prosecutor in a *graphe* suffered a fine of 1000 drachmas and partial *atimia* if he got less than a fifth of the jury's votes.[141]

4 Most private suits were dealt with by arbitrators (*diaitetai*),[142] whereas public prosecutions were taken by the magistrates by means of an *anakrisis*.[143]

5 *Dikai* were judged by 201 or 401 jurors, *graphai* by 501 or more.[144]

6 In *dikai* the parties had a time-limit for their speeches, and a jury dealt with several cases in a day; *graphai* lasted all day.[145]

7 The plaintiff in a private suit always gained a personal advantage from winning his case, since he got either damages or the value of his suit.[146] A public prosecution, on the other hand, brought no personal advantage to the accuser, because the punishment was

---

[132] Bonner and Smith (1930–8) II 7ff.

[133] *M&L* 86.20–3 = Fornara (1977) no. 15B.   [134] Arist. *Ath. Pol.* 9.1.

[135] Ruschenbush (1968) 47–53.

[136] Dem. 46.26; Pl. *Euthyphr.* 2A. Lipsius (1905–15) 239 n. 6.

[137] Isoc. 20.2. Hansen (1981a) 13.   [138] Dem. 59.16. Lipsius (1905–15) 244 n. 16.

[139] Is. 5.17–18; Dem. 37.41.   [140] Dem. 21.47, 103. Hansen (1976) 63–5.

[141] Dem. 53.1–2.   [142] Arist. *Ath. Pol.* 53.2–6. See p. 197.   [143] Dem. 58.8.

[144] Arist. *Ath. Pol.* 53.3; 68.1.   [145] Arist. *Ath. Pol.* 67.1.

[146] Harp. s.v. *hyperemeroi.*

death, exile, loss of rights, confiscation to the state or a fine, which, with a few exceptions, also went to the state.[147]

8 In private suits execution was left to the winning party;[148] in public prosecutions it devolved on the magistrates.[149]

The distinction between *dikai* and *graphai* only partly corresponded with the modern distinction between civil and criminal proceedings;[150] and the Athenians subdivided the two types into a welter of subtypes that seem odd to us: homicide was pursued by a special *dike phonou*,[151] a private suit of murder; defamation with a *dike kakegorias*,[152] a private suit also; desertion with a *graphe lipotaxiou*,[153] a public prosecution; and so on. Yet another idiosyncrasy of the Athenian system was that the types of procedure often overlapped, so that a plaintiff or accuser could choose between a range of different procedures, often with different consequences for both pursuer and pursued.[154] Thus, if a magistrate was alleged to have taken a bribe he could be taken to court in seven different ways.

1 He could be denounced with an *eisangelia* to the Assembly.[155]
2 The Assembly could decide that the case should be dealt with by an *apophasis*,[156] i.e. a request for an investigation and proposal by the Areopagos.
3 An *eisangelia* could be made to the Council instead of the people.[157]
4 The Council could bring the case on its own initiative.[158]
5 Any citizen could bring the case before the *thesmothetai* by an *apographe*,[159] a written statement of the alleged amount of the bribe with a demand for confiscation.
6 Also through the *thesmothetai*, any citizen could initiate a public prosecution for bribery, the *graphe doron*.[160]
7 The magistrate could be accused at his *euthynai*,[161] his rendering of accounts at the end of his yearly term of office.

In some of these cases conviction could result in the death penalty (1–4 and 6), in others at most a fine (7) or merely confiscation of the bribe (5). Some bore no risk for the pursuer (1, 3–4 and 7).[162] *Apographe* could actually bring him a reward for his accusation (one third of the value of

---

[147] Dem. 21.45.
[148] Dem. 30.8.
[149] Plut. *Mor.* 834A. Lipsius (1905–15) 942–52.   [150] Geldart (1959) 188ff.
[151] Arist. *Ath. Pol.* 57.3; Ant. 6.6, 41–2.   [152] Lys. 10.2.   [153] Dem. 21.103.
[154] Dem. 22.25ff.   [155] Lys. 28.9, 29.2. Hansen (1975) cat. no. 73.
[156] Din. 3.1–2.   [157] Ant. 6.35. Hansen (1975) cat. nos 131–3.
[158] Ant. 6.49–50. Hansen (1975) cat. no. 134.
[159] *IG* II² 1631.361ff. Hansen (1980b) 117–19.   [160] Dem. 46.26; Din. 2.17.
[161] Arist. *Ath. Pol.* 54.2.   [162] Hansen (1975) 30.

what was confiscated),[163] while a *graphe doron* or an *apographe* involved the risk of a fine of 1000 drachmas and partial *atimia* if the accuser failed to get a fifth of the votes.[164] It is important to stress, however, that by and large these procedures differed only in the way they were begun and in the consequences of acquittal or conviction: what happened in between, from the preliminary investigation by the magistrate to the vote by the court, was always the same.

It must have been exceedingly difficult for the ordinary Athenian citizen to find his way in this maze of procedures, yet the laws insisted that in both *dikai* and *graphai* people must bring their cases in person:[165] it was forbidden by law to pay another citizen to appear as your advocate in court.[166] You could, if the jury permitted, share your speaking-time with a friend or relative,[167] and in political trials it was almost regular for both accusation and defence to be divided between several speakers from the same group.[168] An advocate of such a kind was called a 'fellow speaker' (*synegoros*).[169] A further way of getting expert help was to turn to a professional speech-writer, explain the case to him and get him to write a speech which you would then rehearse and recite in court: in the course of the fourth century such speech-writers (*logographoi*)[170] became a profession, specialized in by metics as well as citizens. The logographer could also assist his client in preparing the case,[171] so he was the nearest Athenian parallel to the English solicitor. He naturally expected a fee,[172] and in fact logography represented a breach of the Athenians' fundamental principle of protecting the democracy from professionalism and making every citizen present his own case: the law forbade paid *synegoroi* but not paid *logographoi*. But logography was regarded with scepticism and suspicion, and the profession had little standing:[173] several Athenian political leaders, Demosthenes and Hypereides for example, began as logographers, but gave it up as fast as they could and did not like to be reminded of that stage in their careers.[174]

In addition to the logographer the Athenian system threw up a quite different character about the courts, the sycophant (*sykophantes*) or professional accuser.[175] The word means a 'fig-revealer', and is supposed originally to have referred to someone who shakes a fig-tree to get

---

[163] Lewis (1966) 188 with n. 67.   [164] Hansen (1975) 29.

[165] Quintilian *Institutio Oratoria* 2.15.30.   [166] Dem. 46.26.

[167] Hyp. 2.20.   [168] Andoc. 1.92–5, 133 (prosecution), 150 (defence).

[169] Dem. 59.14. Lavency (1964) 84–95.

[170] Aeschin. 1.94; Theophr. *Char.* 17.8. Lavency (1964).

[171] Dem. 58.19.   [172] Din. 1.111.   [173] Hyp. 5.3.

[174] Dem. 32.32; Isoc. 15.36ff.   [175] Lofberg (1917).

down the fruit.[176] It signified someone who used the right of accusation possessed by every citizen to further his own advantage, sometimes legitimately but mostly by plain and simple blackmail. The Athenian system presupposed ideally that a high number of citizens would, without thought of personal advantage, be willing to help other citizens, or the society as such, by coming forward as accusers. But in certain cases they were so anxious to get an illegality into court that they relaxed their ideal and offered a reward for successful accusation, as in the *apographe*[177] described above. That activity on the part of a sycophant, though despised, was not unlawful. But a direct threat to the whole system was represented by the sycophants who used the right of accusation for blackmail, by menacing a lawbreaker with prosecution and obtaining money from him for refraining[178] or by menacing an entirely blameless person with prosecution in the hope that he would sooner pay up than risk defending himself in court against an experienced orator.[179] The Athenians recognized the danger[180] and tried to meet it, partly by creating special procedures against sycophants, particularly the *probole*[181] and *graphe sykophantias*,[182] and partly by the penalty for not getting a fifth of the votes.

When a citizen appeared in court as a public accuser his first anxiety was, therefore, to dispel any suspicion that he was a sycophant. He could stress his public-spiritedness, but that tends to make ordinary folk even more suspicious,[183] and usually there was a much more cogent argument to deploy: he could declare that the accused was his personal enemy and that he was using his citizen right to prosecute for revenge and not for gain.[184] Revenge was regarded as a legitimate motive: an accuser motivated by hate would often demand the maximum penalty against his foe, and even for lesser offences he might recommend the maximum on the ground of its general preventative effect. On the other hand, a lawbreaker with no particular enemy might escape for lack of an accuser – unless a sycophant got him. The combination of stern criminal punishments and chanciness of accusation made Athenian law in this respect regrettably unstable. Mere chance could result in some minor offenders being condemned and put to death *pour encourager les autres*,[185] while more serious crimes went unpunished because nobody brought an accusation[186] or

---

[176] Lofberg (1917) viii.   [177] Dem. 53.1–2.   [178] Dem. 58.12–13.
[179] Lys. 25.3; Isoc. 18.9–10.
[180] Ar. *Plut.* 849–958; Xen. *Hell.* 2.3.38. Lofberg (1917) 25.
[181] Arist. *Ath. Pol.* 43.5.   [182] Isoc. 15.313–14.
[183] Aeschin. 1.1; Lycurg. 1.3.   [184] Lys. 12.2–3.
[185] Dem. 21.182; Thuc. 3.45.   [186] Dem. 59.109. See p. 191.

because the criminal succeeded in buying himself off by bribing possible accusers.[187]

THE ORDER OF EVENTS IN A CASE BEFORE THE PEOPLE'S COURT

Summons and preliminary hearing

Every case began thus: a plaintiff or accuser accompanied by two 'summoners' (*kleteres*) called out his adversary personally by word of mouth;[188] this step, called *prosklesis*, was a summons to appear before the relevant magistrate on an agreed day.[189] On that day the plaintiff or accuser handed in a written charge (*graphe*) to the magistrate and the defendant handed in a written reply (*antigraphe*).[190] The magistrate could reject the written charge if it was not within his sphere of competence, or wrongly formulated, or if the law did not recognize the offence charged;[191] it is not known whether he could reject a charge simply because he thought it unfounded.[192] If the charge was accepted by the magistrate the defendant could always raise a formal objection by *paragraphe*, which had to be judged by a court before the case could go any further.[193] (*Paragraphe* was a type of procedure in its own right, introduced shortly after 403, which dealt only with whether the case in question could be duly brought.) If the jury accepted the *paragraphe* the case could not proceed, but if they threw out the *paragraphe* it took its course.[194]

At the end of the first meeting the magistrate charged the parties to appear at a preliminary hearing (*anakrisis*).[195] He had also to see that the written charge was published in front of the Monument to the Eponymous Heroes.[196]

Simultaneously with the delivery of the written charge both parties had in most private suits to put up a court fee. These *prytaneia*, paid by both sides, were 3 drachmas in minor cases and 30 drachmas in major cases. They fell to the state, and in the last resort were really all paid by the loser, because after the case was over the loser had to reimburse the victor his *prytaneia*.[197] In the majority of public prosecutions what had to be put up was called *parastasis*, but how much it was and what happened to it remains unknown.[198]

[187] Dem. 25.46–8. Hansen (1975) 59 n. 23.   [188] Dem. 34.13; 53.14.
[189] Lys. 23.2.   [190] Dem. 45.45–6.   [191] Dem. 37.34.
[192] Harrison (1971) 90.   [193] Isoc. 18.1–3.
[194] Wolff (1966); Isager and Hansen (1975) 123–31.   [195] Dem. 58.8.
[196] Dem. 21.103.   [197] Poll. 8.38; Dem. 47.64.
[198] Arist. *Ath. Pol.* 59.3.

The *anakrisis* began with the parties swearing an oath (*antomosia*) as to the truth of the written charge and reply,[199] respectively. For public prosecutions the magistrate himself carried out the *anakrisis*,[200] but for most private suits he appointed an official arbitrator.

The duty of arbitrator (*diaitetes*) fell upon all citizens aged fifty-nine, and was connected with military service, because they were the men in the last of the forty-two years of liability to conscription.[201] They were divided into ten groups by tribes, and each group had to deal with the cases in its tribe for the year.[202] The magistrates, namely the Forty, chose the arbitrator for each individual case by lot from the relevant group.[203] The first priority of the arbitrator was to reach a settlement: if he could not, he had to give an award. The parties were required to make available all documents in the case, but otherwise the proceedings were wholly informal. If there was a settlement, or both sides accepted the award, the result merely had to be endorsed by the magistrate[204] and the case was at an end forthwith, but if either party was dissatisifed he could appeal to the court. The arbitrator collected all the documents in two sealed jars, one for each party, and delivered them to the magistrate who had initiated the preliminary hearing.[205] He was entitled to a fee of 1 drachma from each party.[206] When the preliminary hearing was thus completed, the magistrate applied to the *thesmothetai* for a court and for the case to be put on the list.[207]

The selection of jurors by lot

Court proceedings began at dawn[208] with the selection by lot of the day's jurors from those of the eligible 6000 who had turned up. The purpose of the selection by lot was twofold: a democratic procedure to give every citizen the same chance of selection as a juror,[209] and a bar against attempts at bribery (which was a capital offence both for the briber and the bribed).[210] Nevertheless we hear of various bribery scandals at the end of the fifth century and the beginning of the fourth,[211] and the daily selection of jurors by lot was doubtless introduced in the 370s[212] as a

[199] Harp. s.v. *antomosia*; Lys. 23.13.   [200] Is. 6.12.
[201] Arist. *Ath. Pol.* 53.4; *IG* II² 1926.   [202] Dem. 47.12.
[203] Arist. *Ath. Pol.* 53.5.   [204] Dem. 21.84–5.
[205] Arist. *Ath. Pol.* 53.2; Dem. 21.83ff. Boegehold (1982).   [206] Poll. 8.127.
[207] Arist. *Ath. Pol.* 59.1; *SEG* 26 72.26–8.   [208] Ar. *Vesp.* 689–90.
[209] Dem. 39.10–12.   [210] Aeschin. 1.87; Dem. 46.26.
[211] Arist. *Ath. Pol.* 27.5 (Anytos); Isoc. 18.11 (Xenotimos); Aeschin. 1.86 (Demophilos and Nikostratos).
[212] Kroll (1972) 89.

more effective control, since the system ensured that no one knew in advance how the day's jury panels would be manned, nor what cases a given panel would find itself judging.

It was the business of the *thesmothetai* to set the programme for each court day and work out how many jurors and courts were needed.[213] They also decided whether the day should be devoted to smaller private suits with 201 jurors or larger ones with 401, or to public prosecutions with 501 or more.

It seems that in Aristotle's time the courts were all together in the north-east corner of the Agora behind an enclosure, with ten entrances, one per tribe.[214] Early in the morning the potential jurors began arriving. In front of each of the ten entrances there were ten chests, each marked with one of the first ten letters of the alphabet, *alpha* to *kappa*. As people arrived they went to the entrances of their tribes and put their jury plaques in the chest whose letter corresponded to that on the plaque. At nine of the entrances stood an archon ready to supervise the allotment; at the tenth stood the secretary of the *thesmothetai*.[215] Then began the allotment, at each entrance, as follows.

When all potential jurors for one tribe had given up their plaques, the archon took one plaque from each of the ten chests, and the ten persons thus chosen counted at once as jurors; but their first task was to each take the chest with his letter on it and stand in alphabetical order, five at each of the two *kleroteria* set up at the gate.[216] A *kleroterion* was a *stele* of marble, of a man's height, with five columns of slots corresponding to the size of a jury plaque.[217] Each man with a chest was given a column of slots into which he put all the plaques from his chest starting at the top. Beside the *kleroterion* ran a narrow vertical tube, and into this tube were put black balls and white balls (the white balls numbering exactly a fifth of the total of jurors from that tribe needed for the day). The balls were then let out of the bottom of the tube one at a time. If the first ball was white the possessors of the first five plaques from the top were accepted as jurors;[218] if it was black, those five at once got back their plaques and went home.[219] The procedure continued until the last white ball came out, at which point the required number of jurors from that tribe had necessarily been reached. When all ten tribes had completed the procedure the jury list for the day was complete.

As soon as the selection of jurors was over, another selection by lot

[213] Arist. *Ath. Pol.* 59.1.
[214] Arist. *Ath. Pol.* 63.2. See p. 191.
[215] Arist. *Ath. Pol.* 63.1–2, 64.1.   [216] Arist. *Ath. Pol.* 64.1–2.
[217] Arist. *Ath. Pol.* 63.2, 64.2. Dow (1939); Bishop (1970).
[218] Arist. *Ath. Pol.* 62.2–4.   [219] Arist. *Ath. Pol.* 65.3.

began, to distribute them between courts. The entrance to each court had a different coloured lintel, and before the allotment began one of the *thesmothetai* had furnished each court-room with a letter from *lambda* onwards.[220] The jurors now went to a basket with acorns in, each acorn having a letter corresponding to one of the courts, and each juror took an acorn. The archon put the juror's plaque into a chest with the same letter as the acorn.[221] The juror went inside the enclosure, and a public slave handed him a staff of the same colour as the lintel of the entrance that bore the same letter as the acorn,[222] and at the entrance to the court the juror handed over both acorn and staff and received in exchange yet another token.[223]

There followed a third selection by lot, this time between the magistrates themselves: into one tube was placed one ball for each court, marked with that court's colour, and into another tube was placed a ball for each magistrate; a ball was taken from each tube, and so on, and that determined which magistrate was to chair which court.[224]

Lastly, within each court a final selection by lot took place, to choose one juror to control the water-clock, four to carry out the counting of votes, and five to carry out the payment of the jurors when the day's business was over.[225]

No one has ever calculated how long this procedure took;[226] but its frequency ensured that for all concerned it became absolutely routine, and it is a reasonable guess that all four allotments could have been got through in an hour.

The reason for describing the selection of jurors by lot so minutely is not that the details themselves are of much interest but because they illustrate better than anything else the fascination of the Athenians for ingenious devices: more than 2000 citizens, on some 200 days every year, spent at least an hour of their time playing this game, which takes four whole chapters of the *Constitution of Athens* (63–6) to describe. What is more, everywhere in the Athenian constitution we come across traces of equally complicated and time-consuming procedures, even if they cannot be reconstructed from the sources with equal precision.[227]

---

[220] Arist. *Ath. Pol.* 65.1–2; 63.5.   [221] Arist. *Ath. Pol.* 64.4; 63.2.
[222] Arist. *Ath. Pol.* 65.1.   [223] Arist. *Ath. Pol.* 65.2–3. Hommel (1927) 17.
[224] Arist. *Ath. Pol.* 66.1.   [225] Arist. *Ath. Pol.* 66.2–3.
[226] But see Keil (1902) 254–6.
[227] See for instance pp. 35 (ostracism), 250 (selection by lot of the *epistates ton prytaneon*), 220 (voting in *dokimasiai*).

Before the court

The hearing began with the reading aloud of the written charge and the reply of the defendant.[228] The parties were required to take an oath that they would confine themselves to what was relevant to their case,[229] after which they began their speeches – first the plaintiff or accuser and then the defendant. In a public prosecution each party made only one speech, but it could last up to three hours;[230] in a private suit the time was graduated according to the importance of the case, being at most about forty minutes, but in that case the parties were both given a chance to meet each other's points in a short reply and reply-to-reply.[231] As already noted, the parties were required by law to present their cases themselves, but they could share their time with one or more *synegoroi*.[232] A speaker could ask his opponent direct questions, and the opponent was obliged to answer.[233] The timing of speeches was regulated by a water-clock, *klepsydra*:[234] reading aloud of documents was done by a clerk and did not count against the speaker's time;[235] the speaker would ask the clock-keeper to put a stopper in the hole each time he called on the clerk to read.[236]

Requirements of proof

Aristotle in the *Rhetoric* distinguishes between argumentative proofs (proofs involving *techne*, *pisteis entechnoi*) and non-argumentative proofs (*pisteis atechnoi*). The former are the argumentations of the speech itself; the latter are the outside things that support them, comprising (1) laws, (2) witnesses, (3) contracts, (4) testimony under torture, and (5) oath.[237]

    1 Laws had to be put in as evidence, because the parties must discover the relevant laws, presumably in the state archive, and copy them for themselves.[238] In a few cases the laws have come down to us in the surviving speeches as read,[239] but more often we have only the speaker's interpretation of the law concerned.

    2 Witnesses were, naturally, the most important method of proof,[240] which is why people were always called to witness important legal transactions such as marriages, wills and loans of money.[241]

---

[228] Aeschin. 1.2. [229] Arist. *Ath. Pol.* 67.1.
[230] Aeschin. 3.197. Hommel (1927) 89.
[231] Arist. *Ath. Pol.* 67.2; Ant. 2–4. Rhodes (1981a) 719–28. [232] See p. 194.
[233] Lys. 22.5; Pl. *Ap.* 25D. [234] Young (1939) [235] Arist. *Ath. Pol.* 67.2–3.
[236] Dem. 45.8. [237] Arist. *Rhet.* 1355b35ff; 1375a22ff.
[238] Lys. 30.3. [239] Dem. 23.22, 28, 37, etc. Drerup (1898).
[240] Bonner (1905); Leisi (1908). [241] Is. 9.8, 11–13.

All free adults, including non-Athenians, were competent to be witnesses,[242] and not merely competent but required to be so if summoned.[243] From about 380 onwards, all statements were committed to writing and read out by the clerk, but the witness was required to be present in person, to reinforce the truth of his statement by his presence and to face a possible accusation of false witness.[244]

3 Contracts, wills and other documents of private law had far less importance as evidence than in a modern society: the development of law in the fourth century was still at a stage where the vast majority of legal transactions were oral acts reinforced by the presence of witnesses.[245]

4 Testimony by a slave was only valid if it had been given under torture (*basanos*). The examination could only be carried out with the permission of the owner, and for the information so obtained to be accepted as evidence required the consent of both parties.[246] Actual cases of the examination of slaves under torture are known only from public prosecutions,[247] but the possibility of such an examination was used as a rhetorical argument in many private-law speeches.

5 A party could not be a witness in his own case,[248] and women had no entry to the courts at all:[249] if a party,[250] or a woman,[251] had relevant evidence it could only be put to the jury in the form of an oath; like the results of examination under torture, oaths could only be read out as documentary evidence, and with the consent of the opposing party.

It is important that precedent in any formal sense is never adduced as one of the *pisteis atechnoi* and hardly ever referred to in argument: the Athenians held that the right and power to judge a case rested with the jurors for that case, and they were not to be bound by what others, on another day, might have done.

Evidence under points 2–5 could be demanded by a *proklesis* – that is, a call upon someone (usually the opposing party) to enter into a contract in which he obliged himself either to produce the evidence or to permit the demandant to produce it, with the proviso that both parties were obliged to accept the truth of the evidence produced if the opponent had accepted the *proklesis*.[252]

[242] Dem. 35.14.   [243] Is. 9.18–19.
[244] Bonner (1905) 46–7; Calhoun (1919)./
[245] Dem. 35.10–12. Pringsheim (1955); Thomas (1989) 41–4.
[246] Dem. 49.55; Is. 8.12. Thür (1977).   [247] Hyp., *P. Oxy.* 2686.
[248] Dem. 46.9–10.   [249] Dem. 57.67–8. Lipsius (1905–15) 874.
[250] Dem. 49.65.   [251] Dem. 39.3.   [252] Dem. 59.120–5.

When the defendant had completed his speech both parties had to say whether they proposed to accuse any of their opponent's witnesses of false witness.[253]

The final stage   The jurors had no opportunity for discussion during the casting of the votes: on the contrary, it was thought undesirable for them to exchange even a word or two about the case.[254] They were given, by the men in charge of the voting, two bronze voting-disks (about 5 cm in diameter), each with a short axle, one hollow and the other solid.[255] At the same time they received, in exchange for the token they had been given on entry, another token marked with the letter *gamma*, which was a receipt for their participation in the vote.[256] The crier announced that the solid disc was a vote for the defendant and the hollow one a vote for the plaintiff or accuser. Next, the jurors filed past two voting-urns, one of which was of bronze, and into it the juror cast the vote he intended to be valid – either the hollow one for the plaintiff or the solid one for the defendant; the other urn was of wood and into that he cast his other disc. If you held one wheel in each hand with its little axle between first and second finger no one could see how you distributed your vote, and thus the voting was secret. The urns had covers with room for only one voting-disk at a time,[257] to obviate cheating. The votes were counted on a specially prepared board with holes for the axles, and the crier pronounced the result.[258] If the votes were equal (because one or more of the jurors had had to leave the court) the defendant was acquitted,[259] and if the accuser in a public prosecution had not obtained one fifth of the votes he was subject to a fine of 1000 drachmas and partial *atimia*.[260] In certain private suits the unsuccessful plaintiff was liable to *epobelia*, a fine of one sixth of the sum at issue.[261]

Upon condemnation of the defendant, judgement was sometimes for 'specific performance' or for a penalty fixed by law; but in a whole set of cases, *agones timetoi*, the penalty or performance was determined according to the proposals of the parties.[262] In those cases the parties reappeared for a further short speech each, in which each proposed a penalty and justified it.[263] For both it was essential to remain within the realm of the reasonable, because the jurors only had a choice between the two proposals and could not propose any penalty on their own

[253] Arist. *Ath. Pol.* 68.4.   [254] Arist. *Pol.* 1268b8–11.
[255] Arist. *Ath. Pol.* 68.2; Boegehold (1963) 366–74.
[256] Arist. *Ath. Pol.* 68.2. Hommel (1927) 25.   [257] Arist. *Ath. Pol.* 68.3–4.
[258] Arist. *Ath. Pol.* 69.1.   [259] Aeschin. 3.252; Arist. *Ath. Pol.* 69.1.
[260] Dem. 53.1–2. Hansen (1975) 29–30.   [261] Dem. 47.64. Lipsius (1905–15) 937–9.
[262] Harp. s.v. *atimetos agon.* Lipsius (1905–15) 248–57.
[263] Arist. *Ath. Pol.* 69.2. MacDowell (1985) 525–6.

account. The voting on the penalty took place in the same way as that on the case itself, and each juror once more received the coloured staff back as a control mark.[264]

When the final vote had taken place the jurors received their 3 obols by handing in their token or their staff, as the case might be: the payments were organized by the five chosen jurors and were made according to tribes.[265]

THE POLITICAL ROLE OF THE PEOPLE'S COURT

The People's Court was competent to judge every lawsuit and condemn every sort of crime, but in a description of the working of Athenian democracy attention must be focused principally on the control exercised by the People's Court over the other organs of state and over the political leaders.

Given the organization of the courts it follows that all political control had to take the form of a trial based on an accusation by a named person against a named person: therefore the People's Court exercised its political role by giving judgement in political trials, and we must first try to define a 'political trial'.[266] In Attic speech there is no term for a political trial, nor can we, within the procedural system, pick out such trials as a well-defined group. One can begin, however, with the distinction between private suits (*dikai idiai*) and public prosecutions (*dikai demosiai*): in his speech *Against Meidias*, Demosthenes emphasizes that private suits are for offences against private persons, public prosecutions for offences against the *polis* as such.[267] It follows, of course, that such offences as treason naturally fell under the head of public prosecutions, but it must not be concluded that all public trials were also political trials. A glance at the list of known *graphai* and special public prosecutions is sufficient to show that many public prosecutions concerned offences against private persons – for example, the *graphe* (or *eisangelia*) *kakoseos orphanou*, the public prosecution for harming an orphan:[268] in that case the Athenians evidently felt that the offence was against the *polis*. Why? Presumably because an orphan and a minor was in no position to bring the case himself and needed the help of society. A public prosecution took place when the injured party was the *polis*, either directly, as in the case of

---

[264] Arist. *Ath. Pol.* 69.2. Hommel (1927) 100.
[265] Arist. *Ath. Pol.* 66.3; 69.2.
[266] Hansen (1990a) 231–3.
[267] Dem. 21.25–8, 32, 44–5. Cf. Pl. *Lg.* 767B; Arist. *Pol.* 1289a15–20.
[268] Is. 11.31–2.

treason, or indirectly, because the person harmed needed the help of the
polis to have the offence brought to justice.[269] Political trials, therefore,
were only one subgroup amongst public prosecutions: what can be said
is that every political trial was a public prosecution and never a private
suit (unless there was a misuse of procedure, which was by no means out
of the question).[270]

We can come a step nearer if we turn from the injured party to the
offender. As said above, every case had to be against a specific, named
person, so an institution or a collective could not be made defendant in
any prosecution. A charge against a decree of the Assembly had to be
directed at the proposer of the decree,[271] and an attack against a ten-man
board of magistrates had to be pursued as ten separate charges.[272] Thus,
a 'political trial' can be defined as a trial against a 'politician', which is
exactly what Demosthenes says in his speech *Against Timokrates*, where
he reminds the jury that there are two kinds of laws and two kinds of
sanctions for transgressing the laws: one type of law concerns the citizens
as private individuals in their daily mutual relations, and in that type the
sanctions are mild; the other type concerns the politically active citizens,
and in that case the sanctions are ferocious.[273] The recognition here of
political trials as a special category is notable;[274] but who were the
'politicians' in Athens? In its widest sense the term would have to include
everyone who took part in the Assembly, as well as the jurors, the
councillors and all the other magistrates. But we have seen that the
ordinary voter in the Assembly could not be brought to answer for a
decision he had voted for;[275] neither could a juror be made responsible
for a judgement he had voted for.[276] So a political trial could only be
brought either against speakers and proposers (in the Assembly or the
Council or before the *nomothetai*), or against accusers (in public
prosecutions) or against the magistrates, the *archai* (including the
Council).[277]

This analysis is corroborated by Attic linguistic usage. There is no
word corresponding to our word 'politician', only the word-pair *rhetores
kai strategoi*, 'the orators and the generals'.[278] If one scrutinizes all the
types of public prosecution in Athens, there are a number specifically
directed against orators or against *archai*, including the generals,[279] but
they are not all equally important. Several are only known from the
scholia and the lexica and we have not a single example of their use.
Others, however, occur so frequently in the sources that we can assume

---

[269] Ruschenbusch (1968) 47–53.
[270] E.g. Ant. 6.21–2, 35, 37–8 (a *dike phonou*).
[271] Dem. 23.104.
[272] Ant. 5.69–70.   [273] Dem. 24.192–3.
[274] Dem. 18.210, 25.40.   [275] Thuc. 3.43.5.   [276] Ar. *Vesp.* 587.
[277] Hyp. 3.27.   [278] See p. 268.   [279] Hansen (1990a) 236 n. 101.

that they were in constant use. There are three especially important kinds of prosecution that seem to have formed the basis of the political powers of the People's Court: the *graphe paranomon*, the *eisangelia eis ton demon* for treason or bribery, and the *euthynai*, arising out of the accounting given by magistrates at the end of their year of tenure. Each of the three is directed against a particular type of political leader: the *graphe paranomon* against the orators,[280] the *eisangelia* mainly against the generals,[281] and the *euthynai* against all magistrates.[282] These must be further discussed, but it is important to add briefly three more, which, though less important, were pendants to the others. Along with the *graphe paranomon* against decrees must be considered the *graphe nomon me epitedeion theinai* against laws; along with *eisangelia* to the people, usually used against generals, goes *eisangelia* to the Council, which could be employed against any magistrate for any offence; and with the *euthynai* at the end of a magistrate's tenure goes *dokimasia*, the court's preliminary examination of magistrates before their entry into office.

THE *GRAPHE PARANOMON* AND THE *GRAPHE NOMON ME EPITEDEION THEINAI*

Origin

The introduction of the *graphe paranomon* is often connected by historians with Ephialtes' reforms of 462 on the ground that it must have been introduced because the Areopagos had been reduced to a homicide court and had lost its power to supervise the laws.[283] There is, however, no sign of the *graphe paranomon* in the sources before the beginning of the Peloponnesian War,[284] and the first certainly datable example is in 415,[285] shortly after the last ostracism ever held at Athens. That is very likely no coincidence: in the fifth century the state's strongest weapon against its political leaders had been ostracism, but in the fourth it was a trial before the People's Court and, typically, a *graphe paranomon*.

Procedure[286]

A *graphe paranomon* could be brought by any citizen,[287] and was introduced by a *hypomosia*, an allegation under oath that a particular decree was unconstitutional (*paranomon*).[288] The oath could be taken either

---

[280] Aeshin. 3.4–5. [281] Dem. 13.5. [282] Aeschin. 3.15.
[283] Jones (1957) 123. [284] Thuc. 3.43.4–5. Wolff (1970) 21.
[285] Andoc. 1.17, 22. Hansen (1974) cat. no. 1. [286] Wolff (1970); Hansen (1974).
[287] Dem. 23.4; Din. 1.100–1. [288] Dem. 18.103.

before the vote, during the debate on that decree in the Assembly,[289] or after the voting, when the decree had been passed.[290] In the former case the debate was adjourned and in the latter case the decree was suspended until the People's Court had given a verdict in the matter.[291] The man who had sworn the *hypomosia* appeared before the court as accuser of the man who had proposed the decree: once he had sworn the oath he was obliged to pursue his accusation and deliver to the *thesmothetai*[292] a written charge[293] containing the grounds on which he held the decree to be unconstitutional, otherwise he was liable to the usual penalty for abandoning a public prosecution: a fine of 1000 drachmas and a ban on ever again bringing a *graphe paranomon*.[294]

The accusation was either that the decree was unconstitutional, formally or materially, or that it was undesirable and damaging to the interests of the people. A decree was formally unconstitutional if, for example, it was proposed by a citizen who had undergone *atimia*,[295] or if it had been put to the Assembly without a *probouleuma*.[296] An example of material illegality is the decree proposed in 352 for giving special protection to the general Charidemos by prescribing that if anybody killed him the killer should be extradited and put to death without trial. One of the arguments for its illegality was that intentional homicide must be tried by the Areopagos: if the laws prescribed a trial it was contrary to them to propose a decree permitting execution without trial.[297]

The notion of illegality was extended in the course of the fourth century from simple breach of some specific provision to breach of the (democratic) principles underlying the laws,[298] and so to the mere accusation of undesirability. Thus, in some surviving speeches in *graphai paranomon* the accusation is that the proposal is not just unconstitutional but damaging to the interests of the people, e.g. by bestowing honours and privileges on an unworthy person.[299] Historians often claim that, juristically speaking, the actual charge was still only one of illegality, and that the talk about the political consequences of the proposal was only so much rhetoric, designed to get the proposal thrown out, whether unconstitutional or not.[300] It is true that the speeches often contain passages that are juristically irrelevant but cleverly designed to impress a jury of amateurs; but as far as the *graphe paranomon* is concerned it can be shown that both parts of such an accusation had juristic rel-

---

[289] Xen. *Hell.* 1.7.12–14.   [290] Dem. 22.5, 9–10.

[291] Dem. 26.8.   [292] Hyp. 3.6.   [293] Aeschin. 2.14.

[294] Dem. 18.82.   [295] Dem. 22.24, 33; Dem. 59.5 (with Sauppe's conjecture).

[296] Dem. 22.5–7.   [297] Dem. 23. Hansen (1974) cat. no. 14.

[298] Wolff (1970) 45 67.   [299] Dem. 22.35–78; 23.100–214; Aeschin. 3.49–200.

[300] Madvig (1878); Lipsius (1905–15) 393.

evance.[301] For example, the law about grants of citizenship contained a provision that citizen rights must not be bestowed on anyone who had not done something to deserve them;[302] but by relying on that clause any citizenship decree whatsoever could be attacked before the court, with the sole argument that the new citizen was unworthy to become an Athenian, and such a wide interpretation of the idea of unconstitutionality must have had the result that any decree without exception could be attacked as unconstitutional.[303]

A *graphe paranomon* proceeded like any other public prosecution and went before a court with at least 501 jurors; in important cases the court could be enlarged with further panels of 500,[304] and in one famous case all of the 6000 who turned up on the day sat on the case together.[305] Judgement in a *graphe paranomon* had a twofold consequence: the arraigned decree was thereupon null and void, and the proposer was punished, typically with a fine, which sometimes could be merely nominal[306] but was sometimes so great as to put the unlucky man in lifelong debt to the state and in consequence visit him with *atimia*.[307] A third judgement against the same person led to total and permanent *atimia* as an automatic appendage.[308] On the other hand, the liability of proposers was limited to one year,[309] and a *graphe paranomon* brought after that limit had the sole consequence of annulling the decree, with no effect on the proposer.

One may feel surprised at the severity of the penalty when one reflects that a *graphe paranomon* against a decree was often brought after the Assembly had passed it: there seems something absurd about punishing a political leader for a proposal that the people had accepted, possibly unanimously.[310] The philosophy behind the penalty was, however, that the people are never wrong, and will indubitably reach the right decision if a matter is properly put to them, but they can be misled by cunning and corrupt orators and make erroneous decisions against their better judgement.[311] The *graphe paranomon* was actually the procedure by which the People's Court could overthrow decisions of the People's Assembly; but the procedure was directed not against the people but against the orators who had misled them.[312] It was a bulwark against corrupt dema-

---

[301] Hansen (1974); Maio (1983) 36–7; Yunis (1988).   [302] Dem. 59.89–91.
[303] Hansen (1987a) 99, *pace* Yunis (1988) 364–8.
[304] Dem. 25.28 with Weil's emendation, see Hansen (1976) 147.
[305] Andoc. 1.17. Hansen (1989a) 230.   [306] Hyp. 3.18.
[307] Dem. 58.1.   [308] Hyp. 4.11–12.
[309] Dem. 23.104; cf. Dem. 20.144 with *hypoth.* 2.3.   [310] Dem. 59.5.
[311] Thuc. 3.43.4–5; Dem. 23.97.   [312] Aeschin. 3.3–5. Hansen (1974) 54 n. 7, *pace* Bleicken (1984) 395–6.

gogues and sycophants, so a proposer must actually be punished the more savagely, the more people he had persuaded to vote for an unconstitutional decree.[313] Unfortunately, these severe sanctions seem merely to have brought into being a new kind of corruption. If a proposer risked being punished for his decree he naturally preferred to get someone else to make the proposal in that person's name, and then the real proposer could recommend the proposal in the Assembly without being technically responsible for it. Some of the less well-known proposers whose names can be read in the preambles of the surviving decrees may well have been men of straw for political leaders; and in the speech against Neaira we actually hear of sycophants who, for pay, let their names be inscribed on the proposals of others.[314]

Significance of the graphe paranomon

By this procedure, then, the court could overturn any decree passed by the Assembly; but how often was it used? We possess no fewer than thirty-five examples of its use in the period 403–322,[315] and that is a very large number if one thinks how limited our sources are. In two of those thirty-five cases, moreover, we hear of someone being accused a third time of proposing an unconstitutional decree: Demades was condemned three times and temporarily lost all his citizen rights,[316] and Philippides was at risk of a third condemnation in the *graphe paranomon* brought against him by Hypereides.[317] Aristophon, on his own admission, according to Aeschines, had been acquitted in no less than seventy-five prosecutions for proposing unconstitutional decrees in the course of a political career of more than half a century;[318] and in Aeschines' speech he is contrasted with Kephalos, who could congratulate himself on never having been prosecuted for any of the many proposals he had put before the Assembly.[319] The natural conclusion is that seventy-five is an excessively large number of prosecutions of a single political leader and probably an exaggeration on Aeschines' part, but that it was a notable exception for a political leader to escape altogether from exposure to a *graphe paranomon*. Demosthenes says that in the period after the defeat at Chaironeia he had to defend himself almost daily against people trying to accuse him of proposing unconstitutional decrees and attack him for political crimes and maladministration.[320] The vast majority of Athenian political leaders

---

[313] Aeschin. 3.16.   [314] Dem. 59.43; cf. Aeschin. 1.32. See p. 146.
[315] Hansen (1974) cat. nos 4–39 (delete no. 8).   [316] Diod. 18.18.2.
[317] Hyp. 4.11.   [318] Aeschin. 3.194. Whitehead (1986) 313–14.
[319] Aeschin. 3.194.   [320] Dem. 18.250.

must, at least once and often more than once in their careers, have been sent before the courts to defend the proposals they had made in the Assembly; and there is nothing against supposing that the jurors must have judged a *graphe paranomon* something like once every month.

Notwithstanding the obvious differences between ancient and modern societies, the significance of the *graphe paranomon* can best be set in relief by comparing it with the situation in the modern state in which the right of the courts to oversee legislation has been the strongest.[321] The Supreme Court of the United States has had the power to test and overthrow Congressional Acts since 1803.[322] In the period 1803–1986 that power was used 135 times: our sources show that at Athens that figure was nearly reached in two decades, let alone two centuries. In recent years, however, judicial review of laws has risen to Athenian heights both in Germany (constitutional court established in 1949) and in France (constitutional council established in 1958, very active from 1974). In both countries almost every important legislative battle in parliament between the parties will be carried before the constitutional court or council by the losing faction.[323]

No single reason can be given why the Athenians wanted to subject the decisions of their Assembly to a second scrutiny and pass the decision to the courts. The most important reason was, no doubt, the respect all Greeks felt for the superior wisdom and experience of age and for the oath sworn by the jurors; but the actual pattern of debate and manner of voting also helped to augment respect for the courts.

In the first place, the double consideration of a proposal allowed the possibility of coming to a better decision.[324] Presumably the majority of jurors in a *graphe paranomon* would have been present at the Assembly meeting where the proposal had been discussed, and the decree had doubtless been the subject of public argument between the Assembly's decision and the meeting of the court.[325] Dealing with the matter twice gave them a breathing-space to overcome the effects of mass psychosis such as a skilful orator could whip up in a highly charged situation.

Secondly, in the Assembly the decree subject to attack had been only a single item on the agenda, and the fact that every citizen could speak may sometimes have led to chaotic debates. In the court there was a whole day set for dealing with the proposal, the debate was between two parties only, and both sides had prepared their cases fully.

Thirdly, in the Assembly the vote was by show of hands; in the court it was by ballot. Consequently, in the Assembly there was always the

---

[321] Bonner and Smith (1930–8) ii 296.   [322] Abraham (1987) 66–75.
[323] Waltman and Holland (1988) 96–8, 140–4.   [324] Thuc. 3.42.1.
[325] Dem. 22.59.

possibility of group pressure on voters or corrupt misstatement of the result; in the court, by contrast, the method of voting protected the individual citizen and limited the chances of corruption. Thucydides explains that many opponents of the great Sicilian expedition in 415 were quite simply frightened of voting against the popular proposal in a show of hands;[326] and Aeschines insinuates that those in charge of the Assembly had often let themselves be bribed to make a false estimation of the vote[327] – and the charge comes in a passage where Aeschines is criticizing the Assembly and insisting on the courts as a bulwark of democracy.

Finally, the frequent use of the *graphe paranomon* is doubtless due to the fact that in Athens there was often sharp conflict between groups of political leaders. The group that lost a vote in the Assembly often refused to accept defeat and made use of the possibility of appeal to the courts; and thus, through the *graphe paranomon*, the courts gained a greater influence than they would have had if the political climate had been more tranquil.

Graphe paranomon against a proposed decree

A *graphe paranomon*, to repeat, could be brought before as well as after the passing of a decree, and the prosecution resulted in approval or rejection of the proposal.[328] What, then, happened if the court approved a proposed decree that had been stopped by *hypomosia* before being put to the vote in the Assembly? One might expect that the proposal would have had to be discussed anew in the Assembly before it could be passed;[329] but the only detailed description of a *graphe paranomon* of this kind seems to show that the final stage of the affair was approval of the decree by the court.[330] Thus, approval of a proposed decree by the court had the effect not merely that it was constitutional but also that it counted as having been passed. In such a situation the court seems to have appropriated the people's power of decision.

Graphai paranomon as political prosecutions

'Abolition of the *graphe paranomon* is as good as abolition of the democracy':[331] it is no surprise that the doctrine appears in speeches for the prosecution.[332] It is hard to judge how true it was; but abolition of democracy certainly was fatal to the *graphe*: it was suspended by the

---

[326] Thuc. 6.24.3–4.   [327] Aeschin. 3.3.   [328] Hansen (1989a) 271.
[329] Gerner (1949) 1288–9.
[330] Dem. 24.9–14. Hansen (1989a) 274–9, *pace* Hannick (1981).   [331] Dem. 58.34.
[332] Hansen (1974) 55–61.

oligarchs in 411[333] and again by the Thirty in 404,[334] and when Demetrios of Phaleron came to power in 317 he apparently had the right of the courts to test the legality of decrees transferred to a board of guardians of the laws (*nomophylakes*).[335] Under the democracy the *graphe paranomon* was always regarded as the bulwark of the constitution and the only sure defence of the laws.[336]

That may look somewhat less impressive if we examine the content of the decrees that were attacked as unconstitutional. Of the thirty-eight prosecutions on the subject, nineteen are directed against honorary decrees (including citizenship grants) and only thirteen against decrees of other sorts, while in the remaining six cases we do not know what sort of decrees they were brought against.[337] The central place of honorary decrees in relation to the *graphe paranomon* must be considered in conjunction with the fact that honours and grants of citizenship formed a very large part of all the decrees passed by the Assembly in the fourth century: such matters had a greater significance for the democracy, and for Athenian society as a whole, than a modern European might expect.[338] Only a few of the decrees for honours and citizenships that were attacked by *graphai paranomon* had major political resonance – notably Hypereides' proposal to free all the slaves and give citizenship to all the metics;[339] in most cases the attack was against a pretty trivial honorary decree. But the real purpose of the prosecution was not to overturn the decree but to get at the person who had proposed the honours or at the person whom it was proposed to honour. That comes out most clearly in the cases where the decree was for honours for a political leader and the proposer a minor follower: the most famous example is Aischines' *graphe paranomon* against the proposal of Ktesiphon to honour Demosthenes with a golden crown.[340] In such a case, the only person officially penalized was the insignificant author of the proposal, not the stratesman against whom the attack was really directed, and a condemnation by the court can hardly have had only that in view. The scrutiny of the legality of the decree was also only a secondary issue: the real purpose was a stab at the reputation of the political leader the decree was intended to honour. An honorary decree was a sort of vote of confidence by the Assembly, but it could be attacked in the court, and that turned the court into a political forum and its condemnation into a vote of censure.[341] If its vote

---

[333] Arist. *Ath. Pol.* 29.4.   [334] Aeschin. 3.191.
[335] Philoch. fr. 64. Wolff (1970) 25.   [336] Aeschin. 3.3–8.
[337] Hansen (1974) 62 (delete no. 8).   [338] See p. 157.
[339] Hansen (1974) cat. no. 27.   [340] Hansen (1974) cat. no. 30. See p. 8.
[341] Hansen (1974) 62–5.

was favourable, however, that was equivalent to final approval of the decree, so that one can practically say that it was the court and not the Assembly that bestowed the honours.[342]

Graphe nomon me epitedeion theinai

After 403/2 the *graphe paranomon* could be used only against decrees:[343] against laws a new procedure was instituted, the *graphe nomon me epitedeion theinai* or 'public prosecution for having proposed and carried an unsuitable law'.[344] The procedure was exactly the same as that of the *graphe paranomon*, and the consequences for the proposer were also the same: we actually know of one case where the proposer was condemned to death and executed.[345] This *graphe* had the result that a decision taken by those who had sworn the Heliastic Oath in their capacity as *nomothetai* could be overturned by the same set of people in their capacity of *dikastai*. The main difference, perhaps, was that the jurors had available a whole day to consider the *nomos* that had been arraigned, whereas the *nomothetai* could pass several *nomoi* on the same day, so the advantage of the *graphe* was that the law received a renewed and possibly more thorough inspection. In fact, double consideration of the same matter was one of the characteristics of Athenian democracy, particularly in the fourth century. The principle occurs in two variants: the same matter is considered by two different bodies, or the same body considers the same matter twice. The *graphe nomon me epitedeion theinai* seems best regarded as belonging to the latter category, of which another example was *anapsephisis*, the right of the Assembly to overturn a decision of its own at another session.[346] The *graphe nomon me epitedeion theinai* was not nearly as frequently employed as the *graphe paranomon*: in the orators we have only six examples of it[347] as against thirty-five of the *graphe paranomon*. The best-known cases are the prosecution of Leptines in 355/4[348] and of Timokrates in 354/3.[349]

EISANGELIA

The word *eisangelia* means literally 'denunciation', and it was used in legal language as a technical term for a variety of procedures that had in

---

[342] Aeschin. 3.243; Dem. 18.222.   [343] See p. 175.
[344] Dem. 24.33; Arist. *Ath. Pol.* 59.2. Wolff (1970) 31–2.   [345] Dem. 24.138.
[346] See p. 307.   [347] Hansen (1974) 47 n. 21.   [348] Dem. 20.
[349] Dem. 24.

common that they were set in motion by a denunciation. The basic procedure branched out into several varieties, according to which authority the denunciation was made to,[350] but by far the most important variety was that used for political prosecutions, which began with *eisangelia* to the Assembly (*eisangelia eis ton demon*) or to the Council (*eisangelia eis ten boulen*). *Eisangelia* to the Council could only be used against magistrates and for maladministration by magistrates, but *eisangelia* to the people could be used against any citizen who had allegedly committed a political crime.[351] *Eisangelia* to the Council is described in detail below in the chapter on the Council; in what follows we shall concentrate on the much more important *eisangelia* to the people.

The denunciation law

Eisangelia to the people was regulated by a law the main part of which is quoted in Hypereides' speech for Euxenippos.[352] It prescribes that a denunciation (*eisangelia*) may be made to the Assembly

> (1) if anyone tries to overthrow the *demos* of Athens or joins others to overthrow the *demos* or forms a conspiracy (*hetairikon*); (2) if anyone betrays a city or fleet or a force on land or sea; (3) if anyone takes payment, being a speaker [*rhetor*, i.e. in the Assembly], so as not to give the best advice to the *demos* of Athens.

Hypereides is not quoting the whole text of the law, and in the third section, for example, has left out a provision that 'breaking a promise to the people' was a crime for which a man could be charged by *eisangelia*.[353] But all contemporary sources show that *eisangelia* to the people, after the passing of this law at the end of the fifth century,[354] was exclusively used for the three crimes specified in the quotation from Hypereides: attempt to overthrow the constitution, treason, and political corruption.[355] It has sometimes been asserted that *eisangelia* was also permitted against any serious crime not covered by any other law,[356] but that belief is supported only by the lexicographical tradition, which conflicts with the contemporary sources.[357] It is true, however, that *eisangelia* was often abused[358] by the most grotesque interpretations of the sections of the denunciation law

---

[350] Harp. s.v. *eisangelia*.
[351] Hansen (1975) 21–8; (1980) 93–4, *pace* Rhodes (1979) 111–14.
[352] Hyp. 3.7–8.   [353] Dem. 49.67. Hansen (1975) 13–14.
[354] Thalheim (1902, 1906).   [355] Hansen (1975) 19–20.
[356] Rhodes (1972) 163–4; (1979) 107–8.
[357] Harp. s.v. *eisangelia*. Hansen (1980) 91–3.
[358] Hyp. 3.1–3.

quoted by Hypereides. An Athenian citizen who left Athens in panic directly after the defeat at Chaironeia in 338 was eight years later denounced by *eisangelia* and charged with treason;[359] and he was only acquitted by the court because the votes were equal.[360] And a man who was suspected of seducing an Athenian woman was brought into court by an *eisangelia* on the argument that seduction of a freeborn Athenian woman was an attack on the democracy.[361]

Procedure

Eisangelia was a fixed item on the agenda of the Assembly once in every prytany. In an *ekklesia kyria* any citizen could make a denunciation,[362] which led to a debate[363] resulting in a proposal for a decree; the proposal, besides the name of the person denounced, had also to contain an account of the crimes alleged against him, the paragraph of the denunciation law under which he was accused,[364] and, if appropriate, what penalty he ought to suffer.[365] Before 355 the proposal must also have included a suggested decision whether the prosecution should be passed to the People's Court or whether the Assembly should judge the case itself.[366]

An *eisangelia* to the people could, it seems, be carried out without any preparation by the Council[367] as long as it was brought in an *ekklesia kyria*, where *eisangelia* was an obligatory item;[368] it was, on the other hand, a legal requirement to begin with a referral to the Council if the denunciation was to be brought in an ordinary meeting of the Assembly, when *eisangelia* was not automatically on the agenda, so that it needed a *probouleuma* in order to be introduced.[369] The Council would also come into the picture in an *eisangelia eis ton demon* if the Assembly, having received an *eisangelia*, decided that the Council should make a concrete *probouleuma* to be put to it at the next meeting.[370]

It was, of course, the denouncer who put the proposal for a decree to the Assembly,[371] and he was then under a duty to appear as accuser: the citizen who abandoned an *eisangelia* once made was liable to a fine of 1000 drachmas.[372] He was, however, dispensed from the usual further provision that an accuser in a public prosecution was liable to a fine of 1000 drachmas plus partial *atimia* if he obtained less than a fifth of the votes:[373] treason and political corruption were reckoned as such dangerous crimes that the Athenians wanted no obstacle to stand in the way of an

---

[359] Lycurg. 1. Hansen (1975) cat. no. 121.   [360] Aeschin. 3.252.
[361] Hyp. 2; Lycurg. fr. 70. Hansen (1975) cat. no. 119.
[362] Arist. *Ath. Pol.* 43.4.   [363] Dem. 19.116.   [364] Hyp. 3.29–30.
[365] Lycurg. 1.113.   [366] Hansen (1975) 51–3, but cf. 37 n. 2.   [367] Hyp. 2.3.
[368] Arist. *Ath. Pol.* 43.4.   [369] Rhodes (1981a) 525.
[370] *IG* II² 125.6–9 = Tod 154 and Harding (1985) no. 66.   [371] Hyp. 3.29.
[372] Dem. 25 *hypoth.* 2–3; Lycurg. fr. 11.

accuser. It may have been just this favoured position of the accuser in an *eisangelia* that led to abuse of the procedure; and shortly before 330 the Athenians were obliged to apply the customary provision to the case of *eisangelia* as well.[374]

Whereas the accuser was more advantaged in an *eisangelia* than in other prosecutions, the accused was often less so. *Eisangelia* was one of the few public prosecutions that could result in custodial arrest between the denunciation and the trial,[375] and in such a case the accused had to prepare his defence while in prison, with no opportunity to assemble the witnesses or documents he might need. Custody was not, however, obligatory in every case, so an accused person could often remain free, which gave him the chance to escape prosecution by flight into exile.[376]

When the Assembly or the Council had dealt with the case it went to the *thesmothetai*,[377] who carried out the *anakrisis* and summoned a court. In the fifth century and the first half of the fourth, however, the Assembly often resolved to hear the matter itself,[378] in which case it was the duty of the *prytaneis* to summon an extraordinary meeting of the Assembly, whose only agenda of the day was the hearing of that one case, and in which judgement was given by show of hands.[379] In about 355 the Assembly lost its last vestige of judicial power, and after that all prosecutions by *eisangelia* were judged by the People's Court.[380] For such cases the *thesmothetai* normally summoned a court of 501, but for important trials it might be reinforced to up to 1001 or 1501 jurors,[381] and in one case we hear of a court manned by no fewer than 2501.[382] In court the case proceeded like any other public prosecution, with the speech for the prosecution, the speech for the defence, and a vote of 'guilty' or 'not guilty'. *Eisangelia* was an *agon timetos*, so if the verdict was 'guilty' the jury had to vote a second time to choose between the penalties proposed by the accuser and the (now convicted) accused.[383] The sources show that the usual penalty was death, but exceptionally a fine could be imposed: this, however, could be so huge that the convicted man became a state debtor, and so *atimos* for the rest of his life.[384]

Eisangelia as a political prosecution

Denunciation to the people gave the People's Court enormous power over the political leaders of Athens and the magistrates, not just because of

---

[373] Hyp. 2.8. [374] Dem. 18.250; Lycurg. 1.3. [375] Dem. 24.63.
[376] Philoch. fr. 149A. Hansen (1975) 35 n. 54. [377] Dem. 24.63.
[378] Dem. 49.10. Hansen (1975) 51 n. 1. [379] Dem. 19.31.
[380] Lipsius (1905–15) 191–2; Hansen (1975) 53–5. [381] Philoch. fr. 199.
[382] Din. 1.52. [383] Dem. 23.167. Hansen (1975) cat. no. 96.
[384] Din. 1.14. Hansen (1975) 35.

the severity of the penalties but still more because of the frequency of its use. In spite of the limitations of the sources we hear of no less than 130 prosecutions by *eisangelia* in the period 492–322. Sixty of them were directed against private citizens and metics, thirty-four against generals (one against eight generals collectively), ten against other magistrates, nine against citizens holding other public office, such as envoys or trierarchs, and seventeen against speakers in the Assembly.[385] The high figure for prosecutions of private persons by *eisangelia* is largely explained by the scandals of 415, when at least forty-eight citizens and metics were accused and condemned for having profaned the Mysteries[386] and desecrated the city's herms[387], (pillars with a bust of Hermes on top and sculptured genitals on the front, standing in the streets of Athens).

Eisangelia to the people was the weapon especially used against the generals. The Board of Generals comprised only ten men out of a total of roughly 700 annual magistrates; nevertheless, we know of thirty-four *eisangeliai* against generals, whereas the sources refer only to ten *eisangeliai* against all the other magistrates put together. One famous case was the Trial of the Generals after Arginoussai, when eight generals were collectively condemned for treason for failing to pick up the survivors after the battle,[388] and another was that against Timotheos, Iphikrates and Menestheus after the defeat at Embata in the Social War (356/5); in that case the court exhibited a quite exceptional mildness, for Menestheus was acquitted, Iphikrates dismisssed, and Timotheos fined 100 talents.[389] *Eisangelia* to the people was, in fact, the sword of Damocles that hung over the generals, as is shown not just by the large number of prosecutions but also by the way it is described in the orators,[390] as, for example, in Demosthenes' bitter outburst in the *First Philippic*:

> Things are nowadays so scandalous that every single general is judged in your court two and three times on charges of life and death, while not one of them has the guts to fight a single battle against the enemy for life and death. They prefer the death of kidnappers and cutpurses to a proper one: only criminals die by death sentences; generals ought to die in battle.[391]

The first reaction of any historian to this jeremiad is, naturally, that it must be a blatant overstatement – which, of course, it is. But detailed study of the sources suggests that Demosthenes' critique is not entirely beside the mark. He made it in 351, so we can best judge its truth if we

---

[385] Hansen (1975) 58.   [386] Hansen (1975) cat. nos 13–42.
[387] Hansen (1975) nos 43–60.   [388] Xen. *Hell.* 1.7.1–35. See p. 6.
[389] Isoc. 15.129. Hansen (1975) cat. nos 100–2.   [390] Hansen (1975) 59.
[391] Dem. 4.47.

take the period 432–355 and compare the number of all known Athenian generals with the number of *eisangeliai* against generals. From those seventy-seven years we know the names of 143 generals, who filled 289 of the 770 generalships held all told.[392] Of those 143, thirty-five were denounced to the people by *eisangelia*, one of them actually three times and another twice. Now, it is not the case that our sources mention generals especially often because they were denounced by *eisangelia*; rather the opposite.[393] The sources seem to show that at least a fifth of all generals were confronted sooner or later by an *eisangelia*; in other words, in every board of ten generals there were probably at least two who, in the course of their military careers, would be denounced by that procedure.[394] And their first *eisangelia* was usually their last, for it usually ended with condemnation and the death sentence[395] – in the light of which many a general preferred to flee into exile and be condemned in his absence.[396] Since we also know that *eisangelia* to the people was only one of the procedures by which the Athenians put their generals on trial,[397] we must allow that Demosthenes' statement about the frequency of trials of generals is not so far from the truth after all.

There can be no doubt that a general was often denounced to the people for having lost a battle or being unlucky in a campaign,[398] but the sources show that the charge was always framed in terms of corruption or treason, as required by the denunciation law; there exists no single example of a charge framed in terms of incompetence or of a general being brought before a court explicitly to answer for a lost campaign.[399] Nor do the sources usually allow us to decide whether a general was guilty of the crimes for which he was condemned. In fact, the very large number of prosecutions by *eisangelia* faces the historian with an uncomfortable dilemma: either the Athenian Assembly had a notable tendency to elect corrupt and traitorous generals, or else the People's Assembly and the People's Court had a habit of condemning honourable generals on false grounds. There is, naturally, nothing to prevent both explanations from containing part of the truth; but, irrespective of which horn of the dilemma we take, we must conclude that the notably large number of political trials points to a serious defect in the Athenian political system. Athens had 30,000 full citizens: even in a modern nation state with millions of inhabitants such a large number of political prosecutions would be remarkable. It must also be pointed out that the

---

[392] Hansen (1990a) 237 n. 105.   [393] Hansen (1975) 60–2.
[394] Hansen (1990a) 238–9; Sinclair (1988a) 146–52.
[395] Hansen (1975) 64 n. 4.   [396] Hansen (1975) 35 n. 54.
[397] Hansen (1975) 63.   [398] Fornara (1971) 38; Tolbert Roberts (1982) 123.
[399] Hansen (1975) 65.

defect was structurally related to the democratic constitution: ancient democracy was as a rule charactrerized by frequency of political prosecutions, whereas oligarchies suffered from the opposite defect, that leaders were hardly ever called to account at all.

The *graphe paranomon* was directed against the speakers in the Assembly, and *eisangelia eis ton demon* mainly against the generals whom the Assembly had elected; the power of the courts to oversee the 600 or so magistrates selected by lot was exercised mainly through control of them at the point of entry into office (*dokimasia*) and at their rendering of accounts at the end of their period of office (*euthynai*). Generals also were supposed to undergo *dokimasia* and *euthynai*; but generals could be re-elected, even in their absence, and in these circumstances *dokimasia* may have been omitted or become a mere formality, with the general holding office continuously for several years before undergoing proper *euthynai*.[400]

The courts could also call magistrates to account for their administration in the course of their period of office, and that was mainly done through prosecutions raised by *eisangelia* in the Assembly or the Council. *Dokimasia* and *euthynai*, on the other hand, were carried out directly by the courts: the Assembly was not involved at all, and the Council took part only in the case of the coming year's councillors[401] and the nine archons.[402] A candidate rejected by the Council always had the right of appeal to the courts.[403] All other *dokimasiai* were carried out by the courts directly,[404] presided over by the *thesmothetai*.[405]

Dokimasia[406]

This procedure gave the courts the chance to offset the more unfortunate consequences of selection by lot and to control, and if necessary overturn, an election made by the Assembly. It was, however, not an examination of the candidate's competence, but only of his formal qualifications, conduct and political convictions.[407] The Council, or court, was required to reject a candidate if he was not an Athenian citizen or was under thirty or was seeking re-election to the same office, but also if he was guilty of

---

[400] Arist. *Ath. Pol.* 59.2.   [401] Lys. 31.1–2.   [402] Lys. 26.8, 21.
[403] Arist. *Ath. Pol.* 45.3, 55.2.   [404] Arist. *Ath. Pol.* 55.2.
[405] Arist. *Ath. Pol.* 59.4.
[406] Aeschin. 3.14–15. Lipsius (1905–15) 270–8; Kahrstedt (1936) 59–63; Harrison (1971) 201–3; Rhodes (1972) 176–8.
[407] Lys. 26.9. Adeleye (1983).

any crime normally punished with *atimia*.[408] Ane even if he possessed all the formal qualifications he could always be turned down on the ground that he was unworthy to hold office.[409] We possess four speeches in *dokimasia* proceedings, all from the corpus of Lysias,[410] and in all four the charge is of oligarchic sympathies and complicity with the oligarchic regime of 404/3, which the amnesty of 403 had rendered unpunishable but which could very well still disqualify a man at a *dokimasia*.

Dokimasia, whether before the Council or the People's Court, began with a series of questions that the candidate had to answer, with support from witnesses. We hear mostly about the questions addressed to the nine archons,[411] but we know that the same or similar questions were put to all candidates.[412] The candidate had first to state the name and deme of his father, father's father, mother and mother's father; then he had to say whether he worshipped Apollo Patroös and Zeus Herkeios, i.e. testify that he was a member of a phratry, and show that he kept up his family cult; and finally he had to prove that he was kind to his parents, belonged to one of the three highest property classes and had done his military service.[413] When the candidate had answered all these questions and provided witnesses to the truth of his testimony, any citizen could come forward and accuse him, and he had to answer the accusations there and then. After that a vote was held, in the Council by show of hands, in the court by ballot.[414] A vote was obligatory even if no accuser had presented himself,[415] which means that when the votes were counted a candidate might find himself rejected as unworthy without any charge having been made, and without any right of reply.[416]

Dokimasia seems to have had no effects except the rejection of the candidate (*apodokimasia*),[417] and the uncovering of a punishable offence in the course of proceedings only had an effect beyond rejection if the *dokimasia* was followed by a prosecution. The *dokimasia ton archon* was not a specific type, like *graphai* and *eisangeliai* or *euthynai*: there was no summons, no *anakrisis* and no penalty for the accuser if he withdrew the charge or got less than one fifth of the votes.[418] The court was open to all, and any number of accusers might appear, one after another. Several *dokimasiai* took place in a day, so that the time for speeches must have been much less than in true public prosecutions, and we have no information whether the court was manned with 501 jurors as in a normal public case.

---

[408] Arist. *Ath. Pol.* 55.3.   [409] Lys. 16.9.   [410] Lys. 16, 25, 26, 31.
[411] Arist. *Ath. Pol.* 55.3; Xen. *Mem.* 2.2.13.   [412] Din. 2.17.
[413] Arist. *Ath. Pol.* 55.3.   [414] Arist. *Ath. Pol.* 55.4.
[415] Arist. *Ath. Pol.* 55.4; Lys. 26.10.   [416] Hansen (1990a) 235 n. 96.
[417] Arist. *Ath. Pol.* 45.3, 55.4.   [418] Hansen (1975) 30.

Dokimasia took place in the last months of the year, after the election and allotment of magistrates, which happened at the earliest in the seventh prytany. In most cases it was a mere routine, taking only a few minutes per candidate, but even so it was enormously time-consuming. The Council had to handle 509 *dokimasiai* and the courts at least 700, and it had to be done individually, so that in favourable circumstances it must have taken the Council several days and a section of the court several weeks to get through: it is not at all surprising to learn in one of Lysias' speeches that the first part of the *dokimasia* of next year's archon had only been carried out by the Council on the penultimate day of the year, so that the subsequent part, before the court, could not be carried out in time.[419]

There is a surprising contrast between the time-consuming nature of the *dokimasia* and its limited political significance. We know of only eight cases in which a candidate at *dokimasia* was accused and had to answer.[420] In one case only, the *dokimasia* was of an *elected* magistrate: in spring 406 Theramenes was elected general but was accused at his *dokimasia* and rejected on a vote.[421] The other seven known cases are all of magistrates selected by lot. *Dokimasia* must have been virtually always a mere formality, and to our way of thinking it must have been deadly boring; that the Athenians went through it year after year for centuries shows that their attitude to this sort of routine must have been quite different from ours. They evidently enjoyed participation in their political institutions as a value in itself.

Control of magistrates during their tenure

Even after entry into office magistrates had to undergo regular inspection of their administration. Any citizen could at any time impeach a magistrate to the People's Court by one of the usual procedures;[422] but besides that the Athenians possessed several special procedures for maladministration that were set in motion as a matter of routine every prytany. Characteristic of these procedures is that the initiative was taken in the Assembly or the Council but the case had to go to the courts and be judged by a jury.

An obligatory item on the agenda of an *ekklesia kyria* was the 'vote on the magistrates', *epicheirotonia ton archon*.[423] Under that item any citizen could propose a vote of no confidence against any one soever of the 700 or so magistrates,[424] whether elected or selected by lot: it was levelled

---

[419] Lys. 26.6.   [420] Hansen (1987a) 177 n. 655.
[421] Lys. 13.10.   [422] Ant. 6.44–5.
[423] Arist. *Ath. Pol.* 43.4, 61.2. Hansen (1975) 41–4.   [424] Din. 3.15.

sometimes against an entire board of magistrates,[425] and it could be used against magistrates *in absentia*[426] – which shows that the vote was taken without discussion. If the show of hands went against him (*apocheirotonia*) the magistrate was instantly suspended.[427] *Apocheirotonia* was not, however, an independent procedure: it had to be followed up by, for example, an *eisangelia*,[428] which was also a fixed item on the agenda of an *ekklesia kyria*, and came directly after the *epicheirotonia*. But we know of one case in which *epicheirotonia* was followed by an *apophasis*,[429] so *eisangelia* was not the only or the obligatory procedure against a suspended magistrate. In any event, the case was judged by the court.[430] If the jury followed the recommendation of the Assembly, the suspended magistrate was dismissed and punished; but the court could perfectly well decide against the suspension and acquit the accused, whereupon he was at once restored to his office.[431]

In addition to all that, the Council undertook a regular inspection of the accounts of all magistrates. Every year a board of ten inspectors (*logistai*) was selected by lot from amongst the councillors, with the duty, every prytany, to inspect the administration by the magistrates of public funds entrusted to them.[432] Moreover, each individual councillor had a duty to give information and bring a prosecution if he had reason to believe that a magistrate had committed an offence in the course of his duties. If that took place, the councillor concerned, or a committee of the Council, came forward as accuser,[433] and the Council pronounced a provisional judgement; if it found the magistrate guilty, the case had to go to the court, which pronounced the definitive verdict.[434]

By extension of the Council's official jurisdiction against magistrates, any private person had the right to bring an accusation to the Council (*eisangelia eis ten boulen*) on his own account against any magistrate for any offence committed in office.[435] In contrast to the *eisangelia eis ton demon*, this procedure could be used only against magistrates or persons carrying out a public duty,[436] but to make up for that it covered any sort of offence, whereas *eisangelia eis ton demon* could only be used for treason and corruption. The case came first to the Council: the citizen came forward as accuser and the magistrate had an opportunity to defend himself. The Council's hearing resulted in a vote by ballot, and if the

[425] Dem. 58.27–8.   [426] Dem. 50.12.   [427] Arist. *Ath. Pol.* 61.2.
[428] Dem. 23.167–8; Aeschin. 3.52.
[429] Din. 3.1, 16. Hansen (1975) 43 n. 47.
[430] Arist. *Ath. Pol.* 61.2.
[431] Dem. 58.27–8.   [432] Arist. *Ath. Pol.* 48.3.
[433] Ant. 6.49–50.   [434] Arist. *Ath. Pol.* 45.2.
[435] Arist. *Ath. Pol.* 45.2.
[436] Hansen (1975) 21–8; MacDowell (1978) 169–70.

verdict (*katagnosis*) was 'guilty' a second vote was taken by show of hands to decide whether the defendant should be punished with a fine of at most 500 drachmas or with a more severe penalty. If the Council decided for a severer penalty, a new hearing before the court was obligatory; if the Council decided for a penalty of not more than 500 drachmas, the case only came before a court if the defendant appealed.[437] The *thesmothetai* were required to summon a court and preside.[438] The court could overturn or confirm the Council's verdict; if it confirmed it, the jury determined the penalty according to the proposals of the parties: it could vary from a nominal fine[439] to a death sentence.[440]

Euthynai

Not only actual magistrates, but anyone who had carried out a public function or had had charge of public funds was obliged to submit himself to an accounting, *euthynai*.[441] *Euthynai* applied, as a matter of routine, to envoys, priests, trierarchs, and even members of the Areopagos,[442] but they were first and foremost a weapon against the 500 councillors and the 700 or so magistrates, both those elected and those selected by lot.

When magistrates retired from office at the end of the year, they had to submit their accounts to yet another board of ten inspectors (*logistai*), who were assisted by ten advocates (*synegoroi*).[443] Within one month the inspectors caused all the accounts to be inspected,[444] and as the inspection proceeded the magistrates were summoned before a court of 501.[445] The inspectors presided over this court,[446] while the advocates presumably appeared as accusers[447] and reported on the board's audit of the accounts, whereupon any citizen could come forward and accuse the magistrate;[448] and, even if the accounts had been approved by the inspectors and the advocates, the crier still had to ask whether anyone wished to bring an accusation.[449] An accusation had to be either of embezzlement (*klopes*) or of bribery (*doron*) or of some lesser financial offence (*adikiou*).[450] When the accused had made his defence the jury voted;[451] in contrast to *dokimasia*, where a vote had to be taken on every magistrate, it may be taken for granted than in *euthynai* there was only a vote on those magistrates against whom an accusation had been laid.[452] In a conviction for *klopes* or *doron*

---

[437] Dem. 47.42–3; Arist. *Ath. Pol.* 45.2.   [438] Dem. 24.63.

[439] Dem. 47.43.   [440] Dem. 51.8–9. Hansen (1975) cat. no. 142.

[441] Lipsius (1905–15) 286–98; Kahrstedt (1936) 165–80; Harrison (1971) 208–11; Piérart (1971) 526–73; MacDowell (1978) 170–2.

[442] Aeschin. 3.17–20.   [443] Arist. *Ath. Pol.* 54.2.   [444] Harp. s.v. *logistai*.

[445] *Lex. Cant.* s.v. *logistai*.   [446] Dem. 18.117.

[447] Though no explicit evidence. MacDowell (1978) 171.   [448] Dem. 18.117.

[449] Aeschin. 3.23.   [450] Arist. *Ath. Pol.* 54.2.   [451] Aeschin. 3.23.

the penalty was a tenfold fine, in the case of *adikiou* a simple fine.[453]

After the inspection of accounts there followed the second phase of the *euthynai*, in which the magistrates were made to answer for any other offences they might have committed in the exercise of their duties. This phase was activated by a committee of ten correctors (*euthynoi*), one per tribe, and twenty assessors (*paredroi*), two for each corrector. Each corrector had to sit with his assessors at the Monument to the Eponymous Heroes, each in front of the statue of the hero of his tribe; and, within the first three days after the inspectors had completed their examination of a magistrate's accounts, any citizen or metic could go to the corrector for the magistrate's tribe and present a written accusation against him. If the corrector thought the accusation justified, he handed it on to the Board of Forty, if the case needed to be dealt with in a private suit, or to the *thesmothetai* if it was going to involve a public prosecution. The Forty, or the *thesmothetai*, as the case might be, were now responsible for the next state of the case, and for summoning a court to hear it.[454] Of course, the person who had presented the accusation was obliged to appear as accuser before the court. *Euthynai* do seem to have been a specific procedural type,[455] and, unlike the other examination procedures, they could lead either to a private suit before the Forty or to a public prosecution before the *thesmothetai*. A magistrate could, it seems, be accused of any conceivable offence, and the penalty was not confined to a tenfold fine: it was fixed by the court according to the proposals of the parties, and several sources refer to the death penalty as a possibility.[456]

The inspectors had to complete their inspection within the first thirty days of the year, and written accusations had to be handed in to the correctors no more than three days after completion of the inspection. *Euthynai* of magistrates, therefore, were concentrated in the first two months, Hekatombaion and Metageitnion (July–August and August–September); and even magistrates who had been dismissed during the year did not have to submit accounts before the beginning of the following year.[457] Only *euthynai* of envoys and others chosen *ad hoc* for public duties were dealt with as they came up all through the year.[458] *Euthynai* were held for each individual member of a board,[459] and the court presided over by the inspectors must, during Hekatombaion, have got through more than a thousand separate cases. The vast majority of *euthynai* no doubt took only a couple of minutes each, but the time expended must still have been enormous. The number of prosecutions

[452] Hansen (1990a) 236 n. 97.   [453] Arist. *Ath. Pol.* 54.2.
[454] Arist. *Ath. Pol.* 48.4–5.
[455] Dem. 19.103–4; Aeschin. 2.139. Hansen (1975) 45–8.   [456] E.g. Lys. 27.7.
[457] Dem. 49.25. Hansen (1975) 45 n. 63.   [458] Dem. 19.211.
[459] Dem. 22.39.

resulting from *euthynai* was naturally far smaller, but in those circumstances the individual cases were relatively time-consuming: the prosecutions before the *thesmothetai* must have taken a whole day each. It is
astonishing how few actual cases of *euthynai* we know about, with the
name of the magistrate concerned: just fifteen or so in all.[460] And we
have not a single example of a jury passing a death sentence as a result
of *euthynai*. It must be concluded that the submission of accounts, though
without doubt important, did not possess nearly as much importance as
the *eisangelia* or the *graphe paranomon*.

---

[460] Hansen (1989a) 10 n. 32.

9

The Magistrates

At Athens in the time of Demosthenes all important decisions were taken by the Assembly, the *nomothetai* and the People's Court, but it was the magistrates[1] who had to prepare the decisions and implement them.[2] 'Magistrates' is a translation of *hai archai*[3] (a synonym was *hoi archontes*,[4] though that was mainly used to denote the nine archons[5]). The word *arche* actually means a magistracy,[6] but it was used with just about equal frequency of the person holding the magistracy;[7] hence *hai archai*, 'the magistrates', was the collective term for a group of people who constituted a branch of the government on a par with the *ekklesia* and the *dikasteria*.[8]

Administration was the branch of government least easy to accommodate to the notions of direct democracy, in which political freedom consisted in the right of all to participate. That may well be why Aristotle in his list of the essential principles of democracy in the *Politics*[9] says little about the Assembly or the courts, which raised no particular problems in that regard, but gives a whole list of principles about office-holding.

1 All citizens have the right to vote for magistracies and to hold office themselves.
2 Everybody should hold office in turn.
3 All offices should be subject to selection by lot, except the few that demand special skills.
4 Admission to office should not be limited by any property requirement.
5 Except for military posts no one may hold the same office more than once (or at most a few times).
6 Periods of office must be as short as possible.

---

[1] Busolt and Swoboda (1926) 1054–150; Kahrstedt (1936); Develin (1989).
[2] Arist. *Pol.* 1322b12–7   [3] Aeschin. 3.13ff. Hansen (1980c) 152–4.
[4] *SEG* 26 72.24–5 = Harding (1985) no. 45; Is. 1.14.
[5] *IG* II[2] 47.37; Lys. 7.22.   [6] Arist. *Ath. Pol.* 56.2.   [7] Andoc. 1.84.
[8] Arist. *Pol.* 1317b35–6; Dem. 25.20.   [9] Arist. *Pol.* 1317b17–1318a3.

7 Everything must be decided by the Assembly and nothing by the magistrates.

8 Magistrates must receive pay, preferably all, but in any case those who eat together.

9 If a post is by long tradition held for life its powers must be restricted and selection to it must be by lot.

To those principles enumerated by Aristotle must be added two more.

10 The administration of the magistrates must be under the control of the decision-making organs and the magistrates must always be under a duty to account to the Assembly and the courts.[10]

11 Magistrates should exercise their power in boards and not as individuals.[11]

Aristotle insists that the term *archai* does not include all those with public duties chosen by election or by lot: for example, neither priests nor *choregoi* nor criers nor envoys count as *archai* in the proper sense.[12] The *archai* were a well-defined group of state officials, and they were defined in various laws, paraphrased by Aischines in his speech *Against Ktesiphon*, from which we can conclude that the criteria for being a magistrate included being chosen by election or by lot [from amongst those aged not less than thirty]; undergoing a preliminary examination (*dokimasia*) before taking up office; holding office for at least thirty days; and rendering accounts (*euthynai*) on relinquishing office. And their rights included presiding over the courts (*hegemonia tou dikasteriou*), imposing minor fines (*epibolas epiballein*), and controlling public funds and supervising public workers.[13]

A summary of the most important magistracies forms the main part of the second half of the *Constitution of Athens*:[14] Aristotle lists and describes forty-six different magistrates and boards of magistrates.[15] The most noteworthy feature of the list is that Aristotle counts the Council of Five Hundred as a board of magistrates.[16] That corresponds to his general assertion in the *Politics* that the Council is the most important board of magistrates in a democratic city-state;[17] it corresponds also to the Athenians' own perception of their constitution: in many laws *hoi archontes* is used as a common term for magistrates and councillors.[18] Furthermore,

---

[10] Arist. *Pol.* 1298a22, 1318b21-2.   [11] Theophr. *Char.* 26.1-2.

[12] Arist. *Pol.* 1299a14-20. Hansen (1980c) 170-3.

[13] Aeschin. 3.13-15, 28-30. [] not in the source. See p. 227 n. 24.

[14] Arist. *Ath. Pol.* 43-62.   [15] Hansen (1980c) 155.

[16] Arist. *Ath. Pol.* 43.2-49.5. Hansen (1981c) 347-51.

[17] Arist. *Pol.* 1299b30-2, 1317b30-1, 1322b12-17.

[18] Dem. 24.54; *SEG* 26 72.19-26 = Harding (1985) no. 45.

Aischines treats the Council as one of the boards of magistrates selected by lot;[19] and Demosthenes speaks of the selection by lot of 'any *arche*, such as the Council, the *thesmothetai* and the rest'.[20] However, numerous other passages distinguish between the Council and the magistrates,[21] and in the speech *Against Aristogeiton* we meet a fourfold division of the organs of state into the Council, the Assembly, the People's Court, and the boards of magistrates.[22] Naturally, by its size, composition, functions and involvement with the Assembly the Council had a quite special place amongst the boards of magistrates, but that must not be overstressed: in modern accounts of Athenian democracy the authors have been so taken with the differences as virtually to forget that the Council was a board of magistrates at all,[23] and that its real competence (like that of the other boards) was limited to bringing matters before the decision-making organs and carrying out the decisions they made.

QUALIFICATIONS AND FUNCTIONS

Qualifications

The age-limit was the same for magistrates as for the *nomothetai* and the jurors: a candidate must be at least thirty. That principle was maintained throughout the history of the democracy.[24] Formally the old rule still applied in the fourth century that magistrates must be drawn from the top three Solonian classes, but it was a dead letter.[25] Selection was either by election or by lot: magistrates chosen by the Assembly,[26] and in certain exceptional cases by the ten tribal assemblies,[27] were elected on a show of hands; selection by lot was performed in the Sanctuary of Theseus, presided over by the *thesmothetai*.[28] All magistrates (i.e. *archai*, not other officials such as envoys or priests) had to undergo the preliminary *dokimasia*,[29] and, like the jurors, they had to swear an oath to carry out their duties properly and in consonance with the laws. The oath was different according to the board concerned:[30] the surviving fragments of the Council's oath[31] are especially concerned with the Council's jurisdiction,[32] while, according to tradition, the oath of the archons[33] went back to Akastos,[34] a mythical archon of about 1000 BC: it contained an often-

---

[19] Aeschin, 1.106, 109.   [20] Dem. 39.10.   [21] Dem. 24.20.
[22] Dem. 25.20.   [23] Hansen (1981c) 345 n. 2.
[24] Hansen (1980c) 167–9, *pace* Develin (1985).   [25] See pp. 44–5.
[26] See pp. 159–60.   [27] Aeschin. 3.27–30.   [28] Aeschin. 3.13.
[29] See pp. 218–20.   [30] Din. 3.2, 10.
[31] Xen. *Mem.* 1.1.18; Lys. 31.1. Rhodes (1972) 194.
[32] Dem. 24.147, cf. 144.   [33] Arist. *Ath. Pol.* 55.5.   [34] Arist. *Ath. Pol.* 3.3.

quoted passage to the effect that an archon who accepted a bribe had to put up a statue of his own weight in gold[35] at Delphi;[36] but, though Athenian magistrates were often impeached and condemned for corruption, no such statue, as far as we know, was ever erected.

Functions

Hai archai means literally 'the rulers', and in many oligarchical city-states that name was fully justified, for all power lay in the hands of the magistrates,[37] who were chosen from amongst the richest citizens,[38] and assembly and people's court were unknown institutions[39] or mere ciphers.[40] But in democratic states the principle was to give power to the people and prevent the establishment of a magisterial élite: Aristotle states this with his usual clarity in two remarks in the *Politics*: 'the fourth type [of democracy] is this: all meet and take decisions, while the magistrates can decide nothing but only prepare the decisions',[41] and 'even the power of a council is destroyed in such democracies, where the people meet and transact everything'.[42] In accordance with this principle the Athenian *archai*, as the democracy grew up, were reduced from 'rulers' to administrators.

In Athens political power was divided into power of initiative (*legein, graphein*), power to prepare business (*probouleuein, anakrinein*), power to decide (*kyrion einai*), and power to execute (*prostattein, epitattein*). Only Aristotle has any theoretical discussion of this division, but that is not surprising: many of the workings of Athenian democracy can be reconstructed by means of the 'survivals' (inscriptions and speeches), but the only theoretical discussion of the principles underlying them is in the 'accounts', mainly Aristotle's *Politics*.[43]

Every process of political decision-making requires someone to take an initiative, and at Athens that was left to *ho boulomenos*, the citizen volunteer.[44] His initiative, however, was mediated through the magistrates, a group of officials who called the meetings, prepared the business, presided, and put the motions to the vote, but did not themselves possess the power of decision. That was reserved to the citizens, in the Assembly, the boards of *nomothetai* and the courts, which could not take any initiative on their own account[45] and were convened by the Council or by the other boards of magistrates. Herein lay an important division of responsibilities.

---

[35] Arist. *Ath. Pol.* 7.1.   [36] Plut. *Sol.* 25.3.

[37] Arist. *Pol.* 1275b13–17; 1293a28.   [38] Arist. *Pol.* 1292a39–b7.

[39] Arist. *Pol.* 1275b7.   [40] Thuc. 5.84.4.   [41] Arist. *Pol.* 1298a28–32.

[42] Arist. *Pol.* 1299b38–40.

[43] Arist. *Pol.* 1275a22–33, 1299a3–1300b12, 1321b4–1323a10. See pp. 9–10.

[44] Aeschin. 3.220 (Assembly); Ar. *Plut.* 916–19 (courts).   [45] Hansen (1981c) 353.

The Council and the *prytaneis* had the sole right to call meetings of the Assembly[46] and the *nomothetai*,[47] but only very exceptionally did the committees of the Council have the right to preside over the courts:[48] even in cases such as *eisangeliai* to the Council it was the *thesmothetai* who summoned the court and presided over its proceedings.[49] By contrast, the other boards of magistrates had the right to summon and preside over the courts,[50] but no such right over the Assembly or the *nomothetai*. If the *strategoi* wanted an Assembly summoned they had to apply to the *prytaneis* and the Council,[51] and if the *thesmothetai* wanted a board of *nomothetai* appointed they had to go through the Assembly and the Council.[52]

Besides the right to summon and preside over the decision-making bodies the magistrates had another very important task. Government is not just a matter of taking decisions: they have to be executed, and that was at Athens first and foremost the job of the magistrates. Xenophon, Plato and Aristotle all assert that the most important duty of the magistrates is to give orders to the citizens,[53] and the ephebic oath included a promise to obey the magistrates.[54] Many provisions in the surviving laws and decrees are instructions to magistrates to put the decisions into force;[55] and when sentence was passed in a public prosecution it was the magistrates who had to see to its execution.[56]

The magistrates were furnished with the necessary authority by giving them special legal protection and the power to impose minor fines. As a sign of public authority every magistrate wore a myrtle-wreath in the course of his duties,[57] and violence against or defamation of a magistrate on duty was punished more severely than in the case of an ordinary citizen.[58] If anyone refused to obey the command of a magistrate, he could be subject to an inappellable fine of up to, probably, 50 drachmas,[59] and the Council could impose up to 500 drachmas[60] (though in that case there was appeal to the courts).[61]

HOW MAGISTRATES WERE CHOSEN

In a modern European state there tends to be a hierarchy of officials, and officers of state are chosen by their superiors. In a Greek city-state

---

[46] Arist. *Ath. Pol.* 43.3.   [47] Dem. 24.27.
[48] *SEG* 26 72.20, 26 = Harding (1985) no. 45.
[49] Dem. 24.63; Arist. *Ath. Pol.* 45.1.   [50] See p. 189.   [51] See p. 133.
[52] See p. 166.   [53] Xen. *Mem.* 3.9.11; Pl. *Pol.* 260B; Arist. *Pol.* 1299a25–7.
[54] Tod 204.11–12.   [55] *SEG* 26 72 = Harding (1985) no. 45. Hansen (1981c) 357–9.
[56] Dem. 24.80–1.   [57] Dem. 26.5; Poll. 8.86.   [58] Dem. 21.32.
[59] *IG* I³ 82.26.   [60] Dem. 47.43.   [61] Arist. *Ath. Pol.* 45.2.

matters were quite otherwise, in the first place because the administration of the state was not hierarchical in structure,[62] and secondly because the officials were chosen either by election or by lot.[63] The former is not particularly unfamiliar to us: in the United States many officials are elected, and in European democracies election, direct or indirect, is the prescribed procedure for choosing new holders of the highest ranks — direct in the case of the president of a republic, indirect in the case of the ministers in a parliamentary democracy. Selection by lot, on the other hand, is totally unknown today. It was practised in some Swiss cantons[64] and many Italian city republics[65] until the eighteenth century, but to us it sounds crazy,[66] and nothing illustrates better the huge gap between ancient and modern democracies. We can just about imagine a people's assembly or, at a pinch, a people's court, but nobody nowadays would dream of picking a chief of police or an under-secretary of state by putting into a hat the names of all citizens who said they wanted to stand and choosing at random.[67]

True, there was in ancient Greece itself great disagreement whether magistrates should be chosen by election or by lot. Sokrates thought it ridiculous of the Athenians to have magistrates so chosen when they would never have thought of choosing a helmsman or architect or flute-player that way,[68] and Aristotle in the *Politics* underscores the fact that election of magistrates is the oligarchic and selection by lot the democratic way.[69] In fact sortition was the way of 'radical' democracy (Aristotle's type IV), while the original 'moderate' democracy (type I) practised election:[70] this was still democratic because every citizen had the right to vote in the elections and be elected,[71] whereas in oligarchies both were limited by a property census.[72]

Selection by lot

The vast majority of Athenian magistrates were selected by lot; and, since almost all of them held offices that only lasted a year and could not be held by the same person again, the people had to choose something like 1100 persons in that manner every year, i.e. the 500 councillors plus some 600 other magistrates. The remaining 100 or so magistrates were chosen by election. Yet, notwithstanding the very large number of places to be filled, lots were drawn, as a rule, only amongst such such citizens

---

[62] Busolt and Swoboda (1926) 1059.   [63] Aeschin. 1.13; Arist. *Ath. Pol.* 43.1.
[64] E.g. in Basle after 1715.   [65] Najemy (1982) 99–125.   [66] Elster (1989) 78–92.
[67] Headlam (1891) 1–3.   [68] Xen. *Mem.* 1.2.9; Arist. *Rhet.* 1393b4–8. See p. 236.
[69] Arist. *Pol.* 1294b7ff.   [70] Arist. *Pol.* 1298a20, 27. See p. 68.
[71] Arist. *Pol.* 1300a31–4; 1317b18–19.
[72] Arist. *Ath. Pol.* 1300b1–3; 1292a39–b7.

as presented themselves for allotment.[73] In the case of the Council, candidates were nominated in their deme assemblies, while in the remaining cases candidature was based on the tribes. A distinction must also be made between the archons, who were selected by a double procedure of allotment, and the rest, in whose case there was only a single drawing of lots. So there are three different procedures to describe: (1) the selection of archons, (2) the selection of other magistrates, and (3) the selection of the Council; but that third case will be described below when we come to the Council. Common to all the procedures was the use of individual plaques[74] and the *klerotenia* we have met with at the allotment of jurors.[75] Every citizen over thirty who was chosen received a bronze plaque inscribed with his name, patronymic and deme, and stamped with the official stamp (the Gorgon's head):[76] the only difference was that the jury plaques might be obsolete every year as soon as the next body of jurors had been chosen, whereas those for the magisterial elections could be kept for a longer period, often for the whole of a citizen's life.[77]

The archons were selected in two stages: first, each tribe selected ten candidates by lot in its own assembly,[78] and then each group of ten submitted to a second sortition carried out centrally, which produced a final group of ten, one per tribe, to be the nine archons plus the secretary of the *thesmothetai*.[79] Substitutes were chosen, and, if any one of those chosen was rejected at his *dokimasia*, he was automatically replaced and the substitute had to undergo *dokimasia* in his place.[80]

The rest of the magistrates were probably selected by a single central procedure.[81] What was required was often one representative per tribe,[82] and the allotment must have been carried through board by board: at each selection those persons were allowed to stand who had not held that particular office before. Candidates rejected for one post probably had the choice of taking part in one or more subsequent allotments. In this case, too, substitutes were chosen, at least to some extent,[83] though the frequent lacunas in the boards of magistrates[84] show that the arrangement for deputies did not suffice to fill the empty places.

The central selection of the magistrates was no doubt carried out on a single day:[85] it was presided over by the *thesmothetai* and took place in the Sanctuary of Theseus,[86] located near the Prytaneion east of the

---

[73] Isoc. 15.150; Lys. 6.4, 31.33. [74] Dem. 39.10.
[75] Dow (1937) 198–215, (1939) 1–34; Bishop (1970). See p. 198.
[76] Kroll (1972) 53–6, 59–68, 91–4. [77] Kroll (1972) 75–8.
[78] Arist. *Ath. Pol.* 8.1. [79] Arist. *Ath. Pol.* 55.1. [80] Lys. 26.6, 13–15.
[81] Aeschin. 3.13.
[82] Arist. *Ath. Pol.* 47.2, 48.1, etc.; *IG* II² 1388.1–12. Busolt and Swoboda (1926) 1062.
[83] Dem. 58. 29. [84] See p. 233.
[85] *IG* I³ 52.13–15 = *M&L* 58 and Fornara (1977) no. 119. [86] Aeschin. 3.13.

Akropolis.[87] As all 1100 new selected magistrates had to undergo *dokimasia* before entering upon office, the allotment must have taken place a little before the end of the year,[88] probably at the same time as the election of the military magistrates, i.e. in the seventh prytany or later.

Recruitment of magistrates selected by lot

Since magistracies were reserved to citizens over thirty, the 1100 or so magistrates annually selected by lot had to be drawn from a pool of about 20,000 persons. Such a degree of participation of ordinary citizens in the running of the state cannot but cause astonishment, not to say envy, to a supporter of democracy in the twentieth century, where the problem is the dwindling participation of people in the process of government.[89] How was it possible?

Besides the 500 councillors the Athenians had to pick by lot about 600 other magistrates. In spite of the larger total the recruitment of the other magistrates may have made fewer demands on the size of the population than that of the Council, for the following reason: it was forbidden to hold the same magistracy twice,[90] but there was nothing to prevent a man from being appointed to a different one. That could not be done until the magistrate had undergone his *euthynai* for the post he had just left, and that was not till early in the next year;[91] so it was impossible to be an allotted magistrate two years running, but there was nothing to stop someone holding office evey other year. We actually have numerous instances of politically active citizens who were magistrates many times,[92] and it is not beyond all possibility that the offices were in fact concentrated in relatively few hands.

The picture in the literary sources is that there was often competition for offices,[93] and that might induce us to suppose that there were always at least enough candidates for the selection by lot, but the inscriptions show that there were difficulties of recruitment: whereas the lists of the *prytaneis* and the councillors show that the Council always had its full 500 members, it is clear from the accounts and inventories of the other magistrates that there were often vacancies on the other boards.[94] In the inventories of the Treasurers of Athena between 403/2 and 344/3 we get twenty-three boards of treasurers, and they ought to have had ten men each, but only nine are complete, and the other fourteen have only nine

---

[87] Dontas (1983) 60–3.   [88] Lys. 26.6.
[89] Finley (1973b) 33; Holden (1974) 143, 186.   [90] Arist. *Ath. Pol.* 62.3.
[91] Dem. 24.150. Kahrstedt (1936) 140. See p. 292.
[92] Lys. 20.5; Andoc. 1.147; Aeschin. 1.106.
[93] Dem. 39.10–2; Isoc. 7.25; Din. fr. i.2.   [94] Hansen (1980b) 121.

or eight or seven or six members;[95] and similar vacancies can be traced in the *poletai*[96] and the Superintendents of the Dockyards.[97] Although the system allowed for some substitutes, the Athenians in the fourth century could not always fill their boards of magistrates properly; and from that two conclusions can be drawn: that not enough volunteers came forward for the selection process, but that the Athenians did not resort to compulsion to fill the lists. Many boards were supposed to consist of one representative per tribe, and except for the archons there do not seem to have been selection meetings in the tribal assemblies: candidates applied directly to the central meeting. If it then appeared that one tribe or other could not supply enough candidates, a place was left empty on the list.

The fact that the literary sources talk of competition for places while the epigraphical sources reveal vacancies in some boards of magistrates is doubtless to be explained by the considerable difference in nature of the offices to be filled. Some were lucrative,[98] while others actually involved outlay;[99] some gave prestige, others were not highlyregarded: to be the eponymous archon of the year was expensive but a distinction,[100] whereas to be one of the Eleven gave little status but possibly nice perquisites.[101]

Election

The just over 100 magistrates chosen not by lot but by election included all the military commanders,[102] all those who looked after the training of the ephebes,[103] the most weighty financial officers,[104] some persons in charge of sacred affairs, such as the Commissioners for the Eleusinian Mysteries,[105] and a few others, such as the Superintendent of the Water Supply (*epimeletes ton krenon*).[106] Election was not regarded as anti-democratic provided that all citizens could vote and any citizen could in principle be elected;[107] but Athenian history demonstrates that the combination of lot and election did lead, to some degree, to the concentration of power in the hands of the elected magistrates. Originally the state was run by the archons,[108] and they were elected until the reforms of 487/6, after which they were selected by lot and declined in importance.[109] In the rest of the fifth century it was the generals, elected, who

---

[95] Kolbe (1929) 262; Tréheux (1965) 13. Develin (1986) 82–3.
[96] *Hesperia* 10 (1941) 15–27 no. 1.1–5.   [97] *IG* II² 1617.71–80.
[98] Dem. *Prooem.* 48.2; Isoc. 7. 24–5.   [99] Arist. *Ath. Pol.* 56.4.
[100] Dem. 20.28, Lys. 26.11.   [101] Arist. *Pol.* 1322a1–4.
[102] Arist. *Ath. Pol.* 61.1–7.   [103] Arist. *Ath. Pol.* 42.2.
[104] Arist. *Ath. Pol.* 43.1.   [105] Arist. *Ath. Pol.* 57.1.
[106] Arist. *Ath. Pol.* 43.1.   [107] See p. 225.
[108] Thuc. 1.126.8.   [109] Arist. *Ath. Pol.* 22.5.

were the political leaders;[110] and then, in the fourth century, when citizen generals were sometimes replaced by and sometimes behaved like *condottieri* at the head of semi-private mercenary armies,[111] the Athenians found it safer to put civil magistrates at the head of affairs of state:[112] the new financial posts, especially the treasurership of the Military Fund and the Board for the Theoriç Fund, were chosen by election, not by lot, and, what is more, probably for four years at a time.[113] And elected magistrates ran the training of the ephebes, at least after the reforms of the 330s.[114]

The election of magistrates took place in the Assembly by show of hands.[115] The main election meeting (*archairesia*) was held at the earliest possible date after the sixth prytany (February) on which the omens were favourable;[116] there had to be enough time for the *dokimasia* of those elected before their entry into office at the beginning of the next year in July. But only the military commanders were elected at that special meeting,[117] well before the beginning of the campaigning-season; the financial officers, who only took up their posts a month after the beginning of the year, i.e. after the Panathenaic Festival,[118] were probably elected later than the generals[119] – and, as noted above, perhaps only every fourth year; and the officials who ran the ephebic training were also only elected after the new year had begun,[120] to take office in the third month, Boedromion.[121]

The election meeting was called, like other Assembly meetings, by the *prytaneis*, and there had to be the usual *probouleuma* of the Council.[122] Citizens who sought election could advertise themselves before the meeting,[123] and groups such as the *hetaireiai* might canvass for one of their members,[124] but it is improbable that the *probouleuma* contained a list of candidates: candidature took place orally at the meeting. It was not forbidden to propose onself, but usually a candidate was put up by some other citizen present.[125] Any full citizen could be proposed, and there was no rule that the candidate had to have given his consent – a man could even be proposed and elected *in absentia*:[126] to allow oneself to be elected to an office was the moral duty of every citizen, though anyone who had been proposed against his will could decline election by giving a declaration under oath (*exomosia*) that he had a legitimate excuse.[127]

---

[110] Arist. *Ath. Pol.* 28. 2–3, cf. Hansen (1989a) 17 n. 46.   [111] See p. 270.
[112] Hansen (1989a) 31.   [113] *IG* II² 338. Develin (1984) 135–6.
[114] See p. 301.   [115] Aeschin. 3.13. Hansen (1987a) 191 n. 781.
[116] Arist. *Ath. Pol.* 44.4; *IG* II² 892.5–6.   [117] Aeschin. 3.13; Arist. *Ath. Pol.* 44.4.
[118] Arist. *Ath. Pol.* 43.1.   [119] Aeschin. 3.24. Hansen (1987a) 191 n. 786.
[120] *SEG* 28 103.27–8. Hansen (1987a) 191 n. 787.   [121] Golden (1979) 32.
[122] Arist. *Ath. Pol.* 44.4.   [123] Dem. 13.19.
[124] Thuc. 8.54.4; Pl. *Tht.* 173D; Ar. *Lys.* 577–8 with schol.   [125] Piérart (1974A) 139.
[126] Kahrstedt (1936) 40 n. 2.   [127] Theophr. *Char.* 24.5.

Of the actual voting-procedure we know virtually nothing, except that it was by show of hands, which, as usual, implies estimation of the outcome rather than an exact count. But two passages in Plato's *Laws*[128] are probably based on Athens, in which case they furnish four further clues towards a reconstruction.

1 Candidates could be proposed in advance of the meeting, but that did not prevent further names from being introduced after the meeting had begun.
2 Proposing of candidates and voting on them alternated, so new candidates could be proposed even after the voting had begun.
3 In some cases a candidate was proposed specifically to oppose another named candidate.
4 The vote was by a show of hands, in which the electors had either, on the one hand, to accept or reject a candidate, or, on the other, to choose between two specific candidates.

Applying these principles to Athens, the election of a board of ten can be reconstructed in the following way.[129] Candidates were proposed one by one, and after each proposal the people voted for or against that candidate. As soon as ten candidates had secured a majority, any new candidate could only be proposed in opposition to one of those already elected, and the vote was then between those two. If the new candidate got the majority, he ousted his opponent. The proceedings were terminated as soon as no more opposition candidates come to the fore. If a board had to comprise one representative from each tribe, the procedure was possibly as follows. A candidate from tribe I was proposed, and the people voted for or against him. The first candidate to get a majority was elected unless a named opponent to him was proposed, in which case the vote was a vote between the two of them. When no more candidates were proposed, the people proceeded to the next tribe, and so on.

Selection by lot, election and democracy

Why was the lot seen as so particularly characteristic of democracy? Critics of democracy tended to link selection by lot with their notion of the democrats' ideal of equality:[130] if all men are equal you had better draw lots for who shall govern the state. But in fact, as we have seen, democrats never asserted that all men were equal, only that they ought to have equal opportunity.[131] In Perikles' funeral speech the Athenians

---

[128] Pl. *Lg.* 755C–D; 763D–E. Piérart (1974b) 242–6, 291–5.
[129] Piérart (1974a); Hansen (1987a) 44–6.
[130] Isoc. 7.21–2; Pl. *Lg.* 757B. See p. 84.   [131] See pp. 81–4.

are actually praised for laying weight, in the manning of public offices, on the personal merits of individuals and not doing it by mere rotation:[132] Perikles (or Thucydides) thus actually rejects any link between lot and equality. And in the Debate on the Constitutions in Herodotos the selection of magistrates by lot is linked to the sovereignty of the people,[133] which is quite a different matter: the purpose is to reduce the hold of the magistrates on the reins of government. The same idea can be seen in book 6 of Aristotle's *Politics*, where a long series of limitations on the powers of the magistrates is coupled with the principle that all power ought to be exercised by the people.[134] Seen in that light, Sokrates' famous criticism can be seen to be the sophism it is: how absurd it is, says Sokrates, to pick the magistrates by lot when you would not pick a helmsman, or whatever, in that way.[135] The sophism, of course, resides in the unstated premise that the magistrates have the same power to steer the ship of state as a helmsman has to steer his ship. but the Athenians chose their magistrates by lot precisely to ensure that they should *not* be the steersmen of the state: one of the purposes of the lot was to diminish the powers of the magistrates.The lot was based on the idea not that all men were equally expert, but that all men were expert enough at what they were chosen for, and that by the use of the lot magistracies would cease to be attractive as weapons in the struggle for power.

In a democracy the desire to limit the powers of magistrates is coupled with the desire to get everybody to serve as magistrates by turns.[136] Rotation is secured partly by having short periods of office and partly by enlarging the number of posts to the greatest possible extent. If, then, a very large proportion of the citizenry are to hold some office sooner or later, selection by lot is the logical way to do it. Even in a democracy some offices are coveted because they lead to prestige[137] and advantage,[138] and selection by lot ensures that the question of who obtains what post shall be settled by chance,[139] whereas election opens the way for strife and, ultimately, *stasis*: the democrats preferred the lot because it obviated corruption and fractionalism.[140] The critics countered by asserting that the lot might well produce magistrates with oligarchical sympathies, and that the risk of *stasis* was actually aggravated if you had enemies of the regime amongst your magistrates[141] We do not know what the counter-reply of the democrats was, but it can be guessed: that after selection

---

[132] Thuc. 2.37.1. See p. 73.   [133] Hdt. 3.80.6.
[134] Arist. *Pol.* 1317b28–30.
[135] Xen. *Mem.* 1.2.9; Arist. *Rhet.* 1393b4–8. See p. 230.
[136] Ps. Xen. *Ath. Pol.* 1.2; Arist. *Pol.* 1317b2, 19–20.
[137] Lys. 26.3, 11.   [138] Lys. 21.18.   [139] Din. 3.16; Isoc. 7.23.
[140] Arist. *Pol.* 1303a15; *Rhet ad Alex.* 1424a12ff.
[141] Isoc. 7.22–3; *Dissoi Logoi* DK 90.7.

the candidates all had to undergo *dokimasia*, which, after 403/2, was reformed so as to give the People's Court the opportunity to reject on the spot anyone who might be suspected of oligarchical tendencies.[142]

Collegiality

Oligarchs went in for election and the holding of posts by individuals; democrats chose the lot and collegiality. The opposition between collective and individual office-holding is one of the few differences between oligarchy and democracy not explicitly mentioned by Aristotle in the *Politics*; but his pupil Theophrastos in his little book *Characters* hits that nail squarely on the head: his sketch of the 'Oligarchical Man' begins with an Assembly meeting at which a motion is proposed to set up some board of ten, whereupon the Oligarchical Man shouts 'One's enough, as long he's a man', and the only line of Homer he knows is 'More than one ruler is fatal, I say: let one be the ruler'.[143]

Collegiality implied that all members of a board were on an equal footing: there was no fixed chairman and no member had more authority than another. Decisions of a board had to be arrived at by discussion amongst the members, and in case of disagreement they had recourse to a vote and the majority decision bound all.[144] In the laws and decrees it was whole boards that had tasks imposed on them.[145] Boards had to administer the funds at their disposal collectively, and accounts were published, after their period of office was over, in the name of all: for instance, all the Treasurers of Athena,[146] all the Superintendents of the Dockyards[147] or all the *poletai*.[148] Occasionally we meet the phrase 'NN and his colleagues' (*ho deina kai synarchontes*)[149] but there is no indication that the magistrate named had more power than his colleagues.[150] Also the once-widespread view[151] that one of the generals had special powers has been disproved[152] Thus, a board administered as a collectivity; but there was some dissonance between collective administration and the Athenian legal system, which was based on individual responsibility, so that only an individual could be brought into court, not a board of magistrates as such. If a board of ten was required to answer for its administration, that involved ten prosecutions:[153] in the Trial of the

---

[142] See p. 219. [143] Theophr. *Char.* 26.1–2.

[144] Hdt. 6.109–10; Lys. 16.16; Xen. *Hell.* 1.7. 29–30; Aeschin. 2.84. Kahrstedt (1936) 152.

[145] *SEG* 26 72 = Harding (1985) no. 45. [146] *IG* II² 1370.

[147] *IG* II² 1607. [148] *Hesperia* 10 (1941) 15–27 no. 1. [149] *IG* II² 1377.

[150] Kahrstedt (1936) 160–5. [151] Beloch (1884) 274–88; Bloedow (1987) 24–7.

[152] Dover (1960) 61–77; Fornara (1971) 28–39. [153] See p. 204.

Generals that principle was cast to the winds and the generals were sentenced to death collectively,[154] but it was a plain unconstitutionality, of which the people almost at once repented. (A few decades earlier they had behaved quite constitutionally: the *Hellenotamiai* were charged with embezzlement, the board was dismissed, and its members, one by one, were condemned to death and nine of them executed, at which point it was discovered how the deficit had arisen, in time to save the last one.)[155]

But collegiality did not preclude the distribution of particular duties amongst the members of a board. Most boards comprised one representative from each tribe, and the administration was divided amongst the members so that each was given the relevant duty in respect to his own tribe. Thus, the nine archons plus the secretary of the *thesmothetai* constituted a board of ten which oversaw the daily allotment of jurors tribe by tribe, each member dealing with his own;[156] the Forty were divided into ten groups of four, and each group dealt with private suits arising within its own tribe.[157] Division of duties can, in fact, be traced far beyond the range of merely tribal divisions. One general, or a part of the Board of Generals, was often sent out to a campaign;[158] and from the mid fourth century[159] five of the ten generals had individual spheres of duty: one commanded the army in external campaigns (*epi tous hoplitas*), one undertook the defence of Attica (*epi ten choran*), one was responsible for the appointment of trierarchs (*epi tas symmorias*), and two were in charge of the shipyards and the naval harbour (*epi ton Peiraiea*).[160] The division of labour within the Board of Generals was probably introduced at the same time as the reform by which tribal representation was discontinued and the generals were elected *ex hapanton*, from all Athenians.[161] Finally, in laws and decrees a specific task is often imposed on a single member of a board.[162] The division of labour must have reduced the duties of the individual magistrates significantly, and except for the archonships there was no magistracy manned by lot that demanded a citizen's time every day, let alone all day from morning to night.

Modern historians often link collegiality to selection by lot. The argument is this: when the Athenians changed from election to selection by lot they were obliged to put several men in each job in case some of those chosen turned out incompetent or unreliable.[163] A board of ten was usually sure to be big enough to contain a majority of sensible people.

[154] Xen. *Hell.* 1.7.8–11.   [155] Ant. 5.69–70.   [156] Arist. *Ath. Pol.* 63.1.
[157] Arist. *Ath. Pol.* 53.1–2.   [158] Kahrstedt (1936) 149–51.
[159] *IG* II² 204.19–20 = Harding (1985) no. 78.   [160] Arist. *Ath. Pol.* 61.1.
[161] Arist. *Ath. Pol.* 61.1; *P. Oxy.* 1804 fr. 4.4–6. Hansen (1988c).
[162] *SEG* 30 61.34; *IG* II² 1496.120; Is. 1.14. Kahrstedt (1936) 156–60.
[163] Glotz (1929) 213.

Now, there is no doubt some truth in that: Lysias actually remarks in a speech on a *dokimasia* that a bad citizen will do less harm on a board than on his own.[164] But the point must not be stressed out of all proportion. For one thing, boards of magistrates existed long before selection by lot was introduced: the *thesmothetai* were an elected board right down to 487/6. And, for another, three of the most important Athenian magistracies in the classical age were manned by lot but by single individuals, namely the archon, the king archon and the polemarch. Finally, the theory does not square with the division of duties amongst the members of the boards.

No: what the Athenians were doing by setting up so many boards of magistrates was attempting to prevent anyone from acquiring particularly powerful influence, and the ones selected by lot were mostly employed in administrative tasks not requiring a high level of special skill. Then again, the lot was based on voluntary candidature, which helped to eliminate those who had neither the talent nor the taste for administration. However, there must always have been some who had the taste but not the talent; and it would be wrong to imagine that *dokimasia* helped much to sort them out, because that procedure was only concerned with formal qualifications and general loyalty to the democracy – and, in any case, there are astonishingly few examples of people actually being rejected at their *dokimasia*.[165] On the other hand, neither do we hear complaints about incompetent magistrates, and dismissal of magistrates selected by lot during their period of office or condemnation at their *euthynai* at the end of it is far less prominent in the sources than prosecutions for proposal of unconstitutional decrees or than *eisangeliai*, which were mainly directed against one group of elected magistrates, i.e. the generals.[166] And when a magistrate was brought into court the charge was usually bribery or embezzlement, not incompetence.[167] In relation to *euthynai* inexperience is mentioned only once in the forensic speeches, and then as a valid excuse for a poor citizen who had been selected by lot to fill a magistracy.[168] If the sources are to be believed, the administration did work, perhaps even satisfactorily, in spite of the fact that it was mostly carried out by officials chosen by lot who only functioned for a year and would have no opportunity ever to fill the same post again.

Numbers

No less than seventy-one different magistrates and boards of magistrates are attested, and if we add up all our fourth-century references we arrive

[164] Lys. 26.11.   [165] See p. 220.   [166] See pp. 216–18.
[167] See p. 217.   [168] Dem. 24.112.

at a figure of some 450 magistrates, elected and selected by lot.[169] Furthermore, the evidence is anything but exhaustive: a board as important as the Comptrollers of the Mint only became attested with certainty in 1963 with the publication of a new inscription.[170] All over Attica there were sanctuaries administered by boards of state officials who are only randomly attested in our inscriptions,[171] and the Guardians of the Laws (the *nomophylakes*) are only known from two chance references to a lost forensic speech of the 320s.[172] Every time a sizable new inscription emerges from the soil of Attica there is a good chance that the list of known boards of magistrates will acquire an addition.

In the first, historical, half of the *Constitution of Athens* Aristotle states that in the second half of the fifth century the Athenians had some 700 internal magistrates engaged in the administration of Athens and Attica and about another 700 overseas magistrates administering the empire.[173] Both figures have been rejected by scholars as patent exaggerations, and the usual procedure of historians is to halve the total on the mistaken premise that Aristotle's list of magistrates in the fourth century is as near as makes no difference complete:[174] that list includes only about 320 magistrates. Certainly, after the collapse of the Athenian Empire in 404 we need not worry ourselves any more about the accuracy or otherwise of Aristotle's total of overseas magistrates; but it is quite reasonable to suppose that the number of internal posts was the same in the fourth century as in the fifth. The sources point strongly in that direction, and instead of the usually posited 350 or so magistrates we should reckon that, in the fourth century as in the fifth, there were up to 700 *archai*, taking those elected and those selected by lot all together.[175]

Remuneration

In a Greek city-state of radical-democratic complexion it was a basic principle that citizens should be remunerated for the exercise of their political rights,[176] while in oligarchies, naturaly, the principle was the opposite: all who served must do so without financial reward.[177] On that basis the Athenian magistrates were paid for their services in the fifth century,[178] down to the oligarchical revolution of 411, when pay for magistrates was almost totally abolished.[179] When the democracy was restored in 403/2 the Athenians reintroduced pay for the courts[180] and

---

[169] Hansen (1980c) 163.   [170] *SEG* 21 667.   [171] Linders (1975).
[172] Din. fr. vi.11, xiv.2.   [173] Arist. *Ath. Pol.* 24.3.   [174] Jones (1957) 136 n. 9.
[175] Hansen (1980c) 166–7.   [176] Arist. *Pol.* 1317b35–8. Ste Croix (1975).
[177] Arist. *Pol.* 1294a37–41.
[178] Ps. Xen. *Ath. Pol.* 1.3.; *IG* I³ 82.17–21. Hansen (1979a) 12–13.
[179] Arist. *Ath. Pol.* 29.5; Thuc. 8.65.3, 67.3.   [180] Ar. *Eccl.* 687–8; *Plut.* 277.

undoubtedly for the Council as well, and shortly afterwards actually introduced it for the Assembly;[181] yet never, so far as we can tell from the sources, did they return to pay for magistrates. The majority, whether elected or chosen by lot, had thenceforward to serve the state without regular remuneration: the only exceptions were the archons[182] (who had actually been paid even under the oligarchical regime in 411),[183] the overseas magistrates,[184] and a few others.[185]

That magistrates were basically unpaid in the fourth century is, it is true, a supposition, and rests on an argument from silence: pay for magistrates is not referred to in any of the numerous central sources where we should expect it.[186] Arguments from silence are, of course, always liable to be overturned at any time by new evidence; nevertheless, it is flying in the face of the only evidence we have (i.e. the negative evidence) to supppose, as some historians persist in doing, that many magistrates in the fourth century were fully employed and must have got, for example, a drachma a day for every day in the year.[187] The Athenian principle was that political pay must correspond to political activity: many magistrates, especially those concerned with religious affairs, served only a few days in the year, and the few people who did go on receiving pay got it, in any case, only for the days on which they actually performed their duties.[188]

The abolition of pay for magistrates was certainly a retreat from radical-democratic principles and another sign that the Athenians from 403/2 had opted for a more 'moderate' form of democracy. Only for the Council was pay reintroduced, paid on every Council day in the year (at a rate, by the end of the fourth century, of 5 obols a day) to those councillors who turned up;[189] but in that case *misthos* was an unavoidable necessity, because participation by the majority of the citizens was a prerequisite for the functioning of the Council at all.

If magistrates did not generally receive regular remuneration, that is not to say that they might not make some profit out of their offices. Numerous sources show that they were able to obtain various perquisites or other economic advantages.[190] The job of a general might be perilous (and not only in the field), but it was often lucrative: a successful general could acquire booty and receive gifts from foreign states, as well as other sorts of presents seldom specified.[191] Hypereides says that such

---

[181] Arist. *Ath. Pol.* 41.3.   [182] Arist. *Ath. Pol.* 62.2.   [183] Arist. *Ath. Pol.* 29.5.
[184] Arist. *Ath. Pol.* 62.2.   [185] Arist. *Ath. Pol.* 42.3.
[186] Dem. 24.96–101; *IG* II² 1672; Arist. *Ath. Pol.* 62.2. Hansen (1979a) 15–19, *pace* Gabrielsen (1981) 57–87, 97–9.
[187] Jones (1957) 6; Gabrielsen (1981) 146–9 and *passim*.
[188] Hansen (1979a) 7–10.   [189] See p. 253.
[190] Isoc. 7.24–7, 12.145, 15.145–52. Hansen (1980b).   [191] Pritchett (1974) 126–32.

perquisities, though they had no basis in law, were accepted by the Athenians as long as the generals were loyal.[192] Other magistrates, too, had good opportunities for benefit: the Superintendents of the Dockyards could get sweeteners from the trierarchs for supplying ships or tackle;[193] and part of the court fees, it is thought, went to the magistrates who prepared the cases and presided over the courts.[194] Perquisites need not be in money: at the great sacrifices the religious officials often received a fixed portion of the flesh, worth a good many drachmas,[195] and, since the duties of many of the religious officials were only occasional their share in the sacrificial animal was very likely a full remuneration for their pains.

In all such cases it is to be noticed that the magistrate made a gain without the state having to contribute anything: the generals got their perquisites from foreigners, the civil magistrates from private individuals, the religious officials from sacrificial animals already paid for out of state funds. But there were great differences between offices. Some magistrates were obliged to contribute out of their own pockets: the members of the Board for the Festival of Dionysos, for example, had (until *c*.340) to pay the cost of the great procession, which may well have cost them 1000 drachmas apiece.[196] In other cases a magistrate might contribute voluntarily to the duties of his office out of his own fortune.[197] A magistracy could have more or less the character of a liturgy,[198] and for many the expense may have exceeded the profits: if it had really been profitable to be, for example, one of the Treasurers of Athena, there would not have been as many vacancies on the boards as there were.

THE TASKS OF ADMINISTRATION

The large number of magistrates went with a minute distribution of functions. The result was a large bureaucracy, but one characterized more by its numbers than by the extent of the tasks the officials were set to perform. The Athenian citizen differed from the citizen of a modern democratic state in being, on the one hand, much more often a state official of some sort, but, on the other hand, much less frequently under the control of state officials himself. A really thoroughgoing police state existed only at Sparta (and in the fantasies of Plato and Aristotle); it had no counterpart at Athens. After his two-year military service an Athenian citizen was only directly under the control of magistrates when taking

---

[192] Hyp. 1.24–5. Hansen (1980b) 113–14.
[193] Dem. *Prooem.* 48.2–3. Hansen (1980b) 112–13.   [194] Hansen (1980b) 118–19.
[195] *IG* II² 334.10–16.   [196] Arist. *Ath. Pol.* 56.4.
[197] Dem. 18.114.   [198] Andoc. 1.132; Pl. *Resp.* 343E.

part in a political assembly or fighting in the field or celebrating one of the great city festivals; apart from that perhaps his most frequent contact with officials was if he traded in the market-place.

The numerous boards can be divided into groups according to their functions, and we can best avoid an anachronistic interpretation by following Aristotle's classification in Book 6 of the *Politics*. He begins with a quite detailed account of ten typical spheres of functioning of city-state magistrates:

1 control of market trading;
2 surveillance of public and private buildings, roads and water-supplies;
3 oversight of the country districts;
4 management of the state's finances;
5 preparation of trials and chairmanship of courts;
6 execution of sentences;
7 high command of army and navy;
8 control over other magistrates;
9 presidency of political assemblies; and
10 administration of cult and sanctuaries.[199]

In the light of this summary of their duties Aristotle divides magistrates into six main categories:

1 religious magistrates;
2 army and naval commanders;
3 financial magistrates;
4 inspectors (of markets, buildings, roads, water and country districts);
5 judicial magistrates; and
6 steering-committees for the people's assembly.[200]

Then, after those six groups, which every *polis* must have in order to function at all, he names a seventh, necessary if a *polis* is to live up to the ideal of what a society ought to be; and under that heading he puts magistrates to control the women and children and the *gymnasia* – though he at once observes that such officials are not found in democratic states.[201] Hence it is no surprise that in Athens such magistracies only appeared under Demetrios of Phaleron (317–07)[202] after the democracy had been abolished: the nearest parallels before that are the Guardians of the Laws (*nomophylakes*), who are known from the 320s,[203] and the Prefect and Board of Moderators, who supervised the training of ephebes,

---

[199] Arist. *Pol.* 1321b12–1322b29. [200] Arist. *Pol.* 1322b29–37.
[201] Arist. *Pol.* 1292b37–1293a10. [202] Philoch. fr. 65. [203] Din. fr. vi.11, xiv.2.

which was reformed after the defeat at Chaironea in 338.[204] On the whole, Aristotle's theoretical groups correspond well enough with what we learn about Athens in the fourth century, with the proviso that some of the Athenian magistrates combined functions belonging to different Aristotelian categories: the archon, king archon and polemarch were both judicial and religious magistrates,[205] and the generals were not only army commanders but had also judicial[206] and religious functions, so that it was the generals, for example, who brought the annual offering to the goddess Demokratia.[207]

SUBORDINATES

Shortness of tenure, non-repeatability, lack of overlap between one board and the next, and amateur status are the characteristics of Athenian magistracy that are most suprising to us and make us wonder how the administration of Athens ever worked at all. Some of the perfectly sensible reasons why the Athenians chose to organize themselves in that way we have already seen, but the question about efficiency persists. The amateurism is relatively easy to come to terms with if we bear in mind that until quite recent times the tasks of administrators have been very much less specialized than we are used to, so that any such task could be successfully undertaken by anyone of reasonable intelligence and motivation. But the shortness of tenure, non-repeatability and lack of overlap, ensuring that no one could ever get to know any branch of the administration properly, remain baffling. Was there no continuity at all, and no one with expert understanding of executive government in general? Well, perhaps one branch of the administration, relatively unsung, deserves a word by way of epilogue to an account of the administrative officials of Athens: namely their secretaries, the *grammateis*[208] (and the *paredroi* of the archon, the king archon and the polemarch),[209] and the clerical staffs of the secretaries, including a number of under-secretaries (*hypogrammateis*).[210]

The *grammateis* were mostly Athenian citizens, and some of them, such as the secretaries of the Council[211] and the secretary of the *thesmothetai*, counted as magistrates.[212] Those who were not magistrates, however, could be citizens, metics or slaves;[213] they were hired by the magistrates they served and paid for their services.[214] As to continuity, the Athenians

---

[204] Harp. s.v. *Epikrates*.   [205] Arist. *Ath. Pol.* 56–8.   [206] *IG* II² 1629.206–10.
[207] *IG* II² 1496.131–2, 140–1.   [208] Ferguson (1898).   [209] Arist. *Ath. Pol.* 56.1; Dem. 21.178.   [210] *IG* II² 2825.11–12.
[211] Arist. *Ath. Pol.* 54.3–5; *Agora* XV 43.227–31.   [212] Arist. *Ath. Pol.* 55.1–2.
[213] *IG* II²1556.14, 1561.32.   [214] Dem. 19.249.

were relentlessly doctrinaire: Lysias in the speech he wrote for the prosecutor of Nikomachos, the law-codifier, states a rule that not even a *hypogrammateus*, secretary of secretary, could serve the same *arche* twice (which does not, perhaps, exclude him serving the same *arche* later on as full secretary).[215] But the *grammateis* and *hypogrammateis*, by going the rounds of *archai*, could make a career for themselves and acquire some professionalism in the job. Aischines as a young man was *grammateus* or *hypogrammateus* of a number of – in Demosthenes' pejorative description – 'little boards',[216] and subsequently did not like to be reminded of the fact. But Nikomachos himself may be the better paradigm: son, it was alleged, of a public slave, he made himself the professional authority on the statutes and, sitting in his office somewhere in Athens, did the people sterling service over a decade by producing the revised law-code;[217] yet we only really know about him because he became prominent enough to attract a public prosecution.[218] And if he is a paradigm there were, perhaps, at the very base of the system, some mostly humble and disregarded experts (permitted to be experts because they could be disregarded) holding the democratic administration on their shoulders.

---

[215] Lys. 30.29.
[216] Dem. 18.261, 19.200.
[217] Lys. 30.2–3. See pp. 162–4.
[218] Lys. 30. Dow (1959, 1960).

10

The Council of Five Hundred

The most important board of magistrates in a democratic city-state is the council (*boule*). So declares Aristotle in the *Politics*,[1] explaining that the council is the executive and preparatory body for the decision-making organ, the assembly;[2] in an aristocracy the most important magistrates are the guardians of the laws (*nomophylakes*) and in an oligarchy the planning-board (*probouloi*).[3] Sure enough, at Athens the first step in the abolition of democracy after the defeat in Sicily in 413 was the establishment of a board of ten *probouloi*,[4] and in Plato's *Laws* his utopia is governed by a board of thirty-seven *nomophylakes*.[5] Democratic councils were much larger than that, corresponding in numbers more to a modern parliament: in a minor city, Erythrai, there were 120 places on the council,[6] while big states had councils running into hundreds of members.[7] Athens after Kleisthenes had a council consisting of 500 persons, and its official title was 'The Council of Five Hundred', *he boule hoi pentakosioi*[8] (to distinguish it from the Areopagos, *he boule he ex Areiou pagou*).

Evidence of all types points to the central role played by the Council in Athenian democracy. In the structural account of the contemporary democracy in Aristotle's *Constitution of Athens* a quarter of the whole is devoted to the Council.[9] In the Agora it is the Council house and the prytany house (Tholos) of which traces can still be seen,[10] whereas the premises of the other magistrates, and even the courts, can only be

---

[1] Arist. *Pol.* 1322b12–17. [2] Arist. *Pol.* 1299b32–3.

[3] Arist. *Pol.* 1323a6–9, 1299b31–6.

[4] Thuc. 8.1.3; Arist. *Ath. Pol.* 29.2; Lys. 12.65. Gomme, Andrewes and Dover (1981) 6–7.

[5] Pl. *Lg.* 752E–755B. Piérart (1974b) 122–51.

[6] *IG* I[3] 14.9 = *M&L* 40 and Fornara (1977) no. 71.

[7] *IG* II[2] 230.2–4. Oehler (1899) 1034–5. [8] Dem. 19.179; *SEG* 19 133.2.

[9] Arist. *Ath. Pol.* 43.2–49.5. [10] Thompson and Wycherley (1972) 29–38, 41–6.

identified with much uncertainty and were never as prominent anyway. History tells the same story: Kleisthenes' political organization of Attica was closely bound up with creating a Council to his satisfaction,[11] and the Council was the only organ of state in which each individual deme of Attica was represented.[12] And, last but not least, when an Athenian speaker wanted to list the most important institutions of Athens he usually named the Assembly (*ekklesia* or *demos*) the Council (*boule*) and the People's Court (*ta dikasteria*)[13]

The Council was a board of magistrates (*arche*),[14] but it was very unlike the others. In size, obviously, it was quite different from the boards of ten and more like a court with 501 jurors. It met every weekday, and had a far wider range of powers than any other board. Its working-link was with the Assembly and the *nomothetai*, whereas the other boards were linked to the courts. It received all envoys from foreign states and so played a central role in foreign policy. It also ran the financial administration and kept a permanent eye on the other boards: in those two spheres the sources reveal a hierarchy, the Council standing higher than the other magistrates. So, not surprisingly, in the orators and elsewhere a distinction is sometimes made between the Council and the other boards.[15] In contrast to the others the Council even had some decision-making power; but that was very limited and went on being steadily reduced during the two centuries of democracy.[16] It was the Council's probouleutic and administrative functions, not any power of decision-making, that gave it its central place in the democracy: Aristotle was right to say that a council loses its independent powers under a democracy, where the people meet often and are paid for attendance at their meetings.[17]

ORGANIZATION

Selection by lot

There are six things we know from the sources about the selection of members of the Council. We learn that

1 representation on the Council was based on the 139 demes and not merely on the ten tribes;[18]

---

[11] See p. 34. [12] Traill (1975) xiii.
[13] Dem. 20.100; Pl. *Ap.* 24E–25A. Hansen (1983a) 144–5.
[14] *IG* I³ 105.45; Arist. *Ath. Pol.* 43.2, 62.2. Hansen (1981c) 347–9. pp. 226–7.
[15] Lys. 25.14; Dem.24.20. Hansen (1981c) 350–1. [16] See pp. 255–6.
[17] Arist. *Pol.* 1299b38–1300a3. [18] Traill (1986) 123–40.

2 the selection was made from those who presented themselves;[19]

3 notice of intention to stand had to be given in the demes, presumably at a meeting of the deme assembly,[20] but

4 the selection by lot took place centrally and involved the use of the personal bronze plaques,[21] which implies in turn the use of the allotment machines, the *kleroteria*;

5 over and above the 500 councillors a corresponding number of substitutes were selected,[22] each as stand-in for an individual councillor,[23] to take his place if he was rejected at the *dokimasia* or died in office; and

6 the Council was always kept at full strength, but some of the small demes could not always come up with enough candidates, in which case it was necessary to transfer the deme's representation, just for that year, to another deme belonging to the same tribe.[24]

In the light of these sources, selection to the Council can be reconstructed as follows. In all 139 demes there were assembly meetings to put up candidates. A deme entitled to, say, nine seats had to present at least eighteen persons: sometimes a deme could find more than enough, sometimes not so, in which case several councillors would have to share the same stand-in, and in some demes it was hard even to find enough candidates for their actual Council places. There is no evidence that the lot was used at this stage in the selection of candidates. Next, those proposed as candidates took part in a central process of selection by lot, carried out deme by deme with individual plaques and all the apparatus of allotment. In most cases there were probably no more candidates than the deme's permitted representatives times two, in which case the purpose of the drawing of lots was really just to decide who would be the Councillor and who the stand-in. The whole procedure was probably carried out in a single day;[25] it took place in the Sanctuary of Theseus and was run by the *thesmothetai*.[26]

Recruitment

Filling the 500 seats on the Council put such a strain on the population of Athens that they had to retreat from two important points of principle that normally governed magistracies: payment for attendance at the Coun-

[19] Lys. 31.5, 33. Hansen (1985a) 57–8, *pace* Ruschenbusch (1979c).

[20] Arist. *Ath. Pol.* 62.1. Whitehead (1986) 267, 319–22.   [21] Dem. 39.10.

[22] Aeschin. 3.62.   [23] Plato Comicus *Hyperbolus* fr. 166–7. Traill (1981).

[24] Traill (1975) 58.   [25] Dem. 24.150.   [26] Aeschin. 3.13.

cil was kept up in the fourth century[27] although payment for magistrates in general was not,[28] and the rule forbidding iteration was not applied: a citizen could be a councillor twice,[29] though not in successive years.[30] However, the inscriptions show that relatively few citizens exercised their right to be councillor twice,[31] and every year the Athenians must have had to find 375–400 members for the Council who had not been on it before. The sources also show that the average age of first-time members was about forty,[32] so citizens did not usually become councillors at the earliest opportunity, i.e. when they were just past thirty. In the demographic structure of Athens people forty years old must have been only about 2 per cent of all citizens over eighteen, i.e. in the fourth century about 600 persons in any year (out of 30,000).[33] It follows that over a third of all citizens over eighteen, and about two thirds of all citizens over forty, became councillors, some of them twice.

The Council could not have functioned unless a reasonable number of *thetes* (who were formally excluded from all magistracies) had turned up for selection to the Council. On the other hand, the evidence reveals a clear tendency for the 'haves' to be overrepresented on the Council in relation to their proportion of the population.[34] At the same time, the Council was not merely a forum for the politically active and the well-off. Sokrates, in his *Apologia*, tells the jury that he has done his citizen duty faithfully all his life but has never taken an active part in politics;[35] in the same breath he says he was a councillor at the time of the Trial of the Generals in 406/5.[36] It follows that serving on the Council was a citizen duty but not 'active politics'; but should 'citizen duty' be taken to imply a legal duty or a moral duty? Could a citizen be obliged to sit on the Council? Well, we know, on the one hand, that people could volunteer and that there was competition for membership; on the other hand, it is inconceivable that the Council could have been maintained at full strength solely by volunteers, at least as far as some demes were concerned. The distribution of the 500 seats was, as we have seen, related to the population of individual demes, but it can never have worked out exactly, and no adjustments were made for population shifts between 403/2 and 307/6, so at least in some demes – Halimous, for example[37] – group pressure or even compulsory enlistment must have been needed to fill the allotted Council places. Hence the Council was recruited by a mixture of volunteers and – more or less – conscripts; it was, on paper, always at full strength.

---

[27] Arist. *Ath. Pol.* 62.2.   [28] See p. 241.
[29] Arist. *Ath. Pol.* 62.3. Rhodes (1980b, 1981b, 1984).   [30] Hansen (1985a) 51.
[31] Hansen (1985a) 51–5; (1988b) 67–9.   [32] Hansen (1985a) 55–6; (1988b) 67.
[33] Hansen (1985a) 11–13.   [34] Rhodes (1972) 5–6; Hansen (1985a) 58–60.
[35] Pl *Ap.* 31C–D.   [36] Pl. *Ap.* 32A–B.   [37] Dem. 57.9–14, Hansen (1985a) 62–4.

Structure

While the Council differed from all other boards of magistrates in being recruited by demes and not by tribes, the tribal division was basic to its organization and its activities. Each tribe's contingent of fifty had to serve as the executive committee of the Council for a tenth of the year: the members of this committee were called *prytaneis*, and their period of office a 'prytany'.[38] The Council year, it will be recalled, had ten months (*prytaneiai*) as compared with the twelve months of the civil year.[39] The order in which the tribal contingents became *prytaneis* was settled by chance, because only at the end of each prytany were lots drawn to determine which group would be the next 'in prytany'.[40]

The chairman of the *prytaneis* was called *epistates ton prytaneon*. He was picked by lot from the *prytaneis* and held office only for a night and a day; an allotment (amongst those who had not held the post already) took place every day at sunset. The *epistates* held the seal of Athens and the keys of the treasuries in the sanctuaries where the state's money and documents were kept.[41] It was he who counted as the head of the state of Athens in relation to other states and received foreign messengers and envoys.[42] Originally the *prytaneis* and their *epistates* also presided over meetings of the Council[43] and the Assembly;[44] from about 400 the *epistates* had to carry out the selection by lot of the nine *proedroi* (who now presided over the Council and Assembly)[45] and he presided only over meetings of the *prytaneis*. The *prytaneis* must have met every day all the year round; and a third of them, i.e. the members from one of the tribe's three ridings, had to be present continuously in the prytany house, the Tholos, along with the *epistates*.[46] It was only possible to be *epistates* once in a lifetime,[47] which is a marvellous illustration of Aristotle's democratic principle that everyone must take part in the government by turns.

MEETINGS

Meeting-days, summons and agenda

According to Aristotle the *prytaneis* had to summon the Council every day except holidays (*hemerai aphesimoi*).[48] Holidays for the Council

---

[38] *Agora* XV 38; Arist. *Ath. Pol.* 43.2. Rhodes (1972) 16–24; Gschnitzer (1974).

[39] See p. 135.   [40] Arist. *Ath. Pol.* 43.2; *IG* II² 553.16–18.

[41] Arist. *Ath. Pol.* 44.1.   [42] Dem. 18.169.

[43] Ar. *Eq.* 674; *IG* II² 50 = *SEG* 14.38, *IG* I³ p. 196.

[44] Ar. *Ach.* 23; *IG* II² 1.42 = Fornara (1977) no. 166.

[45] Arist. *Ath. Pol.* 44.2. See pp. 140–1.   [46] Arist. *Ath. Pol.* 44.1.

[47] Arist. *Ath. Pol.* 44.1. Rhodes (1981a) 531.   [48] Arist. *Ath. Pol.* 43.3.

were the annual festivals[49] and probably the 'taboo days' (*hemerai apophrades*),[50] in all some seventy-five days in the year; the Council was not let off on the monthly festivals,[51] and on the forty Assembly days it usually met after the Assembly was over.[52] So in a normal year of 354 days the Council met on about 275 of them.

Summoning the Council was the duty of the *prytaneis*,[53] who were also responsible for its agenda,[54] in compliance with any rules laid down by law: thus, at the start of each prytany, state expenditure and income had to be on the agenda on two successive days,[55] and foreign policy had to be discussed at special meetings, as in the Assembly, and could not just be put on any agenda.[56] One more example is that when, in 337, it was decided to improve the fortifications of the Piraeus, it was laid down by a law that one Council meeting in every prytany must be reserved for discussion of the repairs and how to finance them.[57]

Meeting-places

The Council normally met in the *bouleuterion*,[58] the Council house in the Agora, but meetings about the navy might be held in the navy yards in the Piraeus[59] or at the harbour wall,[60] and after the Festival of the Mysteries the Council always met in the Eleusinion[61] (and we even hear of meetings on the Akropolis).[62] Both the Council house and the prytany house stood in the south-west corner of the Agora next to the state archive and the Monument to the Eponymous Heroes, where all business requiring public attention was posted.[63] There is no archaeological trace of a specific Council building before about 460, at which date both a building for the Council and one for the *prytaneis* were erected.[64] If that dating is right, the obvious connection is with the reforms of Ephialtes in 462, when the Council's powers were enlarged at the expense of the Areopagos.[65] That original *bouleuterion* only last as such for about fifty years (after which it housed the archive),[66] As for the prytany house, it

---

[49] Mikalson (1975a) 193–7.   [50] Mikalson (1975b) 26.

[51] Mikalson (1975a) 197.   [52] See p. 136.

[53] Dem. 18.169; *IG* II² 1629.247–51 = Harding (1985) no. 121.

[54] Arist. *Ath. Pol.* 44.2; *IG* II² 120.25–6; *SEG* 18 13.13–14.

[55] Arist. *Ath. Pol.* 48.2.   [56] Dem. 19.185.   [57] *IG* II² 244.36–7.

[58] Dem. 25.23; Arist. *Ath. Pol.* 48.1. *IG* II² 330.30–1. McDonald (1943) 131–3, 138–41.

[59] *IG* I³ 61.53 = *M&L* 65 and Fornara (1977) no. 128.   [60] *IG* II² 1629.248.

[61] Andoc. 1.111.   [62] Xen. *Hell.* 6.4.20.

[63] Thompson and Wycherley (1972) 25–46; Rhodes (1972) 30–6.

[64] Thompson (1978) 63; Francis and Vickers (1988) 154, 159.   [65] See p. 37.

[66] Thompson and Wycherley (1972) 29–31.

was a little circular structure[67] called the Tholos or Skias (the 'Sunshade'). (The area around the Tholos was called *to prytanikon*, which is not to be confused with the Prytaneion.)[68] The *prytaneis* held their meetings in the Tholos and took their meals together there.[69] At the end of the fifth century the Athenians built a new *bouleuterion* immediately behind the old one;[70] it was possibly in the Ionic order, and the Council chamber itself measured 19×20 m, so there was room for all 500 councillors to be seated for meetings[71] and for plenty of listeners[72] (who stood[73]).

The seating for the councillors was probably originally wooden benches; only in the Hellenistic age was a kind of theatre constructed, with stone seats in a semicircle.[74] In Perikles' time councillors could sit where they pleased, but in 410 a law was passed that the members' seats must be determined by lot:[75] during the constitutional crisis of 413–411 there had no doubt been a tendency to form groups in the Council, and but for the law of 410 there might have grown up a 'left' and a 'right', as in the Assemblée Nationale in France at the Revolution. The *prytaneis* sat on special benches, perhaps facing the rest of the Council;[76] and a wooden railing separated the councillors from those who came to listen.[77] There was a speakers' platform (*bema*),[78] and there were altars to Zeus Boulaios and Athena Boulaia[79] and the hearth of the Council (*hestia boulaia*),[80] where members under threat could take refuge if the Council was in a lynching-mood.[81] Round the outside of the *bouleuterion* ran a fence with gateways:[82] when the Council held meetings to discuss state secrets[83] all non-members were kept outside the fence.[84] After the construction of the new *bouleuterion* the old one became the state archive, and was called the Metroön (sanctuary of the Mother) because it housed a shrine of the goddess Demeter.[85]

Procedure

From about 400 onwards[86] meetings of the Council were presided over by a board of nine *proedroi*, chosen each morning by lot from the 450 councillors not in prytany, one from each tribe (except from that in

---

[67] Thompson and Wycherley (1972) 41–6.
[68] Wycherley (1957) 179–84.
[69] Arist. *Ath. Pol*, 43.3; Dem. 18.169.   [70] Thompson and Wycherley (1972) 31–5.
[71] Philoch. fr. 140.   [72] Dem. 19.17; Aeschin. 3.125.
[73] Xen. *Hell*. 2.3.50.   [74] Thompson and Wycherley (1972) 33 n. 44.
[75] Philoch. fr. 140.   [76] Lys.13.37.   [77] Ar. *Eq*. 675.
[78] Ant. 6.40.   [79] Ant. 6.45.   [80] Aeschin. 2.45.
[81] Andoc. 1.44, 2.15; Xen. *Hell*. 2.3.52–5.
[82] Dem. 25.23. Thompson and Wycherley (1972) 34.   [83] Aeschin. 3.125.
[84] Dem. 25.23.   [85] Lycurg. 1.66. Thompson and Wycherley (1972) 33.
[86] See p. 140.

prytany), and then by a second allotment one of the *proedroi* was chosen as their chairman (*epistates ton proedron*). This *epistates* received from the other *epistates* (*ton prytaneon*) the agenda for the forthcoming Council meeting and for the Assembly meeting if there was to be one.[87]

Only councillors had an unconditional right to address the Council and propose motions:[88] any other citizen had to obtain leave of the *prytaneis* to appear before the Council.[89] A citizen could probably demand such leave, but foreigners could be rejected out of hand[90] unless they had been granted access to the Council and the Assembly (*prosodos pros ten boulen kai ton demon*) by a special privilege.[91] At the meeting a citizen who was not a councillor could speak, but, if it led to a motion, that could only be proposed by a councillor in his own name,[92] and it was he who had to take responsibility for a possible *graphe paranomon*.[93] The only exception to this rule was the generals, who at least in the fifth century had a right to propose motions in their own names, and so must have had a right to address the Council.[94] But, since the Council was not only the preparatory body for the Assembly, but also an administrative body working in harness with the other magistrates, when it was dealing with public finances it often had to do so jointly with other magistrates, such as the Board for the Theoric Fund, the Treasurer of the Military Fund, the nine archons, the Board of Receivers (*apodektai*) and the Auctions Board (*poletai*).[95] On the days when revenue was paid in, it was the *apodektai* and not the *proedroi* who presided over the Council.[96]

The Council regularly voted by show of hands and the vote was estimated and not counted.[97] When all items on the agenda had been debated, the *prytaneis*[98] – later the *proedroi*[99] – could declare the meeting over.

Remuneration and participation

After every meeting each councillor received a daily payment, which at the end of the fourth century was 5 obols; each member of the *prytaneis* who took part in the common meal in the Tholos received an extra obol.[100] There is nothing in our sources to suggest that meetings of the

---

[87] Arist. *Ath. Pol.* 44.2.
[88] Swoboda (1890) 310; Rhodes (1972) 42–3, 63.
[89] Ar. *Pax* 907 with schol.; *IG* I³ 46.35–9 = *M&L* 49.   [90] Xen. *Hell.* 6.4.20.
[91] *IG* I³ 65.17–20; II² 86.19–21. Henry (1983) 191–9.
[92] Aeschin. 3.125; *IG* II² 243.6–8. Rhodes (1972) 43 n. 6.
[93] Dem. 47.34. Hansen (1974) cat. nos 3, 14, 30.
[94] *SEG* 10 86.47; *IG* II² 27 = *SEG* 10 109. Rhodes (1972) 43–6.
[95] Arist. *Ath. Pol.* 47.2–48.1.   [96] Arist. *Ath. Pol.* 48.2.
[97] Arist. *Ath. Pol.* 44.3. As in the Assembly, see p. 147.   [98] Ar. *Eq.* 674.
[99] Arist. *Ath. Pol.* 44.3.   [100] Thuc. 8.69.4; Arist. *Ath. Pol.* 62.2.

Council normally went on for more than a few hours, so 5 obols was full compensation for those members who lived not too far from the *bouleuterion*. But how about those who lived in one of the distant coastal or inland demes, perhaps anything from 25 to 40 km from the Agora of Athens? They cannot have taken part in every Council meeting; and one source actually states that people did not turn up to all meetings.[101] Was it, then, a mere farce when Kleisthenes divided the seats in the Council amongst the 139 demes according to their population? After all, in his day every citizen actually lived geographically in the deme he belonged to, and the city-population represented only a minority of the citizen body. We must not forget that in Kleisthenes' time probably far fewer Council meetings were held than in the fourth century, which helped to give most members a reasonable chance of attending most meetings. On the other hand, by the fourth century many people from inland and coastal demes actually lived in Athens and the Piraeus,[102] and so were more easily able to represent their distant demes. The effect was to give overrepresentation to the city population, but not, or not so strongly, to the city demes.[103]

The need for a councillor to be present at meetings was greatest when his tribe was in prytany: the members of one riding of the tribe's *prytaneis* had to be at the Tholos all the time, and in the course of the prytany thirty-five or thirty-six of them would be chosen as *epistates*. We may guess that members from even the remotest demes must have stayed in the city during their prytany, and a detail in Plato's *Laws* confirms the likelihood of that assumption: the 360 councillors in his utopia must normally be allowed to live in the country and till their fields, but the twelfth of them who act as *prytaneis* for a month must stay in the city during that time.[104] Membership of the Council was, up to a point, a citizen duty like military service, and historians have never doubted that it was possible to conscript an Athenian citizen for a campaign that would keep him abroad for a month or more; so there is no reason not to assume that a councillor from a country district was required to stay in the city during the thirty odd days of his tribe's turn to be *prytaneis*. And, be it noted, membership of the Council carried exemption from active service,[105] no small privilege if one thinks how frequently Athens was at war. Demosthenes is for ever criticizing the Athenians for their reluctance to serve on campaigns: the exemption of councillors may have been a considerable stimulus to recruitment to that body. On the assumption that, in a normal year of 354 days, the fifty *prytaneis* were paid 1 drachma

---

[101] Dem. 22.36.   [102] See p. 101.   [103] Hansen (1989a) 83.
[104] Pl. *Lg.* 758B–D. Piérart (1974b) 102. Rhodes (1972) 39.   [105] Lycurg. 1.37.

every day and that some 300 other councillors turned up for the meetings on some 275 days, the Council of Five Hundred must have cost the Athenian state something like 15 talents per year.

Limitations

The Council was much the most important board of magistrates, and to prevent it from becoming too powerful the Athenians set narrow limits to its authority. Three source references are particularly relevant. First, in the bouleutic oath[106] the councillors swore not to imprison any citizen prepared to give bail, except traitors, enemies of the democracy and tax-collectors.[107] Secondly, amongst the laws republished in the codification of the years 410–404 there was one about the limits of the powers of the Council relative to the Assembly;[108] it perhaps goes back to Kleisthenes, but may only have been passed in the first decades of the fifth century.[109] We possess fragments of it: it lists decisions that cannot be taken by the Council without reference to the Assembly: war and peace, sentences of death and impositions of large fines or *atimia*,[110] and the administration of public finances and foreign policy[111] (though the surviving fragments do not permit a closer specification of how far the Council was limited in the last two cases). Thirdly, in the *Constitution of Athens* Aristotle says that once upon a time the Council did have some power to impose fines, imprisonment and execution,[112] but at some date (perhaps as late as 403/2)[113] the people passed a law that all verdicts of the Council must be placed before the courts by the *Themosthetai*, whereupon the Council lost its last vestige of independent judicial authority.

Council decrees

A decision of the Council was called a 'Council Decree', *boules psephisma*, in contradistinction to *demou psephisma*, a decree of the people in their Assembly.[114] Council decrees were either *probouleumata* to be put before the Assembly[115] or independent decrees taking force without further

---

[106] Xen. *Mem.* 1.1.18; Lys. 31.1. Rhodes (1972) 194–8.   [107] Dem. 24.144.

[108] *IG* I³ 105. Rhodes (1972) 194–8; Hansen (1989a) 258, 260, *pace* Ostwald (1986) 31–40.

[109] Cloché (1920) 28–35; Lewis (1967) 132.   [110] *IG* I³ 105.34–42.

[111] *IG* I³ 105.44–5, 49.   [112] Arist. *Ath. Pol.* 45.1.

[113] Hansen (1983a) 168, *contra* Rhodes (1972) 207.

[114] Dem. 19.179. Rhodes (1972) 82–7.

[115] E.g. *IG* II² 337.1–25 = Tod 189 and Harding (1985) no. 111. See p. 138.

ratification.[116] Quite a number of the latter have survived, on inscriptions[117] and in the literary sources;[118] they begin with the formula *edoxe tei boulei*[119] and corroborate Aristotle's general verdict on the position of the Council in a radical democracy: the Athenian Council was only independently competent to settle routine and minor matters, such as instructions to trierarchs to return naval gear to their successors[120] or regulations about how to celebrate a festival.[121] The evidence for significant decisions made by decrees of the *boule* is not impressive, and some of it is inconclusive.[122] But the Council could have some delegated competence in matters normally determined by the Assembly: a decree of the Assembly sometimes ended with a clause saying that additions and amendments might be made by the Council without further reference back.[123] Such delegation of powers came to the fore in the second half of the fourth century, when the number of Assembly meetings was limited to thirty (shortly raised to forty) per year.[124] But it must not be imagined that the Assembly gave up anything important; one example actually says that the Council could only decide on details.[125] Alterations of substance would still have had to go before the Assembly.

Preparation of decrees and laws

The central role of the Council in the decision-making process was, however, its right to prepare the agenda for the Assembly and consider in advance every matter to be put before the people. So far as the Assembly is concerned that role has already been described;[126] it remains to quote the evidence, often overlooked, that the Council was also the preparatory body for the *nomothetai*.

1 The Assembly decided by decree whether *nomothetai* should be set up,[127] and that proposal itself had to have been put on the Assembly's agenda by the Council.[128] The only exception was the first Assembly meeting of the year, on 11 Hekatombaion, when review of the laws was automatically on the agenda.[129]

2 Hence, Demosthenes in his speech *Against Timokrates* says that

---

[116] E.g. *IG* II² 6 = Tod 98.   [117] Rhodes (1972) 271–2.
[118] Hansen (1989a) 69–72.   [119] Rhodes (1972) 64.   [120] Dem. 47.33.
[121] Ath. 171E.
[122] *Hell. Oxy.* 6.1; *IG* II² 16 = Tod 103; *IG* II² 18 = Tod 108 and Harding (1985) no. 20. Hansen (1987a) 184–6 n. 724, *pace* De Laix (1973) 78–84; Connor (1974).
[123] *IG* II² 127.34–5 = Tod 157. Rhodes (1972) 82 n. 3.
[124] Dem. 19.154. See p. 134.
[125] *IG* II² 1629.264–9 = Tod 200 and Harding (1985) no. 121.   [126] See pp. 138–40.
[127] See p. 168.   [128] See p. 169 with n. 62.   [129] See p. 166.

the correct procedure of legislation is to go first to the Council and then to the Assembly and, if the Assembly gives its blessing, finally to the *nomothetai*.[130] Moreover, a legislative proposal had to be discussed in more than one Assembly meeting, so, even if the first one was that of 11 Hekatombaion, the discussion at subsequent meetings must have depended each time on an (open) *probouleuma*.[131]

3 Besides its secretary *kata prytaneian* (the general secretary)[132] the Council had two others, one *epi tous nomous* (the 'legislation secretary') and one *epi ta psephismata* (the 'decrees secretary').[133] Aristotle tells us that the function of the legislation secretary was to sit in the Council and take down all laws:[134] he cannot have sat and endlessly copied the existing laws (which anyone could go and read in the archive), so presumably his job, like that of the decrees secretary, was to make formal copies of the legislative proposals that came before the Council, and it may be inferred that the Council had to discuss all such proposals brought up by ordinary citizens.

4 The *nomothetai* were summoned by the *prytaneis*,[135] and it was the secretary of the Council who had the job of publishing the new laws after the *nomothetai* had passed them.[136]

There can be no doubt, therefore, that the Council prepared the business of legislation just as it did that of Assembly decrees, though the decisions were taken by the *nomothetai* (as by the people in the Assembly) on the basis of motions proposed by ordinary citizens.

ROLE IN JURISIDICTION

The courts worked much less closely with the Council than the Assembly and the *nomethetai* did: jurisdiction was more and more concentrated in the hands of the *dikasteria* and the Areopagos. Nevertheless, five aspects of the Council's role remained of some significance.

1 The Council had the right to imprison or remand any person suspected of treason,[137] and to put tax-collectors in prison for debt

---

[130] Dem. 24.48. De Laix (1973) 66. [131] Hansen (1985b) 354.
[132] *IG* II² 223 = *Agora* XV 34 C 1. [133] *Agora* XV 62.200–2, 235–6.
[134] Arist. *Ath. Pol.* 54.4. [135] Dem. 24.27.
[136] *IG* II² 140.31; *SEG* 12 87.23–4 = Harding (1985) no. 101; *SEG* 26 72.47–8 = Harding (1985) no. 45.
[137] Dem. 24.63, 144–6.

if they had not paid up on the nail.[138]

2 Like other boards of magistrates the Council could impose fines, in the Council's case up to 500 drachmas,[139] though the fine was subject to appeal to the courts.[140]

3 In some exceptional cases (parallel to those dealt with by the Eleven)[141] the Council could impose the death penalty and execute it without reference to the People's Court or the Assembly.[142]

4 But its main jurisdictional power lay in its control over other magistrates and officials.[143] Any councillor could *ex officio* instigate an investigation against a magistrate or an official,[144] and any citizen could denounce a magistrate or an official by an *eisangelia eis ten boulen*.[145] In those cases the Council turned itself into a court of law, heard the parties and voted on verdict and penalty;[146] and for the verdict the councillors voted with voting-disks (*psephoi*)[147] and not by show of hands. On the other hand, the Council could only give a preliminary verdict (*katagnosis*),[148] which, if for more than 500 drachmas, had to be laid before the People's Court, which upon reconsideration could accept it or not; after the *katagnosis* the matter was out of the Council's hands.[149]

5 One aspect of the Council's control over magistrates was that it controlled its own members: an unworthy councillor had to be expelled and judged by a court. The expulsion was carried out in two stages: first there was a vote with olive leaves (*ekphyllophoria*), and if a majority voted against their colleague another vote was taken with *psephoi*. if the second vote went against him he was sent before the People's Court, which examined the case and gave judgement.[150]

In addition to its right to declare provisional or final verdicts as above, the Council also conducted four different kinds of *dokimasia*. In the first place, most magistrates, whether elected or selected by lot, had, before entering office, to undergo a *dokimasia* (*dokimasia ton archon*) before a court; but the nine archons and the 500 councillors had to undergo their *dokimasia* before the Council. Originally the Council's verdict was final, but in the fourth century it was always subject to appeal.[151] Secondly,

---

[138] Andoc. 1.93; Dem. 24.96–101, 144–6.   [139] Dem. 47.43; *IG* I³ 105.32.

[140] Arist. *Ath. Pol.* 45.2. Hansen (1975) 24–5.   [141] See p. 190.

[142] Arist. *Ath. Pol.* 40.2; Isoc. 17.42–3; *IG* II² 111.37–9 = Tod 142. Hansen (1976) 32ff.

[143] Arist. *Ath. Pol.* 45.2.   [144] Ant. 6.49–50.

[145] Arist. *Ath. Pol.* 45.2; Dem. 24.63, 47.42–4. Hansen (1975) 21–8; (1980d) 93–5.

[146] Dem. 47.42–4.   [147] Dem. 47.42.

[148] Arist. *Ath. Pol.* 45.2, 46.2, 59.4; Dem. 24.63.

[149] Dem. 51.8–9. Hansen (1975) cat. no. 142.

[150] Aeschin. 1.110–12. Rhodes (1972) 144–7.   [151] Arist. *Ath. Pol.* 45.3, 55.2.

there was *dokimasia ton ephebon*, by which, annually, the Council had to inquire whether the young citizens who had been registered in their demes during the year were of the age prescribed by the law.[152] The third kind, *dokimasia ton hippon*, concerned the cavalry: the Council inspected both horses and riders, to satisfy itself that the horses were in good condition and the riders in good enough training to take the field. Attica was not agriculturally rich and only the upper class could afford to keep horses, so the cavalry were chosen from the richest citizens, originally members of the two top Solonian classes only; but in the fourth century the state paid for the upkeep of the horses, and at the *dokimasia* the Council could deprive a cavalryman of his fodder allowance of a drachma a day.[153] The Council also, in collaboration with the Mustering Board (*katalogeis*), drew up the muster-roll of the cavalry.[154] Lastly, while by *dokimasia ton hippon* the Council inspected the richest citizens, by *dokimasia ton adynaton* it inspected the poorest: those disabled and thus incapable of earning a living, who owned property worth less than 300 drachmas, had the right to a pension of 2 obols a day, and it was the Council who distributed the pensions by decree and made sure they went to really necessitous cases.[155]

ROLE IN ADMINISTRATION

It is impossible to give a full account here of all the Council's administrative duties and powers; a reading of what Aristotle says about them in the second half of the *Constitution of Athens* will serve to show how few Athenian public pies there were in which it did not have a finger. It was involved in the control of all sanctuaries in Athens and Attica[156] and the running of many of the religious festivals;[157] it had the duty to inspect all public buildings,[158] most notably the defences of the city and the Piraeus;[159] it was responsible for the navy and the naval yards,[160] for the building of new vessels[161] and the equipping and despatch of fleets,[162] and it had oversight of the cavalry.[163] It acted as administrator of the public finances in collaboration with various other boards; and, last but not least, it had daily responsibility for foreign policy. Upon these last

---

[152] Arist. *Ath. Pol.* 42.2.   [153] Arist. *Ath. Pol.* 49.1. Bugh (1988) 15–16, 170–1.
[154] Arist. *Ath. Pol.* 49.2.   [155] Arist. *Ath. Pol.* 49.4; Aeschin. 1.103–4; Lys. 24.
[156] *IG II²* 204.21 = Harding (1985) no. 78.   [157] Arist. *Ath. Pol.* 49.3.
[158] Arist. *Ath. Pol.* 46.2.   [159] *IG II²* 244.36–7.
[160] Arist. *Ath. Pol.* 46.1.   [161] Dem. 22.8.
[162] *IG II²* 1629.242ff = Tod 200 and Harding (1985) no. 121.
[163] Arist. *Ath. Pol.* 49.1–2.

two aspects of the Council's work a little more needs to be said; but first, if the reader wonders how the Council could ever deal with such a mass of business, the answer is that it appointed quite a number of committees to take care of particular duties: we hear, for example, about the *triero-poioi*,[164] the committee for the building of new ships, and the *hieropoioi Eleusini*,[165] who took care of the Council's responsibilities in relation to the Mysteries.

Public finances

In the second half of the fourth century Athens had the folowing sources of revenue,[166] which in her most penurious days, in the 350s, brought in an annual income of some 130 talents,[167] ten years later some 400 talents,[168] and in the period of peace after 338, under the administration of Lykourgos, no less than 1200 talents.[169]

1 Not only the sanctuaries of the various divinities[170] but the state itself[171] owned much (mainly sacred) property, which was let at auction to the highest bidder, usually on ten-year leases. The auction was held in the Council under the direction of the *poletai* and in the presence of the king archon, and rents were paid annually to the *apodektai* in the *bouleuterion*.[172]

2 What lay beneath the soil belonged to the state. The valuable silver-mines in the south-east of Attica were let out in separate concessions to the highest bidders for either three or, perhaps, ten years at a time, and that auction also took place in the Council under the direction of the *poletai*, this time with the treasurer of the Military fund and the Board for the Theoric Fund present; and rents were payable each prytany to the *apodektai* in the *bouleuterion*.[173]

3 The most important customs duty was the *pentekoste*, 2 per cent by value on all imports and exports.[174] Collection was farmed out a year at a time to the highest bidders (who tended to be a consortium). The auction took place in the Council under the direction of the *poletai* with, once again, the treasurer of the Military Fund and the Board for the Theoric Fund in attend-

---

[164] Arist. *Ath. Pol.* 46.1.   [165] *IG* II² 1672.280; *Agora* XV 38.83–7.

[166] Andreades (1931) 285–325.   [167] Dem. 10.37.

[168] Dem. 10.38. Theop. fr. 166.

[169] Plut. *Mor.* 852F; *IG* II² 457. Burke (1985) 251.

[170] *IG* II² 334.16–17. *Hesperia* 52 (1983) 100–35, 177–231.

[171] Andoc. 1.92–3.   [172] Arist. *Ath. Pol.* 47.4. Behrend (1970) 63–7.

[173] Arist. *Ath. Pol.* 47.2.   [174] Andoc. 1.133–6; Dem. 35.29–30.

ance.[175] (In the fourth century the 2 per cent import duty on corn was let out separately.)[176]

4 Collection of the *metoikion*, the personal tax on metics, was farmed out on a yearly basis in the Council by the *poletai*,[177] and so was the *pornikon telos*, the licence fee paid by all prostitutes to carry on their profession.[178]

5 Jurisdiction brought in some income in the form of court fees, fines and confiscations.[179] In private suits both parties paid fees (*prytaneia*),[180] and in disputes of private citizens against the state a citizen deposited a *parakatabole*, a percentage of the value in dispute, which fell to the state if the plaintiff lost.[181] In public prosecutions, as already noted, the accuser forfeited 1000 drachmas if he abandoned the case before the hearing or failed to win more than a fifth of the votes.[182] Fines, again, in public prosecutions went to the state:[183] the magistrate in charge of the court had to inform the *praktores* of the fine imposed,[184] and if the condemned person did not pay at once the *praktores* registered him[185] in the central register of state debtors on the Akropolis.[186] Fines were frequent and could mount up to several talents:[187] they must have represented an important part of the state's income. Finally, confiscations: they were carried out by the Eleven,[188] and the confiscated goods were sold at public auction in the Council under the direction of the *poletai* and in the presence of the nine archons.[189] Confiscations must have been an important source of revenue: the best-known example is perhaps Lykourgos' prosecution of Diphilos, a mining-concessionaire, whose confiscated property is supposed to have brought in 160 talents, more than the state's annual income had been before the mid fourth century.[190]

6 The property tax (*eisphora*) was paid by citizens and metics alike, and the richest of all paid the tax for all contributors in advance (*proeisphora*) and recouped themselves from the others. *Proeisphora* was a liturgy, and in the appointment of *proeispherontes* the Council took a part.[191]

[175] Arist. *Ath. Pol.* 47.2.   [176] Dem. 59.27.   [177] Harp. s.v. *metoikion*.

[178] Aeschin. 1.119–20.   [179] Boeckh (1886) I 415–55.

[180] Poll. 8.38; Dem. 47.64. See p. 196.   [181] Harp. s.v. *parakatabole*.

[182] Dem. 53.1–2. See p. 192.   [183] Dem. 24.50, 43.71.

[184] Dem. 43.71.   [185] Dem. 25.28.   [186] Dem. 25.4. See p. 12.

[187] Dem. 23.167 (5 talents), 21.182 (2 × 10 talents); Din. 1.14 (100 talents).

[188] Arist. *Ath. Pol.* 52.1; *Hesperia* 10 (1941) 15–27 no. 1.10.

[189] Arist. *Ath. Pol.* 47.2; *SEG* 19 133.   [190] Plut. *Mor.* 843D.

[191] Dem. 50.8. Wallace (1989b) 478ff.

State income was thus generated by farming-out or by sale; even the property tax became indirect when *proeisphora* was introduced. The only direct source of revenue was fines levied in public prosecutions. Thus, concessionaires and purchasers, *proeispherontes* and condemned persons were the four categories who risked becoming state debtors if they failed to pay in good time. The sanctions were extremely severe in principle but were administered somewhat randomly,[192] sometimes to the advantage[193] and sometimes the disadvantage of those concerned.[194] A debtor could find his debt doubled[195] (usually in the ninth prytany),[196] he could suffer *atimia*,[197] and the Council could put him in prison till he had paid the whole debt.[198] What is more, heirs inherited liability, so that the sons of a state debtor could find themselves landed with *atimia* or imprisonment the day their father died.[199]

A debt to the state was payable either in instalments on the first day of each prytany or yearly at the beginning of the ninth prytany,[200] though fines were supposed to be paid instantly after sentence had been passed.[201] The sums were handed over in the *bouleuterion* to the Council, which was in this matter under the direction of the Board of Receivers, the *apodektai*, not of the *proedroi*. All outstanding instalments were posted on boards, one for each debtor and each instalment, and as they were paid they were wiped off the board there and then.[202]

On the same day all the sums paid in were allotted to the exchequers of the various boards of magistrates according to the *merismos*,[203] the law that determined the attributions,[204] and handed over at once. (On the following day the *apodektai* gave the Council a general statement of the finances.)[205] The Athenians had no central treasury: each board had its own funds and had to look after them itself.[206] For example, the Assembly seems to have had a yearly grant of 10 talents,[207] used, *inter alia*, for the publication of decrees;[208] the Overseers of the Temples received half a talent a year;[209] the Treasurers of Athena, who had to pay the jurors in the courts, must have received, on that ground alone, at least 15 talents;[210]

---

[192] Dem. 25.85–91. Hansen (1976) 59.   [193] Dem. 58.34–5.
[194] Dem. 21.182.   [195] Arist. *Ath. Pol.* 48.1.   [196] Andoc. 1.73.
[197] Dem. 59.6.   [198] Andoc. 1.92–3; Arist. *Ath. Pol.* 63.3.
[199] Dem. 24.200–1.   [200] Arist. *Ath. Pol.* 47.3.   [201] Dem. 58.48–9.
[202] Arist. *Ath. Pol.* 48.1.   [203] Arist. *Ath. Pol.* 48.2.
[204] *IG* II² 29.18–22 = Tod 116. Hansen (1983a) 192.   [205] Arist. *Ath. Pol.* 48.2.
[206] Rhodes (1972) 103.
[207] *IG* II² 43.68 = Tod 123 and Harding (1985) no. 35. Jones (1957) 154 no. 33.
[208] *IG* II² 106.17–19 = Tod 135. Henry (1989).   [209] Arist. *Ath. Pol.* 50.1.
[210] *IG* II² 1629.213–17 = Tod 200 and Harding (1985) no. 121.

and in the 320s the *thesmothetai* must have got some 15 talents to pay citizens for attending the Assembly.[211]

Given the *merismos*, the job of the Council and the Board of Receivers in relation to the public finances was purely administrative: they had only very limited power to take decisions about the use of the moneys they administered – except for the Council's own allowance under the *merismos*, administered by the two treasurers of the Council (*tamiai tes boules*).[212] If the Council or the Assembly passed a decree the execution of which involved expense to the state, one or other of them, as the case might be, had also to decide which board of magistrates must charge the cost to its annual budget, and if the decree could not be executed within the bounds of the *merismos* the Assembly had to set up *nomothetai* to pass a law sanctioning the increase or at least ratifying a disposition already taken.[213]

If the state could not afford the amounts that needed to be handed over to the various exchequers, it was necessary either to pass an Assembly decree for an extraordinary *eisphora*[214] or to draw on the reserves, i.e. the votive offerings dedicated to the gods and kept in the temple treasuries[215] – or simply to put a moratorium on payments and scale down the state's expenditure. That is why we hear more than once of the courts being shut down because there was no money to pay the jurors.[216] On the other hand, the state might find itself with a surplus after all the exchequers had received their due shares: that was called *ta perionta tes dioikeseos*, 'the sums left over from the administration', and a law required that in time of war the surplus should go to the Military Fund and in peacetime to the Theoric Fund.[217] It, or part of it, could also be handed to the treasurers of Athena and the Other Gods for safekeeping on the Akropolis.[218]

Besides the Council and the Board of Receivers the most important financial magistrates were the treasurer of the Military Fund (*tamias stratiotikon*) and the Board for the Theoric Fund (*hoi epi to theorikon*).[219] After its foundation, probably by Euboulos in the middle of the fourth century,[220] the Theoric Fund gradually acquired more and more responsibilities, such as the financing of public buildings and roads and the administration of the navy.[221] The board was elected, not chosen by lot,[222] and it served for terms of four years[223] from Great Panathenaia to

---

[211] Ar. *Eccl.* 290–3.   [212] *IG* II² 120. 20–2; 223 C 7–9 = *Agora* XV 34.
[213] *IG* II² 222.41–52. See p. 173.   [214] Dem. 19.291, 22.48.
[215] Thuc. 2.13.4; Dem. 22.48; *IG* II² 1493–5. Mitchel (1962) 226.
[216] Dem. 45.4, 39.17. See p. 189.   [217] Dem. 59.4.
[218] Schol. Dem. 24.136; *IG* II²1443.12–13.   [219] Arist. *Ath. Pol.* 43.1.
[220] See p. 98.   [221] Aeschin. 3.25; Harp. s.v. *theorikon*. Ste Croix (1964) 191.
[222] Aeschin. 3.24.   [223] Develin (1984); Havicht (1989).

Great Panathenaia.[224] In the middle of the fourth century the Theoric Board, and not the Board of Receivers, oversaw the finances along with the Council,[225] and at any time one of its members had a particularly close link with the Council in that respect.[226] Euboulos, who was in practice in charge of the finances of Athens at that time, was a member of the Theoric Board,[227] and it was he[228] who secured the passing of a law that forbade anyone on pain of death to propose a change in the *merismos* transferring money from the Theoric Fund to the Military Fund;[229] only in the crisis of 339, after the beginning of the final war with Philip of Macedon, was Demosthenes able to have that law repealed and get all the appropriations concentrated in the Military Fund.[230] After 338 the powers of the Theoric Board were greatly curtailed by a law proposed by one Hegemon,[231] and, when Lykourgos, in the years 336–325, controlled the finances of Athens, it was as incumbent of a new, probably four-year, post, in which he was called *ho epi tei dioikesei*.[232]

Foreign policy

The other extremely important administrative sphere of the Council besides the public finances was foreign policy. It was vital for someone to be able to take various decisions in matters relating to foreign powers without for ever having to put them to the Assembly, and it was equally vital for some matters to be able to be discussed confidentially; and, naturally, there had to be some board of magistrates to represent Athens officially in relation to other states.

Hence, the entire day-to-day direction of relations between Athens and other states was the concern of the Council. When messengers or envoys from foreign powers came to Athens they were directed to the *prytaneis*[233] and given leave to appear before the Council before being introduced to the Assembly:[234] and, what is more, the Council could decline to allow them to be presented to the Assembly at all, as happened in 371 when the Thebans sent a messenger to report their victory over the Spartans at Leuktra.[235] And when Athenian envoys returned at the end of a mission their first duty was to report to the Council.[236] Replies to foreign powers and decisions as to what to do about them were, of course, the

---

[224] Arist. *Ath. Pol.* 43.1.   [225] Aeschin. 3.25.

[226] *IG* II² 223 C 5 = *Agora* XV 34.   [227] Aeschin. 3.25.

[228] Schol. Dem. 1.1 (16.15, Dilts).   [229] Dem. 1 *hypoth.* 5.

[230] Philoch. fr. 56A.   [231] Aeschin. 3.25.   [232] See p. 160.

[233] Dem. 18.169.   [234] Aeschin. 2.58.   [235] Xen. *Hell.* 6.4.20.

[236] Aeschin. 2.45–6.

business of the people in their Assembly, but when a decision had been made it had to go back to the Council for all sorts of consequential measures to be taken: every time Athens despatched a delegation or a fleet, or commissioned an army, the decision of principle had to be followed by a long list of administrative items, which may have been less fundamental but were equally necessary to the execution of the main decision.[237] It was in just such cases that the Assembly delegated decision-making powers to the Council:[238] thus, in 325/4, when a fleet was despatched, we learn that the Council was given authority to take all necessary measures within the framework of the Assembly's overall decision.[239] In numerous cases the Assembly even delegated to the Council the power to choose envoys, which was normally reserved to the people.[240]

Confidential negotiations were quite impossible in the Assembly, but could be held in the Council, though even there not without problems.[241] To that end, the Council could hold confidential (*en aporrhetoi*) meetings, with no non-members present, at which the councillors must have been sworn to secrecy.[242] In 340, not long before the outbreak of war with Philip, Demosthenes, through a member of the Council, outmanoeuvred Aischines by getting the Council, in closed session, to pass a decree which was subsequently ratified by the Assembly;[243] and before the outbreak of the Lamian War in 323 the general Leosthenes held secret meetings with the Council about supplies and financial support.[244]

The confidential discussions in the Council have naturally not left much trace in the sources; but at least on the formal and official level the Council's importance in foreign policy can be perceived in the surviving treaties, in which it is nearly always the Council (usually along with the generals) that takes the oath on behalf of Athens[245] and thus represents the Athenian state to the outside world. As hosts of foreign representatives it was the *prytaneis* and in particular their *epistates* who represented Athens; and when foreign envoys were invited to dinner in the Prytaneion[246] we may imagine that the *epistates* was invited along with them as head of state, and was allowed to exchange residence in the Tholos for a jaunt to the Prytaneion on the other side of the Akropolis.[247]

---

[237] Rhodes (1972) 118.   [238] Ste Croix (1963) 115 n. 2.

[239] *IG* II² 1629.264–9, 272ff = Tod 200 and Harding (1985) no. 121.

[240] *IG* II² 16..17–20 = Tod 103; *IG* II² 117.19–21. Piérart (1974a) 130–7.

[241] Dem. 2.6; Theop. fr. 30. Ste Croix (1963); Griffith (1979) 238–42.

[242] Dem. 25.23.   [243] Aeschin. 3.125–7.   [244] Diod. 17.111.3.   [245] *IG* II² 105.32–4 = Tod 136 and Harding (1985) no. 52.

[246] Dem. 19. 234. Osborne (1981) 156.   [247] Miller (1978) 136–83.

11

The Political Leaders

POLITICAL INITIATIVES

In Athens decisions were taken collectively (by the Assembly, the *nomothetai* or the courts). The work preparatory to the taking of a decision, and responsibility for its execution, lay with the magistrates, but the matter had first to be brought before them by an ordinary, individual Athenian citizen. That is a striking difference between antiquity and today: in modern democracies it is almost always the authorities or the elected politicians who start something. Some ordinary citizen may prompt the authorities to take an initiative, but he does not have to answer for it; and such an initiative is commonly channelled through collective bodies such as interest groups, parties or the mass media.[1] That the initiative in the process of political decision-making was wholly and completely left to the individual citizen seems as odd to us as does the direct democracy's principle that all important decisions must be taken by the votes of large citizen-assemblies.

What was the word for the initiative-taker in Athenian democracy, and what sort of initiatives did he take? Surviving laws and decrees require initiatives to be taken by *Athenaion ho boulomenos hois exestin*, 'any Athenian who wishes from amongst those who may';[2] and in the abbreviated form *ho boulomenos*, 'anyone who wishes', the same phrase occurs in the orators.[3] It was the function of *ho boulomenos* to provide the initiatives for the laws that would be passed by the *nomothetai*,[4] the decrees that would be passed by the Assembly[5] and the prosecutions that

---

[1] Wheare (1968) 43–61; Holden (1974) 69–71.
[2] Dem. 24.63; *SEG* 26 72.34 = Harding (1985) no. 45.
[3] Andoc. 1.23, Dem. 13.11; Aeschin. 2.65. [4] Dem. 24.23.
[5] Aeschin. 1.23.

would be judged by the courts.[6] He was the king-pin of Athenian democracy – and he was, in principle, anybody.[7]

In contrast to the magistrates, *ho boulomenos* had no official status, though there was admittedly nothing to stop a magistrate donning the mantle of *ho boulomenos*. The most important example of this is the councillor who moved a *probouleuma*,[8] for in the resulting decree of the Assembly the proposer is never referred to as a councillor:[9] he is just given his name like the proposer of a non-probouleumatic decree, and he evidently counted as acting not as a councillor but as an ordinary citizen. Neither was *ho boulomenos* subject to *dokimasia* or *euthynai* like the magistrates; but he could always be made to answer for his initiative, even, in extreme cases, be condemned to death for it. There were *graphe paranomon* and *graphe nomon me epitedeion theinai* for his proposals to the Assembly or the *nomothetai*,[10] and as a public prosecutor he risked a fine of 1000 drachmas and partial *atimia* if he withdrew or got less than a fifth of the votes.[11] If suspected of acting as a sycophant he could be brought into court by a *probole* or a *graphe sykophantias*,[12] and if treasonable conduct was added he could be liable to an *eisangelia*.[13] Finally, *ho boulomenos* had to be, if not the Reasonable Man, at any rate the Moral Man: a citizen who stood up to address the people must not have been guilty of any offence under military law, nor have been cruel to his parents, nor have squandered his patrimony, nor have worked as a prostitute,[14] and his conduct in those matters could be subjected to a special procedure of inspection before a court (*dokimasia ton rhetoron*),[15] in which, if found guilty, he was punished with permanent total *atimia*[16] (hence ' . . . of those who may').

There was no law requiring anybody to appear in the role of *ho boulomenos*,[17] and the orators found no fault with the fact that many Athenians never addressed their fellow citizens;[18] but the democratic ideology implied that it was a moral duty to do so from time to time,[19] and ideally the sum of active citizens was equal to the whole body of citizens.[20] In that regard, however, the ideal never matched the reality: a minority came to dominate the field of politics and the majority of citizens never trod the speakers' platform. Judged by political activity the citizens of Athens can be divided into three groups.[21] First there

---

[6] Isoc. 20.2; Ar. *Plut.* 916–19.   [7] Hansen (1981c) 359–65.
[8] See p. 253.   [9] See p. 145.   [10] See p. 175.
[11] See p. 192.   [12] See p. 195.   [13] See p. 213.
[14] Aeschin. 1.28–31.   [15] Aeschin. 1.32. Lipsius (1905–15) 278–82.
[16] Aeschin. 1.134; Dem. 19. 284.   [17] Dem. 19.99.
[18] Dem. 18.308, 22.30.   [19] Aeschin. 3.220.   [20] Pl. *Prt.* 319D.
[21] Hansen (1989a) 11–17.

were the passive ones, who took no part in the Assembly and did not
volunteer for the Heliastic Oath or the selection of magistrates. They are
the ones spoken of disdainfully by Perikles in the funeral speech[22] (though
Plato[23] and Isokrates[24] refer to them respectfully enough). Secondly,
there was a very large group who did participate in the Assembly and
serve as *nomothetai* and as jurors in the courts, but whose participation
was limited to listening and voting and who did not raise their voices in
discussion.[25] And, thirdly, there was the much smaller group of initiative-
takers, who spoke and proposed motions; and even of those the majority
performed the role of *hoi boulomenoi* according to the democratic ideal,
i.e. as private persons taking responsibility for an initiative from time to
time.[26] Only the minority of that group were the really politically active
people who performed more or less professionally as speakers in the
Assembly and legislators and instigators of public prosecutions, and they
are the people whom the history books tend to call the 'politicians' of
Athens.[27]

SPEAKERS AND GENERALS

There is no word in ancient Greek corresponding to our 'politician', only
the pair *rhetores kai strategoi*, 'the speakers and the generals'.[28] The *rhetor*[29]
is the proposer of things in the Assembly[30] or Council[31] or courts[32] or
to the *nomothetai*,[33] though the word can also signify one who supports
or opposes an initiative taken by another.[34] A synonym occasionally used
for *rhetor* was *ho politeuomenos*, the man who made active use of his citizen
rights,[35] and another was *demagogos*, by which democrats meant just
'leader of the people' in a neutral sense,[36] while the critics of democracy
used it in the modern sense of 'demagogue'.[37]

Rhetores were self-selected; the *strategoi* on the other hand were a board
of ten elected magistrates, who, besides their duties as commanders of
the Athenian forces,[38] had important civil functions: they presided over

[22] Thuc. 2.40.2.   [23] Pl. *Tht.* 173C-D.   [24] Isoc. 15.38.
[25] Dem. 22.36; Aeschin. 3.233.   [26] Aeschin. 3.220; Dem. 22.37, 23.4, 24.66.
[27] Perlman (1963); Connor (1971).
[28] Dem. 18.170; Din. 1.71; Hyp. 3.27; Hansen (1989a) 5–7.
[29] Hansen (1981c) 368–70.   [30] Aeschin. 3.55.   [31] Lys. 22.2.
[32] Din. 1.100.   [33] Dem. 24.142.   [34] Aeschin. 1.28–32; Hyp. 3.7–8.
[35] Dem. 3.29–31. Hansen (1989a) 14 n. 38.
[36] Lys. 27.10; Hyp. 1.22. Hansen (1989a) 14 n. 40.
[37] Xen. *Hell.* 2.3.27; Isoc. 8.129; Arist. *Pol.* 1292a7.   [38] Kahrstedt (1936) 241–62.

the People's Court in all cases under military law[39] and in disputes between trierarchs;[40] they seem to have had the right to attend the Council and address it without special leave;[41] and they usually took the oath, along with the councillors, on behalf of the Athenian state in treaties with other states.[42] It might seem surprising that the generals are named side-by-side with the *rhetores* as the political leaders. The Athenians, like the citizens of other democracies, were keen to limit the powers of magistrates, but the generals were the exception: they were elected, not selected by lot, and they could be re-elected without limit.[43] Why did the Athenians allow this? The fact is that in its classical period Athens, like many other city-states, was a society in which war was the norm and peace the exception.[44] In the fourth century, wars were not carried on quite so relentlessly, and years could go by without any actual battles; but the Athenians still almost always had a fleet at sea or an army in the field. So it is not so very surprising after all that the generals were named alongside the *rhetores* as the political leaders of the democracy.

Rhetores and *strategoi* are treated as separate in the sources, because they represent two different kinds of political leadership, but there was nothing to stop one and the same citizen from filling both roles, and in the fifth century that was much the most normal thing: men such as Themistokles, Aristeides, Kimon, Perikles, Kleon, Nikias and Alkibiades were elected and re-elected to the generalship and simultaneously engaged in politics as speakers and proposers in the Assembly. The close relationship between being a *rhetor* and being a general shows that at that period, like Clausewitz, the Athenians regarded war as 'politics continued by other means'.

After the democratic restoration of 403/2[45] a split in political leadership between *rhetores* and *strategoi* began to develop:[46] the generals who won (and lost) wars for the Athenians – Iphikrates, Chabrias, Timotheos, Chares, and so on – very seldom took the platform as speakers, while the political assemblies were dominated by such figures as Euboulos, Demosthenes, Demades, Hypereides and Lykourgos, who were never elected to the generalship. The only statesman of the old style was Phokion,[47] but neither as speaker nor as general did he acquire the same kind of political leadership until the short period 322–318 after the

---

[39] Lys. 15.1–4.   [40] *IG* II² 1629.204–12.   [41] See p. 253.

[42] *IG* II² 124.20–3 = Tod 153.   [43] Arist. *Ath. Pol.* 62.3.

[44] Pl. *Lg.* 625E.   [45] Hansen (1989a) 17 n. 46.

[46] Isoc. 8.54–5; Aeschin. 3.146. Gilbert (1877) 1–93; Mossé (1962) 269–73; Perlman (1963) 347; Davies (1981) 124–31.

[47] Plut. *Phocion* 7.5.

democracy was over. The reason for the split was the growing specializ-
ation of oratory on the one side and military technology on the other.[48]
The Assembly was increasingly dominated by speakers trained in rhetoric,
and the citizen militia increasingly gave way to mercenaries under the
command of professional generals, sometimes even *condottieri*, who often
came from other states.[49] They were granted Athenian citizenship, but
they never enjoyed the people's trust as did the native civilian leaders.[50]
Not that it ever came to open conflict between the civil and the military
leaders; in fact, remarkably, the leading speakers served in the ranks on
campaigns,[51] while the leading generals were mostly content to cast their
vote in the Assembly like ordinary citizens and made as good as no
attempt to speak or make proposals themselves.[52]

The decline in the leadership of the generals in the fourth century is
also bound up with the creation of the new financial offices, filled by
election and for four years at a time: the treasurer of the Military Fund,
the Board for the Theoric Fund and *ho epi tei dioikesei*, the post that
enabled Lykourgos, in the twelve years after the defeat of 338, to put
the state on its feet again.[53] In fact in the period 355–322 there is evident
a tendency for the fifth-century coalescence of *rhetores* and *strategoi* to be
replaced by a coalescence of *rhetores* and elected financial officers.[54]
However, the split must not be exaggerated:[55] there were always numerous generals who appeared as *synegoroi* in the courts[56] or were chosen by
the Assembly as envoys.[57]

In most history books the *rhetores* are called the 'politicians'[58] of Athens,
but the term 'politician' is a misleading modernism, best avoided. Of
course, our word 'politician' is derived from the Greek *politikos*, but that
term is only found in the writings of Xenophon, Plato and Aristotle,[59]
never in the language of the law or in the speeches the Athenians listened
to, and even then it means 'statesman' rather than 'politician'.[60] And
when we turn from language to content there is a world of difference
between the *rhetor* and the modern politician.[61] A politician, today, is a
decision-maker (either individually or in a body) and is elected by the
people, or is at least a candidate for election; he is paid for his activities,
his accountability is often restricted by immunity from prosecution, and

[48] Arist. *Pol.* 1305a7–15.   [49] Pritchett (1974) 59–116.
[50] Dem. 23.65 (Charidemos of Oreos). Hansen (1989a) 19.
[51] Diod. 16.87.1 (Demades); Aeschin. 3.253 (Demosthenes).
[52] Hansen (1989a) 18–19.   [53] Mitchel (1970) 28–36.
[54] Hansen (1989a) 31.   [55] Sealey (1956) 178–9; Hansen (1989a) 19–21.
[56] Aeschin. 3.7.   [57] Xen. *Hell.* 6.2.39, 6.3.3. Hansen (1989a) 20 n. 53.
[58] Jones (1957) 128; Davies (1981) 124.
[59] Xen. *Mem.* 1.6.15; Plat. *Pol. passim*; Arist. *Pol.* 1252a7ff.   [60] Hansen (1989a) 4–5.
[61] Hansen (1989a) 1–4.

he is almost sure to be linked to some political party.[62] In fact the word often has a pejorative ring: in many countries you would not find a political figure willing to stand up and say, 'I am a politician.'[63] The Athenian *rhetores*, by contrast, were not elected but self-appointed; they never took decisions, only made proposals; they risked being penalized if they made money out of their political activity; they were constantly brought to account before the People's Court and, as will be argued below, there were no political parties for them to belong to. Nor was there the same discrepancy between how the political leaders saw themselves and how others saw them: the terms *rhetor* and *ho politeuomenos* could be used pejoratively, but they were quite as often used in a favourable sense, and Demosthenes in *The Crown* prides himself on having been *rhetor* and *politeuomenos*.[64]

So the political leaders in Athens were the group of Assembly speakers, generals and financial officers who did not just from time to time exercise their citizen duty to submit to election or propose decrees or laws, but took regular initiatives in the political assemblies. They came to form something of an elite, and to that extent represent an undemocratic trait in Athenian democracy. Amongst the thousands of Athenians at any time who took part in the Assembly and the courts there were, indeed, several hundred who proposed motions and brought prosecutions occasionally,[65] so that participation in the political life of the state, even at the top level, was astonishingly high; but, all the same, it was a very small group of Athenians who were the political professionals, recruited either from the well-off or from the ambitious who became well-off as a result of their political careers. This dissonance between ideal and reality can be summarized under four catch-phrases, relating to the four things that have always represented a peril for democracy: concentration of power, elite recruitment, political profit and professionalism.

Concentration of power

Such concentration can be seen in respect of the generals who kept being re-elected and the *rhetores* who were for ever proposing motions.

The most popular general of all in the fourth century was actually Phokion, who held the post no less than forty-five times;[66] but a much less important character, Philokles of Eroiadai, was elected more than ten times,[67] which implies that frequent re-election was quite common.[68]

---

[62] Moodie (1964).
[63] Sperber and Trittschuh (1962).
[64] Dem. 18.173, 212.   [65] See p. 144.   [66] Plut. *Phocion*. 8.2.
[67] Din. 3.12.   [68] Develin (1989).

We do not know exactly how many times the great generals in the first half of the century were re-elected, but Iphikrates was general at least thirteen times, Chabrias at least fourteen, Timotheos at least twelve and Chares at least nineteen times.[69]

Timarchos of Sphettos is supposed to have proposed more than 100 decrees,[70] and, according to Aischines, Aristophon of Azenia was acquitted seventy-five times in prosecutions for unconstitutional proposals,[71] so he must actually have proposed far more. He is named alongside Kephalos of Kollytos, who had the reputation of having proposed more decrees than any other Athenian. We only know twelve of Aristophon's decrees, half on stone and half referred to in the literature,[72] and of those of Kephalos only two can be identified;[73] the preservation-rate is evidently very low, so it is impressive that we have knowledge of twenty-two decrees proposed by Demades, eleven by Lykourgos and no fewer than thirty-nine by Demosthenes.[74] A political leader in the course of his career must have proposed hundreds of decrees; but we also hear of quite a number of people who, individually, only proposed one or two. If we compare all that with the likely total number of decrees the Athenians passed in the years of the 'new democracy', it is evident that at any time there were no more than a score or so political leaders, although there must have been several hundred citizens who took the platform on occasion.[75] The inference is that, during the eighty-two years the 'new democracy' lasted, there were fewer than a hundred political leaders but several thousand who were politically active occasionally at the highest level.[76] That conclusion is valid not only for the Assembly: we can tell from the sources that the same small elite also proposed legislation for the *nomothetai* and brought political prosecutions before the courts.

Recruitment

Concentration of power can be offset to some degree by wide recruitment of the elite; but here too it must be admitted that the Athenians, contrary to democratic principle, took their leaders from a narrow group of families that, even if no longer an aristocracy, were still an economic upper class.

From the beginning of democracy under Kleisthenes till the death of Perikles in 429 most of the political leaders of Athens were recruited from the aristocracy and belonged to the very clans who had held power

[69] Hansen (1989a) 49, 60, 63, 64.   [70] *Suda* s.v. *Timarchos.*

[71] Aeschin. 3.194, but see Oost (1977).   [72] Hansen (1989a) 37–8.

[73] Hansen (1989a) 51.   [74] Hansen (1989a) 40, 53–4, 41–2.

[75] Hansen (1989a) 120–2.   [76] Hansen (1989a) 122–4; Ober (1989) 108.

in the days before Kleisthenes:[77] the constitution was changed but the faces were the same; only now the aristocrats had to lead instead of rule, and success depended on persuasion. The Solonian property classes had already paved the way for a 'plutocracy' in which influence was based on wealth rather than birth.[78] That took a while to have effect, but by the Peloponnesian War we can trace a decided change in the recruitment of political leaders: amongst the prominent men who competed for popular favour towards the end of the fifth century there were many 'new men', often perhaps just as much a part of the wealthy class as their predecessors but of less distinguished birth.[79] And that development continued in the fourth century, so that by Demosthenes' time there were very few aristocrats amongst the *rhetores* and *strategoi*: the most notable exceptions were the orator Lykourgos, from the aristocratic clan of the Eteoboutadai,[80] and the generals Iphikrates of the Praxiergidai[81] and Timotheos perhaps of the Kerykes.[82] And in fact aristocratic descent was no longer a card worth playing: Iphikrates' clan had not had a leading role in Athenian history at any time, but all the same it is striking that in a speech in his own defence he proudly declared that 'his clan began with himself'.[83] Only in cult activities and priesthoods did the old aristocratic families preserve their traditional role.

Wealth was a different matter. In the fourth century many of the political leaders were rich enough to have to perform liturgies; many, even, of the lesser ones we hear about belonged to the liturgy-performing class, i.e. the tiny group of 1200 richest citizens, every one of whom must have had a fortune of several talents.[84] We know the names of almost 400 fourth-century orators and generals,[85] of whom more than a hundred are also attested as liturgy-performers or relatives of liturgy-performers.[86] Given the low preservation-rate of the sources, if we knew the names of all the political leaders and all the liturgy-performers, the overlap between the two groups could not help being even more marked. So there was certainly a correlation between wealth and political leadership;[87] but a correlation cannot, of course, show which was cause and which was effect: were the leaders recruited from the economic upper class, or was it political activity that made them rich enough to rise into it? Both: many known Athenian leaders, such as Andokides, Kallias,

---

[77] Connor (1971) 10–12. [78] See p. 30. [79] Connor (1971) 155, 159.
[80] Plut. *Mor.* 841B. MacKendrick (1969) 3–27.
[81] *Hesperia* 7 (1938) 92–3 no. 12. Davies (1971) 248. [82] MacKendrick (1969) 11.
[83] Lys. fr. 43. [84] See pp. 112–15. [85] Hansen (1989a) 32–64.
[86] Davies (1971). [87] Davies (1981).

Timotheos, Meidias, Demosthenes and Apollodoros,[88] were rich men's sons – there was an unmistakable tendency for the rich families to monopolize politics; but the group was not closed. A man could lift himself into the elite by his own bootstraps, and, when he did, he usually made a fortune on the way,[89] as did Demades, Chares and Aischines.[90] So the next question is: how did you make a fortune out of politics?

Political profit

Generals were paid on campaign, but not, apparently, when they were performing civil functions at home in peacetime;[91] and *rhetores* received no remuneration for moving decrees or bringing accusations. So in principle it was not possible to make a living out of political activity. Yet we often hear in the orators of *rhetores*[92] and *strategoi*[93] making fortunes. Hypereides' speech of accusation against Demosthenes in the Harpalos affair in 324/3 sums it up:

> Gentlemen of the jury, you grant the *rhetores* and *strategoi* tremendous perquisites, although the laws do not permit them to receive such benefits, only your mildness and indulgence: your only proviso is that the gains should be for your advantage and not to your harm. Demosthenes and Demades have, I believe, made more than 50 talents each from their decrees at home and from acting as *proxenoi*, quite apart from what they have got from the King of Persia and Alexander.[94]

Hypereides' account of the 'gifts' to *rhetores* and *strategoi* is surely trustworthy: it comes in a speech where it would have been to the accuser's advantage to claim that all 'gifts' were bribes. Most of the other evidence we have of specific 'gifts' to named persons is more dubious because usually unverifiable:[95] for example, the sums that Aischines and Demosthenes accuse each other of accepting. Aischines received money from Philip in 346,[96] plus an estate in Macedonia which in 343 yielded an income of 3000 drachmas (half a talent);[97] he got 2 talents from Demosthenes' opponents in 340 to speak against the latter's new trierarchic law;[98] and finally he acquired an estate in Boiotia.[99] That was

---

[88] Davies (1971) 31, 123, 263, 386, 437, 509.
[89] Lys. 27.9–10; Isoc. 8.124; Dem. 3.29–30. Hansen (1987a) 66; Ober (1989) 233–6.
[90] Davies (1971) 100, 545–7, 568–9.   [91] Ar. *Ach.* 597, cf. Larsen (1946) 91–8.
[92] Dem. 24.123–4; Isoc. 12.12; Din. 1.98–9.   [93] Lys. 29.2. Pritchett (1974) 126–32.
[94] Hyp. 1.24–5. See p. 293.   [95] Wankel (1982); Harvey (1985).   [96] Dem. 19.167.
[97] Dem. 19.145, 314.   [98] Dem. 18.312.   [99] Dem. 18.41.

fine, and raised Aischines from penury to the upper echelons,[100] but Demosthenes operated in a different league even when it came to perquisites.[101] He got vast sums for the decrees he proposed and for his trierarchic law: Hypereides guesses 60 talents.[102] On one occasion Demosthenes is supposed to have made 5 talents just by keeping his mouth shut in the Assembly.[103] He also received money on a huge scale from Persia, though the calculations vary from 10 talents to 70.[104] Only practically at the end of his career was the orator accused and condemned for having accepted 20 talents from Harpalos, Alexander's runaway finance minister.[105]

So the Athenians did tolerate their political figures receiving 'gifts'; and when those persons talked money they tended to talk in talents and minas, whereas the ordinary citizen talked in drachmas. There was, however, another side to the matter: fines in political trials were set in relation to the sums that political leaders got in 'gifts', and condemnation in an *eisangelia* or a *graphe paranomon* could easily result in a fine of 5 or 10 or 50 or up to 100 talents.[106] The higher you climbed the further there was to fall.

It was naturally the leaders who received the largest 'gifts', from foreign states and from their fellow citizens, but the second rank of the politically active also had opportunities for gain: in the courts as sycophants, by blackmail of various sorts,[107] and in the Assembly as men of straw, by accepting the risk of proposing measures really initiated by more powerful people.[108] Of course, not all political leaders accepted 'gifts', and it is only fair to remember that some of them spent their personal fortunes in the service of the state. The general Timotheos had to contribute from his own resources and take up bank-loans in order to finance the campaigns the state had sent him on without providing the means.[109]

The sums that accrued to the political leaders came from widely differing sources and served very different purposes. There were legitimate sources of income, such as the pay of generals on campaign[110] and of envoys on their journeys,[111] the generals' share of booty,[112] and gold crowns worth 500 or 1000 drachmas presented by the people;[113] such crowns were not necessarily dedicated to a god but were often kept by

---

[100] Davies (1971) 547.
[101] Davies (1971) 133–5.   [102] Hyp. 1.25.
[103] Plut. *Mor.* 848B.   [104] Plut. *Mor.* 848A; Aeschin. 3.239.
[105] Din. 1.6. See pp. 293–4.   [106] See pp. 207, 215.
[107] Aeschin. 1.107; Dem. 58.10–13. Lofberg (1917) 32–48.   [108] Dem. 59.43.
[109] Davies (1971) 509–10.   [110] Ar. *Ach.* 597. Larsen (1946).
[111] *IG* II² 102.10–13 = Tod 129 and Harding (1985) no. 43. Mosley (1973) 73–7.
[112] Thuc. 3.114.1. Pritchett (1971) 83–4.   [113] *IG* II² 410.

the honorands as their property.[114] There were more dubious payments, formally perhaps illegal, but to which a blind eye was turned – 'gifts' and perquisites of various sorts.[115] And then there were plain bribes, such as might be associated with corruption and treason.[116] The Athenians drew no sharp distinction between gifts and bribes: it is significant that they only had one word for both, *doron*, 'gift', with 'bribe' as a derived meaning.[117] Thus, a public prosecution for bribery was called simply *graphe doron*, 'prosecution for gifts'.[118] The fact is important, for the imprecise attitude of the Athenians to 'gifts' caused tremendous uncertainty and instability in the political system. A leader could enrich himself with impunity as long as he was trusted by the people or as long as his policy worked, but a shift of politics could change the picture at an instant, and his enemies could strike him down with a prosecution that might reduce him to beggary or drive him into exile, or even lead to his execution.

Professionalism

In the fourth century the circle of political leaders was narrowed not only by their mostly being recruited from the 'haves' but also by the growing demands of professionalism, which made it more and more difficult for the ordinary citizen to assert himself in the political field: the tendency can be found as much in the case of the generals as in that of the *rhetores*.

In Perikles' time the army was still a citizen militia, and the Athenians could elect the dramatist Sophokles to a generalship:[119] a hundred years later the conduct of war had become a specialism of professionals. The citizens underwent a two-year military training in their nineteenth and twentieth years,[120] and the generals were often professionals[121] who could even offer their services to another state in any year when the Athenians did not elect them. The most celebrated were Iphikrates, Timotheos, Chabrias and Chares, who were all native Athenians, and Charidemos, to whom the Athenians gave citizenship so as to be able to elect him general.[122]

Similarly with the *rhetores*. To take the platform in the Assembly or carry through a prosecution in th People's Court demanded an increasing degree of eloquence and rhetorical schooling such as was confined to

---

[114] Aeschin. 3.46–7.   [115] Hyp. 1.24–5.   [116] Dem. 19.191.
[117] Dem. 21.113 (*nomos*), 46.26 (*nomos*), 19.7. MacDowell (1990) 337.
[118] Harp. s.v. *graphe doron*; Aeschin. 3.232.   [119] Androt. fr. 38.
[120] Arist. *Ath. Pol.* 42.2–5. See p. 89.   [121] Dem. 23.139.
[122] Pritchett (1974) 59–116.

professionals. The frequent declaration by speakers that they are 'unac-customed to public speaking' is often couched in terms that make it evident to us that the *soi-disant* 'amateur' is either himself a professional or has got a professional to compose his speech. And professionalism went hand-in-hand with elite recruitment, for the training in political oratory given by the sophists was not to be had for nothing, nor was a speech by a logographer.[123] And, just as foreign *condottieri* could enter Athenian service and wage campaigns on behalf of Athens, so foreign speech-writers could settle in Athens and write, for a fee, speeches to be spoken by citizens, especially in the courts.[124] The two most notable were Lysias from Syracuse and Deinarchos from Corinth: both were metics who made their living at Athens as logographers. They could not take part in the decision-making assemblies of their hosts, but by the speeches they wrote they could influence the politics of Athens indirectly.[125].

PARTY POLITICS?

The concept of a political party

The most hotly disputed question about the Athenian political system is whether or not politically active citizens were divided into parties or political groupings. Some historians, reflecting European experience, will describe the 'four parties, the oligarchs led by Phokion, the pro-pertied moderates represented by Demades, the radicals led by Hyperei-des and the great bulk of the democratic party, who had followed Demosthenes',[126] or will call Euboulos the 'leader of the peace party'[127] or say that Demosthenes controlled the 'anti-Macedonian party'.[128] Others reject this model based on alleged ideologies: they prefer to speak of 'political groups' linked by kinship, friendship or regional connections, and they avoid the word 'party' – American historians take this kind of view, having in mind groups closer to the political parties found in the United States.[129] Yet others reject altogether the idea that Athens had political groupings of any consequence in any sense.[130]

If a considered choice is to be made between these viewpoints it must

---

[123] See p. 194.   [124] Lavency (1964) 42–5.   [125] Plut. *Mor.* 850C.

[126] Tarn (1927) 440.   [127] Glotz and Cohen (1936) 242ff; Perlman (1967) 167, 174.

[128] Cawkwell (1978) 118–19.

[129] Calhoun (1913) 97–147; Sealey (1956a) 202–3; Connor (1971) xi, 5–9; Romilly (1975) 131–81; Funke (1980) 1, 23; Strauss (1986) 28–31.

[130] Reverdin (1945) 201–12; Jones (1957) 130–1; Finley (1962) 15; Seager (1967) 95.

rest first, if not on a definition of a 'political party', at least on some significant criteria. The three criteria on which the analysis that follows will be based are as follows.

1 The evidence must show that there were competing groups, each containing a small number of leaders but also a substantial number of followers.
2 Such a group must exhibit some degree of organization and stability over a period.
3 The groups must be competing to win a majority of votes on the basis of which the winning group will be able to impose its will.

(Political scientists do not nowadays treat as a criterion of a political party the possession of a programme or set of policies, because some groups fully accepted as parties, such as those in the United States, are united only in the attempt to get their candidates elected, and their party lines do not run in accordance with ideology.)[131]

Now, as to the first criterion, it is commonly allowed that there were groups amongst the leading *rhetores*, and that is what is always adduced when historians talk about political parties at Athens. But that is to stop half-way: we must ask whether those leading personalities had substantial numbers of followers in their political train.

As to organization and stability, the fact that all are agreed that ancient city-states did not have political parties exactly in our sense does not necessarily mean that they had none at all, for perhaps their formation was simply less developed. After all, no modern political party is more than a hundred or so years old,[132] yet we do not hesitate to speak of political parties in the late eighteenth and early nineteenth centuries.[133] On the other hand, we must demand a minimum of organization and stability: if changing groups of leaders from day to day and from issue to issue were supported by changing groups of followers, it really would be meaningless to talk about political parties.

Finally, a widely accepted modern definition of a political party runs thus: a party is any political group that puts up candidates for public office at elections and is strong enough to get candidates in.[134] That shows how the modern concept of a party is totally bound up with elections, and so with representative government. So here we might have a syllogism: Athens was a 'direct democracy' and did not have

[131] Schumpeter (1942) 283.   [132] Duverger (1964) xxiii–xxxvii.

[133] E.g. Hattar (Hats) and Mössor (Caps) in Sweden after 1720. Carlsson and Rosén (1961) 104, 200.

[134] Sartori (1976) 63–4.

representative government, therefore Athens cannot have had political parties. That, however, would be simplistic, for although in Athens decisions were made not by representatives but by the whole people in their Assembly, they were made by a vote, and we would still be entitled to look for parties of leaders and followers concerned to win majority votes for this or that proposal.

Terminology

Let us, however, begin with the words they used. Was there in Greek a word or idiom denoting a party or a political group? The answer is yes, if you consult dictionaries and read sources in translation. For example, in the *Constitution of Athens* Aristotle, translated, says, 'there were three parties: first there was the party of the Shore, led by Megakles the son of Alkmaion, the second party was that of the Plain . . .', and so on.[135] But the Greek word here rendered by 'party' is *stasis*. *Stasis* is a very common word, but in historical contexts it almost always means 'civil war' and very rarely 'political group' (never so in the orators);[136] and when it does mean the latter, as in the passage just quoted, the connection with civil war is still obvious, for Aristotle is talking about feuds: a *stasis* is a group trying to gain total power for itself, not just votes. In older English, *stasis* would have been well translated by 'faction', not by 'party'.[137] A modern political party tries to gain or retain power within the civil order: revolutionary groups are not 'parties' in the ordinary sense. Indeed, when historians speak of political parties at Athens in the age of Perikles or Demosthenes they are thinking of constitutionally based groups, not revolutionary ones.

Hetaireia and *hetairikon*, derived from *hetairos*, are other words often translated 'party', but *hetairos* is a 'comrade', and 'comrades' associations' would be a better translation of its derivatives than 'parties'.[138] The words refer, in any case, in so far as they are political, to the time of the oligarchical revolutions in Athens, and are used of the oligarchical action committees that overthrew the democracy.[139] They were not political parties but revolutionary cells, and a law (probably passed in the period 410–404) prescribed that an *eisangelia* should be brought against anyone 'who tries to overthrow the democracy or form a *hetairikon*'.[140] (One further term is *synomosia*: it means people who have joined in swearing

---

[135] Arist. *Ath. Pol.* 13.4–5. Fritz and Kapp (1950).   [136] Aurenche (1974) 10–15.
[137] Sartori (1976) 3–13, 25; Strauss (1986) 17–28.
[138] Calhoun (1913); Aurenche (1974) 15–32.   [139] Calhoun (1913) 21ff.
[140] Hyp. 3.8. Thalheim (1902, 1906).

an oath, i.e. conspirators;[141] and most historians manage to avoid the mistranslation 'party' in that case.)

Attic Greek did not, then, possess a word or word-group corresponding properly to our 'party'. However, terminology is not all, and the historical evidence must be interrogated. Two pieces of evidence must first be dealt with which, on the face of it, powerfully support the belief that political parties existed in Athens, at least in the fifth century, to which they both refer. The first is the story of how Thucydides the son of Melesias separated off the *kaloikagathoi* in the Assembly so as to give them greater weight,[142] and the other is the story of how Nikias and Alkibiades combined their followers to secure the ostracism of the hapless Hyperbolos.[143] Both passages imply institutions that could properly be called political parties in quite a modern sense, and they are the ones on which historians tend to rely. The trouble is, simply, that they both come from Plutarch,[144] who wrote 500 years later, and, unless he says what source a story comes from, so that we can assess that, or is supported by other evidence, he cannot bear the weight historians want to place upon him.[145] He does not quote his sources for these anecdotes, so we must look to more contemporary evidence, and ask of it two questions: (1) do the sources furnish examples of collaboration between *rhetores* resulting in the formation of groups of leaders; and (2) do they furnish examples of substantial numbers of ordinary citizens voting in the Assembly according to the instructions of those groups?

Groups of political leaders?

There is some evidence of collaboration between political leaders. Demosthenes sat in the Assembly where he could discuss his policy with other *rhetores*,[146] and Aischines was surrounded by his group, who at least once succeeded in shouting Demosthenes down.[147] And in the Council the *rhetores* must have attempted to sit in groups, at least in connection with the oligarchic revolution of 411, for when democracy was revived in the following year a law was passed requiring seats in the *bouleuterion* to be assigned by lot.[148] (The same tendency, during the French Revolution, led to the formation of the 'right' and 'left', first in the Legislative Assembly and then in the Convention.) Sources also

---

[141] Aurenche (1974) 32–41.   [142] Plut. *Per.* 11.2. See p. 138.

[143] Plut. *Nicias* 11.5.   [144] Gomme (1945) 59–60; Andrewes (1978) 1–2.

[145] Whibley (1889) 37; Hignett (1952) 256, 267; Connor (1971) 24, 79–80; Strauss (1986) 30.

[146] Aeschin. 2.64, 67–8.   [147] Dem. 18.143.

[148] Philoch. fr. 140. See p. 252.

explicitly state that the *synegoroi* who supported the parties in political trials might be not just friends and relatives but other political leaders, and that such collaboration was not restricted to the circumstances of the particular trial.[149]

Furthermore, the structure of the democracy required co-operation between like-minded political leaders: for example, a man who wanted to get the people in the Assembly to decide something had usually to attend meetings of the Council[150] and find a councillor to propose a *probouleuma* there;[151] or one leader might propose to the people the setting-up of *nomothetai* and his fellow put the motion to the *nomothetai* when set up;[152] or a general in the field might have to find a *rhetor* in Athens to propose a strategy for the people to endorse.[153]

This constitutes adequate evidence for collaboration, at times, between one political leader and another and the formation of small political groups, but it leaves unanswered such important questions as how long-lasting they were, how far they were organized, how large they might be, how many such groups might exist at the same time, and what the members had in common – whether policy or promotion or something else.

Nothing in the evidence so far cited affords any grounds for seeing any uniform or stable organization of political groups. In a political trial one *rhetor* joins his voice to three others; in the Assembly a leader is flanked by some supporters; someone acts as spokesman for a political principal: some active councillors sit together during their year in office; some like-minded persons form a club that can be used for political purposes. Perhaps it is this last item that looks the most promising, and obliges us to return to the *hetaireiai*. We saw them as oligarchical cells at the end of the fifth century,[154] and although they were banned by the law passed between 410 and 404[155] they were still common in the fourth century: just such a club supported Meidias against Demosthenes.[156] In that age, however, they appear mostly in their (probably original) role of social clubs for dinner-parties and mutual aid in the private sphere.[157] Still, English and American historians particularly have seen in the *hetaireiai* the nuclei of political parties.[158] They argue as follows: the *hetaireiai* were clubs of members of the same age[159] and status, mostly

---

[149] Andoc. 1.150; Aeschin. 2.184.   [150] Dem. 8.4, 19.17, 21.116.
[151] Aeschin. 3.125.   [152] Dem. 24.26, 27, 39–40.
[153] Aeschin. 2.71; Pl. *Euthydemus.* 290C–D.
[154] 415: Isoc. 16.6; Andoc. 1.11ff, 54ff. 411: Thuc. 8.65.2; Xen. *Hell.* 2.3.46. 404: Lys. 12.55; Arist. *Ath. Pol.* 34.3. See p. 40.
[155] Hyp. 3.7–8.   [156] Dem. 21.20, 139.   [157] Dem. 54.7, 14–20, 30–40.
[158] Calhoun (1913) 10–39; Connor (1971) 25–9, 55–6; Aurenche (1974).
[159] Pl. *Def.* 413C; Hdt. 5.71.

young and upper-class,[160] and they were private[161] and often secret,[162] with some twenty or thirty members,[163] meeting in each other's houses.[164] The obvious occasions for such meetings were *symposia*,[165] but the members tended to support each other in all aspects of life, for example lawsuits,[166] for they were *philoi*, 'friends'.[167] Most of the *rhetores* were probably members of *hetaireiai*,[168] and for them membership opened up the possibility of turning such a club into a political group supporting the leader – even named after him, as *hoi peri Thrasyboulon kai Aisimon kai Anyton*[169] or *hoi amphi ton Peisandron*,[170] 'the followers of Thrasyboulos, Aisimos and Anytos' or 'the followers of Peisandros'. It seems that there were many *hetaireiai*, and an individual could belong to more than one,[171] so the way was open for coalitions amongst them;[172] but the uniting force was not political programmes but personal relations based on family ties, marriages and regional connections: the keystone was *philia*, 'friendship'.[173] Individual *hetaireiai* may have been reasonably stable,[174] but the coalitions between them were loose and fleeting.[175] On this model, it only appears that politics in Athens were determined in the Assembly by debate and vote of the people: in fact the initiatives were taken by *rhetores* belonging to coalitions of *hetaireiai*, and such a coalition might sometimes be large enough to control the majority vote.[176] The rivalries between the groups turned on power, for on external and internal policy they did not disagree.[177]

There may be some truth in this view, but its limitations are also grave. In the first place its basis is evidence from fifth-century, not fourth-century, Athens, though we know much more about decision-making in the latter period. Secondly, the principal sources supporting it are Plutarch's *Lives* and the accounts of the oligarchical revolutions of 411 and 404. Plutarch, to repeat, is a late source and inadequate unsupported; for the oligarchical revolutions and the *hetaireiai* that were important in them we have excellent contemporary sources such as Thucydides and Lysias, but that was a period of revolutionary activity and cannot be

---

[160] Dem. 21.213.

[161] Pl. *Tht.* 173D; Dem. 54.7.

[162] Pl. *Resp.* 365D.

[163] Andoc. 1.34, 52; Dem. 57.10.   [164] Andoc. 1.11; Dem. 40.57.

[165] Aeschin. 1.58.   [166] Is. fr. 29; Dem. 21.139.

[167] Andoc. 1.53; Lys. 9.13–14.   [168] Calhoun (1913) 18–19; Connor (1971) 27.

[169] *Hell. Oxy.* 6.2.   [170] Thuc. 8.65.1.

[171] Dem. 54.14. Calhoun (1913) 30; Connor (1971) 28, 67–70; Sealey (1956b) 242.

[172] 411: Thuc. 8.54.4. 404: Lys. 12.43–7. 396: *Hell. Oxy.* 6.2.

[173] Connor (1971) 32, 35–82; Bicknell (1972) Preface.   [174] Sealey (1956a) 181.

[175] Connor (1971) 6, 70–2.

[176] Connor (1971) 134–6; Rhodes (1986) 139: Strauss (1986) 28–31.

[177] Sealey (1956a) 202–3.

extrapolated to the subsequent period of political peace and constitutional politics.

And what, finally, of *philia*, 'friendship'? Historians of ancient Greece[178] have here been influenced by an analysis that until recently held sway among historians of the Roman Republic:[179] *amicitia*, 'friendship', meant political grouping – 'party', in fact. Historians of Rome have been retreating from that analysis,[180] and if we abandon Roman Republican history as a parallel and look to contemporary Greek writings we find plenty of philosophical discussion of *philia* in Xenophon and Plato and Aristotle but no sign, either there or in the historians or the orators, that it was an important political concept – unless we go round about and assert that *philoi* were the same as *hetairoi*, and come back to *hetaireiai* as political groupings. But then we are up against the fact that in the fourth century the *hetaireiai* do not seem to have been political clubs. And, finally, it is all very well to say that friendships, family ties and regional connections were what really linked the groups rather than ideologies or programmes; but the best evidence we have for such groups is (once again) that relating to the oligarchical revolutions, and there the differences were in the highest degree ideological and constitutional and programmatic, for they concerned nothing less than whether Athens should be a democracy or an oligarchy. In the *Constitution of Athens*, too, the analysis of political groups in the fourth century focuses on constitutional issues,[181] and in the age of Demosthenes the best-attested controversy between the leaders was as political and ideological as you could get – pro-Macedon and anti-Macedon.[182]

In summary, while there is some evidence that in the fourth century political leaders co-operated and formed small groups, no clear picture can be obtained from the sources as to what character and organization they had.

Groups of political followers?

We now have to consider whether substantial numbers of ordinary Athenian voters followed particular leaders, thereby constituting larger groups or parties. According to the model outlined in the last subsection, a coalition of small groups might sometimes be large enough to control the majority vote,[183] and a leading *rhetor* might enjoy the allegiance of a large

---

[178] Connor (1971) 18, 64; Bicknell (1972); Davies (1981) 2, 97; Finley (1983) 40–1.
[179] E.g. Taylor (1949) 7.   [180] Brunt (1988) 351–81.
[181] Arist. *Ath. Pol.* 28.   [182] Dem. 18.176; Aeschin. 3.130. Cawkwell (1978) 118ff.
[183] Calhoun (1913) 115; Sealey (1956b) 241; Connor (1971) 134–6, 84; Rhodes (1985c) 9.

proportion of the citizenry for some time.[184] Hardly anything at all of the kind is to be found in the sources.

When, after the battle of the Arginoussai in 406, the followers of Theramenes wanted to get the generals convicted for failing to rescue the survivors, they approached, at the Festival of the Apatouria shortly before the crucial Assembly meeting, all those dressed in black and with their hair cut, and urged them to attend the forthcoming meeting and vote against the generals: they were lobbying the relatives of the dead, not rallying regular political supporters.[185] Or take another political tale: Ergokles was a member of the Board of Generals of 390/89. He was indicted by an *eisangelia* for treason, embezzlement and corruption, but before the Assembly met to hear the trial he had – allegedly – succeeded in bribing no fewer than 2100 citizens.[186] Here was another attempt to influence large numbers and secure a majority of votes; but according to the story it was done by bribery, not by the mobilization of supporters or political groups to which Ergokles was affiliated. As for the occasion in 340/39 when Demosthenes was shouted down by Aischines and his followers,[187] twenty or so would have been enough to do that, and we do not have to think of a large Aischinean 'party'. Those two political giants clashed twice in famous trials: first in 343/2, when Demosthenes called Aischines to account for his embassy to Philip in 346;[188] and secondly in 330/29, when Aischines brought a *graphe paranomon* against Ktesiphon for proposing a crown for Demosthenes.[189] On both occasions each of them asserted that the other had touted for support amongst the prospective jurors before the hearing,[190] but there is no indication in any of the four preserved speeches that such an attempt met with any success, and on the second occasion Demosthenes does not even hint that Aischines' acquittal on the first occasion had been due to the court's being packed with his supporters.

The only source that might support packing of the courts is Theophrastos' sketch of the 'Scoundrelly Man', who is said to lead a group of scoundrels and sit with them in the courts[191] – a source never mentioned by those who discuss the problem. Likewise, only one source supports the assumption that followers as well as leaders were sometimes organized:

---

[184] Calhoun (1913) 111ff; Glotz (1929) 176–7; Ehrenberg (1960) 49–50; Connor (1971) 136. *Contra*: Jones (1957) 130–1.

[185] Xen. *Hell.* 1.7.8 (Correct interpretation of the pasage by Büchsenschütz and by Breitenbach).

[186] Lys. 29.12. Cf. Aeschin. 1.86; Isoc. 8.50.   [187] See. p. 280.

[188] Dem. 19 *versus* Aeschin. 2.   [189] Aeschin. 3 *versus* Dem. 18.

[190] Dem. 19.1; Aeschin. 3.1. Cf. Dem. 21.4; Ar. *Vesp* 552ff; Lys. 13.12.

[191] Theophr. *Char.* 29.6.

Demosthenes in his Assembly speeches often criticizes his fellow Athenians for their way of conducting politics, and in two passages he puts his criticisms in identical terms: 'Men of Athens, you used to pay your taxes by symmories, now you conduct your politics by symmories. There is a *rhetor* in charge of each, and a *strategos* as his henchman, and 300 to do the shouting, and the rest of you are divided between them, some in one group and some in another.'[192] The political groups thus described by Demosthenes are very close to what we should call 'parties': each is composed of a small number of leaders and a larger number of followers, all (or most) citizens belong to one or other of them, and the rivalry between them takes place in the Assembly, where the followers vote on proposals moved by the leaders. The passage has not attracted the attention it deserves, and historians who believe in Athenian political parties would be wise to give it the central place in their evidence instead of the all-too-frequently-quoted passages from Plutarch. From what Demosthenes says it must, undeniably, be concluded that groupings of political followers were sometimes to be found at Athens; but a calculated outburst of anger by an orator in an Assembly speech cannot outweigh the silence elsewhere in the thousands of pages of rhetoric in which political rivalry is the theme.

Arguments from silence are, indeed, not without danger: are the sources silent about political parties because there were none or because for some reason it was not thought fitting to mention them? An analogy to the latter might be the Athenian export of olive oil and of silver: the written sources give almost no hint that such exports took place, yet on the basis of a passage or two combined with the archaeological evidence we can infer that the export of olive oil was important and that of silver perhaps the backbone of the Athenian economy.[193] That line of argument does not, however, apply when the question is about political parties. Many passages in the speeches both to the courts and to the Assembly refer to political rivalries: the duel between Aischines and Demosthenes, for example, is the central theme of four speeches amounting to more than 300 pages.[194] In them we hear, indeed, about narrow groups of political leaders, comprising some twenty to thirty people; but never is there any indication that Aischines or Demosthenes belonged to, or controlled, a larger political party. And, when, in the sources, a political leader has to admit and explain a defeat he has suffered in the Assembly or the courts, he may allege that his opponent won a majority of the votes by specious rhetoric;[195] he may claim that his rivals interrupted his

[192] Dem. 2.29 = 13.20.   [193] Isager and Hansen (1975) 37, 45.
[194] Aeschin. 2, 3; Dem. 18, 19.   [195] Aeschin. 3.97–102; Dem. 18.132.

speech and prevented the Assembly from taking proper account of his views;[196] he may allege bribery, of the *proedroi* to estimate the vote wrongly[197] or of a large number of the voters themselves;[198] he may assert that his adversary moved his proposal late in the meeting when many citizens had already gone home.[199] But one argument is never heard: 'My opponent packed the Assembly with his political party: if the voters had been a fair cross-section of the people I'd never have been defeated.' Indeed, if anything, the orators probably exaggerate the importance of factions in order to blacken their opponents. So the silence as to larger political groups is after all significant, and strongly implies that they did not normally exist.

In the nineteenth century European parliaments, groupings amongst the elected politicians regularly developed sooner than the corresponding groupings amongst the voters, but the organization of the leaders always led in the long run to the organization of the followers.[200] If, then, at Athens, there is evidence of some organization into groups of those who initiated matters in the Assembly and other bodies, should it not follow that during the two centuries of the democracy from 507 to 322 their supporters must in the long run also have been organized? Not necessarily, as the experience of the Swiss *Landsgemeinden* may serve to show. Like other contemporary Western societies Switzerland has a developed party system. The elections to the Federal Parliament are completely dominated by the parties, which play a similar role in elections in those cantons which have parliaments and not *Landsgemeinden*. Every spring the political parties in the *Landsgemeinde* cantons arrange political meetings and instruct their supporters how to vote on the crucial issues. Furthermore, many speakers who address the people in the meeting of the *Landsgemeinde* are members of one political party or another and put forward that party's point of view. Nevertheless, party affiliation is weakened to the point of virtual dissolution in the *Landsgemeinde*. At the meeting-place, the voters never group themselves according to parties; relatives, friends and neighbours often stand together, but no faction or party group can be detected. Furthermore, the debate does not follow party lines, and an influential speaker may turn the scales, so the outcome of the vote on a controversial issue is often unpredictable even a few minutes before the show of hands takes place. It would be an exaggeration to say that the political parties have no influence at all in the *Landsgemeinde*: occasionally a matter may be settled on party lines. But it is not the characteristic behaviour of those assemblies.[201]

---

[196] Dem. 19.8, 23–4, 45–6.   [197] Aeschin. 3.3.
[198] Aeschin. 1.86; Lys. 29.12.   [199] Aeschin. 3.126; Dem. 21.193.
[200] Duverger (1964) xxiii–xxx.   [201] Hansen (1983a) 221–2.

If, then, a fully developed modern party system more or less dissolves when several thousand citizens vote directly in an assembly meeting, the same could have been true in Athens. The existence of groups of political leaders does not, in face of the general silence of the sources, necessarily imply corresponding groups of supporters, and the outcome of the vote in the Assembly may have been as unpredictable as it is today in the *Landsgemeinden*. The Assembly behaved in accordance with the democratic ideal: the people did not just vote according to the crack of their leaders' whips.

Interest groups?

Modern experience has induced political scientists to assert that governments are only a screen of institutions masking the real power in the hands of an elite,[202] and historians of antiquity have tended to follow their lead: don't imagine that you understand Athenian democracy when you have read about the workings of the Assembly and the Council and the courts, but look instead for the real power exercised by leaders, influential families and political groups.[203] Of modern societies something of the sort is certainly true, but for Athens it is anachronistic. Of course the orators, when it suits them, go on about how plausible speakers hoodwink the *demos*;[204] but in another context they will be saying how impossible is the job of a *rhetor* because everything is institutionalized and all political decisions are made in the Assembly.[205] We should remind ourselves once more of the way in which policy was formally made at Athens: an initiative taken by *ho boulomenos*; preliminary consideration by a board of magistrates; debate in a decision-making assembly, and a vote taken in that assembly. In the light of our discussion, *ho boulomenos*, though in principle anybody, reveals himself as as political elite; but there is as good as no evidence that behind that formal framework there lay informal organizations corresponding to the political parties and interest groups characteristic of modern democracies. Recently, for example, an attempt has been made to show that there was a 'mining-lobby' in Athens;[206] but scrutiny of the evidence adduced for it leads rather to the opposite conclusion: there is *no* sign of any mining-lobby. Policy was made by debate in the Assembly and not by the back-room negotiations of political leaders on behalf of political parties, because there were no political parties and no organized interest groups.[207]

---

[202] Mosca (1939); Michels (1911); Schumpeter (1942).   [203] Connor (1971) 4–5.
[204] Isoc. 8.124–30; Dem. 3.30–1; Aeschin. 3.250–1.   [205] Dem. 18.236; 19.185.
[206] Rankin (1988).   [207] Hansen (1987a) 86;. Ober (1989) 334.

12

The Council of the Areopagos

In the sixth century the Areopagos had been the most important political body of Athens,[1] but by Ephialtes' reforms in 462[2] it had become mainly a court for cases of homicide in which the victim was an Athenian citizen.[3] After the restoration of democracy in 403/2, however, and all through the fourth century the sphere of activity of the Areopagos was again progressively enlarged. That development was bound up with the desire of the Athenians to create a more 'moderate' democracy than they had had in the fifty years between Ephialtes and the Four Hundred and again in the last years of the Peloponnesian War;[4] in other words it is bound up with their notions of the 'ancestral constitution' or 'golden-age democracy', as it is perhaps better called.[5]

COMPOSITION

The Council of the Areopagos got its name because it met on the *Areios pagos*, the Hill of Ares.[6] In the fourth century it could also assemble in the Stoa Basileios in the Agora,[7] but the Hill of Ares remained its normal meeting-place,[8] both for trials for homicide[9] and when it exercised other functions.[10]

The Areopagos consisted entirely of former archons.[11] When the nine archons laid down office at the end of their year, their conduct in office was scrutinized first by the People's Court at their *euthynai*,[12] but afterwards by the Areopagos itself,[13] which investigated the conduct of

---

[1] See p. 37. [2] Arist. *Ath. Pol.* 25.2. [3] Philoch. fr. 64b.
[4] See p. 151. [5] Din. 1.62. [6] Dem. 23.65–6; Isoc. 7.38.
[7] Dem. 25.23. [8] *SEG* 12 87 = Harding (1985) no. 101.
[9] Lys. 1.30; Aeschin. 3.51. Wallace (1989) 215–16. [10] Dem. 59.90.
[11] Plut. *Sol.* 19.1; Dem. 24.22; Arist. *Ath. Pol.* 60.3. [12] Dem. 26.5.
[13] Hyp. fr. 164; Xen. *Mem* 3.5.20.

each of them, and only after that were they accepted as members of the Areopagos (*Areopagitai*). Acceptance was, however, for life.[14] We have no evidence as to the size of the Areopagos, and are reduced to calculation. A man could not be archon under the age of thirty,[15] and the archons were selected by lot from those who presented themselves.[16] The general prohibition against cumulation of magistracies[17] did not apply to the Areopagos, so having a seat on the Areopagos was no ban on holding another office (Euboulos, for example, was one of the *thesmothetai* in 370/69[18] and after that a member of the Areopagos, but that did not prevent him from being on the Board for the Theoric Fund in the 350s);[19] otherwise, citizens ambitious for office would have had to treat the archonship as a retirement job and wait before presenting themselves for selection, whereas we have several pieces of evidence for 'young' archons.[20] So we can go on the assumption that the candidates for the archonship were a normal cross-section of the male citizen population over thirty, with the proviso that it was mostly the better-off who presented themselves for that office.[21] Taken in conjunction with the demographic structure of Athens,[22] that will give an average number of Areopagites of about 150 persons,[23] and, if so, the Areopagos was indeed a council of elders, for two fifths of them must have been over sixty. Aristotle acknowledges in his account of the *gerousia*, the Spartan council of elders, that mental powers age along with physical,[24] but elsewhere he agrees that wisdom increases with age;[25] and the advanced age of its members did not diminish the respect the Athenians had for the Areopagos: on the contrary, they shared the general admiration all Greeks had for the greater experience and wisdom of age, and the Areopagos was always hailed as the best court Athens had.[26]

Unfortunately, we know very few fourth-century Areopagites; it is true that dated decrees and inventories furnish the names of the archons, but they give them usually without patronymic and demotic, so that precise identification is impossible. As it was regular for the politically active to present themselves for the selection of magistrates and hold one or more offices, it would be tempting to suppose that many political leaders sooner or later must have held an archonship and finished up in the Areopagos.

---

[14] Lys. 26.11; Arist. *Ath. Pol.* 3.6. [15] See p. 227.
[16] Dem. 39.10, 12. [17] Dem. 24.150. [18] *SEG* 19 133.
[19] Aeschin. 3.25, cf. Dem. 26.5.
[20] E.g. Thrasyllos (Is. 7.7, 34). See Hansen (1990c) 74.
[21] Dem. 20.28. Hansen (1990c) 77. [22] See p. 91.
[23] Hansen (1990c) 75, *pace* Wallace (1989a) 96–7. [24] Arist. *Pol.* 1270b35–40.
[25] Arist. *Pol.* 1329a13–17. [26] Dem. 23.65ff; Aeschin. 1.92; Lycurg. 1.12.

Nevertheless, although we can identify thirty-six of all archons between 403 and 322, only five of them are attested as having engaged in other political activities[27] and only one, namely Euboulos, is a known political leader; so it looks as if the Areopagos was not a forum for the political elite, but rather (as could be expected) contained a disproportionate number of the well-to-do,[28] which was far from the same thing.

POWERS

Development, 403–322 BC

From Ephialtes in 462 down to the oligarchical revolution of 404, when the Thirty took power, the Areopagos was exclusively a court for homicide.[29] The Thirty were elected as legislators,[30] and one of their first reforms was to annul the laws of Ephialtes and Archestratos dealing with the Areopagos,[31] so that at one stroke the Areopagos got all its old powers back. However, what the results of that might have been no one was ever to know, because a few months later Athens was in the throes of the civil war which led to the downfall of the Thirty and to the return of the democrats in autumn 403.

At the restoration of democracy the powers of the Areopagos were curtailed once more; but it was not reduced to being only a homicide court as it had been from 462 to 404. After the debacle of the Peloponnesian War even democrats saw eye-to-eye with the Thirty that the Areopagos ought to have some degree of supervision over the laws, the magistrates and the conduct of the citizenry as a whole; and from 403 onward, throughout the fourth century, we can see its powers expanding all the time. (That tendency continued into the Hellenistic age,[32] and came full circle in the age when Athens was a provincial city of the Roman Empire: in the last century of the Roman Republic and in the Principate the Areopagos was once more the most important organ of state in Athens,[33] as it had been in the archaic age before Kleisthenes and Ephialtes.)

In 403/2, in connection with the general revision of the whole corpus of laws, the Assembly decreed that the Areopagos was to supervise the administration of the laws by the magistrates.[34]

---

[27] Hansen (1990c) 77.   [28] Hansen (1990c) 77.
[29] Philoch. fr. 64. MacDowell (1963) 39–47; Wallace (1989a) 97–106.
[30] Xen. *Hell.* 2.3.2.   [31] Arist. *Ath. Pol.* 35.2.
[32] Busolt and Swoboda (1920–6) 935.   [33] Geagan (1967) 41–61.
[34] Andoc. 1.84.

In 352/1 the Assembly ruled that the Areopagos should join with the Council and various other boards in supervising all sanctuaries in Athens and Attica.[35]

In the 340s a new criminal procedure was introduced called *apophasis*, a variant of *eisangelia*, which went in the first instance to the Areopagos.[36]

In the second half of the century the Areopagos seems sometimes to have taken upon itself to intervene in the election by the Assembly of representatives of certain kinds; thus, when Aischines was elected *c*.343 as Athenian advocate in an international law-case about Delos, the Areopagos annulled the election and replaced him by Hypereides.[37] And in 338, after Chaironeia, the Areopagos interfered with the people's election of a new general and secured the appointment of Phokion instead of Charidemos.[38]

After the defeat at Chaironeia in 338 the Areopagos is said to have played a decisive role in the critical period down to the peace with Philip, including the execution, on its own authority, of some defectors.[39] Only then was defection made a capital offence, by a decree of the people which may even have been passed after some at least of the summary trials by the Areopagos.[40]

In the course of that critical period[41] the Assembly, on the motion of Demosthenes, actually passed a decree that the Areopagos should have the right to judge any citizen for any offence.

Of the above reforms two need some further description: the general right of judgement resulting from Demosthenes' decree, and the procedure of *apophasis*.

Judgement

In his speech against Demosthenes, Deinarchos paraphrases Demosthenes' decree thus:

> It was you, Demosthenes, who proposed in the presence of all these people here and the whole of Athens that the Council of the Areopagos, in accordance with the ancestral laws, should have authority to punish a person who broke the laws. And you handed and delivered the city to this council which in a few minutes you will be telling us is an oligarchical body.[42]

---

[35] *IG* II² 204.16–33 = Harding (1985) no. 78. [36] See p. 292.
[37] Dem. 18.134. [38] Plut. *Phocion* 16.4. [39] Lycurg. 1.52; Aeschin. 3.252.
[40] Lycurg. 1.53. [41] Hansen (1983a) 190 with n. 24, *pace* Wallace (1989a) 115ff.
[42] Din. 1.62.

The decree gave the Areopagos authority to judge every breach of the laws and condemn the offender to the severest punishments allowed.[43] Sentence was final and did not have to be laid before the Assembly or the People's Court; and the condemned person was handed over to the executioner straightaway.[44] Given the general way the law worked in Athens, it may be assumed that thereafter an intending prosecutor could choose whether he would lay a charge before the Areopagos or the People's Court: evidently prosecutors sometimes chose the Areopagos, for we have some examples of that body using its new powers. Demosthenes probably got his decree through in the panic days after Chaironeia, but it follows from the speech of Deinarchos that it was still in force fourteen years later.[45]

Apophasis

In sources from the second half of the fourth century we meet a quite new type of public prosecution, *apophasis*,[46] which seems to have been introduced in the 340s[47] and involved the Areopagos, the Assembly and the People's Court. It was a variant of *eisangelia eis ton demon*, and was used, like the latter, to prosecute attempts to overthrow the democracy,[48] treason,[49] and bribery[50] on the part of political leaders. The difference is that *apophasis* was not brought by an individual citizen who was personally responsible but by the Areopagos itself[51] or by the Assembly,[52] which had to elect persons to act as public accusers;[53] and the preliminary investigation was not the responsibility of the accusers but of the Areopagos.[54] The word *apophasis*, usually used for the whole procedure, really signifies the 'report' that the Areopagos made to the Assembly as a result of its investigation.[55] The investigation included summons of witnesses, taking of evidence of slaves under torture, and so on,[56] and it resulted in a verdict of 'guilty' or 'not guilty'; but the verdict was only provisional.[57] When the report had been read and discussed in the Assembly, if the verdict of the Areopagos was for acquittal the case was abandoned, but if it was for condemnation the people could confirm it by a show of hands, *katacheirotonia*, choose a number of public accusers and pass the

---

[43] Din. 1.6, 83.   [44] Din. 1.62.   [45] Din. 1.112.
[46] Hansen (1975) 39–40; Wallace (1989) 113–19.
[47] Dem. 18.134; Din. 1.63 (346–40). Carawan (1985) 124–8.
[48] Din. 1.3, 112; Hyp. 1.2.   [49] Dem. 18.133; Din. 1.58, 63.
[50] Din. 1.1, 3–4.   [51] Dem. 18.133; Din. 1.55–6.
[52] Hyp. in *P. Oxy.* 2686.15; Din. 1.4.   [53] Hyp. 1.38; Din. 1.51, 58.
[54] Hyp. 1.38; Din. 1.3–4.   [55] Din. 1.1.
[56] *P. Oxy.* 2686 (fragments of Hyp. *For Chairephilos*).   [57] Din. 1.54–8.

case to a court,[58] in which the jury heard the parties in the usual way and then voted, first on the question of guilt[59] and then on the penalty:[60] in voting on the guilt of the accused, the court could uphold or overthrow the preliminary verdict of the Areopagos. An *apophasis* was only exceptionally begun by the Areopagos itself; the usual procedure was for the Assembly by decree to call upon the Areopagos to investigate the case and prepare a report.

The sources show that *apophasis* was used with great frequency;[61] and it was the procedure used in the greatest of all fourth-century Athenian political scandals, the Harpalos affair.[62] In January 324[63] Alexander the Great's treasurer, Harpalos, fled from Babylon with 5000 talents and thirty ships, to be out of the way of the king's wrath when he got home from India.[64] After some vicissitudes he was allowed in midsummer 324 to enter the Piraeus with his thirty ships and the 700 talents he had left.[65] Antipater and Alexander's mother Olympias demanded his immediate extradition,[66] and on a motion of Demosthenes the Athenians passed a decree that he should be imprisoned and the money deposited on the Akropolis.[67] Shortly afterwards Harpalos escaped, and of the 700 talents only 350 were to be found;[68] no one doubted that the other 350 had been used to bribe Athenian political leaders, and when suspicion turned on Demosthenes, amongst others, it was he who got another Assembly decree passed that the affair should be investigated by the Areopagos.[69] The resulting *apophasis* was only presented to the people six months later:[70] it contained the names of political figures whom the Areopagos found guilty of taking bribes and an account of the sums each of them was supposed to have received.[71] Nine were found provisionally guilty by the Areopagos,[72] including two outstanding Athenian statesmen, Demosthenes the moralizing patriot and imperialist and the versatile *bon viveur* Demades,[73] who saved Athens four times when it had to make peace after defeats; others were the 'demagogue' Aristogeiton,[74] who prided himself on being the 'people's watchdog',[75] and Philokles, the general for the Piraeus, who had given Harpalos permission to enter.[76] The people passed all nine cases on to a court of 1500 jurors,[77] and elected ten public accusers,[78] among them Hypereides,[79] who had for

---

[58] Din. 2.20.   [59] Din. 1.54–9.   [60] Din. 1.60.   [61] Din. 1.54.

[62] Badian (1961) 31–6; Goldstein (1968) 37–49; Wallace (1989) 198–201.

[63] Worthington (1986).   [64] Diod. 17.108.6; Curtius 10.2.1.

[65] Plut. *Mor.* 846A.   [66] Diod. 17.108.7.   [67] Hyp. 1.8–9; Din. 1.89.

[68] Hyp. 1.10; Plut. *Mor.* 846B.   [69] Din. 1.4, 83–6.   [70] Din. 1.45.

[71] Hyp. 1.6.   [72] Badian (1961) 35 n. 141; Goldstein (1968) 42.

[73] Din. 1.89.   [74] Din. 2.1.   [75] Dem. 25.40.   [76] Din. 3.1–3.

[77] Din. 1.107.   [78] Din. 1.51; 2.6. Badian (1961) 32 n. 113; Goldstein (1968) 42.

years collaborated with Demosthenes in the struggle against Macedon. Hypereides' speech against his old colleague is in part preserved, as are also the three speeches written by the metic Deinarchos for another of the accusers, against Demosthenes, Aristogeiton and Philokles.[80] As far as we know almost all the accused were found guilty, and only Aristogeiton is known to have been acquitted:[81] Demosthenes was condemned to a fine of 50 talents, and since he could not pay he was put in prison – from which he soon escaped.[82]

CHARACTER IN THE FOURTH CENTURY

The Areopagos was a foreign body in Athenian democracy, a remnant from earlier days, and not easily accommodated to the structure of the democracy in Demosthenes' time. In some ways it was like a board of magistrates: Areopagites were all ex-magistrates and still subject to *euthynai*;[83] they had a preparatory function, as in the procedure of *apophasis*, where the Areopagos played the same role as the Council did in an *eisangelia eis ten boulen*;[84] they had administrative duties like other boards – for instance, the supervision of sanctuaries; and, like boards of magistrates, the Areopagos could probably meet on its own initiative without having to be summoned by anybody else.[85] Apparently, meetings of the Areopagos were not presided over by any magistrate, except when it functioned as a court for homicide: then the king archon presided.[86] In matters other than homicide the power of the Areopagos was, down to about 340, limited to exacting minor fines just like the other magistrates.[87] All that makes it understandable that Aristotle, in one solitary passage, calls the Areopagos a magistracy.[88]

In other respects, however, it was very unlike a board of magistrates: Areopagites were neither elected nor selected by lot; they did not have to undergo *dokimasia*; membership was for life; and they could hold other offices – so, as cumulation of magistracies was prohibited, the Areopagos cannot have been a magistracy. And the most important function of the Areopagos was as a court for homicide (after Demosthenes' decree, for other cases also), and under that hat the Areopagites were exactly like the jurors in the People's Court: they were summoned by the king archon, who presided; they listened and voted but did nothing else; and as a

[79] Hyp. 1.   [80] Din. 1, 2, 3.
[81] Din. 3.14; Dem. *Ep.* 3.31, 37, 43. Goldstein (1968) 43–4.
[82] Plut. *Dem.* 26.2. Goldstein (1968) 43 n. 36.   [83] Aeschin. 3.20.
[84] See p. 222.   [85] Inference from *SEG* 12 87 = Harding (1985) no. 101.
[86] Arist. *Ath. Pol.* 57.4.   [87] Dem. 59.80.   [88] Arist. *Ath. Pol.* 3.6.

court they were a decision-making organ, which no board of magistrates was. On the whole, however, the powers the Areopagos received in the course of the fourth century were advisory, preparatory and administrative.

Even in Demosthenes' time the memory lingered of how the Areopagos had once been an oligarchical council of elders like the Spartan *gerousia*.[89] A very clear case is the tyranny law of 337/6, passed by the *nomothetai* on the proposal of one Eukrates.[90] It begins with a clause legalizing self-help against anyone trying to overthrow the democracy, a repeat of Demophantos' tyranny law of 410;[91] but unlike Demophantos' law the whole of the rest of Eukrates' law is directed against the Areopagos. 'If the People or the democracy at Athens are overthrown no member of the Council of the Areopagos shall go up to the Areopagos or meet in the Council or discuss any single thing; and if anyone does . . . he and his descendants shall suffer *atimia* and his property shall be confiscated and a tenth go to the goddess Athena.' When the Areopagos is singled out in this way in a law about the overthrow of the democracy, that indicates that it was considered by some at the time as a powerful body, and one whose members might conceivably be interested in modifying the constitution – perhaps even in overthrowing it. In the 330s it was believed that an emergency usually resulted in an increase in the powers of the Areopagos,[92] so it is only natural that a law against tyranny passed in 336 focused on the Areopagos as the potentially important organ of government after a revolution. But the tyranny law was only one moment in a long story, and in the fourth century in general the Athenians' attitude to the Areopagos was a favourable one, and their willingness to enhance its authority was linked to their fondness for the idea of 'golden-age democracy'.[93]

[89] Isoc. 12.154.
[90] *SEG* 12 87 = Harding (1985) no. 101.
[91] Andoc. 1.96–8.
[92] 508/7: Hdt. 5.72.1 [See Hignett (1952) 93–5]. 480: Arist. *Ath. Pol.* 23.1. 405: Lys. 12.69. 404: Arist. *Ath. Pol.* 35.2. 338: Lycurg. 1.52.
[93] Hansen and Elkrog (1973); Wallace (1989a) 180–4.

13

The Character of Athenian Democracy

Like many Greeks, the Athenians had a soft spot for the 'golden age', the belief that everything was better in olden times and that consequently the road to improvement lay backwards and not forwards.[1] That attitude acquired practical importance for the constitutional debates and, indeed, the constitutional changes of the fourth century at Athens: if you wanted to defend the existing system the way to do so was to anchor it in the past and declare that you were only doing what the forefathers had done;[2] and if you were a reformist you could best get your proposals accepted by claiming that your reform was nothing but a return to the sensible democratic institutions that contemporary leaders had neglected.[3] That democracy itself was sacred went without saying. People such as Plato and Aristotle preferred the rule of the few to the rule of the many,[4] and many other Greek city-states were governed by oligarchs,[5] who regarded democracy as the rule of the mob;[6] but for the politically active citizens at Athens democracy was exclusively a positive value: oligarchy must wear the face of democracy if it was to be acceptable,[7] and 'oligarch' was as much a term of abuse in Athens[8] as 'democrat' was in some other places.[9] The Greeks in general debated whether democracy was good or bad, and, because they looked backwards, the universal 'hurrah word' was not, as with us, 'democracy'[10] but *patrios politeia*, the 'ancestral constitution'.[11] That term could cover any type of constitution whatever

---

[1] Dodds (1973); Dover (1974) 106–8; Hansen (1989c) 71–3.
[2] Dem. 20.153, 24.142.   [3] Aeschin. 1.33–4; Din. 1.62.
[4] Jones (1957) 41–72.   [5] Whibley (1896).
[6] Hdt. 3.81; Xen. *Ath. Pol.*; Arist. *Pol.* 1310a8–12.   [7] Isoc. 7.57.
[8] Dem. 24.75–6; Din. 1.62.   [9] Thuc. 6.89.6.   [10] Holden (1974) 2.
[11] Fuks (1953); Ruschenbusch (1958); Finley (1971); Walters (1976); Lévy (1976) 173–208; Harding (1977); (1978); Mossé (1979a); Hansen (1989c).

– the rule of the one,[12] the few[13] or the many;[14] but whatever it was it was always a Good Thing: the term *patrios politeia* silenced the critics and they could only retaliate by arguing that *their* ideal was the *true* ancestral constitution.[15] However, the Athenians in the fourth century avoided it as a slogan, doubtless because it had been used by the wrong people in the constitutional struggles of 411 and 404;[16] they still anchored their constitutional ideal in the past, but called it by other names, such as *patrios demokratia*,[17] the 'ancestral democracy', or 'the constitution of the forefathers', *he ton progonon politeia*.[18]

By insisting that their 'ancestral constitution', their *patrios politeia*, had been a democracy, the Athenians at once narrowed the range of *patrios politeia* in one sense, but they were still left with a chronological vagueness, because 'ancestral', *patrios*, might refer to any period in the past: the 'ancestors' might be anyone from the grandfathers of living Athenians to Deukalion, the only man who survived the Flood.[19] When, in Demosthenes' time, the Athenians wanted to legitimate the present by the past, how far back did they actually look for the 'golden age'? Well, it depended on what they were talking about. When they debated foreign policy in the Assembly they naturally looked back to the Persian Wars and the great days of the Delian League,[20] and to heroes such as Miltiades, Themistokles, Aristeides and Perikles;[21] but when they were discussing their constitution they always went further back, and the great paradigms were not Ephialtes and Perikles, nor even Kleisthenes, but Solon[22] or the mythical king Theseus.[23] A bronze statue of the lawgiver Solon stood in the Agora,[24] and in the Stoa of Zeus there was a painting by Euphranor of Theseus standing between Demos and Demokratia;[25] but neither Kleisthenes nor Ephialtes nor Perikles was ever commemorated officially in sculpture or painting. And the reason cannot have been an inhibition against commemorating contemporaries, for the general Konon had a bronze statue in the Agora in the early fourth century, perhaps even before he died.[26]

The 'radical' democracy spanned the years 462–404; and if you want to find praise of that you must read the funeral speech of Perikles in

[12] Hdt. 3.82.5; Arist. *Pol.* 1285a24.
[13] Xen. *Hell.* 6.5.6; Arist. *Ath. Pol.* 35.2.   [14] Andoc. 1.83; Lys. 34.
[15] Arist. *Ath. Pol.* 29.3 *versus* Thuc. 8.76.6; Arist. *Ath. Pol.* 34.4 *versus* Lys. 34.
[16] Wallace (1989a) 193.   [17] Arist. *Pol.* 1273b38.
[18] Isoc. 12.114; Dem. 15.33; Din. 3.21.   [19] Hansen (1989c) 76.
[20] Isoc. 4.85ff; Dem. 18.208–10; Lycurg. 1.108–9.
[21] Isoc. 15.234; Dem. 13.21–2; Din. 1.37.
[22] Dem. 22.30–2; Aeschin. 3.257; Hyp. 5.22.
[23] Dem. 59.75; Isoc. 12.128–48; Theophr. *Char.* 26.6.   [24] Dem. 26.23.
[25] Paus. 1.3.3–4.   [26] Dem. 20.70.

Thucydides[27] – or else any item from the modern historical literature, which, since the middle of the nineteenth century, has chosen Periklean democracy as the legitimator of its own liberal-democratic ideals.[28] In the fifth century the Athenians believed that it was Kleisthenes who had started their democracy,[29] but in the fourth they asserted that Kleisthenes had only restored the democracy initiated by Solon after it had been overthrown by Peisistratos[30] (and there was a variant of that, that democracy had really been invented by King Theseus and had developed gradually down to Solon[31]).

If we assemble all the constitutional measures that the fourth century Athenians attributed to Solon they make an impressive list:[32] he created a Council of Four Hundred, 100 from each of the four tribes;[33] he established the People's Court, manned by sworn jurors selected by lot;[34] he invented the difference between laws as general norms and decrees as specific ones[35] and handed the right to make the former to *nomothetai*, also chosen from those who had sworn the oath;[36] he saw to it that magistrates were no longer simply elected but selected by lot from an elected short-list,[37] that they served without pay,[38] and that their judicial powers were limited by the citizen's right of appeal to the People's Court;[39] he extended the right of prosecution by new procedures whereby any citizen, not just the injured party, could bring a charge;[40] he protected the laws by a special 'prosecution for having proposed an unsuitable law',[41] and the constitution by a new *eisangelia* to the Areopagos for attempts to overthrow the democracy;[42] he made it obligatory for every citizen to take sides in the event of *stasis*;[43] and, finally, he imposed special requirements of conduct on those who wanted to be active in politics – he laid down rules for speakers in the Assembly,[44] and was particularly praised for the rule that the oldest should speak first.[45]

'No smoke without fire', of course, and some of those reforms may well belong to the early sixth century and be genuinely Solonian; but in other cases they are demonstrably anachronisms. It is extremely unlikely that Solon produced laws regulating democratic organs of government.[46]

[27] Thuc. 2.35–46. Loraux (1986).
[28] Grote (1846–56) 6.180.
[29] Hdt. 6.131; Arist. *Ath. Pol.* 29.3.   [30] Isoc. 7.16; Arist. *Ath. Pol.* 41.2.
[31] Isoc. 12.131, 148.   [32] Hansen (1989c) 78–9, 91–3.
[33] Arist. *Ath. Pol.* 8.4; Dem. 20.90, 24.148.
[34] Arist. *Ath. Pol.* 9.1; Arist. *Pol.* 1274a3–5; Dem. 24.148.   [35] Hyp. 5.22.
[36] Dem. 20.93; Aeschin. 3.38, cf. 3.257.   [37] Arist. *Ath. Pol.* 8.1; Dem. 20.90.
[38] Isoc. 7.24–5.   [39] Arist. *Ath. Pol.* 9.1.
[40] Arist. *Ath. Pol.* 9.1; Dem. 22.25–30.   [41] Dem. 24.212.
[42] Arist. *Ath. Pol.* 8.4.   [43] Arist. *Ath. Pol.* 8.5. Rhodes (1981a) 157; David (1984).
[44] Aeschin. 1.22–32; Dem. 22.30–2.   [45] Aeschin. 1.23, 3.2.
[46] See p. 50.

The Athenians combined a vast respect for olden times with a very limited historical sense:[47] Demosthenes in the speech against Leptines could assert without batting an eyelid that Solon had invented the *nomothetai*, when it is quite certain that they could not have been in existence for more than half a century when he spoke.[48] What, after all, did the Athenians really know about the history of their own constitution?[49] A hundred years after Kleisthenes no one even knew any more the exact wording of his laws,[50] although they really were the foundation of the democracy. Most Athenians in Demosthenes' time no doubt genuinely believed that their democracy went back to Solon (or even to Theseus); for they made no distinction – as we pride ourselves on doing – between history and myth. Nowadays we put Solon in history books and Theseus in books about mythology, but to the ordinary Athenian they were part of the same story; and that made Theseus more historical than we can accept – and Solon more mythical. Attributing the beginnings of Athenian democracy to Theseus and Solon is of course a nonsense, and nowadays we know as much, but it was a nonsense that the Athenians believed; and before we point out the mote in their eyes we had better not forget the beam in our own: the ideas prevalent in the nineteenth century and the early part of the twentieth about *die germanische Urdemokratie* or the ancient Germanic *gens* were just as mythical and unhistorical as the beliefs of the Athenians about 'Solonian democracy'.[51]

But it is worth taking a closer look at the myth, for, if we do, something striking emerges: the allegedly Solonian constitutional reforms mostly concern the People's Court, the *nomothetai*, the Areopagos and the magistrates: no source connects Solon with the Assembly or the people's right to vote in it on all important matters. The nearest we get to the Assembly is Solon's supposed rules for the conduct of speakers.[52] Now, that idea of democracy is quite different from the constitution the Athenians actually lived under in the fifth century: in Perikles' time there were no *nomothetai* and there was no distinction between laws and decrees, but all important decisions (including some judgements in political trials) were taken in the Assembly. Periklean democracy was an assembly democracy, in which power was exercised directly by the *demos* in the *ekklesia*, whereas the mythical democracy they liked to attribute to Solon was a people's-court democracy, in which the powers of the *demos* in the *ekklesia* was counterbalanced by the sworn jurors, the Areopagos and the magistrates. In Isokrates' speeches and Aristotle's *Politics* it is also pictured as a 'mixed constitution', with the Areopagos as the 'aristocratic'

---

[47] Pearson (1941); Perlman (1961); Nouhaud (1982).   [48] See p. 165.
[49] Thomas (1989) 83–94.   [50] Arist. *Ath. Pol.* 29.3. Hansen (1989c) 85–6. See p. 20.
[51] See p. 2.   [52] Hansen (1989c) 97–9.

element;[53] but admiration for 'mixed constitutions' is to be found only in theorists such as Plato, Aristotle and Isokrates: the orators in general picture 'ancestral democracy' as a 'moderate' democracy, but certainly not as a 'mixed constitution'.

FOURTH-CENTURY DEMOCRACY

Where, then, shall we situate the democracy of the fourth century? Was it a 'radical' democracy as in the fifth or a more 'moderate' democracy like that attributed to Solon? There can be no doubt that the 'ancestral constitution' was the ideal that the Athenians dreamt of re-establishing: the dream recurred with increased intensity every time Athens lost a war – which it often did in the fourth century. The constitutional debate seems almost to be a function of failure in foreign policy: in 404 the Athenians suffered the most serious defeat in their history, and in the years that followed first the Thirty (in pretence) and then the returned democrats themselves attempted to restore the 'ancestral constitution';[54] in 355 Athens lost her war against the Allies who had revolted, and again the dream of the 'ancestral constitution' turns up in the sources;[55] in 338 Athens was finally defeated by Philip, and at once we meet reforms designed to restore the 'ancestral constitution';[56] in 322 Athens was actually captured by the Macedonians, who set about re-creating the 'ancestral constitution' – only this time, since it was dependent on the military power of Macedon, it appeared in an oligarchical guise,[57] whereas changes up to then had never been more than modifications of the democracy.

Let us very summarily remind ourselves of those changes. At the restoration of democracy in 403/2 the laws were recodified and inscribed on stone,[58] and thenceforward a distinction was made between *nomoi* and *psephismata*.[59] *Nomoi* were to be made or changed through a new, special procedure involving the *nomothetai*,[60] and were protected by a new *graphe*;[61] at the same time, the Areopagos was given the role of overseeing their administration by the magistrates.[62] *Dokimasia*[63] and *euthynai*[64] were revised so as to increase the role of the courts in relation to them; but

[53] Arist. *Pol.* 1273b35–41; Isoc. 12.130–2; Pl. *Menex.* 238C–D. Aalders (1968) 52–3; Nippel (1980) 99ff.

[54] See pp. 42, 151.   [55] See p. 159.   [56] See p. 291.

[57] Plut. *Phocion* 27.5; Diod. 18.18.4–5.   [58] See pp. 163–4.   [59] See p. 171.

[60] See p. 167.   [61] See p. 212.   [62] See p. 292.   [63] See p. 237.

[64] Piérart (1971).

the courts were relieved of much first-instance jurisdiction in private lawsuits, which were put into the hands of *diaitetai*.[65] About 400, presidency of the Council and the Assembly was handed over to the *proedroi* (a title that had only previously been used in 411, and so hardly had a 'radical-democratic' ring),[66] and in the 370s (probably) was introduced the selection by lot of jurors for each day at the beginning of the day.[67]

Also to the first half of the fourth century belongs the *merismos*, the fixing by *nomos* of the allocation of public funds,[68] and the creation of new financial offices (plus, after 338, *ho epi tei dikoikesei*);[69] and during that period spheres of individual responsibility were created within the Board of Generals.[70] About 355 (probably) the last jurisdictional powers of the Assembly were withdrawn[71] and the number of Assembly meetings was restricted to thirty (later forty).[72]

To the second half of the century belongs the new procedure of *apophasis*[73] (perhaps after the peace of Philokrates in 346), which further enhanced the powers of the Areopagos, and Demosthenes' decree of 338 giving it a general jurisdiction.[74] Also after Chaironeia the terms of ephebic service were revised, with new officials in charge: a *kosmetes* ('prefect') and a board of *sophronistai* ('moderators'),[75] who were chosen by a double procedure, election from a pre-elected shortlist.[76] Their names are suggestive: very moralizing and Spartan in tone.

Did the Athenians, by means of those various changes, succeed in fulfilling their dream of restoring the 'ancestral democracy' they attributed to Solon? Not if we listen to the philosophers and the critics of democracy, who still classified the constitution of Athens as a 'radical democracy' (Aristotle's type IV). They argued as follows.

1 *Demos* was not the whole people; it was the ordinary people, i.e. the poor, *hoi aporoi*. Since the poor were in the majority in the Assembly and in the courts the philosophers could argue not implausibly that the *demos* had the power in both groups,[77] and diverting functions from the Assembly to the *nomothetai* and the courts made not the slightest difference: it was still the *demos*, i.e. the poor, who had the power.

2 The real prerequisite for a 'moderate' democracy (Aristotle's type I) was that citizen rights should be limited to the hoplites[78] by a

---

[65] See p. 89.   [66] See p. 141.   [67] See p. 197.   [68] See p. 152.
[69] See p. 270.   [70] See p. 238.   [71] See p. 159.   [72] See p. 134.
[73] See pp. 292–4.   [74] See pp. 291–2.   [75] See p. 89.
[76] Arist. *Ath. Pol.* 42.2. Hansen (1986b) 225.
[77] Pl. *Resp.* 565A–C; Arist. *Ath. Pol.* 41.2.
[78] Arist. *Pol.* 1279b3, 1297b1. See p. 68.

(not particularly severe) property qualification:[79] it would exclude, particularly, the day labourers of the city, for 'moderate' democracy ought to be agrarian democracy.[80] By contrast, Athens maintained right down to 322 the rule that all males acquired full citizen rights with adulthood: the agrarian community had no special privilege, and no property qualification prevented the less prosperous from participating. In terms of citizen rights Athens remained a 'radical' democracy, and in that respect there was no change between the fifth and the fourth century – a fact underlined by the formal decision in 403/2 to maintain the Periklean citizenship law of 451.[81] In the second half of the century the Athenians, it is true, tried to create a 'hoplite democracy' by giving all the ephebes a hoplite panoply after their first year's service,[82] but it was only a sort of fiction, for in real hoplite democracy on Aristotle's pattern the hoplites had to pay for their equipment, which automatically excluded the lower classes.

3 In a 'radical' democracy the power of the magistrates was limited to the preparation and execution of decisions: the decisions were taken by the assemblies.[83] In a 'moderate' democracy the people's power was limited to electing the magistrates and calling them to account for their administration,[84] but the decisions were taken by the magistrates.[85] Here, too, Athens remained a 'radical' democracy, and the changes made in the fourth century did not alter that: if at the beginning of the century the Council had some degree of decision-making authority and jurisdiction, it had lost it again by Demosthenes' time.[86]

4 In the 'moderate' democracy of the philosophers pay for the exercise of political rights was kept to a minimum. The Athenians in the fourth century did not reintroduce regular pay for magistrates, but they did encourage participation in the Assembly by newly establishing payment for Assembly meetings,[87] and they also newly established the *theorika* for participation in the great festivals.[88] It is quite plausible to argue that in respect of pay the democracy was more 'radical' in the fourth century than in the fifth.

---

[79] Arist. *Pol.* 1292b29–30, 1318b30–1. See p. 68.
[80] Arist. *Pol.* 1292b25–9, 1318b9–12. See p. 120.   [81] See p. 54.
[82] Arist. *Ath. Pol.* 42.4.   [83] Arist. *Pol.* 1298a28–32, 1299b38–40, 1317b28–31.
[84] Arist. *Pol.* 1318b21–2, 28ff, 1274a15–18.   [85] Arist. *Pol.* 1298a13–24.
[86] Hansen (1987a) 183–4 n. 725. See p. 157.   [87] See p. 150.
[88] See p. 98.

So the constitutional reforms of the Athenians in the fourth century were not enough to persuade the philosophers to classify Athens as a 'moderate' democracy; and we might well agree if we knew as much as they did about the several hundred other democratic city-states that existed at the time: practically our only point of comparison is, unfortunately, Periklean democracy, and Athenian democracy in the time of Aristotle really was in numerous important ways different from that.

If we could travel back to the age of Demosthenes and ask an ordinary Athenian the question 'Who is *kyrios* in Athens?' all the sources indicate that the immediate reply would be 'the laws' (*hoi nomoi*).[89] If asked, however, 'Which persons are *kyrioi*?' he would probably say, 'The *demos* is *kyrios*',[90] but then he would take *demos* to mean the whole of the people, i.e. the state of Athens,[91] and not the common people or the poor as Plato or Aristotle would have told us. But let us suppose that the interrogation was pushed one step further by the question 'How and where does the Athenian *demos* exercise its supreme power?' The expected answer would be: 'In the *ekklesia* on the Pnyx where the people meet and make decisions on all important matters.' That is indeed the answer which Aristophanes suggests in his *Knights*, where the two slaves (the generals Demosthenes and Nikias) call their master Demos Pyknites, 'Mr Demos of Pnyx'.[92] It is also the answer found in other fifth-century sources, for instance in speeches by Antiphon and Andokides,[93] and in Xenophon's description of the Trial of the Generals.[94] But the step from the supreme *demos* to the supreme *demos-in-the-ekklesia* is conspicuously absent from all fourth-century sources. Instead we are told that it is the jurors in the *dikasteria* who are *kyrioi* or *kyrioi panton*.[95] The People's Court is set off against the People's Assembly[96] and is sometimes singled out, at the expense of the *ekklesia*, as the supreme body of government.[97] Occasionally the *dikasteria* are even said to be above the laws.[98]

If the Athenians did not succeed in creating something radically different from 'radical' democracy, maybe that is not what they were trying to do. They simply wanted to modify their constitution and place some controls on the unlimited power of the people. The tendency of the reforms is clear: the Athenians wanted to obviate a return to the political crises and military catastrophes of the Peloponnesian War.[99] In spite of the philosophers it can hardly be denied that the Athenians in the fourth century were weary of extreme 'radical' principles and were trying to set

[89] Aeschin. 3.6; Dem. 25.20; Hyp. 3.5.   [90] Dem. 20.107, 59.89.
[91] Hansen (1987a) 97.   [92] Ar. *Eq.* 42.
[93] Ant. 3.1.1; Andoc. 2.19.   [94] Xen. *Hell.* 1.7.12.
[95] Dem. 24.118; Din. 1.106; Lycurg. 1.3–4.   [96] Dem. 19.297; Aeschin. 3.3–5.
[97] Dem. 57.56.   [98] Dem. 24.78; Isoc. 20.22.   [99] See p. 151.

in their place if not a 'moderate', then a 'modified', democracy, in which the courts and the *nomothetai* were the organ of control for keeping the Assembly and the political leaders in their place and for re-establishing respect for the laws.

With that lack of historical sense which was no doubt due to lack of historical knowledge the Athenians themselves claimed that the fourth-century reforms were an attempt to go back to the 'ancestral constitution', and thus invented the myth of Solonian democracy.[100] And their attempt was not without success, for Athens suffered no *stasis* in the fourth century, and the democracy was not overthown until 322/1, when the Macedonians captured Athens and brought in a constitution in which full rights were limited to a property qualification of 2000 drachmas,[101] thus excluding the ordinary Athenian from participation in the decision-making assemblies. That is why our account ends there.

SOME PRIMARY CHARACTERISTICS

Assembly democracy

All political decisions in Athens were taken by simple majority (such requirements as a two-thirds majority being unknown) in big assemblies of from several hundred to several thousand citizens, after a debate lasting at most a few hours. In the Assembly and the Council all participants had the right both to vote and to speak; in the *nomothetai* and the juries all had the right to vote, but the right to speak was limited to the proposers or prosecutors, as the case might be, and their opponents. Many of the most characteristic features of Athenian democracy can best be appreciated by remembering that Athens was an assembly democracy and not a parliamentary one.

Majority and minority

Democrats maintained the fiction that decisions of the Assembly were taken by the whole citizen body,[102] even if only a minority could be present[103] and even if a large minority might have voted against and others abstained.[104] (As a matter of fact, unanimous votes were almost certainly commoner in assembly democracies than they are in modern parliamentary ones.)[105] They turned a blind eye to the problem of political

---

[100] See p. 298.   [101] Diod. 18.18.4; Plut. *Phocion* 27.5.
[102] Thuc. 6.39.1. See p. 125.   [103] See pp. 131–2.   [104] See p. 147.
[105] Aeschin. 3.13; Dem. 59.5; *SIG*³ 1109.20–4; *IG* II² 2090. Hansen (1983a) 215.

obligation: how far should the decisions of the majority bind those who had voted against or were not even present? The problem is raised by Xenophon in his Socratic discourses,[106] but is never mentioned by the champions of democracy: Perikles in the funeral speech in Thucydides admits that democracy is government by the *majority*,[107] but the remark is not developed and is immediately brushed aside with the assertion that *all* have equal rights and that the *individual* always has the chance to win reputation by being elected to a leading post.

Critics of the democracy insisted that it was not government by the people but government by the majority, specifically by the poor, since they were the majority.[108] The problem of the loyalty of the individual in the face of a decision he thinks unjust is famously handled in Plato's *Crito*, where Sokrates insists on respect for the laws as the force that binds all citizens and, in his own case, requires him to stay in prison and submit to the death sentence imposed on him, even though he believes it to be unjust.[109] But not all the critics of democracy were of that calibre, and Aristotle in the *Politics* points out more than once that the majority decisions of the humble folk may drive the well-to-do minority into rebellion.[110] Yet that never became a problem in Athens, and the oligarchical revolutions had a quite different basis. The advantages of democracy even for the well-to-do[111] evidently outweighed the disadvantage of being sometimes in the minority.

Persuasion

Democracy is a constitution based on argumentation,[112] and debate plays a far more important role in an assembly democracy than in a parliamentary one. In modern democracies there is often a gulf between political debate, which takes place in the media, and decision-making, which is mainly done in offices and committee rooms. In Athens, by contrast, debate took place in the Assembly and led directly to decisions therein. It also took a different form from that of parliamentary democracy: in a meeting with hundreds or thousands of participants discussion was out of the question, and debate took the form of a series of speeches to an audience,[113] which, immediately the speeches were over, voted on the question. Hence rhetoric had a much higher profile at Athens than in democracies nowadays: speeches in a modern parliament are no longer really for the purpose of winning a majority of those present to one's

---

[106] Xen. *Mem.* 1.2.45.   [107] Thuc. 2.37.1, quoted on p. 73.
[108] Pl. *Resp.*; 565A–C; Arist. *Pol.* 1290a30–1.   [109] Pl. *Cri.* 50A–54D. Woozley (1979).
[110] Arist. *Pol.* 1304b19–1305a7.   [111] Lys. 19.57; Dem. 21.62–3; *Prooem.* 55.1.
[112] Dem. 19.184.   [113] See p. 142.

point of view, but to influence the public through the media (especially just before elections). In Athens the political speaker had on every occasion actually to get a majority of those present to vote for his view, and rhetoric, the 'art of persuasion', was the most important weapon in the competition between political leaders. All Athenian statesmen in Demosthenes' time were orators, none any longer generals,[114] and the gift of persuading the people played a much larger part in whatever power they acquired than their ability as administrators or financiers.

Party politics

Assembly democracy is inimical to the formation of parties: parties are a child of modern indirect democracy, because they are bound up with elections to representative bodies.[115] Athenian democracy was characterized by an absence of parties in the modern sense: there were groupings of political leaders, but they did not have behind them corresponding groups amongst the public who listened and voted.[116]

Decision-making

Everybody attending the Assembly had the right to speak and vote; but did it really make sense to put all important political decisions into the hands of a majority of ordinary citizens? Plato's Sokrates thought that absurd, when you wouldn't run a ship by putting everything to a vote of all those sailing in her.[117] Well, the Athenians did believe in the intelligence and sound judgement of the ordinary citizen,[118] but they also insisted that no citizen was required to engage in political activity at the top level.[119] Political activity can be divided into passive participation – that is, listening and voting – and active participation, which means proposing things and taking part in political argument:[120] what the Athenians expected of the ordinary citizen was the former, which demanded enough common sense to choose wisely between the proposals on offer,[121] whereas active participation was left to those who might feel called to it – 'he who wishes', *ho boulomenos*, in fact. Democracy consisted in every citizen having *isegoria*, the genuine possibility to stand up and state his proposal or his objection, but it did not require everyone to do

[114] See p. 270.   [115] See pp. 278–9.   [116] See pp. 283–7.

[117] Pl. *Pol.* 298C–D; *Resp.* 488A–E.

[118] Eur. *Or.* 917–22; Dem. 3.15. Ober (1989) 157–9.   [119] Dem. 19.99, cf. 10.70–4.

[120] Aeschin. 3.233. Sinclair (1988a) 191, 221.

[121] Thuc. 6.39.1; Dem. *Prooem.* 45.1–2; Arist. *Pol.* 1282a16–23.

so[122] – indeed, if every citizen had insisted on making use of his *isegoria*, assembly democracy would have broken down there and then.

Preventing demagogy and mass hysteria

The Athenians knew perfectly well that a skilful demagogue could win the citizens to his proposal irrespective of whether it was really in their best interest:[123] competition among political leaders could lead to their bidding against each other with promises to the people and to the people being seduced by their promises.[124] There was also a risk of the people, in wrath or panic, being persuaded into hasty decisions,[125] as in the Trial of the Generals in 406.[126] The purpose of some Athenian institutions was to counter just such risks. Demagogues were open to all the public prosecutions we have seen: breaking a promise to the people was a crime for which a man could be charged by *eisangelia* or *probole*.[127] As for hasty decisions, the Athenians sought to limit their dangers by two methods. The first was that of handing important areas of decision-making to somewhat smaller bodies dominated by the older and more experienced citizens, i.e. in the fourth century, putting legislation and jurisdiction into the hands of the *nomothetai*[128] and the *dikastai*,[129] who were all over thirty and had sworn the Heliastic Oath.[130] The second method was the introduction of two-stage procedures. Some of those double procedures, by which matters considered had to be reconsidered after a few days or a longer interval, go back to Kleisthenes; others were introduced at the end of the fifth century and in the fourth. Every decree of the People's Assembly, for example, had to have been discussed first in the Council,[131] and was subject to possible reversal by a court for unconstitutionality.[132] Some decrees, such as treaties and conclusions of peace, seem to have required a debate in two successive sessions of the Assembly;[133] others had to be ratified at a second Assembly meeting, on which occasion there had to be a quorum;[134] and it was always possible, through the procedure of *anapsephisis*, to reopen at a subsequent meeting a matter already decided.[135] Legislative proposals were discussed by the Council and in the Assembly before they were put to the *nomothetai*,[136] and *nomoi* themselves could be subject to re-examination by the courts.[137] The big

---

[122] Dem. 18.308, 22.30; Eur. *Supp.* 438–41.
[123] Lys. 18.16; Dem. 3.30–1; Aeschin. 3.250–1.   [124] Dem. 3.22.
[125] Ar. *Eccl.*797–8.   [126] Xen. *Hell.* 1.7.35. See. p. 6.
[127] Dem. 49.67; Arist. *Ath. Pol.* 43.5. Hansen (1975) 13–14, 38.   [128] See p. 167.
[129] See p. 159.   [130] See p. 97.   [131] See p. 138.   [132] See p. 208.
[133] Thuc. 1.44.1; Aeschin. 2.60–1. Hansen (1987a) 88.
[134] Andoc. 1.87; Dem. 24.45; Dem. 59.89–90.   [135] Thuc. 3.38.1, 49.1. Dover (1955).
[136] See p. 169.   [137] See p. 212.

political trials had to be initiated in the Assembly by decree, and only after that were they heard by the courts.[138] And the dismissal of a magistrate was effected in two stages: suspension by the Assembly followed by a trial.[139]

The system of two-stage procedures could sometimes lead to just the opposite result from that intended: instead of over-hasty decision-making the process could become so complicated and slow as to make it difficult, for example, to mount an effective foreign policy.[140] Demosthenes, who could sometimes criticize the democracy of which he was a leader, makes precisely that point,[141] in a criticism still heard today: democracy is an ineffective form of government when confronted by a dictator, who can come to lightning decisions and strike when and where he chooses.[142]

Amateurism

All citizens were to take part, if they wished, in running the state, but all were to be amateurs,[143] or *idiotai* as the Athenians used to say:[144] professionalism and democracy were regarded as, at bottom, contradictory. The Athenians ensured the absence of professionalism in their administration by insisting that most magistrates should be picked by lot and could fill a particular magistracy only once and for one year only;[145] and they prevented continuity in the administration by always replacing all members of a board at the same time (i.e. at the end of the year). Furthermore, it seems to have been normal for magistrates at their *euthynai* to give lack of qualifications as the excuse for their failings in office.[146] Even in the case of political leaders, lack of professionalism actually counted as an advantage: when a modern politician addresses parliament he likes to claim that he is exceptionally well qualified to speak on the matter in hand, whereas Athenian orators liked to begin by explaining that they were just ordinary citizens.[147] In order to make the law democratic, the Athenians saw to it that no bar or bench should grow up: pay for advocates was forbidden[148] and juries were composed of several hundred ordinary citizens.[149] In that they were so successful that the law of Athens never attained to the professionalism of Roman law, and Athenian law has thus never had the influence that Roman law has had on the subsequent law of half the world.

---

[138] See p. 153. [139] See p. 221. [140] Isoc. 8.52.
[141] Dem. 19.184–5, 4.36–7, 13.32, 15.1. [142] Lucas (1976) 253.
[143] Aeschin. 3.220; Dem. 23.4; Isoc. 13.8–9.
[144] Dem. 19.182, 22.37; Hansen (1989a) 13–14. [145] See p. 244.
[146] Dem. 24.112. [147] Dem. *Prooem.* 13. [148] Dem. 46.26.
[149] Aeschin. 3.233.

This whole hostility to professionalism also ties in with the Athenians' idea that people ought to do politics in their spare time: the whole democracy was predicated upon the principle that political activity should be compatible with the ordinary citizen's ordinary job.[150] That is why political activity in Athens could be so widespread and participation so astonishingly high.

The voluntary principle

Assembly democracy rested on the services of volunteers all the way through, from the citizens who voted and the magistrates who administered to the leaders who took the political initiatives: there was no legal obligation to take part in any of it.[151] Undoubtedly there was some group pressure, and in the Funeral Speech Perikles is made to say that the passive citizen is not merely a 'quietist' but a 'good-for-nothing'.[152] Yet simultaneously we meet in the sources just the opposite idea, that a respectable citizen ought to keep clear of the Agora – not just from the shopping-centre but from the Council house and the courts[153] – and not be too keen on turning up to the Assembly.[154] That was the old aristocratic attitude persisting in people's minds into the age of classical democracy:[155] there was nothing to be ashamed of in non-participation,[156] and, even in the public sphere, the Athenians lived up to their ideal that every citizen might live as he chose.[157]

On the level of participation, however, voluntarism carried the risk that there might not be enough people for a quorum in the Assembly or to fill places on the boards of magistrates; and on a higher level there were other risks: if no one was willing to be *ho boulomenos* a prosecution might not be brought,[158] or no one might be willing to take the initiative in making an unpopular proposal in the Assembly.[159] In the law the consequence might be that a citizen would only be willing to act as prosecutor in a public trial if he had a personal feud with the defendant[160] or saw an opportunity for profit.[161] The result was an element of gamble in the criminal law,[162] for a guilty person might escape punishment unless he had personal enemies – or was well-to-do, for in the case of the well-to-do the boot was on the other foot and a quite blameless citizen risked

---

[150] Aeschin. 1.27; Pl. *Prt.* 319C.   [151] See pp. 233, 249, 267.
[152] Thuc. 2.40.2.   [153] Lys. 19.55; Is. 1.1; Isoc. 15.38.
[154] Eur. *Or.* 917ff. Hansen (1989a) 12.   [155] Carter (1986).
[156] Lys. 19.18.   [157] Dem. 10.70.   [158] Lycurg. 1.4; Ar. *Plut.* 916–19.
[159] Dem. 3.10–13, 8.68, 73. Hansen (1989a) 284–5.   [160] Lys. 12.2; Dem. 53.1.
[161] Dem. 25.40–1.   [162] Hansen (1976) 121.

being accused by a sycophant who under the guise of *ho boulomenos* really hoped for personal gain, possibly in the form of blackmail.[163]

Accountability

Voluntarism was combined with the total freedom of anybody to take the initiative in politics, and, except for the generals, political leaders were not filtered through any process of election such as that prevailing in representative democracies. There was thus a risk that undesirable persons might seize political opportunities to promote their own interests rather than those of the people, and that is why the counter-measures were so remarkably severe. We often meet in the sources the idea that reward and punishment are the two main driving-forces of democracy:[164] willingness to take the initiative must be encouraged by rewards, but promoting private interest to the detriment of the common weal must be punished by the law's harshest penalties.

The Athenians had the characteristic of being honest with themselves about themselves. They were deeply suspicious of one another (i.e. of themselves) and quite realistic and unsentimental about people's (i.e. their own) conduct. They went on the basis that, given the chance, every one of them would have his hand in the till and make a profit out of political activity,[165] and they took every possible means to limit the chances. 'Mildness' (*praotes*) was indeed supposed to be one of the democratic virtues,[166] but it belonged to the sphere of private conduct, certainly not when it came to magistrates and political leaders.[167] That is the background for the innumerable kinds of public prosecution and the astonishing frequency of their use. Athenian leaders were called to account more than any other such group in history: to be a *rhetor* or a general was to choose a perilous career that could easily lead to condemnation and execution – if you failed to flee into exile in time.[168]

If we ask how, in that case, the Athenians managed to get any citizens at all to seek political leadership, we come back to the other side of the coin: rewards. Political activity was regarded as a positive value, and ambition and competitiveness were fostered by all the marks of honour that the Athenians bestowed on such as merited their trust.[169] (Other historical examples can be cited to show that it is never difficult to find people whose political ambitions override the risks to life and fortune:

---

[163] See p. 195.   [164] Dem. 20.154; Lycurg. 1.10.
[165] Dem. 25.15–16; *Prooem.* 48.2; Hyp. 1.24–5; Pl. *Resp.* 359B–60D.
[166] Dem. 22.51; Arist. *Ath. Pol.* 22.4.   [167] Dem. 24.192–3.
[168] See pp. 208, 217, 267.   [169] See pp. 157, 211.

one is the period of the Terror in the French Revolution between 1794 and 1795.)

Publicity

Democratic government at Athens was accompanied by publicity to a degree otherwise unheard-of in past societies. Meetings were not only manned by citizens, but surrounded by a further listening public; audiences flocked not only round the courts[170] and the Council[171] but round the Assembly, too, when space was too small for all to participate in the meeting.[172] And, when the proceedings were over, discussion went on in the Agora[173] and in people's workshops.[174] Everything had to be publicized, either orally or in writing: assemblies were not only decision-making organs but the forum where many matters were brought to the notice of as many citizens as possible – for example, the regular statements of the financial situation by the officials,[175] the honorary decrees for those who had deserved well of the community,[176] and announcements about matters of private law such as inheritances and 'heiresses' (*epikleroi*).[177] At the Monument to the Heroes were posted legislative proposals,[178] charge-sheets in public prosecutions,[179] call-up lists,[180] and the like. Laws and decrees and the inventories of magistrates were recorded on stone and set up all over the place in Athens and in the Piraeus: and in the Metroön political leaders could check all the documents they needed for their orations.[181] It was a hallmark of democracy to have a written code of laws available to the public for inspection;[182] and again and again in the inscriptions the formula is repeated that a proposal or decision is to be published so that it can be read by anyone who wishes.[183]

Many democratic institutions rested originally on oral transmission,[184] but writing became more and more important during the classical age,[185] and the rule laid down in 403/2 that in future magistrates must use only the written laws[186] is characteristic of the 'new democracy' down to 322. A speaker in the People's Court takes it for granted that his audience will be capable of reading a family tree he had intended to show them;[187] and in the fourth century both pleas and testimonies had to be in written

---

[170] Ant. 6.24; Aeschin. 2.5. Wycherley (1957) 146.   [171] Dem. 25.23; Aeschin. 3.125.
[172] Ar. *Eccl.* 431–4. Hansen (1983a) 27.   [173] Aeschin. 3.1.
[174] Isoc. 7.15.   [175] Aeschin. 3.25.   [176] Aeschin. 3.32.
[177] Arist. *Ath. Pol.* 43.4.   [178] Dem. 20.94. See p. 168.   [179] Dem. 21.103.
[180] Ar. *Pax* 1180–4 with schol.   [181] Aeschin. 3.75.   [182] Eur. *Supp.* 433–4.
[183] Larfeld (1898–1907) II 720.   [184] Hansen (1989c) 85–7.
[185] Harris (1989) 92–3.   [186] Andoc. 1.87. See p. 170.
[187] Dem. 43.18.

form.[188] At mobilization the names of those called up were published on long lists;[189] and already in the fifth century every citizen was supposed to be able, at an ostracism, to write on a potsherd the name of the person he wanted banished – there was, as far as we know, no institutionalized assistance for possible illiterates. Now there was, of course, a gap between the assumption that the ordinary citizen could read and write and the extent to which that was so in practice. It is generally assumed that most Athenian citizens were literate,[190] but the evidence is thin, and for none except the political leaders was literacy an unavoidable necessity;[191] this was no doubt a factor in the process of elite recruitment and incipient professionalism.[192] Even in Demosthenes' time the main function of the ordinary Athenian citizen was listening and voting, not reading and writing, and no doubt those who could read were often in demand, at the Monument of the Heroes, to read things out to those who could not. As to writing, Plutarch's famous story of Aristeides' agreeing to help an illiterate citizen fill in his potsherd and being asked to write the name of 'that fellow Aristeides' is of course anecdotal,[193] and we are not allowed to believe anecdotes (though, oddly enough, there does survive one *ostrakon* on which the name Aristeides was started in a shaky hand and crossed out and begun again in a firm, legible one).[194] That was a case of one citizen helping another, but there may well have been people who did the same for a consideration. There were certainly people who would distribute for nothing sherds inscribed in advance with the name of some opponent, for 191 sherds, all with the name of Themistokles, were found in a well, all inscribed by only fourteen persons between them.[195] That testifies both to the limits of literacy and to some incipient formation of political groups.

Yet schools were private and perhaps too expensive for poor citizens.[196] It is indeed a paradox that Athenian democracy on the one hand presupposed that its citizens could read and write and on the other hand took no public action to ensure schooling for them. In Plato's and Aristotle's utopias schooling is universal and compulsory[197] and the lack of a public educational system was one of the most insistent criticisms directed by the philosophers against the democracy.

[188] Bonner (1905) 46–7; Calhoun (1919).
[189] Ar. *Pax* 1180–1. Hansen (1985a) 84–6.   [190] Harvey (1966) 628–9.
[191] Harris (1990) 79–80.   [192] See pp. 144, 277.   [193] Plut. *Arist.* 7.7–8.
[194] Agora P 5976. Vanderpool (1973) 229–30.   [195] *Hesperia* 7 (1938) 228–41.
[196] Xen. *Mem.* 2.2.6; Theophr. *Char.* 30.14. Harris (1989) 100–1.
[197] Pl. *Lg.* 804C–E; Arist. *Pol.* 1337a33ff.

Participation

The level of political activity exhibited by the citizens of Athens is unparalleled in world history, in terms of numbers, frequency and level of participation. Let us remind ourselves: an Assembly meeting was normally attended by 6000 citizens,[198] on a normal court day some 2000 citizens were selected by lot,[199] and besides the 500 members of the Council there were 700 other magistrates;[200] and those figures must be taken in conjunction with the fact that there were no more than 30,000 male citizens over eighteen, and of those no more than 20,000 were over thirty.[201] The Assembly met thirty or forty times a year;[202] the courts were summoned on about 200 days;[203] the Council met on at least 250 days;[204] and some boards of magistrates, such as the archons, the market-inspectors and the Eleven, were on duty every day all year round. Most notable of all in comparison with modern democracy is the level at which ordinary folk took part: they were not confined to choosing the decision-makers but, in their hundreds and thousands, prepared decisions, made them, and administered them in person.

Rotation

All must be able to participate: but in a literal sense that principle was unattainable, even in the Assembly, which was not large enough for everyone to attend. So it could only be translated into relative reality in the form that all must be able to participate turn and turn about,[205] 'to be ruled and rule by turns'.[206] Only part of the citizen body turned up to a given Assembly meeting, but as there were thirty or forty a year the circle of participants must have been far larger than the 6000 who were at any given meeting. Similarly, the numerous changes of name on the personal plaques of the jurors testify to a good deal of change in the composition of the panel of 6000 who functioned as jurors and *nomo-thetai*.[207] And, because a man could only be selected by lot for a magistracy every other year, the pool of magistrates must have been well above 1200.[208] The rule that a man could be a councillor no more than twice in a lifetime[209] means that every second citizen above thirty, i.e. something like every third citizen, served at least once as a member of the Council;[210] and three quarters of all councillors in any one year had to

---

[198] See p. 130.   [199] See p. 187.   [200] See p. 240.   [201] See pp. 91–2.
[202] See p. 134.   [203] See p. 186.   [204] See p. 251.   [205] Finley (1983) 74.
[206] Arist. *Pol.* 1317b2; Eur. *Supp.* 406–8; Dem. 19.136.   [207] See p. 182.
[208] See p. 232.   [209] Arist. *Ath. Pol.* 62.3.
[210] See p. 249.

serve for a night and a day as *epistates ton prytaneon* (and never again).[211] Simple calculation leads to this astounding result: every fourth adult male Athenian citizen could say, 'I have been for twenty-four hours President of Athens' – but no Athenian citizen could ever boast of having been so for *more* than twenty-four hours.

Motivation

We return to a point touched on already: for many Greeks political activity was a positive value and participation in the decision-making process an end in itself and not just a means to self-advancement.[212] According to Aristotle, man is a 'political animal', i.e. the very stuff of human life at its most basic is involvement in social organization,[213] or, as we might say nowadays, in the determining and distribution of the community's values.[214] It seems that the Athenians derived actual enjoyment from the formal play with complicated procedures such as sortition and voting.[215] No doubt that was motivation enough for some Athenians to take an active part in political life; nevertheless there were still reasons for providing a stimulus. For one thing, many were too poor to be able to engage in politics during much of their working-time without adequate compensation: hence payment for attendance at the various assemblies. Many magistrates, on the other hand, received no payment, and there was no special payment to those who spoke in the Assembly: if they made anything out of their activities that was sycophancy, and a crime. So in their case the stimulus was different: honorary decrees, and suchlike, for the best board of the year, the best speaker, and so on.[216] Plato divides political pay into two categories: money and honours.[217] Ordinary citizens who took part in the decision-making process anonymously and collectively were paid in good coin, whereas the active citizens who appeared personally as speakers and magistrates were stimulated by the hope of receiving the honours of the year: a golden crown and an invitation to a dinner in the Prytaneion. It would be wrong to underestimate those honours: they were not just the routine they appeared to be, but a vital hormone without which democracy would have languished. Competition for honours was a powerful motivation for all Greeks, in all spheres of life from politics to sport;[218] and at formal dinners in the Prytaneion Olympic victors sat side-by-side with leading orators and magistrates and with the descendants of Harmodios and Aristogeiton.[219]

---

[211] Arist. *Ath. Pol.* 44.1. See p. 250. [212] See p. 60.
[213] Arist. *Pol.* 1253a2–9; *Hist. An.* 487b33–488a14. [214] Easton (1953) 130ff.
[215] See pp. 188, 199, 220. [216] See pp. 111, 157, 211. [217] Pl. *Resp.* 347A.
[218] Dover (1974) 229–34. [219] Miller (1978) 7.

Economic background

Pay for political participation made democracy the most expensive of all forms of constitution.[220] As long as the state was in funds the daily payments could be made without problems, but in times of stringency the risk was that the poor might use their majority to 'soak the rich' in order to keep up the payments – in the Assembly by imposing taxes, which only the rich had to pay, and in the courts by condemning rich citizens and confiscating their wealth.[221] That danger of 'government by the people' was a theme beloved by its critics;[222] but that it had a core of truth is often corroborated by the orators: Lysias, for example, asserts that the Council is not tempted into illegalities as long as there are enough funds for the administration, but 'as soon as it gets into difficulties it is constrained to accept *eisangeliai* and confiscate people's property and follow those of the *rhetores* who make the most wicked proposals'.[223] How dangerous a problem that really was in fourth-century Athens we are not in a position to determine, but that it pertained mainly to crisis periods is made probable by the Third Oration of Hypereides, which was spoken in the period of peace after the settlement of 338: in it there are three examples of how the Athenian courts did *not* fall into the temptation of condemning a number of rich mining-concessionaires, although the accusers' proposals for confiscation were very tempting.[224] On the other hand, we hear from another source that in those very same years the richest of all the mining-concessionaires, Diphilos, was condemned to death and executed and his fortune of 160 talents distributed among the citizens.[225]

But how expensive actually was the democracy?[226] In the 330s, when Aristotle was writing the *Constitution of Athens*, the Assembly cost about 45 talents a year,[227] the Council probably about 15[228] and the courts somewhere between 22 and 37.[229] Payment for magistrates was not a major item,[230] and is not even mentioned by Demosthenes in his list of payments.[231] So Assembly pay, which was only introduced in the fourth century, cost more than the Council and the courts together, and must have been the heaviest item in the budget along with the *theorika*,[232] the size of which is not known and cannot be calculated,[233] but which

---

[220] Arist. *Pol.* 1317b35–8.
[221] Pl. *Resp.* 565A; Arist. *Pol.* 1304b20–4, 1320a4–6; Isoc. 8.130.
[222] Jones (1957) 55–61.   [223] Lys. 30.22. Cf. Lys. 19.11, 27.1.
[224] Hyp. 3.32–8.   [225] Plut. *Mor.* 843D. Hansen (1985a) 45–7.
[226] Jones (1957) 3–20.   [227] See p. 150.   [228] See p. 255.
[229] See p. 189.   [230] See p. 241.
[231] Dem. 24.97–9. Gauthier (1976) 28–9; Hansen (1979a) 16–17.
[232] See p. 98.   [233] Buchanan (1962) 83–8.

Demades referred to vividly as the 'glue of the democracy'.[234] To the daily payments must be added the cost of honorary decrees; they, too, cannot be calculated, but they may well have cost the Athenians between 10 and 20 talents a year, about as much as the Council did.[235]

These figures can be put in perspective by a comparison with the state finances as a whole in the fourth century. Before the middle of the century the entire annual income of Athens was only 130 talents; but at that time expenditure on political pay, especially on the Assembly, was also much less than it became in Demosthenes' time. At the end of the 340s state income had reached 400 talents a year, and in the peace period after 338 it rose to 1200 talents.[236] 100 talents at most out of 400–1200 is hardly overwhelming; and political pay is set even better in relief if we compare it with the military expenditures of Athens. Historians have often asked how on earth Greek city-states, especially Athens, could afford to maintain their democracies, with substantial daily payments to large numbers of citizens: they might with much greater justification ask how those states managed to engage in warfare, as they did pretty well all the time. In 351, for example, Demosthenes moved a decree to fit out a small permanent force of 10 triremes, 2000 hoplites and 200 cavalry: that modest force he reckoned would require an outlay of 92 talents a year – and he was doing his level best to make the bill sound as low as possible.[237] The proposal was turned down, as it happens, but we know that the Athenians often had larger forces than that in the field. It was not, then, the institutions of the democracy that brought Athens to the edge of bankruptcy but the endless wars, which made far greater demands on the budget than all the political payments together. And even in peacetime the military expenses were considerable. After the reform of 336/5 the training of the ephebes cost some 25 talents a year,[238] but the Athenians' real pride and joy was the cavalry, 1000 strong; even the fodder for their mounts cost the state 40 talents a year.[239] Such was the cavalry, exclusively recruited from the upper class, upholders of the aristocratic ideals – yet, all in all, it must have cost the Athenian democracy about as much as did the Assembly of the People.

A further aspect of the economic background remains to be considered: how were the Athenians, rich and poor, able to get the necessary free time to engage in politics to the extent that they did? The commonest answer has always been that they did so by exploiting those who had no

---

[234] Plut. *Mor.* 1011B.   [235] *IG* II² 410. Hansen (1987a) 115.
[236] See p. 260.   [237] Dem. 4.28–9.
[238] Arist. *Ath. Pol.* 42.3. Hansen (1988a) 4.
[239] Xen. *Hipparchicus* 1.19. Bugh (1988) 154–6.

political rights, above all the slaves, and (in the fifth century) by fleecing their allies in the Delian League.

For more than a hundred years controversy has raged amongst ancient historians as to whether Greek democracy was based on slave labour.[240] At one end of the spectrum we have the picture of Athens beloved of the Enlightenment and the Romantic age, as a society in which the citizens engaged in no activity but politics and festivals, while all production was left in the hands of metics and slaves.[241] That picture influenced Marx and Engels[242] and, in a simplified form, it was adopted by later Marxists, who wanted to identify the citizens with the exploiting class and the slaves with the exploited.[243] As a counter to this classic Marxist account there grew up in the present century a liberal-democratic one, in which Athens was a society where virtually everybody had to work for a living and only the middle and upper classes had slaves.[244] Both pictures are wrongly drawn. It is certainly true that most Athenians worked for a living,[245] but the sources also show that the vast majority of them had slaves.[246] The older conception corresponds to the Greeks' own ideal: Aristotle dreamed of a state in which all citizens were exempt from ordinary manual labour so that they could spend all their time in political activity.[247] But the reality in Athens was very different. According to some historians, many Athenian citizens were *de facto* excluded from political activity because they could not afford to leave their work.[248] And at the same time as they minimize the importance of slavery they also assert that it was largely the middle and upper classes who filled the magistracies and attended the Assembly and the courts; but if that was the case then once again it is slave-owners who were active in politics, so that, contrary to what those historians would like, there is still, on their own premises, a relationship between slavery and political activity. In fact the daily pay for attendance at political meetings, in the fourth century at any rate, was adequate to ensure that no citizen was prevented by poverty from exercising his political rights.[249]

Neither of the two extreme points of view claims many supporters nowadays, and a broad spectrum of ancient historians would probably accept the following five points.

---

[240] Finley (1959).
[241] Constant (1819) 499; Boeckh (1886) I 709; Wood (1988) 5–41.
[242] Engels (1884) ch. 5, 139–40.   [243] Thomson (1956) 204.
[244] Ehrenberg (1951) 183–4; Jones (1957) 76–9.
[245] Jones (1957) 18; Ste Croix (1981) 52.
[246] Finley (1959) 150; Lévy (1974) 31–4; Garlan (1988) 60–1.
[247] Arist. *Pol.* 1278a9–11, 1337b4–11.
[248] Cloché (1951) 210; Jones (1957) 17–18; De Laix (1973) 176.   [249] See pp. 185, 242.

1 The great majority of Athenians had to work for a living.

2 Quite a large number of Athenians, and not only the middle and upper classes, took an active part in the government by attending the Assembly or acting as jurors in the courts or sitting on the Council or undertaking magistracies.[250]

3 But political activity only occupied a fraction of the time of the individual citizen: direct democracy meant that most citizens took part in politics as amateurs and only very few as professionals.[251] The number of citizens who spent all their time in political activity was tiny, probably not exceeding one in 1000.[252]

4 Most Athenians owned at least one slave, the possession of whom must have made political activity easier, and that is the sense in which there was a relation between slave labour and democracy.

5 Whether slavery was a *necessary* precondition for the rise and existence of democracy is a question that we cannot at present answer.

Whereas the problem about slave labour as a precondition for democracy has long been a subject of debate, women's labour[253] has never been considered in this context, surprising as that may seem, especially nowadays. In the agrarian societies of the Mediterranean world, from antiquity till today, much of the work has been left to the women: ploughing seems to have been the only task that was reserved to the men.[254] It may well be thought that it was the work of the women even more than that of the slaves that provided the male citizens of Athens with their opportunity to run the political institutions.

The other allegation of historians, since the middle of the nineteenth century, when interest in Athenian democracy began to be concentrated on the age of Perikles, is that the democracy was only possible because of the proceeds from Athens' naval empire[255] – hence, democracy in the fourth century was only a shadow of what it had been a century before.[256] That assertion fits ill with the fact that the two most expensive payments, Assembly pay and the *theorika*, were only introduced in the fourth century when Athens had already lost her empire.[257] Pay for magistrates was doubtless much less in the fourth century than in the fifth, but all in all the democracy in Demosthenes' time was far costlier than in that of Perikles, and the big daily payments of the fourth century support the very opposite assertion, that Athenian democracy was *not* dependent on

---

[250] See pp. 127, 185–6, 249.   [251] See p. 308.   [252] See pp. 144, 271.

[253] E.g. Arist. *Pol.* 1323a5–7; Dem. 57.30.   [254] Hansen (1987a) 150 n. 232.

[255] Arist. *Ath. Pol.* 24.   [256] Finley (1973b) 49–50.

[257] Jones (1957) 5; Hansen (1983a) 19.

the proceeds of empire. However, it was undoubtedly the need to administer the empire, from the middle of the fifth century, plus the proceeds of that empire, that led to the great expansion of democratic institutions and the introduction of the earliest kinds of political pay, for the jury courts and the Council.[258]

Institutions

The characteristics of Athenian democracy described above are almost all bound up with its political institutions; and that is no accident.[259] A general look at states and societies down the ages reveals a spectrum running from societies that have virtually no political institutions to those in which they seem to be the backbone of the society. In medieval Europe one end of the spectrum was represented by Iceland, which had only one magistrate, the 'Lawspeaker',[260] the other by the cities of northern Italy with their vast complex structures of councils and magistrates, elected and selected by lot.[261] In Africa, Rwanda, with an immensely complicated political structure, lies next to Burundi, which has practically none.[262] The Greek *poleis* in general were characterized by the abundance of their political institutions, and democratic Athens was notoriously in the lead; in fact, never before or since has such an elaborate network of institutions been created and developed in order to run a quite small and fairly simple society. And most adult male Athenian citizens were often, and some were regularly, involved in the working of those institutions.

That, of course, is the point, and the great difference between ancient 'direct' democracy and modern 'representative' ones: for 99 per cent of the citizens in a modern democracy, institutionalized participation is restricted to voting once every other year or so,[263] and alongside the state's political institutions entities of another sort absorb more of the time and interest of the citizens and dominate and shape society – party organizations, unions, corporations, the mass media, and other such pressure groups. Also, public opinion nowadays is formed no longer inside parliaments but outside them, by and through the mass media. Accordingly, political science has moved away from what it calls 'political morphology' or 'anatomy'[264] (which means the institutions of the state) and focuses instead on those other sorts of institution that influence political decision-making.

---

[258] Schuller (1984).   [259] Hansen (1989a) 263–9.

[260] Jóhannesson (1969) 40–2.   [261] Waley (1978) 27–51.

[262] Vansina (1973) 166–9.

[263] Rousseau, *Du contrat social* 3, 15. Lucas (1976) 166–74.   [264] Macridis (1955) 8.

Some historians, in the wake of the change of direction by political scientists, are keen to turn analysis of the Greek city-states away from their state institutions towards sociological analysis of the allegedly more fundamental pressure groups and suchlike.[265] This has often cast exciting new light on the history of Athens; but it ought not to induce us to neglect analysis of Athenian state institutions, for at least we have plenty of evidence for those, whereas there is a corresponding lack of information about the other alleged structures, and that situation cannot be attributed merely to the haphazardness of the transmission: it is a part of the very nature of Athenian democracy.[266]

It is also often, and justly, remarked that Athenian democracy was not just a constitution and a set of institutions but a way of life. To the Greek way of thinking, no constitution could be consistently carried through unless it matched the character and life-style of the citizenry,[267] and so to democracy corresponded the 'democratic man' (*demokratikos aner*)[268] and the 'democratic life-style' (*demotikon ethos*).[269] Certainly; but, again to the Greek way of thinking, it was the political institutions that shaped the 'democratic man' and the 'democratic life', not vice versa:[270] the institutions of the *polis* educated and moulded the lives of the citizens,[271] and to have the best life you must have the best institutions[272] and a system of education conforming with the institutions.[273] A clash between, say, a democratic constitution and an oligarchic life-style might occur in a *polis*, but that would typically be after a revolution,[274] and after a while the change of the constitution would change the life-style and restore the correspondence between constitution and life-style – unless a maladjustment of the institutions provoked a new revolution.[275] That is why its state political institutions were, and remain, the most important aspect of Athenian democracy as a historic political system, and that is why they have been the principal subject of the present book.

---

[265] Connor (1971) 4–5.　[266] Hansen (1989a) 265–6. See p. 287.

[267] Pl. *Resp.* 449A.　[268] Pl. *Resp.* 557B.　[269] Arist. *Pol.* 1292b14.

[270] Arist. *Pol.* 1317a10–39.　[271] Simonides fr. 67 (Bergk).

[272] Pl. *Lg. passim*; Arist. *Eth. Nic.* 1181b12–23; *Pol.* 1297a14ff.　[273] Arist. *Pol.* 1310a14ff.

[274] Arist. *Pol.* 1292b11–21.　[275] Arist. *Pol.* 1301b4ff.

Maps and Plans

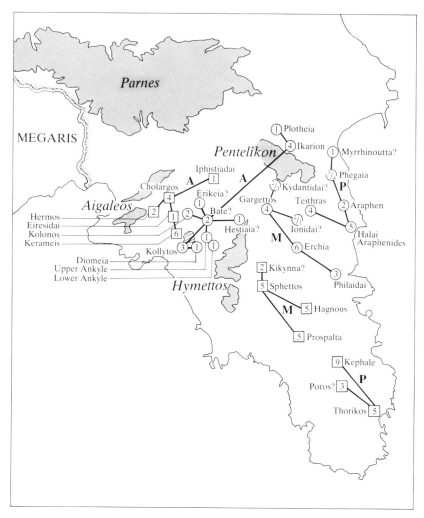

1 The political organization of Attica illustrated by two of the ten Tribes, i.e. Aigeis (II) = ○ and Akamantis (V) = □.
The Ridings are: A: Asty, P: Paralia, M: Mesogeios.
Bouleutic quotas are shown within the circle or square.
Demes of the same Riding are joined by lines.
Location is unknown for two demes (both with two councillors): Otryne (city deme of Aigeis) and Eitea (city deme of Akamantis).
The trittys-affiliation of Diomeia (here a city deme of Aigeis) is still in dispute.
Source: adapted from Traill (1986), Map.

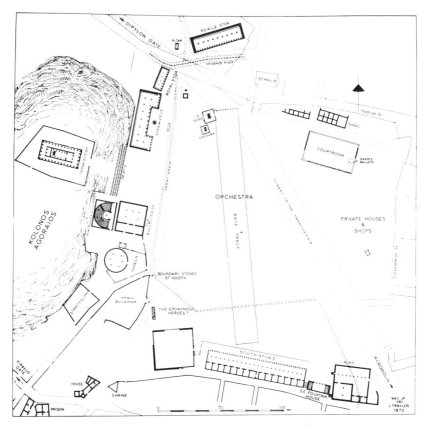

2 Plan of the ancient Athenian agora at the end of the fifth century. (By John Travlos, 1970, Agora Excavations, by kind permission of the American School of Studies at Athens.)

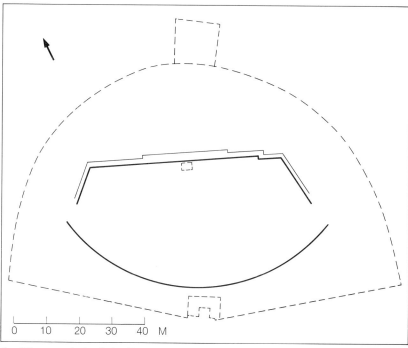

3 First period of the Pnyx, *c*.460 or, perhaps, *c*.500. The Pnyx of the third period is indicated by broken lines. Restored plan.

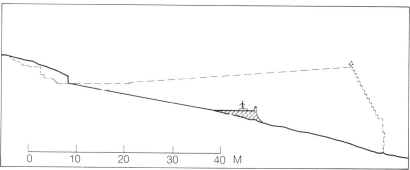

4 The Pnyx of the first period. Restored section on the longitudinal axis.

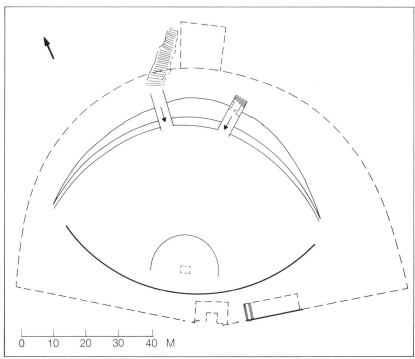

5 Second period of the Pnyx, *c*.400 B.C. Restored plan of the auditorium with broken lines indicating the Pnyx of the third period.

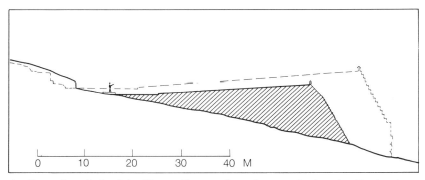

6 Second period of the Pnyx. Restored section on the longitudinal axis.

Bibliography

The following abbreviations are used in this bibliography. They conform to the usage of the *American Journal of Archaeology*.

AC	*L'Antiquité classique*
AHB	*Ancient History Bulletin*
AHR	*American Historical Review*
AJA	*American Journal of Archaeology*
AJAH	*American Journal of Ancient History*
AJP	*American Journal of Philology*
AthMitt	*Mitteilungen des deutschen archäologischen Instituts, athenische Abteilung*
AW	*The Ancient World*
BCH	*Bulletin de correspondance hellénique*
BSE	*Annual of the British School at Athens*
CJ	*Classical Journal*
ClMed	*Classica et Mediaevalia*
CP	*Classical Philology*
CQ	*Classical Quarterly*
CR	*Classical Review*
CSCA	*Californian Studies in Classical Antiquity*
DarSag	Daremberg and Saglio, *Dictionnaire des antiquités grecques et romaines*
GRBS	*Greek, Roman and Byzantine Studies*
G&R	*Greece and Rome*
HSCP	*Harvard Studies in Classical Philology*
JHS	*Journal of Hellenic Studies*
JIAN	*Journal international d'archéologie numismatique*
LCM	*Liverpool Classical Monthly*
MAI	*Mémoires de l'institut national de France, académie des inscriptions et belles-lettres*

MusHelv	*Museum Helveticum*
Njbb	*Neue Jahrbücher für das klassische Altertum*
PP	*La parola del passato*
P&P	*Past and Present*
QUCC	*Quaderni Urbinati di Cultura classica*
RE	Pauly-Wissowa, *Realencyclopädie der klassischen Altertumswissenschaft*
REG	*Revue des études grecques*
RM	*Rheinisches Museum für Philologie*
SB	*Sitzungsberichte* (followed by name of Academy)
SIFC	*Studi Italiani di Filologia classica*
SymbOslo	*Symbolae Osloenses*
TAPA	*Transactions and Proceedings of the American Philological Association*
WS	*Wiener Studien*
YCL	*Yale Classical Studies*
ZPE	*Zeitschrift für Papyrologie und Epigraphik*
ZSav	*Zeitschrift der Savigny-Stiftung für Rechtsgeschichte, romanistische Abteilung*

Aalders, G. J. D. 1968: *Die Theorie der gemischten Verfassung im Altertum*, Amsterdam.

Abel, V. L. S. 1983: *Prokrisis*, Meisenheim am Glan.

Abraham, H. J. 1987: *The Judiciary: the Supreme Court in the governmental process*, 7th edn, Boston, Mass.

Actes du Colloque 1970–3 1972–6: *Actes du Colloque sur l'esclavage 1970, 1971, 1972, 1973*, Paris.

Adams, C. D. 1912: Are the political speeches of Demosthenes to be regarded as political pamphlets? *TAPA* 43, 5–22.

Adelaye, G. 1983: The purpose of *Dokimasia*. *GRBS* 24, 295–306.

Allen, C. K. 1964: *Law in the Making*, Oxford.

Amira, K. von 1913: *Grundriss des germanischen Rechts*, Strasbourg.

Amit, M. 1965: *Athens and the Sea: a study in Athenian sea-power*. Collection Latomus 74.

Andreades, A. 1931: *Geschichte der griechischen Staatswirtschaft*, Munich.

Andrewes, A. 1956: *The Greek Tyrants*, London.

——1961a: Philochoros on phratries. *JHS* 81, 1–15.

——1961b: Phratries in Homer. *Hermes* 89, 129–40.

——1978: The opposition to Perikles. *JHS* 98, 1–8.

——1982: The growth of the Athenian state. *Cambridge Ancient History* III 3, 360–91.

——1982: The tyranny of Pisistratus. *Cambridge Ancient History* III 3, 392–416.

Arterton, F. C. 1987: *Teledemocracy: can technology protect democracy?*, Washington, DC.

Ashton, N. G. 1977: The Naumachia near Amorgos in 322 BC. *BSA* 72, 1–11.

Aurenche, O. 1974: *Les groupes d'Alcibiade, de Léogoras et de Teucros*, Paris.

Austin, M. M. 1981: *The Hellenistic World from Alexander to the Roman Conquest: a selection of ancient sources in translation*, Cambridge.

Austin, M. M. and Vidal Naquet, P. 1977: *Economic and Social History of Ancient Greece*, London.

Badian E. 1961: Harpalus. *JHS* 81, 16–43.

——1971: Archons and *strategoi*. *Antichthon* 5, 1–34.

Baiter, G. and Sauppe, H. 1850: *Oratores Attici* II, Zürich.

Ball, T., Farr, J. and Hanson, R. L. (eds) 1989: *Political Innovation and Conceptual Change*, Cambridge.

Barker, E. 1951: *Principles of Social and Political Theory*, Oxford.

Beloch, K. J. 1884: *Die attische Politik seit Perikles*, Leipzig.

Behrend, D. 1970: *Attische Pachturkunden*. *Vestigia* 12.

Bengtson, H. 1962: *Die Staatsverträge des Altertums II. Die Verträge der griechisch-römischen Welt von 700 bis 338 v. Chr.* Munich.

Bentham, J. 1816: *Chrestomathia*. Repr. in *The Works of Jeremy Bentham*, ed. J. Bowring, Edinburgh, 1843, VIII 1–191.

Berlin, I. 1969. *Four Essays on Liberty*, Oxford.

Bers, V. 1985: Dikastic *Thorubos*. *Crux*, 1–15.

Bertelli, S. 1978: *Il potere oligarchico nello stato-città medievale*, Florence.

Bicknell, P. J. 1971: Herodotos, Kallimachos and the bean. *Acta Classica* 14, 147–9.

——1972: *Studies in Athenian Politics and Genealogy*. *Historia* Einzelschriften 19.

——1989: Athenians politically active in Pnyx II. *GRBS* 30, 83–100.

Billigmeier, J. C. and Dusing, M. S. 1981: The origin and function of the Naukraroi at Athens: an etymological and historical explanation. *TAPA* 111, 11–16.

Bishop, J. D. 1970: The Cleroterium. *JHS* 90, 1–14.

Blass, F. 1898: *Die attische Beredsamkeit* I–III, 2nd edn, Leipzig.

Bleicken, J. 1984: Verfassungsschutz im demokratischen Athen. *Hermes* 112, 383–402.

——1985: *Die athenische Demokratie*, Paderborn.

Bloedow, E. F. 1987: Pericles' powers in the counter-strategy of 431. *Historia* 36, 9–27.

Bobbio, N. 1987: *The Future of Democracy*, Cambridge.

Bogaert, R. 1968: *Banques et banquiers dans les cités grecques*, Leiden.

Boeckh, A. 1886: *Die Staatshaushaltung der Athener* I–II, 3rd edn, Berlin.

Boegehold, A. 1963: Toward a study of Athenian voting procedure. *Hesperia* 32, 366–74.

——1972: The establishment of a central archive at Athens. *AJA* 76, 23–30.

——1982: A lid with depinto. *Hesperia* suppl. 19, 1–6.

Bonner, R. J. 1905: *Evidence in Athenian Courts*, Chicago.

Bonner, R. J. and Smith, G. 1930–8: *The Administration of Justice from Homer to Aristotle* I–II, Chicago.

Bourriot, F. 1976: *Recherches sur la nature du genos*, Lille.

Brickhouse Th. C. and Smith, N. D. 1989: *Socrates on Trial*, Oxford.

Bruck, S. 1894: Über die Organisation der athenischen Heliastengerichte im 4.

Jahrh. v. Chr. *Philologus* 52, 295–317.

Brun, P. 1983: *Eisphora – Syntaxis – Stratiotika. Recherches sur les finances militaires d'Athènes au IVe siècle av. J. C.*, Paris.

Brunnsåker, S. 1955: *The Tyrant-Slayers of Kritias and Nesiotes*, Lund.

Brunt, P. A. 1988: *Amicitia* in the late Roman Republic. *The Fall of the Roman Republic and Related Essays*, Oxford, 351–81.

Buchanan, J. J. 1962: *Theorika*, New York.

Bugh, G. R. 1988: *The Horsemen of Athens*, Princeton, NJ.

Burke, E. M. 1985: Lycurgan finances. *GRBS* 26, 251–64.

Busolt, G. and Swoboda H. 1920–6. *Griechische Staatskunde* I–II, Munich.

Cadoux, T. J. 1948: The Athenian archons from Kreon to Hypsichides. *JHS* 68, 70–123.

Calabi Limentani, I. 1981: Demostene XX 137: a proposito della *graphe nomon me epitedeion theinai*. In *Studi in onore di Arnaldo Biscardi* I, Milan, 357–68.

Calhoun, G. M. 1913: *Athenian Clubs in Politics and Litigation*, Austin, Tex.

——1919: Oral and written pleading in Athenian courts. *TAPA* 50, 177–93.

Cane, P. 1986: *An Introduction to Administrative Law*, Oxford.

Carawan, E. 1984: *Akriton apokteinai*: execution without trial in fourth-century Athens. *GRBS* 25, 111–21.

——1985: *Apophasis* and *eisangelia*: the role of the Areopagus in Athenian political trials. *GRBS* 26, 115–40.

——1987: *Eisangelia* and *euthyna*: the trials of Miltiades, Themistocles and Cimon. *GRBS* 28, 167–208.

Carlen, L. 1976: *Die Landsgemeinde in der Schweiz*, Sigmaringen.

Carlsson, S. and Rosén, J. 1961: *Svensk Historia* II, Stockholm.

Carter, L. B. 1986: *The Quiet Athenian*, Oxford.

Cartledge, P. 1979: *Sparta and Lakonia*, London.

Cassola, F. 1964: Solone, la terra e gli ectemori. *PP* 19, 26–68.

Cawkwell, G. L. 1963: Eubulus. *JHS* 83, 47–67.

——1978: *Philip of Macedon*, London.

Chase, A. H. 1933: The influence of Athenian institutions upon the *Laws* of Plato. *HSCP* 44, 131–92.

Christensen, J. and Hansen, M. H. 1983: What is *syllogos* at Thukydides 2.22.1? *ClMed* 34, 17–31. Repr. in Hansen (1989a) 195–211.

Clemenceau, G. 1924: *Demosthène*, Paris.

Clinton, K. 1982: The nature of the late fifth-century revision of the Athenian law code. *Hesperia* suppl. 19, 27–37.

Cloché, P. 1920: Le conseil athénien des cinq cents et la peine de mort. *REG* 33, 233–65.

——1924: La Boulè d'Athènes en 508/507 avant J. C. *REG* 37, 1–26.

——1951: *La démocratie athénienne*, Paris.

Coale, A. J. and Demeny, P. 1966: *Regional Model Life Tables and Stable Populations*, Princeton, NJ.

Colin, G. 1946: *Hypéride, Discours*, Budé edn, Paris.

Connor, W. R. 1968: *Theopompus and fifth-century Athens*, Washington, DC.

——1971: *The New Politicians of Fifth-Century Athens*, Princeton, NJ.

——1974: The Athenian Council: method and focus in some recent scholarship. *CJ* 70, 32–40.

Constant, B. 1819: *De la liberté des anciens comparée à celle des modernes.* Repr. in *De la liberté chez les modernes*, ed. M. Gauchet (Paris, 1980).

Coulanges, F. de 1864: *La cité antique*, Paris.

——1878: Recherches sur le tirage au sort appliqué à la nomination des archontes athéniens. *Nouvelle revue historique de droit français et étranger* 2, 613ff.

Crux 1985: *Essays Presented to G. E. M. de Ste Croix on his 75th Birthday*, Exeter.

Dahl, R. A. 1963: *Modern Political Analysis*, Englewood Cliffs, NJ.

Damsgaard-Madsen, A. 1973: Le mode de désignation des démarques attiques au quatrième siècle av. J. C. *Classica et Mediaevalia Francisco Blatt Septuagenario Dedicata*, 92–118.

——1988: Attic funeral inscriptions: their use as historical sources and some preliminary results. In *Studies in Ancient History and Numismatics Presented to Rudi Thomsen*, Århus, 55–68.

David, E. 1984: Solon, neutrality and partisan literature of late fifth-century Athens. *MusHelv* 41, 129–38.

Davies, J. K. 1967: Demosthenes on liturgies: a note. *JHS* 87, 33–40.

——1971: *Athenian Propertied Families*, Oxford.

——1977/8: Athenian citizenship: the descent group and the alternatives. *CJ* 73, 105–21.

——1981: *Wealth and the Power of Wealth in Classical Athens*, New York.

Debrunner, A. 1947: Demokratia. In *Festschrift für E. Tièche*, Bern, 11–24.

De Laix, R. A. 1973: *Probouleusis at Athens*, Berkeley, Calif., and Los Angeles.

Derenne, E. 1930: *Les procès d'impiété aux philosophes à Athènes au Ve et au IVe siècles av. J. C.*, Liège.

Deubner, L. 1932: *Attische Feste*, Berlin.

Develin, R. 1984: From Panathenaia to Panathenaia. *ZPE* 57, 133–8.

——1985: Age qualifications for Athenian magistrates. *ZPE* 61, 149–59.

——1986: Prytany systems and eponyms for financial boards in Athens. *Klio* 68, 67–83.

——1989: *Athenian Officials 684–321 BC*, Cambridge.

Dickie, W. W. 1973: Thucydides 1.93.3. *Historia* 22, 758–9.

Dittenberger, W. 1872: Der Vermögenstausch und die Trierarchie des Demosthenes. *Dissertationes: Demosthenes* I, Rudolfstadt.

Dodds, E. R. 1973: *The Ancient Concept of Progress and Other Essays*, Oxford.

Dontas, G. S. 1983: The true Aglaurion. *Hesperia* 52, 48–63.

Dorjahn, A. P. 1935: Anticipation of arguments in Athenian courts. *TAPA* 66, 274–95.

Dover, K. J. 1950: The chronology of Antiphon's speeches. *CQ* 44, 44–60. Repr. in Dover (1988) 13–35.

——1955: *Anapsephisis* in fifth-century Athens. *JHS* 75, 17–20. Repr. in Dover (1988) 187–93.

——1960: *DEKATOS AUTOS. JHS* 80, 61–77. Repr. in Dover (1988) 159–80.

——1963: Androtion on ostracism. *CR* 13, 256–7. Repr. in Dover (1988) 83–5.

——1968: *Lysias and the Corpus Lysiacum*, Berkeley, Calif., and Los Angeles.

——1974: *Greek Popular Morality in the Time of Plato and Aristotle*, Oxford.

——1976: The freedom of the intellectual in Greek society. *Talanta* 7, 24–54. Repr. in Dover (1988) 135–58.

——1988: *The Greeks and their Legacy. Collected Papers* II, Oxford.

Dow, S. 1937: *Prytaneis: a study of the inscriptions honoring Athenian councillors*, *Hesperia* suppl. 1.

——1939: Aristotle, the Kleroteria and the courts. *HSCP* 50, 1–34.

——1959: The law codes of Athens. *Proc. Mass. Hist. Soc.* 71, 1–36.

——1960: The Athenian calendar of sacrifices: the chronology of Nikomakhos' second term. *Historia* 9, 270–93.

Dunsire, A. 1973: *Administration: the word and the science*, London.

Drerup, E. 1898: Über die bei den attischen Rednern eingelegten Urkunden. *Njbb* suppl. 24, 221–365.

——1923: *Demosthenes im Urteile des Altertums*, Würzburg.

Duverger, M. 1964: *Political Parties*, 3rd edn, London.

Easton, D. 1953: *The Political System*, New York.

Eder, W. 1986: The political significance of the codification of law in archaic societies: an unconventional hypothesis. In *Social Struggles in Archaic Rome*, ed. K. Raaflaub, Berkeley, Calif., and Los Angeles.

Edmonds, J. M. 1957–61: *The Fragments of Attic Comedy* I–III, Leiden.

Effenterre, H. van. 1976: Clisthène et les mesures de mobilisation. *REG* 89, 1–17.

Ehrenberg, V. 1921: *Die Rechtsidee im frühen Griechentum*, Leipzig.

——1927: Losung. *RE* XIII, 1451–90.

——1950: Origins of democracy. *Historia* 1, 515–48.

——1951: *The People of Aristophanes*, Oxford.

——1954: *Sophocles and Pericles*, Oxford.

——1960: *The Greek State*, Oxford.

Elster, J. 1989: *Solomonic Judgements: studies in the limitations of rationality*, Cambridge.

Engels, F. 1884: *Der Ursprung der Familie, des Privateigentums und des Staates*, 4th edn, Zürich (repr. Berlin, 1987).

Euben, P. (ed.) 1986: *Greek Tragedy and Political Theory*, Berkeley, Calif., and Los Angeles.

Farrar, C. 1988: *The Origins of Democratic Thinking*, Cambridge.

Feaver, D. D. 1957: The priesthoods of Athens. *YCS* 15, 123–58.

Feraboli, S. 1972: Lingua e stile della orazione Contro Alcibiade attribuita ad Andocide. *SIFC* 44, 5–37.

Ferguson, W. S. 1898: *The Athenian Secretaries*, New York.

Fingarette, A. 1971: A New Look at the Wall of Nikomachos. *Hesperia* 40, 330–35.

Finley, M. I. 1959: Was Greek civilization based on slave labour? *Historia* 8, 145–64.

——1962: Athenian demagogues. *P&P* 21, 3–24. Repr. in Finley (1973b) 2nd edn.

——1971: *The Ancestral Constitution*, Cambridge. Repr. in *The Use and Abuse of History* (London, 1975) 34–59.

——1973a: *The Ancient Economy*, London.

——1973b: *Democracy Ancient and Modern* (2nd edn 1985).

——1976: The freedom of the citizen in the Greek world. *Talanta* 7, 1–23.

——1980: *Ancient Slavery and Modern Ideology*, London.

——1983: *Politics in the Ancient World*, Cambridge.

Flinn, M. W. 1981: *The European Demographic System 1500–1820*, Baltimore.

Flower, M. A. 1985: *IG* II² 2344 and the size of phratries in classical Athens. *CQ* 35, 232–5.

Fornara, Ch. W. 1971: *The Athenian Board of Generals from 501 to 404. Historia* Einzelschriften 16.

——1977: *Translated Documents of Greece and Rome I. Archaic Times to the End of the Peloponnesian War*, Baltimore.

——1983: *The Nature of History in Ancient Greece and Rome*, Berkeley, Calif., and Los Angeles.

Forrest, W. G. 1966: *The Emergence of Greek Democracy*, London.

Fränkel, M. 1878: Der attische Heliasteneid. *Hermes* 13, 452–66.

Francis, E. D. and Vickers, M. 1988: The Agora revisited: Athenian chronology *c*.500–450 BC. *BSA* 83, 143–67.

French, A. 1956: The economic background to Solon's reforms. *CQ* 6, 11–25.

Frier, B. 1982: Roman life expectancy: Ulpian's evidence. *HSCP* 86, 213–51.

——1983: Roman life expectancy: the Pannonian evidence. *Phoenix* 37, 328–44.

Frisch, H. 1942: *The Constitution of the Athenians*, Copenhagen.

Frisk, H. 1970: *Griechisches etymologisches Wörterbuch* II, Heidelberg.

Fritz, K. von 1954: The composition of Aristotle's *Constitution of Athens* and the so-called Draconian constitution. *CP* 49, 73–93.

——1977: Nochmals das solonische Gesetz gegen Neutralität im Bürgerzwist. *Historia* 26, 245–7.

Fritz, K. von and Kapp, E. 1950: *Aristotle's 'Constitution of Athens' and Related Texts*, New York.

Fuks, A. 1951: *Kolonos misthios*: labour exchange in classical Athens. *Eranos* 49, 171–3.

——1953: *The Ancestral Constitution*, London.

Funke, P. 1980: *Homónoia und Arché. Historia* Einzelschriften 37.

Gabrielsen, V. 1981: *Remuneration of State Officials in Fourth-Century BC Athens*, Odense.

——1985: The Naukrariai and the Athenian navy. *ClMed* 36, 21–51.

——1987a: The Antidosis procedure in classical Athens. *ClMed* 38, 7–38.

——1987b: The *Diadikasia*-documents. *ClMed* 38, 39–51.

——1989: The number of Athenian trierarchs after ca. 340 BC *ClMed* 40, 146–59.

Gagarin, M. 1981: *Drakon and Early Athenian Homicide Law*, New Haven, Conn.

Garlan, Y. 1988: *Slavery in Ancient Greece*, Ithaca, NY.

Garland, R. 1982: A first catalogue of Attic Peribolos tombs. *BSA* 77, 125–76.

Gauthier, Ph. 1972: *Symbola: les étrangers et la justice dans les cités grecques*, Nancy.

——1976: *Un commentaire historique des Poroi de Xénophon*, Paris.

——1984: Epigraphie et cité du IVe s. av. J.-C. au IIIe après J.-C. *Acts of the 8th Epigraphical Congress*, Athens 1982, 79–107.

——1988: Métèques, périèques et *paroikoi*: bilan et points d'interrogation. In

L'étranger dans le monde grec, Nancy, 24–46.

Geagan, D. J. 1967: *The Athenian Constitution after Sulla. Hesperia* suppl. 12.

Geldart, W. 1959: *Elements of English Law*, 6th edn, London.

Gerner, E. 1949: *Paranomon graphe. RE* 18, 1281–93.

Gilbert, G. 1877: *Beiträge zur innern Geschichte Athens im Zeitalter des peloponnesischen Krieges*, Leipzig.

Glotz, G. 1904: *L'ordalie dans la Grèce primitive*, Paris.

——1907: Sortitio. *DarSag* IV, 1401–17.

——1926: *Ancient Greece at Work*, London.

——1929: *The Greek City*, London.

Glotz, G. and Cohen, R. 1936: *Histoire grecque* III, Paris.

Golden, M. 1979: Demosthenes and the age of majority at Athens. *Phoenix* 33, 25–38.

——1985: Donatus and Athenian phratries. *CQ* 35, 9–13.

Goldstein, J. A. 1968: *The Letters of Demosthenes*, New York.

Goligher, W. A. 1907: Studies in Attic law II: the Antidosis. *Hermathena* 14, 481–515.

Gomme, A. W. 1933: *The Population of Athens in the Fifth and Fourth Centuries BC*, Oxford.

——1945: *A Historical Commentary on Thucydides* I, Oxford.

——1956: *A Historical Commentary on Thucydides* II, Oxford.

——1962a: The Old Oligarch. *More Essays in Greek History and Literature*, Oxford, 38–69.

——1962b: The working of the Athenian democracy. *More Essays in Greek History and Literature*, Oxford, 177–93.

Gomme, A. W., Andrewes, A. and Dover, K. 1970: *A Historical Commentary on Thucydides* IV, Oxford.

——1981: *A Historical Commentary on Thucydides* V, Oxford.

Gould, J. P. 1980: Law, custom and myth: aspects of the social position of women in classical Athens. *JHS* 100, 38–59.

Graham, A. J. 1982: The colonial expansion of Greece. *Cambridge Ancient History* III 3, 83–162.

Griffeth, R. and Thomas, C. 1981: *The City-State in Five Cultures*, Santa Barbara, Calif.

Griffith, G. T. 1966: *Isegoria* in the Assembly at Athens. *Ancient Society and Institutions*, Oxford, 115–38.

——1979: The reign of Philip the Second. In N. G. L. Hammond, *A History of Macedon* II, Oxford, 203–723.

Grote, G. 1846–56: *A History of Greece* 1–12. Repr. in Everyman's Library.

Gschnitzer, F. 1955: Stammes- und Ortsgemeinden im alten Griechenland. *WS* 68, 120–44.

——1974: *Prytanis. RE* suppl. 13, 730–816.

Gwatkin, W. 1957: The legal arguments in Aischines' *Against Ktesiphon* and Demosthenes' *On the Crown. Hesperia* 26, 129–41.

Habicht, Ch. 1961: Falsche Urkunden zur Geschichte Athens im Zeitalter der Perserkriege. *Hermes* 89, 1–35.

——1989: Pytheas von Alopeke, Aufseher über die Brunnen Attikas. *ZPE* 77, 83–8.

Hampl, F. 1939: Poleis ohne Territorium. *Klio* 32, 1–60.

Hannick, J. M. 1981: Note sur la *graphè Paranomôn*. *AC* 50, 393–7.

Hansen, M. H. 1974: *The Sovereignty of the People's Court in Athens in the Fourth Century BC and the Public Action against Unconstitutional Proposals*, Odense.

——1975: *Eisangelia: the Sovereignty of the People's Court in Athens in the Fourth Century BC and the Impeachment of Generals and Politicians*, Odense.

——1976a: *Apagoge, Endeixis and Ephegesis against Kakourgoi, Atimoi and Pheugontes*, Odense.

——1976b: The Theoric Fund and the *graphe paranomon* against Apollodorus. *GRBS* 17, 235–46.

——1979a: *Misthos* for magistrates in classical Athens. *SymbOslo* 54, 5–22.

——1979b: How often did the Athenian *dicasteria* meet? *GRBS* 20, 243–6.

——1980a: Athenian *nomothesia* in the fourth century BC and Demosthenes' speech against Leptines. *ClMed* 32, 87–104.

——1980b: Perquisites for magistrates in fourth-century Athens. *ClMed* 32, 105–25.

——1980c: Seven hundred *archai* in classical Athens. *GRBS* 21, 151–73.

——1980d: *Eisangelia* at Athens. A reply. *JHS* 100, 89–95.

——1980e: Hvorfor henrettede Athenerne Sokrates? *Museum Tusculanum* 40–3, 55–82.

——1981a: The prosecution of homicide in Athens. *GRBS* 22, 11–30.

——1981b: The number of Athenian hoplites in 431 BC. *SymbOslo* 56, 19–32.

——1981c: Initiative and decision: the separation of powers in fourth-century Athens. *GRBS* 22, 345–70.

——1981d: Two notes on the Athenian *dikai emporikai*. *Symposion* 4, 167–75.

——1982: Demographic reflections on the number of Athenian citizens 451–309. *AJAH* 7, 172–89.

——1983a: *The Athenian Ecclesia. A Collection of Articles 1976–83*, Copenhagen. For contents see list at the end of this bibliography.

——1983b: *Graphe* or *dike traumatos*. *GRBS* 24, 307–20.

——1985a: *Demography and Democracy*, Herning.

——1985b: Athenian *nomothesia*. *GRBS* 26, 345–71.

——1985c: The history of the Athenian constitution [review article]. *CP* 80, 51–66.

——1986a: The origin of the term *demokratia*. *LCM* 11, 35–6.

——1986b: *Klerosis ek prokriton* in fourth-century Athens. *CP* 81, 222–9.

——1987a: *The Athenian Assembly in the Age of Demosthenes*, Oxford.

——1987b: Did Kleisthenes use the lot when Trittyes were allocated to Tribes? *AW* 15, 43–4.

——1988a: *Three Studies in Athenian Demography*. Historisk-Filosofiske Meddelelser Det Kongelige Danske Videnskabernes Selskab 56, Copenhagen.

——1988b: The average age of Athenian *bouleutai* and the proportion of *bouleutai* who served twice. *LCM* 13, 67–9.

——1988c: The Athenian Board of Generals. When was tribal representation replaced by election from all Athenians? In *Studies in Ancient History and Numismatics Presented to Rudi Thomsen*, Århus, 69–70.

——1988d: Demography and democracy once again. *ZPE* 75, 189–93.

——1989a: *The Athenian Ecclesia II. A Collection of Articles 1983–89*, Copenhagen. For contents see list at the end of this bibliography.

——1989b: *Was Athens a Democracy? Popular Rule, Liberty and Equality in Ancient and Modern Political Thought.* Historisk-Filosofiske Meddelelser Det Kongelige Danske Videnskabernes Selskab 59, Copenhagen.

——1989c: Solonian democracy in fourth-century Athens. *ClMed* 40, 71–99.

——1989d: Athenian democracy: institutions and ideology [review article]. *CP* 84, 137–48.

——1989e: Athenian democracy [review of Sinclair (1988a)]. *CR* 39, 69–76.

——1989f: Demography and democracy – a reply to Eberhard Ruschenbusch. *AHB* 3, 40–4.

——1990a: The political powers of the People's Court in fourth-century Athens. In *The Greek City from Homer to Alexander*, ed. O. Murray and S. Price, Oxford, 215–43.

——1990b: Diokles' law (Dem. 24.42) and the revision of the Athenian corpus of laws in the archonship of Eukleides. *ClMed* 41, 63–71.

——1990c: The size of the Council of the Areopagos and its social composition in the fourth century BC. *ClMed* 41, 73–7 (with L. Pedersen).

——1990d: Asty, Mesogeios and Paralia. In defence of Arist. *Ath. Pol.* 21.4. *ClMed* 41, 51–4.

——1990e: When was selection by lot of magistrates introduced in Athens? *ClMed* 41, 55–61.

——1990f: review of Ober (1989). *CR* 40, 348–56.

Hansen, M. H. et al. 1990: The demography of the Attic demes: the evidence of the sepulchral inscriptions. *Analecta Romana* 19, 25–44.

Hansen, M. H. and Elkrog, B. 1973: Areopagosrådets historie i 4. årh. og samtidens forestillinger om Rådets kompetence før Efialtes. *Museum Tusculanum* 23, 17–47.

Harden, D. 1980: *The Phoenicians*, 2nd edn Harmondsworth, Middx.

Harding, Ph. 1977: Atthis and Politeia. *Historia* 26, 148–60.

——1978: Oh Androtion, you fool! *AJAH* 3, 179–83.

——1981: In search of a polypragmatist. In *Classical Contributions . . . Studies . . . McGregor*, New York, 41–50.

——1985: *Translated Documents of Greece and Rome II. From the End of the Peloponnesian War to the Battle of Ipsus.* Cambridge.

Harris, E. M. 1985: The date of the trial of Timarchus. *Hermes* 113, 376–80.

——1986: How often did the Athenian assembly meet? *CQ* 36, 363–77.

——1988: When was Aeschines born? *CP* 83, 211–14.

Harris, W. V. 1989: *Ancient Literacy*, Cambridge, Mass.

Harrison, A. R. W. 1955: Law-making at Athens at the end of the fifth century BC. *JHS* 75, 26–35.

——1968: *The Law of Athens* I, Oxford.

——1971: *The Law of Athens*, II, ed. D. M. MacDowell, Oxford.

Harvey, F. D. 1965: Two kinds of equality. *ClMed* 26, 101–46.

——1966: Literacy in the Athenian democracy. *REG* 79, 585–635.

——1985: Dona Ferentes: some aspects of bribery in Greek politics. *Crux*, 76–117.

Headlam, J. W. 1891: *Election by Lot at Athens*, Cambridge.

Held, D. 1987: *Models of Democracy*, Cambridge.

Henderson, J. 1990: The *demos* and comic competition. In *Nothing to do with Dionysos*, ed. J. J. Winkler and F. I. Zeitlin, Princeton, NJ, 271–313.

Henry, A. S. 1977: *The Prescripts of Athenian Decrees*, Leiden.

——1983: *Honours and Privileges in Athenian Decrees*, Hildesheim.

——1989: Provisions for the payment of Athenian decrees. *ZPE* 78, 247–95.

Hignett, C. 1952: *A History of the Athenian Constitution to the End of the Fifth Century BC*, Oxford.

Hoepfner, W. and Schwandner, E. L. 1987: *Wohnen in der klassischen Polis I. Haus und Stadt im klassischen Griechenland*, Munich.

Holden, B. 1974: *The Nature of Democracy*, London.

——1988: *Understanding Liberal Democracy*, Oxford.

Hommel, H. 1927: *Untersuchungen zur Verfassung und Prozessordnung des athenischen Volksgerichts, inbesondere zum Schlussteil der Athenaion Politeia des Aristoteles. Philologus* suppl. 19.

Hopkins, M. K. 1966: On the probable age structure of the Roman population. *Population Studies* 20, 245–64.

Hopper, R. J. 1953: The Attic silver mines in the fourth century BC. *BSA* 48, 200–54.

——1961: The mines and miners of ancient Athens. *G&R* 8, 138–51.

Hornblower, 1983: *The Greek World 479–323*, London.

——1987: *Thucydides*, London.

Humphreys, S. C. 1974: The Nothoi of Kynosarges. *JHS* 94, 88–95.

——1978: *Anthropology and the Greeks*, London.

Isaac, B. 1986: *The Greek Settlements in Thrace until the Macedonian Conquest*, Leiden.

Isager, S. and Hansen, M. H. 1975: *Aspects of Athenian Society*, Odense.

Jacob, O. 1928: *Les esclaves publics à Athènes*, Paris.

Jacoby, F. 1949: *Atthis: the local chronicles of ancient Athens*, Oxford.

——1959: *Diagoras ho Atheos. SBBerlin*, 3.

Jameson, M. H. 1963: The provisions for mobilization in the decree of Themistokles. *Historia* 12, 385–404.

——1977: Agriculture and slavery in classical Athens. *CJ* 73, 122–41.

Jóhannesson, J. 1969: *Islands Historie i Mellomalderen*, Oslo.

Jones, A. H. M. 1957: *Athenian Democracy*, Oxford.

Jordan, B. 1975: *The Athenian Navy in the Classical Period*. Classical Studies 13, Berkeley, Calif., and Los Angeles.

Kahrstedt, U. 1934: *Staatsgebiet und Staatsangehörige in Athen*, Stuttgart.

——1936: *Untersuchungen zur Magistratur in Athen*, Stuttgart.

——1938: Die Nomotheten und die Legislative in Athen. *Klio* 31, 1–25.

Kajanto, I. (ed.) 1984: *Equality and Inequality of Man in Ancient Thought*, Helsinki.

Katz, F. 1972: *The Ancient American Civilizations*, London.

Keaney, J. J. 1969: Ring Composition in Aristotle's Athenaion Politeia. *AJP* 90, 406–23.

Kearns, E. 1989: *The Heroes of Attica. Bulletin* suppl. 57.

Keil, B. 1902: *Anonymus Argentinensis*, Strasbourg.

Kelsen, H. 1946: *General Theory of Law and State*, Cambridge, Mass.

Kellenberger, M. 1965: *Die Landsgemeinden der schweizerischen Kantone*, Winterthur.

Kenyon, F. G. 1919: Greek papyri and their contribution to classical literature. *JHS* 39, 1–36.

Kennedy, G. 1963: *The Art of Persuasion in Greece*, London.

Kinzl, K. H. 1987: On the consequences of following *AP* 21.4 (on the *trittyes* of Attika). *AHB* 1, 25–33.

——1989: On the consequences of following *AP* 21.3 (on the *phylai* of Attika). *Chiron* 19, 347–65.

Klees, H. 1975: *Herren und Sklaven*, Wiesbaden.

Kluwe, E. 1976: Die soziale Zusammensetzung der athenischen *Ekklesia* und ihr Einfluss auf politische Entscheidungen. *Klio* 58, 295–333.

——1977: Nochmals zum Problem: die soziale Zusammensetzung der athenischen *Ekklesia* und ihr Einfluss auf politische Entscheidungen. *Klio* 59, 45–81.

Kolb, F. 1981: *Agora und Theater, Volks- und Festversammlung*, Berlin.

Kolbe, W. 1929: Zur athenischen Schatzverwaltung im IV. Jahrhundert. *Philologus* 84, 261–7.

Kourouniotes, K. and Thompson, H. A. 1932: The Pnyx in Athens. *Hesperia* 1, 90–217.

Krentz, P. 1982: *The Thirty at Athens*, Ithaca, NY.

Kroll, J. H. 1972: *Athenian Bronze Allotment Plates*. Cambridge, Mass.

Kron, U. 1976: *Die zehn attischen Phylenheroen. MdI Athen* 5. Beiheft.

Kubitschek, W. 1928: *Grundriss der antiken Zeitrechnung*, Munich.

Labarbe, J. 1957: *La loi navale de Thémistocle*, Paris.

Lambert, S. D. 1986: The Ionian Phyle and Phratry in Archaic and Classical Athens. Diss. Oxford.

Lang, M. 1959: Allotment by tokens. *Historia* 8, 80–9.

Lang, M. and Crosby, M. 1964: *The Athenian Agora X: weights, measures and tokens*, Princeton, NJ.

Larfeld, W. 1898 1907: *Handbuch der griechischen Epigraphik* I II, Leipzig.

Larsen, J. A. O. 1946: The Acharnians and pay of taxiarchs. *CP* 41, 91–8.

——1948: Cleisthenes and the development of the theory of democracy at Athens. *Essays in Political Theory . . . Sabine*, New York, 1–16.

Laslett, P. 1956: The face to face society. In *Philosophy, Politics and Society* I, ed. P. Laslett, Oxford, 157–84.

Latte, K. 1939: Orakel. *RE* XVIII 1, 829–66.

Lauffer, S. 1979: *Die Bergwerkssklaven von Laureion*, 2nd edn, Wiesbaden.

Lavency, M. 1964: *Aspects de la logographie judiciaire attique*, Louvain.

Leisi, E. 1908: *Der Zeuge im attischen Recht*, Frauenfeld.

Lenardon, R. J. 1959: The chronology of Themistokles' ostracism and exile. *Historia* 8, 23–48.

Lévêque, P. and Vidal-Naquet, P. 1963: *Clisthène l'athénien*, Paris.

Lévy, E. 1974: Les esclaves chez Aristophane. In *Actes du Colloque 1972 sur l'esclavage*, Paris, 29–46.

——1976: *Athènes devant la défaite de 404*, Paris.

——1983: *Asty* et *polis* dans l'Iliade. *Ktema* 8, 55–73.

——1988: Métèques et droit de résidence. In *L'étranger dans le monde grec*, Nancy, 47–67.

Lewis, D. M. 1954: Notes on Attic inscriptions. *BSA* 49, 30–50.

——1963: Cleisthenes and Attica. *Historia* 12, 22–40.

——1966: After the profanation of the mysteries. *Ancient Society and Institutions*, Oxford, 177–91.

——1967: A Note on *IG* I² 114. *JHS* 87, 132.

——1974a: Entrenchment-clauses in Attic decrees. *Phoros*, New York, 81–9.

——1974b: The Kerameikos ostraka. *ZPE* 14, 1–4.

——1988: The tyranny of the Pisistradidae. *Cambridge Ancient History* V, 287–302.

Linders, T. 1975: *The Treasurers of the Other Gods in Athens and their Functions*, Meisenheim am Glan.

Lipsius, J. H. 1905–15: *Das attische Recht und Rechtsverfahren* I–III, Leipzig.

Lijphart, A. 1984: *Democracies: patterns of majoritarian and consensus government in twenty-one countries*, New Haven, Conn.

Lively, J. 1975: *Democracy*, Oxford.

Lofberg, J. O. 1917: *Sycophancy in Athens*, Chicago.

Loraux, N. 1986: *The Invention of Athens*, Cambridge, Mass.

Lotze, D. 1981: Zum Begriff der Demokratie in Aischylos' Hiketiden. In *Aischylos und Pindar*, ed. E. G. Schmidt, Berlin, 207–16.

——1985: Die Teilhabe des Bürgers an Regierung und Rechtsprechung in der Organen der direkten Demokratie des klassischen Athen. In *Kultur und Fortschritt in der Blütezeit der griechischen Polis*, ed. E. Kluwe, Berlin, 52–76.

Lucas, J. R. 1976: *Democracy and Participation*, Harmondsworth, Middx.

MacDowell, D. M. 1962: *Andokides. On the Mysteries*, Oxford.

——1963: *Athenian Homicide Law*, Manchester.

——1975: Law-making at Athens in the fourth century BC. *JHS* 95, 62–74.

——1976: Bastards as Athenian citizens. *CQ* 26, 87–91.

——1978: *The Law in Classical Athens*, London.

——1985: The length of the speeches on the assessment of the penalty in Athenian courts. *CQ* 35, 525–6.

——1986: The Law of Periandros about Symmories. *CQ* 36, 438–49.

——1990: *Demosthenes against Meidias*, Oxford.

MacKendrick, P. 1969: *The Athenian Aristocracy 399 to 31 BC*, Cambridge, Mass.

Macridis, R. C. 1955: *The Study of Comparative Government*, New York.

Madvig, J. N. 1875: Eine Bemerkung über die Gränze der Competenz des Volkes und der Gerichte bei den Athenaiern. *Kleine Philologische Schriften*, Leipzig, 378–90.

Maio, D. P. 1983: *Politeia* and adjudication in fourth-century BC Athens. *American Journal of Jurisprudence* 28, 16–45.

Mannheim, K. 1951: *Freedom, Power and Democratic Planning*, London.

Markle, M. M. 1985: Jury pay and Assembly pay at Athens. *Crux* 265–97.

Marks, L. F. 1963: Fourteenth-century democracy in Florence. *P&P* 25, 77–85.

Martin, J. 1974: Von Kleisthenes zu Ephialtes. Zur Entstehung der athenischen Demokratie. *Chiron* 4, 5–42.

McCabe, D. F. 1981: *The Prose-Rhythm of Demosthenes*, New York.

McDonald, F. 1985: *Novus Ordo Seclorum: the intellectual origins of the Constitution*, Lawrence, Kansas.

McDonald, W. A. 1943: *The Political Meeting Places of the Greeks*, Baltimore.

McLean, I. 1989: *Democracy and New Technology*, Cambridge.

Meier, Ch. 1975: Freiheit. *Geschichtliche Grundbegriffe* II, Stuttgart, 426–9.

——1989: Politeia. *Historisches Wörterbuch der Philosophie* 7, Basel, 1034–6.

——1990: *The Greek Discovery of Politics*, London.

Meritt, B. D. 1928: *The Athenian Calendar in the Fifth Century*, Cambridge, Mass.

——1952: Law against tyranny. *Hesperia* 21, 355–9.

——1962: *Greek Historical Studies*, Cincinnati.

Mertens, D. 1985: Das Theater-Ekklesiasterion auf der Agora von Metapont. *Architectura* 12, 93–124.

Meyer, E. 1937: *Geschichte des Altertums* III, 2nd edn, Stuttgart.

Michels, R. 1911: *Sur Soziologie des Parteiwesens in der modernen Demokratie*, Leipzig.

Mikalson, J. D. 1975a: *The Sacred and Civil Calendar of the Athenian Year*, Princeton, NJ.

——1975b: *Hemera apophras*. *AJP* 96, 19–27.

Miller, D. 1987: Politics. In *The Blackwell Encyclopaedia of Political Thought*. Oxford, 390–1.

Miller, J. 1984: *Rousseau, Dreamer of Democracy*, New Haven, Conn.

Miller, St G. 1978: *The Prytaneion: its function and architectural form*, Berkeley, Calif., and Los Angeles.

Miro, E. de 1967: L'ekklesiasterion in Contrada san Nicola di Agrigento. *Palladio* 16, 165–6.

Mitchell, F. W. 1962: Demades of Paeania and *IG* II² 1493–5. *TAPA* 93, 213–29.

——1970: *Lycurgan Athens*, Cincinnati.

Montgomery, H. 1983: *The Way to Chaeronea: foreign policy, decision-making and political influence in Demosthenes' speeches*, Oslo.

Moodie, G. C. 1964: Politician. In *A Dictionary of the Social Sciences*, New York.

Morris, I. 1987: *Burial and Ancient Society*, Cambridge.

Morrison, J. S. 1984: *Hyperesia* in naval contexts in the fifth and fourth centuries BC. *JHS* 104, 48–59.

——1987: Athenian sea-power in 323/2 BC: dream and reality. *JHS* 107, 88–97.

Morrow, G. R. 1960: *Plato's Cretan City*, Princeton, NJ.

Mosca, G. 1939: *The Ruling Class*, New York.

Mosley, D. J. 1973: *Envoys and Diplomacy in Ancient Greece. Historia* Einzelschriften 22.

Mossé, Cl. 1962: *La fin de la démocratie athénienne. Aspects sociaux et politiques du déclin de la cité grecque au IVe siècle avant JC.*, Paris.

——1979a: Comment s'élabore un mythe politique: Solon, 'père fondateur' de la démocratie athénienne. *Annales* 34, 425–37.

——1979b: Les symmories athéniennes. In *Points de vue sur la fiscalité antique*, ed. H. van Effenterre, Paris, 31–42.

——1981: La démocratie athénienne et la protection de la propriété. *Symposion* 4, 263–71.

Moysey, R. A. 1981: The thirty and the Pnyx. *AJA* 85, 31–7.

Mulgan, R. G. 1984: Liberty in ancient Greece. In *Conceptions of Liberty in Political Philosophy*, ed. Z. Pelczynski, New York, 7–26.

Murray, G. 1898: *A History of Ancient Greek Literature*, Oxford.

Murray, O. 1980: *Early Greece*, London.

——1987: Cities of reason. *European Journal of Sociology* 28, 325–46. Repr. in *The Greek City from Homer to Aristotle*, ed. O. Murray and S. Price (Oxford, 1990) 1–25.

Musiolek, P. 1981: *Asty* als Bezeichnung der Stadt. In *Soziale Typenbegriffe*, ed. E.Ch. Welskopf, Berlin, III, 368–75.

Musti, D. 1985: Pubblico e privato nella democrazia periclea. *QUCC* 20, 7–17.

Najemy, J. M. 1982: *Corporatism and Consensus in Florentine Electoral Politics, 1280–1400*, Chapel Hill, NC.

Newman, K. S. 1983. *Law and Economic Organization: a comparative study of preindustrial societies*, Oxford.

Newman, W. L. 1887–1902: *The Politics of Aristotle* I–IV, Oxford.

Nicholas, B. 1962: *Roman Law*, Oxford.

Nielsen, Th. H. et al. 1989: Athenian grave monuments and social class. *GRBS* 30, 411–20.

Nilsson, M. P. 1951: *Cults, Myths, Oracles, and Politics in Ancient Greece*, Lund.

Nippel, W. 1980: *Mischverfassungstheorie und Verfassungsrealität in antike und früher Neuzeit*, Stuttgart.

Nouhaud, M. 1982: *L'utilisation de l'histoire par les orateurs attiques*, Paris.

Ober, J. 1989: *Mass and Elite in Democratic Athens*, Princeton, NJ.

Ober, J. and Strauss, B. S. 1990: Drama, political rhetoric, and the discourse of Athenian democracy. In *Nothing to do with Dionysos*, ed. J. J. Winkler and F. I. Zeitlin, Princeton, NJ.

Oehler, J. 1899: *Boule. RE* III 1, 1020–37.

Oost, S. I. 1977: Two notes on Aristophon of Azenia. *CP* 72, 238–42.

Osborne, M. J. 1981: *Naturalization in Athens I. Corpus of Decrees*, Brussels.

——1982: *Naturalization in Athens II. Commentaries on the Decrees*, Brussels.

——1983: *Naturalization in Athens III–IV. Testimonia; The Law and Practice*, Brussels.

Osborne, R. 1985a: *Demos: the discovery of classical Attika*, Cambridge.

——1985b: Law in action in classical Athens. *JHS* 105, 40–58.

——1987: *Classical Landscape with Figures: the ancient Greek city and its countryside*, London.

Ostwald, M. 1968: *Nomos and the Beginnings of the Athenian Democracy*, Oxford.

——1986: *From Popular Sovereignty to the Sovereignty of Law*, Berkeley, Calif., and Los Angeles.

——1988: The reform of the Athenian state by Cleisthenes. *Cambridge Ancient History* V, 303–46.

Pack, R. A. 1965: *The Greek and Latin Literary Texts from Greco-Roman Egypt*,

Ann Arbor, Mich.

Palagia, O. 1982: A colossal statue of a personification from the Agora of Athens. *Hesperia* 51, 99–113.

Pallottino, M. 1975: *The Etruscans*, London.

Papageorgiou, C. I, 1990: Four or five types of democracy in Aristotle? *History of Political Thought* 11, 1–8.

Parke, H. W. 1977: *Festivals of the Athenians*, London.

Parker, R. 1983: *Miasma: pollution and purification in early Greek religion*, Oxford.

Patterson, C. 1981: *Pericles' Citizenship Law of 451–50 BC*, New York.

Pearson, L. 1941: Historical allusions in the Attic orators. *CP* 36, 209–29.

——1942: *The Local Historians of Attica*, Philadelphia.

Pecirka, J. 1966: *The Formula for the Grant of Enktesis in Attic Inscriptions*, Prague.

Pélékidis, Ch. 1962: *Histoire de l'éphébie attique des origines à 31 avant Jésus-Christ*, Paris.

Pelling, C. B. R. 1980: Plutarch's adaptation of his source-material. *JHS* 100, 127–40.

Pennock, J. R. 1979: *Democratic Political Theory*, Princeton, NJ.

Perlman, S. 1961: The historical example, its use and importance as political propaganda in the Attic orators. *Scripta Hierosolymitana* 7, 150–66.

——1963: The politicians in the Athenian democracy of the fourth century BC. *Athenaeum* 41, 327–55.

——1967: Political leadership in Athens in the fourth century BC. *PP* 22, 161–76.

Perotti, E. 1974: Esclaves *choris oikountes*. In *Actes du Colloque sur l'esclavage 1972*, Paris, 47–56.

Pfeiffer, R. 1968: *History of Classical Scholarship from the Beginnings to the End of the Hellenistic Age*, Oxford.

Pickard-Cambridge, A. 1968: *The Dramatic Festivals of Athens*, 2nd edn. ed. J. Gould and D. M. Lewis, Oxford.

Piérart, M. 1971: Les *euthynoi* athéniens. *AC* 40, 526–73.

——1974a: A propos de l'élection des stratèges athéniens. *BCH* 98, 125–46.

——1974b: *Platon et la cité grecque*, Brussels.

Plamenatz, J. 1956: Equality of opportunity. In *Aspects of Human Equality*, ed. G. Bryson et al., New York.

——1963: *Man and Society* I–II, London.

Pleket, H. W. 1972: *Isonomia* and Cleisthenes: A note. *Talanta* 4, 63–81.

Plommer, W. H. 1969: The tyranny of the archon list. *CR* 19, 126–9.

Pringsheim, F. 1955: The transition from witnessed to written transactions in Athens. In *Aequitas und Bona Fides. Festgabe für A. Simonius*, Basel, 287–97.

Pritchett, W. K. 1971: *The Greek State at War* I, Berkeley, Calif., and Los Angeles.

——1974: *The Greek State at War* II, Berkeley, Calif., and Los Angeles.

Pritchett, W. K. and Neugebauer, O. 1947: *The Calendars of Athens*, Cambridge, Mass.

Quass, F. 1971: *Nomos und Psephisma. Untersuchungen zum griechischen Staatsrecht*, Munich.

Raaflaub, K. A. 1980: Des freien Bürgers Recht der freien Rede. In *Studien zur antiken Sozialgeschichte: Festschrift F. Vittinghoff*, Cologne, 7–57.

——1985: *Die Entdeckung der Freiheit. Vestigia* 37.

Rahe, P. A. 1984: The primacy of politics in classical Greece. *AHR* 89, 265–93.

Randall, R. H. 1953: The Erechtheum workers. *AJA* 57, 199–210.

Rankin, D. I. 1988: The mining lobby at Athens. *Ancient Society* 19, 189–205.

Raubitschek, A. 1949: *Dedications from the Athenian Acropolis*, Cambridge, Mass.

——1962: *Demokratia. Hesperia* 31, 238–44.

Rawls, J. 1987: The basic liberties and their priority. In *Liberty, Equality and Law*, Cambridge.

Rawson, E. 1969: *The Spartan Tradition in European Thought*, Oxford.

Reinmuth, O. 1971: *The Ephebic Inscriptions*, Leiden.

Reverdin, O. 1945: Remarques sur la vie politique d'Athènes au Ve siècle. *MusHelv* 2, 201–12.

Reynolds, L. D. and Wilson, N. G. 1974: *Scribes and Scholars*, 2nd edn, Oxford.

Rhodes, P. J. 1972: *The Athenian Boule*, Oxford.

——1979: *Eisangelia* in Athens. *JHS* 99, 103–14.

——1980a: Athenian democracy after 403 BC. *CJ* 75, 305–23.

——1980b: Ephebi, Bouleutae and the population of Athens. *ZPE* 38, 191–201.

——1981a: *A Commentary on the Aristotelian 'Athenaion Politeia'*, Oxford.

——1981b: More members scrving twice in the Athenian Boule. *ZPE* 41, 101–2.

——1984: Members serving in the Athenian Boule and the population of Athens again. *ZPE* 57, 200–2.

——1985a: *Nomothesia* in fourth-century Athens. *CQ* 35, 55–60.

——1985b: Problems in Athenian *Eisphora* and Liturgies. *AJAH* 7 (1982), 1–19.

——1985c: *What Alcibiades Did or What Happened to Him*. Inaugural lecture, Durham.

——1986: Political activity in classical Athens. *JHS* 106, 132–44.

——1987: *Nomothesia* in classical Athens. *L'educazione Giuridica* (Perugia), V2, 5–26.

——1988: *Thucydides History II*, Warminster, Wilts.

Rials, S. (ed.) 1988: *La déclaration des droits de l'homme et du citoyen*, Paris.

Roberts, J. T. 1983: *Accountability in Athenian Government*, Madison, Wis.

Romilly, J. de 1971: *La loi dans la pensée grecque*, Paris.

——1975: *Problèmes de la démocratie grecque*, Paris.

Ross, A. 1946: *Hvorfor demokrati?* Copenhagen. [The section 'Det germanske urdemokrati' (22–4) omitted from the English edn, 1952.]

Roussel, D. 1976: *Tribu et cité*, Paris.

Roussel, P. 1951: *Étude sur le principe de l'ancienneté dans le monde hellénique du Ve siècle av. J. C. à l'époque romaine. MAI* 43 2, 123–227.

Ruschenbusch, E. 1958: *Patrios politeia*. Theseus, Drakon, Solon und Kleisthenes in Publizistik und Geschichtsschreibung des 5. und 4. Jahrhunderts v. Chr. *Historia* 7, 398–424.

——1961. *Ephesis*. Ein Beitrag zur griechischen Rechtsterminologie. *ZSav* 78, 386–90.

——1966: *Solonos Nomoi. Historia* Einzelschriften 9.

——1968: *Untersuchungen zur Geschichte des athenischen Strafrechts*, Cologne.

——1978a: *Untersuchungen zu Staat und Politik in Griechenland vom 7.-4. Jh. v. Chr.*, Bamberg.

——1978b: *Die athenischen Symmorien des 4. Jh. v. Chr. ZPE* 31, 275–84.

——1979a: Die Einführung des Theorikon. *ZPE* 36, 303–8.

——1979b: Die soziale Herkunft der Epheben um 330. *ZPE* 35, 173–6.

——1979c: Die soziale Zusammensetzung des Rates der 500 in Athen im 4. Jh. *ZPE* 35, 177–80.

——1984: Zum letzten Mal: die Bürgerzahl Athens im 4. Jh. v. Chr. *ZPE* 54, 253–69.

——1985a: Drei Beiträge zur öffentlichen *Diaita* in Athen. *Symposion* 5, 32–40.

——1985b: Die Zahl der griechischen Staaten und Arealgrösse und Bürgerzahl der 'Normalpolis'. *ZPE* 59, 253–63.

——1987 Symmorienprobleme. *ZPE* 69, 75–81.

——1988a: Doch noch einmal die Bürgerzahl Athens im 4. Jh. v. Chr. *ZPE* 72, 139–40.

——1988b: Stellungnahme. *ZPE* 75, 194–6.

Ryffel, H. 1903: *Die schweizerischen Landsgemeinden*, Zürich.

Salmon, J. B. 1984: *Wealthy Corinth*, Oxford.

Sargent, R. L. 1927: The use of slaves by the Athenians in warfare. I: in warfare by land. II: in warfare by sea. *CP* 22, 201–12, 264–79.

Sartori, G. 1962: *Democratic Theory*, Westport, Conn.

——1968: Democracy. In *International Encyclopaedia of the Social Sciences*, 112–21.

——1976: *Parties and Party Systems*, Cambridge.

Schläpfer, P. L. 1939: *Untersuchungen zu den attischen Staatsurkunden und den Amphiktyonenbeschlüssen der Demosthenischen Kranzrede*, Paderborn.

Schöll, R. 1886: Über attische Gesetzgebung. *SBMünchen*, 83–139.

Schmidt, K. 1931: *Die Namen der attischen Kriegsschiffe*, Leipzig.

Schreiner, I. 1913: *De Corpore Juris Atheniensium*, Bonn.

Schuller, W. (ed.) 1982: *Korruption im Altertum*, Munich.

——1984: Wirkungen des ersten attischen Seebunds auf die Herausbildung der athenischen Demokratie. *Studien zum attischen Seebund, Xenia* 8, Konstanz, 87–101.

——1985: *Frauen in der griechischen Geschichte*, Konstanz.

——1990: *Griechische Geschichte*, 3rd edn, Munich.

Schumpeter, J. 1942: *Capitalism, Socialism and Democracy*, New York.

Seager, R. 1967: Thrasybulus, Conon and Athenian imperialism 396–86 BC. *JHS* 87, 95–115.

Sealey, R. 1956a: Callistratos of Aphidna and his contemporaries. *Historia* 5, 178–203.

——1956b: The entry of Pericles into history. *Hermes* 84, 234–47.

——1974: The origins of *Demokratia*. *CSCA* 6, 253–95.

——1981: Ephialtes, *Eisangelia*, and the Council. In *Classical Contributions, Studies Presented to Malcolm Francis McGregor*, New York, 125–34.

——1982: On the Athenian concept of law. *CJ* 77, 289–302.

——1987: *The Athenian Republic: democracy or the rule of law?* University Park.

Shear, T. L. Jr 1987: Tax tangle ancient style. *American School of Classical Studies at Athens: Newsletter*, Spring, 8.

Siewert, P. 1982: *Die Trittyen Attikas und die Heeresreform des Kleisthenes. Vestigia* 33.

Sinclair, R. K. 1978: The king's peace and the employment of military and naval forces 387–78. *Chiron* 8, 29–54.

——1988a: *Democracy and Participation in Athens*. Cambridge.

——1988b: Lysias' speeches and the debate about participation in Athenian public life. *Antichthon* 22, 54–66.

Skydsgaard, J. E. 1988: Solon's *tele* and the agrarian history. A note. In *Studies in Ancient History and Numismatics Presented to Rudi Thomsen*, Århus, 50–4.

Sly, J. F. 1930: *Town Government in Massachusetts*, Cambridge, Mass.

Smith, C. F. 1907: What constitutes a state? *CJ* 2, 299–302.

Snell, B. 1935: Zwei Töpfe mit Euripides-Papyri. *Hermes* 70, 119–20.

Snodgrass, A. 1980: *Archaic Greece*, London.

Speyer, W. 1971: *Die literarische Fälschung im heidnischen und christlichen Altertum*, Munich.

Sperber, H. and Trittschuh, T. 1962: *American Political Terms: an historical dictionary*, Detroit.

Stanton, G. R. 1984: The tribal reform of Kleisthenes the Alkmeonid. *Chiron* 14, 1–41.

Stanton, G. R. and Bicknell, P. J. 1987: Voting in tribal groups in the Athenian Assembly. *GRBS* 28, 51–92.

Starke, J. G. 1989: *Introduction to International Law*, 10th edn. London.

Stauffacher, W. 1962: *Die Versammlungsdemokratie im Kanton Glarus*, Zürich.

Staveley, E. S. 1972: *Greek and Roman Voting and Elections*, London.

Ste Croix, G. E. M de 1953: Demosthenes' *timema* and the Athenian *eisphora* in the fourth century BC. *ClMed* 14, 30–70.

——1956: The constitution of the Five Thousand. *Historia* 5, 1–23.

——1963: The alleged secret pact between Athens and Philip II concerning Amphipolis and Pydna. *CQ* 13, 110–19.

——1964: review of Buchanan (1962) *CR* 14, 190–2.

——1975: Political pay outside Athens. *CQ* 25, 48–52.

——1981: *The Class Struggle in the Ancient Greek World*, London.

Stockton, D. 1982: The death of Ephialtes. *CQ* 32, 227–8.

——1990: *The Classical Athenian Democracy*, Oxford.

Stone, I. F. 1987: *The Trial of Socrates*, Boston, Mass.

Strauss, B. S. 1986: *Athens after the Peloponnesian War*, New York.

Stroud, R. S. 1968: *Drakon's Law on Homicide*, Berkeley, Calif., and Los Angeles.

Svoronos, I. N. 1900: *Peri ton eisiterion ton archaion*. *JIAN* 3, 319–43.

Swoboda, H. 1890: Bemerkungen zur politischen Stellung der athenischen Strategen. *RM* 45, 288–310.

Tarn, W. W. 1927: Greece 335 to 321 BC. *Cambridge Ancient History* VI, 438–60.

Taylor, Ch. 1979: What's wrong with negative liberty? In *The Idea of Freedom: essays in honour of Isaiah Berlin*, ed. A. Ryan, Oxford.

Taylor, L. R. 1949: *Party Politics in the Age of Caesar*, Berkeley, Calif., and Los Angeles.

Thalheim, Th. 1902: Zur Eisangelie in Athen. *Hermes* 37, 339–52.

——1906: Eisangelie-Gesetz in Athen. *Hermes* 41, 304–9.

Thomas, R. 1989: *Oral Tradition and Written Record in Classical Athens*, Cambridge.

Thomsen, R. 1964: *Eisphora: a study of direct taxation in ancient Athens*, Copenhagen.

——1972: *The Origin of Ostracism: a synthesis*, Copenhagen.

Thompson, H. A. 1978: review of R. E. Wycherley, *The Stones of Athens*. *Archaeology* 31, 63–5.

——1982: The Pnyx in models. *Hesperia* suppl. 19, 133–47.

Thompson, H. A. and Scranton, R. L. 1943: Stoas and city walls on the Pnyx. *Hesperia* 12, 269–83.

Thompson, H. A. and Wycherley, R. E. 1972: *The Athenian Agora XIV. The Agora of Athens*, Princeton, NJ.

Thompson, W. E. 1966: *Trittys ton prytaneon*. *Historia* 15, 1–10.

——1969: Kleisthenes and Aigeis. *Mnemosyne* 22, 137–52.

——1971: The deme in Kleisthenes' reforms. *SymbOslo* 46, 72–9.

Thomson, G. 1955: *Studies in Ancient Greek Society II. The First Philosophers*, London.

Thür, G. 1977: *Beweisführung vor dem Schwurgerichtshöfen Athens. Die Proklesis zur Basanos*, Vienna.

——1989: Wo wohnen die Metöken? In *Wohnen in der klassischen Polis II. Demokratie und Architektur*, Munich, 117–21.

Toepffer, J. 1989: *Attische Genealogie*, Berlin.

Tracy, St V. 1988: *Ekklesia synkletos*. A note. *ZPE* 75, 186–8.

Traill, J. S. 1975: *The Political Organization of Attica*, *Hesperia* suppl. 14.

——1978: Diakris, the inland trittys of Leontis. *Hesperia* 47, 89–109.

——1981: Athenian bouleutic alternates. *Classical Contributions, Studies Presented to Malcolm Francis McGregor*, New York, 161–9.

——1986: *Demos and Trittys: epigraphical and topographical studies in the organization of Attica*, Toronto.

Tréheux, J. 1965: *Études sur les inventaires attiques*. Études d'archéologie classique III, Paris.

Treu, M. 1967: Ps.-Xenophon, D. *Pol. Ath. RE* IX 2, 1928–82.

Utchenko, S. L. and Diakonoff, I. M. 1970: Social stratification of ancient society. *13th International Congress of Historians*, Moscow.

Vacherot, É. 1860: *La démocratie*, Paris.

Vanderpool, E. 1973: Ostracism at Athens. In *Lectures in Memory of Louise Taft Semple*, 2nd ser. 1966–71, Cincinnati, 217–43.

Vansina, J. 1973: *Oral Tradition*, 2nd edn, Harmondsworth.

Vidal-Naquet, P. 1968: La tradition de l'hoplite athénien. *Problèmes de la guerre en Grèce ancienne*, Paris, 161–81.

Vile, M. J. C. 1967: *Constitutionalism and the Separation of Powers*, Oxford.

Vincent, A. 1987: *Theories of the State*, Oxford.

Vlastos, G. 1953: *Isonomia. AJP* 74, 337–66.

——1964: *Isonomia politike*. In *Isonomia. Studien zur Gleichheitsvorstellung im griechischen Denken*, Berlin, 1–35.

Wade-Gery, H. T. 1958: *Essays in Greek History*, Oxford.

Waley, D. 1978: *The Italian City Republics*, 2nd edn, London.

Walker, E. M. 1927: The Periclean democracy. *Cambridge Ancient History* V, 98–112.

Wallace, 1986: The Date of Isokrates' *Areopagitikos*. *HSCP* 90, 77–84.

——1989a: *The Areopagos Council, to 307 BC* Baltimore.

——1989b: The Athenian *proeispherontes*. *Hesperia* 58, 473–90.

Wallinga, H. T. 1982: The trireme and its crew. In *Actus. Studies in Honour of H. L. W. Nelson*, Utrecht, 453–82.

Walters, K. R. 1976: The 'ancestral constitution' and fourth-century historiography in Athens. *AJAH* 1, 129–44.

Waltman, J. L. and Holland, K. M. (eds) 1988: *The Political Role of Law Courts in Modern Democracies*, London.

Wankel, H. 1982: Die Korruption in der rednerischen Topik und in der Realität des klassischen Athen. In Schuller (1982) 29–53.

Weber, M. 1921: Die Stadt. *Archiv für Sozialwissenschaft* 47, 621–772.

Weil, R. 1960: *Aristote et l'histoire: essai sur la Politique*, Paris.

Welwei, K. W. 1967: Der 'Diapsephismos' nach dem Sturz der Peisistratiden. *Gymnasium* 74, 423–37.

——1974: *Unfreie im antiken Kriegsdienst* I, Wiesbaden.

——1983: *Die griechische Polis*, Stuttgart.

Wheare, K. C. 1966: *Modern Constitutions*, 2nd edn, Oxford.

——1968: *Legislatures*, 2nd edn, Oxford.

Whibley, L. 1889: *Political Parties in Athens during the Peloponnesian War*, Cambridge.

——1896: *Greek Oligarchies: their character and organisation*, Cambridge.

Whitehead, D. 1977: *The Ideology of the Athenian Metic*, Cambridge.

——1981: The archaic Athenian *zeugitai*. *CQ* 31, 282–6.

——1982: Sparta and the Thirty Tyrants. *Ancient Society* 13–14, 105–30.

——1983: Competitive outlay and community profit: *philotimia* in democratic Athens. *ClMed* 34, 55–74.

——1986: *The Demes of Attica 508/7 – ca. 250 BC*, Princeton, NJ.

Will, E. 1972: *Le monde grec et l'Orient. Peuples et civilisations* II 1.

Wilson, W. 1887: The study of administration. *Pol. Sc. Quart.* 2 197–222.

Willetts, R. F. 1967: *The Law Code of Gortyn*, Berlin.

Wolff, H. J. 1966: *Die attische Paragraphe*, Weimar.

——1970: *'Normenkontrolle' und Gesetzesbegriff in der attischen Demokratie*, Heidelberg.

Wood, E. M. 1986: Agricultural slavery in classical Athens. *AJAH* 8 (1983), 1–47.

——1988: *Peasant-Citizen and Slave: the foundations of Athenian democracy*, London.

Woodhead, A. G. 1981: *The Study of Greek Inscriptions*, 2nd edn, Cambridge.

Woozley, A. D. 1979: *Law and Obedience: the arguments of Plato's 'Crito'*, London.

Worthington, I. 1986: The chronology of the Harpalus affair. *SymbOslo* 61, 63–76.

Wrigley, E. A. 1969: *Population and History*, London.

Wycherley, R. E. 1957: *The Athenian Agora III. Literary and Epigraphical Testimonia*, Princeton, NJ.

Wyse, W. 1904: *The Speeches of Isaeus*, Cambridge.

Young, S. H. 1939: An Athenian Klepsydra. *Hesperia* 8, 274–84.

Yunis, H. 1988: Law, politics and the *graphe paranomon* in fourth-century Athens. *GRBS* 29, 361–82.
Zimmermann, H. D. 1974: Freie Arbeit, Preise und Löhne. In *Hellenische Poleis* I, ed. E. Ch. Welskopf, Darmstadt, 92–107.

Hansen (1983a) includes the following articles, listed here with details of first publication.

		Text	Addenda
1	How many Athenians attended the *ecclesia*? *GRBS* 17 (1976) 115–34.	1–20	21–3
2	The Athenian *ecclesia* and the assembly-place on the Pnyx. *GRBS* 23 (1982) 241–9.	25–33	34
3	How often did the *ecclesia* meet? *GRBS* 18 (1977) 43–70.	35–62	62–72
4	*Ekklesia synkletos* in Hellenistic Athens. *GRBS* 20 (1979) 149–56.	73–80	81
5	When did the Athenian *ecclesia* meet? *GRBS* 23 (1982) 331–50.	83–102	102
6	How did the Athenian *ecclesia* vote? *GRBS* 18 (1977) 123–37.	102–17	118–21
7	The *procheirotonia* in the Athenian *ecclesia*.	123–30	
8	The duration of a meeting of the Athenian *ecclesia*. *CP* 74 (1979) 43–9.	131–7	138
9	*Demos, ecclesia*, and *dicasterion* in classical Athens. *GRBS* 19 (1978) 127–46.	139–58	159–60
10	*Nomos* and *psephisma* in fourth-century Athens. *GRBS* 19 (1978) 315–30.	161–76	177
11	Did the Athenian *ecclesia* legislate after 403/2? *GRBS* 20 (1979) 27–53.	179–205	206
12	The Athenian *ecclesia* and the Swiss *Landsgemeinde*.	207–26	

Hansen (1989a) includes the following articles, listed here with details of first publication.

		Text	Addenda
1	The Athenian 'politicians' 403–322 BC. *GRBS* 24 (1983) 33–55.	1–23	24
2	*Rhetores* and *strategoi* in fourth-century Athens. *GRBS* 24 (1983) 151–80.	25–33	34–72
3	Political activity and the organization of Attica in the fourth century BC. *GRBS* 24 (1983) 227–38.	73–84	85–91
4	The number of *rhetores* in the Athenian *ecclesia*, 355–22 BC. *GRBS* 25 (1984) 123–55.	93–125	126–7
5	Two notes on the Pnyx. *GRBS* 26 (1985) 241–50.	129–40	141

6   The construction of Pnyx II and the introduction of   143–52   153
    Assembly pay *ClMed* 37 (1986) 89–98.
7   The organization of the Athenian Assembly. A reply.   155–62   163–5
    GRBS 29 (1988) 51–8.
8   The number of *ecclesiai* in fourth-century Athens [with   167–73   174–5
    F. Mitchel]. *SymbOslo* 59 (1984) 13–19.
9   How often did the Athenian *ekklesia* meet? A reply.   177–92   193–4
    GRBS 28 (1987) 35–50.
10 What is *Syllogos* at Thukydides 2.22.1? [with Johnny   195–209 210–11
    Christensen]. *ClMed* 34 (1983) 17–31.
11 *Demos, ekklesia* and *dikasterion*. A reply to Martin   213–18
    Ostwald and Josiah Ober.
    ClMed 40 (1989) 101–6.
12 The Athenian Heliaia from Solon to Aristotle.   219–57   258–61
    ClMed 33 (1982) 9–47.
13 On the importance of institutions in an analysis of   263–9
    Athenian democracy. *ClMed* 40 (1989) 108–13.
14 *Graphe paranomon* against *psephismata* not yet passed by 271–81
    the *ekklesia*. *ClMed* 38 (1987) 63–73.
15 Two notes on Demosthenes' symbouleutic speeches.   283–96   297
    ClMed 35 (1984) 57–70.

Glossary

Agones timetoi Lawsuits (both private and public) in which the penalty was not fixed by law but had to be determined by the jurors according to the proposals of the parties.

Agora (1) Large open place in Athens, the political and economic centre of the city, situated north of the Akropolis. (2) A political assembly where the members of a deme (*DEMOS* 5) or a *TRITTYS* or a *PHYLE* met to debate and to pass resolutions about local affairs. The *PHYLAI* held their agoras in Athens; the demes held theirs either locally or in Athens.

Anagrapheis ton nomon Board of magistrates set up in 410 to codify the laws of Drakon and Solon. Their work was discontinued at the end of the Peloponnesian War, resumed with the restoration of the democracy in 403 and concluded in 399 with the publication of a calendar of sacrifices.

Anakrisis The preliminary investigation into a lawsuit by the magistrate who would later preside over the section of the People's Court which judged the case.

Anapsephisis Reconsideration and, in particular, a second vote (by show of hands) in the Assembly on an issue which the people had already debated and decided in an earlier session.

Antidosis Exchange of property. If a wealthy citizen believed that he had been nominated unjustifiably to a *LITURGY*, he could challenge another wealthy citizen and demand that the latter undertake the liturgy or exchange his whole property with him. If the other citizen declined the challenge, the People's Court decided which of the two had to undertake the liturgy. It is not known whether an *antidosis* ever resulted in an actual exchange of property.

Antigraphe The defendant's written reply to the prosecutor's *graphe* (*GRAPHE* II).

Antomosia Oath administered by the magistrate at the *ANAKRISIS* and sworn by both parties.

Apagoge Public prosecution which a private citizen initiated with the arrest (*apagoge*) of a person whom he caught committing a serious crime. *Apagoge* was used (1) against *KAKOURGOI* who were caught in the act (*ep'autophoro*); (2) against *ATIMOI* who exercised rights they had been deprived of; (3) against exiles who returned to Athens without reprieve. In (1) and (3) the Eleven (*HOI*

HENDEKA) were empowered to execute the man arrested, if he confessed; in (2) he was held in custody until the case had been heard by a section of the People's Court.

Apatouria Festival celebrated in the PHRATRIES in the month BOEDROMION. On the third day of the festival citizens had their sons registered in their phratries.

Apocheirotonia Vote taken in the Assembly by a show of hands whereby a magistrate was suspended from office until the People's Court had heard the charge brought against him for misconduct in office.

Apodektai Board of financial magistrates composed of one man from each of the tribes (*PHYLAI*) and selected by lot. In collaboration with the COUNCIL OF FIVE HUNDRED the board supervised all state revenue and distributed it to the various boards of magistrates concerned with state expenditures.

Apodokimasia Rejection of a candidate at his *DOKIMASIA*.

Apographe List of property and, in particular, property to be confiscated. The list had to be read out at the *EKKLESIA KYRIA* and, if anyone raised an objection or laid claim to something from the list, a *DIADIKASIA* was held between the state and the claimant. The man who had filed the list acted as prosecutor before the People's Court and, if he won the case, received a third of the value of the disputed property.

Apophasis Public prosecution used in cases of treason, attempts to overthrow the democracy and corruption. The procedure was initiated in the Assembly, occasionally in the COUNCIL OF THE AREOPAGOS. Having heard a denunciation, the people decreed that the Council of the Areopagos should undertake a preliminary investigation of the case and pass a preliminary verdict (*KATAGNOSIS*). The Council of the Areopagos then gave a report (*apophasis*) of its investigation to the Assembly, which in turn referred the matter to a section of the People's Court. The court passed the final judgement and fixed the penalty if the accused was found guilty.

Aporoi The poor, not the destitute but all who had enough to live on but no surplus; opposed to *EUPOROI*, the wealthy.

Archairesia Election of magistrates, specifically the meeting of the Assembly at which the election of (military) magistrates was the most important item on the agenda.

Arche (pl. archai) (1) Magistracy. (2) Especially in plural: magistrates (generic term for all the magistrates i.e. the 500 councillors and about 700 others).

Archon (pl. -ntes) Archon(s). (1) A magistrate (= ARCHE). (2) The plural *hoi archontes* commonly designates the nine highest state officials: the ARCHON, the BASILEUS (King archon), the POLEMARCHOS (polemarch) and the six THESMO-THETAI. (3) The singular *archon* commonly designates the highest state official, after whom the year was named ('in the ARCHONSHIP of N'). He was responsible for organizing state festivals and presided over the People's Court in cases concerning family law and inheritances.

Archonship Term of office (one year) of an ARCHON (3).

Areopagites (pl. -tai) Member of the COUNCIL OF THE AREOPAGOS.

Areopagos (1) The hill of Ares (god of war), situated south of the AGORA, between the Akropolis and the PNYX. (2) Abbreviation for the COUNCIL OF THE AREOPAGOS.

Aristokratia Aristocracy, i.e. rule by the 'best' members of the community.

Assembly EKKLESIA I.

Asty (1) City as opposed to CHORA, land. (2) The third of Attica comprising Athens, the Piraeus and the surrounding plain, bordered by the mountains Aigaleos in the west and Hymettos in the east. One of the three regions (ASTY, PARALIA and MESOGEIOS) into which Attica was divided by the reforms of Kleisthenes.

Astynomoi Board of city magistrates composed of one man from each tribe (PHYLE) selected by lot. Their duties were *inter alia* to ensure that the streets were kept clean and building regulations observed.

Atimia Loss of honour. Penalty imposed on male Athenian citizens principally if they were debtors to the state or had neglected their civic duties. Such citizens (ATIMOI) were deprived of all political rights, the right to legal protection and the right to enter the market-place and the sanctuaries.

Atimos (pl. *-oi*) Person punished with ATIMIA.

Atthidographer The author of an ATTHIS.

Atthis (pl. *-ides*) Chronicles of Athens and Attica.

Autarkeia Self-sufficiency in the economic and human resources necessary to form a 'proper' POLIS.

Axon (pl. *-nes*) Axle. Tall, square wooden block inscribed on all four sides (with the laws of Drakon or Solon). It was placed in a frame and fitted with a pivot so that a reader could turn all four sides towards himself.

Banausos (pl. *-oi*) An artisan or (sometimes) a tradesman. Always a derogatory word, it was, in a political context, used chiefly by the philosophers who criticized democracy.

Basanos Interrogation of a slave under torture, initiated by one of the parties to a case challenging the other party (through a PROKLESIS) and carried out in accordance with a contract between the parties. A *basanos* was obligatory if the testimony of a slave was to be brought before a court as evidence.

Basileia Monarchy.

Basileus (1) King. (2) The king archon, one of the nine ARCHONS. He had charge of state festivals and presided over the COUNCIL OF THE AREOPAGOS in homicide trials.

Bema The speaker's platform (1) in the Assembly, (2) in the COUNCIL OF FIVE HUNDRED, (3) in the People's Court.

Boedromion The third month of the Attic year, September–October.

Boule Council. *Boule* usually refers to the COUNCIL OF FIVE HUNDRED, but can mean also the COUNCIL OF THE AREOPAGOS.

Bouleuterion City hall where the COUNCIL OF FIVE HUNDRED held most of its sessions. Plain rectangular building on the west side of the AGORA near the THOLOS, the METROÖN and the MONUMENT TO THE EPONYMOUS HEROES. It was erected at the end of the fifth-century and had a council chamber measuring 19 x 20 m.

Bouleutes (pl. *-tai*) Councillor, member of a BOULE.

Cheirotonia Vote by show of hands, used in the Assembly, in the COUNCIL OF FIVE HUNDRED and by the NOMOTHETAI.

Chora (1) Land. (2) The countryside, as opposed to the city (ASTY or POLIS).

Choregia A LITURGY where the wealthy liturgist had to equip and train a dramatic or lyric chorus at his own expense for a performance at the DIONYSIA or the THARGELIA. He was then called the *choregos*.

Council of Five Hundred (*he boule hoi pentakosioi*) The Council consisted of fifty citizens from each of the ten PHYLAI, selected by lot for one year from candidates nominated in the 139 demes. The Council met every working day (about 250 times in a year) in the BOULEUTERION in the AGORA. It prepared all business for the Assembly and the NOMOTHETAI and was at the head of the administration of the state.

Council of the Areopagos (*he boule he ex Areiou pagou*) Council of all former ARCHONS, who became members for life after their year of office. The council had about 150 members. It usually met on the AREOPAGOS to pass judgement in homicide trials where the person slain was an Athenian citizen. In the sixth century the council was the most important organ of the Athenian state, but it lost most of its powers by Ephialtes' reforms in 462. After 403 the council won back some of its former powers.

Decree *PSEPHISMA*.

Delian League Alliance of states under the leadership of Athens, founded in 478/7 and originally directed against the Persian king. It developed into an Athenian sea empire and was dissolved after Athens' defeat in the Peloponnesian War in 404. See also SECOND ATHENIAN CONFEDERACY.

***Demagogos* (pl. *-oi*)** Leader of the people, i.e. an orator and proposer of motions in the Assembly. The word was often used in a derogatory sense ('demagogue') by critics of the democracy, and only rarely (in a neutral sense) by the champions of democracy or the political leaders themselves.

Demarchos 'Mayor'. Chief magistrate of a deme (*DEMOS* 5), appointed from the members of the deme by election or lot for one year.

Deme *DEMOS* (5).

Demegoria Speech delivered by a *DEMEGOROS*.

***Demegoros* (pl. *-oi*)** Speaker addressing the people (in the Assembly).

Demos People. The word means (1) the entire Athenian people (= the Athenian state), (2) the common people (= the poor), (3) the People's Assembly (= *EKKLESIA*), (4) rule of the people (= *demokratia*), (5) municipality, i.e. one of the 139 demes created by Kleisthenes in 507 and collected into thirty *TRITTYES*, which were again collected into ten *PHYLAI*.

***Demosios* (pl. *-oi*)** Adjective meaning 'public', as opposed to 'private' (*idios*), used as a noun in the masculine to mean public slaves and in the neuter singular (*to demosion*) to mean the treasury.

***Demotes* (pl. *-tai*)** Member of a deme, i.e. an adult male citizen inscribed in one of the 139 demes (*DEMOS* 5).

Demotikon Third part of the full name of an Athenian citizen, indicating his deme (*DEMOS* 5), e.g. Sokrates Sophroniskou Alopekethen ('of the deme Alopeke').

Diacheirotonia Vote by show of hands in two phases. The vote was either for or against a single proposal or a choice between two proposals.

Diadikasia Lawsuit between two or more parties claiming ownership of the same property. *Diadikasia* was used by claimants in inheritance cases, but also in litigation between a citizen and the *POLIS*.

***Diaitetes* (pl. -*tai*)** Arbiter. Most private suits were referred to an arbiter by the Forty (*HOI TETTARAKONTA*) and only submitted to the People's Court if one of the parties was not prepared to accept the verdict of the arbiter. One arbiter was appointed for each case, and arbiters were selected from men on the military rosters in their sixtieth year.

Diapsephismos General revision of the local citizen registers (the *LEXIARCHIKA GRAMMATEIA*) conducted in all the 139 demes, whereby intruders could be expelled and struck off the list, sometimes after a trial before the People's Court.

Dikasterion I Court, especially the People's Court, where most private suits (*DIKAI*) and public prosecutions (*GRAPHAI*) were heard by sections of several hundred jurors (*DIKASTAI*): 201 or 401 jurors in private suits, 501 in most public prosecutions). In addition to hearing civil and criminal cases, the People's Court examined the magistrates, passed judgements in political trials and sometimes reviewed decrees (*PSEPHISMATA*) passed in the Assembly and laws (*NOMOI*) passed by the NOMOTHETAI. The People's Court met about 200 times a year, under the presidency of the magistrates, most frequently the nine ARCHONS.

Dikasterion II A section (of 500 jurors). Some important public prosecutions, specially prosecutions of political leaders, were heard not by 501 jurors (one *dikasterion*) but by 1001 jurors (two *dikasteria*) or 1501 jurors (three *dikasteria*) or even more.

***Dikastes* (pl. -*tai*)** Juror from the PANEL OF 6000, appointed by lot to serve for one day as a member of a *DIKASTERION*.

Dikastikon Payment of 3 OBOLS which a juror received every day he served in a *DIKASTERION*.

***Dike* (pl. -*kai*)** Private suit which could be brought only by the injured party and could always be settled before the verdict. Most *dikai* were first heard before an arbiter (*DIAITETES*), but it was possible to appeal against this verdict to a section of the People's Court manned by 201 or 401 jurors. The man who won the lawsuit was entitled to get his property back, or to monetary compensation, as the case might be; but he received no help from the public authority in the execution of the judgement.

Dike aprostasiou Private suit against a metic for failing to have a *PROSTATES*.

Dike blabes Private suit for damage incurred.

Dike demosia Public prosecution (*GRAPHE*) as opposed to a private suit (*DIKE* or *DIKE IDIA*).

Dike idia Private suit as opposed to a public prosecution (*GRAPHE* or *DIKE DEMOSIA*).

Dike kakegorias Private suit for defamation.

Dike phonou Private suit for homicide brought by the family of the victim and heard by the COUNCIL OF THE AREOPAGOS if the charge was the premeditated killing (or wounding) of an Athenian citizen.

Dionysia Festival of Dionysos. The most spectacular was the Greater Dionysia held in ELAPHEBOLION for Dionysos Eleuthereus, whose shrine was situated on the south slope of the Akropolis. In addition to phallic and other processions, the Greater Dionysia included performances of tragedies, comedies and dithyrambs.

Dokimasia ton adynaton Examination in the COUNCIL OF FIVE HUNDRED of invalids (*adynatoi*) who owned property worth less than 300 DRACHMAS and applied for a daily pension of 1 OBOL (later 2 obols).

Dokimasia ton archon Examination of a candidate for a magistracy (ARCHE) before he entered office. Most candidates were examined solely before a section of the People's Court, but examinations for the COUNCIL OF FIVE HUNDRED and the nine ARCHONS were held first before the Council of Five Hundred and only then before a section of the People's Court.

Dokimasia ton ephebon Examination of new citizens (EPHEBOI) inscribed during the preceding year in the LEXIARCHIKON GRAMMATEION of their deme. The examination was conducted by the COUNCIL OF FIVE HUNDRED and its purpose was to check that the new citizens had reached the age of eighteen.

Dokimasia ton hippon Examination before the COUNCIL OF FIVE HUNDRED of the horses (*hippoi*) of the cavalrymen.

Dokimasia ton rhetoron Public prosecution brought against a citizen who acted as a RHETOR although guilty of a military offence, of maltreatment of his parents, of squandering his patrimony or of male prostitution. The action was initiated in the Assembly by a denunciation (*epangelia*) and referred to the People's Court.

Drachma (pl. -ai) Unit of weight or money: 4.3 g (of silver). It was minted in coins of 1 drachma and 2 and 4 drachmas.

Edoxe (tei boulei kai) toi demoi 'It was decided (by the Council and) by the people'. Enactment formula used in PROBOULEUMATA ratified by the Assembly.

Eisangelia eis ten boulen Denunciation (to the COUNCIL OF FIVE HUNDRED). Public prosecution brought against an official for misconduct in office. The case was tried first before the Council of Five Hundred, which was empowered to impose a fine of up to 500 DRACHMAS. For more serious offences the case was referred to a DIKASTERION. The Assembly was not involved.

Eisangelia eis ton demon Denunciation to the people (in the Assembly). Public prosecution brought against persons charged with treason, attempts to overthrow the democracy or corruption. It was usually initiated by a denunciation made in an EKKLESIA KYRIA which resulted in a decree by which the case was referred to a DIKASTERION. Before *c*.355 the Assembly could itself sit as a court in these cases. *Eisangeliai* were brought especially against the STRATEGOI.

Eisphora Property tax. Originally it was an extraordinary war tax voted by the Assembly according to need; from 347/6 it was (also) an ordinary tax of 10 TALENTS a year. It was paid by both citizens and METICS on the basis of a property census (TIMEMA), but only by the richest citizens, who for this purpose were divided into 100 SYMMORIES.

Ekklesia (pl. -ai) I The People's Assembly, in which all adult male citizens had the right to speak and vote. In the age of Demosthenes it was held forty times a year, usually on the PNYX, and was generally attended by at least 6000 citizens. The Assembly voted by show of hands on the election of magistrates, on treaties with other states and, in domestic policy, on all important individual issues. The Assembly was summoned by the PRYTANEIS and presided over by the PROEDROI, and it could debate only matters which had first been considered by the COUNCIL OF FIVE HUNDRED.

***Ekklesia* II**   Any meeting of the Assembly that was not an *EKKLESIA KYRIA*.

Ekklesia kyria   Principal assembly: the most important and time-consuming session of the Assembly, held once each PRYTANY.

Ekklesiasterion   Meeting-place of an *EKKLESIA*.

***Ekklesiastes* (pl. *-tai*)**   Citizen attending an *EKKLESIA*.

Ekklesiastikon   Payment for participating in the Assembly, introduced in the decade 403–393, increasing quickly from 1 OBOL to 2 to 3 obols (before 393/2) and standing in the 330s at 1 DRACHMA for an *EKKLESIA* (II) and $1\frac{1}{2}$ drachmas for an *EKKLESIA KYRIA*.

Ekklesia synkletos   Session of the Assembly summoned in an extraordinary way, i.e. with fewer than four days' notice or by decree.

Ekphyllophoria   Vote by olive-leaves taken in the COUNCIL OF FIVE HUNDRED on whether or not to expel an unworthy member from the Council.

Elaphebolion   The ninth month of the Attic year, March–April.

Eleutheria   (1) Autonomy. A political ideal cherished by oligarchs and democrats alike. (2) Liberty. A constitutional ideal closely connected with democracy. In the public sphere *eleutheria* was every citizen's right to participate in the running of the state's institutions; in the private sphere it was every citizen's right to live as he pleased without oppression from others (*zen hos bouletai tis*).

***Eleutheros* (pl. *-oi*)**   Adjective meaning 'free' and denoting (1) a free person, as opposed to a slave (*doulos*); (2) a citizen by birth, as opposed to a free foreigner (*XENOS*) or a slave (*doulos*); (3) an autonomous community (as opposed to a dependency).

Eleven, The   *HOI HENDEKA*.

Endeixis   Denunciation (to *HOI HENDEKA* or the *THESMOTHETAI*). Public prosecution brought especially against *ATIMOI* improperly exercising the rights that they had lost through the *ATIMIA*. The denounced person was usually arrested and held in custody until the trial.

Enktesis ges kai oikias   Acquisition of land and house. A privilege which the Assembly could grant METICS, without which they did not have the right to buy and own real property in Attica.

Ephebe (*ephebos*, pl. *-oi*)   Citizens of eighteen and nineteen years, who received their military training during these two years and in the second year served in garrisons throughout Attica.

Ephegesis   Public prosecution, the same as *APAGOGE*, except that the arrest was carried out by the competent magistrate and not by a private citizen.

Ephetai   Fifty-one men, chosen by lot (?) perhaps from the COUNCIL OF THE AREOPAGOS or perhaps from the PANEL OF 6000. They were the jury in all cases of unintentional or lawful homicide and in cases of premeditated homicide of *XENOI* or slaves.

Epibatai   Marines. Soldiers (HOPLITES) serving on board a *TRIERES*.

Epibole   Fine, usually of up to 50 drachmas, which a magistrate was permitted to impose on anyone who did not obey his orders.

Epicheirotonia ton archon   Vote taken in every *EKKLESIA KYRIA* on any magistrate who was suspected of misconduct in office. A vote of censure

(*APOCHEIROTONIA*) resulted in a trial of the magistrate before a *DIKASTERION*.

Epicheirotonia ton nomon A vote by show of hands taken every year by the Assembly during its first session on whether to uphold the law-code or to change one or more of the laws. If a particular law was voted down and singled out for revision, the matter was referred to a panel of *NOMOTHETAI*, who made a choice between the law in force and one or more alternative proposals.

Epikleros 'Heiress'. If a male left at his death no male offspring but only a daughter, his daughter succeeded to the inheritance (i.e. she became an *epikleros*) in the following way: the nearest male relative had the right (and duty) to marry her off, unless he preferred to marry her himself and to administer the inheritance until the son(s) of the marriage came of age and could take over the inheritance.

Epimeletai tes phyles Board of three presidents of the tribe (*PHYLE*), one from each of the tribe's ridings (*TRITTYES*).

Epimeletai ton neorion Superintendents of the Dockyards: a board of ten which supervised the warships and arsenals of the Athenian fleet. The board presided over the People's Court in cases concerning naval administration.

Epimeletes ton krenon Superintendent of the Fountains: a magistrate elected by show of hands and in charge of Athens' water supply.

Epistates ton proedron President of the *PROEDROI*, appointed by lot from the nine *proedroi* to serve for the day as chairman of the COUNCIL OF FIVE HUNDRED and (forty times the year) of the Assembly.

Epistates ton prytaneon President of the *PRYTANEIS*, appointed by lot from the fifty *prytaneis* to serve as president of the Athenian state for twenty-four hours.

***Epitimos* (pl. -oi)** Citizen in full possession of his rights, as opposed to an *ATIMOS*.

Epobelia Court fee of one sixth of the value of the property in dispute (1 OBOL per DRACHMA) to be paid in certain private suits by the plaintiff. It fell to the defendant if he won the case.

Ethnos People, nation. Term used of societies not organized in *POLEIS*, either large kingdoms such as Macedon or the Persian Empire or the 'backward' regions of Greece, e.g. Aitolia.

Euporoi The wealthy as apposed to the poor (*APOROI*).

Euthynai Rendering of accounts. Public prosecution which all officials (magistrates, envoys, liturgists and others) had to undergo on the expiration of their term of office. It comprised first an obligatory examination of the magistrate's accounts, conducted by the *LOGISTAI* presiding over a section of the People's Court. Next, every citizen had the right to accuse a magistrate (before the *EUTHYNOI*) of any abuse of his office. Any charges presented were heard by a section of the People's Court in a new trial.

Euthynoi Committee of ten members of the COUNCIL OF FIVE HUNDRED who received charges against magistrates on the expiration of their term of office. The *euthynoi* presided over the People's Court in the second phase of the *EUTHYNAI*.

Exomosia Declaration under oath that a person had a legitimate excuse (1) to decline election or (2) to refuse to be a witness.

Forty, the *HOI TETTARAKONTA*.

General *STRATEGOS*.

Genos Clan, i.e. a group of persons claiming descent (in the male line) from a common ancestor. A smaller group than the PHRATRY, of which it formed a part. The members of a *genos* were united in common cults and religious ceremonies.

Gerousia Council of elders, senate. The most famous *gerousia* was the Spartan, composed of twenty-eight Spartiates over sixty and the two kings.

***Grammateus* (pl. *-eis*)** Secretary to a magistrate or a board of magistrates. Occasionally the secretary was himself a magistrate, i.e. a citizen chosen by election or lot to serve for one year. In most cases, however, a *grammateus* was only a paid official, often a slave, appointed by the magistrates themselves.

Grammateus epi ta psephismata Decree secretary: secretary assisting the COUNCIL OF FIVE HUNDRED by taking minutes and making copies of the decrees (*PSEPHISMATA*) that came before the Council.

Grammateus epi tous nomous Legislation secretary: secretary assisting the COUNCIL OF FIVE HUNDRED by taking minutes and making copies of the legislative proposals (*NOMOI*) that came before the Council.

***Grammateus kata prytaneian* (or *grammateus tes boules*)** Secretary of the COUNCIL OF FIVE HUNDRED, responsible for recording, publishing and filing all resolutions passed by the Assembly or the Council or the NOMOTHETAI.

***Grammateus* (*tei boulei kai demoi*)** Secretary of (the Council and) the people: the official who read out all documents to the Assembly and the Council.

***Graphe* I** Public prosecution which any citizen (*HO BOULOMENOS*) could bring in the name of the people. The case was heard by a section of the People's Court, usually manned with 501 jurors (*DIKASTAI*). If the prosecutor withdrew the charge before the trial or received less than one fifth of the votes, he was fined 1000 DRACHMAS and incurred a partial *ATIMIA* (loss of rights). The magistrates were responsible for carrying out the sentence. There were more than fifty different types of *graphe*.

***Graphe* II** The plaintiff's written charge in a private suit or a public prosecution.

Graphe doron Public prosecution for bribery.

Graphe epistatike Public prosecution of the EPISTATES TON PRYTANEON or the EPISTATES TON PROEDRON.

Graphe hybreos Public prosecution for battery, violence, slander, etc.; used if the element of self-indulgence and disregard for others was a prominent feature of the criminal act. Without this element the proper action was a private suit either for battery or violence (*dike aikias*) or for slander (*DIKE KAKEGORIAS*).

Graphe lipotaxiou Public prosecution for not obeying the general's orders or for desertion from the army.

Graphe nomon me epitedeion theinai Public prosecution of a RHETOR who had proposed a NOMOS that was contrary to the laws in force and/or inexpedient. The action was initiated by *HO BOULOMENOS* either before or after the NOMO-THETAI had passed the bill. The case was heard by a section of the People's Court. If convicted, the proposer was punished and the law annulled.

Graphe paranomon Public prosecution of a RHETOR who had proposed a PSEPHISMA of the Council or the Assembly that was contrary to the laws in force and/or inexpedient. The action was initiated by *HO BOULOMENOS* either before or after the *psephisma* had been passed. The *psephisma* was suspended until the case had been heard by the People's Court. If convicted, the proposer was punished and the *psephisma* annulled.

Graphe proedrike Public prosecution of a PROEDROS or of the whole board of *proedroi*.

Graphe sykophantias Public prosecution brought against a SYCOPHANT.

Graphe xenias Public prosecution (1) of a foreigner or a slave who had been falsely inscribed in a deme register as an Athenian citizen, or (2) of a person who had married off a non-Athenian women in his care to an Athenian citizen.

Guardians of the Naval Yards PHROUROI.

Gymnasiarchia A LITURGY in which the liturgist had to meet from his own resources the expense of athletic competitions held at the PANATHENAIA or at the festival of Hephaistos and Prometheus. He was then known as *gymnasiarchos*.

Gymnasion (pl. -ia) Sports grounds outside the city walls. Public institutions open to all citizens. Athens had three *gymnasia*: The Lykeion, the Academy and the Kynosarges, each supervised by a magistrate called the *epistates*.

Harpalos affair, the Bribery scandal in 325/4, caused when Harpalos, the treasurer of Alexander the Great, fled to Athens and tried to bribe the political leaders to obtain asylum for him. The affair resulted in a series of public prosecutions (APOPHASEIS), including one brought against Demosthenes.

Hegemonia dikasteriou The right of a magistrate to preside over a section of the People's Court in cases which fell within his sphere of authority.

Hekatombaion The first month of the Attic year, approximately corresponding to July.

Hektemoroi Small landholders before the age of Solon who had to pay a sixth of the annual produce to their overlords and could be sold as slaves if they defaulted.

Heliaia (1) Solon's term for the People's Court, in the fourth century used synonymously with DIKASTERION. (2) The building where the largest juries (of 1001, 1501 or more DIKASTAI) met to hear important political prosecutions. Not yet located by excavation.

Heliastic Oath Oath which all who served on the PANEL OF 6000 JURORS had to swear at the beginning of the year on the Ardettos hill (which lay south of Athens). By the oath the jurors were bound to give their verdict according to the existing laws and decrees or, if there was no law, to act in accordance with their sense of what was most just.

Hellenotamiai Board of ten, later twenty, treasurers of the DELIAN LEAGUE who in the fifth-century supervised the tribute which the members of the League had to pay to Athens.

Hemerai aphesimoi Holidays for the organs of government, especially the COUNCIL OF FIVE HUNDRED.

Hemerai apophrades 'Taboo days', i.e. 25 THARGELION, when the Plynteria were celebrated, and all the days on which the COUNCIL OF THE AREOPAGOS met to judge homicide cases. The Athenians probably refrained from holding political meetings on these days.

He proedreuousa phyle The presiding tribe, i.e. all members of one PHYLE who attended a session of the Assembly and during the meeting were responsible for the maintenance of order. The *phylai* took turns and the presiding *phyle* was selected by lot.

Herald KERYX.

Hetaireia Society or club of HETAIROI, in the fifth century often of political nature and oligarchic in its views.

Hetairikon = HETAIREIA.

Hetairos (pl. -oi) Comrade, member of a HETAIREIA.

Hiereis Priests, who pronounced prayers, made sacrifices and supervised the rites: distinct from the EPISTATAI, EPIMELETAI and other magistrates who administered the sanctuaries and organized religious festivals. A priest(ess) served a particular deity (e.g. Zeus, Artemis) at a particular shrine. The office was, in some cases, hereditary, but often the *hiereis* were appointed by lot. However, they were never magistrates, nor an integrated part of the state administration, which is why priestesses were allowed.

Hieropoioi Eleusini Committee of ten of the COUNCIL OF FIVE HUNDRED all belonging to the same PHYLE, who assisted in organizing the MYSTERIES held in BOEDROMION.

Hippeis Knights. (1) Members of the second Solonian property class, who produced between 300 and 500 measures of corn, wine and olives a year. (2) Cavalrymen who served in the Athenian cavalry, a force of 1000 men.

Ho boulomenos The volunteer. In political contexts *ho boulomenos* denoted a citizen who took a political initiative: by proposing a decree or a law, by acting as prosecutor or SYNEGOROS in a public action, or by volunteering in the election or sortition of magistrates, envoys and other officials.

Ho epi tei dioikesei Financial administrator. Magistrate elected for a four-year period to superintend the financial administration of Athens. The office was probably introduced in 338, possibly first as an extraordinary magistracy held by Lykourgos.

Hoi epi to theorikon Board for the Theoric Fund. A board whose members were elected for a four-year period. The board was created to administer the theoric payments (THEORIKA), but in the middle of the fourth-century it was the most important board in the financial administration.

Hoi gnorimoi Aristotelian term denoting upper-class citizens, often contrasted with *ho* DEMOS, 'the common people'.

Hoi hendeka Board of eleven men. Magistrates who supervised the prison, carried out sentences in public prosecutions and were responsible for the execution without trial of KAKOURGOI and other criminals.

Hoi omomokotes PANEL OF 6000 JURORS.

Hoi polloi The many, or the majority. A term used synonymously with DEMOS (2) and PLETHOS (2) for the common people who were the majority in the political assemblies.

Hoi tettarakonta Board of forty magistrates who worked in groups of four, one group for each PHYLE. Each group instituted proceedings and presided over the People's Court. The Forty presided in most private suits. Cases with a penalty of less than 10 DRACHMAS were decided by the Forty on their own authority, without appointing an arbiter or convening the People's Court.

Hoplite Foot soldier armed with helmet, shield, greaves and sometimes cuirass (defensive weapons = *hopla*), and with the offensive weapons of spear and short sword.

Horos (pl. -*oi*) Boundary pillar.

Hypogrammateus (pl. -*eis*) Under-secretary, not a magistrate but always a paid official. See GRAMMATEUS.

Hypomosia Sworn objection lodged (1) against a decree (PSEPHISMA), asserting that it was unconstitutional and should be referred to the People's Court under a GRAPHE PARANOMON or (2) against the assessment by the PROEDROI of a vote by show of hands, demanding that the vote be repeated.

Idios Adjective meaning 'private', as opposed to *koinos* or *demosios*, 'public'.

Idiotes (pl. -*tai*) Private citizen. (1) In contrast to POLITEUOMENOS it denoted a citizen who (in accordance with the democratic ideals) participated only occasionally in public affairs, by moving a proposal, initiating a public prosecution, standing for a magistracy, etc. (2) Also, a citizen who (contrary to the democratic ideals) shunned any form of political activity.

Isegoria Equal right of speech. The right of every citizen to speak and move proposals in the political assemblies.

Isonomia The principle of political equality. *Isonomia* does not mean equality before the law, but the equal right of all citizens to exercise their political rights.

Isoteles (pl. -*eis*) A METIC who enjoyed the privilege of *isoteleia*: he was exempted from the tax on metics (METOIKION) and, in time of war, was probably brigaded with the Athenian citizens and not with the metics.

Juror DIKASTES.

Jurors' oath HELIASTIC OATH.

Juror's ticket (*pinakion*) Bronze plaque, about 11 x 2 x 0.2 cm in size, stamped with the state symbol (an owl) and inscribed with the full name of a citizen. A ticket was distributed at the beginning of the year to every one who served on the PANEL OF 6000 JURORS, and was used in the daily allotment of jurors in the People's Court. At the end of the year the 6000 surrendered their tickets but could stand again for selection for the next year's panel. See PINAKION for the wider application of the same term.

Kakourgos (pl. -*oi*) 'Felon'. Category of criminals, especially thieves, robbers, burglars, brigands, etc., but also including adulterers, some types of murderer and others. The Eleven (HOI HENDEKA) were empowered to execute such men without trial if they were caught in the act and confessed.

Kaloikagathoi 'Gentlemen'. Term denoting the noble, honourable, well-educated and often wealthy citizens as opposed to the common people.

Katacheirotonia (1) Condemnation by show of hands in the Assembly when a political trial was heard by the EKKLESIA instead of being referred to a DIKASTERION. (2) Preliminary verdict of guilty passed in the Assembly in response to a PROBOLE.

Katagnosis Preliminary vote (1) of the COUNCIL OF FIVE HUNDRED in an EISANGELIA EIS TEN BOULEN, (2) of the COUNCIL OF THE AREOPAGOS in an APOPHASIS.

Katalogeis Board of ten magistrates responsible for keeping the register of citizens serving in the cavalry.

***Keryx* (pl. *Kerykes*)** Crier. The most important crier in Athens was the *keryx tes boules*, the crier of the COUNCIL OF FIVE HUNDRED, who opened and closed meetings of the Council and the Assembly and called orators to the Speakers' platform (*BEMA*).

King archon *BASILEUS* (2).

Klepsydra Water-clock, used in the People's Court to time litigants' speeches.

***Kleroterion* (pl. *-ia*)** A *STELE* of marble used in the annual allotment of magistrates and in the daily allotment of jurors. A *kleroterion* had vertical columns of slots to hold the *PINAKIA* when inserted. Beside the *kleroterion* ran a narrow tube into which was put the white and black balls used in the sortition.

***Klerouchia* (pl. *-ai*)** Emigré community sent from Athens whose settlers (*KLEROUCHOI*) and their descendants retained their Athenian citizenship. The *klerouchiai* were independent only in local affairs; in foreign and military policy they were governed by Athens.

Klerouchoi Members of a *KLEROUCHIA*, usually selected from the poor citizens.

Klope Theft, which for the Athenians included what we used to call embezzlement.

Kosmetes Magistrate responsible for the training of the EPHEBES, elected for one year by the Assembly.

***Krisis* (pl. *-seis*)** Sentence passed by a *DIKASTERION*, in political actions before *c.*355 sometimes by the Assembly.

Kyrios Master. An adjective which was often used as a noun. As an adjective it had two meanings: (1) empowered, competent; (2) sovereign. As a noun it also had two meanings: (1) guardian of a minor or a woman; (2) owner of a slave.

Law *NOMOS*.

***Lexiarchikon grammateion* (pl. *lexiarchika grammateia*)** Register of all citizens above eighteen, compiled and kept locally in each of the 139 demes.

Lexiarchoi Board of six men who ensured that only citizens participated in the Assembly. Probably replaced in the fourth century by the *SYLLOGEIS TOU DEMOU*.

Lexica Word-lists, compiled in late antiquity or in the Byzantine period, arranged alphabetically, with explanations of difficult words and technical terms from classical literature. The best known are the lexica of Harpokration, Hesychios and Photios, and the *Suda* and the *Etymologicum Magnum*.

Liturgy (*leitourgia*) Public service for the state. Some state expenditures were met not from the state revenues but by requiring a rich man as a civic duty to defray the expenses in question for one year. There were three categories of liturgies: festival liturgies (*CHOREGIA* and *GYMNASIARCHIA*), naval liturgies (*TRIERARCHIA*) and liturgies connected with the property tax (*PROEISPHORA*).

Lochagoi Leaders of *lochoi* (companies) in the army appointed by officers who were magistrates elected by the people.

Logistai (1) Board of magistrates composed of one man from each of the PHYLAI and selected by lot. The *logistai* were auditors who supervised the examination of the magistrates' accounts at the end of the year, and brought them before the People's Court. (2) Committee of ten of the COUNCIL OF FIVE HUNDRED which,

PRYTANY by prytany, inspected the administration of public funds by the magistrates.

Logographos (pl. -oi) Speech-writer. A person who composed forensic speeches for pay, writing to order for people who had to conduct lawsuits before the courts.

Medimnos (pl. -oi) Dry measure of 52 litres by which corn was measured.

Merismos Distribution of the state revenues to the boards of magistrates so that every board had a fixed amount at its disposal. It was regulated by law (*NOMOS*) and supervised by the COUNCIL OF FIVE HUNDRED in collaboration with the *APODEKTAI*.

Mesogeios Inland. One of the three regions (*ASTY, PARALIA* and *MESOGEIOS*) into which Attica was divided by the reforms of Kleisthenes.

Metic (*metoikos*, pl. -oi) When he had been living in Attica for more than one (?) month, a foreigner (*XENOS*) was obliged to find a patron (*PROSTATES*) and with his help to register as a metic and to pay the metic tax (*METOIKION*). Furthermore, after manumission every freed slave held the status of a metic with his former master as his *prostates*. A metic was thus a free foreigner who lived and worked in Attica. He enjoyed legal protection, but had to pay taxes, and perform military service, and had no political rights.

Metoikion METIC tax of 12 DRACHMAS a year for a man and 6 for a woman.

Metra Measures. Dry measures (*MEDIMNOI*) and wet measures (*METRETAI*).

Metretes (pl. -tai) Wet measure of 39 litres in which wine and olive oil were measured.

Metroön Shrine of the Mother, i.e. of Demeter, which lay on the west side of the AGORA, in front of the BOULEUTERION and was used in the fourth century as the state archive.

Metroxenos (pl. -oi) Person whose father was citizen but his mother not. A *metroxenos* was accepted as an Athenian citizen before the introduction in 451 of Perikles' citizenship law.

Mina (*mna* pl. -ai) Unit of weight and money = 100 DRACHMAS = 435 g (of silver).

Misthos Wage paid to a day labourer or a soldier. In political contexts: allowance for those who participated in political meetings. *Misthos* was paid to members of the COUNCIL OF FIVE HUNDRED (5 OBOLS per man per session), the People's Court (3 obols per man per session), the Assembly (1 or $1\frac{1}{2}$ DRACHMAS per man per session) and to some magistrates (especially the nine ARCHONS and magistrates serving abroad).

Monument to the Eponymous Heroes Stone base with bronze statues of the ten heroes of the PHYLAI. Around the base was a fence, on which were posted official documents of all sorts. The Monument stood in the AGORA, before BOULEUTERION and the METROÖN.

Mysteries, the Festival of Demeter and Persephone, celebrated in Athens and Eleusis in the month of BOEDROMION, and restricted to those who had been, or wished to be, initiated into the Mysteries (with no distinction drawn between citizens, foreigners and slaves). The rites were secret, and the secret was so well kept that today we know almost nothing of the details of the Mysteries.

***Naukraria* (pl. -*ai*)**   In the archaic period Athens was subdivided into forty-eight *naukrariai*, twelve for each of the four tribes (*PHYLAI*). Since the tribes were not districts of Attica but organizations of persons, their subdivisions can hardly have been territorial units. Furthermore, the alleged connection between the *naukrariai* and the Attic fleet (*naus* = 'ship') is based on a few lexicographical notes only and has no support in good sources.

Nomophylakes   Board of seven or eleven magistrates allegedly introduced by Ephialtes but not attested until the 320s. The name of the board, 'Guardians of the Laws', reveals that the board must have been entrusted with the protection of the law-code and the observance of the laws, but nothing more can be inferred from the scanty references.

***Nomos* (pl. -*oi*)**   Law. General enactment, intended to be valid for all time, and in the fourth century passed by the *NOMOTHETAI*. A *PSEPHISMA*, by contrast, was an enactment passed by the Assembly, specific in scope and/or applied for a limited period only. The distinction between *NOMOS* and *PSEPHISMA* was introduced in 403/2 in connection with the recodification of the laws of Drakon and Solon.

Nomothetai   Legislative commission, consisting of, for example, 1000 citizens who had been selected by lot from the *PANEL OF 6000 JURORS*. Like the *DIKASTAI* they served for one day only. They listened to a debate on the proposal for a law, and then voted on it by show of hands.

Obol (*obolos*)   Unit of weight and money = 1/6 *DRACHMA* = 0.7 g (of silver). Minted in coins of 1 obol and 2 and 3 obols and in fractions down to 1/8 obol, which was (later) struck in bronze.

Ochlos   Mob or crowd, a word used synonymously with *DEMOS* (2) by the critics of democracy.

***Oiketes* (pl. -*tai*)**   Alongside *doulos* the most common word for a slave, designating specifically a household slave.

Oligarchia   Oligarchy, rule of the few. A form of constitution in which full citizen rights are restricted to the rich through a property census (*TIMEMA*). Power is exercised either by a council and/or by magistrates elected by and from the wealthy. An assembly of the people is either powerless or non-existent, and administration of justice is left to the magistrates.

Ostrakismos   Vote with potsherds (*ostraka*) for the expulsion of a political leader. The procedure was introduced by Kleisthenes *c*.507, and was often used in the period 487–416, but never in the fourth century. If, in the *EKKLESIA KYRIA* of the sixth *PRYTANY*, the people decreed that an ostracism should be held, a day was fixed on which all citizens could assemble in the *AGORA* and vote with potsherds which political leader should go into exile for ten years. The purpose was to avoid rivalry between two leaders which might jeopardize the stability of the state. Every citizen who took part submitted a sherd on which was scratched the name of the person he wished to see exiled. If at least 6000 sherds were cast, the person whose name appeared on most sherds had to go into exile, but he did not incur loss of honour (*ATIMIA*) or confiscation of his property.

Panathenaia   Festival of the goddess Athena, celebrated in the days around her birthday on 28 *HEKATOMBAION*. Athena was honoured with a grand procession and extensive athletic competitions. The Athenians distinguished between the

Great Panathenaia, held every four years, and the Lesser Panathenaia, celebrated in the other three years.

Panel of 6000 Jurors (*hoi omomokotes*) 6000 citizens over thirty, selected by lot from those who applied for one year. Each of the 6000 took the HELIASTIC OATH, was equipped with a JUROR'S TICKET, and had the right to participate in daily allotment of jurors in the DIKASTERIA and the selection of NOMOTHETAI for the boards of legislators.

Paragraphe Formal objection lodged by the defendant in a DIKE, maintaining that the suit was inadmissible because it had already been settled, was brought before the wrong magistrate, or the like. The *paragraphe* was heard separately by a section of the People's Court, which decided whether the original private suit should proceed or be dismissed.

Parakatabole Court fee paid by the plaintiff in a DIADIKASIA.

Paralia Coastal region. One of the three regions (ASTY, PARALIA and MESOGEIOS) into which Attica was divided by the reforms of Kleisthenes.

Parastasis Court fee (1) paid by the prosecutor in a public prosecution; (2) paid by both parties in a private suit to the arbiter who heard the case.

Paredroi (1) assistants of the ARCHON, the BASILEUS and the POLEMARCHOS, two for each. (2) Committee of twenty BOULEUTAI, two from each PHYLE, assisting the EUTHYNOI who were in charge of the second phase of the EUTHYNAI.

Parrhesia Freedom of speech. Every citizen's right to speak his mind in public, both in the political assemblies and in all other fora for public debate.

Patrios politeia Ancestral constitution, i.e. the constitution (monarchy, oligarchy or democracy) under which one's ancestors had supposedly lived. The *patrios politeia* was always portrayed as admirable and in fourth-century Athens it was conceived as a form of original democracy, allegedly introduced by either Solon or Theseus.

Patronymikon Father's name. Second part of the full name of an Athenian citizen, e.g. Sokrates Sophroniskou (= son of Sophroniskos) Alopekethen.

Peltast Light-armed foot soldier, equipped with javelin and a small round shield (*pelte*).

Pentakosiomedimnoi Citizens who produced more than 500 measures (METRA) of corn wine and olives and thus belonged to the first Solonian property class (TELOS).

People's Court DIKASTERION.

Phasis Type of public prosecution used especially for violations of the laws concerning trade, import and export. Usually the action was initiated by the confiscation of some goods pointed out by the prosecutor. The case was brought before a section of the People's Court and, if successful, the prosecutor received a third of the confiscated goods.

Phoros Tribute paid to Athens by those members of the DELIAN LEAGUE who paid in money instead of furnishing triremes (TRIEREIS). The rate seems to have been one TALENT per trireme. In the age of Perikles all but three of the allies had given up sending ships and paid the *phoros* instead.

Phratry (*phratria*, pl. -*ai*) Brotherhood. Association whose members, all Athenian citizens, regarded themselves as (distantly) related to each other. The members of a phratry were united in the cult of Zeus Phratrios, Athena Phratria, Zeus

Herkeios and Apollo Patroös. Before the reforms of Kleisthenes membership of a phratry was probably the criterion that entitled a man to Athenian citizenship, and this requirement seems to have been maintained throughout the classical period, although citizenship was now linked with the demes as well as with the phratries. There must have been at least a hundred phratries altogether, perhaps even more, and the distribution of Athenians into phratries cut across their distribution into PHYLAI, TRITTYES and demes (*DEMOS* 5).

Phrouroi   The 500 Guardians of the Naval Yards, selected by lot in the 139 demes. They must have been watchmen and cannot have been magistrates (*ARCHAI*) in the technical sense.

Phylarchos (pl. -oi)   Commander of the cavalry furnished by each of the ten tribes (PHYLAI).

Phyle (pl. -lai)   Tribe. A subdivision of Attica and of the Athenian citizen body. Before Kleisthenes the Athenians were divided into four *phylai*, each of which was presided over by a *PHYLOBASILEUS*. By the reforms of Kleisthenes Attica was divided into ten *phylai*. Each *phyle* consisted of three geographically distinct ridings (*TRITTYES*), one from the city region (*ASTY*), one from the coastal region (*PARALIA*) and one from the inland region (*MESOGEIOS*). All citizens belonging to the same *phyle* served in the same regiment (*TAXIS*) and served together as PRYTANEIS in the COUNCIL OF FIVE HUNDRED. Each *phyle* was presided over by three elected *EPIMELETAI TES PHYLES*, one from each of the ridings.

Phylobasileus (pl. -eis)   King of a tribe. The leader of one of the four Solonian PHYLAI. In the fourth century his only duties were to perform some ancestral sacrifices and, in the PRYTANEION, to pass sentence in cases of homicide caused by animals or inanimate objects.

Pinakion (pl. -ia)   Bronze plaque inscribed with the full name of a citizen above thirty. Some were stamped with an owl and used in the daily sortition of jurors (see JUROR'S TICKET). Others were stamped with a Gorgon's head and used in the annual sortition of magistrates. Some carried both stamps and could be used for both purposes.

Pinax ekklesiastikos   Register of all citizens who had the right to attend the Assembly. It was compiled and kept locally in each of the 139 demes.

Plousioi   The wealthy as opposed to the poor (*penetes*).

Plethos   The multitude. A term denoting the common people and used synonymously with *DEMOS* (2).

Pnyx   Hill on which the Assembly held most of its meetings in the classical period. It lay about 400 m south-west of the AGORA.

Polemarchos   The Polemarch, one of the nine ARCHONS. He presided over the People's Court in private suits (*DIKAI*) if one of the litigants was a METIC.

Poletai   Board of magistrates composed of one man from each of the ten PHYLAI and selected by lot. The board superintended the auctions in which were leased public and sacred land or concessions to work the silver-mines or the right to collect taxes (*TELE*). The *poletai* also sold confiscated property.

Polis (pl. -leis)   (1) City. (2) City-state. The typical *polis* had a territory of less than 100 sq. km and a citizen population of fewer than 1000 adult males. In addition to the citizens (*POLITAI*) a *polis* was populated by free foreigners (*XENOI*, in some *poleis* called METICS) and slaves (*douloi*). Foreigners and slaves lived in the *polis* but were not members of it. The *polis* usually comprised a city and its hinterland. The city was the political, religious, economic and military centre, even if most of the citizens lived on the land, outside the city walls.

Politeia (1) The political structure of a POLIS, its constitution. (2) Citizenship. (3) The whole citizen body.

Polites (pl. -tai) Citizen. Usually the adult male full citizen, but the term was also used in a wider sense of the wives and children of citizens. After Perikles' citizenship law of 451, an Athenian citizen was a person whose parents were married and were both citizens. In exceptional circumstances a foreigner could become a citizen by a decree (PSEPHISMA) passed by the Assembly.

Politeuomenos (pl. -oi) Politically active citizen, i.e. a citizen who regularly acts as HO BOULOMENOS by addressing the political assemblies, by moving proposals, by bringing public prosecutions and by being a candidate when officials are elected or selected by lot.

Praktores Board of magistrates who kept lists of all debtors to the state and who may have participated in collecting the debts.

Presbeus (pl. -eis) Envoy. Not an ambassador sent out permanently to another POLIS, but a citizen elected *ad hoc* in the Assembly or occasionally in the Council to undertake a specific diplomatic mission. Envoys were usually sent out in groups of three, five or ten *presbeis*. After their mission they had to undergo EUTHYNAI.

Private suit DIKE.

Probole (pl. -lai) Public prosecution against (1) persons who committed a crime during or in connection with a religious festival; (2) citizens and METICS who acted as SYCOPHANTS. The case was judged by the People's Court, but the procedure was initiated in the Assembly by a denunciation. The denunciator asked the people to pronounce a preliminary verdict of guilty (KATACHEIROTONIA). The Assembly's vote was only advisory and did not bind the People's Court.

Probouleuma (pl. -ata) (Preliminary) decree of the COUNCIL OF FIVE HUN-DRED, which was placed before the Assembly for debate and/or ratification. Historians use the term 'open *probouleuma*' for a simple instruction to the Assembly to debate an issue and, if necessary, to pass a decree moved from the floor. A 'specific *probouleuma*' was a detailed proposal worked out by the Council and placed before the people for ratification (sometimes with amendments). If rejected in the Assembly, a specific *probouleuma* could be replaced by a proposal moved from the floor.

Probouleusis Technical term used by modern historians to describe the procedure by which an issue debated in the Assembly was prepared by a PROBOULE-UMA passed by the COUNCIL OF FIVE HUNDRED.

Probouloi (1) An (oligarchic) board of magistrates preparing business for a decision-making organ of government. (2) A board of ten *probouloi* was introduced in Athens in 413 but was probably discontinued in the autumn of 411.

Procheirotonia Initial vote (by show of hands) in the Assembly on whether to ratify or to debate a (specific) PROBOULEUMA. Ratification probably depended on unanimity or at least *nem. con.*, so that debate on a *probouleuma* took place if only one hand was raised against it.

Proedroi Committee of nine of the COUNCIL OF FIVE HUNDRED, selected by lot for one day from the 450 councillors who were not PRYTANEIS. *Proedroi* were introduced in 403/2 or shortly after, and their only function was to preside over meetings of the Council and the Assembly.

Proeispherontes Citizens appointed to perform the PROEISPHORA. They were selected from a panel composed of the 300 most wealthy citizens.

Proeisphora Advance payment of property tax (EISPHORA), a liturgy imposed on the PROEISPHERONTES. The 1200 richest citizens were organized in SYMMORIES and in each of the symmories the most wealthy members were required to pay the tax immediately and then to reimburse themselves later from the other members.

Proklesis Call upon the opposing party in a lawsuit to produce evidence for something or permit the demandant to produce it. A *proklesis* was a necessary condition for having a BASANOS conducted or for presenting an oath as evidence.

Prosklesis Summons to appear before the competent magistrate on an agreed day, issued by the plaintiff (in a DIKE) or by the prosecutor (in a GRAPHE [I]) in the presence of two witnesses.

Prostates Patron. When a foreigner had to become a METIC he was required to choose a citizen as his *prostates* and with his help to be registered in his deme. The relationship between the metic and his *prostates* was permanent, but it is unclear what the *prostates* did for the metic apart from sponsor the registration.

Proxenia A privilege which the Athenian people by decree bestowed on foreigners. By becoming the PROXENOS of the Athenians the foreigner was expected to assist Athenians who visited his city. *Proxenia* could also be bestowed on METICS who had helped Athenians, e.g. by bringing grain to Attica during a famine, but in this case becoming a *proxenos* was a honorific title rather than a privilege. Conversely, another POLIS could bestow *proxenia* on an Athenian and thereby entrust him with helping its citizens when they visited Athens.

Proxenos (pl. -oi) Public guest-friend. A person who in his own city assisted citizens from another city that had appointed him the *proxenos* of its citizens.

Prytaneia Court fee paid by both parties in a DIKE. The litigant who lost the case had to reimburse his opponent his *prytaneia*.

Prytaneion Archaic town hall of Athens located east of the Akropolis. In the *prytaneion* was the public hearth with its ever-burning fire as well as the reception room in which the state's guests were invited to dine with the ARCHONS, Athenian victors in the Olympic games, the descendants of Harmodios and Aristogeiton, and other prominent citizens.

Prytaneis Presiding officers. Fifty councillors belonging to the same PHYLE, i.e. the tribe's contingent in the COUNCIL OF FIVE HUNDRED. Each of the ten groups of *prytaneis* served for one tenth of the year (one PRYTANY) as the executive committee of the Council and the Assembly. The *prytaneis* met and dined together in the THOLOS, and one third of them was always on duty in the Tholos. The *prytaneis* convened the Council and the Assembly and worked out their agenda. In the fifth century they also presided over meetings of the Assembly and the Council, but about 403/2 the PROEDROI took over this duty.

Prytaneis ton naukraron Presidents of the forty-eight NAUKRARIAI.

Prytanikon The office of the fifty PRYTANEIS, i.e. the THOLOS.

Prytany A tenth of the year (in normal years thirty-six or thirty-five days, in leap years thirty-nine or thirty-eight), in which the PRYTANEIS of a PHYLE acted as executive committee of the COUNCIL OF FIVE HUNDRED. A prytany was thus longer than a month, which had twenty-nine or thirty days.

Psephisma (pl. -ata) Decree passed by the Assembly or, in routine business only, by the Council. From 403/2 a *psephisma* was always an enactment specific in scope and/or of limited duration, in contrast to a law (NOMOS), which was a general rule intended to be valid for all time.

Psephophoria Voting with PSEPHOI.

Psephos (pl. -oi) Originally a pebble and, in the fourth century, a small bronze disk, used for voting in the People's Court and in the Assembly when a vote required a quorum of 6000.

Psiloi Light-armed soldiers such as archers or slingers.

Public prosecution GRAPHE I.

Rhetor (pl. -res) Orator. In political contexts a citizen who acts as speaker or proposer before the decision-making organs of government (the Assembly, the Council and the NOMOTHETAI) or as prosecutor or SYNEGOROS before the People's Court.

Riding TRITTYS.

Scholion (pl. -ia) Commentary from the Hellenistic, Roman or Byzantine period on unusual words and phrases in the classical authors. In antiquity the commentaries were often published separately, while in the Middle Ages they were written in the margins of the manuscripts.

Scythian archers Band of 300 public slaves whose duties included the maintenance of law and order in the Assembly. They were armed with bows and were accordingly called 'the bowmen' (TOXOTAI) as well as 'the Scythians' (*hoi Skythoi*). The band seems to have been dissolved before the middle of the fourth century.

Second Athenian Naval Confederacy Defensive alliance of states under Athens' leadership, founded in 378/7 and originally directed against Spartan imperialism. It soon lost its significance, because four leading states seceded in the Social War (357–355). It was dissolved by the peace of 338 between Athens and Philip II of Macedon.

Seisachtheia Shaking-off of the burden. The Athenians' name for Solon's cancellation of the obligations of the HEKTEMOROI towards their overlords.

Skepsis Objection, more specifically an objection raised by a liturgist who claimed to be exempted from undertaking a LITURGY.

Skolion (pl. -ia) Drinking-song performed at a SYMPOSION. The singer held a myrtle-branch and, after his song, passed it on to the guest who had to sing the next song.

Sophist Itinerant teacher. For a fee he taught rhetoric, ethics, politics and often one or more specialist topics (e.g. mathematics).

Sophronistai Moderators. Board of ten magistrates, one from each tribe, elected by the Assembly from citizens above forty. In collaboration with the KOSMETES the *sophronistai* had to supervise the training of the EPHEBES.

Stasis (1) Civil war. (2) Faction, i.e. a political group which by any means – even civil war or revolution – intended to overthrow the constitution.

Stele (pl. -lai) Stone slab, sometimes of marble and often with an inscription, which may be either private (a funerary inscription, a dedication to a deity, a notice of mortgaged land, etc.) or public (a law, a decree, records of a board of magistrates, lists of officials, etc).

Stoa Basileios The administrative office of the BASILEUS; also the meeting-place of the COUNCIL OF THE AREOPAGOS, when it did not meet (on the Areopagos) to hear homicide cases. It lay in the north-western corner of the AGORA.

Strategos (pl. -oi) General. The *strategoi* were a board of ten, appointed by election for one year, with no restrictions on re-election. They were the commanders-in-chief of the army and navy, with extensive authority in the field. In Athens they worked with the COUNCIL OF FIVE HUNDRED and presided over the People's Court in all cases concerning military duties and offences.

Sycophant (sykophantes) Person who gained profit from his political rights. (1) He misused his citizen's right to bring a public prosecution by blackmailing those he prosecuted or threatened to prosecute. (2) He received pay for proposing a decree (PSEPHISMA) which a political leader was unwilling to put forward in his own name.

Syllogeis tou demou Committee of thirty members of the COUNCIL OF FIVE HUNDRED, three from each tribe, responsible before the opening of an Assembly for handing out SYMBOLA to the participants and ensuring that only citizens were admitted.

Symbolon (pl. -la) Token, e.g. a leaden (?) token handed out by the SYLLOGEIS TOU DEMOU to citizens who attended a session of the Assembly. It was handed back after the session in exchange for pay for attendance.

Symboulos (pl. -oi) (1) Adviser. (2) Politically, a citizen who spoke and made proposals in the Assembly.

Symmory (symmoria, pl. -ai) Group of wealthy citizens who shared the obligation to pay EISPHORA or to perform a liturgy, either the PROEISPHORA or the TRIERARCHY. The symmories were introduced in 378/7 in connection with a reform of the *eisphora*: in each symmory the most wealthy members were required to pay the symmory's share of the *eisphora* in advance and later to reimburse themselves from the other members. In about 358/7 the symmory system was extended to the trierarchy: ships were assigned no longer to individual trierarchs or pair of trierarchs, but to whole symmories, whose leaders distributed the burden among the members. A total of some 1200 citizens were members (SYMMORITAI) of the symmories. For payment of *eisphora* they were organized in 100 symmories with some fifteen men per symmory, and for performance of the trierarchy they were organized in twenty symmories with some sixty men per symmory.

Symmorites (pl. -tai) A member of a SYMMORY.

Symposion Male gathering of equals, often friends or HETAIROI, usually upper-class. The *symposion* took place after dinner and could last all night; it was essentially a drinking-party accompanied by all sorts of entertainment, such as songs (SKOLIA), speeches, games, dancing and music.

Synegoros (pl. -oi) Advocate. Friend or relative (supposedly) of a prosecutor or defendant who, with the jurors' approval, acted as counsel and shared the time allotted for speaking with the litigant whom he supported.

Syntaxis The contribution which the members of the SECOND ATHENIAN NAVAL CONFEDERACY had to pay to the League's treasury.

Talent Unit of weight or money = 60 MINAS = 6000 DRACHMAS = 26 kg (of silver).

Tamiai tes Athenas Treasurers of Athena. A board of magistrates composed of one man from each tribe, and selected by lot, nominally from the PENTAKOSI-OMEDIMNOI. In the period 403/2–387/6 the board was amalgamated with the Treasurers of the Other Gods. For the next forty years the two boards existed side by side, but in 347/6 the Treasurers of the Other Gods were dissolved and the Treasurers of Athena took over their functions. The *tamiai tes Athenas* administered the treasures belonging to Athena and deposited on the Akropolis, but they were also active in the state's financial administration, paying the jurors in the People's Court and defraying the costs of publishing decrees, of repairing the walls round the Piraeus, and so on.

Tamias stratiotikon Treasurer of the Military Fund. Magistrate elected for a four-year period to superintend the Military Fund (*ta stratiotika*).

Tamias tou demou Treasurer of the people, i.e. the Assembly. Magistrate elected (?) for one year to administer the people's annual allowance under the *MERISMOS* of ten TALENTS.

Taxiarchos (pl. -oi) The commander of a *TAXIS*. The ten *taxiarchoi*, one from each of the tribes, were elected in the Assembly and, like the *STRATEGOI*, could be re-elected.

Taxis Regiment of HOPLITES. A tribe's contingent of the Athenian field army, led by a *TAXIARCHOS*.

Telos (pl. -le) (1) (Solonian) property class. (2) Custom or duty.

Thargelia Festival to Apollo, celebrated in the month THARGELION. The festival included a procession, offerings to Apollo and choral competitions for choirs of men and boys.

Thargelion The eleventh month of the Attic year, May–June.

Theorikon (pl. -ka) In the singular: the Theoric Fund. In the plural: payments from the Theoric Fund. *Theorika* were properly 'theatre money' and originally the Theoric Fund was a fund from which was paid out 2 OBOLS to every citizen as a grant towards their theatre ticket at the Greater DIONYSIA and other dramatic festivals. The fund was soon expanded, and by the middle of the fourth century it had become a kind of treasury under the control of its administrators, *HOI EPI TO THEORIKON*. They made payments to citizens at an increasing number of festivals, no longer only at festivals which included dramatic performances. The surplus of the revenue each year, if any, was (in time of peace) paid into the Theoric Fund, and the fund also financed public works, naval administration, and so on.

Thesmos (pl. -oi) Enactment, archaic term for what the Athenians later called *NOMOS* and/or *PSEPHISMA*.

Thesmothetai Board of six of the nine ARCHONS. Their principal duties were to convene the People's Court for all lawsuits and to preside over most public prosecutions (*GRAPHAI*).

Thete (thes, pl. thetes) Properly a day labourer, and then a citizen who produced less than 200 measures of corn, wine and olives in a year and thus belonged to the fourth Solonian property class.

Thirty (Tyrants), the (*hoi triakonta*) Oligarchic junta installed with Spartan support in Athens in the summer of 404 after Athens' defeat in the Peloponnesian War. They ruled for about eight months until they were replaced by a new oligarchic group, the Ten, who were, in their turn, overthrown with the restoration of the democracy in the autumn of 403.

Tholos Round building with pointed roof, built *c*.460 on the west side of the AGORA for the PRYTANEIS. The *prytaneis* held their meetings and dined in the Tholos, and a third of them were on duty during the night as well.

Timema (1) In Athens: that part of a (rich) citizen's property which was rated for taxation (EISPHORA). (2) In oligarchies: the amount of property necessary to be a full citizen of the POLIS, i.e. to have political rights.

Toxotai Archers. (1) Light-armed soldiers armed with a bow. (2) Designation of the corps of 300 SCYTHIAN ARCHERS.

Treasurers of Athena TAMIAI TES ATHENAS.

Tribe PHYLE.

Trierarchy (*trierarchia*) LITURGY in which the liturgist had to equip and command a warship (typically a TRIERES) for one year; he was thus known as a trierarch. In the fourth century the duty was often shared between two liturgists.

Trieres (pl. -eis) Galley with three banks of oars, one above the other; it was the most common type of warship in the fifth and fourth centuries. Its crew was 200 men, of whom 170 were rowers.

Trieropoioi Committee of ten of the COUNCIL OF FIVE HUNDRED responsible for the construction of new ships (TRIEREIS) in accordance with the orders of the Assembly.

Trireme TRIERES.

Trittys (pl. -yes) Riding, i.e. a third part of a tribe (PHYLE). By Kleisthenes' reforms Attica was divided into three regions: the city (ASTY), the inland region (PARALIA) and the coast (MESOGEIOS). Each region was subdivided into ten TRITTYES, and a tribe was composed of a *trittys* from each district.

Xenikon telos Fee paid by non-citizens for the right to set up a stall in the market.

Xenos (pl. -oi) Alien without Athenian citizen rights, i.e. any METIC or foreigner in Attica who was free (ELEUTHEROS) and not a slave (*doulos*).

Zeugites (pl. -tai) Citizen who produced between 200 and 300 measures of corn, wine and olives a year and thus belonged to the third Solonian property class.

Index of Passages Cited

General Index